CONFRONTING NEW REALITIES

Reflections on Tanzania's Radical Transformation

Juma V. Mwapachu

E&D Limited

DAR ES SALAAM

E&D Limited
P.O.Box 4460
Dar es Salaam
Email: ed@bol.co.tz

CONFRONTING NEW REALITIES: REFLECTIONS
ON TANZANIA'S RADICAL TRANSFORMATION

Copyright © 2005 Juma Volter Mwapachu

Cover Photo by Eugene Mwassa

ISBN 9987-411-20-7

Printed at Sona Printers Pvt. Ltd. New Delhi, India. www.sona.co.in

To my daughter Hadiyya (Tida) whose love, courage, strength and smile truly makes her a gift from God.

CONTENTS

ACRONYMS

ABSA	Almalgamated Bank of South Africa
ACP	African Caribbean Pacific Countries
ADB	African Development Bank
AEC	African Economic Community
AFC	Africa Football Confederation
AGOA	Africa Growth and Opportunity Act
AMNUT	All Muslim National Union of Tanganyika
APEC	Asia-Pacific Economic Cooperation
ARV	Anti-Retroviral Drugs
ASP	Afro-Shirazi Party
AU	African Union
BAKWATA	Baraza la Waislamu Tanzania
BCCI	Bank of Credit and Commerce International
BEST	Business Environment Strengthening for Tanzania
BET	Board of External Trade
BOT	Bank of Tanzania
BRELA	Business Registration and Licensing Agency
CAADP	Comprehensive Africa Agriculture Development Programme
CAP	Common Agricultural Policy
CARICOM	Caribbean Trade Area
CCE	Centre for Continuing Education
CCG	Creditors Consultative Group
CCL	Computing Centre Limited
CCM	Chama Cha Mapinduzi
CDC	Commonwealth Development Corporation
CED	Centre for Entrepreneurship Development
CEMAC	Economic and Monetary Community of Central Africa and Sao Tome and Principe
CEO	Chief Executive Officer
CHRGG	Commission on Human Rights and Good Governance
CIF	Cost Insurance and Freight
CNN	Cable News Network
COMESA	Common Market for Eastern and Southern Africa
CRDB	Cooperative and Rural Development
CTI	Confederation of Tanzania Industries
CUF	Civic United Front
DAHACO	Dar es Salaam Airport Handling Company
DANIDA	Danish International Development Agency
DAWASA	Dar es Salaam Water Supply and Sewerage Company
DFIS	Development Financial Institutions
DPP	Director of Public Prosecution
DSE	Dar es Salaam Stock Exchange
DTV	Dar es Salaam Television

EAC	East African Community
EACU	East African Customs Union
EADB	East African Development Bank
ECA	Economic Commission for Africa
ECOSOC	Economic and Social Council
ECOWAS	Economic Community of West African States
Ed	Editor
EPA	Economic Partnerships Agreement
EPZ	Export Processing Zone
ERP	Economic Recovery Programme
ESAF	Enhanced Structural Adjustment Facility
EPFAR	Emergency Plan for AIDS Relief
EU	European Union
EWURA	Energy and Water Utilities Regulatory Authority
FAO	Food and Agriculture Organisation
FDI	Foreign Direct Investment
FIDP	Financial Institutions Development Project
FIFA	Federation Internationale de Football Associations
FIS	Islamic Salvation Front. of Algeria)
FMO	Development Bank of the Netherlands
FRG	Federal Republic of Germany
FTA	Free Trade Agreement
GATT	General Agreement on Trade and Tariffs
GDP	Gross Domestic Product
GDR	German Democratic Republic
GNI	Gross National Income
GNP	Gross National Product
GSP	General Scheme of Preferences
H.R.H.	His Royal Highness
HFO	Heavy Finance Oil
HIPC	Highly Indebted Poor Countries
HIV/AIDS	Human Immunodeficiency Virus/Acquired Immunodeficiecy Syndrome
IBRD	International Bank for Reconstruction and Development. (World Bank)
ICTs	Information and Communication Technologies
IDM	Institute of Development Management
IFAD	International Fund for Agricultural Development
IFC	International Finance Corporation
IFF	International Finance Facility
IFM	Institute of Finance Management
IFMS	Integrated Financial Management System
IGU	Income Generating Unit
ILD	Institute for Liberty and Democracy
ILO	International Labour Organisation

IMF	International Monetary Fund
IPI	Institute of Production Innovation
IPO	Initial Public Offering
IPP	Industrial Products Promotion
IRA	Irish Republican Army
IT	Information Technology
JICA	Japanese International Co-operation Agency
KORA	Annual Africa Musical Awards
LART	Loans and Advances Realisation Trust
LDCs	Less Developed Countries
LGPF	Local Government Pensions Fund
MBA	Master of Business Administration
MCA	Millennium Challenge Account
MDGs	Millennium Development Goals
MDVs	Minimum Dutiable Values
MEBO	Management and Employee Buyout
MEIDA	Metal and Allied Industries Association
MFA	Multifibre Agreement
MFIs	Micro Finance Institutions
MFN	Most Favoured Nation Tariff
MIT	Massachusetts Institute of Technology
MNCs	Multinational Corporatons
MPs	Members of Parliament
MTEF	Medium Term Expenditure Framework
NABICO	National Bicycle Company
NAFTA	North American Free Trade Agreement
NASACO	National Shipping Agencies Company
NBC	National Bank of Commerce
NBC	National Business Council
NCA	Ngorongoro Conservation Area
NCCR	National Convention for Construction and Reform Mageuzi. Change)
NDC	National Development Corporation
NEDLAC	National Economic Development and Labour Council
NEMC	National Environment Management Council
NEMC	National Environmental Management Council
NEPAD	New Partnership for Africa's Development
NFC	National and Food Control
NFCC	National Food Control Commission
NGOs	Non-Governmental Organisations
NHS	National Health Service
NIC	National Insurance Corporation
NICO	National Investment Company Limited
NIEs	Newly Industrialising Economies
NIMP	National Irrigation Master Plan

NIPPA	National Investment and Protection Act
NMB	National Micro Finance Bank
NPES	National Poverty Reduction Strategy
NSE	Nairobi Stock Exchange
NSGRP	National Strategy for Growth and Reduction of Poverty
NSSF	National Social Security Fund
OAU	Organisation of African Unity
ODA	Overseas Development Assistance
OECD	Organisation for Economic Co-operation and Development
OIC	Organisation of Islamic Conference
PAYE	Pay as You Earn
PB	Productivity Bargaining
PBFP	Property and Business Formalisation Programme
PCB	Prevention of Corruption Bureau
PCE	Permanent Commission of Enquiry
PER	Public Expenditure Review
PICTA	Pacific Island Countries Trade Agreement
PPF	Parastatal Pension Fund
PRBS	Poverty Reduction Budget Support
PRM	Peer Review Mechanism
PRSP	Poverty Reduction Strategy Paper
PSRC	Presidential Parastatal Sector Reform Commission
PT	Privatisation Trust
PTA	Preferential Trade Area for Eastern and Southern Africa
Q & A	Question and Answer
R & D	Research and Development
SACCOS	Savings and Credit Co-operative Societies
SADC	Southern Africa Development Community
SAPs	Structural Adjustment Programmes
SEDP	Secondary Education Development Plan
SEZs	Special Economic Zones
Shs	Shillings
SID	International Development
SIDP	Sustainable Industrial Development Policy
SMEs	Small and Medium Enterprises
SSA	Sub-Saharan Africa
SUMATRA	Surface and Marine Transport Regulatory Authority
TACAIDS	Tanzania Commission for Aids
TAMWA	Tanzania Media Women Association
TANAPA	Tanzania National Parks Authority
TANESCO	Tanzania Electric Supply Company
TANROADS	Tanzania National Roads Agency
TANU	Tanganyika African National Union
TASAF	Tanzania Social Action Fund
TATEPA	Tanzania Tea Packers Limited

TB	Tuberculosis
TBL	Tanzania Breweries Limited
TBS	Tanzania Bureau of Standards
TCC	Tanzania Cigarettes Company
TCCI&A	Tanzania Chamber of Commerce, Industry and Agriculture
TCRA	Tanzania Communications Regulatory Authority
TDCAs	Trade, Development and Co-operation Agreements
TDFL	Tanganyika Development Finance Company Limited
TFDA	Tanzania Food and Drug Agency
TFTU	Tanzania Federation of Trade Unions
TGARA	Tanzania Government Aviation Regulatory Authority
THA	Tanzania Harbours Authority
TIB	Tanzania Investment Bank
TIC	Tanzania Investment Centre
TIN	Tax Identification Number
TNBC	Tanzania National Business Council
TNCs	Transnational Corporations
TPSF	Tanzania Private Sector Foundation
TRA	Tanzania Revenue Authority
TRC	Tanzania Railways Corporation
TTB	Tanzania Tourism Board
TTCL	Tanzania Telecommunications Company Ltd
TTMA	Tanzania Textile Manufacturers' Association
UDA	Usafiri Dar es Salaam
UK	United Kingdom
UN	United Nations
UNCTAD	United Nations Conference on Trade and Development
UNDP	United Nations Development Programme
UNESCO	United Nations Educational, Scientific and Cultural Organisation
UNICEF	United Nations Children's Fund
UPE	Universal Primary Education
US	United States of America
US$	United States of America Dollar
USAID	United States Aid for International Development
UTT	Unit Trust of Tanzania
VAT	Value Added Tax
VETA	Vocational Education and Training Act
Vs	Versus. (Against)
WSIS	World Summit on Information Society
WTO	World Trade Organisation
WWW	World Wide Web
ZIPA	Zanzibar Investment Promotion Agency)

GLOSSARY

a la carte regionalism	Mixed bag of regionalism system
Afya ni Uhai	Health is life
Al Qaeda	A militant Islamic group based in Afghanistan alleged to be led by Osama bin Laden of Saudi Arabia
Bureau de Change	An establishment for transacting change of foreign currency and financial transactions
Bongo	Brain. actually use your brain to survive in the city setting)
bongoism	Money seeking activities
Bulushi	Baluchi
Bwana	Mr or Master. depending on the context)
Chaggas	Also referred to as Wachagga - an ethnic group from Kilimanjaro Region in north of Tanzania
consensus ad idem	Meeting of the Mind
crème de la crème	The best
DALADALA	Private city commuter transport system in Dar es Salaam
Demokrasia ya Kisiasa na Kiuchumi	The Democracy of Politics and Economics
Eid Ul Fitr	The Festival of Fast-Breaking. A celebration marking the end of the Holy Month of Ramadan for Muslims
El Nino	This is the disruption of the ocean atmosphere system in the Tropical Pacific having important consequences for weather and climate around the globe. El Nino is characterised by unusually warm ocean temperatures in the Equatorial Pacific
esprit de corps	Spirit of belonging to a group especially in an organisation
ex parte injunctions	Court orders granted after hearing one side only in the absence of the other. alleged because of urgency)
ex tempore	Without preparation
Fatwa	Judgement based on Islamic law
fedha si msingi wa maendeleo	Money is not the foundation of development
fimbo ya mbali haiui nyoka	You cannot kill a snake with a stick from a distance

Hamas	A Palestinian "Islamic extremist" group
Harambee	A slogan meaning let us pull together
Hatimaye Wazungu - *wakabidhiwa DAWASA*	Finally the "whites" or Europeans were handed over DAWASA
Heri Wakati wa Mkoloni	Colonial times were better
inter alia	Among other things
Intifada	Uprising. Used in relation to campaigns by Palestinians directed at ending Israel military occupation of their territory
ipso facto	By the fact itself; by nature of the case; by the very act; by the mere fact; the fact itself shows
Jihad	Holy war for Muslims
kandambili	Sandals. related to poverty and failure to afford proper shoes)
Kilimo cha kufa na kupona"	Agricultural production as a matter of life and death
Kwasa Kwasa	Brand or syle of music from the Democratic Republic of the Congo
Laissez-faire	The theory or practice of governmental absention from interference in the workings of the market.
Machingas	Street hawkers
Maduka	Shops
mafuta na minofu	Edible oil and fillet fish processing
Makaburu	Boers of Republic of South Africa
Makuadi wa Soko Huria	The Pimps of the Market Economy
Mali ya Umma	Public property - "un-owned" or people's assets
mambo poa	Cool or everything is alright
Meso	Middle
Mirija	Siphons for sucking the blood, sweat and tears of the people
modus vivendi	Way of living. An accommodation between disputing parties to allow life to go on
Muafaka	Accord or understanding
Mujaheedin	Struggler. Someone who engages in jihad or struggle. Holy warrior
Mwembechai	A suburb of Dar es Salaam City where there were fatal religious clashes between the Police and believers on 13 February 1998
mwenzetu	One of us
Mwongozo wa TANU	TANU Ideology Directive of 1971

Nali	Malawian chilli sauce
njoo kesho	Come tomorrow
nostalagie de la boue	Sentimental yearning for the farm. in the sense of promoting subsidies to farmers)
nouveau riches	New rich class
operation maduka	socialisation of ownership of retail businesses
per se	by itself; taken on its own; taken alone
Papabawa	"The islands' legendary pale-skinned vampire." In Zanzibar Islands and particularly Pemba "popobawa" represents a mystic, sodomite figure, an apparition
prima facie	on the face of it; on the first impression
problematique	problematic
raison d'etre	reason for; reason of; a thing's existence
Ramadhan	The holy month of Ramadhan
Sahib	Master
Salaam za Kheri za Mwaka Mpya	New Year good wishes
Sharia law	traditional Islamic law
Si wangengoja angalau nikafa kwanza?	They should, at least, wait for me to die first. In this context: before they begin to dismantl my legacy)
Siasa ni Kilimo	agriculture is politics
Sine qua non	An indispensable condition or qualification
Status Quo	The existing state of affairs Without which it could not be - an indispensable action Also termed conditio sine qua non - A condition for something to happen
Sungusungu	A form of people's vigilante or militia groups. popular in the Lake Regions of Mwanza, Mara, Shinyanga and Tabora in Tanzania)
Taarab	music with traditional coastal music
Takrima	hospitality
tunakalia uchumi	unproductively sitting on wealth
Tutafika	We shall make it. literally we shall arrive!)
ubepari na unyonyaji	capitalism and exploitation
Ubepari ni unyama	capitalism is barbarism
Ubepari	capitalism

Uhuru na Kazi	Freedom and Work
Uhuru ni Kazi	Freedom is Work
Ujamaa na Kujitegemea	Socialism and Self-Reliance
Ujamaa to Ujangili?	From socialism to survival of the fittest
Ujamaa wa kisasa	Modern socialism
Ujamaa	Socialism
Ujangili	literally means poaching
Ukaripiaji	scold; objugate; reprimand;. bossy attitude) ultra vires beyond the powers; excess of legal powers or authority
unyapala	overseer; headman or foreman attitude
Unyonyaji	Exploitation
Uongozi Wetu na Hatima ya Tanzania	Our Leadership and the Future of Tanzania
Utavuna ulichopanda	whatsoever a man soweth, that shall he also reap
Uzawa	indigenisation
Uzungunization	Europeanisation
Vice Versa	the other way round or with the terms or conditions reversed
vis-à-vis	in relation to; compared with
Wachagga	An ethnic group from the Kilimanjaro region in Tanzania
Wafadhili	Sponsors. Also donors
Wahisani	donors
Wananchi	Citizens
Wapemba	People from Pemba Island in Zanzibar
WaZanzibara	Zanzibaris who originated from Mainland Tanzania
WaZanzibaris	People who are indigenous to Zanzibar Islands
Wazawa	Indigenous people to place or country
Zama za Uwazi Na Ukweli	The era of transparency and truth

ABOUT THE AUTHOR

Juma Volter Mwapachu, a Tanzanian lawyer and Fellow of the Chartered Management Institute (UK) has had a varied career, embracing government, the parastatal sector and the private sector. In the past two decades, he has been closely involved in the political and economic transformation of Tanzania, having been a member of several key Presidential Commissions of Enquiry, notably the Mtei and Nyalali Commissions that respectively recommended a more prudent system of taxation and expenditure management and the re-introduction of a multi-party political system. He has also served as Commissioner of the Presidential Parastatal Sector Reform Commission, an institution that has managed the privatisation process. Ambassador Mwapachu was one of the Members of the Team of Experts that crafted the Tanzania Development Vision 2025. In the parastatal sector, he has served as Chair of the Boards of Directors of Tanzania Railways Corporation and Tanzania Investment Bank. He has also been closely involved in the leadership of the University of Dar es Salaam, both as President of the Convocation for fifteen years and Vice Chair of the Governing Council for 12 years during a period when the University went through a radical transformation. At the level of the private sector, Ambassador Mwapachu was founder member and Secretary General of the Tanzania Chamber of Commerce, Industry and Agriculture when first constituted in 1988. Later, in 1991, he became founder member of the Confederation of Tanzania Industries, an organisation he led as Chair between 1986 and 2000. He was Chairman of the East African Business Council in 1998/1999.

Ambassador Mwapachu is author of many published academic articles and a book: *Management of Public Enterprises in Developing Countries: The Tanzania Experience*. He is also co-editor of two books on *Local Perspectives of Globalisation: The African Case* and *Towards a New Millennium: Perspectives on Tanzania's Vision 2025*. He is presently Tanzania's Ambassador to France.

PREFACE

This book encapsulates a journey of reflection about Tanzania's transformation. It is a reflection on how, since the mid 1980s, Tanzania has strived to confront new, national, regional and global economic and political realities, by taking radical shifts in its domestic political structures and economic policies. At the heart of these reflections and perspectives lie two goals. First, to forge a deeper understanding of the dynamics behind the changes and transformations that have taken place and which continue to evolve. Second, to place these dynamics of change in the battle arena of ideas with a view to promoting informed dialogue and debate about Tanzania's vision of the future and the challenges that have to be met in realising the objectives of the vision.

This is an ambitious book. It casts its net over a wide range of issues: political, economic, and social and within the local, regional and global perspectives. The underlying reason for this hybrid approach is that the book itself is a coagulation of thinking, interrogations and positions drawn from diverse disciplinary perspectives and insights developed over a decade as I closely and intimately watched the political and economic ideological transformations evolve in Tanzania.

Many of the perspectives are unique in the context of available literature on Tanzania. In this light, the book makes an important breakthrough and contribution in the sense that it fills a yawning gap in the literature about Tanzania's recent transformations from a holistic and inter-disciplinary perspective. These perspectives revolve around the following salient issues:

- economic policy reform, especially involving fiscal and taxation, in the context of how the Tanzanian economic environment has broadly been made more attractive to investment over time.
- the on-going process of democratic reform wherein important questions about the entry of religion in politics, the reform of the electoral system and the Tanzania Union Question take pre-eminence.
- the national challenge of leadership and governance in a globalising economic environment is undertaken.
- economic empowerment of the majority of Tanzanians, a subject catapulted by the ardent clamour for the "indigenisation" of the

economy in the wake of the opening up of the Tanzania economy to inward investment and the massive privatisation of state-owned enterprises.

- where to strike a balance between the state and the market, an evidently contentious subject in most developing economies especially those, such as Tanzania, that have been under a socialist economic system for a considerable period of time.
- mindset transformation as a key success factor in influencing radical change and development. The concept is crystallised within the broad context of how Tanzania would be able to ingrain the core philosophy that underpins its Development Vision 2025 as well as master the challenges envisioned in the Vision.
- the role of education and knowledge, contextualised within the framework of promoting a new mindset and the building of a new citizenship, especially among the youth, ingrained by tolerance and respect of diversity, critical fundamentals and building blocks for promoting national peace, stability and development.
- the challenges confronting the private sector as the new engine of growth within the backdrop of three decades of socialist economic policy and management. So is the challenge of building what the former Malaysian Prime Minister, Mahathir Mohammad has termed "smart partnership" among different stakeholders in the Tanzanian society and how public-private partnership can become an important vehicle for sharing the burdens of social and economic development in a market economy environment.
- the role of regionalism and of globalisation and their impacts on Tanzanian public policy, within the overall context of Africa's challenges to realise renaissance and competitiveness.

The first part of the book is devoted to paying homage to the late Mwalimu Julius Kambarage Nyerere, the architect of the Tanzanian psyche. His vision of peace, unity and development lies at the heart of many issues covered in this book. It remains a central feature of and a reference point in the passionate debate about democracy, governance, the union, and the role of the state and the market, particularly in the context of the Tanzania Development Vision 2025. Indeed, what underlies the core thesis of confronting new realities embodied in this book centres on what is viewed as a radical paradigm shift from Nyerere's political oligarchy and economic socialist systems to a liberal democratic and economic system. In this light, I have found it necessary that the book should commence with a close examination of Mwalimu Nyerere's style of leadership, ideas, vision and development strategic choices in order to lay bare the precise political and economic transformations that have taken place in the last two decades as well as interrogate the relevance and plausibility of such transformations in the context of new political and economic realities that are clearly confronting all nations, poor and rich alike.

Though the topics covered in the book are diverse, there is a crosscutting and all-embracing theme. This centres on how Tanzania is responding to and confronting new political and economic realities to construct a new future at a time when globalisation and the challenges of regional integration are intensifying. The book uses ideas that featured in several think pieces written between the mid 1990s and early 2000. Those essays were published in a weekly column in a Tanzania daily newspaper, The African, under the title, The Sounding Board, and in a Tanzanian business and political magazine called Change. Most of the material has necessarily been re-written, updated and fine-tuned to incorporate new developments, data and perspectives. However, I have attempted to retain some of the original focus and thrust in order to capture and retain the original thinking. I believe that this is important as it enables the continuities and discontinuities in the Tanzanian political and economic environment to be brought to the fore. One is thus able to capture the process of change and reform from the vantage point of a historical process. This structure is more particularly important for countries like Tanzania that are still going through a profoundly complex and fragile transition, from an environment ruled by a monolithic party political system and a socialist command economic regime to an environment driven by plural and liberal political and economic systems.

Overall, this book helps the reader to reflect and imbibe that sense of a movement, of a country in transition, and of the key factors that underlie and influence Tanzania's process of change and transformation. My hope is that the book will provide cutting edge raw material to all those committed to exploring the myriad challenges that confront many developing countries in the context of a brave new world. These are the challenges that underpin the capacity of poor countries to deepen democratisation, confront the new realities of global capitalism and to liberate themselves from the shackles of poverty, ignorance and pandemic diseases such as malaria, TB and HIV/AIDS.

The manuscript was ably copyedited by Professor Chris Maina Peter of the Faculty of Law, University of Dar es Salaam. He made several useful proposals on structure, consistency and text refinement. To him, my sincere thanks. I also wish to thank my publishers, E & D Limited of Dar es Salaam for their commitment and encouragement which has been indispensable in bringing this project to completion.

Finally, I would like to note the ardent help of loved ones, notably my wife Rose for having been a close companion, supporter, motivator and catalyst in my effort to write this book. My adult children have been a source of encouragement and inspiration, bringing their diverse professional knowledge and experiences to bear on many issues covered in this book. I thank them all for their contribution. This book is dedicated to my daughter, Hadiyya.

Juma V. Mwapachu
Paris
August, 2005.

Part one

HOMAGE TO MWALIMU JULIUS NYERERE

-We are poorer for his death, richer for his life-- John Atkin.

-Riveting end of an era; it's the silencing of a voice, which, uninterrupted for five decades, never abandoned principle, never abandoned purpose, never abandoned vision. -UNICEF.

Chapter

1 NYERERE: THE GLORY AND THE LEGACY

The heart that loves, the brain that contemplates,
The life that wears, the spirit that creates.
One object, and one form, and builds thereby
A sepulchre for its eternity.

-P B Shelley: **To Divide Is Not To Take Away.**

It could never be an easy task at any moment to write about the departed beloved Mwalimu Nyerere, Tanzania's liberator; the teacher; the peace builder; the inspirer; the galvaniser and unifier; the soul of the Tanzanian nation who sadly passed away on 14 October 1999. Nyerere was an icon for Tanzania. Yet in real life, he refused to be identified as an icon. He could not be as he drew power from the people. His words, vision, actions and ethical leadership most profoundly affected Tanzania.

John W Gardner (1968) wrote in *No Easy Victories* that, "leaders have a significant role in creating the state of mind that is the society. They can serve as symbols of the moral unity of the society. They can express the values that hold the society together. Most important, they can conceive and articulate goals that lift people out of their petty pre-occupations carry them above the conflicts that tear society apart, and unite them in pursuit of objectives worthy of their best efforts." How true of Mwalimu. It is as if Gardiner was writing specifically about the deceased Father of the Tanzanian Nation. Mwalimu himself, as early as December 1962, in his *Presidential Inaugural Address*, affirmed: "it is the dignity and well being of all the people which is the beginning and the end of all our efforts." He consistently, until his death, worked tirelessly to realise and sustain this objective. To him, human dignity underlined everything - social, economic and political. It underpinned his fundamental philosophy, his beliefs, and his actions.

Nyerere: Man of Principles

Nyerere was a visionary of the rare kind; everything he thought about and acted upon was premised on clarity of pre-determined goals, objectives and convictions. Opening the University College Dar es Salaam Campus in August 1964, he said, "Only when we are clear about what we are trying to do can we begin to think about the way of doing it." It was a loaded statement indeed. How often, in Nyerere's retirement from leadership and active politics have Tanzanians reflected on whether what they are doing, in their different walks of life and in their plans, is truly predicated on or informed by a clarity of what they strive to achieve? Often, as leader, Nyerere was confronted by a paradox, a dilemma, as he led Tanzania through thick and thin, on how he should respond to serious national economic problems. Leaders, like the late Kamuzu Banda of Malawi, decided to surrender to the "devil". namely, apartheid South Africa), than, ostensibly, allow their people to die of hunger! Weak leaders were prepared to sacrifice principles at the altar of survival even at the loss of dignity. To Mwalimu, a poor free man was always better than a wealthy slave.

Nyerere did not therefore hesitate to break off diplomatic relations with the then Government of West Germany in 1966 to prove this point. Social principles, in his view, were, by definition, "ideals of which to strive and by which to exercise self-esteem." He consistently disputed the deemed virtue of pragmatism when linked to social and economic issues and to the ostensible viability of achievement of fundamental social principles. To him, social principles were simply sacrosanct. To argue about their viability was, prima facie, absurd. In his view, the key question was "whether a society of freemen can do without" social principles. The belief, the philosophy, was the end goal.

Nyerere was obsessed with the importance of doing what he believed was the right thing. Precisely for this reason, in the introduction to his first book, *Freedom and Unity*, Nyerere unequivocally asserted, "for those with the courage to aspire, to believe, and to work, Tanzania is a challenging and exciting land." Nyerere knew, from very early on after independence, that the realisation of his vision for Tanzania, a country that had to be built on the basis of principles of human dignity and social justice, hinged on the success of inspiring and imbibing an ethic of courage, belief and work. His early galvanising slogans of *Uhuru Na Kazi*. Freedom and Work) and, later, *Uhuru Ni Kazi*. Freedom is Work), were not mere political gimmicks or polemics for power's sake. Nyerere used them to cultivate and exhort a new sense of purpose and meaning, centred on the lofty objective of creating a new society, a society based on human respect and putting people first in development policy and decisions.

His ardent commitment to human dignity is what inspired Mwalimu to espouse his version of socialism and self-reliance. It also inspired his aversion to colonialism, apartheid and racism of any kind, minority racial rule and imperialism. Nyerere strongly believed that the Tanzanian society could not acquiesce in the abasement or humiliation of its own purpose, namely that of upholding human dignity. In adopting a single party political system and the Arusha Declaration, whose basic thrusts he had developed in his papers, *Democracy and the One Party State*. 1963) and *Ujamaa: The Basis of African Socialism*. 1962), he was clear in his own mind that it would have been difficult to spearhead the realisation of human dignity in a political environment of political pluralism, underpinned by capitalism. He wrote in the *Introduction* to his book *Freedom and Socialism*, "A political democracy which exists in a society of gross economic inequalities, or of social inequality, is at best imperfect, and at worst a hollow sham." Nyerere saw in socialism the appropriate vehicle for enlarging the real freedom of the people and the expansion of their opportunity to live in dignity and prosperity.

The failure of public ownership and the consequent adoption of the market economy disturbed Nyerere up until his death. He constantly raised his voice to caution about the dangers of departing from the principles of human dignity. He feared that had such principles been sidelined and sacrificed in the name of pursuing the inevitable logic of global capitalism, the future peace and stability of Tanzania could have been undermined. Besides, it is not as if that he never reconciled himself to the failure of some of his socialist economic policies. He did. Nevertheless, he knew, as some of us do, that the core values that he strived to realise remained valid and would be for a long time to come.

In this context, the emergence, for example, of ideas centred on indigenisation, or *"uzawa"* literally angered him because they were symptomatic of apartheid, a proposition that he had castigated back in 1968 when he exclaimed whether "exploitation was only wrong when carried out upon the masses by people of a different race." To him, exploitation was race neutral. The wealth divide coinciding with the racial divide perceived to continue after the collapse of the public ownership system that Nyerere had conceived as part of the Arusha Declaration as a key vehicle for bridging that divide, had to be dealt with, from Mwalimu's standpoint, outside race-based policies and measures. He feared that the clamour for indigenisation would extend beyond the race divide and thereby destabilise unity and peace.

As stated earlier, the commitment to human dignity, and not mere altruism, also greatly influenced Mwalimu's struggle against all forms of oppression and domination. He was instrumental in the establishment of the *Organisation of African Unity*. OAU) as a dynamic force that would lead the fight against apartheid, colonialism and minority racial rule in Africa. In hosting the OAU Liberation Committee in Dar es Salaam, Mwalimu took the risk of exposing Tanzania to military attacks and subversion from the very oppressive regimes that Africa sought to topple. Tanzania also became the launching territory for most wars of liberation as well as the haven for freedom fighters and refugees, not just for *Southern* Africa, but also for Palestine and the Western Sahara. Frequent justifications by

Mwalimu that the price of freedom that Tanzanians had to pay for was the political liberation of Africa from colonial and minority racial rule became the mantra.

Nyerere and African Unity

Few critics of Nyerere saw power mongerism in him. Often such perception is derived from their association of Mwalimu with the introduction of the One Party Political System in 1965. Yet, that perception belittles Mwalimu's commitment to African unity, which, in his view, was not for the sake of size, but for "strength and power to defend the real freedoms of the ordinary man and to help him progress in his freedom." Evidently, some Zanzibaris may doubt if this is what has truly turned out to be as far as the Tanzania Union is concerned. Indeed, some Tanzanian Mainlanders may equally think otherwise pointing out that the Mainland 35 million population have surrendered too much political power to a small Island of less than one million people! Such views are a disservice to Mwalimu. What has become of the Union, its weaknesses and the fragilities on the economic and political fronts, should not override the fundamental rationale that has underpinned it.

In this light, I am often amazed, when studying Nyerere's character and his writings, by the acuity of his mind. How many Tanzanians, concerned about the state of a relatively young Tanzania Union, know that Mwalimu had discussed the on-set of globalisation, in its modern sense, as opposed to its historical context of the slave trade and imperialism, and the challenges of realising a World Government, as early as 1966? The Japanese management guru, Kenichi Ohmae, one of the leading minds on the concept of globalisation and author of the famous book, *The Borderless World* would be amazed by Nyerere's foresight. In the *Introduction* to his book *Freedom and Unity*, written in 1966, Nyerere observes, "the technology of the twentieth century straddles the world and yet we try to operate social relations as if national boundaries created impenetrable barriers between different peoples. It is essential that our concept of society be adapted to the present day." In the same Introduction, Nyerere further points out: "throughout the world, nation states have been so successful in creating concepts of an exclusive internal unity that almost all peoples are now terrified by the thought that someone from 'outside' will have power over them; they do not seem able to realise that they will also have power over others."

Nyerere all along believed in integration - political and economic. Zanzibar was evidently a natural and historical ally to become the pilot integration case. At the same time, it should also be realised that it was Nyerere who had earlier proposed to postpone the independence of Tanganyika had Kenya and Uganda agreed to form a political federation, with Mzee Jomo Kenyatta, becoming the first President. Therefore, Mwalimu was not simply driven by power as perceived from his move to introduce the One Party Political System. Where unity was at issue, Nyerere was prepared to surrender power. I always like to cite my favourite historian, AJP Taylor on contentious matters of this nature. As if in response to Nyerere's critics, the late Professor Taylor (1996) wrote, in his book, *The Origins of the Second World War:* "Historians often dislike what happened or wish that it had happened differently. There is nothing they can do about it. They have to state the truth as they see it without worrying whether this shocks or confirms existing prejudices."

Thus, Nyerere had pursued the Union of Tanganyika and Zanzibar because he believed that the only way Zanzibar could succeed to defend its revolution and the freedoms as well as the progress of ordinary Zanzibaris was through the establishment of the United Republic of Tanzania. As recent as 1995, Nyerere reiterated his caution about the emerging contentious views about the Union. Specifically, he reminded Zanzibaris that theirs was not a homogenous political entity; that not only was Pemba and Unguja politically split, but also that the whole of Zanzibar was a melting pot, comprising what he described as *"WaZanzibaris"* and *"WaZanzibara"*. As Tanzanians face the future without Nyerere, it is vital that Nyerere's foresight and wisdom continues to inform our decisions and our actions in a new and unfolding regional and global political and economic environment.

Nyerere's Internationalism

Nyerere's internationalism was driven by his quest for human dignity whose critical underpinning was the pursuit of a just and equitable global economic order. His election to the position of Chairman of the South Commission, which, in 1990, came up with a Manifesto titled *The Challenge to the South*, was a clear recognition of Nyerere's tenacity and life-long struggle to inject human equality in international economics. His internationalism also extended to the politics and conflicts of Africa. At the OAU founding meeting in Addis Ababa in 1963, Nyerere moved a resolution on the respect of colonial borders. It was evident to Nyerere that without respecting inherited colonial borders the African nation-state would find it difficult to exist and conflict would rule endlessly.

His nomination as the Facilitator for the Burundi Peace Process in 1997 was testimony to his success in building a cohesive, unified and peaceful Tanzania. One of the tragedies of Mwalimu's premature death is his inability to complete his mission of conflict resolution for Burundi. However, after his death, much has been achieved in forging a peace accord in Burundi, though a looming cloud of uncertainty remains over the political destiny of this politically fragile nation. Africa will certainly miss this great son of rare ability, commitment and foresight.

Unifier and Builder

Nyerere was always cognisant of the fragility of the African nation-state. In abolishing the chiefdoms in Tanganyika at the eve of independence, he knew well that unifying 120 different tribes would be a difficult task were the chiefdoms to be allowed to survive. As a son of a chief himself, he was prepared to betray his own background in the interest of building a firm foundation for national unity. As he later wrote in the book, *Freedom and Unity*, "In Africa now the social ethic is changing, and has to change, from one appropriate to a tribal society to one appropriate to a national society."

At home, Mwalimu was a skilful politician. He used political power and authority to achieve his set vision and goals. Many of the critics of his leadership locate their criticisms of him largely in this area of governance. Thus decisions like the abolition of local government in 1972, the abolition of Co-operatives in 1976, and the implementation of the villagisation programme, 1973-76, have been isolated for particular chastisement, having been politically rather than economically motivated, and, thus for having undermined the country's progress. Mwalimu himself has been honest enough to absorb some of the blame. It is evident though, that Nyerere did not effect any of the decisions that he is accused of out of poor judgement or hunger for power, as some of his critics would like us to believe. On the contrary, in all the above three referred areas of decisions, Nyerere's objective was primarily to transform the social and economic structure of rural life for the better. My reading of Nyerere is that he never saw or used power for its own sake. To him, power was, to borrow Richard Nixon's words, "the opportunity to build, to create, to nudge history in a different direction."

For those who better understood Nyerere's thesis of socialism, they would know that for quite sometime, Nyerere was closely influenced by the Maoist strategy of rural transformation. Nyerere saw the peasant, not the proletariat, as the fountain and the key vehicle for spearheading a national socialist revolution. Thus, the following measures that he effected, were intended to put the peasant in command in the quest for spearheading radical rural socialism and transformation:

decentralisation, effected in 1972, which was, in effect, the re-centralisation of power of local government at the central government level so as to achieve policy coherence and a common pursuit of economic strategies, villagisation programme, and the abolition of the democratic co-operatives and their replacement with village socialist co-operatives.

What is significant to recognise is that, in spite of the drawbacks manifested by these specific policy measures, Tanzania has remained peaceful and stable. In many other African countries, instability and tumult could have erupted from such drawbacks. The reason for such stability is not far to seek. Nyerere was considered by the people to be a man of the people, such that, even where he committed mistakes, his credibility, integrity, honesty and his commitment to providing the basic needs and welfare of the people stood him in good stead. At no time did Nyerere abuse his greatness; to him the feeling of guilt, regret and compassion always formed part of power that he wielded. He was, after all, a very religious person.

Power of leadership

Nyerere's mastery of language, both Kiswahili and English, his use of symbols and images that made meaning to ordinary people and his unique eloquence and oration, constituted powerful tools of political and social influence, mobilisation as well as legitimacy. He used these tools to reach out to the people, inspiring them and galvanising them behind his vision. They also became his key pillars for exercising power effectively.

One of the key lessons of leadership that present leaders and leadership aspirants should learn from Mwalimu is how to stay and remain close to the people. Nyerere, the man and the leader was the antithesis of the leader that Brutus eloquently captures in his famous soliloquy in Shakespeare's Julius Caesar, one of Mwalimu's favourite readings and which he translated into Kiswahili: *"But 'tis a common proof, that lowliness is young ambition's ladder, whereto the climber upward turns his face; But when he once attains the upmost round, He then unto the ladder turns his back, looks in the clouds, scorning the base degrees by which he did ascend."* Nyerere's strongest attribute was his simplicity and his accessibility. His wants in life were basic. He sought nothing materialistic in leadership and in his own private life. Thus, he was able to rise above and overcome the human frailties which power of office often attracts, tempts and corrupts. To him, corruption was evil; he compared it to an act of treason.

The secret of Nyerere's power and authority and its broad acceptance lay in the way he inspired his lieutenants. He had a unique ability to set both the terms of a debate or discussion and the framework for subsequent decision. He always left his lieutenants intimidated and awe-struck by his mastery of facts and his brilliance. His sense of timing for effecting decisions and his capability at manipulating and presenting facts made him a master of power management. Nyerere also had remarkable energy, stamina and endurance. He rarely fell ill. Therefore, his sudden illness and death came as a major shock to all.

Man of Ideas

Mwalimu was not simply a teacher in the ordinary parlance of the word. He was a man of ideas, an intellectual of the highest order. He was not constrained by statism. He once wrote, "There is no stability in stagnation in this twentieth century; stability can only be achieved through maintaining balance during rapid change." Thus, whilst he was responsible for justifying the relevance of the One Party State in his paper *Democracy and the One Party State*, he is the one, at the 1990 CCM Congress, that voluntarily relinquished the post of Chairman of the ruling party-CCM, and first mooted that multiparty politics was an idea whose time had come. Moreover, going by the Tanzanian political orthodoxy that had entrenched during his leadership, Mwalimu had to move the idea for the new thinking not to be considered taboo. Few else would have dared to bell the cat. The late Alec Nove wrote in his book *Economics of Feasible Socialism:* "ideas evolve, ideas can be re-interpreted, elements of doctrine can be dropped, in response to circumstances, even while men seek to shape circumstances in the light of their ideas." To Nyerere, as long as orthodoxy was not predicated on principles whose validity was for all time, then ideas had to evolve and be changed in the light of objective conditions. Nyerere was not as dogmatic as often presented in some quarters of public opinion. Indeed, whilst Tanzanian political orthodoxy for a long time frustrated the fertility of ideas, because ideas had to conform to the conventional thinking of the ruling party, Nyerere was one person that broke the rules. Thus, whilst he sent down almost all the students of the University College, Dar es Salaam for demonstrating against the introduction of National Service in October 1966, very much a reflection of his intolerance for unorthodox thinking, he is the one that showed deep inclination in allowing opposing ideas in the country to contend. In his address at the University of Dar es Salaam during the 25th Anniversary of the University's founding, in July 1995, Nyerere underscored the importance of staff and students having "untrammelled freedom to think, and to exchange thoughts, even if the thinking leads some of its members to become unorthodox in their conclusions. Orthodoxies change; as knowledge expands, the understanding of truth develops."

9

To be a man of ideas, Nyerere had to develop a strong appetite for books and reading. Indeed, the respect that he enjoyed internationally was, to a large degree, an outcome of his ability to engage anybody in the industrialised and developing world alike on almost any social, economic or political issue because he kept abreast of new ideas and new thinking over most burning issues of intellectual discourse. He thus confounded conventional thinking on issues such as democracy, debt, privatisation and globalisation. I recall an interesting encounter where Mwalimu Nyerere was involved as a Panellist at an International Conference of the Society for International Development in Amsterdam in mid 1991. The Panellists included Mrs. Olof Palme, Madam Bruntland, the late Mahboub Ul Haq and Jan Pronk. The subject was the "Peace Dividend" after the end of the cold war. When the turn for Nyerere to speak came, he started off with his characteristic cracking laugh. The assembly hall, with about 2000 delegates, went into a temporary trance. Then Nyerere said: "In Africa, we have a saying that when elephants fight, it is the grass that suffers. But the other day, a friend of mine came up with something that I had not heard before. He said, but Mwalimu, do you know, when elephants make love, the grass suffers even more!"

That intervention more or else closed the debate. To Nyerere, the cold war had ended but a new global relationship, between the cold war opponents, was bound to emerge, a relationship based on "love". In other words, in the post-cold war era, with new love in place, the grass, namely the poor, would inevitably suffer even more. Mwalimu has more or else been proven right; there has been no notable peace dividend to the poor. This story, in many ways, captures the warm sense of humour that characterised Mwalimu's personality and the manner in which he so intimately connected with the people.

Nyerere was a powerful educator. Many Tanzanians have questioned the reversals that experienced in the field of Universal Primary Education. UPE) and the slippages in literacy and adult education, particularly in the period between 1986 and 1997. The question is who is to blame? Mwalimu's strategy in promoting UPE and mass literacy was through nation building. He looked upon the promotion of education as a political rather than an economic process. As a result, he succeeded to improve primary education without injecting significant financial resources. Literacy rate shot up above 90% during his leadership. More significant is the fact that Mwalimu gave special attention to the education of the girl child and women. He knew well that gender inequality was caused by gaps in education among girls and women and that such gap accentuated the duality of cultures, economic levels, in terms of gender exploitation and consumption standards, especially in rural Tanzania. It was only through raising education levels of girls and women that a major process of social and economic transformation could be unleashed in Tanzania.

At another level, Nyerere gave great priority to promoting gender equality. The fruits of his labour were evident in politics and in government administration. This goal has been sustained by his successors, especially so by President Mkapa's administration. However, its scope and depth is yet to permeate right across the national social strata. This legacy should be given a shot in the arm.

There are those who would wish to judge Mwalimu from the point of view of his failures. Fair is fair. Humans make mistakes. But rather than dwell on Nyerere's failures and shortcomings, Tanzanians should remember Mwalimu for his vision for Tanzania; a vision for all time.

Conclusion

Tanzania's beloved Mwalimu is gone. Tanzanians have suffered an irreparable loss. It is a loss to live with. Mwalimu is only gone in soul; his spirit lives, the spirit that has given Tanzanians love, social harmony, religious tolerance, unity and peace and a hope of a future of prosperity. He has left behind a formidable legacy. Tanzanians should strive to uphold and sustain the legacy. The best way to remember Mwalimu is therefore for all Tanzanians to re-dedicate themselves to his worthy legacy and, collectively, make it work for their national benefit and that of the future generations.

Chapter

2 NYERERE AND CONVENTIONAL WISDOM

*It is now "conventional wisdom" in Washington. even in the IMF, at least in
terms of its rhetoric) and in donor capitals that poverty needs to be addressed
as a matter of highest priority; that political stability and good governance.
notably reduced corruption) are prerequisites for development; and that national
ownership of programmes is critical to their success. It has taken them a long
time to reach these positions. But Julius Nyerere was espousing them and trying
to build practice upon them 30 years ago ... he was decades ahead of his time
in these matters.*

Gerald Helleiner: **The Legacies of Julius Nyerere: An Economist's
Reflections.**

Mwalimu Julius Kambarage Nyerere's greatest influence and
inspiration to me featured in his intellectual refusal to fall captive
and be prisoner to what the western liberal orthodoxy promoted
as the conventional wisdom- political, social or economic. On the
afternoon when I was presenting this personal reflection on the late
Mwalimu at a University of Dar es Salaam Colloquium, President Benjamin
Mkapa was also coincidentally, in his State Funeral Address, making
reference to the World Bank President's condolence message on Nyerere's
death. That message featured Nyerere's rejection of some of the World
Bank's conventional wisdom, particularly the one about using Gross
National Product. GNP) as primary criteria for determining the level of
development of a country. With the benefit of hindsight, people like
Nyerere have led to the recent burial of the "Washington Consensus."
To Nyerere, the fundamental test of effective leadership centred on
autonomous conscience; in other words, the high degree of personal
conviction and independence of mind based on a firm commitment to
core beliefs and social values rooted in one's culture and objective realities.
As I grew up and became intensely and passionately sensitive to the large
presence of Mwalimu Nyerere in an emerging independent nation, in the
struggle for consolidation of national freedom and in the quest to confront
the daunting challenges of development in a politically and economically
fragile nation-state, the depth of Mwalimu's independent thinking
capacity struck me. As a law student at the University College in Dar es
Salaam, in the mid to late 1960s, and as a TANU Youth League cadre and

leader, I became even more aware of Mwalimu's core strength as a national leader, that of thinking and acting on the basis of what he believed to be in the best interest of the Tanzanian people. Nothing swerved him from that position and direction.

Much has stuck deep in my mind from Mwalimu's influence. This has had a marked impact on my own thinking, and in my attitude towards leadership and in how to view the challenges of underdevelopment that still shackle our economy and society. Mwalimu Nyerere presented himself to me as a leader with the force of mind and the mental versatility to understand the state of our national condition and the dynamic of change. He was able to churn out, as a matter of course, policy responses that confounded the best of global and national conventional thinking.

Nyerere had the capacity to battle ideas. His mind and brain was a battleground of ideas. These days, in tune with the so-called conventional thinking, such battleground is described as a marketplace of ideas - as if ideas are traded! To Mwalimu, ideas about freedom, democracy, equality, human dignity and respect, about the creation of a global economic order that sets out fair and equitable rules involving trade, income re-distribution, and the sharing of power in international governance- were not tradable ideas as in a negotiation for sale and purchase! On the contrary, they constituted a new battleground for the creation of a world founded on social justice. To him, political independence depended on economic independence not in autarky terms, but rather in getting a country to win self-respect and dignity by relying largely on itself for national development.

Thus, Mwalimu Nyerere knew, from the on-set of political independence, that falling prey to the conventional wisdom which the western liberal orthodoxy champions, whether in politics or economics, would stifle and even undermine the very political independence that had been achieved as well as the fundamental economic philosophy that was driven by principles of equality and social justice. Little wonder that on the eve of independence, Nyerere clearly discerned the existence of an ideological conflict between the so-called egalitarian foundations of democracy and the inegalitarian reality of capitalism, more so for a poor emerging political entity.

Nyerere and Liberal Democracy

Therefore, the earliest conventional wisdom Nyerere challenged and immediately overhauled was the Anglo-Saxon model of democracy. Nyerere even saw the existence of tribal chiefdoms, which he was part and which the British had turned into a surrogate political system, as an extension of the Anglo-Saxon model of democracy. The Anglo-Saxon model of democracy was the antithesis of the foundations of a united and egalitarian society that a newly independent nation needed to promote. Nyerere did not therefore introduce the one party political system as a means of creating an authoritarian dictatorship as adduced in certain quarters of intellectual and political discourse. On the contrary, Nyerere's objective in taking Tanzania on the path of the monolithic political party system was informed by the reality that the liberal conventional wisdom, if allowed to take root, would have resulted in the failure to build a new society united behind a vision of harmony, dignity, equality and peace.

Democracy and Socialism Are Inseparable

To Nyerere, democracy and socialism were inseparable; they mutually reinforced each other. In the Introduction to his book, *Freedom and Socialism*, he was unequivocal when he posited, "a political democracy which exists in a society of gross economic inequalities, or of social inequality, is at best imperfect, and at worst a hollow sham." In advocating the adoption of socialism, as early as 1962, though it's actual promulgation took place later in 1967, through the Arusha Declaration, Nyerere was cognisant of the inherent destructive character of the capitalist system. Interpreting the capitalist system, Nyerere wrote, "individual wealth is the most important single criterion for respect, and the competitive spirit is acclaimed as a paramount social virtue -in practice if not in theory." To him, such conventional wisdom was illogical. Human respect and social virtue could not be realised through capitalism. Nyerere died with this belief anchored in his heart and soul. Neither of these views, which Nyerere espoused about the indivisibility of democracy from socialism and the destructive character of capitalism on human respect, dignity and social virtue, fit into the western liberal conventional wisdom. Thus, Nyerere was bold, courageous and intelligent enough to refuse to graft onto the Tanzanian body politic an orthodoxy that was foreign to Tanzanian cultural roots and objective national realities manifested by stark poverty, tribal and religious cleavages and allegiances, the absence of a political culture and the fragile state of the private sector.

Since the introduction of liberalisation, deregulation and privatisation, in the mid 1980s, Nyerere had been at the forefront to denigrate the so-called conventional wisdom of free market; what the Washington Consensus for so long prescribed as the necessary prescription for realising sustainable economic growth in poor economies. In his view, there was nothing "universal" about the benefits of free market. The Fukuyama thesis about the "end of history", namely that the end of communism marked the inevitable ascendancy of liberal political and economic ideas, was hubris to Nyerere. Indeed, the rancidity of the market in a poor country evoked an irascible response from Nyerere. His core thinking in this regard is well captured in an article written by the French socialist, Jacques Attali, titled: *The Crash of Western Civilisation: The Limits of the Market and Democracy*: Attali posited: "The frantic search for money to fund elections and the scale of the criminal economy are signs of the ascendancy of the market economy over democratic ethics." Mwalimu Nyerere would have been honoured where it mattered most to him were the right to representation of the people to be socialised rather than allowed to fall to the dictates of the market. This is why a proportional representation electoral system is best suited to ethical politics in a poor and emerging plural society.

Nyerere and Political Corruption

Many Tanzanians, who listened attentively to Mwalimu Nyerere's 1995 May Day Speech delivered in Mbeya, would recollect Mwalimu's fears about the corruption of democratic values that was entrenching in Tanzanian society and how it could undermine peace and stability. Attali's view of the foreboding outcome of such an environment would have captivated Mwalimu Nyerere. Attali (1991) has further asserted: "Eventually, democracy will fade away, having been replaced by market mechanisms and corruption. We will have a kind of market dictatorship, a 'lumpen market', without strong democratic institutions to serve as countervailing powers. Political outcomes will be bought and sold, and the market economy will rule every element of public life, from police protection, justice, education, and health to the very air we breathe, paving the way for the final victory of 'corporate economic rights' over individual human rights." Are we not experiencing a semblance of such type of environment in Tanzania? Put differently, are the threats of such environment not looming?

Is it not perverse, in a country where social status is increasingly associated with material wealth, that Tanzanian politics and, particularly when connected to party and parliamentary elections, should be transformed into what Mwalimu Nyerere in the Introduction to his book *Freedom and Unity*, surmised as an imperceptible "merchant and client relationship," the merchant, in this case, taking the shape of wealthy political candidates and or their benefactors? When it comes to questions about the equality of all citizens, especially in their participation in public affairs, universities and civil society have a key role to play in configuring a framework for ethical politics. Nyerere constantly urged these segments of society to play an oversight role in promoting and ensuring ethical politics. The challenge remains alive.

Finally, an American author on the science of personal achievement, Anthony Robbins, wrote in his book, *Unlimited Power*, "the quality of our lives is determined not by what happens to us, but rather by what we do about what happens." These are powerful words. Nyerere saw this philosophy as reflecting a typically ridiculous conventional wisdom. Nyerere's legacy, on the contrary, is that Tanzanians should strive to respond not to what happens to them because to do so would tantamount to their lives being shaped on the basis of orthodox political and economic prescriptions of others. His central thesis was that Tanzanians should instead shape their own destiny and build the kind of society *they* wanted. Thus, what happened to them should be of their own making. Such an approach could only be achieved where, as a nation, Tanzanians would be guided by shared principles and core values which they genuinely believe in and which they are committed to uphold, promote and apply as the building blocks for the construction of the society they envision.

This is what would translate into national success; the success, despite all the shortcomings a mortal and fallible person would commit, that Mwalimu Nyerere achieved. The American essayist and poet, Ralph Waldo Emerson once wrote: "To laugh often and much; to win the respect of intelligent people and the affection of children; to earn the appreciation of honest critics and endure the betrayal of false friends; to appreciate beauty, to find the best in others; to leave the world a bit better, whether by a healthy child, a garden patch or a redeemed social condition; to know even one life has breathed easier because you have lived. This is to have succeeded."

Going by Emerson's wisdom, Mwalimu Julius Kambarage Nyerere *truly* succeeded. The burden of his legacy to us all is can we, as individuals, as institutions of higher learning, as the national leadership and as a whole people, succeed within the framework of Mwalimu Nyerere's success? Are we sufficiently bold and courageous; are we ingrained with the same level of autonomous conscience, the high degree of conviction based on principles, beliefs and core values, to be able to honour, rise and live up to Mwalimu Nyerere's expectations? Are we able to challenge the global conventional wisdom that poor countries are subjected to accept readily? To succeed, the bedrock of Mwalimu's legacy should inform the national direction.

Chapter

3 TANZANIA AFTER OR WITHOUT NYERERE

He was so much to everyone, a pillar of what Tanzania is today, a repository of wisdom, counsel and guidance. He has left us, but we shall not let slip his legacy. We shall safeguard his cachievements and hold high the torch of struggle and freedom he has bequeathed us.

Benjamin W. Mkapa: Address at the State Funeral for Mwalimu Julius Kambarage Nyerere, 21 October, 1999.

Immediately following the death of Mwalimu Julius Nyerere, an intellectual debate emerged in Tanzania revolving around the question: Tanzania without Nyerere. At the core of that agonising debate were two scenarios: First, the broad view that Nyerere was the principal architect of all that is good in Tanzania: love, peace, racial and religious harmony, unity, improvement in gender sensitivity and equality and human dignity. The question that arose was what happens to the country now that he was dead. Second, there was the general concern that all may not be well in the Tanzanian State. Yes, the Nyerere legacy is there. Yet even such perception or belief was and is debatable. As Nyerere himself warned, early in 1995, there were cracks appearing in the house that is Tanzania; cracks in the walls, on the ceiling and even in the foundation. Cracks which, in his view, threatened to undermine some of the key pillars of his legacy. These cracks are examined below.

However, the main burden here is to present the argument that it is not as if the legacy of Nyerere has suddenly taken the centre stage because Mwalimu Nyerere is dead. That would tantamount to begging the question. The legacy of Nyerere was there as he lived. 14 years after his retirement from the Presidency, late in 1985, Nyerere sat, watched, listened, assessed and saw how his legacy was handled, treated, respected, hailed, chipped away, dismantled, remoulded and even abandoned. I would submit, therefore, that the question before Tanzanians, yesterday, today and tomorrow, is not so much what of Tanzania *without* Nyerere as much as what of Tanzania *after* Nyerere.

In other words, the central question to what extent Tanzanians, as leaders

17

and as citizens, would treasure, cherish and uphold the legacy of Nyerere may have little to do with Mwalimu's death, his absence from the Tanzanian political scene. Rather, it has more to do with how Tanzania went through the travails and experiences of managing or mismanaging Mwalimu's legacy during Mwalimu's lifetime in the first place. What makes Mwalimu's death a decisive moment is precisely whether Tanzanians would behave differently after Nyerere's death from how they behaved *after* Nyerere had retired from public office?

At the outset, it should be noted that most Tanzanians would locate Nyerere's legacy on what he believed in, what he did and what he achieved or what he may not have achieved as President and as a political leader. It is from such a standpoint that the foundations of unity, social harmony, equality and human dignity, which Mwalimu created and fought hard to sustain, obtain a relevant context. Whichever instruments of policy and power Nyerere used- the one party state, public ownership or the villagisation programme- all these, at their core, were driven by the primacy of core social values and virtues which, in Nyerere's wisdom, were vital to the creation of a united and peaceful land.

Understandably, after Mwalimu's death, there is an emotional re-dedication to the ideals and principles that Mwalimu professed and pursued to galvanise, empower and inspire Tanzanians to rise beyond the mundane and commit them to lofty goals. Such ideals could have been over the liberation of countries still under colonial and minority racial regimes or accepting a non-pluralistic political and economic system. At the same time, Tanzanians often forget, may be too hastily and regrettably so, that re-dedication to Nyerere's legacy and vision may not be enough and that the time to walk the talk is nigh.

The test of leadership could not be more onerous than now. During the 14 years when Nyerere was out of power, it could be asked to what extent a passionate commitment to Mwalimu's ideals and virtues existed. And it is not as if that Nyerere did not try to make his presence felt. From time to time, he intervened to share his views over what he thought were processes of national derailment taking place. Indeed, if one goes merely by Mwalimu's own concerns and trepidations, which he often revealed publicly, about how the pillars of national unity and peace were slowly but consistently undermined through various policies and leadership behaviour, particularly in the period between 1990 and 1995, then clearly a problem existed about adhering to Nyerere's legacy as he lived.

It is notable that during this period, Mwalimu Nyerere became particularly disturbed and perturbed by the emergence of cracks in his legacy. He often said that the national guiding purpose was getting lost. He anguished at the fast pace in which the masses were losing an anchor in their lives, in the wake of the erosion of the welfare state. In one of his early 1995 speeches, he painfully revealed a true story about an epileptic young woman from his own village of Butiama who had fallen and badly knocked her forehead on a wall suffering serious injury that required simple surgery. The poor woman failed to get hospital treatment because she could not pay for it.

Nyerere also became highly critical of the integrity of leaders and institutions during this period. He was particularly critical of a leadership that had become prisoner to the conventional wisdom of the IMF and the World Bank. In his view, national core values were sacrificed at the altar of the market economy. Nyerere often wondered, in disbelief, if the IMF and the World Bank were gods; that what they said sounded like religious sermon. Jenerali Ulimwengu was correct in positing, in one of his weekly essays in the column of the Tanzania weekly newspaper, *Rai,* that peace and stability were not *seeds* that could be re-planted. On the contrary, they constituted *harvests* for feeding and nourishing Tanzanians. Nyerere was always focused on sustaining peace and stability. To him, everything else depended on them. If the market economy would reinforce them, then that was well and good. However, if it subverted them, then something was seriously wrong. For a poor country, where the economic system was wrong it had to be addressed quickly to avert instability. The entry of the market and of political pluralism did not take place when Nyerere was in political power. Yet, part of his legacy centres on those changes.

Central to Nyerere's legacy is the question about leadership integrity. Nyerere anguished at the ascendancy of corruption, and the way it undermined the integrity of leaders and institutions. He admonished the emergence of the rule based on personal whims rather than on the constitution and the rule of law. In his epoch 1995 May Day Speech at Mbeya, he showed mad indignation at the government decision to amend the constitution in order to set aside a High Court judgement that recognised the constitutional validity of independent candidates in national elections. That decision, which catapulted a clash between a legislature under the virtual control of the executive, since the government in power had a monopoly of representation in the legislature, and the judiciary, was as underhand and as irresponsible as any other move, by anybody, that subverts the sanctity of the constitution to suit the political ends of those in power. In that move by the government, Nyerere saw one of his core legacies mauled before his eyes.

However, there were other "cracks" that equally disturbed Mwalimu Nyerere. They included the re-emergence of tribalism; the rise in religious bigotry and intolerance and the birth of "racist" polemics centred on the concept of "*Uzawa*". In his view, the pillars of his legacy were slowly being chipped away as he lived. He often wondered what would happen after he was gone! Sometimes, with a light touch but still communicating a painful message across, Nyerere would joke about how his legacy being subverted right before his own eyes. He would say "*Si wangengoja angalau nikafa kwanza?*. meaning that they could, at least, wait for me to die first before they began to dismantle my legacy).

All the actions that precipitated these concerns took place in Tanzania without Nyerere being in power, but alive. Imagine then, Tanzania *after* Nyerere; that is, after his death. Clearly, Tanzanians have a daunting challenge ahead of them. First, in understanding more clearly what Nyerere's legacy embodied. Secondly, in upholding and cherishing Nyerere's legacy if they can. For Tanzania *without* Nyerere may indeed prove to be a haunting experience; more like the Ghost of Banquo confronting Macbeth.

Chapter

4 HOW TO REMEMBER MWALIMU NYERERE

Do not go where the path may lead, go instead where there is no path and leave a trail.

-Ralph Waldo Emerson.

Since his death in October 1999, it is as if the world has lost its vigorous and spiritual conscience. The world has gone topsy-turvy, reminding us of the popular song of yesteryears: "Stop the world, I wanna get off." The world, especially the poor world, misses Nyerere's cracking laughter, often a cynical one, directed at the abuses against the pursuit of a global shared political and economic destiny. The third world has lost Nyerere's powerful and fearless voice of integrity and wisdom.

We live in a world where, for example, Israel's Sharon ridicules even the power and authority of the United States by executing a bloody and destructive war against a weak and defenceless Palestine. Traditional African-Arab solidarity over Palestine, on the other hand, has suffered a tragic loss of direction and radicalism. A philosophy of everybody to himself and God for us all seems to have taken over in the context of the grim poverty afflicting poor nations whose amelioration crucially depends on poor nations playing surrogate to rich countries.

Such is the world that Nyerere would not have stood idly by and passively accept. Such is the world that misses the leadership of the Poor's greatest warrior. This is how we should remember Mwalimu Nyerere. We miss him for his hard-headiness and for his awesome capacity to dream about Tanzania's destiny and to reason and articulate. In his absence, the poor world increasingly finds itself powerless. You sense a sad dislocation in the political ethos and culture of the poor world, as we knew of it in Nyerere's life.

With Nyerere gone, the intensification of arrogance of the powerful nations passes without serious criticism. Yes, you have Mandela's voice around. But it is more respected for its moral authority, it lacks, in my view, the political intellectual tenacity and depth of Nyerere's. Thus, the poor are today constantly reminded of Fukuyama's "end of history," the celebrated on-set of neo-liberal capitalism under the leadership of the US, and of the "new liberal imperialism", a term used by Robert Cooper, Tony Blair's close associate. In an article in UK's the *Guardian* of 6 April 2002, Mr. Cooper postulated, that precisely because of the death of imperialism, the world was witnessing the emergence of "failed states"; of a "pre-modern world" characterised by chaos, wars, drugs, crime and terrorism. He argued a case for a world in which the efficient and the well governed export stability and liberty, what he describes as "cosmopolitan values". Listening to President Bush's State of Union Address in February 2005, you would think that Mr Cooper wrote it! President Bush said, "We are all part of a great venture: to extend the promise of freedom in our country, to renew the values that sustain our liberty, and to spread the peace that freedom brings." What an amazing coincidence of thought.

However, Mwalimu Nyerere would certainly have challenged the manner in which this thesis of force of freedom was being advanced. For who determines who is "efficient and well governed" and who constitutes a "failed State"? How would the so-called "stability and liberty" be exported? Does Israel's Sharon, for example, qualify as a leader of an efficient and well-governed state? Was Arafat leading a "failed state"? What effective difference would President Mahmood Abbas bring to the situation? Could a state that is virtually captive, under siege and occupation be able to behave and act as a state at all? Is Israeli's military might often unleashed on a defenceless Palestine the qualification for exportation of peace and stability? What is particularly *liberal* about such form of intimidation in the name of promoting democracy and security?

There is today a worrying timidness and lack of radicalism on the part of the leadership of the poor world to condemn, unreservedly, what, for example, has clearly been a deliberate military onslaught in the past four years to destabilise the emergence of a Palestinian state. Diplomatic initiatives such as the Road Map and President George W. Bush's other initiatives which were undertaken at the back of the late Arafat or with the deliberate isolation of Arafat, could not change the stark and horrifying state of abdication by the leadership of the South and Africa in particular, in confronting what has clearly been a new form of neo-colonialism against Palestine. The courage of Egypt and Jordan in recalling their Ambassadors at the height of Arafat's isolation manifested acts of unique and bold leadership. But which African countries did the same? In the case of Mwalimu Nyerere, even out of formal political leadership, he would have stood tall and firm against Sharon and all those that have prosecuted war mongerism and acts of violence against the Palestinian people.

Throughout his political life and leadership, Mwalimu Nyerere refused to accept any form of "imperial" or big brother leadership posture or culture. At the height of excellent Tanzania - China relations, at a Beijing State

Banquet in June 1968, Nyerere spoke, for the first time, of a relationship between *"unequal equals"*. Nyerere believed in and was committed to building and realising a shared vision of global solidarity in which mutual respect, trust, sovereign equality, peace, stability and prosperity thrived. Sovereign equality is the defining relationship of states irrespective of unequal size, military power and wealth. He rejected any notion of a "new liberal imperialism" where military might became the basis for global governance. He did so, in agreement with what Amartya Sen observed in his article titled, *Freedom's Market,* published in *The Observer.* UK) of 25 June, 2000, that there is "inequality of power, for which there is much less tolerance now than in the world that emerged at the end of the Second World War."

Nyerere was also circumspect about the realisation of the lofty ideal of North-South solidarity. Of course, as Africans, we are all hopeful about the NEPAD initiative. Some of the world leaders from rich nations are committed to the initiative. Nevertheless, it is important, as we celebrate the life of Mwalimu Nyerere, to recall the caution Nyerere made, in this context, in his address to the South African Parliament in October 1997. He said: "There is no internal urge in the US, in Europe or in Japan to help Africa. None. And, I think, to some extent, the urge of imperialism has gone. So you could be easily forgotten. Africa is of interest when we are killing one another. Then we arouse a lot of interest - *Africa is on its own - totally on its own"..* Emphasis added)

Africa is indeed largely on its own. The implications of this stark reality elude many African leaders. Nyerere always spoke of African nation-states as being "a creation of colonialism" and that their economic salvation lay in rising above such hangover *and be African.* The general belief is that Africa now has NEPAD, though still infant. However, and without appearing to be a pessimist, can Africa truly make NEPAD work? In other words, is there a clear resolve on the part of African leaders to marshal and galvanise Africa's public and private sector behind NEPAD? The World Economic Forum meeting in Durban in early June 2002 focused attention on this subject. The Second African Union Summit in Maputo in July 2003 also put significant attention on how to make NEPAD work effectively. Yet, one has the dreadful sense, informed by a looming, deep-seated perception on the ground, that Africa is yet to rise above its colonial legacy; namely that of a continent of nation-states. There is still mistrust all around. At the Algiers meeting of the NEPAD Steering Committee on the Peer Review Mechanism, in November, 2004, and at the Extraordinary AU Summit in Abuja late January/early February, 2005, a non issue about where the location of the NEPAD Secretariat now in South Africa should be and why it should not shift to Addis Ababa, ostensibly to integrate it in the AU Commission Secretariat, was a burning point of discussion and cause of unnecessary disunity. There seems to be little appreciation about the work being done by the NEPAD Secretariat and the Steering Committee in South Africa and with the enormous support extended to it by the South African government and above all that NEPAD is not an institution but a programme Thus, how could the mere location of NEPAD be considered so important, if it is not for cheap, divisive politics? Professor Onora O'Neill in her 2002 *BBC Reith Lectures* advises us in this context, "without trust we cannot stand." And Africa without trust, within itself, it surely cannot move ahead. Unfortunately, few African leaders seem to play surrogate to their ex-colonial masters. They close their eyes to African priorities and play to the tune of these latter countries and thereby undermining Africa's focus and direction.

So how does Africa build trust? How does it develop and ingrain the kind of trust that builds bridges across the several divides that now consume Africa and fuel racial, religious, ethnic and tribal divides? How does Africa make civil wars disappear, political power based on ethnicity become history, coups, even in small states like Sao Tome and Principe disappear? How does it make regional integration become another level of political liberation rather than a loss of national sovereignty? How can elections be held without rigging and corruption determining results? All these are questions that haunt Africa. They also haunt NEPAD and the lofty goals it stands to achieve.

In Tanzania, one sees how such state of mistrust is being ingrained and, unashamedly, done even by way of deception. Take the issue about South African investments. Some Tanzanian political leaders, intellectuals and the media have used deception to mislead ordinary Tanzanians about these investments. "Tanzania has been taken over by South Africans", they exclaim! You ask yourself, are these people honest and truthful about what they say or are they merely violently venting out their frustrated self-interests? Alternatively, and perhaps more importantly, are they patriotic Africans who understand and appreciate what Nyerere warned, "Africa is on its own - totally on its own".

It was Mwalimu Nyerere, as if already seized of such wave of deception and sheer ignorance, who, in his address to the South African Parliament in October 1997, said: "South Africa, because of its infrastructure, can attract more investment from Europe, from North America than Tanzania can, fine go ahead. Do it, use your capacity to get as much investment as you can. That's good. But then don't be isolated from the rest of Africa. What you build here because of your infrastructure and the relative strength of your economy, you are building for all of us here."

If such negative attitudes by a few amongst us persist, it is not Africa that would find itself on its own, it will be Tanzania. Tanzania should not fool itself about the potential of non-African foreign direct investment. The record of such investment flow into Africa is little and far between. In this context, on the occasion to mark the Tenth Anniversary of the joint venture between the Tanzania Government and South African Breweries on 6 November 2003, President Benjamin Mkapa correctly posited, "South Africans have an equal right as any other foreign investor in bidding for companies scheduled for privatisation, or in looking for opportunities for investment. It is unrealistic to expect that this government can put in place a mechanism to filter out South African investors. It is not only impractical: it is utterly unconscionable." It is precisely for this reason that NEPAD is viewed as part of the solution to Africa's deprivation and poverty. It is also why globalisation is increasingly under attack by the poor; not because they reject the importance of markets and of transfer of technology, skills and best practices, which globalisation is associated with, but rather because Africa cannot *confidently*, based on experience, expect the rich nations to help them adequately and sustainably.

This is what troubled Mwalimu Nyerere to the point of his being the leading advocate, not only of national, but also of collective self-reliance of the poor. In espousing the "trade union of the poor", Nyerere went beyond a call to arms by the poor world in confronting global inequality, in power and distribution of resources. He was also advocating the imperativeness of greater co-operation between and among poor nations. Yet some Tanzanians would dare insult South African investments and even use derogatory words like *"Makaburu"*. Boers) to describe the investors from South Africa. Tanzanians who are concerned about their development should seriously ask who are behind such machinations and whose interests do they serve? Mwalimu Nyerere would be restless where he lies if such people would lead Tanzania.

Chapter

5 MWALIMU NYERERE'S BIRTHDAY

So many worlds, so much to do,
So little done, such things to be,
How know I what had need of thee,
For thou wert strong as thou wert true?

Alfred Lord Tennyson: So Many Worlds, So Much to Do.

Celebrating birthdays is a kind of ritual to most people. It is an occasion of fun, joy and entertainment, especially for younger persons. It provides annual opportunities for people to renew friendships and develop new acquaintances. Mwalimu Nyerere began to celebrate his birthday, at least to the knowledge of the Tanzanian nation, only when he turned seventy-five, that is, in 1997. At his last birthday, on April 13, 1999, the usual drinking and being merry climaxed the birthday of Mwalimu. Yet Mwalimu Nyerere was no ordinary person, in life and in death. Celebration of his birthday should not be treated as an ordinary occasion for fun and joy. Tanzanians should celebrate the birthday of this great son of Tanzania, Africa and the poor South, in a fashion befitting and deserving his enormous contribution to a philosophy of political and economic independence and collective self-reliance for Tanzania and the poor world and to the quest for equity and equality in North-South relations.

Though Nyerere is dead, Tanzanians still identify him as their Father of the Nation. Yet this title is almost a cliché, especially to young Tanzanians. Mwalimu's birthday should therefore provide an annual occasion when Tanzanians should reflect on the life and role of the founder of independent Tanganyika, the co-architect of their Tanzania Union and a leading global figure in fighting for the rights of the oppressed, the colonised, and the poor. Indeed, Mwalimu Nyerere's birthday should be marked by a day of national reflection and re-dedication to the beliefs, the ideals, and the principles that Mwalimu articulated, symbolised and used to inspire and galvanise millions of Tanzanians to rise above self and build a peaceful, united and proud nation. Why, as a nation, should we celebrate Mwalimu's birthday with honour, pride and a sense of gratitude? John,

Stuart Mill once wrote, "One person with a belief is equal to a force of ninety-nine who have only interests." Mwalimu Nyerere should be remembered annually as a person who had a dream, a vision for Tanzania, who lived a life as a model of the vision that he enunciated and committed his life to its realisation. That vision was driven by several core beliefs that gave Tanzanians a sense of hope about a better future for them. At no time during his entire leadership of Tanzania and his own life did Nyerere depart from focusing on and adhering to his beliefs, largely captured in the Arusha Declaration.

In the Introduction to his book, *Freedom and Unity* in which Nyerere thought through the basic philosophy that underlined his guiding beliefs, Mwalimu argues that "social principles. such as love, sharing and work) are by definition, ideals at which to strive and by which to exercise self-criticism. The question to ask is not whether they are capable of achievement, which is absurd, but whether a society of free men can do without them." Put differently, Nyerere postulated that core values or principles stood the test of all time. They could be difficult to achieve, depending on obtaining circumstances, but their validity was not impaired by mere non-achievement. For example, some of the criticisms that levelled against Mwalimu Nyerere's development philosophies have missed this particular point. Nyerere's socialism as core values of society lives even when Tanzania embraces the market. Tanzanian society could not survive without them. What failed was the vehicle that used to realise those values that underlined Nyerere's socialist beliefs.

It is important to delve further into some of Nyerere's celebrated core beliefs. It is those beliefs that we must return to annually and re-dedicate ourselves. In my view, what stood out as Nyerere's foremost belief was integrity. Nyerere strongly believed that if the people felt that the leadership lacked integrity, then trust and, therefore, followership would evaporate. Integrity fed on trust and he underscored the imperativeness of the moral and social ethic. When debating the budget in Parliament in May 1960, before he became Chief Minister, he referred to corruption and bribery as "a greater enemy to the welfare of a people in peace time than war". Nyerere added that "if people cannot have confidence in their own government, if people can feel that justice can be bought, and then what hope are you leaving with the people? The only thing they can do is to take up arms and remove that silly government. They have no other hope."

Another aspect of the moral or social ethic that Nyerere stood for and which he advocated and fought for throughout his life was the equality of human beings, in their rights and duties as human beings and as citizens. In his December, 1962 President's Inaugural Address Nyerere reaffirmed that "It is the dignity and well being of all our people which is the beginning and the end of all our efforts. For the freedom we demanded was not mere independence from colonialism; what we sought was personal freedom for all the people of Tanganyika." Mwalimu decried divisions based on rulers and the ruled, rich and poor, educated and illiterate, and economically disadvantaged versus those living in idle comfort.

Through socialist ownership as an instrument of economic control and management, Nyerere believed that human dignity could best be realised. He was right in his ideal. Unfortunately, he was wrong in assuming the viability and robustness of the vehicle chosen for realising that belief. Even then, Tanzanians should give due credit to him for two important decisions that reflected the kind of leadership qualities Tanzanians should emulate. First, he was prepared to eat his own pride, after throwing the IMF out of Tanzania in 1981, by starting the economic liberalisation process in 1984. Second, he realised, by 1984, that Tanzania needed new leadership better able to try out new models of development but which would not destroy the core values that he believed in and worked hard to ingrain. He wanted to stand on the side and allow change to take its course and not be a burden. This is why he quit the Presidency in 1985.

A celebrated academic in the field of leadership, Warren Bennis, (1990), in his book *On Becoming A Leader* examined what distinguishes a leader from others. He wrote: "Competence or knowledge, without vision and virtue, breeds technocrats. Virtue, without mission and knowledge, breeds ideologues. Vision, without virtue and knowledge breeds demagogues." Where does Nyerere fit in this description? Neither. Nyerere was able to balance competence, vision and virtue. It is such attributes that enabled Nyerere to galvanise and inspire Tanzanians and win their reverence and support even when out of public office. It is such profound attributes that we must acclaim and celebrate as part of Nyerere's birthdays. However, there is another thing that many Tanzanians do not know about Mwalimu Nyerere. This is that leaders are not born, they are made. The key question is who makes them? The answer is themselves. The secret behind leadership development is self-learning. Mwalimu was the role model for all Tanzanians in continuous learning. To a good, effective and aspiring leader, knowledge is endless. Leaders pursue knowledge, to borrow Tennyson's stanza from the poem, Ulysses, "like a sinking star". Indeed, to cite Eric Hoffer, in the context of the modern era, "in a time of drastic change, it is the learners who inherit the future; the learned find themselves equipped to live in a world that no longer exists."
Without continuous learning, Nyerere would not have achieved the respectability that he enjoyed around the world as a global political leader and as an intellectual of the highest order. Thus, our leaders should be challenged to learn. To understand and master the nature of the dynamics

of global change and transformation, there could be no choice but for leaders to learn and learn all the time. Tanzanian youth, in particular, should be challenged to adopt reading as pleasure. Let Mwalimu Nyerere's birthday be a day dedicated to renewing a national commitment to learning as a continuous process and as a basis for improving the quality of national leadership and the quality of national response to the challenges that confront Tanzania at the individual and the collective level.

Finally, Tanzanians should celebrate not only Mwalimu Nyerere's vision but also, and more importantly, his determined and confident approach to staying a course that he believed in. Mwalimu was never afraid to take risks and make mistakes. He was always bold and courageous. The height of such leadership style was reflected when he asked the Embassy of the Federal Republic of Germany. FRG) to pack up and leave Tanzania in 1966 upon the threat by the FRG government to withdraw aid to Tanzania after Tanzania recognised the then German Democratic Republic. GDR). In his Memorandum to the then TANU, Tanzania's sole political party before its merger with Zanzibar's Afro-Shirazi Party in 1977, Nyerere wrote that Tanzania could either accept "dictation" from West Germany and thus be its "puppet state" and continue to receive economic aid, or it could maintain its principles and suffer loss of aid. He concluded that it was better to be poor than to be a rich slave. The lesson is that leaders should, all the time, be led by an overarching purpose, principle and vision. That should not mean that leaders be inflexible. On the contrary, as Nyerere himself admitted, whilst goals are sacrosanct, the way to achieve them need not be. Tanzania would sometimes have to run "straight ahead and fighting through obstacles; at other times it will mean manoeuvring to find a better and easier way through", so wrote Nyerere in his essay, *Principles and Development*.

What lessons do we draw from this style of leadership? Recent experience indicates that external forces are driving many leaders to the point that few actually lead their economies independently. Evidently, we live in a more troubled and unsettling world; an environment that is ever reshaping itself and changing in complex ways. Such a world demands a different leadership style from that of Nyerere. This is fine. However, it should still be acknowledged that what would profoundly propel a leader's chance of successfully confronting the global and domestic economic tumult is the ability to craft a compelling vision of the type that Nyerere developed and then move on to sustain it. The trust and commitment of the people rests on the existence of a compelling vision. Departure from it can erode such trust. Little wonder that Mwalimu Nyerere, even in death, continues to command so much respect of the Tanzanian people. It is because they still believe in his vision and the core social values he upheld that Tanzania continues to be a proud nation. This is also the reason why Tanzanians should celebrate Nyerere's birthday rather than mourn his death. It is regrettable that the government declared the day of his death rather than his birthday a public holiday. The decision deserves revision.

Chapter

6 NOBEL PEACE PRIZE: FOR WHAT PEACE?

As we embark upon this new century, for the Nobel Prizes and for the world, let us do everything in our power to make it a century of generosity, humility and tolerance, of solidarity, compassion and respect. It is my hope that the Nobel Prize in this new century will continue to recognise these values and the actions that flow from them, and thus continue to give support to people who are struggling to bring light into a world that at times seems very dark indeed.

-Oscar Arias: *The World and the Nobel Peace Prize in the 21st Century: Old and New Dimensions,* December 8, 2001.

For sometime now, I have been concerned and critical about the underlying factors that inform the decisions of the Norwegian Nobel Committee on whom to award the most distinguished prize in the world - the Nobel Peace Prize. Evidently, it is often difficult not to accept the choice made. After all, we live in a world that is often afflicted by tension, conflict and instability. It is these events, these social and political conditions, unfolding and invariably in an evolving state of flux, that appear to attract the greater attention of the Nobel Committee. Such events shape the direction of the decisions taken.

Those who have earned the Peace Prize have deserved the acknowledgement of their efforts, their commitment and even of the dangers that they have often faced as they have pursued the goal of peace. They are people who have played pivotal and frontal roles in brokering peace. In some cases, they have directly been a part of the peace making effort itself. Mandela and de Clerk, Arafat, Peres and Rabin, were, indeed, part of both a conflict and part of the peace effort. They were responsible for a protracted war as well as of the peace that ensued.

Of course, in the case of South Africa we could proudly speak of a final peace - an end to the guerrilla war and the apartheid system. South Africa is now a truly democratic, non-racial nation. The same could not be said of the Israel - Palestine quagmire. Arafat, Peres and Rabin created the foundation and the path for realising durable peace and stability in their region. Their predecessors, Henry Kissinger and Anwar Sadat won the

Peace Prize for the Camp David Peace Initiative - much less of a peace realisation really, with the benefit of hindsight. More recently, in 1998, the Nobel Peace Prize was awarded to Northern Ireland political leaders, Mr. Hume and Mr. Trimble for their role in enabling a process - a complex process - towards peace to take concrete shape. However, peace is yet to be fully realised in Northern Ireland in terms of its end objective, namely the final resolution of the political future of Northern Ireland. Obviously, in pursuing such a critical approach about the manner in which the Peace Prizes are awarded, it is not my intention to belittle the arduous and onerous tasks and the work that goes into kick starting peace processes or enabling peace to be finally achieved wherever that occurs. Getting political opponents to talk is an achievement in itself, as it happened in Zanzibar over the *Muafaka*. Clearly, those who make such breakthroughs should be honoured.

Evidently, the Norwegian Nobel Committee has a strict if narrow definition of peace and of the criteria used to recognise someone as deserving the award of the Nobel Peace Prize. This is the very question I wish to tackle, notwithstanding the 2004 apparent departure in honouring the Kenyan Green Belt Movement leader, Wangari Maathai. The burden of my argument is that the term 'peace' should be given meaning that recognises its broad character. Recognition should be given to those individuals who have openly and tirelessly worked to create the conditions that nurture and cherish peace, people who have succeeded in assuring durable peace, in their societies and nations.

It appears to me, with due respect to the distinguished Norwegian Nobel Committee, that to focus attention only on those who prevail in conflict situations overlooks the importance of work that goes into creating the circumstances that inhibit instability and conflict in the first place. At present, it is as if conflict and war are given some kind of recognition, as inevitabilities, if you will, whose resolution should be rewarded for. Surely, peace is not God endowed or created. People, as individuals, create peace. Indeed, they often create peace, and durable peace at that, by confronting all kinds of dangers and challenges through resolving and removing the adverse conditions and systems that potentially fuel and fertilise conflict.

Today, instability rules in South Africa. Violent crime is threatening the very peace that Mandela and de Clerk worked for and achieved. Nevertheless, what South Africa achieved in 1994, was, in reality, a "political settlement" that destroyed and buried apartheid. A peace ushered in a new political dispensation of racial equality and political pluralism. The challenge, more formidable, however, is how the South African leadership would achieve post - apartheid peace. Herein lies the main point of this discussion. The Nobel Committee appears overly focused, in its Peace Prize awards, on the "political" side of peace, not on the social dimensions of peace.

Interestingly, the 1998 Nobel Prize for Economics was awarded to the Indian academic Amartya Sen for his work on welfare economics that focused on famine and poverty issues. In most developing countries, questions that relate to addressing poverty reflect a deeper connection to peace and stability. Somebody once wrote, "Hunger is rage in the belly." But Professor Sen's Prize was for economics, not for peace. The resulting question is why is it that the Nobel Committee has not so far awarded, to the best of my knowledge, the Peace Prize to a person or persons who have worked for promoting peace in their societies in ways other than resolving conflicts? In other words, should peace prizes not be awarded for actual peace, real peace?

I believe that it would not have been as satisfying to Tanzanians to witness, for example, Mwalimu Julius Nyerere being awarded the Nobel Peace Prize for brokering peace in the ethnically war-torn Burundi than in his being awarded such a Prize for creating a firm foundation for a peaceful and stable Tanzania. Tanzania is truly a model and a citadel of durable peace, a haven of peace. And it is a country where refugees also find a home and even new citizenship. It is a country in the forefront in promoting peace in troubled neighbouring countries, the Great Lakes region as a whole.

Tanzania did not achieve such state of peace and stability on a platter, like manna from heaven. Nyerere worked for it, right from the on-set of political independence in December 1961. His initial action to abolish tribal chiefdoms was a bold and courageous step. It was a risky decision that could easily have sparked off resistance and instability. In political management, Nyerere's governance style was driven by the quest to unify the country across the tribal, racial and religious divides. He deliberately ensured that his government leadership characterised such unity.

At the economic level, on the other hand, Nyerere saw capitalism, in a predominantly poor country, as a serious source of social stratification and a potential cause of tension and conflict. He viewed the wealth divide along racial lines as a time bomb, which over time, would explode with disastrous impact on national peace and stability. Thus, the economic measures that he unleashed in the form of "Ujamaa" were directed at building a society that would be at peace with itself.

To-day, Tanzania has strong roots of peace and stability. So strong are the roots that the convulsive market policies presently being implemented are embraced by the people without some of the destabilising consequences normally experienced elsewhere in Africa. Nyerere was the architect of this state of peace and order. The central question then is: is this not the kind of peace that the Norwegian Nobel Committee would also consider for awarding the Peace Prize? In how many parts of the world, especially developing countries, would you find Tanzania's kind and level of peace and Tanzania's zealous contribution to forging peace to others?

The Norwegian Nobel Committee should re-think its concept of peace and the criteria it uses to award the Nobel Peace Prize. My hope is that people like Mwalimu Julius Nyerere would be rewarded with the recognition for having being responsible for creating the foundations for durable peace to thrive in their societies.

Part two

THE RADICAL TRANSFORMATION

The courses of action open to us can be discerned. And so can those, which, however popular, will be futile, if not counterproductive. The realities are different from the issues on which politicians, economists, scholars, businessmen, union leaders, still fix their attention... The convincing proof of this is the profound sense of unreality, which characterizes so much of today's politics and today's economics.

-Peter F. Drucker: *The New Realities.*

Chapter

7 OVERVIEW OF PROGRESS AND CHALLENGES

The radical decision is usually the right one. The right decision is usually the hardest one. And the hardest decisions are often the least popular at the time. We are at our best when we are at our boldest.

-Tony Blair: *Labour Party Conference, October 2002.*

In this overview, I outline some of the salient features of the social, political and economic transformations that have taken place in Tanzania since the commencement of economic reforms in 1986 and political reforms in 1992 underlining key achievements so far realised and putting forward selected challenges that continue to confront the country and which require attention in the days ahead. At the heart of this overview, is the point that Tanzania can realise beneficial change and development where there is boldness in leadership to take right decisions even when seemingly unpopular and where leaders are able to discern that we live in a brave new world where there is discontinuous change and that new realities are ever unfolding.

Since 1986, Tanzania has experienced a gradual but radical change in its social, political and economic systems and policies. The country has seen the lives of the people affected in different ways. Their values, beliefs and relationships have come under serious pressure and are in a state of flux. The driving force behind these changes is the on-set of the new world economic order which is shaped, on the one hand, by globalisation- the ascendancy of a fundamentalist market ideology, and, on the other hand, by a wave of liberal democracy. This brave new world has been catapulted by two main factors. First, the collapse of communism in 1989, an event that marked what many regard as the failure of the ideology of the one party political system and of the socialist, planned economic system. Second, the unprecedented expansion and dominance of multinational and transnational companies in global trade, largely powered by breakthroughs in information and communications technologies and by the opening up of global markets. The *World Investment Report, 2002*, the Report of the United Nations Conference on Trade and Development. UNCTAD), shows that 65,000 parent transnational and multinational companies had more than 850,000 subsidiaries and affiliates around the world, employing 54 million people. More than 50,000 of these parent companies were located in developing countries. It is also noteworthy that the sales of the subsidiaries and affiliates alone, in 2001, were US$19 trillion, in other words, more than twice as high as total world exports in 2001.

These changes emerged at a time when Tanzanian policies and outlook, from both political and economic angles, were still rooted in socialism and a system of political oligarchy. It would be recalled that for many years, especially between the mid 1960s and the mid 1980s, Tanzania was the African citadel of the one party political system and of African socialism. *Ujamaa*). In 1965, the one party political system was legislated. The socialist system, on the other hand, was promulgated in February 1967 following the adoption of the Arusha Declaration. This Declaration was a blueprint for Tanzania's socialist development as well as a vision of the new society Tanzania desires to construct.

Tanzania's experience as a one party state and as a socialist economy has been widely recorded with different perspectives and ideological discourses. It is not my intention to re-state those different positions, though in various sections of this book, I attempt to examine and analyse them. Suffice it to state, at this juncture, that Tanzania has not been insulated from the impact of political and economic global changes that have often been dislocating, particularly in the early 1980's. These global changes continue to influence the political and economic direction of Tanzanian-type polities. In this overview part, I broadly examine how Tanzania has confronted the challenges of transforming its fragile economy and making it more vibrant and robust. Central issues relating to how the process of radical transformation has been managed are scrutinised, pointing out the key progress made, achievements realised and the challenges that lie ahead. I also examine the political challenges as an introduction to what is later analysed in greater depth.

Economic Reforms

In the 1970s, the World Bank and external donors, especially the Scandinavian welfare states, Netherlands, Germany and the United Kingdom, largely underwrote the Tanzanian socialist model of development. However, that model came under intense pressure in the early to mid 1980s. As a result, Tanzania was put under enormous pressure to reform radically, as confidence in the efficacy and effectiveness of the state enterprise-driven economic system eroded, leading to serious aid fatigue on the part of donors. Tanzania's own efforts to pursue a self-reliant economic structural adjustment strategy between 1981 and 1984 faced daunting challenges given the backdrop of a costly war against the invasion of Tanzania by Uganda's Idi Amin army in 1978/79, the second oil price shock in 1979 and the end of the global coffee price boom in 1978.

In this light, an internally driven and financed restructuring of an economy whose growth had become negative and whose treasury was largely empty proved to be an exercise in futility. Admittedly, the internally generated reforms undertaken did not seek to dismantle the state enterprise system, a system largely responsible for devouring scarce resources and undermining the market incentives that were necessary to spur economic growth. Naturally, and with the advantage of change in the top leadership, following Mwalimu Julius Nyerere's retirement as President in October 1985, Tanzania woke up to confront new economic realities with greater boldness and an open mind. The adoption of an *Economic Recovery Programme. ERP)* in June 1986 supported by the International Monetary Fund. IMF), the World Bank and donor countries, marked the beginning in the turn of events for the Tanzanian economy. Through the ERP, the process of dismantling the socialist economic system and building a new market-driven economy was put into gear.

Between mid 1986 and presently, Tanzania's economic reforms have encountered several difficulties. In a spate of literature written by astute economists, nationals and foreigners, these reforms have been examined and critiqued. Thus, I need not belabour this area. Moreover, Tanzania has continued to be a fertile ground for debate about the character, process and the costs and benefits of a market economic system that is evolving. There are Tanzanian academics like Issa Shivji and Seithy Chachage who hold the view that Tanzania has become a surrogate economy, a neo-colony, so to speak. They contend that Tanzania has lost the capacity for self-reliance and the viability to stand on its own feet. To them, arguments put forward by political leaders about how best to confront economic realities like globalisation are nothing but a surrogate submission to an imperialistic conventional wisdom socked into the throats of poor nations. In a recent think piece titled, *"Tanzania: What Kind Of Country Are We Building?* Professor Shivji postulates that national consensus in Tanzania cannot be built "on the basis of imported or imposed metapolitical values of political pluralism and hedonistic individualism." He sees a new material reality in place characterised by "extreme class and social divisions". Professor Chachage, on the other hand, in a political satire entitled, *"Makuadi wa Soko Huria".* The Pimps of the Market Economy), tells a story of how the Tanzanian economy and resources have been hijacked and plundered by the local bourgeoisie in cohort with foreigners and of the insidious tyranny embedded in the market economy. The trouble with such views is that they offer no plausible and viable alternatives in the context of global new realities. In contrast, whilst Tanzania has not been able to reverse income poverty levels, the reforms it has effected, especially in the last decade, have realised significant achievements in stabilising the macro-economic fundamentals and in putting the economy on a growth trajectory. I examine these achievements in various sections of this book.

In Part three of the book, I examine the process of economic reform from the standpoint of the Annual Budgets and Finance Acts that the government effected from fiscal year 1997/1998. Whilst the reform programme commenced in June 1986, it is from financial year 1997/1998 that Tanzania *seriously* began to take great leaps forward in pursuing bold and radical economic reforms, including privatisation. It is through the Budgets and the Finance Acts that one is able to sift the extent and depth of reforms. The reforms have covered fiscal reform, reform of the taxation regime and putting in place structures for improving tax collection and administration. They have also covered the following broad areas:

domestic debt management and management of the fiscal deficit through controlling expenditure, introduction of mechanisms for more effective financial management and control, reduction of inflation, creation of a more conducive environment for promoting domestic and attracting foreign investments, bolstering domestic investment and opening up the economy to competition, establishment of robust regulatory systems and structures, and introduction of measures to protect the domestic industry as it adjusted to a new market environment.

Macro-economic Achievements

The macro economic achievements as at June 2005 were most commendable and should be celebrated. Real GDP growth of 6.7% was the highest achieved since the on-set of economic reforms in 1986. The brief setback recorded in fiscal year 2003/2004 when GDP growth declined to 5.6% was a result of two consecutive years of serious drought that affected agricultural productivity. On the other hand, overall inflation, at 32.5% in 1994, drastically declined to 4.0% in June 2005. What is significant to observe is that the high-level inflation rate reached in 1994, almost a decade since the on-set of economic reforms, is explained by serious reverses in macro-economic policy stability in the period between 1991 and 1995. Such macro-economic mal-performances underline the imperativeness of sustaining prudent and sound economic policies notwithstanding short-term hardships that resultantly impinge on the people. Revenue growth per month, on the other hand, increased from Shs.25 billion in 1995 to Shs.160 billion in February, 2005 largely due to the good performance of *Value Added Tax. VAT),* introduced in July 1997, and to improved tax administration. Average monthly collection for fiscal year 2004/05 was Shs 145 billion. It is important to note though, that as a percentage of GDP, the revenue yield only slightly shot up from 12.6% in 1997 to 13.4 % in 2004. Tanzania is thus still far from achieving self-reliance, even in its finances, since 41 % of its budget, as at June 2005, remained dependent on external aid. External grants and concessional loans to Tanzania increased from Shs. 187 billion in 1995/96 to Shs. 1.7 trillion in 2005. However, Tanzania's external debt burden, of some US$ 7.9 billion in April 2004 remains a serious impediment to the country's quest to achieve self-reliance, this notwithstanding that under HIPC Tanzania has benefited from debt cancellation amounting to Shs. 1.3 trillion which would span a period of 20 years. In this context, the reports emanating from the G8 Finance Ministers' Meeting in London in June, 2005 that Tanzania is one of 18 poor countries that would have its total multilateral debt. owed to the IMF, the World Bank and the African Development Bank) cancelled may be manna from heaven. This was ratified by the G8 Summit at Gleneagles, Scotland in July 2005. The overall debt in question has a face value of around US$ 40 billion. Its cancellation would remove an average debt service payment of about US$ 1.0 to 1.5 billion annually for all the countries affected put together.

However, as poor countries celebrate what such debt cancellation may hold for them in tackling abject poverty, the emergence of an oil shock poses serious challenges. A report of the International Energy Agency released in the fourth week of August 2005 estimates that the oil prices which hover around US$ 65 per barrel would cost African economies US$ 10.5 billion a year, which is more than ten times the benefit of the debt relief that the G8 Geneagles Summit approved. In other words, for poor nations, the struggle for economic emancipation and making poverty history continues. It is for this reason that the poor nations like Tanzania have to search for more sustainable ways to address their economic condition.

Performance in the area of foreign exchange reserves, which stood at US$ 2.1 billion as at December 2004, has been particularly noteworthy. In months of imports of goods and services, these reserves have risen from 1.6 months in 1995 to 8.3 months at the end of March 2005. This cover has declined to 7.0 months in June 2005. What raises concern, however, is the state of Tanzania's exports. Tanzania's trade balance registered a deficit of US$ 948.2 million in 2004 compared to US$ 804.2 million in 2003. The decline is reflected in the poor performance of exports. Total merchandise exports have risen from US$ 682.9 million in 1995 to only US$ 1,333.5 million as at June 2004. Out of this figure, non-traditional exports accounted for US$ 1,042.2 million. However, US$ 686.5 million or 65.87.0% of these exports represents gold exports alone. Therefore much has to be done to boost exports of manufactured goods and traditional exports in particular. In 2004, traditional exports stood at a paltry US$ 292.3 million. The upsurge in tourism and its contribution to export receipts is a shot in the arm for Tanzania's economic fortunes thanks to an improved investment environment the government has put in place since 1998. Official figures show that as at June, 2004, tourism contributed 16% of GDP and brought into Tanzania close to US$ 700 million. However, the earnings figure is problematic. Surely, if that much was earned from tourism alone, then the figure for non-traditional exports should be much higher than US$ 947.0 billion. Nevertheless, according to an IMF Working Paper published in February 2005 by Volker Treichel titled *Tanzania's Growth Process and Success in Reducing Poverty*, receipts from tourism rose from US$ 65 million in 1990 to only US$ 446 million in 2003.

Nevertheless, much remains to be done to give the tourism sector greater competitive advantage *vis a vis* competing countries in the region, notably Kenya, Zimbabwe and South Africa. The first Tourism Investment Forum ever held in Tanzania took place in Arusha at the end of 2002 and President Benjamin Mkapa addressed it. It is critical to continue to engage investors at special forums like this one and to openly discuss ways and means to promote their confidence and thereby bolster investments. Agriculture is one key sector that cries out aloud for serious commercial investment. Lately, especially since 2001, the government has begun to direct greater attention to this key sector. Thus, the fiscal incentives extended to investments made in agriculture and related sectors, as embodied in the Finance Act, 2004, reflect the government's serious resolve at bolstering agricultural production and productivity.

For a country like Tanzania, with limited domestic capital for investment, higher economic growth and the creation of jobs heavily depends on inward investment. In the tourism industry, for example, more investments in hotels and lodges as well as in infrastructure, especially railways, airports and roads, are necessary if tourists that are more discerning would visit Tanzania's world famous wildlife parks and historic sites. Arguably, since 1997, there have been serious and well thought out policies and measures taken to promote Tanzania as an economy of choice for foreign direct investment. FDI). Thus, FDI has grown from US$150.8 million in 1995 to US$ 260.2 million in 2004. Between 1997 and 2002, Tanzania attracted almost US$1.0 billion in FDI making it one of sub-Saharan Africa's leading investment destinations. However, gold is now making a higher contribution to export receipts, largely because of the higher gold prices in the global market, especially since late 2002. Since 1998, following the Mining Investment Forum held in Arusha in 1997 and the enactment of the Mining Act in 1998, mining has constituted the single largest sector for FDI in Tanzania. This sector grew by 15% in 2002 and its contribution to GDP in 2003 stood at 3.0%. Total investment, as a percentage of GDP, increased from 14.7% in 1997 to 18.5% in 2003. These significant investments have been largely catalysed by the legislative restructuring of the organisation responsible for investment promotion, giving birth to the Tanzania Investment Centre. TIC) in mid 1997. Since 1998, TIC has been able to build capacity and insight, learning from other more successful experiences, and undertaking well-planned and executed investment promotion programmes in Tanzania and around the world. Between 1990 and December 2003, TIC approved 2,527 investment projects that created an estimated 497,539 jobs. 44.0 % of the projects are owned by Tanzanians, 24% are foreign owned whilst 32. % are jointly owned jointly between locals and foreigners. It is also noteworthy that in 2001 President Mkapa established an Investors' Roundtable, for both foreign and domestic investors. The Roundtable meets annually to exchange views about how best to promote Tanzania as an investment destination embracing different sectors of the economy. The 5th Roundtable met in May, 2005.

Several other economic achievements have also been made in recent years. However, what stands out is the privatisation policy and programme. As at the end of December 2004, Tanzania had privatised 312 state owned enterprises, about 82% of the total, and 499 non-core assets. The perception that the Tanzanian leadership has sold almost all state-owned assets to foreigners is not correct. 160 privatised companies have in fact been sold to Tanzanian citizens. 16 of which under the management and workers buy-out scheme or MEBO). Only 24 companies were sold to foreign investors directly and 128 were sold under a joint venture arrangement involving foreign investors, the government and Tanzanian investors. 407 no-core assets were sold in the open market, whilst 47 companies were liquidated under the Loans and Advances Realisation Trust. LART). There are clear benefits that accrued to the country from privatisation. Suffice it to cite one lucid example of Tanzania Breweries. At the time of its privatisation in 1993, the pre-tax profit of this company was Shillings 11.03 billion, the equivalent of US$ 24.4 million, at the exchange rate ruling at that time of Shillings 450 to one US$. In 2004, net profit after tax profits was Shillings 44 billion or US$ 40 million at the ruling exchange rate of Shillings 1100 to one US$. This excellent performance should equally be viewed from the perspective that the shilling was heavily overvalued in 1993 in contrast to the position in 2004, thus not reflecting the true value of earnings at the time of privatisation. At the same time, the performance has had huge multiplier effect in the economy. For example, barley farming whose productivity drastically declined between the early and late 1990s has seen significant improvement in recent years. Increase in the production of beer has also created thousands of jobs largely benefiting small and informal business sectors.

Reform and Poverty Reduction

The adoption of the Poverty Reduction Strategy Paper. PRSP) in September 2000 enabled Tanzania to fulfil the conditions that entitled it to debt relief under the enhanced Highly Indebted Poor Countries. HIPC) Initiative. Between financial year 2002/2003 and March 2003, debt relief amounted to shillings 80.0 billion up from Shillings 46.0 billion in 2001/2002. It is through such debt relief that the government has been able to begin to address non-income poverty more determinedly. It is important to give this debt relief the objective picture it deserves because there have been consistent criticisms in the Tanzania media, civil society and academia that economic reforms have not improved the lives of ordinary Tanzanians. Such concerns and criticisms deserve objective responses. According to the Household Budget Survey of 2000/01, the proportion of Tanzanians below the national food poverty line is 18.7%. On the other hand, Tanzanians below the national basic needs poverty line is a high of 35.7%. However, nominal national per capita income has risen from US$ 161.0 in June 1990 to US$ 277.0 in January 2003 in real terms. What is disturbing is that Tanzania's external debt burden at almost US$ 8 billion in 2004 continues to constitute a serious bottleneck to the achievement of sustainable economic growth.

As for criticism levelled at the mismatch between macro-economic performance and improved livelihood of the people, it is important to point out that for economic reforms to improve the livelihood of the people it is essential that the fundamentals of the economy be put right first. Though the reforms commenced in 1986, prudent and predictable economic reforms started, in effect, in 1997. For example, the serious economic reversals that Tanzania suffered in the period 1991-1995 almost totally undermined the gains that had been achieved between 1986 and 1990. Clearly, the lesson here is that persistence in upholding difficult reforms is a virtue and that building is often more complex than destroying. With such policy improvements, Tanzania is now beginning to see a major shift in resource allocations, targeting those sectors that directly affect the welfare of the people, especially the poor and the vulnerable. In fiscal year 2001/2002 alone, the primary education sector, under the framework of the Primary Education Development Plan, saw its budgetary allocations increase by 29.4% or 2.2% GDP. As a result, there has been a dramatic increase in the enrolment in primary schools. standard one to seven as a whole) in Tanzania Mainland from 4.2 million in 2000 to 6.5 million in 2003. The gross enrolment ratio reached 105.3% in 2003. Improvement of basic education has clearly taken the centre stage of economic and social reform.

Poverty reduction under the PSRP ended in June 2003. Effective July 2005, the government has introduced a new five year National Strategy for Growth and Reduction of Poverty. (NSGRP). The NSGRP was tabled before the National Assembly in April 2005 for debate, as it should be. Various stakeholders in the social milieu had also earlier debated the Strategy Programme. The strategy will end in 2009/10. It is significant to note that in the preparation of the NSGRP, the Development Vision 2025, the National Poverty Reduction Strategy. (NPRS), 2010 and the targets set by the MDGs by 2015 were taken on board. The central features of the NSGRP are:

- maintaining macro-economic stability.
- promotion of economic growth to reach 8.0% of GDP by 2010.
- increasing domestic revenue to reach 15.5% of GDP by 2008/09.
- scaling up investments towards SMEs and large scale agriculture and agro-processing.
- promoting jobs creation by supporting fast growing sectors such as tourism and mining.
- containing external debt to GDP ratio at 50% or less by 2010.
- reducing budget and other external support from 11.0% of GDP in 2004/05 to 8.6% in 2007/08.
- increasing food crop production from 9.0 million tons in 2003/04 to 12 million tons in 2010.
- reducing the proportion of rural population below the basic needs poverty line from 38.6% in 2000/01 to 24% by 2010, and food poverty line from 27% to 14% in the same period.
- reducing the proportion of urban population below the basic needs poverty line from 25.8% in 2000/01 to 12.9% by 2010 and below the food poverty line from 13.2% to 6.6% in the same period.
- improving accessibility to health services such that household to be within five kilometres of health service unit.
- reducing number of illiterate adults from 3.8 million in 2004/05 to 1.8 million in 2007/08.
- ensuring that at least 80% of adults, especially women in rural areas are literate by 2010.
- enrolling at least 50% of boys and girls aged 14-17 in ordinary level secondary schools by 2010.
- increasing proportion of rural population with access to clean and safe water from 53% in 2003 to 80% and for urban population from 73% to 90%, by 2010.
- reducing infant mortality from 95 in 2002 to 50 in 2010 per 1,000 live births.
- Arrest the spread of HIV and Aids and render effective health support to those afflicted by the pandemic.

The implementation vehicle of the NSGRP, structured within the overall framework of the Tanzania Development Vision 2025, will be the formulated Tanzania Mini-Tiger Plan 2020. The Plan, which is inspired by the experiences of the Asian tiger economies, encapsulates three main planks:

- Improving the climate and conditions for promoting domestic and foreign investments through the establishment of Special Economic Zones. SEZs) which will have adequate supporting infrastructure.
- Improving the legal and regulatory framework.
- Promoting the SEZs around the world with a view to bolstering investments.

The importance attached to labour intensive industries, especially textiles and garments as well as gemstones and wood products which would enjoy readily available raw materials, tourism and agriculture, within the SEZ concept, is timely.

Education is Key

Evidently, a central challenge in reducing poverty and in promoting sustainable economic development generally lies in addressing weaknesses in the education sector. The challenge, on the one hand, is to increase the percentage in enrolment for pupils in the age group from 7 to 13 years, which, though up from 58.8% in 2000 to 88.5% in 2003, it is still below regional standards, and, on the other hand, to upgrade the quality of teachers' education. Improvements in standards of education in Tanzania crucially hinge on improved education delivery in the classroom. At present, the teachers' education system is dogged by limited facilities, low quality of teachers, devastating impact of HIV/AIDS, limited and largely poor quality intake of would be teachers as good students always aspire to proceed for tertiary education, poor living conditions of teachers in school environments, both in urban and rural areas, and low salaries. In a paper for the Copenhagen Consensus project, written by Harvard Professor Lant Pritchett, a reference of which is made in *The Economist* of April 22nd 2004 it is pointed out that "what is the point of `universal enrolment` if schools and teachers are unable to provide a decent education?" It is important for countries like Tanzania that are now allocating significant sums of money into bolstering enrolment at primary school level to evaluate the value realised from such investments. The educational deficit could not be reduced by simply increasing enrolment. That would be too simplistic an expectation. It is schools with good quality teaching that have to be worked for.

Another challenge is the current extremely low intake of primary school leavers into secondary schools due to inadequate numbers of secondary schools. Much as the enrolment in secondary schools has increased by 120.3% between 1995 and 2004, the transition rate on the other hand from primary to secondary school has only gone up from 14.6% to 30.1%. As at June 2003, there were only 893 O'level secondary schools, of which 569 were government and 324 private, including seminaries and 190 A'level secondary schools, of which 80 were government and 110 were private. This is an area of serious inadequacy demanding the urgent intervention of public-private partnership at its best. It is shown in the Ministry of Education Basic Statistics in Education publication of June 2003, that, two years after independence, in 1963, the percentage of primary school leavers entering secondary education was 29.2%. That percentage declined into single digits between 1977 and 1987. It is only since 1996 that the percentage started to climb again. In 2002, it stood at 21.7%, still a far cry from the standards achieved in neighbouring countries like Kenya and Uganda. The present Secondary Education Development Plan. SEDP) envisages increasing this proportion of students transiting to secondary education from 22% in 2002 to 50% by 2010. The success of this ambitious programme hinges on external support. During fiscal year 2004/2005, the World Bank extended to Tanzania a total of US$ 150 million in soft loan and grant. US$ 123.6 million as loan payable over 40 years with 10 years grace period at low interest rate and US$ 26.10 million as grant) to support SEDP.

A key component of this programme is the reduction of fees payable by students studying in day public secondary schools by 50% that is from Shs 40,000 to Shs. 20,000 per student per annum with effect from January 2005. The Minister for Education, in his Ministry's Budget Speech for fiscal year 2004/2005, pronounced this objective. The government will cough up the differential in fees as a subsidy. However, it remains vague how the transition rate from primary to secondary education would increase from the mere lowering of fees given that public secondary schools are few as opposed to a major injection of public funds and the promotion of private sector investment in secondary education. For example, over 6000 students who passed Form Four examinations in 2005 could not obtain admission into Form Five due to lack of adequate facilities. In addition, there is the more onerous challenge of how to improve the quality of secondary education when the primary education "raw material" suffers from a serious quality malaise. Evidently improving teacher training is proving to be a matter of major concern necessitating urgent attention. Equally important is the challenge to renew attention in addressing the state of illiteracy. Presently, about 28.6% of Tanzanians cannot read and write in any language. 36% of them are women. Clearly, the capacity to respond to challenges of poverty and development, particularly in rural areas, hinges a great deal on bringing about quick and massive improvement in literacy levels, especially among girls and women. Equally important and urgent is the need to expand technical and especially vocational training institutions around then country. It is this kind of education that would crucially unlock the entrepreneurial potential for economic empowerment and self development. Current data shows that enrolment in technical institutions increased by a mere 11% between 1995 and 2004.

Social Action Fund

The poverty reduction goal is also directed at how to improve income levels of the poor. In this context, a notable development participatory programme targeting poverty reduction has been underpinned through the creation of the Tanzania Social Action Fund. TASAF). The World Bank, through a concessional loan of US$ 60 million, supported this Fund during the first phase. In November 2004, the World Bank extended another credit of US$ 129 million and a grant of US$ 21.0 million for the second phase. Through TASAF, the people in rural areas are able to determine their own needs in social services such as sanitation, water supply, feeder roads, classrooms, teachers' houses, health facilities, agricultural seed nurseries etc. 87% of the Fund reached the grassroots as at June 2003. The funding is projects-focused with only a minor fraction of it extended towards administration. The challenge is how to make the Fund sustainable, in other words making it significantly non-dependent on the World Bank and the donors. This means that the private sector in Tanzania would have to play a bigger role in supporting the Fund. Such corporate philanthropy would go down well with the less endowed in society and thereby provide greater legitimacy to private sector role in the economy at a time when the state is taking a different role from the hitherto dominant one of being the lead provider of social services. I am reminded, in this context, of what Charles Dickens wrote in the novel, *Hard Times*: "The whole moral is that capitalists should be kind, not that workers should be rebellious."

Building Government Capacity

Macro-economic achievements have also much to do with the performance of the government itself. Thus, to improve the capacity of the government, efforts began in 1992 to restructure public services and address the capacity deficit of the central and local government system. There has been a 30% reduction of the workforce from 335,000 in 1992/1993 to 260,000 in 1999/2000. The wages of public servants in turn have increased by 75% from Shs. 12,000 in 1992 to Shs. 54,000 in 1997. In the 2002/2003 Budget, wages were put up by 15.5%. Salary adjustment appears to be of continuous character as reflected in the Budget Speeches of the Ministry responsible for public service for financial years 2003/2004 and 2004/2005.

There are also attempts to improve the capacity and effectiveness of human resources in the public service. It is not clear though how the government is going to train its key staff in public management in the absence of specialised training institutions catering specifically for this requirement, the type that you find in the United Kingdom and the United States. Clearly, it is time that the government seriously considers to create Polytechnics of the type that the UK had for many years most of which have since become Universities in their own right. Paradoxically, though, there is now a move to introduce e-government. Of course, given the emergence of information and communications technologies. ICTs), it is critical that such tools and systems drive the operations of and decision-making in the government. The wide geographical spread of Tanzania with the attendant poor transport infrastructure justifies that ICTs become the strategic vehicles for bolstering improved decision making and getting many government services online for the citizens capable to access them to benefit from them. In this connection, it is noteworthy that since May 2004 the Tanzania government has introduced e-government. However, e-government requires profound changes in the way the government functions. Simply introducing such technology may not bear beneficial results. The system demands well-trained public servants to deliver the envisioned performance of government. Better training of public servants to equip them with expertise of computer-based processes of communications and of knowledge search and sharing should thus be given urgent priority.

Needless to state, e-governance has great potential in deepening democratisation in the country, as the internet can become an effective platform for massifying information on political rights and responsibilities. As Ahmed Mohiddin (2004) has pointed out in his article, the *Challenges of e-Democracy: Opportunities and Risks,* "e-Democracy is unlikely to succeed if the basic fundamentals of e-government are not in place. The latter is possible only in a situation where there are widespread understanding of the role of governments in a democracy, and the duties and responsibilities of those in governance positions." As civil society becomes more computer literate, it can galvanise, through e-democracy, and reach out to as well as engage the government more effectively on the needs and aspirations of the people. Professor Mohiddin is wary about the impact of e-governance given its impersonal character that erodes the traditional communitarian culture of communication, through community halls, public places, and group meetings. At the same time, however, he acknowledges its positive contribution in exposing Africans to the global marketplace of ideas, information, knowledge, experiences and best practices, so crucial in promoting democracy, human rights and development. It could be added that e-democracy can have profound impact in the electoral process. The massive vote that Jakaya Kikwete received at the CCM Special Congress in May 2005 at Chimwaga, Dodoma as CCM's candidate for the October 2005 Presidential election was apparently professionally organised and managed through a nation-wide network linked by electronic communications using SMS and mobile phone technology.

Improvement of government capacity to manage the process of development takes a more serious dimension at local government level. At this level, there is an even greater need to enhance capacities and capabilities. Local government presently exhibits several weaknesses, notably in financial and general management. Of course, this is not a problem that affects Tanzania alone. Many poor countries face a similar weak system of local government. Yet the on-going local government reform does not seem to be driven by a vision of making this system of governance a primary one in promoting participatory democracy- in politics and development. Tanzania should take the cue from the Report of the ILO World Commission on Social Dimension of Globalisation: *A Fair Globalisation: Creating Opportunities For All*. The Report asserts, "There are often major obstacles to local government development. Greater decentralisation is needed, but to be effective increased capacities and resources, and effective frameworks for democracy and participation must accompany it. National governments have critical role in ensuring redistribution from richer to poorer regions, and in raising the capacities of local governments and other actions."

In Tanzania, local government remains heavily dependent on central government resources to the extent that it has become disempowered. It is little wonder that the decision of the central government, reflected in the Finance Act, 2003 to abolish several local government taxes and levies, including the development levy, which was the key revenue earner for local authorities, has been poorly received at local levels. Evidently, local government taxes had been on the increase with debilitating impact on business and economic activities at district and regional levels. Yet it is equally pertinent to point out that local authorities have not had adequate funding sources of local tax revenue. This means, therefore, that the success envisioned in propelling a more monolithic fiscal regime would crucially depend on the extent to which the central government would bridge the shortfalls in revenue that local authorities would inevitably incur. In this context, one needs to recognise the positive moves taken to empower local government. For example, subsidies extended to local government have shot up from Shillings 12.3 billion in fiscal year 1995/1996 to Shillings 292.0 billion in 2003/2004.

Are Reforms lacking in Vision?

A central troubling question since the on-set of initial trade liberalisation in 1984 and the adoption of ERP in June 1986 and, indeed, up until 1999 when the Development Vision 2025 was adopted, remains: where does the pursued economic reform lead Tanzania? As the reform takes shape and is deepened, the vision of Tanzania ostensibly remains as enunciated in *The Arusha Declaration,* namely the construction of a socialist society. As such, the large question that has inevitably taken the centre stage of public debate has become whether capitalism as manifested by the market-driven reform under implementation, and, notably, by the privatisation of state-owned enterprises, leads to the building of a socialist society? This question first emerged when the ruling political party, *Chama Cha Mapinduzi. CCM)* National Executive Committee in 1991 adopted the Zanzibar Resolution that threw out of the window the Arusha Declaration's *Leadership Code.* That Code initially prohibited CCM leaders and all the CCM members later, from undertaking any form of private enterprise activity. The Code is considered to have been singularly responsible for undermining any form of entrepreneurship from emerging among the majority African Tanzanians after 1967. Indeed, the central tenet of the clamour for *"uzawa"* or indigenisation of the economy centres on the very notion that the Arusha Declaration's Leadership Code disenfranchised the majority Tanzanians from wealth creation activities. The argument now posed is that some form of redress is required by way of a deliberate government policy of affirmative action being effected. Part eight of the book dwells on this subject at length.

Following the Zanzibar Resolution, the CCM appointed a committee. which I was privileged to be a member) to review CCM's socialist economic policies and advise on the appropriateness of adopting new policies in keeping with the new realities of the 1990s and beyond. In December 1992, at a CCM National Congress at Chimwaga, Dodoma, the Committee presented its report titled *Policy and Direction of the CCM in the 1990s and beyond.* The core thrust of the policy was that past development policies, strategies and institutions that CCM had adopted and put in place, under the one party regime, and informed by the Arusha Declaration had become surrealistic and retrogressive. The Committee recommended the adoption of a new policy that put the market and the individual as well as co-operative enterprises as the central vehicles for leading the economic development process. The Congress unanimously adopted the Report.

That policy marked by a major ideological shift by the ruling party, the custodian of the Arusha Declaration, precipitated a more heightened concern about the economic direction Tanzania was taking. The concern is well captured and articulated by a Kenyan Professor, Ahmed Mohiddin, in an article in a Tanzania intellectual magazine called *Change*, published in the November/December 1993 issue. The article is titled, *Tanzania in Transition: From Ujamaa to Ujangili?*. loosely translates into: Tanzania in transition: From socialism to survival of the fittest). Mohiddin's central thesis is posed in the question: is "there not a danger, that in the absence of a clearly articulated vision, the appropriate policy-statements, the institutions that are supportive of that vision, and an intellectual and moral leadership to steer the people towards the vision, that the change could very well be that of from a projected society of harmony – *ujamaa* – to that of conflict - *ujangili*"?

It was in that context that President Ali Hassan Mwinyi, before he completed his final second term of office, appointed, in mid 1995, a Team of Experts to construct a new Development Vision for Tanzania through a broad participatory approach. The team completed its work at the end of 1998. In 1999, the government formally adopted *Tanzania Development Vision 2025*. The Vision articulates the kind of a country Tanzania should be in 2025. It is discussed at length in Part six of the book. Suffice it to state that the Vision now underpins national development goals and strategies. However, there are a number of Tanzanians who point out that the Vision is neither compelling nor inspirational in the manner the Arusha Declaration was or continues to be. As recent as end February 2004, at a dialogue session sponsored by the NGO Forum, *Business Times* and Haki-Elimu, whose key elements were reported in the *Guardian* of 29 February 2004, it was generally argued that Vision 2025 was not a people's vision; that it benefited few elites leaving the majority of Tanzanians in severe economic and social distress. The dialogue session further held that the vision could only be relevant if it benefited the majority of the people. In sum, the dialogue meeting reinforced the view held in certain quarters of Tanzanian society that Vision 2025 is not compelling.

Such views, unfortunately, miss the centrepiece of the Vision, namely that it is inspired by the same core values of the Arusha Declaration, a blueprint that does not seem to arouse much conflicting opinion in Tanzanian society. The key point of departure between the Vision 2025 and the Arusha Declaration is located mainly on the impact of the changed global political and economic environment and the shift from state commandist economic system to private ownership. In other words, the driving vehicles of economic transformation have changed. It would seem that the opponents of Vision 2025 would wish to see Tanzania reverting to socialist ownership. One wonders though whether socialist ownership would today meet the approval of majority Tanzanians. In addition, the criticisms against the Vision fail to appreciate the clear proposition embodied in the Vision that a strong state is an absolute necessity in ensuring that the market does not create a market society, but, rather, a welfare society. This debate is well captured in Parts three and six of the book.

Smart Partnership

As market reforms have entrenched, so has the urge by the private sector been to play a greater role in ensuring that reforms worked in the best interests of the economy. In this context, a notable feature of the reform process, especially since 1997, has been the move by the government to develop a smart partnership arrangement with the private sector. Since fiscal year 1997/98, the government has closely involved the organised private sector, through the Tax Policy Task Force, in offering its views over several policies, notably fiscal and the budget. The high watermark in the process of building such smart partnership was the establishment of the Tanzania National Business Council. TNBC) in April 2001 through a Presidential Order. The TNBC brings together representatives of key business associations, public economic agencies such as the Tanzania Revenue Authority. TRA) and the Tanzania Investment Centre. TIC), and key economic ministries. The President is the chair of the TNBC. The mandate of the council is wide. However, its immediate focus is on policies and strategies that need to be adopted or fine-tuned in order to improve the competitiveness of the Tanzanian economy. This is important if the economy is to attract and promote more investments and garner the much-needed competitive edge in the regional and global markets.

On the occasion of the meeting of the Tanzania National Business Council. TNBC) on 15 March 2005, the last one before he completes his mandate in November 2005, President Benjamin William Mkapa hailed the decision to establish the TNBC. He noted that the institution had heralded a unique smart partnership between the government and the private business sector since formation. Few Tanzanians would doubt the historic importance of the TNBC and the achievements the resulting partnership has realised through constructive dialogue. Yet, four years after, time has probably come to examine whether the TNBC is the ideal body for promoting a more inclusive smart partnership in the Tanzanian society. In discussing this question, a brief background of the salient reasons that catapulted the establishment of the TNBC is necessary.

The period between 1992 and 2000 was marked by a heightened concern within the Tanzanian business community that the government was formulating economic policies and effecting measures predominantly based on the conventional wisdom and directives of the IMF, the World Bank and key donor nations. It was apparent to the Tanzanian private business sector that local ownership of the development process was being sacrificed largely because the economy was in doldrums and that the domestic capacity to redress the situation was low. Put differently, it was as if Tanzania was left with little choice but to absorb whatever prescription given by external agencies. In this light, a burning view prevailed that left on its own, the government could not effectively negotiate policies with the international multilateral financial institutions and donors that, necessarily, had to reflect and embody a national social compact. Inevitably, such an environment fertilised suspicions and recriminations between the government and the private business sector, the latter regarding itself as worse affected by the structural adjustment measures that were effected. The recriminations were manifested by rhetorical confrontations over fiscal and tax policies and measures adopted by the government, especially between 1997 and 2000. In his above referred speech, President Mkapa captured the mood of that time in the following words: "It would seem that we almost lost the sense that all of us in Tanzania-the people, civil society, business and government-are in fact one people, sharing a common destiny." To some extent, the establishment of the Tax Policy Review Task Force helped to dampen the heated passions of the business community.

On a positive note, the prevalence of the mood of suspicion and recrimination and, indeed, of the lack of a shared destiny, is what gave birth to the TNBC. Thanks to President Mkapa's involvement and intimate engagement in former Malaysian Prime Minister Mahathir Mohammad's led `smart partnership` dialogues for Southern Africa between 1997 and 2000, a new and more positive mindset emerged and ingrained in the Tanzanian top political leadership about the importance of institutionalising smart partnership between the government and non-state business actors in Tanzania. Since its establishment, the TNBC has been able to address several policy issues mainly centred on how best to improve the Tanzanian business and economic environment to bolster both inward and domestic investments and make economic activities more viable and profitable. Little wonder, therefore, that President Mkapa should surmise, in this light, that "one of the greatest achievements under the TNBC has been our acceptance-government as well as the private sector-of enhanced roles as members of `Corporate Tanzania.`" But then, here lies the rub. Should Tanzanian smart partnership be viewed from such a narrow scope of a `Tanzania Incorporated`? Should Tanzanians not think in terms of a wider-angle view embracing how smart partnership should become a platform of national solidarity?

Constructing A Broader Smart Partnership

Now that TNBC has found its feet and the private business sector has its act together on how best to engage the government on matters of its specific concern and interest, time has come to think of how to promote a loftier participation by the broader society in national social and economic matters. In my view, if one of the central objectives of the TNBC is "to promote the goals of economic growth with social equity and even development" and to "encourage and promote the formulation of coordinated policies on social and economic matters", as enunciated by President Mkapa when launching the TNBC in 2001, then the TNBC, as presently constituted, cannot rise to higher and loftier goals and tasks. This is because the TNBC is presently overly representative of the private business sector and its interests are more dominantly influenced by economic efficiency and less by social justice. Yes, TNBC still has a role to play. However, Tanzania needs a more inclusionary participatory platform able to move beyond narrow sectional interests of non-state actors.

It should be recognised that the underlying ethos of smart partnership was originally enunciated in the South Commission Report, *The Challenge To The South*. In that report which had a lead inspiration from the late Father of the Tanzania Nation, Mwalimu Julius Nyerere as Chair of the Commission, it is stipulated that "the State is best able to perform its demanding functions when there is a national consensus on the goals and purposes of development, and on the apportionment of the costs as well as the benefits of development. Democratic institutions, which allow full participation and through which such consensus can be reached, are therefore not only an objective of people-centred development, but its very means as well." The Report further observes that a self-sustaining economy within a stable society is inconceivable if the society is not imbued with an integrative and cohesive spirit of social justice. Achieving a delicate balance and trade off between the needs for economic efficiency and social equity is what many would regard to be the national consensus on development. Such a consensus could not be realised within the present framework of the TNBC.

Evidently, the Mkapa administration in recent years has strived to engage the broader Tanzanian stakeholder community in a series of dialogues involving social and economic issues. Therefore, yes, there has been an element of more inclusive smart partnership outside the framework of the TNBC. Notable examples include deliberations involving public sector reforms, privatisation and poverty reduction. However, such stakeholder dialogues have largely been informal and unstructured. In fact, it could be said that they have been used more as "bouncing walls" to enable the government to sense the mood of key non-state actors in society than as concrete platforms for arriving at shared decisions and directions. This shortcoming or deficiency has been acknowledged in the National Strategy for Growth and Reduction of Poverty. NSGRP) 2005/06-2009/10. From this perspective, it is clear that time has come for smart partnership to be deepened if Tanzania will collectively and more vigorously pursue the goals of Development Vision 2025. This is an inevitable and natural course in deepening democratisation in the country. In this quest, Tanzania could borrow a leaf on how South Africa has succeeded to construct a more inclusionary system of smart partnership.

South Africa has a broad based organ of smart partnership where non-state actors are widely represented. This organ, the National Economic Development and Labour Council. NEDLAC), was established in February 1995 following the NEDLAC Act being passed by Parliament in 1994, as South Africa's primary institution for social dialogue between organized business, government, trade unions, employers' organizations and civil society or community on broad issues of social and economic policy. Its core objective is to promote the realisation of social and economic compact through more inclusive dialogue. NEDLAC's principal objectives are:

- promote the goals of economic growth, participation in economic decision-making and social equity.
- seek to reach consensus and conclude agreements pertaining to social and economic policy.
- consider all proposed labour legislation relating to labour-market policy before submission to Parliament.
- consider all significant changes to social and economic policy before implementation or submission to Parliament.
- encourage and promote the formulation of coordinated policy on social and economic matters.

More than a decade since the re-establishment of multi-party democracy, Tanzania is now poised to deepen democratisation beyond political parties and parliamentary representativeness. Introducing a broad based inclusive smart partnership participatory system of the NEDLAC type would go a long way in bridging the present Tanzanian democratic deficit. Tanzanian civil society hungers for a formal platform, best established through force of law that would offer it the opportunity for strategic reflection and decision making on broader interests and needs of society.

Public-Private Partnership

Public-Private Partnership has now become a buzzword, particularly in transition economies. In many of these countries, such partnership has taken the form of the private sector negotiating with governments to secure a more supportive and enabling environment to do business. For a while, this focus is understandable since these economies are reforming and have only recently opened up to the outside world. What is important to note, however, is that the burden of sharing responsibilities between the government and the private sector in promoting development has to be appreciated quickly. The expectation of governments has been that in consideration for the private sector being enabled to enjoy a conducive environment to invest, compete and be profitable they, in turn, would respond by being ethical and responsible especially over tax compliance and generally in improving corporate governance.

The experience of gross corporate malfeasance that the industrialised countries went through in 2002 involving firms such as *Enron* and *WorldCom* in the United States of America, and later *Parmalat* in Italy, in late 2003, amongst several other firms before them, as far back as the BCCI mega fraud in the early 1990s, could not be allowed to take place in fragile transitional economies. The impact would simply be devastating. In this particular context, it is interesting to observe that the entry of firms into Tanzania having a global touch and concern about corporate governance is beginning to take effect in making corporate ethics the hallmark of corporate conduct. In August 2003, the National Bank of Commerce. NBC), for example, decided to shed off one of its members of the Board of Directors on grounds of abuse of insider information relating to the bank's obligations to the government and the bank workers' strike that took place in July 2003. That decision constituted the birth of corporate governance in line with the *Cadbury Report* in the UK and the *King Reports*. 1 and 2) in South Africa. In July 2004, Tanzania acceded to the NEPAD Peer Review Mechanism. PRM) that requires that African countries implement fundamental standards of political and corporate governance. The PRM encapsulates agreed codes and standards in four main areas: democracy, good governance, economic governance and management, socio-economic development and corporate governance.

In Part three of the book, a close review is made of economic governance and some aspects of socio-economic development. Part four of the book examines in detail aspects relating to democracy and good political governance. In part seven, an analysis is made of Tanzania's response to requirements of corporate governance.

Public-Private Partnership crucially means that since the private sector is now positioned as the new motive power of economic growth, it is imperative that it be seen to play a role beyond mere making profits and paying taxes. In particular, it needs to put greater attention on investing in human capital and in social services. The corporate philanthropy examples displayed by global foundations of leading firms such as Microsoft, Ford, Carnegie, Clinton and so many other private sector trusts and endowments, should jolt the hearts and minds of leading Tanzanian private companies in their own ways and capacities, to equally come out in support of worthy social and economic causes. In this context, when officially opening Afrika Mashariki Gold Mines Limited operations in Tarime Tanzania, in September 2002, President Mkapa hailed the company's corporate responsibility in the area where the mines were located. He referred to an investment of US$ 3.1 million that the Company had spent on putting up roads, a police station, health centre and in providing student scholarships. These are commendable efforts. However, it is important to distinguish corporate responsibility that benefits the area within a gold mining precinct and the support extended for broad national benefit. The decision of Resolute. Tanzania) Limited to surrender free of charge all immovable structures and facilities at its gold mine site at Lusu, in Nzega District at the end of its mining activity, for the purpose of establishing a University College of Mines as a Constituent College of the University of Dar es Salaam is a good example of corporate social responsibility per excellence.

In July 2003, the Standard Chartered Bank, Africa Region also made an announcement in Tanzania that the bank had decided to use part of its yearly profits to fund development projects that would go towards improving the living standards of the people in countries where they operate. This is a welcome departure from the conventional corporate responsibility that has so far been seen in Tanzania where one time, *ad hoc* assistance is offered. There is a lesson to be learned here by all business lobby organisations in Tanzania, about how to balance their work and concerns between policy dialogue with the government on fiscal and tax issues and embarking on prompting their members to become more involved in developmental issues of a *national* character. The decision of the Tanzania CEO Club to constitute a scholarship programme for deserving students seeking to pursue higher education is the kind of developmental activity I have in mind.

At the end of July 2003, *Fortune,* the famous global magazine, held in Aspen, Colorado, USA, what they called *"Brainstorm 2003"*. This was the third annual gathering of business leaders of global companies and of lead thinkers from around the world. The purpose of the gatherings is to exchange ideas on different global issues of concern to humanity. "Brainstorm" proceeds from the premise that business is as much part of the problem as of the solution in the world and the challenge is to strike the right balance between the quest for making corporate profits and being corporate citizen. For business to dialogue with other national stakeholders as to how to improve the business image is a rare phenomenon in Tanzania. Instead, you have a situation where the media, often with a negative spin, portrays the picture that business firms are in an endless quest to secure special favours from the government. In the post-socialist era, and at a time when there is acrimony about the underlining justification for privatisation of state-owned enterprises and a twisted sense that the economy is being taken over by or even sold to foreigners for cheap, such stance by the media only helps to undermine the legitimacy of business in society.

Therefore, time has come for Tanzanian business organisations to move seriously beyond their immediate parochial interests. They should address the need for people's development and determine how business can play a part. In this context, *Fortune's* type of Annual Brainstorms could constitute the kind of powerful platforms which Tanzania's private sector lobby institutions could use to dialogue with other national stakeholders, including the government, on how to move the economy forward. Such platforms, moreover, could help business institutions to re-invent themselves as they reach a plateau in terms of what they can further engage the government on, especially on matters that are of primary concern to them during the transition period from a socialist to a market economy. Secondly, they would enable them to reach out to the broad mass of the people on how the private sector can respond to the challenges posed by the poverty that engulfs the majority of the people. In Part seven of the book, I review in greater depth public-private partnership and the challenges that lie ahead in consolidating and deepening such partnership.

Leadership Matters

"We recognise that failures of political and economic leadership in many African countries impede the effective mobilisation and utilisation of scarce resources into productive areas of activity in order to attract and facilitate domestic and foreign investment".

-The New Partnership For Africa's Development. NEPAD), October 2001.

Tanzania has achieved positive results in its economic reform efforts, particularly since 1997. For this, President Mkapa deserves positive reinforcement and accolades from all Tanzanians. This record of success confirms the mantra that leadership matters. Having said this, one should quickly point out that a more determined struggle for Tanzania's quest for emancipation from scourges of poverty, ignorance and disease has now only started. It may sound strange to say this after over forty years since Tanzania obtained its independence. At the dawn of independence in December 1961, Mwalimu Julius Nyerere had identified poverty, ignorance and disease as the triple enemies of the newly born country. Regrettably, these enemies continue to ravage the lives of the majority of Tanzanians today. In this light, economic reforms have recently come under attack for having failed to bring about relief to the people. Suddenly, there is the sense that economic reforms are, in themselves, some kind of a panacea for improving the living standards of the people. However, as President Mkapa perceptively noted in his address at the first *Tanzania Development Forum* in April 2003, "economic reforms are not expected to directly solve our growth, unemployment and poverty problems. The *raison d'etre* for economic reform is to create a domestic structural and policy environment that can make it possible for activities to take place that ultimately increase growth, reduce unemployment, and is conducive to poverty reduction."

Yet, there are other factors having direct impact on bolstering economic growth, creating more jobs and reducing poverty. The challenge of effective and visionary *leadership* stands out as one of them. In the same manner in which President Mkapa's leadership has enabled Tanzania to pursue sound and prudent economic policies that are consistent and predictable and whose results, at the macro-economic level, have been clearly discernible, so also would good leadership, *generally*, drive Tanzanians to respond with determination to the challenges having direct bearing on improving the quality of their lives. In other words, visionary and inspiring leadership is essential in galvanising and sparking the resourcefulness of the people behind a mission.

In this context, I have watched President Mkapa with admiration, consistently pursuing with strong commitment, an ethos directed at national renewal, modernisation of the state and in infusing, probably not too successfully as yet, a new mindset within his own political party leadership. He has also strived to lead the country beyond dogmatic ideas and outmoded attitudes. In recent times, this posture has not been well understood and received in some quarters of his ruling party and even in the opposition political parties. The recent emergence of an inchoate, "nationalistic", not necessarily "left," populism in Tanzania, so well manifested in the Parliamentary debates in 2003 over the privatisation of the NMB and the whole subject of the amendment of the land law and commercialisation of agriculture are evidence of such phenomenon. It is a phenomenon that is a product of weak understanding of what President Mkapa views as Tanzania's new vision driven by the realities of globalisation.

In the light of such backdrop, of the emergence of an apparent ideological cleavage within CCM, it is incumbent upon the CCM to soul search about where it stands ideologically, especially as the General Elections of October 2005 draw close. One gets the sense that for the CCM it is the trajectory of progress that matters more and that what remains to be shaped and realised has thus more to do with pace and speed. Such posture may not reflect the reality and could be misleading. As alluded to above, there are worrying stances that clearly reflect the existence of stresses and strains within the party. It is dangerous for any political party to hold a dogmatic view about what is the current reality in Tanzania and what holds in store. As I wrote in the Foreword to a recent booklet, *Tutafika: Imagining Our Future Tanzania*, many Tanzanians have become captive to the "tyranny of the present". The CCM leadership is no exception. Since the departure of Mwalimu Nyerere from the leadership of CCM, the party has consistently thrown itself behind a Presidential candidate in the belief that the candidate would forge electoral success. This scenario has reflected the visible lack of a political "movement" within CCM. It is important to ask therefore whether the party has a coherent ideology that unifies the membership, the way *ujamaa* did in the 1970s and 1980s.

Evidently, President Benjamin Mkapa, more in the mould of Tony Blair and Bill Clinton, has been able to transform CCM into "New CCM" and pursuing "Third Way"-type of policies. He has strived to reposition CCM from the left towards the "centre". Whether such a shift constitutes or represents a new political movement for CCM is debatable, let alone whether what has been unleashed would endure. A political movement has to derive its durability from clarity of convictions. Yet you often wonder whether CCM has such clarity across the breadth of its leadership, followers and members. Therefore, the modernisation of CCM and its renewal, as well as the type of leadership that the party proceeds to identify and propel for national leadership in 2005, crucially hinge on such clarity of convictions. It would appear that as far as President Mkapa is concerned, the evident fleeting plaudits in his party could count for little against what he awaits as the judgement of history on his radical reforms. However, his openly strong support for the CCM candidature of Jakaya Kikwete at the party elections in early May 2005 points to a plausible direction that CCM may indeed be working towards its reinvigoration and a more bold redefinition and refinement of its core policies.

It is not as if such move would be novel for political parties in countries such as Tanzania. Even in the rich western countries, there is growing concern about relevance and efficacy of party policies. Peter Mandelson pertinently observed at the 2003 Progressive Politics Conference in London, "Renewal is what keeps progressive political movements alive. Parties survive for long periods as defenders of particular social interests, as standard-bearers of once powerful ideologies, and as instruments of individual political ambition. They may even from time to time get elected. But without a relevant governing project, in touch with constantly changing social and political challenges, they will not prosper". During his term of administration, President Mkapa has attempted to generate such governing project. However, many within his party and without are not clear what ideology informs the project. There is little doubt that the policies that Mkapa has vigorously pursued are market oriented. However, could they be based on any ideology such as liberal capitalism? If yes, then it could be asked why CCM in its Guidelines and Manifestos continues to identify itself with socialism and self-reliance; what socialism?

Coincidentally, a similar question bedevils New Labour in the UK. The former General Secretary of the Fabian Society, Michael Jacobs, writing in the British magazine *Prospect* of October 2002, under the title, *Reason to Believe*, observes in this context: "Ideology gives a government roots. In providing voters with a strong sense of a government's purpose, it gives them something to grip on. Policies are often weak instruments for attracting public support. They are complex; they must be designed to satisfy different, even conflicting, interests; they take a long time to have visible effect; they sometimes fail. A clearly articulated philosophy cannot only explain the aim of policy to the public, it reassures them that the government has a purpose and direction when its policies are not making this evident." In contrast, Prince Aga Khan believes that ideology has become irrelevant in the modern day. Speaking at the Foundation Ceremony of the Aga Khan Academy in Maputo, Mozambique, on 25 June 2004, His Highness talked of the "triumph of pragmatism and professional expertise over ideology". He added that this triumphalism was now "accepted wisdom". Has ideology become irrelevant? In my view, it has not.

Thus what is CCM's ideology? Does Vision 2005 constitute *that* ideology? But then is Vision 2005 not a *national* Vision in the sense that all the people irrespective of their political affiliation own it? In turn, is it possible in the world today to have an ideology different from liberal capitalism? What then happens to the enchantment with radical idealism that has inspired the hearts and minds of Tanzanians since the Arusha Declaration, a Declaration that pushed mainstream politics towards a grand project for social transformation of the masses. Has radical idealism become irrelevant? What possibly could distinguish the different political parties in Tanzania today apart from their leadership quality and financial capacity? In similar vein, this is what the Conservative party leader, Michael Portillo, called upon the Tories in Britain to do following yet another change in its top leadership in late 2003. In an article in *The Sunday Times* of January 4, 2004 titled, "Howard reinvented himself now he has to reinvent a party," Portillo postulated that if the conservative party were to remove the labour party from power, its leadership had to lift its sights, its mind and its heart "above the baying audience of the party faithful and speak to the nation in all its diversity." It is interesting to examine Portillo's remarks in the context of the defeat of the Tories in the May 2005 elections and the resignation of Michael Howard. In our view, what Portillo meant was that the Tories should have returned to the ideological core values of the Conservative party, which, in essence, are driven by neo-liberal economic freedom and private initiative. Unfortunately, in this past election, there was a strategic failure on their part to shift the ideological pendulum to the extreme right and thereby failing to question the dominance of the state in key sectors of the social-economy.

In the case of the CCM, the party is in power all right. However, to remain in power, it should constantly respond to new challenges that are in no way different from those confronting any party that seeks to grab power. Trust lies at the heart of electoral victory. Often, such trust is bolstered through parties re-inventing themselves. The days of electoral victories based on the charisma and adoration of a leader, as it happened under Mwalimu Nyerere now seem over. New Labour in Britain, for example, saw its electoral fortunes in 2005 diminish significantly largely because of erosion of trust. CCM must work for such trust. Re-inventing a party also means promoting values that resonate with the people. In this instance one notes the mantra that CCM has adopted from Jakaya Kikwete's campaign slogan, *"nguvu mpya, ari mpya na kasi mpya."*. new impetus, new zeal, new momentum). In my view, what is missing in this new perspective to pursuing deeper national transformation is *"fikra mpya"* or new thinking. Surely, the onerous challenges that Tanzania faces in a fast changing world crucially require adaptive minds and new policy directions. There is still much room for improving ideas and strategies in realising a higher growth goal for Tanzania. In the next section, I highlight some of the immediate challenges that should be addressed if Tanzania is to reduce poverty and bolster higher economic growth.

Challenges to Confront

There are several challenges that Tanzanians, in their collective wisdom and actions, and in partnership with their government, should respond with vigour, new thinking, ingenuity and hard work if Tanzania is to prosper. What follows does not constitute an exhaustive review of the challenges in the least. It is only an attempt to capture some of them.

Agriculture as Backbone

It is important and urgent to transform the agriculture sector. Tanzanians have to be able to feed themselves and to have adequate food security. Even though Tanzanian agriculture sector in 2003 contributed 45% of GDP and 60% of export earnings, it remains, in absence of a better term, primitive. Since 1999, this sector has grown, on average, only by 5.0%. This growth declined to 4.0% in 2003 due to drought. This sector is heavily rain-fed and peasant-based; it is technologically backward and extremely vulnerable to domestic weather conditions and the volatilities of commodity prices in the global marketplace. Only 8% of Tanzania's arable land is under agriculture and, of which, only about 1% of it is under permanent crops. Out of total land area of 886,040 square kilometres, only 1,530 square kilometres or 0.2% is under irrigation. Yes, the government is now addressing the irrigation question more seriously. Indeed, under the framework of the National Irrigation Master Plan prepared in collaboration with Japan's JICA in 2002/2002, 29.4 million hectares have been identified as suitable for irrigation, of which 2.3 million hectares are the most viable for development. The aim of the Plan is to put 30,000 hectares of land under irrigation per annum. For this objective to be realised, the government needs to allocate Shs.30 billion per annum. Yet, the average budget allocation between 2001/2002 and 2004/2005 is only 21.57% of what is needed.

What has thus happened is that between 1999/2000 and 2003/2004 the agricultural land under irrigation has risen only from 157,000 hectares to 227,000 hectares, or a 44.89% increase. The land under irrigation therefore represents only 10% of the land identified as most viable for irrigation. It is a far cry from making a difference. This is why Tanzanians should be bold enough to accept that, for a long time, peasant agriculture would not contribute to any significant national growth and prosperity. Modernisation of agriculture is an urgent imperative. In this light, the opening up rural farmlands to investment, domestic and foreign, has to be taken up more seriously. It also means viewing agriculture as an important source of creating jobs and not simply as a sector whose objective is premised on the "rural socialism"- lopsided self-employment ideology.

What all this means is that the ideological legacy from the "rural socialism" era, that commercial agriculture constitutes some form of feudalism and could undermine traditional rural forms of social and economic capital, is irrelevant today given the existence of a strong State and an effective regulatory regime. Samir Amin (2003) contests this view in his article, *World Poverty: Pauperisation & Capital Accumulation.* He argues a case for macro policies that protect peasant food production from the "unequal competition of modernised farmers and agribusiness corporations-local and international". Interestingly, he does not refer to non-food crops. Yet even on food crops, the logic of his argument begs the fundamental issue about how food shortages and frequent famine happen in most poor countries.

Commercialisation of Agriculture

In my view, commercialisation of agriculture is the best strategy to bolster economic growth and attack rural poverty. However, it may not be the solution to the rural-urban migration A World Bank report: *Cities: The New Frontier,* 2003 indicates that the world is going through a major population shift. It is estimated to move from 47% urban in 2000 to 60% urban in 2030. In fact, as far as the developing countries are concerned, more than half of the population will be living in cities by year 2020. Jeffrey Sachs regards this shift as a positive development in the fight against poverty. His argument rests on the fact that urban areas have outperformed rural areas during the past one century on almost all facets of economic development. Nevertheless, it is also a reality that migration from rural areas may decline when well-paid jobs are created in rural areas themselves through commercialisation of agriculture. Standards of welfare would thus conceivably improve. Indeed, such improved quality of life in rural areas may be less financially engaging to the exchequer than improving the social and economic infrastructures in urban areas that would be necessary to meet the needs of an explosive urbanisation.

Specifically, agricultural commercialisation needs to embrace greenfield investments in non-food agriculture. Privatisation of the sugar industry as shown by the success stories of Kilombero, Mtibwa, Arusha Chini, and, more recently in Kagera, shows the huge benefits of "corporatising" agriculture, whether through the privatisation route or greenfield investments. For example, Kilombero Sugar Company has increased sugar production from 42,000 tons at the time of privatisation in 1998 to 126,743 tons in 2003. Data from the *Tanzania Economic Survey, 2002* shows that privatised sugar companies have made substantial tax revenue contributions to the Exchequer. The companies have also created thousands new formal jobs. More importantly, thousands of peasants in the precincts of the Sugar Mills have improved their incomes and living standards through sugar cane out-grower activities that have benefited significantly from seed supplies and extension advisory support services from the sugar industry corporate bodies. For example, sugar cane out-growers around Mtibwa Sugar Mill have expanded production from 80,000 tons in 1997/1998 when Mtibwa sugar Mill was privatised, to 240,000 tons in the 2003/2004 crop season. Overall, sugar cane production has increased from 423,000 metric tonnes in 2002/03 season to 752,000 metric tonnes in 2004/05 season. It is equally notable that social services in the areas where sugar mills are located in the form of schools, health centres, potable water supplies and urban-type amenities have flung up and improving the quality of livelihoods.

Mistakes may earlier have been made in allocating some of the land to the sugar companies that may have been part of village land or even land adjoining national parks. There is need to correct such mistakes. However, the mistakes should not be viewed, unnecessarily, in the kind of negative light projected in isolated quarters whose aim seems to promote an ideological war against commercial agriculture. Such mindset, founded on rural socialism, continues to inform this posture. It should also be appreciated that the agricultural sector as it exists today largely falls outside the tax-net. In other words, 45% of GDP does not contribute to tax revenue. Imagine what revenue in GDP terms would be were even 25% of this sector to be brought into the tax net. This proposition could work out were most of the current fallow arable land to be put under more productive, commercial-based farming. Incremental revenue could be as much as 5% of GDP.

Therefore, the challenge is to change the mindset of Tanzanians about why it is so crucial to open up agriculture to private investment and to mobilise and attract more investment, domestic and foreign, into the sector as well as related sub-sectors, like beef ranching, dairy and fishing. The preparation and adoption of the *Agricultural Sector Development Programme* and the *Rural Development Strategy* in 2002, belated as they are, are welcome policy developments. In this context, the decision by the government, announced in the Minister for Finance's Budget Speech in June 2003, to introduce subsidies for high yielding seeds and fertilizer for farmers, starting with the main maize producing regions of Tanzania as part of the strategy to promote food security, was as historic a decision as it was timely and imperative. More elaborately, the government has now been able to secure loans and grants from the African Development Bank. ADB) and the International Fund for Agricultural Development. IFAD) to the tune of Tanzania shillings 135 billion to finance poverty reducing agricultural development activities in five regions of Tanzania between 2005 and 2011. Clearly, Tanzania's organic economic growth will emanate from agriculture.

Fiscal Incentives for Promoting Agriculture

The policy steps taken by the government since 2003 and more so since the fiscal budget of 2004/2005 wherein several fiscal incentives have been extended to investments in agriculture and to the procurement of equipment for the agricultural, fishing and livestock sectors reinforce this strategic policy direction of putting agriculture at the centre of the drive to boost economic growth and reduce poverty. These incentives include the introduction of capital allowances. some at 100% and some at 50% with accelerated allowances for the balance) for costs relating to clearing of land, for irrigation, equipment systems, planting of permanent crops, environmental protection of land, procurement of agricultural, livestock and fishing machinery and accessories. Customs duties have been exempted on agricultural implements and inputs, whilst VAT is not levied on raw materials and inputs for agricultural, fishing and livestock purposes. Above all, income taxation for agricultural activities, unlike for other businesses, would not be subjected to quarterly payments but to the end of the year following harvests. These are revolutionary fiscal measures and with a more congenial land law in place, the response to investment in the agriculture, livestock and fishing industry can only be robust. Tanzanians should take advantage of these supporting incentives. I still believe though that Tanzania should use the platform of an Investment

Forum, similar to what was held in 1997 for the mining sector, if investments in commercial agriculture are to be bolstered on a massive scale. The special investment forums held at Vodaworld in Midrand, South Africa at the end of October 2004 and London, hosted by Standard Chartered Bank, at the end of November 2004, were something close to what we are proposing. However, in both cases, agriculture was mixed up in a whole bag of investment proposals presented to potential investors and may not have received the pronounced attention I am proposing.

Financing Agriculture

The move mooted by the government to establish a specialised bank that would extend loans to the agricultural, livestock and natural resources sectors, catering for both the large and small borrower needs, is an equally important one. However, the proposal may be unwarranted in terms of its underlying justification. In my view, the state should not move back into business, least of all, banking, much as the government appears to be moving more in the direction of promoting a bank that would be owned by the private sector, international organisations like the IFC and the government itself. Interestingly, the idea to promote a state-owned agriculture bank has arisen against the backdrop of successful lending to Cooperatives for crop procurement by some of the mainstream banks, notably Co-operative and Rural Development Bank. CRDB) Bank and Exim Bank.

Based on the Budget Speech of the Ministry responsible for Cooperatives and Marketing for 2003/04, it would appear that even without a specialised bank for agriculture being created, it is possible for existing mainstream banks to lend to the agriculture sector, though such lending, at this stage, has concentrated on crop procurement and mainly for cotton and coffee. The Budget report shows that following the establishment of the Export Credit Guarantee Facility in fiscal year 2002/03 with an initial seed capital of Shs 6.5 billion. the guarantee sum has since been increased to Shs. 15.0 billion in 2004), banks have become more positively inclined to lend for crop procurement. The report further disclosed that CRDB Bank had set aside Shs 11.86 billion of which 8.87 billion was utilised in 2002/03 and that, as at June 2003, Shs 8.5 billion, or 95.6% of the liability, had been paid back. The credit guarantee scheme appears to work well. CRDB alone approved loans amounting to a total of Shs. 15.9 billion during its financial year 2003/2004 favouring 12 Cooperative Unions and 5 Cooperative Societies.

In the light of this positive experience in financing agriculture, it stands to logic that the next challenge is how the government would extend additional guarantees to secure what is riskier lending, for whichever bank, state or private, namely lending for agricultural production as opposed to lending merely for crop procurement. This challenge has partly been addressed by the newly introduced fiscal incentives extended to the agricultural sector and by the amendment of the land law that hitherto proved an encumbrance to banks to extend loans to the agricultural sector.

Bolstering Investments

Tanzania should not be oblivious of the reality about the overall state of domestic investment. Risk capital is not readily available in Tanzania. Yet in recent times, especially during 2002/2003, there have been vitriolic attacks against foreign investment in Tanzania. To these critics, foreign investment is viewed as the jagged fang of savage, anti-people capitalism. Data from economic surveys shows that the ratio of investment in the GDP that was 30% in 1991 declined to 19.7% in 1995. It is down to 17.4% in 2002. This decline is partly explained by the government's withdrawal as an investor from the economy, a process that was necessary following the debacle of the state enterprise business sector. In this context, Tanzania has little choice but to increase the ratio of total investment as a percentage of GDP if it wishes to reduce poverty and raise the living standards of its people. The FDI ratio has to rise to at least 25%, the benchmark that has been set by the UN Economic Commission for Africa for the realisation of economic growth rates of around 8% on sustainable basis.

Much has been done to make the Tanzanian environment more conducive to attracting FDI. The increase of FDI from US$ 50.2 million in 1994 to US$ 250.0 million in 2004 is clear evidence. In fact, between 1998 and 2003, Tanzania was able to attract an annual average of US$ 356 million in FDI. The challenge to enhance the level of investments remains. Several factors, as outlined below, would require government's direct involvement if higher levels of investments are to be realised, more jobs created and higher economic growth achieved, especially through bolstering higher consumption of locally manufactured products.

First, the government has to address the problem of high costs of doing business. These costs are much higher than those in the sub-region. They subvert higher inflow of investments and de-motivate expansion of domestic investments. Take the costs of electricity as an example. These are simply too high. Even after their reduction by 22% early in 2004. though they have since been increased again from end 2004), at US cents 9.0 per Khw. compared to 3.5 cents in South Africa and 7.0 cents in Kenya, they are too high. Worse still, the power is erratic. Besides, the cost of transportation, especially by railway, is equally uncompetitive because infrastructure is rundown. Water supply for industrial use in urban centres and Dar es Salaam especially, is intermittent and seriously inadequate. Above all, whilst accepting the fact that Tanzania's tax revenue base is still low compared to that of Kenya, for example, the higher rate of VAT at 20% compared to Kenya's 16.0% is rather high.

Second, banks in Tanzania are highly risk averse to lending. Evidently, there may be good reasons for such stance. As a start, the socialist banking culture left behind a misconceived legacy that borrowing did not entail paying back. This explains why state-owned banks were encumbered with huge non-performing portfolios before their privatisation. Banks have also found it difficult to realise defaulted loans through foreclosure or other legal avenues. Part of the problem is the weak contract enforcement legal system. The establishment of a Commercial Court in Dar es Salaam in 2000 and Arusha in 2004 have proved useful in this regard. Nevertheless, the legal process itself still suffers from an ambivalent injunctions regime, which, whilst within the requirements of due process, is abused to the point where, sometimes, judicial corruption is tooted as one of the underlying reasons for the abuse.

Third, there has also been the contentious question about the Land Act, 1999 that has overprotected land-based security of borrowers to the disadvantage of banks. It remains to be seen what the amendment of this law in 2004 would generate. However, there have been encouraging developments in the monetary regime as a whole. The proportion of credit allocated to the private sector in relation to total credit has risen significantly between April 2003 and June 2004, from 67.8% to 85%. Moreover, total lending to the private sector as a proportion of total deposits rose from 37.5% in April 2003, to 48% in June 2004.

However, the interest rate regime remains of concern as it reflects continued risk averseness on the part of the commercial banks. As at June 2005, interest rates on loans averaged 14.0% whilst the rates for fixed deposits were at an average low of 2.8%. The huge interest margin in lending and deposit rates whilst declined to 9.9 % in June 2004, is still too wide for borrowers, depositors and regulators. It also appears to be explained by the equally huge risk in lending. Of course, this may explanation may not capture the whole truth. Some corporate customers enjoy as low as 11% borrowing rates and even much lower rates for trade finance facilities denominated in foreign currency. The people worst affected are those whose businesses must necessarily be backed by land-based securities. These suffer interest rates even as high as 20% to offset the cost of risk. Part eight of the book examines these issues more deeply.

Dynamising the Informal Sector

One of the key challenges confronting Tanzania is how to deal with its growing informal sector. This sector is estimated to contribute almost 30% of Tanzania GDP. The non-agricultural part of it also accounts for 12% of the urban employed. However, this is yet another sector, as *is* agriculture that is also largely outside the tax net. The Peruvian experience so well captured in Hernando de Soto's books, *The Other Path* and *The Mystery of Capital* provides insightful lessons for policy makers on how best to transform the informal sector and make it contribute more to economic growth. The key factor lies in empowering the sector-organisationally, entrepreneurially and legally, to have access to credit from banks and financial institutions. Hernando de Soto points out that real estate accounts for some 50% of the national wealth of advanced nations. In developing countries, it is close to 75%. By "uncoupling the economic features of an asset from its rigid, physical state, a representation makes the asset `fungible`-able to be fashioned to suit any transaction." The simple reason for this is that you need a legal title to any asset to be able to make money. The challenge for countries like Tanzania is therefore to make this process of "uncoupling" possible and simple.

Ghana has been able to make headway in this instance. Former US President Bill Clinton has helped Hernando de Soto set up the Foundation for Building the Capital of the Poor in Ghana. This Foundation is now helping moving poor people's assets into the legal regime. Through this process, such assets would be available as collateral for securing bank credit. This is where the Tanzanian economic empowerment policy should put its focus upon, namely, how to get the legal system to be reformed to respond to such innovative empowering policy interventions. Professor de Soto was invited by President Mkapa to visit Tanzania in September 2003 and interact with policy makers, parliamentarians and other key stakeholders in the Tanzania economy and share with them his experience in making the poor access capital and unleashing a new form of capitalism. Since then, de Soto's institution has been retained by the Tanzania government, with the financial backing of the Norwegian government, to work out a system that would enable Tanzanians transform their physical assets more easily into capital. Much of de Soto's advice would ultimately depend on how the government takes bold and radical decisions to shift from a land title registration and ownership regime that has subsisted in Tanzania since the colonial times. This subject is discussed at length in chapter twenty nine.

On liberalising micro-credit facilities, it is important to take note that CRDB Bank has made significant headway in supporting the informal sector. Between January 2000 and March 2003, the bank disbursed more than Shs.5.1 billion in loans to several *Savings and Credit Co-operative Societies. SACCOS).* 37.2% of the loan portfolio benefited the agricultural sector, 40.4% went to the commercial sector, which, by definition, is where "the informal sector" falls. The balance, 21.1%, was loaned for development projects, mainly in the education sector and in the construction of houses. Only 0.3% went to the processing industry, primarily agricultural processing. The moral of the CRDB bank's important on-lending venture is that Tanzania has to promote more and more viable SACCOS as micro-finance vehicles for lending to small borrowers. In other words, it is to, and through SACCOS and other micro-finance institutions, such as Pride Africa, that mainstream banks can more cost effectively and prudentially extend loans the way CRDB is doing. It should be noted, however, that as recent as June 2004, as reported by *Nipashe Newspaper* of 10 June, 2004, the CRDB Director of Customer Services, Joseph Witts, was quoted saying that only 5% of loans extended to SACCOS were being utilised for economic productive activities, the balance going towards consumption and education fees. This is a regrettable phenomenon as it shows a lack or shortage of the entrepreneurial spirit. The good news, on the other hand, is that the number of SACCOS has shot up from 803 in June 2000 to 1,375 at March 2003. Moreover, the value of shares and savings in these SACCOS has increased from Shillings 14.0 billion to Shillings 27.3 billion between June 2000 and March 2004.

Addressing the Fiscal Deficit

The fiscal deficit is still a problem for Tanzania. In fiscal year 2003/04 the deficit as a percentage of GDP before grants was 11.2%. After considering grants it was 4.0%. It has to be curtailed to a minimum. Tanzania cannot achieve economic self-reliance and truly own its development agenda when its total domestic revenue, in June 2004, was a mere 13.5% of GDP. Tanzania is not meeting its own needs. In the financial year 2003/2004, foreign aid and grants were Shs 625.1 million compared to total domestic revenue collections. tax and non-tax) of Shs 1.27 billion or 51% of the total government budget. Foreign aid and grants as a percentage of GDP have risen from 2.5% in 1997/98 to 11.9% in 2004/2005. The dependency on foreign assistance is neither sustainable nor is it in the security interest of the country. There are positive signs in having the reliance on foreign aid and grants reduced. In fiscal year 2003/2004 it came down to 45% and the budget for 2004/2005 forecast a reduction to 41%. The dependency would still be high and there is little doubt, in the light of a difficult global economic environment whose central focus, notwithstanding the polemics about the Millennium Development Goals, is the fight against terrorism that it is simply dangerous to continue to rely on aid and grants. The radio statement made by President Mkapa addressed to Tanzanians at the end of May about self-reliance reflects the bold reality and Tanzanians have to come to terms with that reality. In this regard, it is paradoxical that an astute economist like Professor Ibrahim Lipumba, the Chairman of the Civic United Front political party, would question, following the Budget Speech for fiscal year 2004/2005, the benefits of the cash budget system that the Tanzania government has so successfully used over the past seven years to ensure prudent expenditure management.

HIV/AIDS: The Battle for a New Liberation

Tanzania must vigorously combat HIV/AIDS. An HIV/AIDS Indicator Survey sponsored by the Tanzania Commission for Aids. TACAIDS) and undertaken by the National Bureau of Statistics reveals that in 2004, 7% of Tanzanians or about 2.2 million were infected with the deadly virus. Thus, whilst Tanzania's average life expectancy was a high 51 years in 1987, it had declined to 49 years in 2000. HIV/AIDS has a strong negative impact on human capital and national development. The World Bank estimates that Tanzania's GDP by 2015 could come down by 15-20% due to the HIV/AIDS pandemic if no appropriate programmes and institutional arrangements are put in place quickly. President Mkapa is deeply committed to the task of mobilising and sensitising the population and especially the youth on the certain death that faces the country with all its devastating consequences on national development. Tanzanians cannot afford to continue to lead lives as if everything was normal in human sexual relationships. Sex life has to change. It *must* change. No area of greater concern exists in the Tanzanian society that demands total partnership in firm action, across all sectors of society, than attacking the multifaceted character of the AIDS pandemic. No amount of money in medication and sensitisation would save the nation. It is the character and the sheer dogged resolve of every person that would prove to be the salvation. Nevertheless, here also lies the challenge for public-private partnership.

The private sector as well as the civil society and NGOs must use their workplaces and communities as sensitivity laboratories for promoting behavioural change. The lead example shown by South Africa's Anglo American Corporation in underwriting the costs of medical treatment of all their workers infected with HIV or suffering from AIDS should be replicated by the Tanzania business sector. There is also need to recognise the health delivery intervention in this area of the William J. Clinton Foundation through which a deal with Indian pharmaceutical companies was struck in October 2003 for halving the prices of anti-retroviral drugs for treatment of AIDS. Under the deal, the price of the ARV formulations were expected to fall from around US $ 418 and US $ 300 to less than 50% per person per annum. This is the kind of public-private partnership that needs to be deepened in Tanzania if marked improvement in addressing the pandemic would be realised.

The Crisis of Jobs

Labour in Tanzania gained significantly from the expansion of "populist" economic policies flowing from the adoption of the Arusha Declaration in 1967. The rapid growth of the parastatal sector and of the public administration particularly following the adoption of the 1972 Decentralisation Programme, created thousands of jobs, direct and indirect. Indirect jobs were created in the sense that big government meant, on the one hand, big consumption whose spill over or multiplier effect was also huge. On the other hand, the expanding parastatal sector, notably in the 1970s, gave birth to several new corporate jobs in the economy. It is significant to note that until the mid 1980s, the government and state-owned enterprises absorbed all graduates from institutions of higher learning annually as a deliberate policy. However, a different employment environment emerged with the on-set of deep economic reforms as part of the re-definition of the role of the state in the post-command economy era and as a move to transform the government into a better-focused and more efficient administration. Moreover, parastatals had to layoff workers as part of their restructuring, closure and privatisation. Economic liberalisation has generally unleashed a new business management discipline centred on the principle: compete or die. These measures have also catapulted a painful quest for a jobs recovery programme.

The crisis of jobs has inevitably fuelled a debate. There are those who view the loss of thousands of jobs as an abdication of people-centred development policies identified with the Arusha Declaration. Another group views job losses as a capitulation by the government to liberal economic policies advanced by the IMF and the World Bank. They surmise that these policies have not proven themselves anywhere without causing turmoil. However, is it not the reality that these job losses have in fact been an inevitable result of a new environment of competitiveness that has been catapulted by globalisation? How else would one rationalise the jobs conundrum of the 1990s and early 2000 in the highly industrialised countries? For example, both Germany and France in 2004 had unemployment rates of close to 10%, the highest in decades. Even the US economy is confronted by a jobs crisis, with 6.1% unemployment rate in 2003, representing almost 9 million unemployed. It is important to take note, that since the 1980s, the global economy has come face to face with increased competition at international and national levels. This new form of competition has not only been spearheaded by the rise of transnational and multinational corporations in global trade and investment but also by the entry of new technologies.

In a pioneering book, *The End of Work: The Decline of the Global Labour Force and the Dawn of the Post-Market Era*, Jeremy Rifkin (1995) paints a bleak picture of jobs and employment. In his view, technology breakthroughs are precipitating "an era of near worker less production" at a time when the global population is surging to unprecedented levels. His foresight is that the "the clash between rising population pressures and falling job opportunities will shape the geopolitics of the jobs emerging high-tech global economy well into the next century". Rifkin is not the only voice of jobs future shock. Peter Drucker in his book *Post Capitalist Society* equally warned that "the disappearance of labour as a key factor of production" is going to emerge as the critical "unfinished business of capitalist society". The Editor of the US *New Perspectives Quarterly*, Nathan Gardels also wrote in the *Washington Post* of April 11,1993 under the title, *Capitalism's New Order*, that "from the standpoint of the market, the ever swelling ranks of the unemployed face a fate worse than colonialism: economic irrelevance". These are disturbing scenarios. Yet, they are not completely unforeseen. In fact, in the *First Volume of Das Kapital* published in 1867, Karl Marx forecasted the steady elimination of workers by machines. He observed that each new technological breakthrough "transforms the worker's operations more and more into mechanical operations, so that at a certain point the mechanism can step into his place — hence we have the struggle of the worker against machinery. What used to be the activity of the workers' labour becomes that of the machine." Jacques Attali, the late President Mitterand's Minister and technology consultant, in his book *Millennium: Winners and Losers in the Coming World Order* describes machines as "the new proletariat."

For the industrialised countries, there is a serious policy commitment to addressing the problem of job loss. They have little choice as the problem is precipitating political upheaval marked by severe restrictions in migrant labour and the rise to political power of right wing parties in Western Europe. Their focus of attention is on the question: how does the powerful technology revolution translate into a promise for a great transformation for the people? Social scientists like Rifkin warn that failure to ensure equitable sharing of the productivity gains resulting from high-tech revolution would reinforce the growing gap between the rich and poor and would lead to social and political turmoil *"on a global scale."* These countries have therefore called for the re-definition of opportunities and responsibilities for millions of their people.

However, how do such redefinitions of opportunities in the developed world spill over to poor countries? Do poor countries have any choice but to follow the economic model of the industrialised world? Is such a model relevant given the fact that the third world is yet to incorporate state of the art technologies that significantly replace people with machines? Yet poor countries have little choice but to promote international competitiveness. Their business firms have to cut back middle management layers, retrench unskilled and semi-skilled personnel, decouple business activities by shedding off unprofitable lines and place greater focus on core activities in which firms enjoy distinctive competence and competitiveness. Such process of downsizing or right sizing is inevitable. In fact, economic reforms being implemented have unleashed a new business discipline that requires firms to be lean, fit and flexible. Firms should moreover design strategies that counteract growing competition and high transaction costs. Consequently, loss of jobs would intensify rather than regress in the future.

In such an environment, there is need to revisit the obtaining industrial relations regime in place. The traditional management. employer) - worker adversarial model of industrial relations has become outmoded and a shackle on competitiveness. In the industrialised world, trade unionism is fast departing from its confrontational mode. In fact, they are experiencing a decline in trade union membership and use of strikes as a weapon for negotiations. In its place, there is now emerging what is described as "business unionism" whose central thrust is the improvement of total work and income security through the enhancement of workers' mobility and skills development across jobs within and across companies.

It is disappointing that little is taking place in Tanzania at such labour-management front. The Tanzania Federation of Trade Unions. TFTU) is still more involved in protection of workers' rights, especially during retrenchment and in bargaining higher wages than in helping industries to prosper and thereby secure better benefits for the workers. Time has come for the TFTU to change its management culture and adopt "business unionism." It must quickly shift its strategy from collective bargaining to productivity bargaining. PB). PB, amongst other strategies, addresses problems of loss of business turnover as such outcome leads to loss of jobs. The TFTU and associated unions should now face the reality that the tough economic situation in place embodies competition, privatisation and deregulation and should thus be willing to discuss long-term measures to address such challenges. Joint problem solving between the unions and employers is the way forward.

Tanzanian business firms are now increasingly driven by competitiveness and bottom line considerations. They have few options but to move fast and adapt, introduce modern technology and upgrade the skills of workers. This should be the trend. Growth of jobs will come through higher economic growth, deeper industrialisation and higher investments. Even then, the crisis of jobs in Tanzania will remain for a long time to come. Tanzania should therefore brace itself to manage the crisis of jobs and craft innovative policies to address it. It is noteworthy that the National Strategy for Economic Growth and Reduction of Poverty which becomes operational in July, 2005 targets job creation as one of the key programmes it will focus upon within the over all national quest to realise the MDGs by 2015.

Youth in Crisis

Such a quest to promote sustainable sources of employment especially for the youth is paramount. In 2002, Tanzania had about 46% of its population below the age of 15 years, of whom only 10% had post-primary school education and training compared to 20% in the OECD countries and 30% in the Asian countries. This youth demographic profile poses serious challenges to policy makers and to the private sector in Tanzania as it imposes huge burdens on the economy, the environment, urbanisation, peace and tolerance. There are two important aspects to ponder. First, the demographic profile manifests itself in rural-urban migration. This has serious implications on the immediate and future capacity of peasant agriculture development, on the ground of displacement of able-bodied human-power and literate persons better able to absorb modern farm methods. Second, it manifests itself in a crisis of employment. Almost 650,000 youth enter the labour market each year. Based on data on the growth sectors of the economy for the next few years, employment will increase by between 50,000 to 60,000 a year, covering less than 10% of job entrants. The report in the Economic Survey, 2003 shows that the unemployment rate is estimated at 12.9% of total labour force, which is given as 17.8 million of whom 75% live in rural areas. *The Tanzania Poverty and Human Development Report 2002* points out that unemployment increased from 3.5% in 1990/91 to 5% in 2000/2001 with the most affected being in the age group of 15 to 34 years.

The most critical challenge in addressing the unemployment problem is the improvement of education standards and widening the scope of vocational training. There is wide consensus among new investors in Tanzania that the quality of our graduates, at different levels of education, is far below that of neighbouring countries like Kenya and Uganda. Whilst Tanzania trained a large pool of managers in the socialist era, who are still available in the job market, their training and experience was largely rooted in the monopoly state enterprise system. In such circumstances, it is sometimes easier to train a novice than to change somebody's mindset influenced under a different social and economic environment. This situation could explain why some ex-parastatal executives have failed to secure jobs in the post economic liberalisation period. Evidently, the quality of education should be improved. The curricula should also change to respond to skills needed by the market. Part nine of the book addresses some of these issues.

Transforming Mindsets

The challenge Tanzania faces if it is to pursue a successful, consistent and forward-looking economic policy is that of the state of the mindset of its people. It is all too easy to heap opprobrium that the achievements so far attained at the macro-economic level have not benefited the majority or reduced poverty of Tanzanians. It is as if this is a response to somebody having postulated that macro-economic stability automatically breeds prosperity. That would be ludicrous. On the other hand, to think that there exists a different route, a more direct one to bolstering higher living standards of the majority of Tanzanians by short-circuiting the reform process under implementation is at best illusory and deceptive at worst.

Yet, recently there has emerged in Tanzania a strong plank involving leading politicians and even business leaders, brandishing the argument that macro-economic stability has not reduced poverty. This stance has sometimes been drummed up to a demagoguery crescendo. This is a concerning stance. It manifests a mindset directed at dovetailing the privatisation process, especially its momentum. Moreover, it has used derogatory expressions against privatisation, describing it as *"uzungunization"*. loosely meaning, in racial terms, as "Europeanisation"). In other words, privatisation is the selling off of state enterprises to foreigners. A Tanzania local Kiswahili daily newspaper, *Nipashe* of August 2, 2003, reporting on the official hand over of the Dar es Salaam Water Supply and Sewage Company. DAWASA) to a British firm, Biowater, under a ten year management concession, printed as its headline story: *"Hatimaye Wazungu wakabidhiwa DAWASA"*. meaning that finally the "whites" or Europeans are handed over DAWASA). The fact that the government has terminated the contract with Biowater for apparent malperformance is not sufficient ground to give credence to such racist reporting.

In fact, non-Tanzanian investors have even been accused of buying state enterprises using "black" and "illicit drugs money." Is this not going overboard? The sudden upsurge of this mindset appears to be driven by the revival of sentiments and passions about the "indigenisation" of the economy that call for the economy to be largely owned by Tanzanians of African origin. It is critical to demolish this myth being propagated that foreign participation in business in Tanzania is not in the interests of Tanzania. This I seek to do in Part eight of the book.

"Indigenisation" of the Economy

The clamour for the economic empowerment of Tanzanians. of African origin) has more recently re-emerged more vociferously, taking more of a political stance than economic. The clamour is also directly linked to privatisation. In fact, the move to present a Bill for the privatisation of the National Micro-Finance Bank. NMB) early in 2003 was undermined by Parliamentarians precisely for the reason that the bank was viewed to be more of a vehicle for propelling economic empowerment of majority Tanzanians than being an ordinary commercial bank. Its privatisation, especially where foreigners are involved, was regarded as almost certainly destined to undermine the core objective of ensuring that the NMB served micro-finance interests. Sensing the Bill's defeat in the House, the government tactically withdrew it, ostensibly to "fine-tune" it. Since that debacle, the government has been debating whether NMB should be privatised through an *IPO*, with the majority government shares being ultimately sold to Tanzanians through the DSE or going along with a foreign strategic investor with minority shares being retained by the government.

A notification released on the PSRC website in December 2003, indicated that the government had decided to sell 49% of NMB's shares to a consortium of strategic investors led by a commercial bank having proven experience in banking business. The sale did not specifically involve Tanzanian ownership. By requiring proven banking experience for the strategic investors, it could impute that the government was seeking the involvement, apart from that of a commercial bank, of institutions such as the Development Bank of the Netherlands. FMO), the Commonwealth Development Corporation. CDC), the International Finance Corporation. IFC), TDFL and the like. It was inconceivable that such shareholding would have qualified the Tanzanian pension and social security funds. The notification also provided that upon strategic investors showing interest, 21% of the shares of NMB would be sold to citizens of Tanzania or to companies in which citizens of Tanzania own 100%. The residual 30% shares would be retained by the government and subsequently offloaded, through an IPO, to the Tanzanian public at large. However, more recent events, since the fourth quarter of 2004, indicate a move to sell 49% of the NMB shares to a consortium of Tanzanian investors who have collaboration with a first class local or foreign commercial bank. The distribution of the shares would be 24% citizens and 5% the bank. This is part of the context in which some Tanzanians under a financial corporate vehicle called *National Investment Company Limited.* NICO) have raised capital. NICO, a Unit Trust type of institution, was one of the institutions that bid successfully for NMB in collaboration with Rabo Bank of Holland. Under the NMB privatisation plan, the government would retain 51% of NMB shares. These would, in due course, be sold to the Tanzanian public under an IPO framework.

The changes adopted by the government as to the form of privatisation of NMB do not mark any departure from earlier government position encapsulated in the Bill that was earlier frustrated by a cluster of MPs who had read "foreignisation" of NMB's ownership in that Bill. The government's intention was and continues to be that NMB has to come under a significant ownership and control of a bank or bank- linked institutions to ensure viability. Nevertheless, my position has a different twist. In my view, the key issue in the privatisation of the NMB is not so much the *form of ownership* as the *objective of the bank*. In other words, would NMB be a micro-finance bank? If yes, as the underpinning of the passion that has driven the form of privatisation appears to be, the resulting question is whether the NMB would then be viable. With 104 branches and 4 agencies around the country, NMB's viability would be questionable if retained as a holistic, homogeneous bank. The pre-privatisation NBC is well aware of the burden it carried on its overall profitability because of its huge size. Most rural and district branches of NBC had to be subsidised by the cosmopolitan branches. It is for that reason that NBC was unbundled into two segments after Mwalimu Nyerere's intervention, driven by the logic that a third segment comprising rural branches would not have attracted a serious investor for lack of viability. Otherwise, ideally, NBC was to be restructured, as proposed by the Nyirabu Banking Commission, into three separate banks. It would be interesting to find out how the consortium of strategic investors, local and foreign, would structure NMB in the context of our view that the objective of the bank should be overriding.

As argued later in this overview, I seriously doubt that structured exclusively as a micro finance bank, NMB would be viable. The Tanzanian public have to be cautioned, and the prospectus has to be very transparent in exposing the full facts relating to the viability of the bank in its totality, about what they may get themselves into under an NMB IPO as now proposed. It should not be forgotten how many Tanzanians have lost substantial amounts of their capital through purchase of shares in Tanzania Oxygen Limited. Such eventuality should not be allowed to recur as it could have serious political repercussions.

However, these concerns notwithstanding, I should make it clear that nobody in his right senses would question the logic, the imperativeness and the urgency to work out systems and mechanisms to empower all nationals, of all racial backgrounds, that lack the resources to participate effectively in the wealth creation process. The passion for nationals to control their own economy could not be faltered even when the prevailing logic is that national economies are increasingly becoming microcosms of the global economy. Such logic holds that the nature of ownership is increasingly becoming obsolete particularly for countries whose economic growth is heavily dependent on foreign investments. But this should not infer that nationals should sit idly by and be sidelined in owning part, a large part at that, of their economy. Indeed, the formation of NICO and similar vehicles as the one put in place by TCCIA, and their quest to enable the majority of Tanzanians participate in business ownership formation and creation has to be hailed as a positive move in this direction. Such quest is as valid as it is urgent. A brilliant article in *Harvard Business Review* of August 2003, titled, *Making the world safe for markets,* which features in the book *World On Fire* by Amy Chua, captures well the dangers of not addressing such empowerment. The Yale Law School Professor posits, "— the most formidable problem the developing world faces is structural-and it's one the West has little experience with. It's the phenomenon of the market-dominant minority, ethnic minorities who, for widely varying reasons, tend under market conditions to dominate economically the impoverished "indigenous" majorities around them. They're the Chinese in Southeast-Asia, Indians in East Africa and parts of Caribbean, Lebanese in West Africa, and whites in Zimbabwe, South Africa, and Bolivia, to name just a few".

In countries with a market-dominant minority, the rich are not just rich but also invariably belong to a resented "outsider" ethnic group. In free-market environments, such minorities, together with foreign investors. who are often their business partners), tend to accumulate starkly disproportionate wealth, fuelling ethnic envy and resentment among the poor majorities. When democratic reforms give voice to this previously silenced majority, opportunistic demagogues can swiftly marshal majoritarian animosity into powerful ethno-nationalist movements that can subvert both markets and democracy." It is important to note, though, that the economies that Professor Chua refers to, notably where the Chinese are the minorities, namely Indonesia and Malaysia, those minorities, especially in the specific case of Indonesia, control as much as 70% of the private economy. In Tanzania, in contrast, probably not more than 15% of GDP contributed by the private economy could be directly under the control of the national racial minority. In fact, 30% of GDP is in the informal sector that is controlled by the national ethnic majority. Therefore, yes, Tanzanians of Asian origin have a disproportionate control of *individual* wealth. However, they do not have the kind of disproportionate control of the economy the way white South Africans do in South Africa.

The key point in my concern with the over drummed up indigenisation policy is that it could perversely de-credentialise indigenous economic achievers like Reginald Mengi and Mwita Gachuma who have risen to business success almost entirely through self-driven entrepreneurial enterprise and diligence. They have not succeeded by using state "crutches," a notion wrongly promoted to underpin the concept of indigenisation. The fact that Tanzanians of indigenous origin were left behind in wealth creation and ownership during the implementation of *Ujamaa* should not, in itself, constitute, in my view, the core reason for the state to firm up affirmative action programmes to leverage indigenous Tanzanians. There are those who would disagree with me and hold that the approach is politically correct. However, one may question such a position in terms of results. Business and economic success have distinctive underpinnings that do not necessarily coincide with political correctness of empowerment programmes. This is what Mahathir has described as *The Second Malay Dilemma,* an issue I revert to in the next section and more elaborately in chapter twenty eight.

Suffice it to state that it is debatable whether, in fact, there had been a deliberate policy under *Ujamaa* of disempowering "indigenous" Tanzanians in the same manner that the Bumiputra in Malaysia were under colonialism and black South Africans under apartheid. In Malaysian and South African cases, disempowerment provided strong moral and political grounds for justifying the introduction of affirmative action. Even then, the disempowerment in these two countries could not be viewed in the narrow sense of wealth ownership. The more critical concerns centred on unequal access to land, education, jobs, health facilities and other economic benefits. In contrast, indigenous Tanzanians were and have not been disempowered or unequally treated under *Ujamaa*. By the policies it pursued, CCM. and its predecessor party, TANU), had hoped that the nationalisation of the commanding heights of the economy and the establishment of a robust state owned enterprise sector would, over time, significantly reduce the role and impact of private enterprise to a level where it would not cause the type of wealth divides and sensitivities that now seem to incite the clamour for affirmative action for indigenous Tanzanians.

It is in this context that Iddi Simba's thesis, published in June 2003 under the title, *The Concept of Indigenisation,* should be critically examined. Indigenisation could not be viewed as some kind of magic bullet, a panacea for successful mainstreaming of majority Tanzanians in wealth creation and ownership. That would be an illusion. Thus, the real challenge before the economic empowerment movement in Tanzania is how to enable the national majorities who have control over the major economic factor of the economy, namely land ownership, to turn such control into wealth. Equally imperative is what Professor Chua has described as the need for an "act of enlightened self-interest to launch and promote local corporate responsibility initiatives and innovative profit-sharing programmes." Such programmes could involve, for example, extending grants to TASAF that support programmes at grassroots levels targeting poverty reduction and small scale economic ventures. Private sector businesses particularly owned by Tanzanians of Asian origin should take this form of corporate responsibility as a challenge to them. At the same time, the opening up of agriculture to commercial investments could be planned in such a way as to enable joint ventures between foreign investors and Tanzanians to take place. I for one do not believe that a return to the 1990 investment promotion legal regime that spelt out areas to be strictly reserved for Tanzanian nationals to invest in is the solution to empowering nationals economically. This is a subject we examine briefly in the next section and more elaborately later in this book.

Chapter

8 WEALTH CREATION AND CULTURE

"A race of people is like an individual man: until it uses its own talent, takes pride in its history, expresses its own culture and affirm its own selfhood, it cannot fulfil itself."

-Malcolm X

Economic empowerment is a complex issue. There are no easy conventional formulas for addressing it. Lessons seem to show that, at root, successful empowerment is self-driven, not externally driven. Thus, In Malaysia, the architect of positive discrimination for the Bumiputras has had second thoughts about the policy that he introduced in 1971 as part of a New Economic Policy. In a Speech to the Harvard Club of Malaysia, in July 2002 titled *The New Malay Dilemma*, Mahathir Mohammad noted that affirmative action gave "crutches" to the Malay indigenous people who had since failed to use them effectively. He pointed out that time had come for the government to take away the crutches from them as they had abused them and had failed to develop a "no crutches" mindset.

In Mahathir's view, it is the culture of business and entrepreneurship that matters in wealth creation and empowerment itself. Wealth creation and business success are not about race. In Mahathir's view, if the Malay Bumiputras failed to change their culture- towards work, quality, and pride- there could be no progress. This is a lesson Tanzanians who are overly passionate about economic empowerment should learn. Indigenisation or *Uzawa* is not and could never be a policy panacea for wealth creation. In fact, it could politically be a recipe for national economic disaster. Tanzanians should therefore dispassionately address the core root of their incapacity to be effective wealth creators. They should shun shortcuts, including those introduced through the legislative process. It is not feasible to effect successful entrepreneurship or the aspiration to get rich through law. Poverty is a state of mind as much as wealth is equally a state of mind. Yes, some Tanzanians would argue that poverty in Tanzania is not a consequence of indolence; it is a product of the social-economic system. This could be so. However, it does not override the reality that there exists a poverty of entrepreneurship in the social milieu.

Poverty of entrepreneurship has its historical basis. Individual wealth was disparaged under *ujamaa*. Yet, there is no policy today that denies Tanzanians equal opportunity to go ahead and become rich. Moreover, based on the experience I have had working in rural Tanzania, I believes that there is a culture of poverty ingrained in Tanzanians and particularly in the rural population. This is a culture that is resistant to change and unable, at this stage, to take full advantage of the changing conditions in the economy and of the opportunities that are available. Tanzania faces a cruel dichotomy between having "able-bodied" people and a people who are not "able-minded" or "able-cultured," from a development perspective. This dichotomy cannot be addressed simply through an indigenisation policy or by making bank credit more readily available to peasants and the urban informal sector players. Addressing the dichotomy requires a bold and inspiring leadership, a leadership that is able to connect with ordinary people in metaphors and symbols that touch their hearts and minds and thus ingrain a new culture that sees hard and productive work as the basis for their economic renewal and prosperity. From the mid 1960s to mid 1970s, Nyerere was able to inculcate a culture of nation building and self-reliance.

Thus, in an environment where people suffer from a culture of poverty, easier availability of or access to bank credit may not be the answer to economic empowerment. As Fareed Zakaria (1994) wrote in his article *Culture is Destiny* in the journal *Foreign Affairs*, based on his conversation with Lee Kuan Yew, if you have a culture that does not place much value in learning, scholarship, hard work, thrift and deferment of present enjoyment for future gain, the going will become slower. In other words, culture of wealth creation is destiny. The South Commission Report, *The Challenge to the South*, affirmed this view when it observed, "the broad environment for the effectiveness of capital formation is a society's culture." Changing a culture is evidently more difficult than changing the policies of government. It is simpler for a government to propose an empowerment policy in the manner in which the Tanzania government has done with its National Economic Empowerment Policy. This policy has been translated into a National Economic Empowerment Act, passed by Parliament in November 2004. However, the key test of a successful policy and legislation lies in implementation. Success in this case would crucially hinge on the state of attitudes and business or entrepreneurial culture of the people. Creating a Fund, as envisaged by the law, which would be a financing vehicle to assist Tanzanians of no or little means and unable to borrow from banks on commercial terms is only the beginning in empowering people. The greater challenge will be in getting those empowered to use the funds well and thereby uplifting their capacities to create wealth. This is where accountability would be needed in managing the Fund.

The Stock Market and Empowerment

One of the viable avenues of economic empowerment is the use of the stock market. Much as the majority of Tanzanians may not yet have shares in companies floated on the DSE for lack of adequate disposable income, the success story of the present uptake of shares shows that it is possible for the stock market to become a key avenue of economic empowerment. However, one of the drawbacks is that the stock market itself is yet to be sufficiently developed. However, it can. In fact, it can also become the catalyst for promoting greenfield investments, playing an important source of risk capital. Available data shows, that as at end June 2002, the amount of financial resources sourced by private firms through the Dar es Salaam Stock Exchange. DSE) was only shillings 4.3 billion or 0.07% of GDP. At the same time, only 0.21% of the Tanzanian population or 72,776 individuals participated in trading shares at the DSE as at 9th February 2005. Total market capitalisation, on the other hand, increased from Tanzania shillings 500 billion in 2002 to Shillings 790.43 billion. equivalent of US$ 712.95) as at 15 April 2005, constituting about 31.96 of GDP. PPP). In Kenya, market capitalisation is much higher. As at 15 April 2005, the Nairobi Stock Exchange. NSE) had a total market capitalisation of Kenyan Shillings 326.94 billion or US$ 4.3 billion. The market capitalisation constituted 60.5% of GDP. PPP). Uganda on the other hand had a market capitalisation on 15 April 2005 of Shs. 2.17 trillion equivalent to US$ 1.21 billion or 32.5% of GDP. PPP). Clearly the DSE remains the thinnest in East Africa.

If one compares the thinness of the DSE with what India has achieved in the same area, one then senses the enormity of the challenge that lies before Tanzania in promoting higher domestic savings and investments. In September 2004, Reliance Industries as a group had a market capitalisation of US$ 19.0 billion. In the United States, about 45% of Americans own shares directly or through mutual funds. In 2004 America's stock market capitalisation was roughly US 10 trillion equivalent to 108% it's GDP. PPP). What is significant to note about Tanzania's stock market listing is that out of the presently seven listed companies, two of them, namely Tanzania Breweries and Tanzania Cigarettes Company, controlled 72.77% of the total market capitalisation as at 7th January 2005. The challenge is clearly to deepen market capitalisation by having more companies transforming themselves from private, family owned, to publicly held ones. Apparently, such transformation is hindered by the unpreparedness of many private firms to get their operations to fall under strict and stringent corporate governance disclosure requirements applied to listed companies. Yet the stock market constitutes a key avenue for economic empowerment of everybody in society if well stimulated regulated.

Part of the process of stimulating the stock market and thereby opening up more robust sources for investment, was the government decision to allow the DSE to trade in securities and bonds. The East African Development Bank was the first institution to exploit such opportunity in 2001 and has twice participated in trading its bonds to raise capital for project financing. Another positive move was the decision of the government to allow the partial liberalisation of the capital account, with effect from May 2003. That step has enabled cross listing of shares from other bourses, starting with those in East Africa. So far, Kenya Airways has had its stocks cross-listed on the DSE, as of September 2004. It is likely that East African Breweries would soon follow. South Africa has applied to have its stocks traded on the Johannesburg stock exchange to be cross-listed on the DSE. It is noteworthy that the decision to allow foreign participation in the secondary shares market at the DSE as well as the trading in shares, up to 60% of shares floated, would almost certainly invigorate the Tanzania national bourse.

Following the lead taken by Tanzania Tea Packers Limited. TATEPA), hitherto a 100% private owned company, in floating its shares on the DSE, the challenge is now to see more and more private companies, notably the family owned ones, using the DSE to raise non-debt capital. Such move would also broaden the base of ownership of business, a move in keeping with the national objective of mainstreaming the majority Tanzanians in the ownership process. Tanzania needs to see a quick departure from the present system where the government is the main player at the DSE through the process of off-loading state shares of parastatal bodies. In this context, the birth of the Tanzania Unit Trust in June 2003 and the formation of NICO in mid 2004 herald a historic opportunity in the quest to promote mobilisation and investment of personal savings for investment. The challenge that the Unit Trust and NICO will face in the initial period is the present thinness of the DSE. In time, however, with cross listing of stocks picking momentum, the constraint may be short lived. At the same time, the challenge can be viewed in the context of the creativity of these institutions and those like them, including the SACCOS, to invest in greenfield projects.

Micro-Credit and Empowerment

Another avenue for economic empowerment is easy access to micro-credit. Little wonder that the United Nations has decided to declare 2005 as the International Year of Micro credit. However, what boggles the mind is the rather simplistic attempt made from some quarters in Tanzanian society to link, for example, the privatisation of NMB with the goal of economic empowerment of majority Tanzanians. The form of ownership of NMB, in itself, cannot determine how the bank would operate in order to ensure viability. This is not the picture one gathers from banks such as the CRDB Bank and AKIBA Bank that have sizeable Tanzanian ownership. Therefore, lest we dramatise and drum up illusory expectations to the "wananchi," the people, about the potential availability of "easier credit access" from NMB and such similar banks and financial institutions, in the same manner that small loans are obtained from SACCOS and Pride Africa-type of micro-finance institutions, it is imperative to check the loan portfolios of these banks. They would clearly present a different picture from what many think. Thus, whatever ownership structure NMB finally takes, we should remain cautious about the expectation some Tanzanians hold about NMB's role in economic empowerment of majority Tanzanians. It is not my wish or that of any Tanzanian to see NMB collapse simply through acts of economic populism. In this context, CRDB, for example, has decided to establish a subsidiary bank specifically to promote economic empowerment precisely because it knows that the mainstream CRDB Bank could not cater for basic loan needs of majority Tanzanians that fall within the framework of economic empowerment policy.

It would appear that the populism surrounding the link of NMB's privatisation with economic empowerment is its institutional association with micro-finance from the time of its establishment. Yet NMB is not *truly* a micro-finance bank. Its charter of incorporation may describe it so, but its structure and nature of operations do not reflect such objective. Micro-finance banks that are well known in the world, such as the Grameen Bank in Bangladesh as well as institutions such as the Mindanao Enterprise Development Foundation in the Philippines that operate as micro-finance banks provide loans based on group lending. There is no collateral attached to such loans. Neighbours guarantee one another's loans and interest rates are invariably much higher than those charged by commercial banks. Such higher interest rates offset the huge transaction costs associated with such forms of lending.

As conceived, following its being hived off from the National Bank of Commerce, NMB could not operate on similar basis. Its part metropolitan character, branch-location wise, and given the form and character of the loan portfolio envisaged by those who promote its being made a bank for economic empowerment of the so-called *"Wazawa,"* would not allow it to be a viable micro-finance bank. Above all, it is inconceivable that a foreign investor would bid to acquire a significant share in a bank like NMB that is required, by law, to offer micro-credit facilities directly. This I say notwithstanding the reports that the prospectus released for NMB's privatisation shows that the bank is highly profitable notwithstanding the apparent huge losses made by several of its rural branches. The key point is that NMB has so far not operated as a micro-finance bank. Thus, its profitability may be misleading when considered in the context of its being required to operate as a micro-finance bank after privatisation. CRDB Bank, Akiba and Exim Banks, are examples of banks that are not micro-finance banks but which promote lending to small borrowers by using micro-finance institutions at grassroots levels, such as SACCOS. In Kenya, Cooperative Banks have for years been key avenues for such on-lending transactions that cater for micro- credit needs of small borrowers in rural and urban areas. In other words, mainstream banks can indeed be strategic supporters of micro-finance lending without their being directly involved. In this context, NMB can equally support micro-finance lending. However, given its wide and expansive branch network, character and diversity of clientele, it is doubtful that it could operate profitably as a micro-finance bank.

In addition, another dimension to be looked into in sifting the philosophy of indigenisation is the culture of saving, accumulation and investment that still eludes many Tanzanians, especially the indigenous ones. There is a preponderant propensity to consume in our culture that explains why the savings ratio to GDP in 2002 was only 11.1% compared to Kenya's 17.0%. Even Uganda had a higher ratio of 14.7%. Total deposits of all commercial banks in Tanzania as at April 2003 accounted for only 14% of GDP. The comparative figures for Kenya, South Africa and Mauritius are 37%, 55% and 74% respectively. Tanzania therefore needs to save more and achieve higher savings rates of around 25%. That is when bank deposits would also rise and crucially support lending. Of course, one could pose the point whether an enabling incentive for people to open deposit accounts in banks exists in the light of current low interest rates. This would be a plausible question. Even then, the more probable explanation for the current state of low deposits in banks is the savings culture that obtains in the society, a culture aggravated by the extreme low base of income generation by the majority of Tanzanians. This dilemma about a poor culture of savings and investments flies in the face of the whole ethos and thrust of economic empowerment of majority or indigenous Tanzanians. Money begets money as they say. You cannot therefore become wealthy if you do not save and invest at the same time. Herein lies the challenge of entrepreneurship promotion.

Entrepreneurship is Paramount

David Landes (1998) writes in his magisterial treatise, *The Wealth and Poverty of Nations*, "We live in a world of inequality and diversity. This world is divided roughly into three kinds of nations. Those that spend lots of money to keep their weight down; those whose people eat to live; and those whose people don't know where the next meal is coming from."

The central debilitating malaise that afflicts Tanzania and Africa generally and which undermines development is entrepreneurial constipation. The majority of Tanzanians and Africans still work to live. They largely lack the achievement motivation and the greed for social and economic advancement. They tend to devour capital, not to create it and invest it profitably. Conventional wisdom would attribute Africa's low level of entrepreneurship that is the capacity to perceive profitable opportunities and intelligently seizing them by taking risks, to weak national governance. However, the reality is different. The Tanzania government and most African governments have committed themselves to improving the business and economic environment through enabling macro-economic policies and measures. Equally, micro economic bottlenecks that constrain the buoyancy of economic enterprise are being attended to. In other words, there are deliberate efforts directed at bolstering the growth of entrepreneurship. Evidently, African governments, and Tanzania is no exception, cannot claim to have done all that is necessary to catalyse entrepreneurship to an ideal level. There are both compelling and competing challenges that face African governments, like addressing basic education and health needs, much as these also feed into enabling entrepreneurship to take shape and grow. Fundamentally, there is an intimate nexus between rising levels of entrepreneurship and optimum mobilisation of domestic resources. Yet, the nexus faces the chicken and egg quandary. What is important to note is that the doors of the Tanzania government have been open to an active and vital engagement with entrepreneurs to identify and effect the strategic measures necessary to further leverage business and economic activity.

However, to what extent the improvement in the business environment necessarily spurs entrepreneurship is debatable. Just as the world is ruled by rapid change and knowledge-driven innovation, so is entrepreneurship. Entrepreneurship is not static; it is dynamic. In this context, individuals, not governments, are better placed to take initiatives to respond and to stay ahead of change. Thus, when we think in terms of scales of operation, modern technology, scarcity of capital, total quality productivity, best practices, organisational competence, profits and investments, it is the entrepreneur, not the government, that is primarily responsible for making the success factors of business possible. In other words, entrepreneurship lies at the heart of the spirit of enterprise and should become the ideological mantra of poor countries like Tanzania.

The key challenge that confronts entrepreneurs in Tanzania today and tomorrow is to discover the competitive space to be seized in the national, regional and international markets. Like most Sub-Saharan African countries, Tanzania today trades less with itself and with other nations than it did ten years ago. Lack of market access is part of the problem.

However, it is also a fact that Africa's capacity to produce quality products in large quantities remains a quagmire. Indeed, what is further disturbing is that the value adding business opportunity horizon has become more orthodox and myopic. Tanzanian industries are still predominantly import substituting, not export-oriented. Such business culture could be the main reason for Tanzania's low exports outturn rather than, necessarily, the market fortresses erected in the industrialised economies. Tanzania's exports earnings during 2002/2003 show a skewed character. 38% of the receipts were from gold, with manufactured goods contributing only 7.5%, below fish and fish products whose share was 12.5%. Agricultural commodities. coffee, cotton, tobacco, cashew nuts and other crops) contributed altogether 22.3%. Other exports, which are not agricultural or manufactures, contributed 15.1%. Tourism is a significant contributor of this last segment. It is because of such skewed structure of exports performance that Jagdish Bhagwati has argued that whilst market access is indeed a problem for developing countries, the larger problem is market penetration. In other words, a country may have market access and yet be unable to exploit it. Such dichotomy constitutes the main economic malaise of most African countries. Entrepreneurship should therefore involve the capacity, not only to produce more, but also to produce products that have a market and that can enjoy competitiveness in the global marketplace. Today, many Tanzanian industrialists as well as other economic actors, in the service industry, like tourism, are gripped in grave apprehension about the on-set of the East African Community Customs Union. The main reason for such concern is precisely the state of a mindset that is not well prepared to confront the realities of regional and global business competition.

Yes, Kenyans are equally concerned. However, their concern is more focused on how best to exploit the customs union to take advantage of lower tariffs *vis a vis* imported goods which Uganda and Tanzania may seek to buy from non ECA countries. Even then, it is ludicrous to think that the judgement day for the opening up of the Tanzanian economy could wait until all the perceived costs of doing business in Tanzania would have come down to the levels applicable in Kenya or South Africa. The levels of industrialisation are already overly so skewed in favour of these competing countries that it would not make much difference if the costs of doing business in Tanzania were significantly lowered. On the contrary, it is the broader opening up of the economy, in my view, that would in fact attract the much-needed investment in improving and upgrading infrastructure like energy and transport, thereby lowering the costs of doing business.

Tanzanian entrepreneurs should therefore quickly escape the import substitution mental entrapment. They should chart out a new path and build a strategic business architecture that enables them to venture into and compete in the national, regional and global marketplace. Only then can Tanzania liberate itself, in a more sustainable manner, from the deleterious uncertainty of where the next meal would come from. The opening up of the economy to inward investment is a strategic decision Tanzania should fully embrace as is discuss next.

Who Is "Us" and Who Is "Them"?

*"Post-apartheid South Africa has the most developed and the most dynamic private sector on the continent. It is white, so what? So forget it is white, it is South African, dynamic, highly developed. If the investors of the South Africa begin a new form trekking, you **have** to accept it. It will be ridiculous, absolutely ridiculous, for Africans to go out to seek investment from North America, from Japan, from Europe, from Russia, and then, when these investors come from South Africa to invest in your own country you say, a! a! These fellows now want to take over our economy- this is nonsense. You can't have it both ways. You want foreign investors or you don't want foreign investors."*
-Julius K. Nyerere: Speech at the Conference on **Reflections on Leadership in Africa: Forty years after Independence,** Dar es Salaam, 15 December 1997.

The key point underlying this debate, about who is "us" and who is "them," to borrow the terms of Robert Reich from his outstanding work, *The Work of Nations*, has to be examined closely in the context of the realities of the global economy and thereby debunking the fear of foreign investment. It is evident that a striking feature of the economies of poor countries in the past decade has been the pervasive and vigorous attempt at promoting FDI. The reasons are self-evident. In the past two decades, global FDI flows have exceeded growth rates of world exports of goods and non-factor services and even of world GDP, at current prices. According to the UNCTAD World Investment Report, 2003, the stock of outward FDI was US$ 6.6 trillion in 2001, up from 1.7 trillion 1990. Foreign affiliates of transnational companies, many of which operate in developing countries, accounted for one third of global GDP in 2001 as well as one third of global exports in the same year.

Therefore, to poor countries like Tanzania, FDI has to become one of the key magic bullets for promoting higher and faster economic growth and transformation. FDI is also an important enabling vehicle for transfer of technology, cutting edge skills, best management practices and a culture of competition. There are several examples that can be cited. The excellent performance turnarounds in the beer, cigarettes, cement, tea and sugar industries are proof of the positive impact FDI has had in the Tanzanian economy in recent years. Inevitably, these benefits have unleashed a battleground of competition for investments: direct investment, portfolio investment, cross-border mergers and acquisitions, cross listing of corporate shares in regional and sub-regional stock exchanges and bank lending. Since most poor countries have now more proactively embraced liberal economic policies, the battleground has become fiercer because the critical determinants for attracting FDI have equally become increasingly commonplace. Little wonder, therefore, that the distribution of FDI flows is uneven. But so is the character and quality of investment. For this reason, the challenges confronting poor countries like Tanzania in attracting FDI have become more onerous. Moreover, as the impacts of investment promotion are often benign, countries are necessarily called upon to be more creative and innovative in their strategies and methods of differentiating the products they promote for investment and in broadly exploiting their national distinctive advantages.

Tanzania should question itself: what can it do differently what it is doing now? There is now a near ritual-type of promotion whether it is for investments, trade or tourism. Attendance of Exhibition Fairs around the world has become the conventional wisdom in this endeavour. Yet there are countries that do not rely so much on Fairs. They reach the world stage through other more effective avenues. One such avenue is branding of nations. *"Malaysia, truly Asia,"* is one such powerful brand, effectively conveyed with a logo and sound using global satellite television. Tanzania should equally brand itself. The pertinent question is how one brands Tanzania as a marketable product for investment; how investment promotion is actually undertaken, mindful of who is targeted as potential customer and how the competition is isolated and attacked with the right set of weapons, such as product differentiation, the country in this case being the product, in order to weaken the competition. Finally, there is the question about how investors are assisted and facilitated before and after they set up their business. All these strategies constitute critical distinctive advantages that should be explored and exploited. Tanzania needs to have a visual identity of itself, which a brand logo that departs from the conventional ones depicting Mount Kilimanjaro or the giraffe, should capture and project. Such logo should encapsulate a country that is vibrant and on the move; a country that is united, that is at peace with itself and with the rest of the world; a country rich in natural resources, endowments, rich in diverse cultural values and heritage, and a country with a vision of hope for prosperity. In chapter eleven , I dwell on some of these issues about branding in more detail.

Yet, in spite of the massive challenges that demand a collective purpose and drive about promoting FDI, a troubling and paradoxical situation is emerging in Tanzania. On the one hand, FDI, which has embraced privatisation as one of its core targets, has proven to be an important strategic vehicle in enabling Tanzania to promote higher economic growth. It has also enabled the introduction of new technology and skills as well as a culture of competition in many key economic sectors. It has helped to reverse the trend in job losses following a collapse of a moribund state-owned enterprise sector. Yet, on the other hand, FDI has become a target of attack. An attitude, of wariness, half-heartedness and even hate of FDI, has taken shape. This attitude views FDI as an instrument of economic disenfranchisement of the majority Tanzanians, of loss of right to economic sovereignty, marginalisation of indigenous Tanzanians from wealth ownership, income inequality, job losses and deepening external dependency. It is an attitude that promotes economic insularity. It dominantly focuses on who is *"us"* and belittles the importance of who is *"them"* in Tanzania's economic development. In a recent article on the Pambazuka website, Professor Issa Shivji even dares associate the upsurge of South African investments in Africa and notably in Tanzania as "The Second Great Boer Trek"! It is a dangerous attitude for Tanzania. What many of us know of the Boer Trek has to do with colonialism, apartheid and economic imperialism. To attempt to associate South African investments, whether by white or black investors, with neo-colonial intentions is at best an insult to Tanzania's political capacity to determine and regulate its future.

Law and the Market

Since 1984, Tanzania has been on the road to transform its huge state-owned and controlled economic system into a market driven one. Whilst the new ideology embraces privatisation of state-owned assets, this goal, in itself, has not entailed the total abandonment of the importance and selected role of state entrepreneurship and intervention in the economy. The critical point to note is that the economic reform programme is underlined by the thrust of unleashing market forces to determine the allocation of resources and the performance of economic activities, whether state or private.

A great deal has been done in catapulting market forces to drive economic activities. Indeed, Tanzania's success story in economic reform has centred largely in this area. In the past few years, serious efforts have been directed at stabilising the macro-economic fundamentals. Specifically, fiscal stabilisation has been a major success. This has been achieved in spite of the debt overhang which does not seem to abate in spite of the HIPC initiative coming on stream. Tanzania's external debt stock in 1997/98 was US$ 7.6 billion. In 2003/04, the debt was still US$ 7.9 billion in spite of debt cancellations under HIPC that commenced in 2000/01. One of the important driving forces for achieving fiscal stabilisation is evidently the positive revenue collection administration and prudent expenditure management. Other fundamentals have also been put right. They include price stability, stable and real exchange rate, reform of the tax structure, financial sector reform, privatisation and public service reform.

Consolidating and improving these fundamentals is the challenge that lies ahead. It is clear though that a shift from one form of economic system to another, dramatically different, necessitates a review of laws and institutions to ensure a sound and stable framework for interactions of economic actors in a new environment. This is of significance considering that at the core of the ideological shift are the ascendancy of the market and its discipline and the descendancy of the state to a new role of guardian, referee and regulator. In his book, *The Morality of Law,* Professor Lon Fuller *(1977)* captured this situation as follows: "Law is not like management, a matter of directing other persons on how to accomplish tasks set up by a superior but is basically a matter of providing the citizens with sound and stable framework for their interactions with one another, the role of government being that of standing as a guardian of the integrity of this system." Contrary to Professor Fuller's thesis, under the state ownership system, law was very much like management. The laws enacted to establish parastatals and to regulate the conduct of economic activities in the economy were directed at managing the accomplishment of tasks as defined by the state. Some of these laws, evidently, have been repealed. A good example is the Regulation of Trade Act that had confined both import and domestic trade to a state owned parastatal, the Board of Internal Trade. In this context, it is not surprising that the Tanzania Legal Task Force, which was headed by Mark Bomani in the mid 1990s, had one of its consultancy reports written by Professor Patrick McAuslan, pointedly asserting that "the legal and regulatory framework with which most of the commercial activities are to be conducted is too inadequate to cater for the needs of transacting modern business." The underlying thrust of that report was that a market economy is likely to need more law and regulation.

To what extent then are efforts being taken to create a robust legal and regulatory regime in Tanzania that would not only spur but also effectively regulate investments, including the conduct of business? In fact, in the context of Tanzania's membership in sub-regional economic groupings such as the East African Community. EAC), Southern African Development Community. SADC) and the World Trade Organisation. WTO), at the global level, the urgency and importance of putting in place an appropriate legal and regulatory framework has become urgent. Already, one of the crucial steps to be taken at the East African Community level following the operationalisation of the Customs Union at the in January 2005 is to forge an agreement on a competition law that would ensure a level playing field for business enterprises in East Africa. National competition laws would have to apply in tandem with that of the EAC.

Attempts were taken by the Tanzania government in recent years to enact legislations that are more relevant and appropriate to the market economy. One such law was the Fair Trade Practices Act of 1994. That piece of legislation was the closest that one could relate to a competition law. However, it failed to encapsulate the broad intricacies involved in ensuring fair competition. Thus, the legal requirements relating to restrictive trade practices, anti-competitive practices, regulation of monopolies, acquisitions and mergers and collective resale price maintenance, were not well clarified in the context of a competitive market economy. However, as noted heretofore, the government has made some serious headway in addressing these shortcomings by enacting in August 2003 a full-fledged Fair Competition law. Regulations to enable the enforceability of the law are under formulation. It may also be pointed out that on the labour market front, a new labour law that seeks to create a more flexible labour market regime has been promulgated in 2004. However, whilst the Employment and labour Relations Act is clear about the freedom of association, the right to organise and collective bargaining, more relevant to trade union roles, it does not adequately respond to the broader concerns of a market economy, particularly in removing political involvement in the industrial dispute legal machinery and making it easier for management of organisations to hire and fire. At a different level, a new environment management and protection law is also under review by Parliament and is expected to become law early in 2005. What so far has been far reaching is the establishment of regulatory authorities underpinned by well thought out laws in sectors such as surface and marine transport, water and energy, communications and civil aviation.

It is important to note, however, that having a law in place is one thing, enforcing it is yet another. Indeed, it would appear that a central problem that features prominently in Tanzania lies with the institutional capacities of regulatory bodies charged with the task of law enforcement. Experience has shown that the capacity of the regulatory bodies, be they in fair trade, weights and measures, shipping freight, bureau of standards, or environment, is weak at the levels of technology, finance and human capital. These shortcomings have to be addressed if the market is to be objectively regulated. For example, most of the current hue and cry in the domestic industrial economy abut unfair competition from imports, dumping, sub-standard imports, abuse of form of packaging. weights instead of volume and *vice versa*), is driven, not by the non-existence of laws as such but rather by the serious inadequacies in their enforcement. The absence of tribunals as provided for in some of the laws, or their ineffectiveness, is a serious setback to due process. Specific reference may be made here to the Tax Appeals Tribunal and the Housing Rent Tribunal. The birth of the Commercial Court in 1999 has been a shot in the arm for contracts enforcement. However, the sustainability and improvement of its performance rests on the commitment by the government to its important role. Clearly, the Commercial Court cannot continue to survive and thrive based on foreign aid support of the Danish Government, its main benefactor.

At the same time, Tanzania continues to hear much about the existence of a stable and predictable policy environment as the key driver for promoting investments. But policies have from time to time been changed when stability is imperative for business confidence building. The key point here is that where law underpins policy, the task of ensuring stability takes a more onerous dimension. This is what makes a legal regime such an important vehicle of economic development. In 1999/2000, Tanzania experienced the first unnecessary conflict between the VAT law and the Tanzania Investment law on the question of tax on capital goods imported by investors who had already fallen under the investment law regime. The fracas that emerged gave Tanzania a bad investment image. It was not proper to shift the goal posts for investors midstream as they had already injected capital into the country. As recent as September 2003, a legal wrangle emerged between the Tanzania Investment Centre. TIC) and the Tanzania Revenue Authority. TRA) over the new Income Tax Act 2004. The tax bill had sought to repeal Section 19(2) of the Act establishing the TIC that ensures the sanctity of tax benefits that are granted to investors. Such step would have been contrary to the Tanzania Investment Promotion Policy, which, under Clause 4.3, spells out that the TIC law would be self-protecting and would only be amended under its own law. The TIC described the tax bill as anti-business and anti-investments. The predictability of the investment tax regime was being put to a test and the evident loser in the eyes of potential investors would have been Tanzania. The government had to back paddle on this issue.

At another level, the local government taxation regime has not been in tune with the national taxation policy framework especially in areas such as the promotion of investments. Local Government should be made to understand and appreciate the importance and sanctity of national economic policies and strategies and be required to support them when enacting their own by-laws that affect economic activities in their areas of fiscal competence. The TRA in June 2001 released a *Study Report on Harmonisation of Central and Local Government Taxes*. That report led the government, in the 2003/2004 Budget, to take bold steps in unifying the fiscal regime by abolishing many local government taxes and levies that had been responsible for undermining growth of investment at local levels. The problem is yet to be fully sorted out since the harmonisation has yet to recognise fiscal centralisation. Tanzania needs to move towards some form of the Indian fiscal system where every two or three years an independent Finance Commission, comprising of retired senior judges and public officials, sits and determines the allocation of revenue resources from the Centre to the States. The system makes a great deal of sense because not all regions in Tanzania are equally endowed with sources of tax revenue to meet their most basic needs for development. As the situation stands today, Tanzania is seeing a "North" and "South" emerging, development wise. There is higher level of development in regions that are better endowed with industrial, mining and tourism activities than in areas that merely rely on agriculture as the only tax revenue source.

The market economy is inevitable in Tanzania. The government appears to have the right policies to promote it for national social and economic transformation. However, the legal and regulatory framework for a sound and stable environment for conduct of business under market conditions needs to be further improved. The government should work closely with the business community and other key stakeholders to enact such an enabling legal and regulatory environment.

Democratisation and Political Challenges

On the political front, Tanzania has equally not been immune from the global winds of change. The collapse of Communism in 1989 immediately ushered in a re-examination of the one party political system around the world. In August 1990, the late Mwalimu Julius Nyerere, the architect of the one party system, provoked a debate whether Tanzania was not "mature" enough to revert to multi-party democracy. At that time, Nyerere was still chair of the only political party in Tanzania, *Chama Cha Mapinduzi*. CCM). Voicing such a view, on what was then considered a taboo, indeed almost an act of treason, was enough call to arms for political reform. Thus, early in 1991, the then President, Ali Hassan Mwinyi, constituted a Presidential Commission under the chairmanship of the late Justice Francis Nyalali, then Chief Justice, to solicit views from the people on whether Tanzania should remain a one party state or whether a multi-party democracy should be re-instituted.

The Report of the Commission was submitted early in 1992. It recommended the re-introduction of a multi-party political system. The recommendation was immediately accepted. The Commission also made several other recommendations embracing constitutional, electoral and law reforms with the aim of transforming Tanzania into an effective plural society guided by the rule of law. Many of the recommendations are yet to be effected. One of the boldest and controversial recommendations made related to the modification of the Tanzanian Union. The Commission recommended a federation of three governments: a government for Zanzibar, a government for Tanganyika and a federal government. The recommendation was summarily rejected.

As in the economic front, the political transformation of Tanzania is equally in a state of transition. The last decade has witnessed a patchwork of constitutional and electoral law reforms. However, notwithstanding the lack of such "overhaul" of the constitution and the electoral law, which remain an agenda of debate among the opposition parties, civil society and academia, the reforms that have been undertaken so far have been able to "midwife" the multi-party democracy system and the baby, everything considered, is quite well and healthy. For example, the enactment in 1998 of the Sexual Offences. Special Provisions) Act that provides for greater protection against women and children against sexual abuse and exploitation was a milestone human rights law score. An electoral law change in 2000 deepened democracy by increasing the representation of women in parliament to 20% and in local authorities' councils to 33.3%. Women now account for 22.3% of Members of Parliament compared to the global average, in 2000, of 14.7%. The 14th Union Constitutional Amendment has now increased the representation of women in the Union Parliament to 30% through a proportional representation electoral system which will operate with effect from the 2005 General Elections.

The promulgation of the Commission for Human Rights and Good Governance legislation in March 2001, following the 13th Amendment of the Constitution in 2000 and the establishment of the Commission under the leadership of Justice Robert Kisanga as the first Chairman is also viewed as one of the historical cornerstones in the quest to deepen democratisation and promote human rights in Tanzania. At another level, but equally important, is the transformation of the *modus operandi* of Parliament, intended to make it a more responsive, representative and effective institution *vis a vis* the executive. In March 2003, The Speaker, Honourable Pius Msekwa, created ten new parliamentary committees whose role and focus would be to check the efficiency, effectiveness and conduct of the Executive, including its ministries, enterprises and agencies. This new function is pursuant to Article 63(3) of the Tanzania Constitution. The Committees have been structured on ministerial basis, each Committee handling not more than three ministries. Judging from recent performances of these committees, one senses that Parliament is now exercising greater role in ensuring that the executive is more accountable for its acts and omissions. Examples coming to mind include the rejection of a proposed Bill that was intended to determine the form of privatisation of NMB, the directions put forward to regulate the exportation of gemstones, and even proposals to have the Constitution amended to allow private candidates to contest for seats in Parliament and in Local Councils. Part four of the book examines in detail the challenges that confront Tanzania in the field of democratic reform and, specifically, on the Union.

Two Nations, One State: The Union Question

The Union Question remains a taboo within certain quarters of Tanzanian society. The attempt made by the Kisanga Committee to raise it again met with same negative decision that befell the Nyalali Commission proposal. It is important to point out, however, that it is not as if the Union Question is necessarily focused or centred on what the Nyalali Commission had recommended. Apparently, this is the stance that draws the response of debating the Union question as taboo. Yet, the Union Question is much broader than structure. In this context, few examples may be cited. In the 2002 /03 Union Budget, there was an historic and transparent allocation to Zanzibar of 4.5% of total programme aid granted to Tanzania. I cannot recall a similar circumstance before, though it could be possible that such allocation could have been made. What is more fundamental to quiz, however, is how the 4.5% benchmark was determined? This question remains a moot. Apparently, it would be a subject of negotiations between the Union Government and the Revolutionary Government of Zanzibar. That Budget Speech, however, does not offer much help in alleviating the perceptions that have existed, for a long time, especially in Zanzibar that Zanzibar was for example not equitably benefiting from Programme Aid and HIPC "dividends" granted to Tanzania as a Union. The speech refers to the allocation being "in line with the consensus reached in the past as a transitional arrangement pending the formation of a Joint Finance Commission." The statement begs the question why the Commission that was supposed to have been established in the immediate aftermath of the signing of the Articles of Union in April 1964, has come to be established only in March 2003. The delay in its establishment has certainly caused concerns in the Union.

Therefore, it is not surprising that as recent as early April, 2003 before the first session of the newly established Commission on Human Rights and Good Governance, which has members from both the Mainland and Zanzibar, held in Zanzibar, the Zanzibar Director of Public Prosecution. DPP), a very senior law officer of the Revolutionary Government of Zanzibar, exclaimed that political leaders were behind the failure to solve the union problems. The DPP observed that, for too long, the Zanzibar government had suffered economically because of union problems. He referred to delays in amending both the Union and Zanzibar constitutions are allowing legal contradictions to persist. What contradictions? The DPP referred, as an example, to the applicability of the law that created the Commission on Human Rights and Good Governance. In the view of the DPP, human rights and good governance did not form part of the 1964 Articles of the Union, even as amended and, thus presumably, was *ultra vires* the Articles?

More important to recognise about the DPP's remarks is not whether his remarks were correct or not. It is the mere fact that if a senior official of the Zanzibar Government could be so openly disturbed about the *character* of the union, what then of ordinary Zanzibaris or Mainlanders? The state of the union continues to be in flux and its discussion could not and should not be treated as taboo. At the same time, it is important to recognise and pay tribute to the manner in which the democratic values of tolerance and mutual respect have been successfully marshalled to forge the *Muafaka*. political accord) between the CCM and the Civic United Front. CUF) in 2001. The achievement of the *Muafaka* reflects the potential political maturity holds for Tanzania. The key precedent that has now been set in motion is that political conflict should henceforth be resolved, not through confrontation, but through dialogue. Such spirit of *modus vivendi* augurs well for a democratic Tanzania, especially at a time when Tanzania begins to witness social fractures emerging along religious and other social and economic divides.

Deepening Democratisation

This is not to say that the challenges confronting the Tanzanian democratic system have abated. In fact, several challenges on the political front still need to be addressed if Tanzania is going to deepen democratisation. One of the challenges is whether Tanzania should not adopt a proportional electoral system for its parliamentary and local government systems. The election results, especially in the 1995 multi party general elections, clearly pointed to the fact that Tanzania could have a better representative system of government were a proportional representation electoral system adopted, even if it were to cover 50% of the parliamentary and local government council seats. Democracy deepening would clearly emerge from such development. Moreover, it would also be deepened if the electoral law were to be changed to allow private candidates to contest all electoral positions in the land. There are those who feel that the post of President should be excluded from private candidature. The reasons for the exception may not stand the test of core principles of democracy and of constitutional rights of the individual. Yet, in my view, Tanzania may not have come to the stage where it can risk allowing a private candidate to stand for the highest office in the land. A poor country like Tanzania may find itself electing a President who uses his wealth to corrupt poor voters.

There is also the challenge to see the Tanzanian media, the fourth estate, becoming more responsible, professional, ethical and independent. Yes, transparency destroys secrecy. Yet, it may not reduce the level of deception and misinformation that sometimes features in our societies, thereby undermining the crucial trust that drives collective pursuits of shared values and goals. Evidently, the health of democracy lies in the media becoming a tool of the people and not a tool of the state. At the same time, however, for the media to strive or attempt to manufacture consent of the people and colour public opinion, particularly in a society where the majority of the people are uninformed due to their high levels of illiteracy, undermines the very ethos and primacy of democratic ethics. Informed consent has to be the lynchpin of trust. The recent case involving the United States veteran CBS main news anchor, Dan Rather, is a case in point, even in a highly literate society as that of the US. Mr Rather was embroiled in the 2004 US presidential pre-election scandal involving a story challenging President George W. Bush's military service. Rather had to decide to retire as from March 2005 after being accused of political bias; for having "deliberately" misled the American people over the authenticity of documents relating to President Bush's military service. In spite of Rather's claim that he had made "an error in good faith", he has had to suffer the consequences of overreaching in manufacturing consent of the people.

The *United Nations Human Development Report, 2002* correctly and aptly observes: "informed debate is the lifeblood of democracies." Without it, citizens are "disempowered". Of particular concern is that the media sometimes tramples on the democratic space of the citizens by destabilising, dovetailing, undermining, befogging and misdirecting them, deliberately or often due to the weak capacity of the journalists to fully understand the issues being presented or, worse still, by promoting vested interests. The media coverage of the privatisation of the NBC and, later, the NMB, for instance, was, in my view, driven more by "populist politics" than by economic logic and realities. What is distressing about such media role is that the people tend to be led by what the media says rather than responding to the signals that emanate, to use symbolism from the corporate world, from corporate performance data and what the Alan Greenspans of this world say. Thomas Friedman, in his celebrated book: *The Lexus and the Olive Tree* defines such capital market phenomenon as "electronic herd". To him, it constitutes the Fifth Estate. However, such market countervailing mechanism does not exist in the media field.

This is a serious weakness especially in the arena of politics where the absence of an effective instrument to balance the role of the media is highly pronounced. In such a situation, the media should transform itself, especially so in fragile economic and political environments, by becoming more responsible. For it is in such environments that the media is expected to play a robust and rational whistle blower role and be the instrument that the people can rely upon in ensuring that the government is accountable beyond reliance on the electoral organs that often fall victim to party whip politics. Many of these issues are further examined in Part four of the book that focuses on democracy as well as the Union Question.

Poverty and Democracy

The challenge to make the principles of democracy internalised by all the people is paramount. In a poor country, like Tanzania, democracy can easily become a luxury unworthy the attention and concern of ordinary people. However, as opposed to what is happening in the rich countries where there is growing apathy and cynicism about democracy, since it has insignificant impact on people's livelihoods, so well reflected in growing low turnouts at national and federal elections, in poor countries, on the other hand, such a negative fall out would be disastrous. In poor countries, most of the poor, almost 70-80% of them, live in rural areas. About 48% of them live in abject poverty. Yet these are the people that constitute the bedrock of the electoral process. It is they that ultimately determine who represents them and who leads the nation. This means, in effect, that the process of deepening democracy critically hinges on eradicating poverty. A democracy that fails to fight poverty in earnest and showing positive results is a mockery.

In this context, I am in agreement with President Benjamin Mkapa when he says, "poverty is an extremely weak foundation on which to build democracy. Democratic governance for us must be an integral part of the war on poverty." However, it could also be asked what comes first: democracy as a right, even under an environment of abject poverty, or democratic governance, ostensibly to rid poverty? Immediately after independence, Nyerere had argued a case for the adoption of a one party political system in order to have a system of governance, which, in his view, could have enabled development, namely socialist development, to be realised much faster. Tanzanians may debate the consequences of the choice Nyerere made but Mwalimu knew why it was necessary to avoid a multiparty system.

The key issue here is who defines what democratic governance entails and how it is enforced? In addition, it could be asked whether it is correct to posit that because a people are poor then they inevitably lack the capacity to appreciate and exercise their rights. Is it also possible that we are dealing here with a paradox, a chicken and egg issue, as it were? Indeed, the 1998 Nobel Laureate for Economics, Amartya Sen, argues that "most fundamentally, political liberty and civil freedoms are directly important on their own and do not have to be justified indirectly in terms of their effects on the economy. Even when people without political liberty or civil rights do not lack adequate economic security...they are deprived of important freedoms in leading their lives and denied the opportunity to take part in crucial decisions regarding public affairs." Professor Sen cites an example of Cape Verde and Tanzania positing that in relation to disasters and famine, during the one party state era, "often absence of opposition and the suppression of free newspapers gave the respective governments immunity from criticism and political pressure that translated into thoroughly insensitive and callous policies."

Then there is also the worrying element slowly creeping into the Tanzanian body politic as far as electoral politics are concerned. This relates to the choice of candidates based on striking a balance of representation on religious lines and geographical zones. In the early 2002 elections to select Tanzania's representatives to the East African Legislative Assembly it was quite clear that apart from money being used to influence votes, Members of Parliament appeared to determine the choice of candidates on the basis of how many Moslems should be elected. especially bearing in mind that Zanzibar had its fixed quota of representation and the candidates were predominantly Moslems) and on the basis of zonal representation for the Mainland representatives. What transpired was a serious setback for democratic politics. Surely, representation should be determined on the basis of merit. Such trend, if allowed to take hold, could divide the country.

Challenges Facing Civil Society

The civil society in Tanzania has a key role in arresting the democratic deficit, a deficit that is broadly manifested by politics of political parties than by a broader politics of the people as represented by political parties and civil society. Because of close to three decades of one party rule, civil society in Tanzania suffered serious damage. The abolition of cooperatives in 1976. reinstated in 1984) removed from the political mainstream a voice that represented the people at grassroots level. Trade Unions had also been absorbed into the political party structure, and so were women and youth organisations. To re-build civil society after the destruction of the environment upon which civil society breeds, nourishes and thrives has been an awesome and arduous challenge. Thus, even with the re-entry of multi-party political system in 1992, Tanzania is yet to build organs of civil society that are strong and bold. The new trade unions, now free from association with any political party are yet to re-discover themselves. They are still haunted by their past connections driven by the socialist command economic system and being "surrogate" to a single political party.

Little wonder, that no national civil society comprising women or youth organisations worthy of repute and impact have so far emerged. Yes, there is the Tanzania Media Women Association. TAMWA) that has been an active civil society women's organisation and has played a notable role in mobilising women over issues such as human rights and which has also been able to successfully push the enactment of the Sexual Offences. Special Provisions) Act referred to earlier. They have also sensitised women and mobilised action against female genital mutilation as well as unwanton killings of old women suspected of engaging in occult practices such as witchcraft. TAMWA, by any standards, is a strong, vocal and effective organ of women. However, it is more of an association of professional women in contrast to a national organisation of women.

There are also several professional civil society organisations such as the Tanganyika Law Society, HAKIARDHI, HAKIELIMU and the Society for International Development. SID) to give a few examples. These are important. Just as there are lobby business associations like the Tanzania Chamber of Commerce, Industry and Agriculture. TCCIA), Confederation of Tanzania Industries. CTI), Chamber of Mines, of Agriculture, and Confederation of Tanzania Tourism Operators. All these institutions perform important functions and roles. Many of them have succeeded to influence public policy, promote the rights of economic actors in a new market-driven environment and engage the government on several issues of national importance based on smart partnership. Unfortunately, many of these organisations are disjointed. Apart from business lobby organisations that have a loose and not yet financially viable and sustainable co-ordinating institution, most of the civil society institutions lack effective co-ordination. They are thus not able to rise beyond their own parochial or sectoral interests. Therefore, the political space that civil society is supposed to step into and be engaged in as well as apply collective voice on fundamental issues such as the constitution, the nature of the Union, the weaknesses of political parties, the state of the economy, globalisation, is yet to be well structured and exploited. Mature democracies can probably afford a dissipation of roles and collaboration by civil society bodies. A nascent democracy, on the other hand, needs to forge a coalition of forces, of voices and platforms, from amongst various civil society actors, and play a role that the state cannot afford or risk to marginalise.

Diversity Within Unity

A key challenge confronting Tanzanian civil society is how to build bridges across the national diverse cultures, beliefs, values, religion, race and even tribes. Earlier, I alluded to the emergence of attitudes that foment bigotry and various intolerances in Tanzanian society, including identities based on tribe, religion and geographical zones of origin. These are worrying developments. Tanzanians need to begin a serious dialogue on this emergent situation and foster respect for diversity within unity, in all its forms and manifestations.

In a Special April- June 1997, issue of the Journal, *Alternatives,* which sed on the theme *Social Transformation and Humane Governance*, Rajni Kothari outlines the emergence of opposing global dynamics. He outlines these dynamics to be the quick spread of globalisation, with the ostensible thrust of integration, and the emergent rush of human diversity, held in check, probably until lately, by the strong and centralised nation - state. The emergent diversity is now increasingly characterised by social fractures, intolerance and fragmentation. Witness the intensification of ethnic civil wars and other social convulsions, class identities, racial and tribal identities, sexual diversity tensions, anti-semitism, religions fundamentalisms and militancy, neo- fascism and the rise to political influence by political parties of the extreme right, not only in the rich western world, but in the South as well. Kothari's conclusion regarding this conflicting global dynamic is that the end of the cold war which was characterised by the collapse of communism and the waning of Marxism, as an ideology, may curiously have created a more unstable and violent world. This is a world where, *inter alia*, basic identities and resources of a social and cultural character would become matters of growing conflict and confrontation. One may not fully agree with Professor Kothari's ideological plank of thinking. It is clear, though, that many poor countries, including Tanzania, which for many years have enjoyed enviable cohesion and tolerance among and between diversities, are now beginning to face destabilising forces of diversity. Evidently, it is not possible to address objectively how dialogue can be fostered and facilitated between diversities unless the underlying factors that have made diversity a destabilising phenomenon are more clearly understood.

Some of the key questions that may be asked are: have globalisation and the entry of the market economy in hitherto socialist- oriented poor countries forced into those societies, new and, probably, conventional global, western society features which ignore or undervalue their core diversities? Has the political paradigm shift from political oligarchic systems, the one party state, as it were, to new forms of liberal democratic systems, contributed to intolerant diversities? In her recent brilliant book, *World On Fire: How Exporting Free Market Democracy Breeds Ethnic Hatred And Global Instability*, Amy Chua (2003) explores in depth the emergence of intolerance and hatred for diversity in the context of these political and economic paradigm shifts. She writes, —"the global spread of markets and democracy is a principal, aggravating cause of group hatred and ethnic violence throughout the non-western world. In the numerous societies around the world that have a market-dominant minority, markets and democracy are not mutually reinforcing. Because markets and democracy benefit different ethnic groups in such societies, the pursuit of free market democracy produces highly unstable and combustible conditions."

However, could the legacy of colonialism also be a factor in undermining tolerance for diversity? As far back as 1951, Mwalimu Julius Nyerere had written an essay, whilst studying at the University of Edinburgh, titled, *The Race Problem in East Africa*, where he linked intolerance to diversity with a wealth divide based on racial lines. In that essay, still relevant today, Nyerere posited, "A world seething with hatred is an intolerable place to live in. But we cannot reach the goal by hypocrisy or wishful thinking. We can only do it by honest thinking, honest talking and honest living." Later, in December 1962 in his Presidential Inaugural Address, Nyerere pointed at differences over education opportunities between Christians and Moslems, on the one hand, and between and among tribes, on the other hand, as a source of social conflict. Colonialism contributed to these divisions. These questions are dealt with in Part five and eight of the book.

All these issues are complex and could not be easily wished away. President George W Bush Jr, for instance, talks of "universal values" cutting across diversities. Yet, are human values not intrinsically unique and particularistic? If they are, how then does society forge harmony and tolerance where beliefs and values are different? In reference to the meaning of diversity within unity, the respected Professor Amitai Etzioni, in an article in the *International Herald Tribune* of January 2, 2004 titled *Diversity within unity: Immigrants can belong and be themselves,* posits that the idea is illustrated by the image of a mosaic, which has pieces of different shapes and colours but also a shared framework that may be reordered. In his view, "there are some basics that should be viewed as sacrosanct, but other cultural and social differences should be not just tolerated but welcomed as enriching." Is it therefore possible that we can be inspired, in this context, by the integrative picture of diversity painted by the African -American Poet, Maya Angelou as we search for vehicles that can help us to foster dialogue among diversities: "Human beings are more like than unlike, and what is true anywhere is true everywhere. Perhaps travel cannot prevent bigotry but demonstrating that all people laugh, cry, eat, worry and die. It can introduce an idea that if we try to understand each other, we may even become friends." To Angelou, travel is viewed as one vehicle that can bring about the process of humanity to understand each other, to discover what one may describe not as universal values, but "universal human commonalities" and to appreciate the diversity of the human family. The challenge is to view diversity or "otherness" as something that is not competitive and isolating but complementary.

The central task in fostering and facilitating dialogue between diversities in Tanzania is primarily to promote diversity issues and to get them onto the centre stage of our work and conversations. Tanzanians should strive to engineer an environment that nourishes and catalyses harmony in a world of deepening diversity. They should consistently sensitise and challenge the national, regional and world community to increase awareness over diversity issues. Specifically, Tanzanians should identify, at different levels of society, the structural barriers- legal, social, gender, cultural, political and environmental- that work against or undermine the realisation of harmony among diversities. Such barriers inform the *very* process of dialogue and identify the different diversity constituencies that should be engaged. It is critical, in this context, that the sources of "stereotyping" and "groupthink", at all levels of Tanzanian communities - national, local and village - are identified in order to engage them in a dispassionate dialogue. The aim should be to build bridges of greater understanding in the spirit of promoting societal harmony.

This is a challenge that particularly concerns the youth. Young women and men should be proactively engaged in creative conversations and explorations about their future in an environment of growing diversity. Such process of exploration should be holistic. In other words, it should cover the geographical, cultural, racial, ethnic/tribal, religious, wealth and sexual boundaries. In fact, such process recently began in Tanzania through the auspices of the Society for International Development. Between 2001 and 2002, a group of young Tanzanians engaged themselves in a scenarios project directed at imagining the future of Tanzania in the next 20 to 30 years. The result of their effort is a booklet titled, *Tutafika: Imagining Our Future Tanzania*. The publication constructs three scenarios that depict different paths that Tanzania may take into the future and the possible outcomes. The pertinent part of the introduction of the booklet is telling: "The ability of Tanzania to face the future as a united country will be decided by the skill with which we manage emerging divisions along class, racial, religious and ethnic lines. It is not beyond the realm of possibility that these divisions spiral out of control and threaten the very fabric of our society." Thus, it is the younger generation who can best master a broader and deeper understanding of the power of diversity. They are the ones who can boldly challenge the contextual assumptions that militate against appreciating diverse human identities and qualities and forge the inevitable processes of change.

After the tragic events of 11th September, 2001, the question about human diversity has become extremely sensitive. Often, it has caused much agony and conflict. It would be tragic to humanity were Tanzania, until now the pride of Africa for sustaining peace, cohesion and stability, to fail to restore and cultivate a new hope of human understanding and tolerance. The late Dr. Martin Luther King Jr reminds us, "an individual has not started living until he can rise above the narrow confines of his individualistic concerns to the broader concerns of all humanity". After all, in the context of religion, a respectful religious pluralism is not simply a liberal idea or a hope as often visualised. More importantly, it constitutes an urgent factor and catalyst for the realisation of peace and cohesion.

Part Three

DIMENSIONS OF RADICAL ECONOMIC REFORM

The gardener who tries to grab a thorn bush timidly won't have a grip strong enough to pull it from the earth. Each attempt to grab it will lead to more wounds, and the wounds won't get a chance to heal. The pain will go on forever. The ground will never be cleared for a new burst of productive growth. The unproductive thorn bush will just grow bigger, stronger, and harder to remove the longer the period of timidity lasts.

-Lester Thurow: *Creating Wealth: The New Rules For Individuals, Companies and Countries In A Knowledge-Based Economy*

The hardest part of defending free markets is the need to stress their long-term systematic benefits while refusing to give in to the immense short-term political pressures from inevitable casualties of market institutions. It takes patience to see tomorrow's returns from today's investments.

-Richard Epstein: *Free Markets Demand Protection,*
Financial Times, 13 October 2003.

Chapter

9 LIBERALISATION, EQUITY AND EXCLUSION

History has proven that capitalism, like all social systems, is able at each stage of its expansion to overcome its own permanent contradictions, but not without worsening the violence with which they will be experienced by succeeding generations—More than ever humanity is confronted with two choices; to let itself be led by capitalism's unfolding logic to a fate of collective suicide or, on the contrary, to give birth to the enormous human possibilities carried by that world-haunting spectre of communism.

-Samir Amin: ***Spectres of Capitalism: A Critique of Current Intellectual Fashions.***

Introduction:

The questions about equity, exclusion and liberalisation are pointedly relevant for taking a historical stock of development theory and practice of the four decades of African independence from colonial rule. History has shown, that the development theory of the 1960s, which centred on the so- called "modernisation" and premised on maximisation of economic growth, failed to achieve the expected trickle down. On the other hand, the 1970s and early 1980s saw development theory focused on social and economic justice based on the basic needs approach. Again, history has evidenced that this Welfare State theory failed in most developing countries because it was predominantly consumptionist; it relied too much on foreign aid and it led to dissaving as well as keeping investment at bay. It is notable however, that the prescription for attacking these crises of development, described as structural adjustment programmes. SAPs), which has underpinned development theory from the mid 1980s and well into the 1990s through the courtesy of the International Monetary Fund. IMF) and the World Bank, appears to have generally accentuated rather than alleviated patterns of economic backwardness and social injustice in the developing world. John Loxley and David Seddon have described these SAPs as an attempt by the international financial institutions to force their "ideological hegemony on development history, theory and policy".

However, as if these failures of development theory, to-date, were inadequate, poor nations are now, additionally, confronted by destabilising global forces of change. These forces, social, cultural, economic, political and technological, are challenging the dominant philosophies that have underpinned the development of poor societies, including those driven by SAPs. At their heart, is the notion that the nation-state is increasingly becoming irrelevant in determining development theory and strategy. Samir Amin, in his article, *In favour of a Polycentric World*, has ridiculed these forces castigating them as constituting the global expansion of capitalism. Amin contends that globalisation is a process that "excludes Africa from the future". It is a view shared by the recent Report of the World Commission on Social Dimension of Globalisation titled *A Fair Globalisation: Creating Opportunities For All*. This report postulates that in the absence of a fair and inclusive globalisation that puts people first, sustains human values and promotes their well-being, in terms of their freedom, prosperity and security, globalisation would continue to be equated with traditional domination and exploitation of the imperialism era.

The Vision of Equity and Inclusion

Few people today would imagine the excitement and enthusiasm of Tanganyikans. now Tanzanians) when President Julius Nyerere, in his President's Inaugural Address in December 1962, articulated the vision for his newly born independent state. In reference to the question what kind of a Tanganyika he would seek to build, Nyerere asserted: "It is dignity and well being of all our people which is the beginning and the end of all our efforts. For the freedom we demanded was not mere independence from colonialism. What we sought was personal freedom for all the people of Tanganyika, freedom for every individual, and the chance to make use of that freedom, in cooperation with his fellows - to provide for his own needs and theirs and so live a life of human dignity. We determined to build a country in which all her citizens are equal, where there is no division between the rulers and ruled, rich and poor, educated and illiterate, those in distress and those in idle comfort. We determined that in this country all would be equal in dignity, and would have an equal right to respect, to the opportunity of acquiring a good education and the necessities of life, and all her citizens should have an equal opportunity of serving their country to the limit of their ability".

The Rise of Socialism and Policies of Inclusion

In the same Address, Nyerere underscored that the new Tanganyika to be built would be "a true socialist society" whose key instruments would be the government itself and the cooperative movement. These lofty ideals were later encapsulated in the *Arusha Declaration* adopted in February 1967. Briefly, the thrust of the Arusha Declaration was a commitment to eradicating poverty, disease and ignorance. The declaration embodied a concern for the realisation of equity and a commitment to addressing and reducing gross inequalities through a fairer sharing of national opportunities and resources. The inequalities coincided, on the one hand, with the racial divide, principally Asian versus African. On the other hand, they coincided with tribal-based and religion-based disparities in education opportunities. The Arusha Declaration viewed equity and social justice as indispensable human values for the existence of peace, stability, national cohesion and a humane society.

Over time, however, and as evidenced by Tanzania's development history, the legitimate concerns for a frontal attack on poverty and inequity degenerated into a dogmatic rejection of alternative development strategies that could probably have been more appropriate to sustaining and reinforcing the very attack on poverty and inequity. The rejection of alternative strategies of development emanated from the firm resolve of the Nyerere Administration to use state intervention as the principal vehicle for promoting economic growth and equity. State intervention embraced the nationalisation of the major means of production, exchange and distribution, the moving of the rural population into planned villages between 1973 and 1976, and the expansion of social services- education, health and potable water. Self-reliance that formed a key element of the Arusha Declaration fell prey to an increasingly foreign aid dependency syndrome and thus failed to ensure sustainable growth.

The Ascendancy of Social Exclusion

It is in this context that Frederick Kaijage and Anna Tibaijuka have observed in their book *Poverty and Social Exclusion in Tanzania,* that the Arusha Declaration's "attempts at achieving social inclusion were progressively eroded by the poor performance of the economy from the late 1970s." The poor performance was characterised by a balance of payments crisis, declines in agricultural and industrial production, high rates of inflation, decline in incomes in real terms, chronic shortages of essential goods and a general fall in living standards. A few statistics would help to clarify the character of the economic crisis that ushered in inequity and social exclusion. Most of the data reflected below is sourced from Kaijage and Tibaijuka's book.

Overall, the share of basic social services in the annual budget declined from 25% in 1970/71 to 11% in 1986-87. In the field of education, apart from literacy education, the sector was generally in poor state, manifesting a serious decline in standards. Not only was the student - textbook ratio at a ludicrous level of 10:1, but gross primary school enrolment declined from 98% in 1981 to 78% in 1987. Cumulative drop-out rates in primary schools shot up from 16% in 1977 to 27% in 1980. the drop out rates for girls being 35% and that of boys 29%). Kaijage and Tibaijuka have interpreted the higher drop out of girls as resulting from "a pattern of social exclusion resulting from a conjecture of economic decline and cultural imperatives". Real incomes, on the other hand, declined severely. The real minimum wage. 1969 prices) declined from a peak of Shs. 211/= in 1972 to Shs. 57/= in 1985, a devastating decline. This erosion in purchasing power meant that many urban workers failed to access the most basic means of livelihood. It is also noted that during this period Tanzania experienced a distressing wave of brain drain. Many medical doctors and University teachers left the country for countries in Southern Africa to take up lucrative posts. In the field of health, the national health system was affected by shortages of basic drugs. Basic infrastructure facilities fell into disrepair for lack of maintenance.

The Villagisation Programme, on the other hand, destabilised agricultural production. This situation was aggravated by the dissolution of Co-operatives. which, as noted earlier, Nyerere had viewed as one of the twin instrumentalities for the construction of a socialist state) and the exploitation of peasants who were not paid fair prices for their commodities by the monopolistic state-owned crop marketing institutions.

Clearly then, the history of the development theory applied in the 1960s, the 1970s and early 1980s shows that all was not well in the Tanzanian State. The hailed egalitarian, *ujamaa*. socialist) policies, did not achieve the envisioned levels of social and economic justice. On the contrary, the performance of the state in achieving inclusionary lofty goals was put to question. As Kaijage and Tibaijuka have concluded, a big shadow of doubt was cast on the acclaimed inclusionary role of the Tanzania State during that period. Thus, as at 1984, Tanzania was virtually on the throes of social tension and conflict. What seems to have kept the nation united and, ostensibly, peaceful was the perceived unrealised Nyerere's vision for Tanzania, a vision that gave hope to the people and which the people generally believed in. Thus, the majority of Tanzanians were not disturbed by the set backs which they viewed as transitory. This belief was particularly reinforced by the ethical leadership displayed by Nyerere.

Why the Economic Crisis?

What underlined the Tanzanian economic crisis? Anne Krueger has identified four typical policy failures of developing countries that catapulted economic crises in the 1970s and 1980s. These failures were also contributory to Tanzania's development set backs and they catapulted the economic reforms adopted from 1986 They were failures to:

(i) ensure macroeconomic stability, particularly control of inflation;

(ii) provide adequate and quality soft and hard infrastructure services. education, health, roads, railways, ports, canals, communications, power, water etc) which are essential to productive activity;

(iii) arrest state intervention in economic activities that are best undertaken by the private sector.

(iv) remove administered controls, exchange controls, protection of local industries, import controls, and prices on commodities that misallocate resources in the economy.

In the specific case of Tanzania, the economic crisis was also caused by several other factors, namely poor terms of trade, the break up of the East African Community in 1977, the second oil shock in 1973, the war against Uganda's Idi Amin in 1978/1979 and poor weather conditions. The hostile international economic environment marked by the emergence of a world economy increasingly consuming less and less traditional agricultural based raw materials thereby adversely affecting commodity market prices, also contributed to the Tanzanian economic crisis. In particular, the economic crisis was predominantly a precipitate of the failures of a developmentalist state. However, it is the structural problems in the economy, as outlined by Krueger, which were more responsible for the Tanzanian economic crisis.

Enter Economic Liberalisation

It is from that failure that broad-based economic liberalisation took the centre stage of Tanzania's development theory from mid 1986. Liberalisation, a policy engineered by the IMF and the World Bank, for a significant period in Tanzania's reform process, embraced the conventional prescriptions given for a country in economic distress. These included freeing prices, opening up imports trading, removal of domestic and external subsidies, devaluation of the currency, adoption of positive real interest rates, credit squeeze, and privatisation of state-owned firms. This is the mantra of the *"Washington Consensus"* as it was known.

The rationale of these neo-classical, free market policy recipes is that limiting the role of the state and freeing markets sets the economic fundamentals right, a process that enables the economy to become more productive, resilient and competitive. Such an economy, it is argued, creates more jobs, enlarges markets and stimulates purchasing power. Interestingly, this neo-liberal economic philosophy has also been the dominant operating rationale in addressing economic malaise in the industrialised countries and what the IMF and the World Bank are doing is basically grafting it onto the body economic of developing countries as the right prescription for addressing development maladies.

Unfortunately, however, such conventional wisdom, of neo-economic liberalism, can accentuate rather than alleviate patterns of economic backwardness, social injustice and political domination, a view succinctly postulated by Rajni Kothari in his eloquent essay, *Redesigning the Development Strategy*. Equally, in the view of Adebayo Adedeji, whatever the positive aspects of orthodox structural adjustment, such policies tend to appear as sparks rather than as sustained combustions and, eventually, result in even greater structural and social distortions. Thus, two decades since the on-set of economic reforms, Tanzania, like many countries that have pursued such policies, is still witnessing high levels of income poverty, a precipitous erosion of consumer purchasing power, inequality and the activation of the roots of social tension evidenced in the emergence of the clamour for indigenisation of the economy.

SAPs and Growing Inequity

The focus of SAPs on achieving sustainable fiscal balance of payments at the expense of internal social equilibrium has failed to address the pillars of a poverty eradication strategy which revolved around, the promotion of labour-intensive growth, investment in human capital development, putting in place an industrial policy, creating a system for the intensive and broad delivery of social services, and the establishment of reasonable and working social safety nets. It is in this context that *The Challenge to The South* castigated SAPs for having failed to reconcile "the demands of efficiency and equity". At the root of the failure of SAPs is what the distinguished historian, Basil Davidson, described as the West's plans and proposals for economic recovery based, wrongly in his view, on Africa's history at the stage of "dispossession". He notes: "Read or re-read any of these great schemes for adjustment and re-adjustment and you will be reminded that they all assume that useful or visible history in this continent starts from colonial take over. Before that? A void, a tumult, a panoply of ornamental titles at best."

Moreover, the dominant focus of SAPs on the efficacy and capability of domestic policies reflected a major policy failure in not recognising that the global economic environment, as it exists, defeats the fundamental principles of equity and inclusion. Consider the following:

(i) owing to high levels of debt servicing and the decline in commodity and terms of trade, the net flow of resources continue to be from the South to the North and not vice versa. A great proportion of the inflows of aid and new borrowings are off -set by outflows to service and repay past debts and by the losses resulting from falling commodity prices. It is noted that most commodity market prices are today at levels comparable, in real terms, to those that prevailed in the 1930s.

(ii) protectionist barriers to manufactured exports of developing countries are still in place in spite of the entry of the World Trade Organisation. Global Economic Prospects, 2003, a World Bank Publication, posits in this context as follows: "In Canada, the European Union. EU), Japan and the United States, average ad valorem-equivalent tariffs for manufactures are roughly twice as high for developing countries as they are for members of the Organisation for Economic Co-operation and Development." It is in the light of this state of marginalisation of developing countries that Rajni Kothari, in his book, *Politics And The People: In Search of a Humane India* argues that a distinct shift is taking place: "—from the earlier optimistic theory of progress in which the fruits of science and technology could be made available to all nations and all peoples to a pessimistic view that there isn't enough to go round, that the central issue before the world is security and stability in the face of rapid change and demands for still more rapid change rather than development and expansion of opportunities in which both change and demands for change were to be seen as spurs to a comprehensive process of democratisation and transformation of the world at large. It is the transfer of this changed perspective on the human condition to defensive elites within the Third World and a simultaneous transfer of doctrines of liberalisation and privatisation through technological modernisation that has set the stage for exclusivist tendencies. whose basic cultural disposition was for so long eclectic and inclusive of various diversities and new demands and challenges as and when they arose."

SAPs and the Tanzania Experience

In the Tanzanian context, inequity and exclusion resulting from SAPs manifested in the following:

i) the neglect, over a long period, indeed until as recent as 2002, to direct adequate resources into agriculture. Clearly, if an equitable social order is to be established, the prime concern of economic policy should centre on generating employment. In a poor country that is predominantly rural-based, employment generation can only be best achieved through the transformation of the agricultural sector and the promotion of rural agro-based industrialisation.

ii) growing regional development disparities. These disparities reflected a clear dimension of social injustice. The failure of SAPs to provide adequate support in the area of social services through its policies of deficit reduction as well as developing economic infrastructure constituted one of the central causes of the social exclusion of regions such as Mtwara, Lindi, Rukwa and Kigoma from the national mainstream and thereby narrowing the social and community base of the Tanzanian nation. It is only through PRSP and HIPC, since 2000/01, that these negative effects have received serious attention.

iii) growing inequality in the domestic distribution of income. This phenomenon deepened at the time when cost recovery and cost sharing policies had been put in place in the social service sector. This entrenching inequality precipitated what Ralf Dahrendorf has described as the "valley of tears" wherein crime, broken families, drug abuse and prostitution thrive. It is a situation that is prone to increasing states of confrontation and violence leading to the erosion of national cohesion and stability.

iv) consumption culture has been catapulted into the society, and, in a large measure, on the lines of Western values. This lust for things and for more and more things has, to borrow the words of Rajni Kothari, given rise "to all kinds of unethical practices, chief among them being a large incidence of corruption among public officials and a thriving black economy that is sustained by the availability of a large array of consumer goods." Consumerism seriously undermines the culture of savings and capital accumulation and contributes to the erosion of the national capacity to generate employment and provide adequate social services. In Tanzania, the consequence has been growing inequity and corruption.

v) stabilisation policies, whose principal thrust is cutting government spending, has had a devastating impact on the urban working families as subsidies, through taxation, on food, transport and medical care have either been withdrawn or have become largely taxable.

vi) virtual absence of equity financing for economic projects coupled with unrealistic bank borrowing interest rates, where such funds are available, has accentuated rather than diminished what Nyerere, in 1962, saw as a time bomb, namely the wide wealth differential occurring on racial lines. This state of exclusion of the majority of Tanzanians from the wealth ownership and wealth creation process has precipitated racial intolerance against the minority Asian business class with ardent calls for indigenisation of the economy and an unpopular response to privatisation policy that is viewed to favour those already endowed with capital.

vii) unlike countries like India where the government has made deliberate effort to ensure that the burden of fiscal adjustment does not fall heavily on social programmes, especially those that affect the poor, Tanzania did not, until the advent of the PRSP, equally make provision for creating social safety nets. Specific anti-poverty programmes of the type that India introduced to shock absorb the gravity of fiscal contraction, such as subsidised food and housing, mid-day meals for school children, support to peasants to acquire income-generating assets such as ploughs and milk cows, and promoting rural public works programmes, such as construction of rural roads, wells, irrigation canals, electrification to create rural jobs and bolster productivity- enhancing infrastructure, are yet to be mainstreamed in Tanzanian rural development policy. Attempts in this direction are under consideration within the framework of the new NSGRP slated to take off in July 2005.

Does History Offer a Solution?

I have so far shown that the Tanzanian economy, in the 1970s and the early 1980s, was faced by rapidly growing domestic and external imbalances, severe balance of payments problems and near zero growth. During that period, population was increasing at an unsustainable average rate of 3.3% per annum. The poor suffered the brunt of this economic morass. On the other hand, whilst the economic reforms adopted since 1984, and, more robustly since 1986, under the auspices of the IMF and the World Bank, have succeeded to get the economy on a higher growth trajectory, they have not alleviated poverty. Indeed, the living standards of the poor have deteriorated. The challenge arising out of this history is what next? Can countries like Tanzania unshackle themselves from the growing state of inequity and exclusion at both international and national fronts?

Harvard Professor Emeritus John Kenneth Galbraith (1989) in an essay on *Ideology and Economic Reality* confronts the question as follows: "I do not believe that we can understand the process of change today unless we see it as emerging from the conflict between continuing economic, political and social transformation, on the one hand, and the rules by which both the capitalist and the socialist countries have sought to be guided in all recent times, on the other hand." Put differently, Galbraith postulates that the conflict between ideology and reality, or what he describes as the dynamic of change, is "the dialectic of our time". More or else echoing the same message, Professor Anne Krueger, (1992) now First Deputy Managing Director of the IMF, has contended that, in many instances, "reform programmes fail because of the infeasibility of undertaking some of the measures, thus demanding improved understanding of the political motivations and constraints that affect the choice of economic policies".

It is important to note, in the context of Anne Krueger's postulation, how, for example, the choice of deficit reduction, as an across the board economic policy, could fail to achieve intended results. Yet we learn from the Nobel Laureate, Yale's James Tobin that "deficit reduction is not an end in itself." Its rationale is to improve the productivity, real wages, and living standards of our children and their children. He adds, "If the measures taken to cut deficits actually diminish GDP, raise unemployment and reduce future oriented activities of governments, business and households, they do not advance the goals that are their raisons d'etre; rather, they retard them." In Professor Tobin's view, perverse consequences are likely where deficit reduction measures are effected "at a time when the economy is weak." In addition, "if public sector-future oriented expenditures are the victims of such mistimed and misplaced fiscal austerity, the contradiction between rationale and actual consequences is compounded," In other words, the underlying structure of an economy should inform the choice and sequencing of reform measures.

Nobody in his right senses questions the imperativeness of structural policy reforms, *per se*. In fact, poor countries have little choice in this respect. As the June 1987 Abuja Conference on the *Challenge of Economic Recovery and Accelerated Development* noted, "African countries must continue to pursue structural policy reform measures". It cautioned, however, that they must do so taking into account "the need to minimise the adverse social impact of such measures and take into account the human dimension of adjustment." The Conference urged increased levels of investment in agriculture, low-cost transportation and promotion of agro-allied industries. However, central to a reform programme that seeks to promote equity and social inclusion is the need to strengthen the building blocks of the economy. These are the education system, the productive capacity of the public and private sectors and incentives for entrepreneurship and innovation. The achievement of these measures hinges a great deal on easing the debt and debt service burden as alluded to in the previous chapter. There is no way that a country like Tanzania can successfully strengthen such building blocks of the economy critical in bringing about what Adebayo Adedeji has termed "fundamental structural change and transformation" if it would have to continue with a debilitating debt-service commitment it presently faces.

Globalisation and the Crisis of the Nation-State

How poor countries face the challenge of the debt overhang and poverty has increasingly come face to face with what the industrialised G.8 nations describe as global realities. Poor countries, on the other hand, view such realities as a systematic process of exclusion of peripheral areas. One of the most articulate expose of the view that nation states cannot avoid liberalisation and the pursuit of policies which are more consistent with the changing global economic setting is presented in a the book, *Market Unbound: Unleashing Global Capitalism.* The authors, Lowell Bryan and Diana Farrel, both Senior Consultants with McKinsey & Co, paint the following bleak picture: "We have all grown up in a world where the critical economic decisions for nations have been made by a small group of people at the centre of each national government. These national political elites have played the decision - making roles in setting interest rates and foreign exchange rates and in allocating capital within the nation. The power of the political elites to control the flow of capital within their nations has been directly derived from the historic province of the nation state to regulate, to print money, to tax, to subsidise, and to borrow money largely without restraint. We are witnessing the transfer of this power away from these small elite groups to a global capital market that is only now beginning to flex its muscles— We are moving towards a world where the capital markets constrain what governments can do - not the other way round. In this environment, government policy is influenced in real time by whether or not it makes economic sense. Bad policies will be quickly rewarded."

The two authors go on to prescribe the kind of leaders the new global capitalist order needs: leaders who will tell the people that achieving prosperity demands cutting off unsustainable entitlements, cutting off subsidies to industries, elimination of unproductive jobs and that "individuals who want security take responsibility for creating it for themselves". This picture is devoid of the realities obtaining in poor countries. In fact, Samir Amin has questioned how the market could indeed be a liberating force, arguing that such a neo-liberal solution has not been able to suppress social and political tensions anywhere. On the other hand, The British Yale History Professor, Paul Kennedy, in his book

Preparing For the Twenty-First Century, whilst accepting the virtues of the market and the difficulties that have arisen from heavy-handed state interventionism, However, he admonishes the "Washington Consensus" claiming that "the advocates of free-market forces often ignore the massive political difficulties which governments in developing countries would encounter in abolishing price controls, selling off national industries, and reducing food subsidies. They also forget that the spectacular commercial expansion of Japan and East Asian economies was carried out by strong states that 'eschewed *laissez-faire'.*" Even more fundamental are the blunt questions which Kennedy poses: "with the global scene less welcoming to industrialising newcomers, how likely are they to achieve the same degree of success as the East Asian NIEs. newly industrialising economies) did, when they took off a quarter of a century ago? Even if, by an economic miracle, the world's poorest fifty nations did adopt the Korean style of export-led growth in manufactures. which, incidentally, underpins the IMF/ World Bank policy reform prescription), would they not create the same crisis of industrial overproduction as exists in the commodity markets to-day?"

In a well acclaimed speech, *One World or Several or One World and Many,* delivered at the 20th World Conference of the Society for International Development in Amsterdam in May 1991, the late H.R.H. Prince Claus also observed that "the much advocated 'free market' cannot, whatever its many values, solve the problem of hunger and poverty, the destruction of the environment —Nor is it alone able to respond to legitimate aspirations for economic justice, political freedom and equality of opportunity."

Whither Poor Economies

Therefore, poor countries like Tanzania find themselves in an economic policy quandary. What they cannot escape from is the pursuit of development policies that enable the people to realise their potential, build self-confidence and lead lives of dignity and fulfilment. The critical challenge is how to go about achieving such development objectives in the context of a marginalising global economy. John Loxley and David Seddon argue a case for "selective state intervention within a framework of a clearly articulated industrial strategy —- the very antithesis of liberalisation." However, it is I G Patel, in his paper *Employment, Growth and Basic Needs* that puts the policy dilemma more pointedly. He asserts, "it is tempting to seek a new social balance or equilibrium which prescribes a certain basic or once-for-all social transformation which could then be left alone in favour of market forces, incentives and the ordinary but universal instincts of mankind. Whether such a middle path exists and whether such a fine balance can be struck through normal processes of social evolution aided no doubt by men and women of goodwill and goaded by forms of organisations such as trade unions and political parties is as yet an unanswered question of history." Here then lies a challenge for both historians of development and economists to come up with relevant paradigms that respond to distribution of opportunity and wealth, both between and within nations. It is a challenge similar, if not more important, to the struggle to attain political independence from colonialism.

Chapter

10 PERSPECTIVES ON ECONOMIC REFORMS

A stable macroeconomic framework is necessary if we are to be attractive to investment, if we are to have a growing economy, if we are to increase job opportunities, if we are to increase exports, if we are to enhance Government revenues and attract more development assistance including concessionary loans.

-Benjamin W. Mkapa: *State of the Nation Address to the Parliament of the United Republic of Tanzania*, 12 February 2004.

Introduction

Since mid 1986, Tanzania has steadfastly pursued a programme of radical economic reforms. The adoption of the Economic Recovery Program. ERP) in June 1986 marked a major economic paradigm shift, from that of a socialist command economy and welfare state system, the brainchild of the Arusha Declaration, a blueprint for socialist construction, adopted in February 1967, to a liberal and market oriented social and economic system. At the heart of that paradigm shift laid the core thrust to build a market economy. This new objective demanded the adoption of several measures directed at getting the economy out of the doldrums it found itself in by the mid 1980s and putting it onto a robust and sustainable growth trajectory. The initial core measures that were taken are embodied in three sets of economic reform frameworks: the ERP I. June 1986-June 1989), ERP II. June 1989-June 1991), which is also known as the Economic and Social Action Programme, and the Enhanced Structural Adjustment Facility. ESAF) which took effect from fiscal year 1995/96.

Literature abounds on all these reform measures. An excellent summary is captured in a World Bank Country Study published in February 2002 titled: *Tanzania at the Turn of the Century: Background Papers*. Suffice to state, however, that the reform measures focused on the following:
- promoting price stability,
- liberalisation of trade. both external and domestic),
- removal of administered prices on agricultural and industrial products,
- realigning the exchange rate,

- rehabilitation of physical infrastructure,
- restructuring parastatals, including initiating privatisation of state-owned enterprises,
- improving capacity utilization of industries,
- improving balance of payments through stimulating exports
- ameliorating economic pressure on vulnerable groups in society,
- liberalise the financial banking and insurance sectors,
- create a more conducive environment for inducing investments. both foreign and domestic) and
- putting the private sector at the heart of the national economic life.

The combination of all these reform measures have, overtime, produced appreciable economic recovery and stabilisation especially price stability and increased availability of goods and services. It is of note that the improvement in the health of the economy has been particularly spectacular since 1997. Comparative data would help to show how the reform programme in Tanzania has performed. Thus, whilst real GDP growth averaged 1.1% between 1980 and 1985, it rose to an average of 4.1% between 1986 and 1996. However, this performance improvement came at the backdrop of serious reform slippages during the period 1991 to 1994. These slippages have important lessons attached to them. They clearly show that without strong and bold leadership, able to withstand the pressures against fiscal austerity and prudence, it is difficult to sustain a reform programme whose fruits are not realizable in the short term.

In the Tanzanian case, the top leadership during the period 1991-1995 became gripped with apprehension that the reforms that were being pursued were hurting the majority of Tanzanians disproportionately. As a result, reform slippages stepped is, characterised by indiscipline in public finance management, tax exemptions and rising rates of corruption. Revenue declined in the process; budget deficit in fiscal year 1994/95 clocked 10% of GDP, whilst inflation rose sharply from 21.8% in 1992 to 35.5% in 1994, driven largely by the government reverting to excessive borrowing from the banking system. In 1995, GDP growth declined to 3%. Those reform slippages have been arrested since 1997. Tanzania now prides itself of having achieved a growth rate of 6.2% in 2003 whilst the inflation rate declined to 4.0% as at June 2005. Other achievements include foreign exchange reserves which have risen from 1.7 worth of imports cover in 1994 to about 7.0 months cover in June 2005. Government revenue collection per month has shot up from shillings 25 billion in 1995 to shillings 160 billion in February 2005. At the same time, because of fiscal prudence, good governance and greater accountability on the part of the government in expenditure management, Tanzania has since November

2001 qualified for HIPC debt relief. This relief has enabled it to benefit from debt dividends that have supported budget allocations to poverty reducing priority sectors. By early 2005, Tanzania had saved a total of shillings 900 billion or US$ 858.7 million because of the debt relief which it would otherwise have spent to service loans falling under the Paris Club framework. The sectors that have benefited include basic education, primary health care, HIV/AIDS, water and sanitation, agriculture, rural roads, and research and extension in agriculture

Evidently, Tanzania is still confronted by serious economic challenges. For example, the reasonably good gross official reserves of the Bank of Tanzania have more to do with stringent monetary control of expenditure than the performance of the country's export sector. Indeed, President Mkapa admitted this in his State to the Nation address delivered before the Parliament on 12 February 2004, positing that he would have been happier if the reserves "had accrued from the export of products and services by our own people". Thus, whilst the reserves are on the up swing, the trade deficit is still at a high level of 7.1% of GDP in 2003. In the ensuing sections, Tanzania's achievements and the challenges that continue to confront economic reform are examined in detail. Specifically, two areas are selected to form the basis of the examination: promoting macro-economic stability and promoting enabling environment for business.

Promoting Macro-economic Stability

This broad policy dimension is examined from the following perspectives: price stability, stability of the exchange rate and liberalisation of the financial, banking and insurance sectors and privatisation of state-owned enterprises.

Price Stability

A defining feature of Tanzania's success in implementing economic reforms has been the realisation of price stability. In this specific context, inflation has been brought down from an average of 30.9% in 1980-1990 to 26.6% in 1991-1996. As at December 2003, and in spite of the drought conditions that afflicted Tanzania from the end of 2002 and for the great part of the key rain seasons in 2003, inflation had declined to 4.6%. Three policy thrusts can be attributed to the realisation of price stability. Firstly, the strict prudential control of money supply by the Central Bank, the Bank of Tanzania. It is of particular significance to note that despite negative net foreign financing of the fiscal budget, which has shot up from 22% in 1992-1994 to 45% in 2003-2004; external inflation has equally been well contained. The key challenge ahead is how to make low inflation stimulate higher economic growth. Where low inflation is not able to influence robust investment propensity, the inference would be that there are other key economic policy variables at play or absent and which undermine economic stimulation. Such variables would then have to be addressed. I shall examine some of these variables later.

Second, there has been a disciplined control and management of public finances through a vigorous cash-budget system. The Public Finance Act and the Public Procurement Act, both enacted in 2001, put in place a legal and regulatory framework for strict and transparent management of public finances. It is in this context that Tanzania now boasts of a balanced budget. It is important to note also that government expenditure management has been brought into the public domain. Through the mechanism of the *Public Expenditure Review. PER)*, Tanzania boasts of a unique open budgetary process under which donors, business and civil society organisations as well as individual citizens interact with public officials on how the fiscal budget is structured, its premises determined and the priorities it encapsulates. Following the adoption of the *Poverty Reduction Strategy Paper. PRSP)* in 2000, supported by the *Poverty Reduction Budget Support. PRBS)*, the modalities for policy dialogue with respect to programme aid have been laid down enabling shared priorities to be established.

However, it is also important to note that whilst the PRSP process has opened new spaces for dialogue on economic and social policy, the process, so far, has remained largely consultative, not participative. In other words, governments remain in the driving seat as far as the determination of policy content and the structure underpinning dialogue. The situation is probably worse as portrayed in the 2004 Oxfam Report, *Oxfam: From `Donorship` to Ownership? Moving Towards PRSP Round Two.* In that report, Oxfam postulates "policy prescriptions within PRSPs do not come from PRSP participation process, and instead continue to reflect the backstage influence of the donors' own agenda." In the case of Tanzania, it would appear that lessons from the PRSP process have led to a positive change in the determination of poverty reduction plans and strategies. At least this is the picture one gets from the manner in which the government has proceeded to frame the new five years *National Strategy for Growth and Reduction of Poverty. NSGRP)*, 2005-2010 that replaces the PRSP. Equally significant, has been the introduction of the *Medium Term Expenditure Framework. MTEF)* and the computer- based *Integrated Financial Management System. IFMS)*. The MTEF is used to shift budgeting from annual consistencies to objective demand and results-oriented service delivery programmes with clearly set out goals and spending priorities. The IFMS, on the other hand, targets efficiency and integrity of public finance management. These financial systems have generated greater donor confidence in the management of state scarce resources. Indeed, it is because of these prudent public management achievements that Tanzania became one of the first four countries to reach the completion point for debt relief under the *Enhanced HIPC Debt Relief Initiative* in 2001. Following the debt relief, Tanzania external debt service, as alluded to above, has declined from 9.4% of GDP in 1997 to 1.7% in 2001 and from 17.5% of exports to 10.2% in the same period.

Third, improved measures directed towards improving revenue collection have been put in place. The establishment of the Tanzania Revenue Authority. TRA) in July 1996 has been the main driving force in the laudable achievements made in revenue collection. In nominal Tanzania shillings, revenue collection from tax and non-tax sources has shot up from an average monthly level of shillings 37 billion in fiscal year 1995/1996 to shillings 133 billion during November 2004. Whilst tax collection administration has improved greatly, the revenue increase is also attributable to the introduction of *Value Added Tax*. VAT) in July 1998 and the *Tax Identification Number. TIN)* for all registered taxpayers and businesses in July 2000. However, notwithstanding the good revenue performance, Tanzania's revenue generation as a percentage of GDP is still at a low level of 13%, one of the lowest in Africa. The average tax revenue yield for Sub-Saharan Africa is 21%. Kenya's yield, for example, is 22%. Fiscal experts believe that Tanzania's revenue potential is about 5-7% points higher that what is presently collected. At the same time, however, Tanzania's low yield is largely accounted for by a big non-monetised informal sector output, estimated at 30% of GDP. This situation may change as the government adopts fiscal and regulatory measures, as it has done in the Budget of 2004/2005, to correct the root causes of business informality. These measures include abolishing business license fees for businesses with turnover of less than Shillings 20 million.

The IMF is seriously concerned about the revenue low yield. In recent years, especially since fiscal year 1999/2000, it has pushed hard for fiscal and tax reforms to address the shortcoming. Unfortunately, the IMF's drive has often threatened to upset the very policy stability, consistency and predictability that it preaches. As a result, investors' confidence has also been adversely affected along the way. One case needs to be examined to clarify this point. During the period 2000-2001 and 2002-2003 and as lately as end 2003 with specific respect to the proposed new Income Tax Act, 2004, the IMF played a high profile role in getting the Tanzania Government to revise the tax incentives offered to investors under the investment promotion regime. The IMF, and to some degree, the TRA. which has been under constant pressure to deliver higher and higher revenue outturns), have orchestrated the stance that the Tanzania Investment Act, 1997 offers tax incentives to investors which are over generous with adverse impact on revenue buoyancy. Specifically, two tax incentives have been targeted for revision: tax holidays and tax deferrals. In order to have a clear understanding of the implications such revisions have had and would have, it is necessary to give a brief historical outline of tax incentives offered to investors in Tanzania.

The National Investment and Protection Act. NIPPA) enacted by Parliament in 1990 offered generous tax incentives to investors, domestic and foreign. The incentives included five years corporate tax holiday, full remission of import taxes on project specific list of capital goods, exemption from withholding taxes and remission of import duty on start-up raw materials and inputs. Unfortunately, much of the decision-making under NIPPA was discretionary, raising fears that corruption was the key factor in investors obtaining certificates of approved enterprise. Thus, the credibility of the institution managing investment promotion was put on the line. Moreover, in spite of the excellent incentives that NIPPA offered, the Investment Promotion Centre, as it was then called, lacked teeth. It was not a truly "One Stop Centre" in dealing with investors. In the light of such weaknesses, a new investment promotion law was enacted in 1997 setting up the *Tanzania Investment Centre.* TIC) with a well-defined mandate to act as "One Stop Centre" in promoting and facilitating investments. Section 19(2) of the Act assured investors who obtain a certificate of investment *stability* in respect of all tax incentives granted. One such tax incentive was 100% capital deduction, for tax purposes, during the first year of investment. To the IMF, this specific incentive was viewed as a perpetual tax holiday for many enterprises. In fact, the position of the IMF is documented in the *IMF Report: Tanzania: Reforming the Income Tax and Selected Indirect Taxes,* December 1998.

Thus between 1998 and 2002, the government came under constant pressure from the IMF to revise the capital deduction tax incentive. Ultimately, the pressure led to the current position. This is that expenditure on buildings is excluded from any tax relief and replaced by a conventional straight-line annual depreciation rate of 5%. In the case of plant and machinery, capital deduction has been reduced to 50% in the first year, followed by annual wear and tear allowance rates of 37.5%, 25% or 12.5%, applied on reducing basis, the rate applied being contingent on the class of asset being depreciated. On the positive side, tax losses can be carried forward indefinitely thus removing the five years' cap that existed before. Moreover, companies can now claim full relief for interest charges on capital loans. Moreover, pursuant to the Income Tax Act, they are also entitled to a one-time investment deduction of 20% for tax purposes. In as much as these tax incentive changes shift the goal posts, in terms of investment incentives already offered to some investors being changed, they are in line with the prevailing tax legislations in both Kenya and Uganda. They should therefore be taken in good stride by investors in

Tanzania, particularly now that the East African Customs Union has been operationalised.

What was troubling on the tax incentives front is that, in its quest to bolster Tanzania's revenue to GDP ratio, the IMF, since mid 2003, promoted the enactment of a new Income Tax Act that sought to abolish altogether the 50% immediate capital deduction, the 20% investment deduction and existing agricultural and mining tax relief. There was also a provision in the tax bill that sought to revise the indefinite carry forward of tax losses conditioning it only to a situation where there was no change in ownership control of the asset or business. Above all, the law had sought to abolish Section 19(2) of the TIC Act that guaranteed the stability of tax incentives granted to investors holding investment certificates. Such a move would have eroded the key underpinning of the Tanzania National Investment Promotion Policy of 1996, which stipulated, under clause 4.3 that "the Investment Code of 1997 will be self protecting and cannot be changed by any other law except itself." Putting it mildly, what the new Income Tax Act would have done had it not been amended following bold moves taken to block several of its repugnant clauses was to send the wrong signal to new investors that you could not rely on consistency and predictability of investment incentives offered in Tanzania. The intervention of the Tanzania business community supported by the Tanzania Investment Centre led to a more business supportive Income Tax law being enacted in mid 2004. In many respects, the government reflected an excellent attitude of smart partnership in allowing an open and transparent dialogue to take place between itself and the business lobby in arriving at a taxation regime that is largely based on a *consensus ad idem*.

Stabilisation of the Exchange Rate

Since the adoption of the ERP in mid 1986, Tanzania has pursued a bold and vigorous adjustment of the exchange rate. In the initial years, the adjustment was characterised by fast and huge devaluations of the shilling in an effort to bring the local currency in line with real or market rates. Significantly, under ERP I. July 1986 to June 1989), the value of the shilling against the dollar was depreciated by 338% in nominal terms and 111% in real terms. Clearly, if there is one policy measure that injected radical economic reality especially in the state-owned business sector, it was the massive devaluation of the shilling. Particularly so in the period between 1986 and 1995 when Tanzania went through what, most domestic industries, was a destabilising exchange rate adjustment. It may be noted, for instance, that as at the end of 1985, the parallel exchange rate of the shilling to US dollar was 800%. This fell to 50% by 1990 and 10% by August 1993. During that period, many business enterprises, state-owned and private, that had borrowed huge equity loans and had also taken huge overdrafts from the banking sector for working capital, evidently cheaply because of the very low ruling interest rates and the overvalued shilling, suddenly found themselves entrapped with ballooned loans to service.

The challenge of confronting a huge debt service obligation was adversely accentuated by the entry of competition in the domestic economy following the liberalisation of international trade. A hitherto overprotected domestic industry suddenly found itself overexposed to competition from what were, at that time, better quality and more competitively priced goods. Ordinarily, the domestic industry should have competed on an even keel. However, many industries failed to import or buy raw materials locally because they had busted their bank working capital limits following the grave impact of devaluations. Banks had also become strictly concerned about the capacity of their corporate borrowers to adjust to a new competitive environment and thus being able to service their loan outstandings. Indeed, many Tanzanian businesses folded during that time. State-owned enterprises continued for a while, due to subsidisation from the state, but only for a while. Later, privatisation of these industries had to be a natural recourse.

In recent years, the Bank of Tanzania has consistently managed a market-determined exchange rate, driven by the inter-bank market with a small premium extending to the *bureaux de change* operations. It was in August 1993 that the foreign exchange market became unified upon the introduction of the bureaux de change and the liberalisation of almost all current account foreign exchange transactions. The dynamism in the exchange rate market is well reflected in its movement. Between 1994 and October 2004, the bureaux de change exchange rate has moved from shillings 500 to one United States dollar to shillings 1080. Since 2002, the Bank of Tanzania has particularly pursued a monetary policy directed at arresting the appreciation of the shilling whilst, at the same time, closely managing inflation in line with the level applicable in the economies of key trading partner nations. At the heart of such policy is the objective to stimulate export growth in order to achieve external balance.

Following Tanzania's accession to Article Viii of the IMF, the Bank of Tanzania decided to effect partial liberalisation of the capital account in May 2003. That decision enabled Tanzania to benefit from foreign equity and portfolio investments as well as the cross listing of corporate shares. It was a timely move when considered in the context of the coming into effect of the East African Customs Union in January 2005 and the reinforcement of closer economic cooperation on the SADC front. Clearly, the liberalisation of the capital account should help to deepen Tanzania's domestic capital market and to spur more investments. Since the enactment of the *Capital Market and Securities Act* in 1994, a legislation that puts in place a legal and regulatory framework enabling a capital market to operate efficiently, it has been the desire of the Tanzania government to create the environment that would bolster confidence in investors to transfer capital into Tanzania. Partial liberalisation of the capital account falls in line with these objectives.

It is important to recognise though that, historically, growth benefits from capital account have been insignificant in the developing world. In many cases, financial openness has been characterised by dysfunctional speculative short-term financial flows. The report of the World Commission on the Social Dimension of Globalisation titled, *A Fair Globalisation: Creating Opportunities for All* cogently highlights the dangers posed by capital account liberalisation. It posits that a "dogmatic approach" should not be taken, adding that the experience that led to the financial crises in East Asia in the late 1990s has shown "that countries with underdeveloped and poorly regulated financial systems should adopt a more cautious and gradual approach". It is therefore important that monetary authorities in Tanzania keep a close tap on the operations of the capital market. Indeed, the reason behind Tanzania allowing only partial liberalisation is precisely to ensure that the openness allowed is within the capacity of the regulatory regime to effectively manage and control.

Liberalisation of the Financial and Banking Sectors

Prior to the licensing of private banks in 1992/1993, only two state-owned commercial banks dominated in the Tanzanian economy: the National Bank of Commerce and the Cooperative and Rural Development Bank. CRDB). During the past decade, however, a number of excellent international and regional banks have set up operations in Tanzania. Overall, there are 27 commercial banks now operating in Tanzania. They include:

Standard Chartered Bank, Citibank, Stanbic Bank. which is part of the Standard Bank Group of South Africa), ABSA which has acquired 70% of the shares of the privatised National Bank of Commerce, CRDB Bank, Bank of Baroda, Barclays Bank, Kenya Commercial Bank, Eurafrican Bank, African Banking Corporation, Diamond Trust Bank, Postal Bank. state-owned), Exim Bank, International Bank of Malaysia, Akiba Bank, People's Bank of Zanzibar. state-owned), United Bank of Africa, CF Union Bank and Habib African Bank. More recently, since 2000, Community as well as Cooperative Banks have also emerged in Dar es Salaam, Kilimanjaro, Kagera and Ruvuma regions. The remaining state-owned commercial banks are the National Microfinance Bank. NMB), which is in the process of being privatised, and the National Bureau de Change Bank, which since July 2004, has acquired a new name: Twiga Bankcorp Limited.

The expansion of commercial banking activity of international standard has had a telling impact on the Tanzanian economy. As a start, it has bolstered confidence of foreign investment. More importantly, however, it has brought in foreign capital into the economy enabling many key business operations to kick-start and expand. According to the IMF/ World Bank Joint Report: *Financial Sector Assessments Tanzania*, of August 2003, commercial bank credit to the private sector has expanded from shillings 156.9 billion in 1990 to shillings 310 billion in 1994 and to shillings 848.0 billion in March 2004. Of course, the expansion of credit is yet to reach appreciable levels and the challenge remains how to enable greater expansion to take effect. According to the Bank of Tanzania Monthly Economic Review for June 2004, commercial credit to the private sector represented 85.0% of total credit, as at June 2004, compared to 43% in 1999/ 2000. However, the share of private sector credit to total deposits remains low, at 48.0% as at end of June 2004.

An area of greater concern in the liberalisation of the financial and banking sector is the continuing imbalance in the margin between the lending and saving deposits rates. Though the prime-lending rate has dropped from 40% in 1995 to an overall weighted average rate of 9.9% in June 2004, the spread between the prime lending rate and the level of deposit interest rate remains high. Indeed, the IMF / World Bank Joint Report referred above, observes that whilst this spread has shown a state of decline, particularly in the period 2001-2002, it remains high. The report cites weighted average lending rate of 14-15% in early 2003 while the deposit rates averaged only 3%. Whilst conceding that banks allocate high-risk premium to credit risk and the existence of weak contract enforcement. notwithstanding the establishment of a designated Commercial Court in September 1999 which has in fact speeded up the process of adjudication of commercial disputes), the report still finds the spread to be too wide. Given the intensity of competition that presently exists in the banking sector, the continuing high cost of borrowing appears to lack logic other than sheer risk averseness to lend, a risk factor attributed to Tanzania's poor history of non-performing bank portfolios in state-owned banks.

Insurance Industry

The liberalisation of the insurance industry was effected in 1997 following the enactment of the *Insurance Act. No. 18) of 1996*. Whilst the former monopoly insurance company, the state-owned National Insurance Corporation. NIC) is still in the process of being privatised, several private insurance companies have been registered and set up since 1998. As at 31st December 2002, they stood at 10. inclusive of NIC and the state-owned Zanzibar Insurance Corporation). It is notable, however, that Tanzindia Assurance, a consortium of Indian, Kenyan and Tanzanian investors led by the Indian General Insurance Corporation and Life Insurance Corporation, entered the Tanzanian insurance market towards the end of 2003. Presently, the insurance industry in Tanzania is characterised by a highly oligopolistic structure with about four companies controlling the lion's share of the market. The situation is more pronounced at the level of Brokers' participation in insurance underwriting with two, largely foreign-owned insurance brokers, controlling over 50% of the underwriting portfolio which, in 2002, was 46.4% of total insurance premiums written. Notwithstanding such highly concentrated character of business control by insurance companies and brokers, the industry as a whole is highly competitive and operates with reasonable efficiency and profitability. In this regard, the National Insurance Supervising Board which was established by the Insurance Act as a supervisory and regulatory institution has strived to ensure good prudential management of insurance companies.

The Insurance sector plays an important role in the economy and its liberalisation should be viewed in this light. According to the Insurance Supervising Department's *Annual Insurance Market Performance Report for the year ended 31st December 2002,* during 2002, all classes of long term and general insurance business collectively generated gross premium income totalling shillings 53.76 billion or 0.61% of GDP. at current prices). In turn, the industry's contribution to the finance and insurance sectors' GDP. at current prices) was 23.21% in 2002. The level of the industry's contribution to the development of the national economy can be sensed from the data on investments. Total investments in insurance companies rose by 4% from Shillings 71.4 billion in 2001 to Shillings 74 billion in 2002. As at December 2002, their investments in government securities and bank deposits amounted to Shillings 16.9 billion, shares in the stock exchange and other unit trusts amounted to Shillings 4.2 billion and investments in land and buildings. other than those occupied by insurance companies for their own operations) totalled Shillings 4.6 billion. The Annual Insurance Market Performance Report unfortunately does not disaggregate the investment portfolio for government securities and bank deposits. Such disaggregation would have helped to show how the insurance industry participates in bolstering the banks' sources of loanable funds. There is also the perspective of participation in the contractual savings market. Mauritius, for example, is one of the few developing countries. which include South Africa and Malaysia) where contractual savings, that is savings with insurance companies and pension funds, exceed 40% of GDP and represents an important engine to the domestic financial system.

Amongst the major challenges that confront the Tanzanian insurance industry is how to deepen the industry participation in the economy. In 2002, the total assets of all the insurance companies totalled 106 billion shillings, representing a meagre 1.3% of GDP. Evidently, a higher contribution is contingent on the growth of the economy. It also crucially hinges on the state of the people's mindset towards insurance. Unsurprisingly, even amongst the educated Tanzanians, few of them have private medical insurance let alone life insurance. Part of the problem in this area has been, on the one hand, the poor record of the National Insurance Company in promoting these insurance products, and on the other hand, NIC's poor payments record. The liberalisation of the insurance industry poses new set of challenges not only to change people's attitudes towards insurance but also to offer price competitive premiums for products that bolster the assets of the industry and thereby energising the industry to play a more robust role in the economy.

In an effort to deepen the domestic insurance business, the National Insurance Board has been deeply engaged in promoting the establishment of the Tanzania Reinsurance Corporation, Tan Re. It is observed, for instance, in the Statement of the Chairman of the National Insurance Board, which accompanies the Annual Insurance Market Performance Report of the Insurance Supervisory Department for the year ended 31st December 2002, that though the ratio of re-insurance premiums ceded to gross premiums written, increased from 44% in 2001 to 49% in 2002, the increase, it is contended, could have been higher had a Tanzanian re-insurance facility existed to underwrite risks. The underlying thrust of the argument for the establishment of Tan Re is that the net premiums retained in Tanzania have been decreasing due to more re-insurance premiums being ceded to foreign re-insurance companies. However, the popular argument that foreign re-insurance is a back door means for enabling capital flight by insurance companies operating in Tanzania is not supported by data. Indeed, even with Tan Re coming on stream, it would be essential for external re-insurance to be taken to ensure viable protection. In a way, therefore, Tan Re would act as a de facto "middleman," adding to the overheads of insurance companies which would have to passed over to policy holders. In this context, it is imperative that Tan Re walks before it runs and avoids imposing huge percentages of insurance policy cessions from its on-set. In sum, whilst one would wish to be nationalistic and thus promote domestic re-insurance as one way to deepen the insurance assets in Tanzania with positive concomitant spill over into the rest of the economy, caution is called for. Re-insurance business, like the wholesale liberalisation of the capital account, is a highly risky business. You need to have in place mature and well-regulated insurance systems in order to take such a leap forward. With leading global companies investing in Tanzania, such as South African Breweries, Coca-Cola, AngloGold and other mining companies, South African Airways, Japan Tobacco, Unilever, the Banks, Serena Group etc, an insurance business that is not supported by reliable re-insurance could dampen the confidence of major economic players. It is critical that Tan Re, a private company but paradoxically established by Presidential Order as if it were a state-owned enterprise, acts prudently and collegially by involving insurance companies in determining reasonable share treaties and facultative acceptances.

Privatisation Policy and Process

Privatisation of state-owned enterprises constituted a key component of Tanzania's economic reform. Whilst there is a view that privatisation policy has been dominantly driven by an ideological shift from socialism to the market economy, hard economic facts on the ground point to different reasons. In a brilliant expose by Richard Mushi titled, *Fiscal Impact of the Parastatal Sector in Tanzania: 1984 – 1995*, we note that between 1984/85 and 1995/96, net outflows, in real terms, from the government to the parastatal sector grew from shillings 6.3 billion to shillings 18.1 billion. Mushi's study shows that in any one year at least one third of the parastatals made losses during the period examined. In 1991, 50% of 41 parastatals, whose accounts had been audited, made losses. Indeed, accumulated losses of state-owned institutions rose, in real terms, from shillings 5.4 billion in 1990 to shillings 13.3 billion in 1993. The losses were incurred at the backdrop of various measures of support extended to parastatals between 1984 and 1994. The support measures included subsidies, fresh equity injections, grants, subventions and exemptions from payments of sales taxes and customs duties assessed on goods imported or domestically purchased by parastatals. Mushi records that between 1984 and 1994 the support measures amounted to shillings 49.2 billion. What was recovered was only shillings 10.6 billion or 21.6%. Moreover, because of the readjustment of the exchange rate and borrowing interest rates, key components of the structural adjustment programme, parastatal loans ballooned from shillings 6.0 billion in 1987/88 to shillings 18.0 billion in 1993/94. As a result, loan defaults by parastatals alone averaged shillings 14.0 billion between 1998/90 and 1991/92.

Clearly, under such circumstances, where parastatals were not only disproportionately gobbling up huge amounts of government revenue and taxes paid by the people, but also artificially surviving, a radical surgery had to be undertaken. Whilst privatisation may not be a panacea, in circumstances as those that obtained in Tanzania in the early 1990s, it was the only prudent strategy to pursue. It is in the context of the dismal condition that parastatals were in that the government decided to establish the *Presidential Parastatal Sector Reform Commission. PSRC)* in 1993 to oversee the restructuring and privatisation of parastatals that numbered close to 450. As a prelude to the privatisation exercise, and in the light of the large non-performing portfolio loans within the state-owned commercial banking sector, notably involving the NBC and CRDB, a law was enacted in 1991 establishing the Loans and Advances Realisation Trust. LART). LART was mandated to assume and, subsequently, to realise the non-performing loans of the NBC and CRDB in order to clean up their balance sheets in preparation for privatisation. Initially, LART issued bonds to NBC and CRDB in 1992 and 1993 in place of the bad debts. However, later, LART took up the responsibility of liquidating insolvent parastatals, supporting the role of the PSRC in restructuring state-owned enterprises.

The privatisation process picked up steam since 1997 partly because Tanzania's benchmarks with the IMF and the World Bank were partly contingent on realising a given level of privatisation performance. They were also partly contingent on the Exchequer not being able to sustain paying for losses incurred by parastatals. Thus, until June 2004, 307 parastatals had been privatised as outlined in the overview section. Of these, 47 are parastatals assigned to LART either for liquidation or for disposal. Out of the total privatised enterprises, 156 were sold to Tanzanian nationals. 16 of them to nationals through the management and employees' buy out or MEBO) on 100% shares basis, 23 were sold to foreigners on 100% shares basis and 128 were privatised on joint venture basis involving foreigners and Tanzanians with varying share ownerships. At the same time, 417 stand-alone non-core assets were also sold off.

The next stage of the privatisation process is crucial. It involves the privatisation of two key financial sector institutions: the National Insurance Corporation. NIC) and the National Microfinance Bank. NMB). Politics have come in the way of early privatisation of these two institutions. However, it would now appear that time, not the resolve, is the main factor. Even more complex would be the privatisation of the infrastructure parastatals, namely the Tanzania Railways Corporation. TRC), Tanzania Harbours Authority. THA) and the Power Utility Company, TANESCO. TRC is already in the process of being privatised through a concession agreement. For THA, studies have been completed on the best methodology to be adopted in concessioning it. Equally, studies have been undertaken on how to unbundle TANESCO so that power generating is separated from power pool distribution and marketing. For sometime, between 2001 and 2004, it appeared that the government was sold to the idea of unbundling TANESCO and proceeding with privatisation in 2005. It now appears that the government has reneged on this approach. At the end of October 2004, the government announced that it would be necessary to turn around the performance of the utility company first, through the management contract it had assigned to a South African company, Net Solutions, before deciding on unbundling and privatisation. It would be interesting to learn the reaction of the World Bank that has provided funding for studies on how best to unbundle TANESCO and privatise it.

In the following section, Tanzania's achievements and challenges in the economic reform arena are examined in the context of how the government has promoted an enabling environment for investments and business to grow and thrive.

Promoting Enabling Environment for Business

Many nations have gone through the process of macro-economic stabilisation and liberalisation. Yet sound macro-economic policies and a stable political context are necessary but not sufficient to ensure a prosperous economy. As important- or even more so- are the micro-economic foundations of economic development, rooted in firm operating practices and strategies as well as in the business inputs, infrastructure, institutions and policies that constitute the environment in which firms compete. Unless there is appropriate improvement at the micro-economic level, political and macro-economic reform will not bear full fruit.

-Michael Porter: *The Micro-economic Foundations of Economic Development*, 1998.

One of the defining features of Tanzania's economic reform agenda has been how to create an enabling environment that would not only promote investments but also ensure the viability and robustness of existing business enterprises and economic activities. In the previous section of this chapter, I have alluded to the critical challenge that has confronted the Tanzania government in the past two decades in striking a complex balance between realising a balanced budget enabled by revenue fundamentalism and promoting an economic stimulus fiscal and tax policy. Evidently, in an environment where the IMF and the World Bank, with clear intentions of getting the Tanzania economy to adjust, stabilise and grow, have subjected economic reform to close supervision, scrutiny and monitoring, the domestic space for exercising policy sovereignty has often been constricted. Indeed, sometimes it has actually been undermined. It is little wonder, in this context, that Tanzania went through dramatic and negatively serious reform slippages in the period 1991 to 1995. During that period, former President Ali Hassan Mwinyi was prompted to exercise greater sovereignty vis-à-vis policies of the IMF and the World Bank, and, consequently, with the donor community as a whole, over the determination of the form and pace of economic reform. At that time, it was perceived that the depth of the reform programme pursued was hurting the poor with adverse political consequences especially on the part of the ruling political party that was then gearing up for the first multi-party general elections in 1995. The policy reversal shows that the pursuit of radical economic reform demands broad ownership of the reform programme as well as bold and courageous leadership prepared to put itself on the line for short-term hardships that arose.

In this specific section, as is examine how the government has responded, over time, to the challenge of delicately balancing economic reforms that seek to generate more revenue for the exchequer whilst at the same time promoting investment by creating a more conducive and enabling business environment. Of particular focus is the question how the government has responded to concerns of the domestic economic sector about protection against unfair competition unleashed by trade liberalisation and about reducing the high costs of doing business or what is described as combating competitive disinflation. As is also examine how the government and the business sector have been able to promote a smart partnership in policymaking.

The quality of any national business environment crucially hinges on the nature of fiscal policy and the tax measures that are imposed on economic activities. In the Tanzanian context, from the on-set of IMF-driven economic reforms in mid 1986 there lacked a comprehensive policy on selective protection of domestic economic activities. This deficit occurred in spite of the fact that the Confederation of Tanzania Industries. CTI) prepared and submitted, in 1993, an Industrial Policy proposal to the government. The proposal was subsequently fine-tuned by the government and published in 1995 as the *Sustainable Industrial Development Policy. SIDP).* As shall be observed later, there has always been a lag response between the time a proposal is submitted to the government on policy change or new measure being effected and decision taken. Thus, the good intentions of SIDP notwithstanding, there were insignificant implementation of the lofty goals. Take the case of dumping which the CTI called upon the government to take action on as far as back as 1994. It was only in February 2004 that a bill to enact an anti-dumping law was tabled before Parliament. Of course, the law marked an important development, belated as it was since many domestic industries have had to and continue to compete against shoddy, sub-standard and under-priced imported products. Even then, the lofty objectives of *The Anti-Dumping and Countervailing Measures Act, 2004* would be ineffective if the government fails to address the whole gamut of factors that undermine the capacity of domestic industries to be viable and competitive. Some of these factors are examined below.

Since the mid 1990s, the Tanzania business sector has consistently presented a case before the government for the stimulation and protection of domestic industries as well as for the creation of an enabling environment that spurs investments. The case has centred on the following key areas:

- high import tariffs and other taxes especially those levied on critical industrial raw materials, inputs and spares.

- high payroll taxes
- nuisance taxes
- Local Government taxation
- massive tax evasion
- abuse of discretionary powers by public officials.
- Export Processing Zones. EPZ)

High Customs Tariffs

The English proverb that a stitch in time saves nine is apt in examining how the question of customs tariffs and other key taxes has been handled in Tanzania over time. At the same time, it is also evident that better late than never. It is notable that the government has positively responded to adjusting the customs tariff in so far as import taxes on industrial raw materials and spares are concerned especially in the period between fiscal year 1998/1999 and 2002/2003. Of course, a few industries had already suffered irreparable loss, in income as well as in the capacity to upgrade themselves technologically to meet the challenges of new competition. The reform of the customs tariff is clearly one area where the government came under a heavy dose of influence, even pressure and direction from the IMF. In this specific area, and for a long time, the IMF missed the point in terms of appreciating what was the right policy to influence within the objective realities in place. Conventional wisdom in public finance holds that it is income, not capital, that should attract taxation. Raw materials, inputs, industrial spares and capital goods do not constitute income. They only enable income to be created. As such, they should not be taxed at all. Yet, in the interest of bolstering revenue generation, the Tanzanian business sector was prepared to depart from the conventional wisdom and allow a taxation regime that works based on manufacturing degree of processing to form the basis for determining tariff rates. Of course, manufacturing degree of processing had to be considered from a relative point of view. In other words, its logic could not be treated as sacrosanct. It had to be informed by the stage of technological development a country was in. Equally, the nature of manufacturing degree of processing had to be industry-specific. In this context, what is semi-processed raw material in Kenya, for instance, is a basic raw material in Tanzania and the tariff should recognise such reality.

For several years, from the late 1990s to 2001, the government hesitated, clearly under IMF influence, to take bold and independent decisions to effect a tariff proposal based on manufacturing degree of processing. The large national economic picture was sacrificed on the tomb of short-term revenue fundamentalism. The government was blinded from seeing that revenue collection would actually increase from a more reliable and tax compliant domestic industry. Put differently, tax evasion on imports was never seriously included in the equation in examining the tariff proposal put forward by the Tanzania manufacturing business sector. It was as if Tanzania's import substituting industries were perceived to be inherently inefficient and uncompetitive and thus could not benefit from whatever lower tariffs put in place for imported industrial raw materials and other inputs.

The idea of applying manufacturing degree of processing in guiding fiscal policy took four fiscal years-1999/2000 to 2002/2003- to be comprehensively appreciated and endorsed in the form of new tax measures. The delay was mainly caused by disagreement on the definition of what constituted raw materials. Given Tanzania's low stage of industrialisation, industrial raw materials needed a broader definition than conventionally defined. As noted earlier, semi-processed products imported for manufacturing value addition had to be considered as industrial raw material. To cite an example, tin plates are semi-processed materials. However, they constitute basic raw materials in the manufacture of dry cell batteries and crown corks. Were a maximum customs tariff of 25% of CIF value to be imposed on tin plates as opposed to 5% or 0%, the cost of production of end products would be that much higher and would undermine the competitiveness of those products vis-à-vis equivalent imported finished products. In the end, the respective domestic industries would be forced to shut down with consequential loss of jobs.

Indeed, this is the situation that beset a leading national bicycle manufacturing company, National Bicycle Company. NABICO), which was privatised and taken over by Avon Cycles of India. In fiscal year 1999/2000, the company issued notice of closure and 120 workers would have lost their jobs. The reason was simple. The company manufactures frames, forks and mudguards in Tanzania. The remaining bicycle inputs are imported from India. For the imported inputs, like rims, the company was required to pay 20% import duty for what to it constituted basic raw materials. To the Tanzania Revenue Authority, on the other hand, these inputs were regarded as finished products and thus could not enjoy a lower tariff of 5 or 10%. Yet import duty levied on a full-assembled imported bicycle was a mere 25%. In other words, the objective of bicycle manufacturing technology transfer to Tanzania and in creating more local jobs was being frustrated by an illogical tariff structure. It is only in fiscal year 2001/2002 that the government came round to treating bicycle rims and steel pipes as basic raw materials for assembly of bicycles.

There are several other industries in Tanzania that suffered because the concept of manufacturing degree of processing did not fit into the IMF conventional definition in determining the tax structure. They include packaging. where the differential tariff of 25% for coated paper *vis a vis*

20% for finished imported paper products was ludicrous), kiln refractory bricks and kiln coolers for the manufacture of glass bottles, leaf springs. where alloy steel bars usable, in Tanzania, only for the manufacture of motor vehicle springs, attracted 20% duty), clinker. a product mix of gypsum, sand and water) for the cement industry which is imported only when cement plants close kilns for maintenance, attracted 25% import duty, the same tariff levied on imported packaged cement!

It is the fiscal budgets of 2001/2002 and 2002/2003 that finally realised the importance of the concept of manufacturing degree of processing as a vital policy in protecting and bolstering the competitiveness of Tanzanian industries and in promoting job creation. A much clearer customs tariff structure now exists with four bands: 0, 10, and 15 and 25%. Since January 2005, the EAC Customs Union has three external customs tariff bands: 0, 10 and 25%. These tariffs apply to goods entering the Community from outside. The two fiscal budgets referred above also broadly addressed other taxes that had had an adverse impact on domestic industries. Of particular note is the tax element on heavy finance oil. HFO) which, for several years, had eroded the competitiveness of the cement and glass industries especially when the additional element of high cost of electricity is included. For example, in 2000, the cost of producing a metric tonne of cement in Tanzania was US$ 36 compared to US$ 18 in Kenya. The production cost differential was caused largely by the huge differential in the cost of HFO and electricity applying in the two countries. The *IMF 2003 Country Report on Tanzania* shows that based on year 2000 data, US$ cost per kilowatt-hour of electricity in Tanzania was 0.105 compared to Kenya's 0.093. The US$ cost of HFO per litre was 0.626 for Tanzania compared to 0.440 for Kenya. The differential on fuel dollar cost lay in the tax element: 0.353 for Tanzania compared to 0.167 for Kenya. In the fiscal budget 2002/2003, the government lowered the tax element on HFO from shillings 26.50 per litre to shillings 13.50 per litre. It was an important shot in the arm for major HFO users.

High Payroll Taxes

As part of the overall economic reform, Tanzania has undertaken a radical restructuring of income taxation- personal and corporate. The current highest marginal rate of PAYE and corporate tax is 30%. All fringe benefits are monetised and form part of taxable income. This move has had a positive revenue impact on PAYE collections. However, the tax-free monthly income threshold in Tanzania is still much lower than that in Kenya and Uganda. In Tanzania, from July 2005 it is at Shs. 80,000 or US$ 60. In contrast, the tax-free threshold on monthly income, equivalent in Tanzania shillings, is Shs 156,000 or US$ 140, in Kenya. In Uganda, it is equivalent to US$ 84. Clearly, the Tanzania threshold needs to be further jerked up to at least Shs 120,000 if it is to motivate payment of higher salaries especially to low wage earners as well as stimulate consumer demand. Moreover, the present low tax-free threshold on salaries accentuates the serious concern that exists among employers in Tanzania with respect to payroll taxes. Tanzania has the highest payroll taxes in the Eastern, Central and Southern African regions. The composition of these payroll taxes is as follows:

Type of Tax	Rate
NSSF. employer contribution)	10%
NSSF. employee contribution)	10%
Skills and Development Levy	6%

In the light of the monetisation of all fringe benefits into salary and the low tax-free threshold on salaries, the cost of payroll contributions has become punitive because, unlike in Kenya and Uganda, there is no cap on the NSSF contributions. The skills levy has to be brought down to about 4%. Inevitably, job creation has suffered at a time when the government is seriously committed to stimulating jobs and bolstering incomes in its effort to reduce poverty. Many employers resort to recruiting casual workers to circumvent payment of payroll taxes. Without imposing a maximum salary cap to base payroll contributions, job creation would continue to suffer and so would the competitiveness of Tanzanian producers.

Nuisance Taxes

Of the most hated nuisance taxes has been withholding tax on goods and services. This tax was introduced in the 1991/1992 fiscal year for payments made by the government and its agencies to suppliers of food and services to the government. It was expanded in the 1993/1994-budget year to cover payments made by private companies. The tax was based on turnover: any payment exceeding shillings 100,000 per transaction had to be taxed at the rate of 2% excluding VAT and the revenue there from remitted to the Income Tax Department. The supplier of goods and/or services was entitled to claim tax withheld as credit against the annual income tax liability. However, and logically, following the introduction of VAT in July 1998, the imposition of withholding tax was rendered superfluous. Yet the Tanzania Revenue Authority rejected arguments for its withdrawal, clearly for good reasons. In fiscal year 1999/2000, Tanzania Revenue Authority collected some 19 billion shillings from this tax source alone. The private sector, on the other hand, objected to the imposition of the tax because it constituted a nuisance tax. Four reasons were adduced in support: One, record keeping of withholding tax deducted by customers was an administrative nightmare. Two, the quarterly provisional tax payment system ran parallel with withholding tax, in other words, a system duplication. Three, the Income Tax Department failed to honour refund claims of taxpayers enjoying a five years' tax holiday or whose companies made losses. Four, withholding tax undermined the cash flows of companies.

In the fiscal budget 2001/2002, the government abolished withholding tax on goods and services for all TIN registered companies. However, it had taken the government ten years to realise and appreciate the dysfunction of the nuisance tax. Evidently, revenue fundamentalism overrode the nuisance character of the tax. The burden of the argument here is that it is always important for the government to have the big picture in matters of fiscal and tax policy rather than being driven by short-term revenue interests that may damage the environment for attracting and promoting investments. In this context, it could be observed, that since fiscal year 2000/01, the government, in certain fiscal aspects, has embraced this posture as manifested by the harmonisation of withholding tax on dividends at 10% and on interest at 15% applicable to both holders and non-holders of TIC approved investment certificates. Withholding tax on interest for TIC certificate holders prior to July 2000 remains at 0%. In addition, in order to promote tourism, withholding tax on leased aircraft has been abolished. Effective fiscal year 2001/2002, withholding tax on interest on foreign loans for investments has also been abolished. Moreover, in the fiscal budget for 2005/2006, stamp duty on various transfer instruments. bills of sale, exchange of property, transfer of lease etc) has been reduced from 4% to 1%

The remaining challenge is for the government to harmonise withholding tax rates with Kenya and Uganda on management and professional fees, royalties, rent, branch dividends and interest. However, at the same time, the government should be mindful of the pressure put on her to introduce new negative withholding taxes such as those that had been envisaged in the Income Tax Bill, 2004. The earlier proposed taxes included 20% withholding tax on payment of interest to non-residents. This has now been reduced to 10% in the Income tax Act 2004. However, at a time when equity finance is in short supply in Tanzania, as commercial banks concentrate more on short term lending, it would be a retrogressive step to undermine term finance borrowing from regional development banks, such as the East African Development Bank and the PTA Bank, by sustaining withholding tax on interest payable. Such a measure would accentuate the cost of short-term borrowing and further reinforce revenue fundamentalism in contrast to the quest to promote economic growth. The virtues of policy stability, consistency, and predictability should be upheld and sustained.

Business Licensing

The government decision in the fiscal budget 2004/2005 to abolish the requirement for annual renewal of business licences has come as a major relief to businesses operating in Tanzania. For several years, the Tanzania business community had urged the government to abolish this nuisance requirement. The government had turned the requirement into a revenue measure when, in fact, it should have treated it as a regulatory one. The imposition of such licence renewal meant that an investor was under a state of uncertainty at the beginning of each year as to whether his or her business would be allowed to continue to operate, a most ridiculous situation. Why would the government, on the one hand, promote investments and then retain a discretionary authority, exercised annually, to decide whether or not to renew a business licence. Business licences issued under the Business Licensing Act of 1972 will now be issued only once, at the time of the establishment of a business. However, this positive change notwithstanding, it is now provided that after the initial payment for registration, "no business fee shall be charged under the Business Licensing Act of 1972 where a business is regulated by another law in a specific sector." What is left uncertain by this provision is whether once a business licence is issued under the Business Licensing Act, 1972, which is the "mother" law, a regulatory organ in a particular sector can override such license and disallow a particular company from operating and on what grounds. What remedy or recourse would an affected company have in such cases? This is a key question in an environment where the politics of "uzawa" are creeping into some sectors of the economy and where some regulatory bodies attempt to condition issuance of sector business licenses to payment of extortionary annual fees to help them meet their overhead costs. Put differently, it would be ludicrous and defeatist were the change effected to remove the requirement of annual renewal of business licenses under the Business Licensing Act, 1972, to be replaced by yet another revenue driven annual licence fee paid to regulatory bodies.

Local Government Taxation

Though the Public Finance Act 2001 centralises fiscal authority in the Minister for Finance, local government taxation continues to reflect serious weaknesses in and dissipation of that authority. In all the fiscal budgets from 1999/2000 to 2003/2004, the Minister for Finance directed that cesses and different levies imposed on agricultural produce by local authorities should be capped at 5% of the farm gate price. The directive has not been enforced. Cashew farmers, for example, have been gravely impacted by cess and levies imposed by local authorities in the past six years. The cumulative taxes have often been as high as 35% of the farm gate price. The total tax burden, on average, has varied between 20-25% of farm gate prices. This taxation regime erodes the incomes of peasants and is a mockery for a poor country like Tanzania, 48% of whose GDP depends on agriculture. Rich countries subsidise agriculture. Tanzania, on the other hand, marginalises it through a non-enforced fiscal policy regime. How to enforce the fiscal authority of the central government remains a huge challenge.

Massive Tax Evasion

Since the on-set of trade liberalisation in 1984, Tanzania has become a huge market for all kinds of imported goods, most of which are dumped, smuggled or enter the country without proper taxes being paid on them. For example, in 2001, it was estimated that between 30% and 40% of the processed tea market in Tanzania was controlled by smuggled imports of tea from the sub-region. On the other hand, the severity of dumping of cheap and sub-standard products, especially motor vehicle tyres, dry cell batteries, safety matches, bath sandals. "*kandambili*"), shoes, toilet soap, motor vehicle spares, GCI sheets and petroleum products has been extremely worrisome. Moreover, tax evasion has embraced a whole host of imported products including sugar, rice, wines and spirits, electronic goods, textiles and garments. The most common method of tax evasion has been under-invoicing, false classification of goods, false declaration of quantities and outright smuggling where no tax at all is paid. This is an area where even pre-shipment inspection, undertaken by global inspection companies, failed to have an impact. The result has been revenue foregone in billions of shillings annually.

In a November 2003 report titled, *A Review of Business Environment in Tanzania* prepared by Ravi Chande for the Tanzania National Business Council, it is reported, for example, that annual loss caused by dumping of petroleum products in recent years had been of the order of shillings 94 billion. At the same time, the government has been forfeiting about shillings 34 billion per annum on account of tax exemptions. This loophole would probably have been plugged following the wise government decision, taken in fiscal year 2002/2003, to require the government itself to pay customs and excise duties for all its imports. Interestingly though, it took over ten years for the government to effect such move which was part of the recommendations embodied in the Mtei Commission Report of 1991. Overall, estimates on total revenue loss from international trade range between shillings 318 billion and 414 billion in 2001. This revenue loss translates to between 4.2% and 5.4% of GDP. In the report, Mr Chande observes that falsification of VAT returns is rampant, especially in the hotel and catering services, retail and wholesale trading business, building contracts and transporters. Tax revenue losses through such falsifications are thought to be huge though precise data is unavailable.

In another report prepared by Ravi Chande for the Tanzania Ministry of Industry and Trade in November 2001 titled, *Comparative Analysis of Prevailing and Emerging Macro-economic and sectoral policies and their Impact on the Industry and Trade Sector,* we learn that tax evasion in Tanzania has been undertaken through a number of routes. Over the years, these routes have acquired names: the Zanzibar route, Mombasa route, Lake Victoria route, Transit trade route, tax exemption route and bonded warehouse route. Each of these routes has its own risk factors and it is these factors that determine the premium for corruption to be paid to public officials, largely tax officials but also to border police and immigration personnel. Since fiscal year 1999/2000, the government has done much to arrest dumping and tax evasion. However, the minimum dutiable values. MDVs) that had been imposed did not last long as they were deemed to be outside the framework of "countervailing duties" stipulated in the World Trade Organization. WTO) rules. The reversal in tax policy was considered retrogressive especially in the context of how best to deal with imported products such as jute cloth and jute bags that are heavily subsidised in their countries of origin, notably Bangladesh and India. The Government of Bangladesh has a deliberate policy of subsidising its largely state-owned jute industry because it creates thousands of jobs and bolsters export receipts. Part of the subsidy is in the form of 10% cash payment based on the FOB export price. A more substantial subsidy is in the form of the government absorbing all losses made by the jute mills.

The jute case presents a highly paradoxical policy question for Tanzania. Tanzania is a producer of sisal. In the 1960s and 1970s, it was a world leader in sisal production. Sisal fibre is best suited for the manufacture of bulk crop packaging, namely sisal bags. In fact, sisal bags are preferred for packaging export products such as coffee, cashew nuts and beans. However, Tanzania has not been able to sustain sisal production and the manufacture of sisal bags because cheap imported jute bags have taken over the domestic packaging market. The argument against restricting importation of jute bags is that such decision would erode the competitiveness of exports of agricultural commodities as they would have to be packed or bagged in more expensive sisal bags. What is not put to question is why Tanzania is not subsidising the sisal industry and sisal bags in the same manner that Bangladesh does for the jute industry and jute bags? Yet were the Tanzania government to take a deliberate policy decision to protect and promote the sisal bag industry, several benefits would accrue to the national economy. These include boosting employment in sisal plantations and in sisal bag manufacturing, generation of almost shillings one billion in annual tax revenue, and churning export receipts of between US$ 10-12 million per annum from export of sisal fibre, rope yarn, carpet yarn and fine yarn. Exports of sisal bags themselves would be of the order of US$ 3 million a year whilst still importing the most essential jute bags.

At the same time, it is important to clarify that protection and promotion of domestic industries is a double-edged sword policy question. Such protection cannot always be at the expense of other economic players within the national economy. In the case of sisal bags, there is a clear case for the state to intervene to bolster the domestic sisal industry as explained above. With respect to the sugar industry, on the other hand, the case is not as clear-cut. Imported industrial cane sugar, also called refined sugar that is used as raw material in the manufacture of beverages, beer and some pharmaceutical products is not subsidised. As such, it would not make economic sense were the government to fold its hands and stay on the fence where new domestic producers of industrial sugar seek to price their products way above international prices. Evidently, the new investors would argue that they have only recently acquired, through privatisation, inefficient sugar plantations and mills and that they have had to inject significant capital to turnaround those enterprises and thus, rightly, they have to recover their cost of capital. Such argument, in my view, would not override the necessity to keep sugar prices at reasonable levels. For example, it was reported in the Tanzania media that a leading domestic sugar producer, Kilombero Sugar Company, was moving towards invoking a price for industrial sugar of US$ 460 per metric tonne in contrast to the going international price of between US$ 320 and 350 per metric tonne. The argument in support of such higher prices should not be allowed to hold because its implications to the rest of the economy would be disastrous in terms of higher, less affordable prices of beverages, beer and medicines and in reduced exchequer revenues.

To conclude, it is tax administration that ultimately needs to be improved if dumping, smuggling and all forms of tax evasion are to be contained. Mere passing new legislations and imposing punitive taxes cannot realise desired results. However, and in fairness to the TRA, its performance has been spectacular considered against the background of the tax system and administration it inherited in 1997. Incompetent and corrupt staff have been weeded out of the tax administration system and, in the past few years, there has been considerable capacity building in training and in appropriate computerisation to transform the TRA into a more efficient and effective institution. The mission of the TRA is better clarified and improved revenue collection is proof of a dramatic improvement in tax management. Yet the challenges remain, especially when the government continues to be under pressure to improve the revenue to GDP ratio. The temptation to go for easy solutions in boosting tax collection is evident.

However, it would be the wrong approach to take. Plugging the loopholes mentioned above and addressing the challenge of broadening the tax base more robustly by promoting selected protection of domestic industries and formalising the huge informal sector could raise more revenue.

Abuse of Discretionary Powers

A critical factor that undermines the quality of the environment in which business operates is how public officials, especially those who closely connect with economic and business actors, exercise their responsibilities and authority. During the past decade and particularly since the establishment of the TRA, Tanzania has witnessed increased cases of overzealous exercise and abuse of discretionary powers. Not just tax collectors have been involved. Other public officials, from police on the beat to municipal and other local authority officials, health officials, factory ordinance inspectors, National and Food Control officials, to immigration officials, all of them, in one way or another, have equally been responsible for harassing business people. Invariably, the abuse of discretionary power has taken the form of threatening closure of business premises or factory when a public health official, for instance, discovers one soft drink bottle on the bottling line containing some form of precipitate or a cockroach, or sheer harassment like asking why a Business Licensing Certificate is not displayed on the wall of a business premise. The abuse is driven not as much by legal uprightness as by the simple objective of corruption.

The period between 1997 and 2000 experienced numerous acts of such abuse and harassment. What was particularly regrettable was that factories were indeed closed down without the respective owners even being allowed the right to natural justice. In addition, even where the right of natural justice existed, the legal process was lengthy and costly. At the end of the day, businesspeople found corruption to be the best solution in dealing with the situation, rather than exercising their legal rights in courts. Though there has recently been some improvement in countering these abuses of powers because the anti-corruption movement and public sensitisation about corruption have picked up steam, it is still important to keep these lessons in mind and especially the importance about ensuring that regulation is undertaken with fairness. It is not enough to create regulatory institutions. It is how the government ensures that such institutions perform their tasks transparently and judicially that would create the requisite confidence in business and other economic actors in the economy.

Export Processing Zones

The idea about establishing export-processing zones. EPZs) in Tanzania was born in the early 1990s. It was largely by the declining state of the textile industry. It is noteworthy, that the Tanzania textile industry, at its pinnacle in the early 1980s, when it was mainly state-owned, boasted of over US$ 500 million in investments and employed over 37,000 workers. One of Tanzania's major paradoxes is that a country that is a net producer of cotton, has failed to become a giant textile country. The principal cause for this paradox is the manner in which the government implemented the trade liberalisation policy took little account of the importance of protecting an industry that was also one of the four largest tax revenue contributors to the exchequer. Left open to external competition in an environment where the regulatory regime was weak in combating dumping, smuggling and tax evasion, the domestic textile industry was virtually left to collapse. From the early 1990s, the Tanzania Textile Manufacturers' Association and the CTI put a great deal of pressure on the government to protect the textile industry and, in turn, promote cotton production. Different fiscal policy scenarios were put forward for consideration including allowing textile mills to manufacture "under bond" and allowing EPZs to come on stream. The example of Mauritius, a non-cotton producer, should be emulated. It has become a leading textile exporter through exploitation of the benefits of EPZs. However, the response from the government, at that time, was negative. If there is one good example where an opportunity of massive economic benefit at the time when the government was implementing intensive economic reforms it is that of the textile industry. Though a law to allow EPZs to operate was finally enacted in June 2002, more than two decades have been lost and the process of recovery for the textile industry would be long and difficult.

The driving force behind the establishment of EPZs in Tanzania is not the clamour by the Tanzania textile business community for a search for more effective solutions to resuscitate the domestic textile industry and putting it on a growth and more competitive trajectory. On the contrary, domestic textile companies have in fact been marginalised by the law establishing EPZs much as Friendship Textile Mills, a Tanzania-Chinese joint venture company, has since been given EPZ status. Rather, it is the success stories of countries like Mauritius and Kenya in attracting new investments generally and textiles in particular following AGOA coming on stream. It would appear that the decision to marginalise domestic textile mills was made as a trade off with the World Bank whose concern has been that EPZs erode tax revenue. In its report, *Global Economic Prospects and the Developing countries, 2003*, the World Bank posits, "governments may hope to make up for an unfriendly investments environment through incentive mechanisms. But while there are clear examples in which targeted incentives such as fiscal incentives, export processing zones. EPZs) or support for economic clusters – may indeed lead to higher investment levels. and the jobs and related spillovers that go along with then), *"there is, unfortunately, little evidence that such initiatives can be systematically successful"*.. emphasis added).

Put differently, the World Bank does not favour EPZs. Yet, it begs logic that at a time when President Benjamin Mkapa is seriously concerned that Tanzania's foreign exchange reserves are not strongly supported by national exports, the government, at the same time, should shy away from exploiting opportunities presented more broadly by EPZs in bolstering exports. After all, the impact on tax revenue generation would be negligible since the domestic textile industry has for decades been in doldrums. The perceived revenue loss even if all the mills were to enjoy EPZ status would thus be insignificant. However, the benefits to the economy, in terms of the cotton industry being bolstered, more jobs created and competitive productivities enhanced for higher export outturns, would be significant. There is a policy lesson to be learned here. In his book, *Why Globalization Works,* Martin Wolf posits, "all evidence suggests that EPZs work best when they are integrated with the rest of the domestic economy——it is best if they can obtain the full range of backward linkages into the economy." EPZs grafted onto Tanzania territory with most inputs imported does not offer economic stability and have little multiplier effect in the economy. In turn, EPZs that rely on local raw materials have a higher propensity to stimulate the national economy as a whole and more sustainably.

The Tanzania EPZ law provides extensive incentives to exporters that include a 10 years tax holiday, remission of import duty and VAT on imported inputs, exemption from withholding tax on interest, dividends, local government taxes and stamp duty. These incentives are far more generous than currently granted under the Tanzania Investment Centre law. Nevertheless, they only favour <u>new</u> investments. In this context, and having been disallowed EPZ status, domestic economic players have naturally not been favourably disposed to the EPZ law. There are two main concerns about the EPZ regime in Tanzania. The first one relates to the EPZ mandate being placed outside the TIC framework. Many investors are wary whether the National Development Corporation. NDC) that has been charged with the responsibility to manage the EPZ regime has the experience and expertise to perform its task well. In fact, some observers perceive such assignment of responsibility to the NDC as having more to do with power politics between ministries of government than with policy effectiveness. The EPZ is a brainchild of the Ministry of Industries and Trade. Thus to ensure that the ministry continues to be involved in the programme its rightful parent institution is that ministry. TIC, on the other hand, falls under the President's Office though, in practical terms, under the Ministry responsible for Planning and Privatisation. From an objective point of view, all investment matters should ideally be centralised under one institution and that is the TIC. Dissipation of authority manifested in putting EPZs under NDC may raise difficulties of policy coordination.

The second concern centres on the state of EPZ infrastructure in Tanzania. Unlike in countries like Kenya and Mauritius where industrial parks were set aside and fully equipped with modern hard and soft infrastructure, power, water, telephones, and internet connections, the EPZ regime in Tanzania has not been well pre-packaged. Thus, investors in EPZs are expected to invest risk capital up front in such infrastructure. Clearly, this is a disincentive much as Tanzania offers unique opportunities that still attract investors. Tanzania would probably have mobilised and attracted more investors EPZs been provided with ready infrastructure. Nevertheless, the EPZ experience in Kenya captured in the Financial Times of January 15, 2005, shows that over reliance on foreign enterprises in EPZs anyhow have serious drawbacks. It is observed that many of these enterprises are footloose, ever on the move in search of facilities and incentives that are more conducive and seeking to exploit trade preferences offered by rich countries to poor countries, such as AGOA. As such, they cannot be relied upon to invest long term. Kenya is already experiencing investor turnover in EPZs, ostensibly because the investors are finding costs of operations to be high. If Kenya is going through such a bad experience, then Tanzania, that has even higher operating costs, has to watch out. The long-term benefit of EPZs is clearly to promote more Tanzanian export oriented companies operating under its regime.

In the next section, I turn my attention to examining the evolution of smart partnership between the government and the business sector in Tanzania. This partnership has had positive impact in policymaking, especially over fiscal budget formulation. The concept of smart partnership itself is examined in detail in Chapter twenty four.

Building Partnership in Tax Policy Making

Participatory budgeting shows that even the veil of technical complexity that has protected budgets from open questioning can be lifted once citizen groups have time, skills and access to information. These new forms of people's participation – from influencing agendas through protests to increasing collaboration in decision-making are reinforcing democratic institutions.

-UN Human Development Report, 2002: **Deepening Democracy in a Fragmented World**.

At a time when many developing countries engaged in economic reforms have tended to be overly critical of the role of the IMF and the World Bank in influencing economic policies, it is also important to take note that some governments have made serious attempts at enabling citizen groups, mainly from the private sector, to be closely involved in policy making. Since 1996, President Mkapa's administration has been in the forefront in broadening the base of participation in policymaking. Indeed, most policies and legislations in recent years have not seen the light of day without their being subjected to prior stakeholder scrutiny and critique. There are several examples: Tanzania Development Vision 2025, PER, PRSP, NSGRP, the Competition Law, EPZ Law, Shipping Agency Law, the process of unbundling TANESCO, and the EAC Customs Union adoption process. Moreover, President Mkapa has encouraged the establishment of Investors' Round Tables, for foreign and local investors. He has personally participated in the deliberations of these bodies whose principal objective is to promote dialogue between the government and the private sector with a view to improving the business environment. The launch of the Tanzania National Business Council in March 2001 was the hallmark of President Mkapa's quest to build a strong foundation for smart partnership between the government and the private sector in Tanzania. Unfortunately, the TNBC has only met twice between the time of its formation and December 2004. One would have thought that the Council could meet at least once a year if its objectives are to make a real difference.

Perhaps the most important institution of smart partnership that the government has constituted has been the Task Force for Tax Reform. Formed in December 1996, this Task Force, which is an assembly of Treasury and TRA officials, on the one hand, and of private sector representatives, on the other hand, has since 1997 been responsible for critically reviewing, analysing and recommending fiscal policies and tax measures to guide and inform decisions which relate to annual fiscal budgets of the government. Though the role of the Task Force has always been advisory, as it should be, its record, so far, in terms of the achievements made in getting fiscal policies changed and new tax measures adopted, is clear proof of the seriousness the government attaches to the partnership. No doubt, the Task Force, and especially its private sector representatives, have sometimes faced all kinds of frustrations for not being able to have most of their recommendations adopted and adopted on a timely basis. However, over time, most of the recommendations of the Task Force have actually been effected. What is important is the fact that a dialogue and consultative process between the government and the private sector over key fiscal and tax policy issues has entrenched in the system of state governance. This, in itself, is a historic breakthrough. This achievement has to be seen in the broader context of the government's *Business Environment Strengthening for Tanzania*, **BEST** in abbreviation. Under this programme the partnership between the government and different stakeholders has extended to reviews and enactments of legislations in areas such as land, regulation and labour market.

Conclusion

Tanzania has recorded impressive macro-economic performance since 1996. GDP growth rose to 6.7% in June 2005. In spite of drought conditions in 2003/04 inflation rate has been contained at 4.0% as at June 2005. Foreign reserves as at December 2004 covered 8.9 months of imports. Foreign investment has grown from US$ 50.2 million in 1994 to US$ 260 million in 2004. Challenges remain especially in expanding merchandise exports. Tanzania trade deficit, according to the ADB/OECD African Economic Outlook 2004, was 7.1% of GDP in 2003. It is projected to reach 8.0% in 2005. The costs of doing business also remain high especially in the energy sector. However, there are clear moves towards addressing this problem, through unbundling and part privatisation of TANESCO, using gas and coal reserves for power generation and connecting the Tanzania power grid to the South African power pool through Zambia. Already, the operationalisation of the Songas gas to electricity project, took effect at the end of 2004.

The remaining hurdle is in changing the mindset of public officials to become more proactive and responsive to a new environment. As Professors Benno Ndulu and Samuel Wangwe wrote back in May 1997 in their paper, *Managing Tanzania's Economy in Transition to Sustained Development*, "government's attitude of control has not yet fully come to terms with the need for facilitating and providing efficient service to business—-the transition from the culture and attitudes of an administratively controlled economy to the culture and attitudes of a competitive economy has turned to be more challenging than anticipated". The consultative mechanism put in place to facilitate dialogue between the government and the private sector should further be reinforced and deepened, as it constitutes a key building block in transforming the mindset of both public officials and business people.

Chapter

11 THE STATE AND THE MARKET

Throughout history, ideas with policy consequences have been the subject of a cycle of emergence-adoption-rejection. and sometimes re-emergence). But that cycle is now accelerating, contributing to policy instability that may retard the adoption of more effective solutions or, worse, increase the probability that bad ideas become influential. Proven policies that take too long to have an effect are also more vulnerable to being replaced by new, untested initiatives that promise rapid results, often falsely.

-Moises Naim: *Misguided Ideas in a Dangerous World.*

—the seeming failure of market socialism has led many to conclude that there is no third way between the two extremes of markets and state enterprises—The fact of the matter is that government plays a prominent role in all societies. The question is not whether there will be government involvement in economic activity but what that role should be.

-Joseph E. Stiglitz: *Whither Socialism?*

Overview

What should constitute the balance of responsibility between the state and the market in Tanzania? Can there be an ideal, albeit static, balance? In introducing this debate, it is essential that certain "basics" be flagged. First, there is the question regarding the reasons that motivated the preponderance of state intervention in the economies of the third world and whether those reasons remain valid, semi-valid or have now become irrelevant.

Such clarification is important because it could all be too easy for a poor country to fall prey to economic liberalisation policies that may not be exactly homegrown and thus fail, in the end, to achieve the kind of society that thrives on social compact and national consensus. It is probably in this particular context that the leading US economist, Professor John Kenneth Galbraith, writing in the French Magazine *L'Expansion*, warned, "we must avoid believing that the more the shock. of a transition to a market economy) is rude and brutal, the more quickly the economy will improve. In that view, difficulty in itself takes on a therapeutic value. But those who will have to put up with the difficulties won't be as easily convinced into making a virtue out of pain as those who speak of it from a comfortable distance". Addressing the question regarding the driving force for the growth of state capitalism in developing countries, *The Challenge to the South*, has noted, that in some developing nations, "colonial policies had been biased against the involvement of the majority of indigenous people in commercial activity, giving rise to the establishment of economic elites. These policies left a legacy of patronage, economic disparities, political contradictions and social divisions. Some newly independent countries had no domestic entrepreneurial class that could mobilize capital and develop the economy; in others, its existence was not perceived. Thus governments felt impelled to do virtually everything themselves; the more ambitious they were to establish their country's economic independence and overcome poverty, the greater the burden they assumed in terms of regulating the economy and direct intervention in productive activities." In the light of such observations, it is pertinent to ask whether, in a country like Tanzania, the reasons that the South Commission has attributed to massive state involvement in the economies of the South have lost validity and have become inconsequential. In turn, it is also critical to examine whether an objective discussion of the role of the state and of the market could avoid addressing the pillars of the dominant state intervention policies of the past and determine whether the objectives of those pillars have been realised or not.

The second question, which flows from the first, should necessarily deal with the predominant failure of state intervention policies and also lead to the next question, whether it would be proper to sacrifice the well being of Tanzanians on the tombstone of the objectives that motivated such massive state intervention in the first place. This is a highly volatile question. Whilst the period 1998 to 2003 witnessed massive privatisation of key state-owned enterprises across most sectors of the Tanzanian economy, this question remains as critical. It thus necessitates close examination. After all, it is also a question that lingers on even in some of the most developed market economies.

Are State-Owned Enterprises Inherently Inefficient?

To start with, there is a dominant view, including in Tanzania that state-owned enterprises. parastatals) are not necessarily inefficient. This view holds that there are parastatals in Singapore, France and the UK that are models of corporate excellence and international competitiveness. To them, parastatal failure is more attributed to unclarified objectives, particularly in relation to profit and commercialisation objectives, and to stifling of corporate management from operating autonomously and in a business minded fashion. In the context of such positions, privatisation is viewed as a policy decision of the last resort in tackling parastatal malaise. What is argued here is that it could be possible to turnaround poor performing parastatals by transforming the traditional and dysfunctional modus of government-parastatal relationship. For example, parastatals could more elaborately be subjected to the discipline of the marketplace. Indeed, in an influential book, *Innovative Corporate Turnarounds*, Professor Pradip Khandwalla, concluded after analysing 65 parastatal cases in India that the dramatic turnarounds of the enterprises reviewed "question one's faith in privatisation as a master remedy for the ills of the public sector". However, there are also those that feel that the loss-making propensity and poor service delivery of much of the parastatal sector seems incurable. They contend that parastatals would always tend towards inefficiency since they could neither go bankrupt, being government owned, nor be compelled to be competitive. They are equally doubtful that deregulation or liberalisation is adequate solution to prod parastatals to excel.

The third question centres on harsh realities, namely how feasible it is for adequate resources to be marshalled by a government to recapitalise sick parastatals and thus enable them to review and improve their operations on a firmer footing. In the Tanzanian context, it would appear that not only was the government unable to raise the required financial resources to bail out all sick parastatals, as and when the situation demanded, but that it also became necessary, at some point, to dispose parastatals in order to raise revenues to finance current spending. Above all, the government also appeared to be under a policy siege in the sense that future support of the World Bank, the IMF and the international donor community appeared predicated, inter alia, on a time-phased framework of privatisations.

Privatisation, Competition and Efficiency

The fourth question to examine is whether there is a direct linkage between privatisation and the encouragement of competition and efficiency. The logic runs that if firms in public ownership can be subjected to competition and efficiency criteria, in the same way as private firms are, then they need not, prima facie, be privatised. In a path setting book, *Reinventing Government: How The Entrepreneurial Spirit is Transforming the Public Sector*, David Osborne and Ted Gaebler have contended that privatisation was simply the wrong starting point for a discussion of the role of government and that "ownership of a good or service- whether public or private- is far less important than the dynamics of the market or institution that produces it." The American authors hold the view that the determining factors for ownership, whether public or private, had more to do with the incentives that drove those within the enterprise system to succeed than the mere form of ownership. They cite the following questions as the basis for determining incentives:

- is the enterprise motivated to excel?
- is the enterprise accountable for its results?
- is the enterprise free from overly restrictive rules and regulations?
- is authority within the enterprise sufficiently decentralised to allow adequate flexibility?
- do rewards within the enterprise reflect the quality of performance?
- is the enterprise exposed to competition?

Taking a similar approach, Harvard Business School Professors, John Goodman and Gary Loveman have argued that the debate over privatisation should be viewed in a larger context. In their article, *Does Privatisation Serve the Public Interest?* the authors postulate, "managerial accountability to the public's interest is what counts most, not the form of ownership." Their conclusions are:-

- neither public nor private managers will always act in the best interest of their shareholders. Privatisation will be effective only if private managers have incentives to act in public interest, which includes, but is not limited to, efficiency.

- profits and the public interest overlap best when the privatised service or asset is in a competitive market. It takes competition to discipline managerial behaviour.

- when these conditions. that is one and two above) are not met, continued governmental intervention will likely be necessary.

Putting it bluntly, the central question to consider is whether the Tanzania government has been predisposed to determining whether to opt for or restrain from proceeding to privatisation in part or fully? In my view, the Tanzanian situation that gave rise to privatisation is easily contrasted from many examples. The majority of the parastatals had reached a point of no return in terms of profitable performance and survival and in a competitive environment. The choice whether to privatise or not did not arise. The government could simply not continue to carry the huge cost of losses incurred by its state owned institutions.

Disillusionment with the Market in Rich Economies

Finally, there is the dimension about the disillusionment with the market economy in some of the industrialised countries and the lessons to be learned by developing countries like Tanzania. *The Economist* of November 21st 1992 reported, for instance, that based on an annual study of British public opinion, British Social Attitudes showed a marked shift in views away from free enterprise and towards state intervention in the economy. It was reported that only one British national in three, out of those interviewed, agreed that private enterprise was the best way to solve economic problems. The reason for the change of hearts and minds was attributed to the state of economic recession at the material time. Needless to ramify, this disillusionment remains deep-seated in France even in 2003. Measures to privatise or deepen privatisation of leading French state-owned enterprises like France Electricity and Gas, Air France and Railways have met with stiff opposition not only from trade union groups but also from the public as a whole.

Of course, the industrialised world is quick to the draw in distinguishing the slide towards state activism in their countries, a situation interpreted as "after the market" problematique, from the kind and level of state intervention that exists in developing countries where the market is considered to be at its embryonic stage. Thus responding to the question whether market capitalism had its day, an *Editorial of the Economist* of November 14, 1992 boldly retorted, "thankfully, not in the developing countries-whose governments tested the limits of economic activism in the 1970s and early 1980s with results they and their electorates are unlikely to forget." Is this position not paradoxical in that it ostensibly promotes the maximisation of market economics for developing countries even when the experience of the rich world shows that at some stage in the development of the market, state intervention has been necessary? Should not the industrialised countries be passing over the lessons of their experience with the free market model and, accordingly, advise developing countries on how best to strike an effective balance between the market and state intervention?

Conventional Thinking on the Market

Such an approach, of sharing the experiences of the market economies with developing countries apparently would be difficult to pursue considering that the international lending agencies that support economic reforms in developing countries are invariably under pressure to adapt their thinking and philosophies of development to current economic orthodoxy of the OECD countries that control their purse strings. Thus, the thrust of advice from the international lending agencies and most donor countries with respect to addressing the role of the state in developing countries overly centres on privatisation rather than on restructuring to transform the productive factors as a way to foster operational efficiency and profitability. I say unfortunate because how else would one-treat reports that the World Bank had "directed" the Tanzania government to privatise a specific number of parastatals, in a time-phased manner as the operation has been. Is such a number-specific directive, if true, in congruence with what World Bank Officials Mary Shirley and John Nellis posited in their World Bank Study: *The Reform of Public Sector Management: Lessons from Experience*. 1991) that "what is involved. in the reform of public sector management) is nothing less that the re-dimensioning of the state, as attempts are made to manage less, but manage it better"? Is managing less necessarily quantitative? Would improvement of management of parastatals not imply less government involvement, particularly after the adoption of new hands off or arm's length relationship between government and parastatals? The over-emphasis on applying market economics *vis a vis* state intervention could probably not serve the goals Tanzania strives to achieve. In this connection, heed should be taken from Professor Robert B. Reich's advice. In a paper titled: *Of Market and Myths,* he argued, "When almost every discussion about the unwanted or the desirable side effects of corporate activity become shoehorned into a debate over the merits of centralized planning or a decentralized market, we lose the capacity to design the market in accordance with our values. We thus miss opportunities to match corporate conduct to public goals through the market. Our cycles of righteous fulmination against, in turn, meddling bureaucrats and irresponsible executive, have tended to elicit the worst of both world- a rigid tangle of rules that fails to enforce effective accountability. This is particularly lamentable, since it is actually within our organizational and analytic power to achieve a good deal more of the best of both".

How to design the market to fit national values is probably the critical challenge. It is a challenge that demands that government takes into account the need for sustained public support for its decisions on what is a highly sensitive matter. In the ensuing sections, I examine how the question regarding the balance between the state and the market has been approached and addressed in Tanzania. Specifically, I outline some of the nagging questions that have emerged following the adoption of market reforms. One of the questions is whether Tanzania remains socialist even while it pursues market policies and what kind of socialism then would that be.

Which And What Socialism?

In a special Tanzania TV Programme aired by DTV on 23 February 1998, two leading Tanzanian social critics, Iddi Simba and Jenerali Ulimwengu debated the subject whether the CCM's policy of socialism and self-reliance was still in place or had been abandoned. Mr Ulimwengu held the view that, by all accounts, CCM was no longer committed to socialism. He argued that the social and economic policies it was pursuing were the antithesis of the basic tenets of Nyererean socialism. Mr Simba, on the other hand, was quick to point out that Mr Ulimwengu had confused the means from the ends. In sum, the debate revolved around the question: was socialism a *condition* of society, a *vehicle* or both. As a corollary, a question arose whether, if socialism were both a condition and a vehicle, then was the *instrumentality* of socialism indispensable in realising the avowed condition? That debate was important and remains so. This is evidenced by the on-going conflicting stances on the ethos and the ideological thrust behind Tanzania Development Vision 2025. As such, the debate needed to be brought onto a wider public stage.

At the outset, it should be pointed out that the debate is not a politically partisan one. In other words, it is not necessarily linked to the CCM. In fact, many Tanzanians do not belong to any political party, and yet are unclear about the development paradigm Tanzania is pursuing. This is not a strange phenomenon. Professor Joseph Stiglitz has noted in his book, *The Roaring Nineties: Seeds of Destruction*, "markets are means to obtain certain ends-most notably, higher living standards. They are not ends in themselves". In other words, markets are not part of an ideology. They merely constitute part of the growth and efficiency agenda. Some Tanzanians may therefore properly feel that the pursuit of the market economy does not represent a new vision of development. Indeed, some Tanzanians view the adoption of market-driven policies as being a process that abandons a pro- poor thrust. They also believe that the consequences of pursuing market policies are bound to be regressive and may even constitute the foundation for the emergence of social tension and instability in society. Privatisation of state assets, for example, is viewed in some Tanzanian quarters as being anti-people and a move directed at bringing about the economic re-colonisation of Tanzania. However, does private ownership necessarily infer a policy that is anti- people and anti-socialism in terms of creating a society wherein the virtues of socialism are absent?

What are the key issues involved in this debate? First, there is the broad mindset that sees dangers in the market system currently being pursued. This mindset is predominantly informed by a conventional and ideological view that a market economy could never build a society that enjoys social justice, freedom, human dignity and equal opportunities for all. The mindset views the market economy as being essentially capitalist whose principal attribute is the existence of a society controlled by two opposing social classes: the capitalist, who owns and controls the means of production, on the one hand, and, on the other hand, the worker or proletariat in the Marxist jargon, who is an alienated, exploited and dependant. Under this system, human equality, which Mwalimu Julius Nyerere described as the "basic assumption" of socialism, is perceived as fundamentally undermined by the existence of private property, a major means of exploitation. In the context of such an ideological view, a government that purports that the conditions inherent in a socialist economy. e.g. human equality) could be realised through the vehicle of the invisible hand of the market, is, at best, ignorant and, at worst, deceitful.

The converse view, which is what CCM holds, is that Tanzania remains committed to building a socialist society, the same kind of society that the architect of Tanzania's *Ujamaa*, Mwalimu Julius Nyerere, had in mind. The CCM Zanzibar Resolution, the CCM Policies and Strategies for the 1990s and the CCM policy 2000-2010, all them restate and reaffirm the commitment to the construction of an *Ujamaa* society that enshrines freedom, social justice, human dignity and equal opportunities for all. At the same time, CCM acknowledges that the instrument or vehicle for constructing such socialist society need not be state control of the "commanding heights" of the economy. This distinction was a central theme that engaged Nyerere's intellect during the formative days of the Arusha Declaration. In his acceptance speech of an honorary doctorate degree at the University of Cairo in February 1967, titled, *The Varied Paths to Socialism*, Nyerere observed that the principle of social ownership and control did not provide a detailed answer to every problem. In fact, he contended that it was possible for group. collective) ownership to result in the "stultification" of development. He cautioned that whilst he preferred alternative methods of public control in case public ownership proved ineffective, ultimately the purpose of public ownership was the central factor and *that* was the service of the people. To quote him: "You do not often serve the people by actions which outrage their feelings, even if those actions are intended to give them collective control over a vital element of their livelihood".

These were the views of Nyerere who had turned more radical after five years of a testing leadership of a poor country devoid of adequate external assistance to kick-start his nascent economy following Tanzania's independence. In this context, it is important to refer to his seminal work that encapsulated his original thesis of *Ujamaa*. In the paper, *Ujamaa: The Basis of African Socialism*, Nyerere analysed the distinguishing factors or values of a socialist society in which the essentiality of public ownership was indeed absent. He posited, "The basic difference between a socialist society and a capitalist society does not lie in their methods of producing wealth but in the way that wealth is distributed." It is not surprising, therefore, that even as far back as March 1994, when addressing the African Business Roundtable in Arusha, Tanzania, Nyerere pointed out that he had talked to a number of Tanzanians to the effect that Tanzanians could, in his view, throw away the *"Ujamaa"* part of the Arusha Declaration but retain self reliance if they so wished. However, he introduced a caveat, namely provided that they went on to convince the mass of Tanzanians that the benefits of collective efforts would still be equitably shared. In other words, Nyerere was reinforcing his mantra that it was equitable wealth distribution rather than public ownership per se that lay at the heart of his concept of socialism. It is thus clear that what emerges from Nyerere's earlier or original thinking about socialism is that socialism should be defined by its goals and not by its dogmatic philosophy.

The appropriateness of such goals could be realised by taking a flexible approach towards the vehicle to be used for its realisation. This specific standpoint is reflected in the CCM's new policies since the early 1990s. Incidentally, the approach has also informed the economic policies that have been pursued by most of the welfare states in Europe and East Asia. The "Welfare States" of Scandinavia, for example, have not had to describe themselves as "socialist" to celebrate the pride of credible achievements using capitalism to create societies that enjoy enviable social justice, gender equality, high living standards and equal opportunities in education and wealth creation. The moral here is that markets depend on government. Markets are mere instruments, evaluated by their performance and impacts. In this context, Professor Cass Sunstein in his book *Free Markets and Social Justice* has pointed out that "achievement of social justice is a higher value than the protection of free markets". Put differently, the state has a central role to play in structuring a place for markets and for the system that is committed to promoting social justice. This process demands that a market system be seen as a vehicle that is subject to constant effective regulation to ensure that it meets social objectives.

Another interesting experience that also constitutes a paradox is the emergence of what Peter Drucker has described as "post-capitalism". In the book, *Post Capitalist Society*, Professor Drucker has posited that developed countries were fast moving out of the system that Karl Marx described as capitalist. In the new society, post-capitalist, "the market remains that effective integrator of economic activity". In the Marxian society, two social classes dominated the society: the capitalist, who controlled the means of production and the proletariat, or the workers, who were exploited for their labour. In the new society, post- capitalist, the society as a whole becomes one of the new "classes". It is the type of society many developed countries have in place. The centre of gravity, to cite Drucker, is different from what Karl Marx identified. He posits, "The social and economic dynamics, its social classes and social problems are different from those that dominated the last 250 years, and defined the issues around which political parties, social groups, social value systems, and personal political systems crystallized." On the other hand, the capitalist has become faceless, as workers, through pension and mutual funds, have increasingly come to own the means of production. This new phenomenon has transformed the shape of American capitalism. In fact, Peter Drucker has asserted that socialism as defined by Marx has become irrelevant in the light of the fact that the ownership of the means of production is now in the hands of the mass of people, the proletariat if you like. This phenomenon is taking place in the US whilst it remains at the same time the most capitalist nation on earth.

Another fundamental change is that the core economic resources of development, or the means of production, have ceased to be the traditional ones, namely, capital, land and labour. Now it is knowledge. Again, evidence abounds in this context. Witness the amazing economic growth of the East Asian tiger economies and the fast growing middle class in India, flowing primarily from mastering new information and communications technologies. In these economies, pension and mutual funds largely control the supply and the allocation of capital. Tanzania, like the rest of the developing world, is changing and should change. It has to build its economy based more on knowledge. Moreover, it should be clearer about the kind of society it seeks to construct. That goal should inform the measures it takes on the economic policy front.

Thus, the debate about "which and what socialism" should be more informed by current realities. These realities suggest the imperative of adopting private entrepreneurialism, as opposed to imperial-feudal capitalism, as the new model of labour - management relations as well as the new economic mode of production, distribution and exchange. Private ownership or the market economy need not mean abdication of government intervention. Indeed, markets should be used to promote the basic goals of the "socialist society". Yes, the government ideally should not interfere in the functioning of markets. However, as Nyerere postulated, the government should closely manage the process of wealth distribution and, in that light, correct market imperfections as they occur. This role is easier said than done. It is for this reason that the second area of concern for Tanzanians has been whether the entry of the market has necessarily marked the exit of the welfare state. I turn to this subject next.

Is the End of the Welfare State Nigh?

At a public rally meeting in Dodoma in March 1998 before a large congregation of Tanzanians meeting to discuss poverty and environmental issues, Nyerere reiterated his position on the adverse impact that capitalism had had on the broad mass of people in developing countries generally and Tanzania in particular and how important and imperative it was for governments to put in place social safety nets, driven by a welfare state system, to mitigate those negative effects. What is interesting to note is that much as we may wish to think that the debate between the state and the market is more pertinent and of particular burning sensitivity and relevance to poor countries such as Tanzania, in fact this is not so. The debate has now taken a global dimension. In his seminal book titled, *The Commanding Heights: The Battle Between Government and The Marketplace that is Remaking The Modern World*, Harvard's Daniel Yergin posits, "where the frontier between the state and market is to be drawn has never been a matter that could be settled, once and for all, at some grand peace conference. Instead, it has been subject, over the course of this century, of massive intellectual and political battles as well as constant skirmishes. In its entirety, the struggle constitutes one of the great defining dramas of the twentieth century. Today the clash is so far-reaching and so encompassing that it is remaking our world and preparing the canvas for the twenty first century." Indeed, a close examination of Tony Blair's *The Third Way: New Politics For The New Century*, shows that, yes, the ideological struggle between the "left" and the "right" continues. For what "The Third Way" dominantly represents, is a middle course between the market and the state. However, how close to the market, how further from the state, and vice versa, remains a paradox. Tony Blair himself views his "new" socio-economic philosophy as embodying "permanent revisionism", meaning a continuing search for more effective and pragmatic means for achieving set goals. He often likes to posit that, to him, "what matters is what works." A Columnist with London's The Sunday Times, Robert Harris, in an article in the *Sunday Times* of 20th September 1998, defined the "Third way" as "some endlessly shifting" third way. Here lies the fundamental question, namely, whether it is viable for national economies to be static in their socio-economic policies given the present ever-changing global economic environment?

The 'Third Way' has also caught up in the United States and in Germany. In fact, most of the Welfare States of the world are now attracted to this new version of capitalism with a human face. This is what Mwalimu Nyerere had equally urged Tanzanians to embrace. However, what Nyerere may not have realised is that the Welfare State under the "Third Way" is, at the same time, undergoing a major transformation, a reform or overhaul. Part of the reason behind this reform is that the important element of the Welfare State, namely, social security, is increasingly under pressure. A dominant question that now pervades public policy debate in the rich welfare states is whether social security, as it exists, is a good investment for the people and a solid basis for the retirement of workers. Blair thinks that there has to be a balance. This is where the idea about Foundation Hospitals and Top up College fees crept into the equation. There is also serious concern about the efficacy of unemployment insurance that is also being viewed as more of an incentive for people to stay off work than to return to work. At another level, the costs of Medicare, in the US, and of the National Health Service. NHS), in Britain, are viewed to be too high for governments to cope. In Britain, Tony Blair has been pushing for reform of the NHS and propelling more public-private partnership in health service delivery including the establishment of Foundation Hospitals.

Yet Nyerere was also right, in a way. The reform of the Welfare State in the industrialised countries is a different ball game compared to Tanzania. Tanzania is at a different historical juncture in development terms. Tanzanians are much poorer to be left to fend for themselves. Thus attacking poverty, as a national goal, could not make meaning, least of all have the envisaged impact, without a strong welfare state being put in place and sustained. In fact, the danger to peace and stability could crucially hinge on how the government frontally addresses poverty. Nyerere put it correctly when he said that poverty was best fought through education, education for all. Question is where is Tanzania on this front? In 2000, the University of Dar es Salaam Convocation organised a brainstorm on *The Crisis of Education in Tanzania*. The debate took place against the backdrop of the Form IV Examinations leakage, a growing feature in the corruption that engulfs the system of education administration and a manifestation generally of declining education standards. What many Tanzanians failed to consider was that public education was not simply a basic service to be provided effectively and efficiently. This service is basic and vital to Tanzania's future. Yet it is presently tangled up with the same contentious issues of wealth, tribe and religion that Nyerere discerned as early as 1962 and which he committed himself to addressing and curbing.

The denationalisation of education and deepening privatisation of education in recent years has relieved the government of a heavy budgetary burden. However, rather than reducing social stratification and the intolerances and bigotry of all types, which existed in pre-independent Tanzania Mainland, private education has accentuated these very sensitivities to the point where the "divides" that characterised the Tanzanian society during the colonial era may now pose greater risks to national unity and social cohesion. Evidently, the economic reforms that the government has had to undertake over the last two decades have necessitated the need for fiscal reforms and reducing the role of the state in the public domain. However, as Nyerere correctly cautioned in his article, *Good Governance For Africa*, reducing the role of the state did not infer dieting and slimming when one is already emaciated and starving. In other words, the state should become stronger in its economic role in society, particularly in fighting poverty, ignorance, disease and in fighting corruption.

Economic reform revolves around the fundamental question how the government prioritises the allocation of resources by always giving greater priority to those areas that target poverty. In this context, education is *the* central sector; it is the principal liberator from poverty and disease. Education also promotes entrepreneurship, one of the motive powers of the market economy. Therefore, it should be given first priority. It is notable, in this instance, that beginning financial year 2000/2001, the composition of government expenditure has gradually but steadily shifted in favour of poverty reduction programmes, in tune with the PRSP Paper adopted in September 2000. As a result, there has been significant increase in expenditure on goods and services targeting poverty from 4.5% of GDP in 1997/1998 to almost 9% of GDP in 2003. At the same time, according to the IMF *Tanzania Country Report* No. 03/0/2 of January 2003, non-wage recurrent expenditure on priority sectors for poverty reduction had increased from 1.3% of GDP in 1997/1998 to 3.2% of GDP in 2001/2002. This is a positive change in focus and should be consolidated.

More broadly, however, it could be asked how realistic is it to expect that the market economy in a poor country would adequately respond to the challenges of poverty eradication. In the rich world, such challenge has become a topical issue in the sense that there is a curious debate, even within the labour and social democratic governments, about the extent to which the state could be the main provider of welfare. At the Labour Party Congress in November 2002, Tony Blair surmised: "From the 1940s to the 1970s—social democrats in Britain and the US who held liberal a view of the `permissive society` divorced fairness from personal responsibility. They believed that the state had an unconditional obligation to provide welfare and security."

In Blair's view, times had changed and that increasingly personal responsibility had to take command in providing welfare and social security. That view he underscored in his Speech at Beveridge Hall, University of London on 11 October, 2004 in these words: "The vision of a true opportunity society replacing the traditional welfare state can be realised only if we deepen the changes we have made to the country and have the courage to see them through." It is a vision based "on the belief that today people want the power to change their lives in their own hands, not those of an old-fashioned state and government. All of it pervaded by a strong commitment to the values of social justice, equality and opportunity for all." It is a challenge that poor countries with scarce resources would necessarily have to seriously ponder about. It is also a question that raises other more fundamental issues, importantly about privatisation, not only of social service delivery but also generally of how the management of the economy as a whole is undertaken. Blair has probably been vindicated by the recent reaction of the French and the Dutch and probably several other Europeans in the context of the rejection of the EU Constitution Treaty . European masses are increasingly viewing the EU as some kind of a social Frankenstein on the ready to strangle them by abolishing the welfare state as they have know of it from the 1950s. This is part of the context that should be examined in interrogating whether privatisation is a panacea.

Privatisation: Is it a Panacea?

Privatisation is now widely seen as conducive to economic efficiency. This view is not ideological, as it was when we were embarking on development and many of us had not pondered the deep-seated incentive problems that public enterprises would face, given the political context within which they would be operating, especially in developing countries. Political staffing, often excessive and of middling quality, the ability to ride out losses by resorting to subsidies and the absence of effective incentives for workers and managers to perform are among the key and in eradicable defects of public enterprises. Some unreformed proponents of the Marxist and Fabian preference for public ownership insist that suitable reforms could still salvage public enterprises as efficient economic entities. This logic, however, is like saying that if we put stripes on an elephant, it will become a zebra.

-Jagdish Bhagwati: *Poverty and Reforms: Friends or Foes?*

*Privatisation is one arrow in government's quiver. But just as obviously, privatisation is not **the** solution. Those who advocate it on ideological grounds-because they believe business is always superior to government-are selling the American people snake oil.*

-David Osborne & Ted Gaebler: *Re-inventing Government*

Watching the international TV coverage of the head-on collision of two London commuter trains near Paddington Station on 5th October 1999 one theme featured prominently. This was about the cost and benefit of the privatisation of British Rail and what some people, in Britain at that time, wished to see, namely the return to State-owned and operated train services. The thrust of the media coverage then was that two serious and fatal train accidents had occurred within a spell of two years, a rare phenomenon during the prime days of the state-owned British Rail. One leading commentator on Sky Television argued that because of the accidents, commercialisation of rail transport management had been put to a test. Evidently, the accidents had shown that there was a serious need to strike a balance between the urge for commercialisation, on the one hand, and the importance to assure public safety, on the other hand. Other equally important questions arose. For instance, the level of fares charged for railway transportation, post privatisation. However, in the particular case of the Paddington Station train accident and the one that had taken place two years earlier on the same railway line and near the same spot, the question of safety clearly stood out.

Interestingly, Britain has recently been moving back towards what has been described as "creeping re-nationalisation" of rail track maintenance, a function that, for years, had been contracted out to private firms. On October 24, 2003, a private technology company which, however, has no shareholders and operates exclusively in the public interest, Network Rail, employed by the British Government to oversee railway maintenance and contract private firms to perform maintenance works, decided to take over rail track maintenance from Javis, the biggest private engineering rail track maintenance contractor on Britain's railways. Rail transport and maintenance had been partly privatised during John Major's government in 1996. In this context, the larger question inevitably asked is whether, in the circumstances, privatisation is necessary. What is of particular interest is that such a question is not only asked in Tanzania but in mature market economies such as Germany, France and Britain as well.

For countries that are in transition from socialist command economies to market-led ones, the question about the necessity of privatisation has taken an even more serious, if political, dimension. There is a curious ideological overtone to it. In sum, there is a common concern in both sets of economic systems about whether privatisation is a panacea to the ills associated with state ownership. Such concern inevitably poses serious danger to the coherence and sustainability of economic reforms in pre-socialist economies that are beginning to get out of the economic morass that they had been in. The same is not the case for the mature, free market economies, whether of the social market variety or, those, like Britain, which, for decades since the end of the Second World War touted with state ownership. Liberal capitalism in these countries has already taken root.

In the specific case of Tanzania, it seems that opinions are divided on this issue, even at this stage when the privatisation exercise has almost reached its climax. Evidently, there is a view which is discernible within certain quarters of intellectual discourse and public debate that all is yet to be lost; that privatisation could somewhat fail to meet the expectations of the mass of people, especially the poor, and thus inevitably bounce public ownership back. What is interesting, though troubling about this line of thinking, is that it is not far removed from other influential voices at the international level as well. For example, the renowned American academic and consultant Daniel Yergin, has focused on this specific ideological "battlefield". In his book: *The Commanding Heights: The Battle between Government and the Marketplace that Is Remaking the Modern World,* which we have cited earlier, Yergin postulates that the frontier between the state and the market "is not neat and well defined". In his view, the clash between the state and market is far-reaching. Put differently, what is posed is that it would be difficult to determine whether privatisation is a panacea, or, conversely, that state ownership is a panacea. *The Challenge To The South* took a more pragmatic stance in addressing this vexatious question by postulating that: "Developing countries have recently been under strong pressure to privatise state-owned enterprises as a means of curing inefficiency, and several countries have gone some way in this direction. The issue needs to be addressed without ideological bias. Rather, there needs to be in each case a careful consideration both of the costs and of the benefits of alternative policies, the social role that a public enterprise is discharging, and the capabilities of private enterprises within the country".

The conclusion of the South Commission Report was that privatisation did not offer "an across-the-board-solution". This means, in effect, that privatisation is not a panacea. This policy debate is topical and Tanzanians need to be clear in their own minds about it lest the society splinters and collides over it even after privatisation has taken deep root. The first point that needs to be considered is that Tanzania is an economic system that has already shifted from the dominance of state ownership to an ownership system that is more market driven and that the question whether privatisation is a panacea equally applies to whether state ownership is a panacea.

There was a time in recent political economic history when the East-West confrontation centred on the clash over the universality of either socialism or capitalism as the remedy for the social and economic ills of society. On the one hand, countries of the West considered capitalism as the panacea for sustainable economic growth and freedom of the individual. On the other hand, the Ex-Soviet and East European countries viewed capitalism or privatisation of the economy as the driving force of exploitation, inequality and social conflict. In the view of the latter, state ownership was *the* vehicle for building an economy based on social justice and human dignity. However, the decade of the 1990s, following the 1989 Revolution in Eastern Europe and the former Soviet Union, the ideological clash between socialism and capitalism has gone through a sea change. Increasingly, a view has taken root that public ownership as an economic system, failed to deliver the Promised Land in the former Soviet Union, viewed to be a socialist global superpower as well as in the poor countries of the South that had been inspired by the ideology of socialism.

Indeed, countries like Britain that had experimented with state capitalism for decades since 1945 also saw, in this period, a consistent demolition of the structures of public ownership. It is notable to observe that the British Fabian movement, which was responsible for articulating a democratic socialist model of national development in Britain, was largely responsible for inspiring the new political independence leadership of Anglophone Africa. Mwalimu Julius Nyerere, in particular, embraced the Fabian version of socialism as opposed to the Marxist variety, in articulating his own philosophy of *"Ujamaa na Kujitegemea"*. socialism and self-reliance). However, it is Britain, under a Labour Party leadership that is presently at the centre of re-defining economic philosophies in line with new realities. In his manifesto, The Third Way, Tony Blair postulated, "The Third way stands for a modernised social democracy, passionate in its commitment to social justice and the goals of the centre-left, but flexible, innovative and forward looking in the means to achieve them. It is founded on the values that have guided progressive politics for more than a century - democracy, liberty, justice, mutual obligation and internationalism. But it is a third way because it moves decisively beyond an old left preoccupied by state control, high taxation and producer interests; and a New Right treating public investment, and often the very notions of 'society' and collective endeavour, as evils to be undone".

In Tanzania as well, the question whether privatisation is a panacea has a philosophical context. When Mwalimu Nyerere enunciated the philosophy of *Ujamaa*, he did not view nationalisation and public ownership as ends in themselves. He was quite clear in his own mind as to the purpose of public ownership. Whilst *Ujamaa* to Nyerere was an end goal, the vision, as it were, of the new society to be built and which to many Tanzanians, remains sacrosanct, Nyerere did not view the vehicle of public ownership as a goal. To him public ownership was never a panacea. In other words, in Nyerere's view, the realisation of a socialist society did not necessarily depend on the form of the economic system. Mwalimu Nyerere was clear in his own mind that public ownership, as a socialist organisation and an instrument or vehicle, was good and appropriate as long as it delivered the results that met the people's basic needs and expectations. He never saw the principle of social ownership and control as a panacea to every societal problem. In the context of what may appear to be a paradoxical position with respect to Nyerere's thinking on a complex issue, Tanzania has been able to objectively soul search the performance of its public ownership and to make a rational shift from the economics of socialist ownership to those of the market economy, in large part, driven by privatisation. One could ask whether policy makers view the shift, driven by privatisation, as necessarily a panacea to Tanzania's economic woes. Evidently, this question has attracted conflicting perceptions and views. It has catapulted the debate in Tanzania about whether privatisation is a panacea. What is important to note is that the debate is not in any way located or restricted to the economies that are emerging from socialist command economic systems.

Private Property Drives Economic Prosperity

The debate whether privatisation is a panacea has featured prominently in most Western European nations, France, Britain and the US. The dominant view that has emerged from such debate is that private property helps to bring about economic prosperity. Professor, Cass Sunstein, in his book, *Free Markets And Social Justice* has adduced four reasons for this conclusion:

First, the institution of private property creates and takes advantage of the powerful human inclination to bring goods and services to oneself and to people one cares about. In his view, an economic system without private property stifles incentives and can induce sloth and waste.

Second, a system of private property performs a crucial co-ordinating function in the sense that it ensures that "the multiple desires of societal consumers are reflected in market outcomes." This, in his view, protects society from "the perverse forms of scarcity produced by a command economy."

Third, the institution of private property solves, all at once, a serious collective problem faced by people in any system that lacks such institution. The problem is that when property is seemingly "un-owned", in other words, where ownership is not identified with an individual or group of individuals,. at the height of public ownership in Tanzania, this problem manifested itself in the derogatory expression *"Mali ya Umma"*, meaning public property or literally, "un-owned" assets and had specific reference to the theft and squander of parastatal assets and resources in the late1970s and early 1980s), no one seems to have sufficient incentive to use it to its full capacity and proper advantage or to protect it against exploitation or abuse.

Fourth, a system of private property creates stability and protection based on expectations that are preconditions for investment and initiative, both from international and domestic sources.

However, without exception, a view has remained in place in almost all rich countries that it is almost impossible to create a just society under open, free market conditions. It is held that the active, though balanced role and intervention of the state, a reformist state at that, is imperative.

Privatisation and the Mindset

In Tanzania, on the other hand, the debate about whether privatisation is a panacea or not has emerged largely from the context of the implementation of economic reforms that have been associated with external agencies, like the IMF, the World Bank and donor countries. In other words, rather than privatisation as a policy measure being critiqued from the context of a failed public ownership system and, thereby, attracting a more balanced opinion, it has been presented and viewed as a *prima facie* prescription based on some universal doctrine to be applied, regardless of relevance, appropriateness or necessity in an economy. What has engendered such skewed perception about privatisation is partly the methodology that has underlined the privatisation process itself. It is not as if the methodology used has been patently dysfunctional. However, after almost three decades of public ownership, there has ingrained in the Tanzanian mindset a view that state-owned enterprises constituted the family silver and that valuable assets should not be disposed of in a conventional market fashion. The continuing wealth divide along racial lines in Tanzania has contributed to the negative attitude directed at privatisation for evident but not always the correct reasons.

Whilst public ownership had been associated with the construction of a society based on social justice, privatisation, on the other hand, has come to signify the entrenchment of the wealth divide along racial lines. The better endowed Tanzanians of Asian origin have been seen as better able to acquire assets being privatised whilst the impoverished majority nationals have ostensibly become more economically marginalized in their own land of ancestry. Acquisition of state-owned enterprises by foreign companies and individuals has reinforced the negative perception and response. Yet what is missing in this mindset is the more fundamental question Nyerere had addressed in his paper, *The Varied Paths to Socialism*. Nyerere postulated that the purpose of an economic organisation, socialist or capitalist, was service to the people. Thus, the key question to be asked in the context of privatisation is not who buys the assets being privatised but rather whether privatisation would be in the broad national interest. At the same time, in a poor country like Tanzania, privatisation should never infer the abdication by the state of its core responsibility to provide basic social services to the people especially those who are disadvantaged and vulnerable. Privatisation should not entail the total end of the welfare state.

In his policy paper, *The Third Way*, Tony Blair described the divorce between democratic socialism and liberalism as the main cause for the weakening of progressive politics across the West during the 20th century. In his view, there is no necessary conflict between the primacy of individual liberty in the market economy, centred on private property and social justice, with the state as its main agent. Blair further asserted, "State power is one means to achieve our goals, but not the only one and emphatically not an end in itself." Put differently, one should always strike an effective balance of roles between state power and the power of the market characterised by privatisation policy and market driven policy measures. Tanzania and the rest of the poor South no longer live in isolation. The global economy is here. William Greider, an American, in an ultra liberal book: *One World Ready or Not: The Manic Logic of Global Capitalism* asserts, in the chapter titled *"The Storm Upon Us"*, "imagine a wondrous new machine, strong and supple, a machine that reaps as it destroys. It is huge and mobile, something like the machines of modern agriculture but vastly more complicated and powerful. Think of this awesome machine running over open terrain and ignoring familiar boundaries. It plows across fields and fencerows with a fierce momentum that is exhilarating to behold and also frightening. As it goes, the machine throws off enormous mows of wealth and bounty while it leaves behind great furrows of wreckage. Now imagine that there are skilful hands on board, but no one is at the wheel. In fact, this machine has no wheel or any internal governor to control the speed and direction. It is sustained by its own forward motion guided mainly by its own appetites. And it is accelerating."

Greider describes this machine as modern capitalism driven by the imperatives of global industrial revolution. Though he admits of the imperfectness of his metaphor, he nevertheless pointedly asserts that the world is confronted by a free-running economic system that is reordering the world. Therefore, as Tanzanians continue to debate whether privatisation is a panacea or not, they should equally be mindful of the new realities that engulf their economy. Privatisation has taken a sensitive dimension mainly because Tanzania is poor. Not underrating the logic behind the forces against privatisation in the rich countries, it is noteworthy though, that in their case, the dimensions, including the social structure, are different. Tanzanians appear to fail and even refuse to recognise how privatisation could liberate them economically. At the same time, some of them also forget, perhaps all too easily, that public ownership, from its most lofty goals, gave hope and expectations to millions of Tanzanians that never came to fruition. Yet in spite of the failure of state capitalism, Tanzanians have not openly questioned whether public ownership was a panacea. Could this be because of the reverence for Mwalimu Nyerere who had moved the idea and had inspired the people to accept it unreservedly?

In this debate, it is questionable whether *ujamaa*, the value condition of a just society, rather than mere public ownership that has failed. There are exceptions, of course, and we see them mostly where there has been an injection of private management in investments jointly owned by the state and the private sector. DAHACO, Tanzania Breweries, Tanzania Cigarettes Company, all these enterprises, have proven that joint ventures between the State and the private sector can succeed. They prove the point that privatisation need not be 100%; it can be quasi and succeed. The ownership structure may equally not involve the state at all. Ownership of privatised companies, which involves the public through IPOs, is also in vogue and is a form of "public ownership." Yet even these forms of ownership have also raised controversy simply because some Tanzanians still find any form of foreign ownership a travesty of economic independence.

Thus, the central challenge that confronts the leadership of countries like Tanzania centres on recasting the beliefs, thinking and values of some people away from the traditional faith in the sanctity of state ownership toward greater trust and confidence in the market. Dr. Yargin has concluded in his book, *The Commanding Heights* by observing that "perhaps, then, what will really determine whether this change will persist, or whether there will be a swing back, is the quality and character of the confidence that underpins the marketplace. Confidence is more likely to endure if it is tempered by a realistic appraisal of risk and uncertainty, and of the benefits and limits of the market and its values." This confidence about the limits and benefits of the market is crucially dependent on the role of the state. Indeed, Martin Wolf is right to postulate in his recent book, *Why Globalization Works: The Case For The Global Economy*, that whilst the market is the most powerful institution ever for raising living standards, "markets need states; just as states need markets." Making a strong state possible is a key responsibility of national leadership. It can be realised where leadership does the right thing.

Leadership: Doing the Right Thing

A central feature of matching the role of the state to capability and effectiveness is the boldness required to choose what the state must continue to do and what it must elect not to do. It is also a critical choice about how best to deliver basic services and regulate the economy. In recent years, since the mid 1990s, the Tanzanian Government has strived to come to terms with doing the right things-social, political and economic. Much has been done and realised at the levels of democratisation, liberalisation and privatisation. Tanzania is today proud of it's achievements at the macro-economic front. The government has stood firm, resisting what the South Commission Report describes as the buying off "social unrest through soft options". Yet more work confronts the government in getting its apparatus to move beyond the basics of adjustment and stabilisation. Of course, financial deepening and outreach remain an urgent task for which the privatisation of the National Bank of Commerce was the *sine qua non*. The privatisation of NMB will cement the process. Getting the bureaucracy *to see and think* about the big picture of the economy, and move beyond short terms, and not holding on to outlived regulatory powers are challenges that need urgent attention. The inflexibility of the labour market regime is another policy area that requires overhaul.

More broadly, Tanzanians should generally transform their mindsets and face the new realities, realities that focus more on ends and much less on the means. Tanzanians should urgently release themselves from the cocoon of issues of yesteryears that continue to confine that vision. Thus, even at the end of the inevitable reforms that Tanzania should undertake, the country, regrettably, continues to be stifled by a confined vision; the lack of a clear understanding about where, as a country, Tanzania is moving to, why and how. In this context, it has been distressing to witness some change of heart in the liberalisation and deregulation of the economy. The hullabaloo that featured in the mass media about the deregulation of shipping business in Tanzania, between 1999 and 2000 smacked of lack of clarity about government policy direction. Surely, the *Usafiri Dar es Salaam.* UDA) - the Dar es Salaam city commuter transport system, had been deregulated years before with the opening up of the business to DALADALA, the private city commuter transport system. UDA still exists, though limping. Monopoly is dead or dying. The people now have a better, more efficient and cost effective service, the traffic jams and constant accidents notwithstanding. The same feature has characterised the field of crop marketing. The monopoly, hitherto vested in the Cooperatives and the state crop authorities, is now history.

As in every historical epoch, there are still some, amongst us, who view liberalisation and deregulation as a return to the exploitation of the peasant and the worker. They fail to understand and appreciate the dynamics of the market, particularly the close relationship that exists between the domestic and the global market system. Fostering markets through privatisation, liberalisation and deregulation is the way forward for most of national economic activities. In an article published by the

Business Times titled, *Is NASACO's Future Bright or Doomed, the* author, Ali Mwambola, commendably addresses some of the critical issues that revolve around the assumed orthodoxy of state ownership. The core thrust of his views is that he saw nothing wrong, for instance, in the decision taken by the then Minister for Industry and Trade, Honourable Iddi Simba, late in 1998, in deregulating the shipping agency management industry. He admonished monopoly and took a strong contrary position to that of the national shipping agency company, NASACO, and of some Tanzanians, that sought the abrogation by the President of Minister Simba's action. A review of this saga is important if only to show that the mindset about transforming public ownership and better understanding of the workings of the market economy is yet to ingrain in Tanzania.

The NASACO Saga: Politics or Empowerment?

The government, through the Ministry of Industry and Trade, tabled before the 2002 April Parliament Session a Bill titled the Shipping Agency Act 2002. Its main objective was to de-license all foreign shipping companies that had been operating as shipping agencies in Tanzania since 1998 and confine majority ownership of shipping agency business to Tanzanian nationals, whilst excluding, curiously, shipping companies from the ownership structure. On the face of it, the legislation sought to create history: that it was possible for a government to legislate economic empowerment of its citizens, a process now encapsulated in the Economic Empowerment Act, 2004. Many Tanzanians cheered this step as a revolutionary breakthrough. However, for whom was the assumed breakthrough meant to benefit? Was it really for the benefit of the broad masses of Tanzanians?

Some Tanzanians regard shipping agency investments and operations as mundane and not, from their constricted view, as qualifying entitlement under the investment law. Evidently, their concept of investment is narrowly conceived in terms of huge cash inflows, machines, and brick and mortar. It is such skewed mindset that appears to have informed the objects and reasons incorporated in the Shipping Agency legislation, namely, that there was little, in terms of capital and management involved in running a shipping agency business as to justify such business being allowed to fall under total foreign ownership and especially ownership by foreign shipping companies. In other words, any Tanzanian could undertake such investment and operation. It is this view, it would be recalled, that drove the agenda behind restricting ownership of specialised cuisine restaurant business to Tanzanians in 1998. That view, to say the least, was simply mischievous and misguided. It is a view anchored in the "old economy" mindset where investment was never seen in the context of *knowledge work* but rather in the productivity of manual work. Yet, we now live in a new digital economy where the key resource and investment is knowledge. Knowledge work, unlike manual work, which is considered a cost, is a capital asset. The sooner Tanzanian public policy and mindset comes to terms with this reality the better for the direction of the Tanzania economy.

In my view, it would be an act of serious folly to enact legislation in the name of a lofty goal about economic empowerment that lacks a coherent national economic philosophy or ideological underpinning. In other words, it is questionable whether the policy of economic empowerment of majority Tanzanians has a supporting policy framework that is cogent, coherent and transparent. It could be asked, for instance, why is the government, in similar vein, not confining airline agent business to Tanzanians? What is the rationale of empowering Tanzanian ownership of shipping agency operations and not airline agency operations? How far does the government go in this case? It is difficult, in the absence of such clarity of policy, to make sense of what appears to be a more politically-driven measure, of the goal of empowerment other than, I may dare to conjecture, to undo what the government has all along pursued, namely opening up the economy wide to investments that create jobs, train Tanzanians, introduce best practices and bolster revenue to the government that helps in uplifting the living standards of the masses. Therefore, it jolts the mind if the rationale of the economic empowerment programme, as reflected in the Shipping Agency Act, indeed justifies the means. In further amplification of this apparent policy fuzziness, taking the tourism industry as another example, it is noted that most of the tour operator companies operating ex- Arusha and elsewhere in Tanzania are in fact foreign-owned. Many of these companies operate with only a few combi and four wheel-drive vehicles. Should the government then proceed to confine such businesses to Tanzanians as well? What would the state of Tanzanian tourism be? The key question posed here is where would the government draw the line on what should or should not be confined to Tanzanian ownership? Are the principles clearly laid out? In addition, have we seriously considered the benefits and costs within the context of a globalising world?

Tanzania, thanks to the able leadership of President Mkapa, is at the stage where leadership is operating based on exploiting success. It is at the stage where the government often boldly starves problems in order to feed opportunities. Such pragmatism has enabled the country to enjoy the confidence of the international community. In addition, it is the only rational way to promote a growth-led economy. What the Shipping Agency Act has done, unfortunately, is to undo the successes that the foreign-owned shipping companies, through their own locally registered offices, had achieved in a matter of few years. In my view, what the

Shipping Agency Act fundamentally failed to appreciate, within the overall context of the new global competitive environment, is the fact that the term "Agent," as defined in the Act, namely a person or company providing shipping agency services on behalf of the principal, is itself also an aberration. Surely, if one acts on his own behalf, as in a court case, it is totally different from somebody else acting on his behalf. Thus, from a strictly legal standpoint, what should the underlying reason be for a government to stop a global shipping company from having its own office in Tanzania to serve its own corporate interests and those of its customers? Strictly, such companies are not using a third party to act for them except where they elect to do so. In fact, there are several shipping lines, which, for sheer reasons of size of operations and of cost, have third party agents. They accept the risk of vulnerability to competition. For them, it is a considered risk decision. It is important for the government to know that some of these shipping companies serve their customers through a network of their own offices and container terminals in more than 100 countries, including neighbouring Kenya and Uganda, though landlocked. These countries are not subjecting shipping companies to ownership laws as Tanzania does. The respected Japanese management guru, Kenichi Ohmae (1995) wrote in the celebrated book, *The End Of The Nation-State:* "so long as nation-states continue to view themselves as the essential prime movers in economic affairs; so long as they resist - in the name of national interest - any erosion of central control as a threat to sovereignty, neither they nor their people will be able to harness the full resources of the global economy."

It would be interesting to see what the reaction of the government would be were large internet commerce sites, such as *E-bay,* and *Amazon.com,* to apply to set up business in Tanzania. Their investment, after all, is primarily knowledge. This is also what Microsoft is all about. Would such *dot.com* companies qualify for certificates of approved enterprise from the Tanzania Investment Centre or would they be viewed as operations that do not bring in substantial *financial* capital and thus do not warrant obtaining approved status? Shipping agency business is also more knowledge than removing containers from ships. It has undergone major information technological transformations. With growing intense global competition in the service industry, shipping companies are increasingly operating their own offices worldwide rather than using third party agents. This is partly because of confidentiality and partly because of cost-effective efficiency. Modern communications networks form the strategic lifelines of these companies. As such, they are of a high security nature.

Since the onset of economic reforms in Tanzania the government and the citizens have been driven by the authority of reason and reality, not by the authority of perception and passion. The rationale behind these radical reforms has been, and remains, to build a robust and efficient economy able to deliver improved livelihoods of Tanzanians. The reforms have not and could not have been intended to protect a parastatal-type activity out of tune with the new global economy. Surely, you could not shield such activity, like a flower garden, from natural cold winds by building a wall around it and using economic empowerment as the pretext. As the management guru, Peter Drucker has written in *Management Challenges for the 21st Century*, "Such walls no longer protect institutions and especially businesses that do not perform up to world standards. It will only make them more vulnerable".

Economic Empowerment and Ownership

Early in 1998, there was a government attempt to de-licence all foreign-owned restaurants in the name of economic empowerment of Tanzanians and some of us questioned the underlying objective since you find Chinese and Indian cuisine restaurants around the world owned and managed by Chinese and Indians. So what was the big deal? Would Tanzanians develop by merely taking over ownership of such special cuisine restaurants? Would they offer the standards expected by international discerning clients? Why should Tanzania bog itself down with such basic, mundane issues of ownership insignificance to the general improvement of the peoples' lives?

In his address to the nation on 31st August 2003, President Mkapa observed that Tanzanians were not adequately disposed to saving and investing. Therefore, when foreigners enter Tanzania they easily exploit opportunities, which Tanzanians do not seemingly, perceive. Yet, when foreigners exploit such opportunities, Tanzanians show dismay. The President quizzed: but where have Tanzanians been all these years and especially following the liberalisation of the economy to allow opportunities to be exploited by others in front of their eyes? Such shortcomings in entrepreneurship, the President regretted, were not dispassionately discussed in the public domain. Instead, Tanzanians complain and refuse to change their mindsets. Tanzanians should be honest to themselves. When a foreigner enters Tanzania and establishes a supermarket or opens a restaurant, what that means is that a market for such services has not been adequately filled. Had nationals responded to exploiting such markets, no foreigners would presumably have gone into those areas.Thus, the challenge is not to shut the door to such foreign investors. Those days are history. Tanzania is now a member of an East African Customs Union and is in the process of opening up its economy to a big SADC market as from 2007. Shortly, there will be greater freedom in cross-border movements of people, goods, capital and services in the sub-region. In such an environment, the right prescription is to build a culture of saving, entrepreneurship and investment in Tanzanians with the aim of building investment capacity that enables nationals to invest in projects either on their own or through joint ventures with foreigners, from the sub-region and way yonder! The establishment of NICO is one robust avenue in building the kind of capacity I am suggesting. Tanzanians should not close their eyes to the reality that the world is going through a massive structural change and uncertainty. In such an environment, there is growing incongruence between economic reality *and* political reality.

Conclusion

The success of business will flow from an environment in which a government is rationally seized of the critical distinction between the definitions of scope that is nation-restrictive and that which is global. The latter scope increases the productivity of capital and, in turn, results in a veritable explosion in productivity and investments in other sectors of the economy. The former, insulates the economy from the entry of firms that clearly define what "herd instinct" is all about in attracting investments. This is the economic reality. Tanzania defies it at its own peril. The nation state in a poor country has a large role to play, no doubt. However, in a globalised economy, the state should equally be intimately sensitive about its limits, especially over matters of economic nature, which could have serious and adverse consequences to economic growth. It is time that Tanzania public policy became more sensitive about the character of the global economy and its complexities.

Chapter

12 BRANDING TANZANIA: PROMOTING A UNIQUE IDENTITY AND IMAGE

The challenge of national economic development has gone beyond the limits of public policy. The new economic order has transformed economic development into a market challenge as well. Nations compete with other nations and strive to devise sources of competitive advantage. Thus todat there are more reasons why nations must manage and control their branding. The need to attract tourists, factories, companies, and talented people and to find markets for their exports requires that countries adopt strategic marketing tools and conscious branding.

Philip Kotler et al: ***Country as Brand, Product, and Beyond: A Place Marketing and Brand Management Perspective.***

The world is caught in frenzy about branding. Every country, developed and developing, is learning from the lessons of how successful companies have become global leaders in the provision of products and services through branding. A brand has become the key source of market power, competitive advantage and higher returns. This is because the global marketplace is now spoiled by choice. The advent of globalisation, marked by the collapse of territorial borders and the contraction of space and time, has ushered in a brave new world for both companies and countries making consumer behaviour and choice global. In such an environment, the brave shall make it; the weak shall falter and be marginalised. It is not military might that defines strength in this new marketplace. The brave new world is defined by new rules of competition, driven by innovation, creativity, entrepreneurship and aggressiveness to promote ever changing and differentiated products and services, and delivering them at a faster speed to consumers.

Every Nation a Brand

In to-day's global village, every nation is already a brand. Many people do not realise this reality. The nation as brand already exists in the minds of people around the world. It is enabled and empowered by 24 hours internet, television and radio. The perception of the world about a country, now, more than ever before, determines the form of political and economic relations between and among nations. In this context, competition for inward investments, tourism, development aid. especially for poor countries, though in the European Union the competition for regional funds equally exists), debt forgiveness and cancellations, buyers of products and services, human skills and special talents. in arts, music and film) has not only taken the centre stage, it has also become extremely intense. This new form of competition has catapulted the ardent quest for national branding. Since every nation is already a brand, for what it is and what it represents, as an identity and as an image, the move towards branding, in effect, is a process of re-branding. Nation branding is predominantly a reconfiguration of the current brand. The aim is to raise the profile of a country. In this light, branding. or re-branding) is informed by national long-term strategic objectives or vision. It is not driven by a time and money wasting image tweaking.

The Tanzania Branding Initiative

Early in 2004, the Tanzania Government decided to promote an initiative to brand Tanzania. The President, Benjamin W. Mkapa, constituted a Task Force, under the chair of Honourable Dr. Abdulkadir Shareef, the Deputy Minister for Foreign Affairs and International Cooperation, to work towards the development of a Tanzania brand. The source of the decision is the repeated observation made by foreign and local investors as well as by informed Tanzanians generally, that Tanzania is not adequately marketing itself to maximise returns from its huge potential, ranging from enviable natural resource endowments, language, culture, peace, and stability. The action taken by the government, belated as it is, is significantly important.

However, the challenge to brand Tanzania, or any poor nation, for that matter, is a complex one. It requires insight, creativity and seriousness. Inevitably, and because of the complexity involved, the process of branding Tanzania should be as broadly participatory as feasible. The Task Force itself has to be broadly representative of public and private sectors. The civil society and the media, in its holistic sense, should particularly be closely involved in the work of the Task Force. Consultation alone would be inadequate. Above all, Tanzanians from all sectors of society and at all levels- urban and rural- should be given the opportunity to express an opinion in what the Tanzania umbrella or master brand and the sub-brands should be. This involvement is paramount because an important component of a brand is *identity;* that is how Tanzanians view themselves in contrast to *image*, which is how non-Tanzanians view Tanzania. Precisely for this reason, a brand should reflect the values, character, hopes and aspirations of the people. A brand should resonate with both citizens and foreigners alike. This distinction is often neglected and is often a subject of confusion. Branding has two audiences: the nation's citizens and foreigners. A brand should therefore encapsulate both identity and image. A brand should enable a country to identify itself from amongst other nations of the world. It is important to recognise that branding goes beyond advertising and marketing.

Firms, Not Nations Compete

The entry of the idea of *"Country as Brand"*, as alluded to, is easier perceived than realised. Indeed, there is a view that holds that the whole idea of branding a country is frivolous because nations after all, do not compete. Harvard Professor Michael E. Porter in his seminal book, *The Competitive Advantage of Nations.* 1990), discusses the notion of a "Competitive Nation" which, in his view, arises out of confusion with the concept of "National Productivity". Porter argues that the challenge confronting nations in competing for global markets hinges on upgrading quality of products and services, improving product technology and bolstering production efficiency. In other words, "firms, not nations compete in international markets". Porter ramifies this view by asserting that firms or companies in fact do not have to be confined to their home. national) territory. They can compete from any location or locations. Little wonder then that the world to-day, and especially the rich countries, should find themselves "outsourcing" services and "offshoring" manufacturing locations. So, where then lies the relevance of "Nation as Brand" in such circumstances?

However, Professor Porter may be missing an important perspective in his discourse, especially in the context of poor countries. To the extent that a brand has the power to change the perception of the world, in other words, how other nations elect to choose to deal with one country in contrast to another, then arguably, nations do compete. New global realities founded on the so-called new global order where issues about democracy, the rule of law, good governance, prudent economic management and terrorism take pre-eminence, there is increasingly a direct link between a country's image and identity and its ability to market its products and services. If a country has a bad image, and however subjective that view or perception may be, its products and services inevitably suffer from isolation and thus loss or erosion of market. There is an inevitable backlash.

The world has already experienced such inevitabilities. Suffice to cite political actions taken to impose economic embargoes on Cuba and on Iraq under Sadaam Hussein. The world has also witnessed how one of the leading tourism destinations in Africa, namely Zimbabwe, has gravely suffered in the past few years because the rich world has decided to isolate

President Robert Mugabe, pronouncing Zimbabwe as a rogue state. Closer to Tanzania, we have also seen how tourism in Kenya has suffered due to a perception ingrained in the western world that Islamic terrorists operate along its coastal areas. Recent reports also indicate that Uganda's tourism has equally declined because of the rebel war in the north of that country. In contrast, however, a country like Colombia, in spite of a poor country image, has been able to promote, very successfully, a Colombian Coffee brand under the famous image of Juan Valdez with his mule since 1981. It is important to underscore this distinction, between what has happened in Zimbabwe or Kenya, on the one hand, and Colombia on the other, because branding of an export product *vis a vis* branding a nation, where tourism comes into play and people have to visit the country, plays out differently. Sometimes nation branding and product branding have to be approached differently.

In sum, the nation brand, the umbrella or master brand, often determines the fate of other sub-brands however well branded they may independently be. In this context, it is of particular importance that the National Brand takes the lead especially where issues about foreign aid, debt cancellation, tourism and inward investment feature. The dynamics of competition for these key factors of development, particularly for poor countries, are different from those that apply to products and services of a commercial character. As noted earlier, for them competition is largely driven by factors such as peace and stability, good governance, democracy, macro-economic stability, good financial systems, flexible labour markets, fiscal incentives and availability of skilled but cheap labour. Kenya, for instance, failed to attract aid and inward investment in the decade between 1992 and 2002 mainly because of a bad image fuelled by allegations of deep-seated corruption in the government system. Yes, nations invariably fall victim to varying degrees of prejudice and bias. Yet the losers, unfortunately, are those countries that pay a deaf ear to what is said about them, however biased! The response by such countries should not be anger, abuse and reclusiveness. Rather, they should be positive in image building or re-building.

Challenges for Brand Distinctiveness

Most of the factors that underpin competitive advantage arising from a positive umbrella national brand are increasingly becoming benign. Many poor nations are radically reforming themselves at the political and economic fronts, embracing the liberal economic orthodoxy. Under such circumstances, competition based on national brand is taking a more challenging dimension. Thus, how to brand a nation to reflect distinctiveness and uniqueness becomes the key core strategy in bolstering competitive advantage. Harvard Professor Joseph Nye has posited, "The greatest source of power in international affairs to-day may lie in persuading other nations to see your interests as their interests." Branding Tanzania so that her interests are projected to other nations and become perceived as their own lies at the heart of promoting such distinctiveness. Good public diplomacy alone may not be adequate. The strategic starting point has to do with whether Tanzania, in the first place, has identified its interests and what those "interests" mean to itself and to outsiders. Does Tanzania, for example, have an identity that is nationally recognised, one that evokes a sense of pride, hope and belonging? Does Tanzania have a sense of place – a nation where diversity, in all its manifestations, is not only tolerated but, more importantly, celebrated as well? What is Tanzania's unifying vision to which everyone or most Tanzanians are committed to?

For almost two decades following the adoption of the Arusha Declaration in February 1967, the pursuit of socialism and self-reliance constituted the unifying vision of Tanzanians. What is the position to-day? Does Development Vision 2025 and what it embodies constitute a new unifying mission? This is an important question to address since for a brand to be credible and plausible it has to mirror a national vision. A brand should moreover enable Tanzanians to speak and act in a co-ordinated and repetitive way about themes that make Tanzania distinctive; themes that represent the *essence* of the country or its "one-ness".

Branding Underpinned by Country's Essence

The essence of Tanzania is what underpins its core competitive advantage. The essence, above all, has to be real, not a facade. In my view, the essence of Tanzania could be summed up as a country that:

- has a unique and unifying national language, Kiswahili.
- believes in peace, unity, tolerance, diversity and human dignity.
- is committed to social and economic justice.
- is haven to refugees.
- is at peace with the world and with its neighbours.
- acts as a peace broker.
- is modernising with vibrant economic opportunities.
- protects its national culture, heritage and natural resource endowments.
- is open to the world.
- offers unforgettable holiday experiences to visitors.
- enjoys the most unique strategic transport and logistics location in the whole of Africa.
- is home to the world famous Tanzanite Germ, the Kilimanjaro Mountain, the "Serengeti Shall Never Die" National Park, The

Selous- the largest game reserve in the world, the Ngorongoro Wildlife National Park- world's crater of ecological and natural wonder, second largest fresh water lake in the world. Lake Victoria) and deepest lake in the world. Lake Tanganyika).

Such essence should be captured in the Tanzania umbrella brand and in the sub-brands as well. Evidently, the sub-brands would be more product or service- specific promotion brands. In other words, they would focus on tourism and on exports of raw and manufactured products or what are called "country of origin" effects.

Prioritising Branding Theme

In determining national branding, it is essential that Tanzania prioritises the key areas it seeks to target and promote more powerfully with maximum benefit. I mentioned earlier that branding can target areas such as improving the country's image for public diplomacy purposes, promoting tourism, bolstering exports, attracting inward investments, lobbying for more foreign aid and debt cancellation. All these targets are important. However, branding is an expensive venture. As such, it is important to prioritise the country's targets, always aiming at targets that would reap maximum value for cost incurred. It is always important to ensure that the selected target, tourism promotion for example, has positive spill over into the other targets such as attracting more inward investment. Nevertheless, most of the targets are complementary. The key task is to sift and isolate the ones with highest synergies and exploiting them to maximum advantage.

Developing a Brand Title

Once the prioritisation has been done, it is then important to develop a brand title. Such process is imperative because it is directly linked to clarifying what the brand is intended for, in other words, to whom it is directed and to realise what? Put differently, there has to be a market segmentation to drive the message of the brand title and the accompanying imagery, through, for instance, television and the branding theme sound. Such process has much to do with understanding target customers, articulating differentiated value propositions and focus on quality, not marketing. The best examples are the following TV footage featured on global TV Networks such as CNN: *"Malaysia, Truly Asia"* *"Incredible India"* and *"Amazing Thailand"*.

In the Tanzanian case, the record so far in developing brand titles has been mixed. Take the case of tourism. The Tanzania Tourism Board first marketed Tanzania tourism under the brand *"The Land of the Kilimanjaro and Zanzibar"*. The question that arises is to whom was the brand targeted and to realise what? Many foreigners may know of Mount Kilimanjaro. But would they visit Tanzania simply because of the unique, snow capped mountain on the equator? Moreover, what does Zanzibar represent in the brand? The channel of communication has also been ineffective because of lack of sound-based imagery. All promotional materials are in booklet forms, brochures, posters and soundless CD ROMs. It is noteworthy, however, that towards the end of 2004, the Tanzania Tourism Board released a globally well acclaimed DVD on Tanzanian tourism extravaganza. This is a major milestone. The key challenge is how the DVD would be put to maximum benefit.

Branding is not Marketing or Advertising

The worst part of the tourism brand, *Tanzania: the Land of the Kilimanjaro and Zanzibar* was to link *"Kilimanjaro"* and *"Zanzibar"*. Clearly, Zanzibar is a unique and powerful brand by and of itself. The politics of the Union should not creep into the commercial arena or ventures. What I referred earlier as the nation's essence is the key determinant in branding a country. Zanzibar has its own distinctive essence and mysticism. This is well captured internationally in novels such as *Zanzibar* by Giles Foden, *The Zanzibar Chest: A Story of Life, Love, and Death in Foreign Lands* by Aiden Hartley, and in an international ladies' perfume, *"Zanzibar"* by Van Cleef & Arpels of Paris. For example, in the novel, *Zanzibar*, it is narrated, "the ghosts of Zanzibar and Pemba live not in thalassia, or any other pavilion of ocean. They live in the flagrant orchards of clove and ylang-ylang that cover the islands like a shroud. It is through these that nightly predations are said to be made by the *papabawa*, the islands' legendary pale-skinned vampire." Of course, *"papabawa"* in Zanzibar is not a vampire. It represents a mystic, sodomite figure, an apparition. Yet the novel, *Zanzibar,* does well in capturing some of Zanzibar's unique essence. This essence is built around the slave market, the historic Stone Town, spice tours, magical lagoons and islands, narrow one-way streets, medieval Arab architecture, unique *taarab* music with traditional coastal music legends like the 93-year-old lady singer, Bibi Kidude, who features in The Economist's *The World in 2005* and described therein as one of "Africa's music treasures

The second shortcoming in branding Tanzanian Tourism happened in 2003 when the Tanzania Tourism Board changed the old brand title to *"Tanzania: Authentic Africa"*. The rationale for the change remains unclear; so was its underlying purpose and target market. Incidentally, Senegal has used this brand for several years. Moreover, there is a licensed company with the name *l'Afrique Authentique* which promotes tourism for Mali, Burkina-Faso, Mauritania, Benin, Niger, Cameroon and Algeria. Its website is: www.afrique-authentique.com. The problem, as I see it, in sporadic playing around with different brand statements, is that branding is confused with marketing and advertising. As observed earlier, a brand should enable a country to identify itself from amongst the crowd. It should have distinctiveness; differentiation, the way "*Volvo,*" the car, is identified with safety. In the case of Tanzania, what is it that sets it apart from competing countries? Changes in brand titles, not well thought out and not arrived at through broad participation of key stakeholders, cannot be effective. In this context, therefore, scarce financial resources have not been well spent especially in branding Tanzanian Mainland tourism. Thus, a distinctive brand for tourism has to be more seriously worked out. In my view, a tourism promotion brand like "*TANZANIA: Experience God's Ultimate Natural Heritage,*" could be the starting point.

Marketing Populism

I may also mention that, recently, a marketing slogan from yesteryears, "*Be Tanzanian, Buy Tanzanian*" has been revived, with strong political back up. This slogan is not a brand. At best, it is marketing populism. As consumers, Tanzanians have to believe in the quality of domestically manufactured products and services delivered. Simply because one is Tanzanian should not mean that he or she should drink Tanzanian "*Safari Lager*" instead of Kenyan "*Tusker lager*" or use Tanzanian "*Foma*" detergent instead of Kenyan manufactured global brand "*Surf*". Tanzanian products must achieve high quality brands that would make the Tanzanian consumer feel proud of the product. The product achieves acceptance not because of its being Tanzanian but because of its quality. Nationalist passion is irrelevant. Let me give an example of a South African product familiar to Tanzanians. South Africa produces tomato ketchup branded "*All Gold*". Because of its high quality and excellent packaging, it easily competes with global brands such as "*Heinz*". One could also mention the Malawian chilli sauce "*Nali*", an emergent brand of international standard. Tanzania's "*Premier Cashew*" could also become a global brand if it were better packaged to meet different discerning markets. Recently, on board British Airways "Club World", I was somewhat distressed to be offered an aperitif with a packet of salted cashew nuts packaged especially for BA. by a Kenyan company. The packaging was first class. However, Kenya is not really a cashew producing country! No doubt, Planters, a global food packaging company, also packages cashew nuts. Therefore, it is not Kenya, as a country, that I am targeting on in this concern. Rather, the point I am making is that here is a country, namely Tanzania, a leading world producer of cashew nuts that is unable to develop a global brand for its product.

Brand Promotion and Management

Finally, the initiative to brand Tanzania should go hand in glove with brand promotion and management. Building brand awareness, the way Tanzania Breweries. TBL) has so successfully done in the last few years is the kind of lesson to be embraced and copied. TBL has improved its product transportation, its warehousing. depots) around the country, its distribution systems, media promotion, including using billboards supporting various social causes including sponsoring major sports events and competitions. It would be disastrous to promote a powerful brand, for tourism, for example, when the country has serious deficiencies in the areas of ground transportation, hotels and lodges, and well trained people in hospitality management. Thus, infrastructure investment is important to branding Tanzania as a tourism destination. The decision taken in the Budget for fiscal year 2005/2006 to amend the Value Added Tax Act by exempting railway locomotives, rolling stock, spare parts and accessories from VAT, abolishing transport license fees for cargo haulage vehicles as well as exempting VAT and excise duty on aviation fuel for domestic air transport would inject greater competitiveness in the transport sector and induce more investments.

It is equally important to come to grips with the reality that when you brand a country or a product you should be well prepared to put your money where your mouth is. Money begets money. Brand promotion is an expensive affair. South Africa knows, for example, that in hosting of the World Cup 2010 the SA brand would be hugely promoted. Yet, it will also be at a huge cost. On the other hand, the returns, over time, would be enormous. For all that it wishes to bring to the living rooms of homes around the world, South Africa would exploit the World Cup to market its brand. South Africa has also been able to realise brand promotion by hosting a number of important events. Examples include the Annual Africa Musical Awards. KORA) at Sun City and the Annual INDABA Tourism Fair in Durban.

Cape Town Jazz has also become a brand in itself, embodying the pinnacle of contemporary African Jazz comparable to the best Jazz of the United States. Not since the Democratic Republic of the Congo, then Zaire, especially from the mid 1960s to the late 1980s, has an African country succeeded to use music to brand itself as powerfully as South Africa has done. With all its instabilities, Zaire became better known for its *"Kwasa Kwasa"* music than for anything else. SA Jazz, on the other hand, through accomplished musicians like Hugh Masekela, Abdullah Ibrahim, Jonathan Butler and Caiphus Semenya, not to speak of the legendary popular musician, Miriam Makeba, has helped to enrich the SA brand image. SA Jazz is unique in that it links South Africa's past of resistance against the apartheid regime and the present of reconciliation, hope, racial harmony and prosperity. In mid 2004, South Africa successfully promoted its SA brand logo, the rainbow flag, with *"ALIVE WITH POSSIBILITY"* as a catch phrase by using the London Cab as a billboard. South African Airways is also being used as another platform in the promotion of the SA brand.

Closer to Tanzania, Kenyan long distance and marathon runners have made Kenya a household name on a global scale. Unfortunately, Kenya has yet to exploit this brand to its maximum benefit because of its liabilities on the governance front. For Tanzania, the challenge is to conceive what brand to promote. Undoubtedly, at the political front, the picture of Tanzania as haven of peace, peace broker and haven for refugees could be one avenue to exploit in promoting the Tanzania umbrella brand. On the business and economic fronts, on the other hand, much more work has to be done because the brand itself is yet to be conceived. However, efforts have begun in the direction of putting Tanzania on the global map as a gem country for investments. The interview on Sunday 7 November, 2004, of the Tanzania Prime Minister, Frederick Sumaye, on CNBC Europe, a global business TV network, explaining the objectives of Tanzania's special Investment Promotion Forum in Midrand, South Africa, and painting a credible and attractive image of Tanzania's abundant investment opportunities in a land of peace and stability, was a major publicity and promotion coup for Tanzania. Tanzania has to be more aggressive in exploiting such global platforms to promote its national brand.

Brand Logo

It is in this area of brand promotion that the *Logo* becomes relevant. A Logo helps the execution of a brand. Tanzania needs an umbrella logo as well as specific sub-logos for the promotion of exports and tourism. Could the Tanzania umbrella logo take either of the following proposals?

Platforms For Brand Promotion

The next stage is the determination of avenues or platforms that Tanzania can use to promote its umbrella and sub-brands. Experience gained so far shows, that specifically in the tourism sector, the Tanzania brand has been promoted at Tourism Fairs in several countries of the world particularly South Africa, Japan, UK, France, Germany, Italy and Spain. Customised publications and posters with pictures and narrative have supported physical participation at such Fairs and what Tanzania offers, especially for what may be described as *"Safari Holidays"*. Zanzibar has also featured at such Fairs, within Tanzania pavilions but promoting its own brand. More recently, Tanzania National Parks Authority. TANAPA) and the Ngorongoro Conservation Area have produced multi-media CD ROMs on Tanzanian wildlife and ecology for promoting tourism.

An important platform for brand promotion is the website. Too many websites, a current feature, can only be dysfunctional. There is need to borrow a leaf from South Africa where not only have they created one organisation to promote the South African brand, namely *The International Marketing Council of South Africa*, but have also, under the control and management of that Council, produced an all-embracing website, *www.southafrica.info*. In my view, the Tanzania Task Force charged with the responsibility of proposing how Tanzania should be branded has to propose the establishment of a National Council similar to that of South Africa, representing public-private partnership, to take full charge of managing the Tanzanian brand. Such Council would need good leadership, excellent management systems and adequate resources to enable fulfil its onerous task. The Task Force should also come up with an umbrella Tanzania Brand Website. This is not the same as the Tanzania National Website that exists presently. It is a specific *brand* website. Everything to do with branding Tanzania, in all its facets: peace and stability, language, cultural heritage, diversity, unity, world heritage sites in Tanzania, natural endowments, strategic geographical location, the Tanzania Union and Zanzibar's own brand, should feature on this special website. Finally, the task Force should challenge Tanzanians to propose an umbrella national brand logo and the sub-brand logos, specifically for the promotion of tourism and exports. The challenge should be fashioned in a framework of competition with attractive prizes and rewards offered to winning proposals. It is essential though that the Task Force initially defines the essence of Tanzania that should then be captured in the logos later to be developed.

Conclusion

It is said that when the going gets tough, the tough get going. In a brave new world, driven by globalisation, the tough will be those nations better able to use soft power to promote themselves as unique and distinctive in what they offer, be they products or services. Nation branding is one strategic vehicle that can promote such unique identity and image. However, it is important to caution that branding is neither marketing nor advertising. A brand has to capture a nation's reality. Therefore, it has to be holistic and credible. In this light, branding a nation is a complex task because it is not simply about developing logos as many people perceive. It is thus critically important that the Task Force does not rush in finalising its work. A brand and sub-brands have to outlive changes of government. To that extent, they should enjoy broad national legitimacy. Such objective can best be realised where the exercise of nation branding takes a broad and intensely participatory approach.

LIGHTING BOUNDLESS
OPPORTUNITIES
special logo

HAVEN OF OPPORTUNITY IN
STABILITY

GEM OF THE WORLD

EXPERIENCE GOD'S
ULTIMATE NATURAL
HERITAGE

For promoting exports, Tanzania
could consider this Logo:

For promoting tourism Tanzania
could consider this Logo:

Part Four

DEMOCRACY, LEADERSHIP AND GOVERNANCE

—direct popular government is not what democracy is about. It is true that any administration should have reasonable time to develop its policies, but this is not the same thing as the current uncritical belief in the importance of "strong government": certainly one hopes that a good government will be strong, but a government that is both strong and bad—is almost the worst possible public evil.

-Raymond Williams: Towards 2000.

We have increasingly come to understand that good governance is the key that unlocks the door to development. But what exactly is good governance and how do poor countries acquire it? If it were simply a matter of adopting institutional blueprints from abroad, development would hardly be as challenging as it surely is. Striking the right balance between institutional imitation and innovation is at the core of the problem.

-Dani Rodrik, *9th Annual Harvard International Development Conference, April 2003.*

Chapter

13 CHALLENGES TO DEEPEN DEMOCRATISATION

For the real cultural conflict of our time is between those who believe that you can change our society and those who think that, at best, you can only hope to make changes within that society.

*-Daniel Singer: **Whose Millennium? Theirs or Ours?***

Tanzania has traversed an interesting, if radical, political path, transforming itself from an oligarchic, one party system, which it had legally enforced in 1965, only four years after gaining political independence, to a multi-party system in mid 1992. The challenges of political reform have been onerous, even debilitating at times, particularly as far as Zanzibar politics are concerned. Generally, this radical shift has necessitated changes in the constitution, in the electoral law and in the whole outlook towards the place and role of separation of powers and the role of civil society in national governance. Whilst there is a view, especially within the current ruling party, the CCM, that changes of these kinds could not be episodic, that they have to evolve over time as the country matures politically, there is also an opposing view that posits that Tanzania needed a radical surgery in its constitution which is still regarded to represent a one party environment. Thus the calls and demands for a new constitution to be drafted. In this chapter, I takes a close look at some of the key issues that lie at the heart of Tanzania's political changes in the past decade. A critical review is made of the challenges that confront the country in deepening democratisation, in addressing concerns over the Tanzania Union, and on improving governance and public service delivery. At the outset, I examines the nature of civil society in Tanzania.

Civil Society: Instrument of Political Action

Civil society and the one party political system, as the Swahili saying would put it, "cannot be cooked in the same pot." Tanzania's 27 years of monolithic party system vindicated this adage. Not only were the organs of civil society, the voluntary organisations established by the people outside the framework of party politics deliberately made inept and apathetic during the era of one party system, many of them were in fact heavily politicised and turned into organs of the party system itself.

It is in the light of this historical context that the re-birth of civil society in Tanzania following the re-entry of political pluralism in 1992 is such a complex development and a challenge for all democracy-loving Tanzanians. Many Tanzanians would understand and probably rationalise the concept of a political party and its role in the democratic system of government. Very few of them, however, would even have heard of the term civil society, least of all know what it constitutes. Indeed, those who purport to know what it means have only a vague idea of its portent force in society. Therefore, when Rajni Kothari, the distinguished Indian social scientist, contends that to restore to the people their sovereignty is not to undermine the role of the state but to transform it and that such transformation can be achieved only through the transformation of the civil society and not the other way round, many Tanzanians would most likely fail to appreciate the postulated logic. To them, the multi-party political system is what would restore and guarantee sovereignty to the people. This is the pervasive rhetoric and the ground for celebrating the re-entry of the multi-party system in the body politic.

Few Tanzanians would also appreciate the logic that participation in the political process means much more than the opportunity to exercise the vote. The reason is not difficult to find. The so-called political climate that not only tolerates dissent but also welcomes it and which puts dissent at the heart of participation, a position so forcefully advocated by the South Commission's Report, *The Challenge to the South,* had never really existed in Tanzania during the period of One-Party rule. Moreover, only a few Tanzanians would be adequately conscientised and sensitised to appreciate the concept of political participation underpinned by an ethic that allows all ideas, from the formal political opposition to the society as a whole, to contend. Electoral and legislative politics as pointed out by Rajni Kothari "have led to a virtual exclusion of the mass of the people from the processes of power". These are important issues to consider because the viability of civil society in any country is driven by dialogue of the people. Dialogue is the essence of the democratic process. It widens the arena of politics beyond electoral and legislative politics. It is dialogue based on voluntarism. Moreover, whilst it is non-political, as political parties are, it is political without the aim of seizing state power.

Tanzania virtually occupies a virgin territory as far as the context and role of civil society is concerned. In this light, not only should the role of the state be transformed a' la Rajni Kothari's thesis, but, more importantly, such transformation should also embody the renewal of civil society itself. This means that the key societal organs of civil society should be enabled to organise and strengthen, on the one hand, to provide a broad platform for debate and dissemination of ideas and, on the other hand, to be enabled to play a frontal role in restoring the spaces which belong to civil society but which the state and the single political party had encroached upon. These spaces embrace not only political and fundamental human rights, but also such rights that emanate from social, economic, ecological, gender and ethical dimensions of the cultural plurality in society. Experience of mature multi-party political systems is testimony to the need for consistent search for new instruments of political action to fill the ever-growing vacuum in political space. Tanzania has witnessed, particularly in the past decade how the media, as an organ of civil society, can become an effective instrument of political action in the areas of public evaluation of government conduct and in enabling the public to secure information on the activities and omissions of the government.

These civil society instruments of political action are becoming more critically essential day by day especially where a growing vacuum in political space has to do with the intensification of fundamentalist perversions and obscurantist advocacy which are undermining and eroding the tenacious ethic and religious plurality through which the organic unity and tranquillity of the country has until now thrived upon. So critical was the vacuum that some Tanzanians, including the parliamentarians, in the period 1990 to 1995 related it to the decline in authority of the state. In India, for example, it is generally held that reactionary forces of communalism, sectarianism and religious bigotry have always swung into play in periods of decline of the political process.

Here then lies a crucial role for civil society. The challenge is onerous and tormenting. However, it should be boldly responded to. Unfortunately, Tanzanian elites, professionals and intellectuals, appear to lack a sense of purpose and direction. It is as if, suddenly, the whole society is driven by a mood of expediency and self-interest. This is a great pity. Intellectuals who, in the late 1960s and throughout the 1970s, provided a larger intellectual perspective to the goals and directions of the national body politic now appear to have lost their moorings. This is not to underrate the role that REDET and the Uongozi Institute at the University of Dar es Salaam have been doing. Not only has REDET performed well in elections monitoring, but has also played a signal role in civic education. The Uongozi Institute Annual State of Politics Symposia, on the other hand, have contributed a great deal in addressing some of the topical issues that relate to democratisation, the Union, religion and politics and the role of civil society. But the role of these organs is not mainstreamed into the daily life of the University. The point that I am making is that the intellectual fervour and militancy that existed in the late 60s and early 70s that were part of the daily life of the University and whose ideas and thinking permeated into the public domain have virtually disappeared. Indeed, at a

University of Dar es Salaam seminar in mid February 2005, on Academic Freedom, Social Responsibility and the State of Academia, Professor Issa Shivji lamented that the management of the University of Dar es Salaam had become so overly influenced by market fundamentalism that it had turned the university into "a kiosk for selling education wares." He went on to castigate what he described as "university mandarins" for becoming surrogates of donors and for allowing state interference in the core mission of the university with the result that "debates and intellectual discourse, which is the life-line of any vibrant university community, has virtually disappeared." Shivji was grappling with a question that has become extremely topical even in developed societies.

In a recent powerful book, *Where have All The Intellectuals Gone?* Professor Frank Furedi cogently surmises that knowledge is increasingly conceptualised as a "ready-made digestible product" that can be marketed and that academic institutions have virtually become a "catering industry" with students queuing up to be given correct amounts of food. Furedi concludes, "The knowledge that is peddled by the merchants of the Knowledge Economy is in fact a mundane caricature of itself." The reason behind this argument is that "without a relationship to Truth, knowledge has no intrinsic meaning. It becomes an abstract insight that is more likely to be transmitted than valued, and can be recycled in its most mundane form." But is higher education indeed being merchandised or is it a case of our losing a sense of balance about the realities of a new world that require higher education to respond to both the professionalisation of different forms of academic discourses and the development of what Professor Georges Haddad of UNESCO has described as the development of "aptitude necessary for intellectual entrepreneurship?" Professor Haddad distinguishes two fundamental aspects of history of mankind in examining the idea of merchandisation of education, a derogatory concept in his view. First, there is the "adventure of the mind, arts, science, education." Second, there is the "commercial adventure: trade, industry and new worlds, today of an economic nature and essential for progress through the creation of wealth and jobs. Both these adventures characterise the human adventure and cross-fertilise each other." In other words then, the role of universities cannot be reduced to the mere conventional search of truth. The interests of the market which increasingly have a direct bearing on the development or welfare of the person have to be equally considered.

Reverting to the subject of civil society, it needs to be underlined that without an effervescent intellectual role in a situation where it is also well supported by a constructive and informed media, civil society in Tanzania would not be able to play a forceful role in national affairs. As the new political chapter of Tanzania's development unfolds, the call for mass politics should be heeded and translated into a formidable platform for a dialogue of the people. The first call to arms, involves the intellectual class of Tanzania and I now turn to examine the challenges that confront it.

Intellectuals and the Democratisation Process

On October 22nd, 1966, President Julius K. Nyerere rusticated for one year virtually 90% of Tanzanian students studying at the then University College, Dar es Salaam. One year after the promulgation of the One Party State, the students' demonstration against the introduction of a two-year compulsory National Service was the first test on Mwalimu Nyerere's system of political oligarchy and the response had to be decisive, swift and drastic. That incident is now history. Yet there are lessons to be drawn from it. First, and this is partly to correct historical distortions: the students did not demonstrate against the National Service as such, much as they agonized and protested about foregoing a large percentage of their would be remuneration as part of the "self-sacrifice spirit" embodied in the National Service requirement and even angrily displaying an isolated placard which read "*Heri Wakati wa Mkoloni*". colonial times were better). Of course, Mwalimu Nyerere, in a typical Machiavellian style, defended his action by harping on the words of the isolated placard that was independently prepared by a single student. The support for Nyerere's decision from all walks of Tanzanian society was inevitably resounding.

What in fact precipitated the demonstration was what the students perceived as the abuse by the One Party Executive and Legislature of an important democratic process enshrined in democratic norms and procedures for policy decisions to be given the force of law. The student leadership had previously been informed that the government would present a *White Paper* on the introduction of National Service and that the views of the students and other youth groups would be solicited and considered before a Bill on the matter was finally put before the Legislature. That procedure did not take place. Thus, the so- called demonstration against the National Service was, in effect, the first and pioneering intellectual challenge against the undermining of a democratic order even under a one party political system.

The second lesson learned was the ruthless action that befell legally elected parliamentarians who defended the actions of the students. They were expelled both from the party, TANU, and from the Legislature. It could be asked, whether the actions taken against them were indeed democratic? Were they constitutional? However, what is important to note, with the benefit of hindsight, is that because of the punitive actions that had been taken against those parliamentarians, the democratic process and ethos in terms of parliamentarians sticking their necks out on matters of national import were thereafter inhibited, and, increasingly, a sense of powerlessness pervaded the legislative establishment. The legislature became surrogate to the Executive. One could pose a question to what extent such character of legislative "powerlessness" has changed since the adoption of the multi-party system, at least as far as the CCM is concerned? There are those who would say, that in recent years, particularly between 2001 and 2004, the legislature has reflected a great deal of independence to the point of even frustrating the Executive's policy programmes, notably privatisation. Yet, from the perspective of promoting the separation of powers, such independence may signal the right direction.

Nyerere: Was he anti Intellectuals?

Professor Ali Mazrui characterised President Nyerere's harsh action against the University Students in 1966 in an article published in the magazine *Transition* in 1967 titled *Tanzaphilia: A Political Diagnosis* as "treason" to his own intellectual class. In fact, Mazrui went as far as describing Nyerere as an intellectual who was, at root, anti-intellectualism. Nyerere's own response to this accusation came in an address to the University of Liberia in February 1968 titled: *The Intellectual Needs Society*. In that address, Nyerere argued that for saying that the University is justified in Africa only if it were geared to the satisfaction of the needs of the society, that University graduates were servants who had more duties and responsibilities to society, not more privileges or rights than those members of society who did not have any education, "I have been accused of turning on my own kind - of being a kind of intellectual cannibal"!

That said, the problem with Nyerere's position about the role of intellectuals in society is largely its linkage to what he describes as the needs of society. It is important to analyse this position because it marks the critical starting point if one proceeds to discussing the role of intellectuals in the democratisation process. The key issue revolves around the question: who determines the needs of society? Is it the people? Is it the leadership? If leadership, which leadership? Experience has shown that since the onset of political independence, Nyerere had been the *principal determinant* of the core national values and direction of society. Admittedly, he used the instrument of the party oligarchy and the controlled, single party legislature, to determine sanction those values and direction. There is little doubt, however, that he was always at the helm of such decisions.

Indeed, there is adequate evidence to prove that Nyerere singly formulated the policies that determined the values of Tanzanians-social, economic and political-embracing education, rural development, state enterprises, cooperatives, villagisation, decentralisation of government, foreign policy, the one party system were almost singly formulated by Nyerere. An ideological institution, the Kivukoni College, was specifically established in 1961 to ingrain the emerging political leadership with the defined values of society. The Institute of Development Studies at the University of Dar es Salaam, from the late 1960s to mid 1980s, was virtually "infiltrated" by the political party, under Mwalimu Nyerere's inspiration and turned into a Centre of Ideological Excellence, promoting a political and economic philosophy in line with Nyerere's perceived "values" and guiding ideological philosophies to underpin the development of Tanzanian society.

Intellectual Monopoly and Intellectual Conformism

No, Nyerere was clearly not an intellectual cannibal. However, he was certainly an intellectual monopolist; not out of malice or power mongerism but out of genuine or even dogmatic commitment to what he perceived to be in the best interest of Tanzania. What is regrettable about Nyerere's intellectual monopolistic posture was its consequences and impact on the mental state of the Tanzanian intellectual. Intellectuals fell short of the signal distinction of being the drivers of the nature and depth of social and political change. The quality of intellectuals, as fearless social critics, eroded over time. The period between the late 1960s and early 1980s, witnessed discussions of public policies on a ritual basis to rationalise what was considered popular and acceptable ideas propounded by Nyerere. However, there were few exceptions, notably when the late Professor Walter Rodney, who taught History at the University College, Dar es Salaam in the late 1960's and early 1970's, pointedly challenged Nyerere's socialist philosophy and policies as not being doctrinaire and thus reactionary. Nyerere responded "violently" in the ruling party newspaper, *The Nationalist,* then edited by Benjamin Mkapa, describing Rodney's think piece as "revolutionary hot air". The net result of Nyerere's monopoly of ideas was the creation of an environment where some leading intellectuals, almost frustratedly, decided to take a back seat and thereby failed to contribute to the improvement of the political and economic process in Tanzania. Many intellectuals, during that period, pitifully acquiesced or succumbed to sycophancy. In this context, and as the role of intellectuals in the democratisation process continues to be critically challenged, Tanzania should be mindful of such past conformist intellectualism. It is somewhat paradoxical that Professor Shivji should lament about the commercialisation of the University of Dar es Salaam, positing that the university mandarins were not allowing academia to enjoy the space for robust public debate. Should we take it that academics have decided to lie back and not challenge such an environment? Should we also believe that academics could not reclaim the autonomy they enjoyed under more difficult political conditions that obtained in the 1960s and 1970s? In the view of Professor Furedi, which we endorse, intellectuals inside and outside the university "must face up to the uncomfortable truth that they risk making themselves irrelevant if they allow current institutional pressures to dominate their work."

What is interesting to note, however, is that once Nyerere vacated the high office of State President in 1985, Tanzania witnessed once again some efflorescence in intellectual activity. The resurgent vibrancy in non-conformist intellectualism coincided with the on-set of lukewarm economic reform policies initiated by Nyerere in 1984 and more vigorously pursued and executed by President Ali Hassan Mwinyi from 1986 and by President Benjamin Mkapa since 1995. During President Mwinyi's administration, the role of intellectuals centred mostly on generating and disseminating ideas bearing on socio-economic progress of Tanzania and, more marginally, on arousing public consciousness on matters relating to political change. Such focus changed during President Mkapa's administration. In this context, the political science department of the University of Dar es Salaam has to be commended for taking a lead in addressing issues more focused on political transformation. It is correct to observe though, that intellectuals have generally been overly engrossed in their own specialist intellectual moorings. This is to be regretted because, to be able to face the new tasks unleashed by the challenges of democratisation, tasks that particularly call for giving voice to the conscience of the nation, intellectuals, to cite Rajni Kothari's view from his book: *Politics and the People: In Search of a Humane India*, have to "stop treating knowledge as a process of accumulation unrelated to political tasks."

The New Challenge for Intellectuals

Tanzania is ripe for intellectuals to launch a massive process of social learning with a focus on placing strategic pressure on the existing constitutional, electoral and juridical order in order to bring about critical political changes. Alvin Toffler, the American social critic warns in his book, *The Third Wave: The Revolution That Will Change Our Lives*, that "we should not expect many of to-day's nominal leaders, presidents and politicians, senators and central committee members to challenge the very institutions that, no matter how obsolete, give them prestige, money and the illusion, if not the reality, of power". Like many African nations, Tanzania has been on the threshold of a major political transformation from three decades of a monolithic political party rule to political pluralism. Yet many informed Tanzanians seem little concerned whether such political transformation would indeed bring about a democratic polity, a polity wherein the executive arm of the state and the people as a whole create an open and vibrant civil society with the people participating, not simply in electoral processes, but more significantly, in the creation of a common shared future.

Evidently, as the formal institutions of governance, social service delivery, dispensation of justice and law and order are shaken by the measures of economic transformation and reduction of poverty as well as by the erosion of the moral fabric, the dynamics of democracy inevitably take the centre stage. Tanzania should necessarily witness convulsions of human consciousness, even strands of struggle and conflict from such challenges. These are the inevitable directions and bearings of the democratisation process. Their basic character is politics of the people rather than mere politics of the parties. It is in this context that some concerned Tanzanians have posed the question whether a serious constitutional engineering is taking place able to deepen the democratic system as opposed to merely reinforcing party politics.

Therefore, the challenge before Tanzanian intellectuals is to participate actively in mobilising, organising and sensitising the people to build a people - centred democracy. For as Professor Arthur M. Schlesinger Jr. posited in his book, *The Cycles of American History,* "Democracy is not self executing." Those who wield the power of the spoken and the written word should lead the task in voicing the conscience of Tanzanians and promote the norms and values that should underpin democratic change. Unlike the "corrupted" intellectualism of the past years, a key attribute of intellectualism today should be its egalitarian, liberal and pluralistic character. Indeed, if "knowledge is the most democratic source of power," as Alvin Toffler surmised in his book *Powershift*, then clearly a real intellectual process in this arena should accentuate and deepen freedom of opinion and dissent and castigate all forms of autocracy, dogma and blind subservience. The process of democratisation cannot realistically be separated from the agents of democratisation. Yet the agents of democratisation could not be limited to the state, the political parties and a few powerful individuals. The whole society has to be viewed as the driving force of democratisation. Otherwise, as the *Challenge To The South* warned, the result would be "widespread apathy within the society, alienation from organised social and political structures, and even conflict." Tanzanian intellectuals should not allow democratisation to be monopolised by the state and the political parties. In the following sections, I examine the central issues and perspectives that need to be considered and pursued in deepening democratisation in Tanzania.

Is a New Constitutional Dispensation Necessary?

We may have a multi-party political system, and our Parliament may have opposition Members of Parliament. However, it is Chama Cha Mapinduzi policies that will be implemented even when nourished by the advice or criticism of the Opposition. That is a fundamental principle of multi-party democracy.

-President Benjamin William Mkapa: *Speech to the Parliament of the United Republic of Tanzania, July 14, 2000.*

Democratisation does not guarantee social justice any more than it guarantees economic growth, social peace, administrative efficiency, political harmony, free markets or the end of ideology. But the institutions, practices and ideals of democracy have the capacity to challenge the concentration of political power and prevent the emergence of tyranny. Thus they play a role in building governance that is by the people as well as for the people.

-Human Development Report 2002: **Deepening Democracy in a Fragmented World.**

The need for a new constitutional dispensation and electoral system continues to raise a great deal of passion and heat. Two strands of opinion dominate the Tanzanian national debate. The first one holds the view that Tanzania has quite successfully gone through multi- party general elections in 1995 and 2000 based on the present Constitution and the Electoral Law, as they presently exist. Of course, the argument runs, the current framework may not be the most ideal. Moreover, it is questioned whether perfection, by definition, is not something that is inherently and probably dangerously static in character. Indeed, unlike democracy that reflects a definitive, almost static status, democratisation, on the other hand, is dynamic in that it captures a character of an on-going process. Incremental improvements on the existing constitutional framework present a more practical approach towards democratisation as opposed to viewing such approach as symptomatic of patch working and thus a distortion in the quest for realising the big picture.

The opposing view, which partly stems from the recommendations of the 1992 Nyalali Presidential Commission Report on One Party or Multi-party System, holds that the underlying democratic value systems that underpin the present Constitution and the Electoral law, suffer from deep-seated one party cultural and ideological traits. The central thrust of this view seems to be that Tanzania rode the tide of global democratisation, which was predominantly precipitated by the 1989 Soviet and Eastern European Revolution, without seriously considering the form of democracy and its machinery that fits Tanzania's history, cultural norms and diversity as well as other important factors such as the nature of the Tanzania Union whose constitutional forte was the One Party state. It is interesting, in this context, that President Benjamin Mkapa should suggest, as he did in February 2004, that there is need to bring about a national dialogue in Zanzibar on the question of its future. Evidently, President Mkapa kept his word as manifested by the dialogue meetings that have taken place in Zanzibar between in June and July 2005 embracing all political parties and not simply those governed by the Muafaka, namely CUF and CCM. These dialogue meetings provide a ground breaking path towards building a culture of political tolerance and promoting cordial relationships within the arena of political actors in Tanzania. It is important, however, that such dialogue be comprehensive from the political, constitutional and economic perspectives.

Going Beyond Liberal Democracy

The on-going debate about Tanzania's constitutional dispensation is fundamental. It goes to the root of the need to entrench a culture of pluralism. We could debate for or against the need for a new Constitution and a new Electoral law. What would not be debatable, however, is that a new political reality has dawned in Tanzania, that the liberal view that democracy is predominantly anchored in representativeness through political parties inside and outside electoral organs is inadequate and outmoded. Social movements within the civil society equally have an important role in influencing the form, depth and character of social, economic and political change. In the latter area, the challenge is more onerous for intellectuals as a section of social movement. After all, intellectuals and professionals are cast in a distinctive role of being better able to perceive social and political reality from their holistic and historical contexts. In this context, the distinguished American Marxist intellectual, Paul Baran, wrote, back in 1961, that intellectuals have "the greatest responsibility for exploring and assimilating historical experience and for providing society with such human orientation and such intelligent guidance as may be obtainable at every concrete junction on its historical journey". However, even at the broader societal level, Tanzania needs a vibrant community of thinking citizens. It would be dangerous, in my view, in the interest of Tanzania's development, were citizens to remain in a mental trance. The need and urgency for collective role and participation of all Tanzanians, through their various civil societies, in the governance of the country, has thus never been greater and urgent.

One of the shortcomings of Tanzania's political transformation is that the country still suffers from very strong political impulses and even illusions conditioned by priorities of the polity as it is rather than as it ought to be. Whether it is over socio-economic issues, politics or the constitution, the country still lacks the mindset and the courage to dare to question, challenge, and accept change; not change for its own sake, but change for promoting a better political and economic dispensation. "Fundamentalist" beliefs, of diverse origins and character, invariably foreclose genuine and open debate and dialogue. They represent the antithesis of democracy. However, it needs to be acknowledged that the usefulness of any idea increases in direct proportion to an appreciation of its limitations. Yet, limitations should not be allowed to undermine change. For whilst change, as Mwalimu Julius Nyerere postulated in his 1969 Speech, *Stability and Change in Africa*, "causes disturbance and thus upsets stability", stability itself is impossible to achieve without change. Indeed, the challenge that Mwalimu Nyerere posed was that of striving to achieve a difficult balance between the often conflicting and complementary needs for change and stability. This is the challenge that should inform, for example, a genuine democratic debate about the need for a new Constitution and Electoral Law in Tanzania.

Building Political Compacts

Rational politics demand that Tanzanians and political leaders move away from politics of confrontation and polarisation to politics of consensus and tolerance. Politics of consensus, by definition, should be based on fundamental values and goals and these have to be formulated on a bipartisan basis. The promotion of such a coalition of interests is the *sine qua non* for achieving a true political and economic democracy. This has been clearly evidenced in the Zanzibar *"Muafaka"*. In this light, the challenging starting point for Tanzanians, leaders and followers alike, is to jettison their shibboleths and illusions about the need for a comprehensive, as opposed to an incremental, constitutional and electoral reform. The vision of the Nyalali Commission could not be more respected and warranted. One could argue for or against the efficacy of a Constitutional Conference. What baffles logic, however, is the apparent insensitivity to appreciating the need for a systematic and broad participative approach, beyond Parliament, to undertaking even the most incremental constitutional and electoral law changes that have taken and are taking place. Such a position is well manifested in the constitutional and electoral law reforms tabled before Parliament in November 2004, which include the introduction of a symbolic element of proportional representation. The government had also sought to introduce a constitutional amendment directed at making the Electoral Commission enjoy, at least, some semblance of independence. However, the proposal failed the test of genuineness and was not presented before Parliament.

The coalition of interests I am advancing can best be achieved through the avenue of a specially appointed Constitutional and Electoral Law Commission comprising distinguished and bipartisan experts from the legal, political and civil society spectrum. Such a commission can identify critical points of convergence as well as points of divergence within the political parties and the civil society as a whole that relate to the fundamental principles to be enshrined in the Constitution and the Electoral Law. Unfortunately, this idea of setting up a Commission has failed to secure from the leadership of the political party in power the objective appreciation it critically deserves.

The constitution is the fundamental law of the country. Tanzania's development is importantly influenced by the nature and content of the Constitution. The importance of such legal pinnacles of the country demands that the constitution be put to public scrutiny. It is in this context that *The Challenge to the South* postulated, "political systems need to be understood by the people they serve and suited to their own value systems." The Report of the South Commission goes further to posit that periodic elections, however free and fair, are insufficient criteria for pursuing genuine development and that it is the continual questioning of citizens, whose freedom of expression should be total, that can stimulate reforms essential for maintaining a country's democratic effectiveness as a society transforms. The following examination of the need for Tanzania to move to a different electoral system fits into this idea of stimulating democratic reforms and deepening democratisation.

Needed: A Proportional Electoral Representation System

An objective examination of the need for the introduction of a proportional representation electoral system, necessarily demands a review of the background of Tanzania's peace, unity and stability and what would it take to sustain such an environment.

Throughout its four decades of political history, Tanzania has enjoyed enviable unity, stability, peace and tranquillity. In spite of years of dismal economic performance, Tanzania has come to be recognised and saluted by the western world as a model of what the key stuff of politics is primarily about, namely the achievement of national harmony and national commitment to basic human values. It is for these noble goals and achievements that Tanzania owes so much to one person, namely, Mwalimu Julius Kambarage Nyerere. For whilst *Ujamaa* as a philosophy of wealth creation in a world driven more by individual and corporate rather than by human or societal interests is, undoubtedly, outmoded, '*Ujamaa*', as a philosophy of unity, redistribution, social justice, brotherhood, love and tolerance should be cherished, strengthened and died for. What has been the contribution of *ujamaa* to the realisation of these values?

Ujamaa, One Party and Peace

The One Party political system, which Tanzania embraced for over three-decades. from 1965 to 1992), was able to survive and, in many respects, enjoy legitimacy, not because there was no political opposition during this period or because it was illegal to organise politically in opposition to the CCM. On the contrary, political opposition, centrifugal as it may have largely been, has all along existed from within the CCM itself and from without. What is important to observe is that political opposition and civil society strife failed to take root and to master grassroots support mainly because the values, which *Ujamaa* epitomised, were strong and neutralising. However, the large question that now faces most Tanzanians and particularly those that are more intelligently exposed to the realities and experiences of multiparty politics in Africa, is whether the *Ujamaa* philosophy would provide the divine spark of creative power for forging unity, brotherhood and tolerance in a different, ostensibly 'divisive' political environment. This question is important. Yet the drawback is that it is not receiving the level of attention it urgently deserves in the sense of the country seriously debating what should be the ideal electoral system.

For it would be a great pity, indeed a setback for peaceful Tanzania, that the new system of multi-party politics should unleash turmoil rather than, as intended, greater societal cohesiveness, tolerance and collective mission. Clearly, competitive politics should not usher in societal disintegration or anarchy! Competitive politics in developing countries where the economic ideological divide should be negligible because it is the development of the poor people that is paramount, provides the medium for consensual as opposed to the western world-type adversarial politics. This means, therefore, that the electoral system should be such that consensual politics stands as the ethos and thrust of competitive politics. In this context, a historic and purposeful challenge as well as mission lies before the CCM, a political party that has been governing Tanzania, you could literally say, since independence, to make this new politics possible. In the next sections of this chapter, I review the pros and cons of different electoral systems. I also propose why I believe that a clear and bold move towards the adoption of a broad based proportional representation electoral system is imperative and of national interest.

Winner Takes All Electoral System

The Constitution currently in place incorporates a "winner takes all" electoral system. This system has, worked well under a one party political system. It is debatable, however, whether it can breed the same equitable results under a multi-party political system environment re-introduced in 1992, after thirty years. Evidently, it would be difficult to change quickly the one party culture ingrained in the people. Yet it is a system incapable of breeding consensual politics. As such, the "winner takes all" electoral system, if introduced, may not bring about the envisioned consensual democratic politics Tanzanians wish to have. On the contrary, the country may witness the re-birth of yet another one party system, only de facto this time around! As in 1965, CCM may celebrate such a re-birth by championing CCM as the party of the people in a country where illiteracy is still quite high. Change may be difficult to come by. A well functioning democratic system needs a credible and worthwhile 'opposition', particularly in countries of the Tanzanian- type where civil society is still nascent and cannot act as a "third force" in the national political framework. In this context, CCM has the noble and role of kindling the flame of creative instinct for Tanzanians to attain a truly inspirational and consensual democratic system. It would be difficult to fulfil this role if it adheres to the present "winner takes all" electoral system. What CCM should do is to pioneer the promulgation of a proportional electoral representation system. There are several reasons in support of such a move viewed in the context of a pluralistic and divisive Tanzanian society. What are the characteristics of this divisiveness? They include:

- widening disparity of wealth across the racial divide and within the indigenous population itself.

- deepening poverty and racial convulsions and, even conflict. A major development is entrenching between rural and urban areas.

- religious bigotry that has now extended to the media level.

- emergence of intervention by religious groups in national politics as a response to an ostensible failure of leadership and a state of drift over vital political, social and economic issues.

- an unemployed urban population that is increasingly amenable to mob psychosis and demagogic manipulation.

- sharp rise in criminality, drug abuse, prostitution. male and female) and an astounding decline in standards of moral rectitude.

- intensification of politics of patronage and patronage of politics underlined by a perceived unholy alliance between the super-rich national minorities and the ruling class- political and the bureaucracy.

These characteristics explain the nature of the national polity and society. They also may likely be responsible for moulding the dynamics of the political process. Thus, in the context of the present electoral system based on constituency winner takes all system, the following dangers could be imminent given the present state of Tanzania:

a) victory in constituency election can be money driven. In other words, those who corrupt the electorate to get their candidates through would become the virtual constituency, not the people. As such, patronage of politics would in this case give birth to politics of patronage.

b) politics based on religion. Moslems voting Moslems and Christians voting Christians) may emerge and polarise society. The result would be patronage of politics on religious grounds thereby breeding politics of religious patronage.

c) subversion and vulgarisation of the democratic system can arise where issues of race, tribe or ethnicity take the centre stage instead of the people being afforded the right to exercise their vote freely.

d) the rich who wish to be elected can use their money to buy votes thus making democracy a tool for the rich to protect and promote their interests. Haiti fell to this system and, seemingly, paradoxical, capitalist America liberated the Haitian broad masses from the shackles of a subverted democracy.

e) demagogues who lack the leadership qualities to build a racially and ethnically homogeneous and tolerant society may rise to power with serious consequences to peace and harmony.

There is no doubt that the type of an electoral system, the process of achieving power that is adopted, can either aggravate the cracks and divisions that threaten to tear Tanzania apart, or can transcend them. Therefore, the historic mission and opportunity before the country and particularly before the present national leadership is to devise an electoral system that is appropriate to the prevailing troubling circumstances with the overarching objective being to regenerate national identity and solidarity while introducing real competitive politics.

Characteristics of a Proportional Representation System

Several characteristics lie at the heart of the system of proportional representation. I will only refer to a few key ones. First, a proportional representation system, such as the one that has been applied in the democratic elections in countries such as South Africa, Namibia,

Mozambique, and Lesotho, would mean that the distribution of seats in the National Assembly would correspond exactly with the proportional distribution of votes. We are all too familiar with the precipitating reason that propelled the Afro-Shirazi Party. ASP) in Zanzibar to stage a Revolution in 1964. It was because the elections, under the "winner takes all" electoral system, failed to reflect the distribution of popular votes, nation-wide, in determining the political party that won the elections and thus legitimately required to form the government. Whilst the ASP won fewer constituent seats, it won more popular votes. At the same time, we are also seized of the situation ruling under the one party or the British electoral system for that matter where a candidate loses a seat by a narrow margin, even of as few as ten votes. Clearly, in a nascent multiparty political system, it would not be advisable to disregard such narrow margins in arriving at parliamentary or local council representation. To do otherwise, would be equivalent to constructing a house on a weak foundation. It is the nation and not the contending political parties that would pay the price were the national political house to collapse. A democratic system should honour the broad popular will of the people by basing parliamentary representation on proportional distribution of popular votes.

How the proportional representation system itself should be structured would be a matter of detail to be worked out. The Nyalali Presidential Commission that recommended the reintroduction of the multi-party political system in 1992 had collected a great deal of information on the different types proportional representation system applied in different countries. The fact that it did not recommend the system when it submitted its Report, simply because it was an issue that was outside its terms of reference, should not block or delay creative instinct to examine its positive elements.

Voting for Parties, Not Candidates

Second, a proportional representation electoral system enables the electorate to vote for political parties as opposed to voting for individual party candidates. Each political party puts up a roll of candidates. However the candidates do not 'fight it out' at a constituency level as is the practice under the present Tanzania or British electoral system. Rather, the list of candidates is primarily used to enable voters to have a feel of the quality of candidates staged by the political parties for ultimate nomination into Parliament. In other words, the list is national, not constituency based. Such an electoral system goes a long way in ensuring that elections are focused more on policy issues and manifestos than on candidates. It is a system that would crucially de-tribalise elections and minimise religious and ethnic sentiments over electoral choices. Such an electoral change to a proportional representation system would be radical given the orthodox electoral political culture ingrained in the country. The electorate has been used to voting for candidates.

In a multiparty electoral system, it is not so much the candidate as what the policies of the party are that matters more. Therein lies the rub. The CCM has been in the forefront in pointing out that political parties should not use the argument of force but the force of argument in promoting themselves. In other words, the CCM has been urging that parties should prepare and pronounce their party policies that would constitute election manifestos. The logic here, in its ultimate conclusion, is that elections should be fought based on party policies, and not simply on candidates. Nyerere was truly right when he said, in the 1970s, that Members of Parliament were not strictly constituency MPs; they were, in every sense, national MPs. The constituency system merely enables an electoral process to take place. Indeed, in a developing economy that is poor in financial and human resources, the multi-party structure of Parliament would not necessarily change this reality about the national character of parliamentary representatives. MPs would remain *national* in their parliamentary roles. For this reason, it is the voting for parties with good policies and presenting a list of good potential candidates that would make greater sense.

Arresting Tribalism, Ethnicity and anti-Secularism

Third, a proportional representation electoral system is bound to reverse rather than sustain or even enhance tribalism, ethnicity and religion bias in the voting pattern. Earlier, I underscored the attributes and benefits of *Ujamaa*. Granted, under the one party political System constituency elections were fundamentally, with few exceptions, influenced by a tribal bias. This was not an electoral policy. Yet it turned into an unwitting convention. It was difficult for a person not belonging to the tribe in a given constituency to be elected as an MP. Some years ago in the Arusha urban parliamentary election, a local, Maasai candidate campaigned on the slogan that "*fimbo ya mbali haiui nyoka*". you cannot kill a snake with a stick from a distance). The opponent from the same party was an "immigrant" in Arusha, a "Mpare" by tribe, from the then Same District. In other words, he was not an indigenous Arushan. What happened was tribal warfare but the one party system insulated such negative consequences.

Contrast this situation with what has happened in the Kenya multi-party general elections. Since 1992, they have all been, through and through, tribal-based. In Malawi, an even worse result! These are guiding lessons. Tanzanians should not allow the multi-party system to be an unwitting recipe for tribalisation of its democracy or, indeed, of its development. Beyond tribalism, issues about ethnicity and religion have also recently entered Tanzanian politics. Azim Premji, the CCM Parliamentary by-election candidate for Kigoma did not have an easy victory in the first multi-party by-elections after 1992 simply because he was a Tanzanian of Asian origin. Equally, some local newspapers had castigated Rostam Sakkari,. now known as Rostam Aziz), the CCM candidate for the Igunga constituency by-election, as a *"Bulushi"*. a Baluchi) as if racial origin of a Tanzanian mattered in a multi-racial society. The election process in those instances was intended to "tribalise" choice of the MP. One may thus pose and question whether "indigenisation of politics" was emerging under the banner of multiparty politics? If so, it is a dangerous phenomenon and its solution partly lies in moving away from candidate-based elections to proportional representation where voting is base on competing political parties.

The religion issue is even more sensitive and potentially explosive. Some political pundits posit that Ibrahim Kaduma, for instance, may have lost the 1990 election in one of the Njombe constituencies because he was a Moslem while the majority of the electorate were Catholics. These are politics of disunity and of destabilisation. If Tanzania were not careful, its hard won unity and stability would be compromised on the tombstone of religious intolerance and differences. Tanzania should arrest such eventualities and one way to do so is to introduce a proportional electoral representation system.

The Danger of Money Buying Votes

The "winner takes all electoral system" under multi-partyism poses additional and serious dangers in the quest to promote ethical elections. There is no doubt that candidates with the financial means may use money to influence the electorate and even to out rightly buy votes, directly or indirectly. The electoral process within CCM in 2005 already indicates the emergence of such phenomenon. Evidently, it would be extremely difficult to legislate controls on the use of funds in the primaries and election campaigns as well as effectively administer such controls given the obtaining pervasiveness of poverty. Tanzania cannot allow the choice of its parliamentary or local government council representatives be based on financial ability to corrupt the electorate, wittingly or indirectly. Democracy would be a sham in such a situation.

In contrast, in a proportional representation electoral system, there are no constituency- based candidates. As such, the possibility of personal wealth being used to buy votes would not exist or would be minimised. Of course, rich candidates selected by various political parties to constitute the roll of candidates may, and probably would contribute significant sums of money to their parties to ensure electoral success. In such a system, it would be easier to legislate and control the use of funds beyond determined maxima in an election campaign than in the winner takes all system. Above all, it would be more difficult for a party to administer voter corruption as the electorate may not be as disposed to respond to incentives. *takrima,* in Kiswahili) as it would normally be in a candidate-based electoral system.

Securing Representatives of Talent and Experience

Fourth, I believe that the proportional electoral representation system, if well exploited by the political parties, should enable Parliament to get people of greater talent and experience. This would make Parliament a more effective instrument for enacting development-focused legislations and promoting measures that make the government better accountable to the people for its acts and omissions. The key question here is how the parties would democratically assemble the list of candidates or party rolls. This may not prove to be such a difficult task for the newer parties. For CCM, on the other hand, "vested interests" and loyalty developed over several decades. the *"mwenzetu"* syndrome) by existing parliamentarians and other CCM leaders may cloud the choice process. However, choice of candidates should not be a *national* electoral issue in the first instance. Each party should conceive its most appropriate methodology for getting the right kind of candidates capable of winning the confidence of the electorate.

Equally, under the proportional representation system it may be possible to have a more professional cabinet, a critical requirement for a government facing discontinuous change and challenges in a complex global economic environment. It is evident that the choice of cabinet ministers in Tanzania has invariably suffered from an acute shortage of able, and more importantly well exposed, individuals. This deficit has existed mainly because better people avoid getting into politics through the "front door", that is, by standing for elections. The risks of losing elections to lesser able but probably more popular or wealthy individuals has been the prime reason for this situation. Yet the country stands to gain by getting the *crème de la crème* into parliament and the cabinet through the "backdoor", if you like, where the proportional representation system is adopted.

More Effective Representation for Women and Youth

Fifth, the proportional representation system would make matters easier in selecting women and youth candidates to enter Parliament as these would be part of each Party's roll of candidates. What would be required is that a percentage of representation would have to be fixed for women and youth candidates. Indeed, the proportional representation system being introduced by the CCM government for the 2005 General Elections is more directed at bolstering the number of women representatives in Parliament to meet the SADC target of 30% rather than a wholesale promotion of the electoral system in the context of the need to deepen democratisation in Tanzania. Postponing the adoption of a more broad based proportional representation, at least to the extent of 50% of all the Parliamentary seats, merely reinforces the polarisation that the first past the post electoral system creates in society. As the values of democracy mature in Tanzania's rural settings where extreme poverty is pervasive, such polarisation may, in the end, breed social tension and even conflict.

In his discussions with the British Minister for International Development in London at the end of February 2004, President Mkapa showed a positive inclination towards the introduction of a proportional representation electoral system. What a huge legacy of democracy would he have left were such commitment turned into reality in the 2005 general elections. However, it would now appear, as alluded to above, that the system he had in mind was a highly limited one in scope.

Conclusion

Tanzanian unity is paramount; it should be sustained and reinforced. The British electoral system of "winner takes all" has serious shortcomings for a country, which, for thirty years, was under one party rule. In spite of thirteen years of a multi-party system, the majority of the rural population still identify the political leadership and national governance of Tanzania with the CCM. This is partly because the voice of the plurality of Tanzanians is not well provided for in the winner takes all electoral system. Moreover, most of the political parties formed since 1992 are yet to find their feet given their meagre resources, financial and human, to stage effective candidate-based national election campaigns as required under the winner takes all electoral system, much as weak leadership in these parties has evidently accentuated such weakness. CCM should neither be happy with such an environment nor should it seek to exploit the deficit. On the contrary, CCM has the responsibility to build a solid foundation for an effective multiparty democracy to thrive. To do otherwise would tantamount to dislodging the Tanzanian culture of comradeship and tolerance built since independence.

CCM should realise that it is presently in the driving seat and that the security and comfort of everybody in Tanzania ultimately depends on its stewardship. As such, it should kindle into flame the divine spark of creative power and strive to attain the central lofty goal of national human endeavour, namely the sustenance of a stable, peaceful and truly democratic Tanzania. To borrow the words of the leading American critic, Alvin Toffler, CCM should not close its mind prematurely to the novel, the surprising, and the seemingly radical. For, as he put it, "like the generation of the revolutionary dead", CCM has "a destiny to create".

Chapter

14 THE UNION QUESTION

Tanzania has shown over the last 40 years that Afican unity is feasible where there is political will. No one can dispute the political risk borne, and the political will shown, by the Founding Fathers of the Union in 1964, in the heat of the Cold War. Today, it is easier simply to maintain what they built. If we were half as courageous as they were, we could have taken our unity to an even higher level. The very least we can do is to keep the union going instead of magnifying the inevitable problems that can realistically be expected now and then. Political union is an ideal in its own right.

Benjamin W. Mkapa: Speech at the Climax of Celebrations Marking the 40th Anniversary of the Union, 26 April, 2004.

The Context

In July 1993, I had suggested, in an editorial in the magazine *Change*, which featured the theme: *Tanzania: Disintegration of the Union?* that the future of the Tanzania Union was on the rocks. I was concerned, at that material time, about the lack of an objective response on the part of the then one party state government to what, in my considered view, appeared to be the growing fragility of the Union that had been formed in 1964 between the then Tanganyika and the Zanzibar independent states. The fragility featured prominently in Parliamentary debates. propelled by the so-called Group of 55 Members of Parliament) and in the Nyalali Presidential Commission Report which, in 1992, recommended the reinstatement of multi-party democracy as well as the restructuring of the Union by creating a Federation.

Writing in the same issue of *Change Magazine*, as a rejoinder to Professor Haroub Othman's article entitled, *Tanzania: The Withering Away Of The Union?*, Mark Bomani observed, "it is totally unrealistic to expect the present arrangement to work any more. Conditions and perceptions have changed drastically. The spectre of the cold war is behind us. The romanticism of African Unity is no longer a guiding factor. The on-set of a multi-party state can no longer accommodate the hegemonic behaviour of the heady days of the one party state. The ostensible exploitation, for commercial purposes, of the present set-up has made many people so disillusioned that any attempt to maintain the *status quo* would not be credible." Bomani raised a number of issues requiring attention, which included the Union Vice President issue, which I address later and on which Bomani became involved in securing a "dispensation" as well as the sensitivity about realising equitable balance in the Union Parliamentary representation. However, the most interesting prophetic comment made by Mark Bomani at that time was, "at times, I have been apprehensive whether the vocal style of some of the national leaders reflects the kind of temperament and suavity critically needed to pilot the Union through the choppy seas ahead. But I could be wrong."

In the light of this situation, I had cited Hamlet's famous soliloquy at what appeared to me to reflect the government's frailty and indecisiveness at a critical moment when a new vision for the Union could be seized and articulated:

> *And thus the native hue of resolution*
> *Is sicklied o'er with the pale cast of thought;*
> *And enterprises of great pith and moment,*
> *With this regard, their currents awry;*
> *And lose the name of action.*

Yet, so much water has flowed under the bridge since July 1993. The deemed "evil pursuits" of the G. 55 were quashed, thanks to the interventionist powerful voice and the "magic stick" of the late Mwalimu Nyerere. The majority opinion of the Nyalali Commission that had recommended the introduction a new federal government to replace the union structure had in 1992 been summarily rejected. Later, early in 1995, as a decisive prelude to the Multiparty General Elections, after a breather of 30 years, Mwalimu Nyerere delivered a stinker about Tanzania's top political leadership with respect to the Union Question in a booklet titled *Uongozi Wetu na Hatima ya Tanzania*. Our Leadership and the Future of Tanzania). In that booklet not only did the wisdom of the Father of the Nation 'stabilise' the Union by making any discussion of the structure of the Union virtually sacrilegious, it also precipitated a historic 'purge' of some CCM veteran leaders from the ruling party's electoral process for the Party's Presidential candidature nomination that took place in the third quarter of 1995. The Prime Minister was forced to resign following the revelations in the book, the key admonition against him being his ostensible lack of a clear stand against the G.55. His Presidential ambitions were equally quashed. The CCM Secretary General, now deceased, equally lost his job along with a chance to become a Presidential candidate. The affected leaders were roundly condemned for having abdicated responsibility to put an effective stop to the "treasonable" pursuits of the G55!

Interestingly, the "pale cast of thought" over the Union Question, which was further weakened by Nyerere's views on the Union as encapsulated in the booklet referred above came under test in 1998. That test was reflected in the release of the *Government White Paper. Government Circular No.1 of 1998)* on 17th July, 1998. Among other constitutional issues, the *White Paper* re-introduced the Union Question by putting it on the centre stage of national political debate. It was a welcome democratic move. Welcome in the sense that the Union Question constitutes part of the Union Constitution and, *ipso facto*, if the Constitution itself is a subject of review, it logically follows that the Union should equally form part of the review. In fact, democratic values would demand that the *White Paper* should have called for peoples' views on the Union without the government itself having to advance its own position, *ex ante*, on the *White Paper* as was the case.

The Structure of the White Paper

At the outset, therefore, criticism should be levelled against the *White Paper* for not having created the environment under which free will and the desires of the majority of Tanzanians could have been expressed. The *White Paper* took a prejudicial and presumptuous position on several issues whose intention, ostensibly, was to influence and drum up the support of a population largely accustomed to giving ready credence to what the government enunciates. Evidently, guided democracy has its benefits but as long as it is objective. In other words, guidance should be informed guidance. It is important to underscore the imperativeness of enabling a society to generate a citizenry that is free from and democratically resists even moral coercion. In a truly plural society, the government should avoid viewing itself as the sole agent for promoting and being a custodian of a higher good. Indeed, what I have discerned to be a failing on the part of the Union Government, over the years, with regard to the debate or discussion about the Union is a paradoxical position of inflexibility. Discussion of the Union Question cannot and should not be a taboo.

Status quoism is never a virtue. In fact, in the modern world, such a stance is increasingly becoming a liability almost in all spheres of public life. This is not to say, of course, that any change should be embraced for its own sake. On the contrary, change has to reflect the genuine needs, wishes and desires of a people even where such change leads to what may be perceived to be perpetrating instability in the eyes of those who associate stability, necessarily, with the *status quo*. Such position contrasts with the positive manner in which a government flexibly approaches and decides matters of social and economic character. In this light, we are always enriched by the powerful wisdom of the late Alec Nove, who, in his powerful treatise: *The Economics of Feasible Socialism* attests to the logic of rational and purposeful change. He postulates: "Ideas evolve, ideas can be reinterpreted, elements of doctrine can be dropped, in response to circumstances, even while men seek to shape circumstances in the light of their ideas".

Thus generally and specifically, in the context of the Union Question, the *White Paper* failed, in my view, to rise beyond *status quoism*. It failed to come to terms with the concrete reality that however lofty an ideal, its ultimate litmus test is its being able to work and meet the desires and expectations of those it is supposed to serve. The burning question about any Constitution is not what is, but what it ought to be, constantly reflecting the concrete desires of the people. In this context, the central question to ask is: does the Union, in its present form and substance, satisfy the desires and expectations of the Zanzibaris and the Tanzanian Mainlanders? This is the material question that should have featured in the *White Paper*; not a discussion of the different forms of Union available around the world and the specific form that the government preferred. Such a discussion necessarily presumed that the problem with the Union, if at all, was based on the structure when, indeed, the problem could have been very different. As a result, the views that were made on the Union were constricted. They became largely confined to structure which is a highly volatile question and which the CCM government had already ruled upon, in 1992, in reply to the Nyalali Commission recommendation to transform the Union into a federation.

Zanzibar's Status in the Union

So what are the central issues that confront the Union today that demand an open, frank and free discussion to inform a new Union dispensation? First, is the question regarding Zanzibar's autonomy and its status in the Union. Is Zanzibar truly in the Union governance system today? This is a debatable question. The Vice President of the Union today hails from Zanzibar. However, it could be questioned if such status places on such high office any authority over Zanzibar except over matters that, constitutionally, are of a Union character. The President of Zanzibar, on the other hand, is not strictly part of the Union apart from enjoying a few Union protocol privileges on ceremonial occasions!

Consider the status of the Zanzibar President whenever he makes a visit to a foreign country. In accordance with the Union constitution, Tanzania and Zanzibar constitute a *"one sovereign republic"*. All matters relating to international relations thus fall within the jurisdiction of the Union Government. When the President of Zanzibar was the Union First or Second Vice-President, prior to the 1995 multi-party general elections, depending on whether the Union President was from the Mainland or from Zanzibar, respectively, he or she could travel abroad under the Union status. This cannot happen now. So how can he or she travel to the Comoros or South Africa as the President of Zanzibar and be accorded the status of a visiting head of "State" or even that of equivalent of Vice President or Prime Minister? As much as Zanzibar Presidents since 1995 have been able to make state visits abroad, the visits have not been viewed or regarded as state visits in strict diplomatic sense. Indeed, in several cases, receiving states have had to go out of their way to make special arrangements to accord the Zanzibar President ceremonial status. This should not be so. Since 1995, the Zanzibar President, as opposed to Zanzibar itself, paradoxically, is not part of the "one sovereign republic." It is a constitutional drawback.

Moreover, the whole idea about the Zanzibar President attending Union Cabinet meetings, ostensibly to provide a link, liaison and information as well as decision making participation appears, at best, ludicrous and, at worst, a vivid manifestation of Zanzibar's loss of legal autonomy and political identity within the Union. Clearly, such a system would not work where the Zanzibar President would originate from a party other than the one that has put the Union President into power. Constitutionally, this is a troublesome issue. Unfortunately, it is being treated as if election results would never bring the arrangement to a head and cause a crisis. Yet even soothsayers are never perfect in their predictions.

Consider another perspective. Zanzibar has exclusive powers and authority over what are described as *"non-Union matters,"* namely health, education, commerce and industry, tourism, agriculture, marketing, trade, works, good governance, lands, transport and communications, labour, sports, culture, youth, gender and community development, economic planning, and non-customs revenue. Yet, from a constitutional point of view, it has no authority on external relations that relate to these matters, except sports, and that is only since early 2004 when Zanzibar was finally allowed separate membership of **Africa Football Confederation.** AFC). Paradoxically, Zanzibar is yet to be allowed to be member of the International Football Federation. FIFA). All external relations are thus vested in the Union Government even where such relations relate to Zanzibar's *non-Union* matters. It could be asked, purely from a juridical angle, on what moral grounds Zanzibar should be constrained from having external relations where they relate to non-Union matters? Put differently: who is responsible for promoting Zanzibar's "Non-Union Matters" at regional and international bilateral and multilateral levels? To argue that all types of external relations fall under Union jurisdiction would appear to rid Zanzibar of its fundamental "constitutional rights" as embodied in the Articles of Union. On the other hand, to give Zanzibar external relations powers over its own internal matters may amount to eroding the sovereign character of the Union. What this issue and that of the status of the Zanzibar President in the Union present is a challenge of constitutional work in progress. But it should more seriously be embarked upon rather than allowing a state of constitutional *status quoism* to rule as reflected in the present situation.

In this light, the leaders and the people should ask whether Tanzania could seriously attest to a celebration of the present status of the Union. Is the Union constitution honoured to the letter? Put differently, is the Union Government strictly enforcing Zanzibar's respect of the Union Constitution? For, if all matters relating to external trade, foreign exchange. outflows and inflows and thus embracing foreign investment as well) and taxation on imports are Union matters, then why does Zanzibar have its own Investment Promotion Agency. ZIPA)? On what legal basis would Zanzibar also proceed to establish a free port without the Union Parliament sanctioning the move? Other questions of autonomy still loom large, as in what is regarded, probably unnecessarily, to be a sensitive subject, namely Zanzibar's wish to become member of the Organisation of Islamic Conference. OIC). Because of such lack of effective autonomy, how could it be inconceivable to conjecture that the Zanzibar economy is surrogate to the Mainland economy, the "Union economy"? On the other hand, is there anything like a "Union economy"? If yes, why do we often hear Mainlanders, politicians, bureaucrats and even citizens, point out that without the Union support, Zanzibar would not survive on its own? As if Zanzibar was not part of the Union! Those who promote such statements, often privately, hold that the solution to Zanzibar's economic woes is for her to reconcile itself to the reality of a monolithic State, namely acceptance of the formation of the Republic of Tanzania as opposed to the United Republic of Tanzania.

Union Financing Zanzibar's Social Sectors

A more sensitive matter about the Union centres on the continued strict interpretation of what matters are Union and what are within Zanzibar's autonomy. I may sound as contradicting myself in what I may postulate. However, time has come, in my view, for the Union Government to shoulder some of Zanzibar's non-Union financial commitments, notably those that fall within the objective of poverty reduction. I have in mind sectors such as primary and secondary education, health, water, rural roads and electrification. Knowing the base of the Zanzibar economy, I do not envision a day soon when Zanzibar could leapfrog economically as to be able to meet the budgetary requirements of some of the basic poverty reducing activities. It is in this context that I have argued a case for the Zanzibar Vision 2020 and the Tanzania Vision 2025 to be rationalised and enjoined particularly in those areas where policies and strategies of poverty reduction are concerned. The Union could suffer where Zanzibaris come to feel that Tanzanian Mainlanders are prospering and their qualities of lives are improving in contrast. certainly not at the expense of) to them. The Union should avoid a situation where a North and a South. rich and poor, relative as it may be) could manifest itself in the structure of the Union. The wisdom of the leadership in the Union Government and Zanzibar should come to terms with these realities and quickly work towards a different policy dispensation where Zanzibar's social sectors of the economy would be fully financed by the Union budget without the management of those sectors being brought under the domain of the Union.

Constitutional Realities Should Rule

In sum, what Tanzania has in place today is more of a *political* dispensation governing specific Union interests rather than a dispensation informed by an ideal framework that guarantees Zanzibar real autonomy and which grants the Zanzibar Presidency the status it deserves within the Union. Tanzanians should stop being overly simplistic about this matter. The umbilical cord that underpinned the 1964 Articles of Union has been weakened by the current constitutional dispensation. The *White Paper* was silent over this situation. The central issue that the government is somehow avoiding coming to terms with is that the entry of multiparty politics has radically changed the ideal preconditions of a two-government system as envisioned under a one party state. If the two-government structure is to be sustained and there are valid reasons for it, then it has to respond to new constitutional realities imposed by the multi-party structure. This is not the case presently.

Tanzania is a single sovereign republic with two governments. However, one of the governments is not as effectively part of the sovereign republic as it should be. Zanzibar should evidently be finding it more and more difficult to operate within the confines of the Union Constitution. This is a reality and it serves no useful purpose trying to shy away from it or to pretend that no problems exist. The reality is that the original character of the Union, as conceived by its Founding Fathers, is no longer in place. What has replaced it, in order to accommodate a multi-party democratic system, is problematic. The *White Paper* neither recognised nor presented this fact and of the need to revisit the Union's legal and constitutional framework.

Thus, Tanzanians should continue to discuss the state of their Union. An honest and dispassionate discussion is imperative if the Union is to meet the expectations and desires of the Tanzanian people. The Kisanga Committee had offered a unique opportunity for such a discussion to take place. But was the opportunity seized or was it squandered? I examine this question next.

The Kisanga Report: A New Democratic Epoch?

To many Tanzanians who had attached significant importance to the work of the Kisanga Committee, a foreboding mood of anxiety loomed large early in 1999 as they awaited the submission of the *Committee's Report* to President Mkapa. A decisive moment had arrived. The British novelist, Graham Greene, once wrote, "There always comes a moment in time when a door opens and lets the future in". Did the *Kisanga Report* open the door and allow the future in? Did it respond to national expectations for a higher level of democratisation and the unleashing of other equally important political dispensations upon which Tanzania's unity, peace and stability hinge upon?

Evidently, democratisation is a process; it is never an episodic event. Thus, the *Kisanga Report* cannot be fairly judged if its recommendations would be viewed from a narrow sense, that of episodic characterisation. Indeed, in this context, the Nyalali Commission Report itself could best be viewed as having only set the stage for a process of democratisation and political pluralism to commence. The maturity of Tanzanian democracy can only realistically be achieved over time, as Tanzanians acquire greater political maturity. As Toynbee wrote in *A Study of History*, "the divine spark of creative power is instinct in ourselves, and if we have the grace to kindle it into flame, then the stars in their courses cannot defeat our efforts to attain the goal of human endeavours". Tanzanians continue to face the challenge of ingraining the "instinct" that is crucial for the attainment of a greater goal of democratisation. Such a challenge would equally be responded to over time.

Did the *Kisanga Report* Deepen Democratisation?

Ever since the *Nyalali Report* ushered in multiparty politics, Tanzania has walked the democratisation high road in such a manner that the spark of creative power has slowly but surely been lighting. With each mile covered, so has the instinct that aspires for a higher form of democratisation been kindled into flame. There is now an even greater appetite for political change, an appetite that realises that whilst the *Nyalali Report* had been ground breaking, the *Kisanga Report* should have built upon its success and shortcomings. In several respects, the mere promulgation of the *Constitutional White Paper*, the recriminations surrounding its form and substance notwithstanding, was a clear and positive testimony of the national urge to move beyond the *Nyalali Report*. It is important to recognise this fact and to salute the boldness and the courage of the national political leadership in realising and affirming that there is a lofty democratisation vision that Tanzania should grapple with and work to attain.

The large question, of course, is, did the *Kisanga Report* move Tanzania forward on the high road towards such political vision? The fact that the *White Paper* raised some fundamental issues that related to the state of Tanzania's political pluralism, democratic structures and the Union Question, amongst others, is a sufficient pointer to a political situation that could have been unsatisfactory and which should, therefore, have been addressed or clarified. Indeed, prior to the appointment of the Kisanga Committee, debates had taken place within the civil society and the political parties about many of the issues that formed part of the terms of reference of the Kisanga Committee. In this context, the expectations from the Kisanga Committee were, inevitably, more sensitive than those that had been expected from the Nyalali Commission. With the role of the Nyalali Commission, there was the almost obvious expectation, indeed, the wish, that Tanzania had to move into a multiparty political system. After all, Mwalimu Nyerere had already uttered, as early as end 1989 that multipartyism was an idea whose time had come. Thus, even if there had been any serious opposition to multipartyism before Mwalimu voiced his opinion, the opposition for change had retreated and vanished.

With respect to the role of the Kisanga Committee, on the other hand, the situation was dramatically different. The issues before it were perceptively more complex and more politically daunting. They were issues that demanded a higher level of independence and a greater dispassionate mindset on those charged with the onerous task to elicit people's views and to make recommendations. There was also the challenge to make history as well as transform legacies. In this light, the distinguished British historian, AJP Taylor wrote in his book, *The Origins of the Second World War* that "historians often dislike what happened or wish that it had happened differently. There is nothing they can do about it. They have to state the truth as they see it without worrying whether this shocks or confirms existing prejudices". The Kisanga Committee was expected to have heeded such wise words. Judge Kisanga and his team did not need to be historians. However, it was hoped that their work would not have been unduly influenced by the conventional thinking of historians and, more in line with the late Professor Taylor's advice, would have stated the truth without worrying whether their Report's recommendations "would shock or confirm existing prejudices".

Kisanga Report and the Union Question

One of the more difficult issues that the Kisanga Committee was to address was the present structure of the Tanzania Union. How the Committee approached the views of the people on such a controversial subject and the position it would have taken on it would probably have constituted the most important part of the *Kisanga Report* considering that the recommendations of the Nyalali Commission had been turned down in 1992. In addition, to say so is not necessary to infer that the central issue about the Union is the structure, namely a Union or Federation. However, from 1992 and especially after the 1995 general elections, the political environment surrounding the Union has become more sensitive particularly in the context of the status of the Zanzibar Presidency in the Union. As it is, the Kisanga Committee was constituted at a time when Tanzania had already experienced the emergence of the G. 55 of Parliamentarians who had clamoured for the formation of a federation, a move that Nyerere demolished.

The Kisanga Committee was also formed after Zanzibar had attempted to join the Organisation of Islamic Conference. OIC), ostensibly unilaterally and contrary to the Union Constitution. Zanzibar was equally admonished by Nyerere for its action and was forced to quit the OIC. In his booklet, *Uongozi Wetu na Hatima ya Tanzania*, Nyerere made reference to the mooted amendment of the Union Constitution as Tanzania moved towards the 1995 General Elections. How to fit the structure of the Union in a new democratic dispensation was a critical aspect of the amendment. The Nyalali Commission had already pondered over the issue and had failed to resolve it within a two-government system. This time around President Mwinyi had constituted a Committee under the Chair of Judge Mark Bomani specifically to recommend how the Zanzibar Presidency would feature in the Union. Mark Bomani's report recommended the creation of a post of Union Vice-President who would feature in the electoral process as a running mate of the Union Presidential candidate. The running mate would be from Zanzibar if the Presidential candidate was from the Mainland and vice versa. However, as for the status of the Zanzibar President, the report proposed the formation of a State Council that would comprise the Union President, the Union Vice President, the Prime Minister and the Zanzibar President. The Mwinyi Government adopted Mark Bomani's recommendations except the one on the introduction of the state Council. In its place, and irrespective of his or her political affiliation, the Union Government resolved that the Zanzibar President would be invited to sit in the Union Cabinet and would have to be sworn-in by the Union President to be able to sit in the Union Cabinet.

The Bomani recommendation suited Nyerere partly because it meant that his legacy of the two- Union Government system would remain sacrosanct. Thus his above referred to booklet rallied support behind Mark Bomani's constitutional proposal to introduce a Vice Presidential candidate of the US variety. That is what Tanzania has in place to day. However, even Mr. Bomani now admits, in retrospect, that his Committee's advice did not respond adequately to the political complexity of the Union dynamic within the period they had at their disposal in putting forward their recommendations. It is easy to see why. The recommendation has created an apparent bad taste in Zanzibar in that the Zanzibar President has been left out from playing a constitutional role in the Union, as clearly envisioned in the Articles of Union of 1964. As a result, intellectual Zanzibaris, like Professor Abdul Sheriff, have openly declared, "the Zanzibar President has been illegally deprived of his constitutional right to be a Vice President of Tanzania, contrary to the agreement that led to the formation of the Union". The Kisanga Committee did not address this question directly, presumably because their core recommendation was in line with that of the Nyalali Commission, namely that Tanzania should consider adopting a federal system of government.

The Kisanga Report and the Electoral System

The second critical issue that the Kisanga Committee could have addressed was the electoral system. It did not. Clearly, Tanzania cannot afford an expensive electoral system of by-elections. This is now evident to everybody. More importantly, Tanzania has to improve and consolidate its democratic electoral process. It could do so by adopting an electoral system that would determine the composition of its elected Parliament in terms of the actual distribution of popular votes. As a start, the system could be divided 50-50 between the present winner-takes-all and the proportional representation system. I have already addressed the unnecessity of having special seats for women. This aspect has been addressed by the 14th Constitutional Amendment. Moreover, there could also be an added advantage in adopting the proportional representation system, namely, that it would not be necessary for the President to nominate ten persons that he or she deems suitable to be Members of Parliament. Further, the present constitutional limitation that the Prime Minister should be chosen only from among the directly elected Members of Parliament would also become irrelevant since every MP would be treated as having been directly elected even if the electoral system is half winner past the post and half proportional representation.

The Kisanga Committee could also have addressed other important constitutional issues. These include a better-clarified system of separation of powers, the independence and membership of the Electoral Commission and the fundamental human right of allowing independent candidates to stand for parliamentary and local authority seats under the current electoral system. However, I believe that such a right should not be extended to presidential elections. There are clear reasons to back this position, including and importantly, the corruption it may embody, with rich individuals attempting to take undue advantage in a poor country where voters could easily be bought. It is noteworthy that the question about allowing independent candidates to stand for constitutional electoral seats arose in Parliament during the debate of the 14th Constitutional Amendment Bill in February 2005. What is curious about the sudden positive stance of MPs, especially those from the ruling party, CCM, in favour of allowing independent candidates to stand, is the timing. It would be recalled that Mwalimu Nyerere had supported this idea back in early 1995 following the famous High Court of Tanzania decision of the late Justice Kahwa Lugakingira, in the Reverend Mtikila case, which held that the constitution did not debar independent candidates from standing for elections to all positions in the land. The government had then proceeded to change the constitution to tighten the section that had provided the loophole leading to the position taken by Lugakingira. However, since 1995 and in spite of a passionate demand for amendment of the constitution to allow private candidates to stand, MPs have never taken interest in the matter. So why now? In my view, it would seem that within the CCM there is increasing concern and worry that the chances of some MPs being nominated by their party to stand in future elections is becoming delicate and uncertain. The reason is evident. In recent years, especially since 2000, several MPs from CCM have turned into "rebels". In other words, they have not been supportive of some of their own government's policies and programmes tabled in the House. They are now worried of what they deem as "victimisation" when it comes to the stage of the party deciding who should be nominated to stand as a CCM candidate in parliamentary constituencies. In clamouring for the allowing private candidates, they are, in effect, seeking to create "safety valves" for themselves. Indeed, in this context, it makes sense that MPs from CCM have shown little interest about the proportional representation system. How could they, when such system would make the requirement of independent candidates as well as constituency-based MPs irrelevant?

Finally, there was the question about who should have decided whether and, in some cases, to what extent, the recommendations of the Kisanga Committee should have been adopted and effected? This is a critical question for a democracy. There was a foul rumour, for example, that some CCM Members of Parliament had not been positively inclined to vote for a constitutional amendment that would have enabled the President to nominate ten people as MPs apparently because many of those MPs had previously gone on to become Cabinet Ministers. Surely, such a step would have been treacherous. Fortunately, it did not take place and the constitution was successfully amended to allow the President to nominate ten MPs who, coincidentally, have not necessarily become ministers.

The fundamental point about how Judge Kisanga Committee's recommendations should have been dealt with centres on the problem of defining the scope and powers of elected "representatives" over matters that enjoy popular will. It would be dangerous to democracy, in my view, were the will and wishes of the people, as embodied in a Public Commission of Enquiry Report, to be manipulated, disregarded or overridden using the very representative democratic system as a crutch. In fact, such a situation would clearly vindicate the importance and imperativeness of introducing a system of referenda. Charles Handy, in his book, *The Hungry Spirit* has aptly posited, in this context, "referenda make the symbolic point that some decisions are too important to be left to politicians, and that the people can be trusted to be responsible for their own future as a society". So what does this situation portend? Can we conjecture that Tanzania is facing a crisis in its multiparty system? What are the challenges that confront Tanzania in the desire to deepen democratisation? I address these questions in the ensuing chapter.

Chapter

15 THE CHALLENGES OF MULTI-PARTY DEMOCRACY

The general enhancement of political and civil freedoms is central to the process of development itself. The relevant freedoms include the liberty of acting as citizens who matter and whose voices count, rather than living as well-fed, well-clothed, and well-entertained vassals.

Amartya Sen: **Development As Freedom.**

M ore than a decade has passed since the respected Nyalali Commission boldly recommended the re-introduction of a multiparty democracy Tanzania. It could be argued that ten years experience of political pluralism is probably too brief to justify and attract a reasonably objective assessment of the new system, particularly so when one considers that the re-entry of a multiparty system in 1992 was preceded by a near three decades of a deeply rooted and ingrained culture of a monolithic political system. Indeed, it could further be argued that such assessment could suffer from the very fact that the one party political system had been powered by charismatic and ardently people-loved leaders, namely Mwalimu Nyerere and, for sometime, until his premature death, Sheikh Abeid Amani Karume. This is a context that presumably should not escape Tanzanians if they are to undertake a serious and objective assessment of the state of the current democratic system.

"Coca Cola" Democracy

Indeed, after the experience of the past two General Elections, there could be no conceivable reason why Tanzanians should not critically take stock of the state of health and condition of their nascent democracy. This, in spite of being reminded that democracy, to borrow the words of a European academic, Yes Meny, is "a long path, a fight on all fronts, a continuous adjustment to new aspirations". This is quite pertinent. Indeed, as the late Mwalimu Nyerere said in response to a question about what he thought of the wild west wind of change that was spreading democracy in Africa in the early 1990s, democracy could not be equated to the marketing of Coca Cola. If it were, it would almost certainly be "Coca

Cola" democracy, devoid of local roots and values. In an interview printed in the *International Herald Tribune* of 13 January 2004, John le Carre, the famous British novelist of spy books, notably the 1963 famous novel *The Spy Who came in from the Cold*, is quoted saying aptly that there was now "a virtual crusade in which we. the western world,) are exporting democracy by military means" These views coincide, in many respects, with a Report written under the auspices of The German Marshall Fund of the United States and the Turkish Economic and Social Studies Foundation, under the title: *Democracy and Human Development in the Broader Middle East: A Transatlantic Strategy for Partnership. Istanbul Paper # 1, June 25-27, 2004).* That Report notes "Democratisation and human development in the region. the broader Middle East) must spring from indigenous roots. Western democracies should not seek to impose any formula for democratic change. But they can and must help from the outside-morally, politically, and, materially." Elsewhere in the Report, it is observed, "the impetus for change in the broader Middle East must come from within societies in the region. The West cannot export democracy as such."

There is a huge debate, rife in the Arab world today, about democratisation. It is particularly being tooted following the overthrow of Sadaam Hussein in Iraq. Fareed Zakaria, in a brilliant article, *Islam, Democracy, and Constitutional Liberalism*, points out that "the Arab world today is trapped between autocratic states and illiberal societies, neither of them fertile ground for liberal democracy. The dangerous dynamic between these two forces has produced a political climate filled with religious extremism and violence." He continues to observe, "The task of reform in the Middle East must fall to the peoples of the region. No one can make democracy, liberalism, or secularism take root in these societies without their own search, efforts, and achievements". An even more scathing attack in this direction has recently come from the distinguished University of London Emeritus Professor, Eric J. Hobsbawm. In an article in the *US Foreign Policy Journal* of September/October, 2004 titled, *Spreading Democracy*, Hobsbawm notes: "We are at present engaged in what purports to be a planned reordering of the world by the powerful states. The wars in Iraq and Afghanistan are but one part of a supposedly universal effort to create world order by "spreading democracy". This idea is not merely quixotic-it is dangerous. The rhetoric surrounding this crusade implies the system is applicable in a standardised. western) form, that it can succeed everywhere, that it can remedy today's transnational dilemmas, and that it can bring peace, rather than sow disorder. It cannot."

So important and controversial is the debate that CNN put it at a global centre stage. In a special *CNN Programme* cast on 21 June 2004 and moderated by Jim Clancy, involving leading Media Executives from the

Arab world, there was a chilling consensus that the US "crusade" to impose. even if by military means) democracy in the Middle East and the greater Arab region would fail and that the experiment undertaken in Iraq would, in fact, show the way to such failure. The CNN Programmes that followed on 24 and 25 June and moderated by Richard Quest and Jonathan Mann respectively, under the themes, *The European Pulse* and *The American Pulse,* equally brought out similar fears about the potential for realising a stable and democratic Iraq from the approach which the US administration had implanted. One of the panellists, a leading German journalist, Joffe, even cited the goals of the insurgency led by the terrorist leader, Abu Mussa El Zaqawi in reflecting his worries, pointing out that real democratisation of Iraq would probably crucially hinge on the total withdrawal of US and Allied military forces from and the end of the occupation of Iraq.

Catalysing Democracy in Tanzania

In the case of Tanzania, positive transformations have taken place recently. In the last decade there has been a monumental drive for change. It is change that has spawned the complete ideological map, of politics and economics. However, having said that, it is also worth noting that Tanzania remains in the throes of creating a new political and economic order; a regime that would adequately respond to and satisfy the needs and aspirations of all the people in a fast globalising environment driven by the knowledge economy. In this context, Tanzania faces stupendous tasks and challenges. Universities and the national intelligentsia evidently have a leading duty to seize the moment. It is to them, largely, that the bell specifically tolls. For as the respected Indian social scientist Rajni Kothari surmised, it is the intellectuals who should "catalyse the myriad strands in national consciousness". In this respect, symposia and other forms of dialogue can help to open up valuable spaces for a process of "catalyisation" to take effect. As the Nobel Laureate Amaryta Sen cogently argued in his book *Development as Freedom,* public debates and dialogues are not only one of the correlates of democracy. Where cultivated, they also "make democracy itself function better".

In advancing the case for debates and discussions in reinforcing democratisation, Professor Sen postulates that "in a democracy, people tend to get what they demand, and more crucially, do not typically get what they do not demand". A nation needs to allow free conversation to take place in society if democracy is to take root. Those who condemn the emergence of seminars, workshops and symposiums on national issues miss the point. Yes, there are promoters of such dialogues that seek avenues for making money for themselves. However, generally, such dialogues and debates are the fountains for promoting a democratic culture. What is of particular significance to note is that, even in the heydays of the one party state, the late Mwalimu Nyerere was very clear about the critical role of the Tanzanian University and of intellectuals generally in the society. He saw the University as an important platform of resistance to orthodoxy and dogma to what was generally taking place in the national body politic. Speaking on *Relevance and Dar es Salaam University*, in August 1970, Mwalimu Nyerere argued that the University could only be able to serve the national purpose if its staff and students were allowed, "to think and speak their thoughts freely". It is what Michel Foucault describes in his article *The Concern for Truth,* as the role "to question over and over again what is postulated as self-evident, to disturb people's mental habits, as the way they do and think things, to dissipate what is familiar and accepted, to re-examine rules and institutions." It is through such processes that Tanzania can deepen democratisation.

Democratic Competitiveness and Spaces

The very essence of democracy is its competitive character. No person, irrespective of status, could justifiably claim to enjoy a monopoly of knowledge or power. It follows therefore, that competition between ideas, undertaken in the public domain, is healthy and nourishes democracy. In the words of the Fourth President of the United States, James Madison, "it is such competition between ideas that enables the society to move towards better rather than worse outcomes." This democratic spirit is captured in the Report of the South Commission *The Challenge to the South*. In that report, which derived historic and able leadership of Mwalimu Nyerere, it is observed that what critically undergirds democracy is wider participation by a people in the political process beyond the traditional opportunity to exercise the vote. The idea of freely allowing all ideas to contend is a powerful one. It is powerful because it calls for a new breed of politics, a politics that opens up broad spaces of political engagement. For how could the hope to "democratise our democracy," to borrow Professor Anthony Gidden's phrase, if, as nationals, across the spectrum of status and roles, the idea of a non-political party process in national governance is shunned?

It is evident that not all Tanzanians affiliate to political parties. Should they, in that light, be restricted from exercising their citizen rights and responsibilities? A good democratic environment should recognise and accept the objective reality of the existence of dual spaces of political participation in a body politic. One space is essentially driven by constitutional elections and legislative politics. The other, however, is driven by civil society and what are now generally called social movements. Civil society encompasses groups embracing the media, women, peasants, environmentalists, human and civil rights, activists, educational institutions, business associations and religious institutions. The role of this non-party group is essentially to deepen the democratic process through consciousness mobilisation, sensitisation, promoting alternative social and economic development strategies and, to use Francis Fukuyama's words, to act as an instrument "by which people are socialised into their culture". In his book *TRUST: The Social Virtues and The Creation of Prosperity*, Fukuyama postulates that a "thriving civil society depends on a people's habits, customs and ethics - attributes that can be nourished indirectly through conscious political action and must otherwise be nourished through an increased awareness and respect for culture".

It is this role of civil society that generates within the society informed public choices. At the same time, however, it is important to note that civil society could not offer a substitute for democratic government. An assemblage of diverse interest groups could not govern any nation. Yet, an open government stands to benefit much from civil society. For this reason, governments have the responsibility to contribute directly in building the capacities of civil society while, necessarily, maintaining its boundaries from it. Needless to state, freedom exercised through broad-based people participation in the political process, carries with it responsibilities that fall within constitutional demands. This is why instruments of the state exist. These instruments of law enforcement and adjudication are there to promote and safeguard the very rights of the citizens the Constitution provides. However, to what extent and how the Constitutional framework in place satisfies the aspirations for an effective and constant interaction between the state and the people, on the one hand, and promotes and safeguards the people's freedoms and needs, on the other hand, could be a matter for serious and contentious debate.

Political Leadership and Civil Society

I believe that it was Edmund Burke who, in this particular context, insisted that neither a democratic majority nor the best of constitutions was any guarantee of rights or liberties. It would thus be sheer dogmatism to believe that Tanzania has attained an ideal system of democratic effectiveness. There could be no such ideal. In fact, we are in agreement with the celebrated English philosopher, Isaiah Berlin, who, in his monumental treatise, *The Proper Study of Mankind*, perceptively observed: "Happy are those who have, by their own methods, arrived at clear and unshakeable convictions about what to do and what to be that brook no possible doubt. I can only say that those who rest on such comfortable beds of dogma are victims of forms of self-indulged myopia, blinkers that may make for contentment, but not for understanding of what it is to be human".

It is evident that the Constitution and its strategic organs as well as the whole idea of the separation of powers, should importantly inform and respond to developments and changes in the social milieu. Of course, we should guard against an idealistic view of that form of democracy whose vision is the self-organising society. Such a vision is a nirvana beyond reach on earth. Well functioning democratic societies have to have leaders who stand above and beyond the people who elect them. Hierarchy and authority remain imperative in a democratic system. What is invariably problematic is when leaders do not embody widely shared values and virtues are elected leaders. Such leaders are not driven by a sense of duty, a national calling. Tanzania should always aspire to have leaders, to borrow an analogy from Shakespeare's Measure for Measure, who, even when they "have a giant's strength" are not "tyrannous" in the way they utilise that strength and do not lead through brute power.

Democracy in Tanzania should demand that the government, the civil society and non-governmental organisations rise in unison to the onerous challenge to make Tanzanians more tolerant, responsible and understanding. These critical mentalities should be built through open dialogue. If they were not, politics and democracy would atrophy into mutual distrust. In addition, it should be underscored that trust lies at the heart of good politics. As Francis Fukuyama has observed, "a nation's well being as well as its ability to compete is conditioned by a single, pervasive cultural characteristic: the level of trust inherent in the society". The core values of the legacy of our founding fathers are trust, peace, goodwill and unity. These would inevitably be affronted if, as a nation, Tanzania sacrifices the opportunity to regenerate and consolidate trust as a way of life. It is thus incumbent upon all Tanzanians in different occupations to engender trust.

Democracy and Tolerance

For several years, since the on-set of multiparty politics in 1992, Zanzibar has learnt the bitter way on this question of tolerance and trust. Zanzibar now knows that an organic society, predominantly Muslim yet secular, divided geographically between Pemba and Unguja Islands, yet one in history and in culture, can achieve political reconciliation, "Muafaka". Such reconciliation could moreover be achieved not by suppressing or shunning differences, but rather by acknowledging them. We constantly learn from political sociologists that democratic societies learn through their conflicts how to negotiate, empathise and better resolve conflicts. Zanzibar has learnt that a culture of dialogue, driven by trust, is what underpins and nourishes its democracy as well as that of Tanzania overall. Thus, Tanzanians should be optimistic about the future of a peaceful and democratic Zanzibar. I believe that Zanzibar would confidently rise to an enviable unity from its newly discovered culture of dialogue, tolerance and mutual trust. The challenge is to deepen this culture across the whole Tanzanian nation.

231

The Fragilities in a Democracy

Whenever the state of multiparty politics in Tanzania is discussed, Tanzanians should not be oblivious of their past. Success stories of yesteryears stare them in the face as they begin to see some cracks develop in what was a solid national social foundation that the founding fathers bequeathed to us. Mwalimu Nyerere and Sheikh Karume played a major role in mobilising Tanzanians and used powerful metaphors and symbols to galvanise and unify them. They succeeded to develop a Tanzanian psyche that was immune to the divides that today consume and destroy other societies in Africa. For a long time, Tanzania prided itself of overcoming racial, tribal, wealth and religion divides. Can it still stand tall today with similar pride? It is a troubling question.

In this context, what strikes and often troubles the mind of many a Tanzanian is whether the spirit of nationalism that Tanzania was able to inculcate and imbibe over many years was an attribute of the political oligarchy system, the one party system, and of socialism? Otherwise, why is Tanzania experiencing cracks in its social fabric? This question is not posed to belittle the envious peace and stability Tanzania enjoys and which may still be the rare in Africa. However, should Tanzanians lie back and take it that all is well and would continue to be so? Tanzanians would not be able to commit with certainty that the degree of the present national cohesion and strength and distinctiveness, as a social and political polity, reflect the conditions they enjoyed in the 1970's or the early 1980's. In fact, only recently, in 2002, President Mkapa took up this issue during the Mwalimu Nyerere Memorial event in Bagamoyo. In his speech, he referred to the regrettable resurgence in tribal affiliations, to the growth of regional and supra-regional identities, driven by political interests; to the re-birth of racial identities; to the emergence of obscure negative sensitivities to foreign investments and to the rise in religious bigotry.

The religion question is a particularly worrying one. For example, it was puzzling that the decision to locate the office of the Mufti, the spiritual leader of Moslems of Zanzibar, sometime in 2001, under the Ministry of Justice and Constitutional Affairs that happened to be headed, at the time, by a Christian cabinet minister, should have turned offensive to some Zanzibaris, notably, the Imams. Yet Zanzibar is and remains a constitutional secular state. Moreover, the President of the United Republic is a Catholic! More recently, in December 2004, some Moslem leaders in Zanzibar even called upon the Revolutionary Government of Zanzibar to amend the Constitution and turn Zanzibar into an Islamic state. Such religious stirrings may reflect changed circumstances, the emergence, if you like, of what Harvard's Samuel Huntington (1996) has described as "clash of civilisations". Moreover, after the tragic events of 11th September, 2001 in the United States, the emergence of such passions in Zanzibar could point to a dangerous development. It is critical, therefore, that Tanzanians ask: what are the circumstances that spur and ignite such negative religious passions and why? Is the ideology of Tanzanian nationalism upon which a strong pluralistic democracy could only be built now falling prey to an encroaching globalisation political culture that is probably incongruent with Tanzanian culture? After all, political pundits such as James Dale Davidson and William Rees-Mogg have cautioned in their book, *The Great Reckoning: How the World Will Change Before the Year 2000:* now that megapolitical conditions have changed in a way that undermines social order and weakens economies, an upsurge of religious fundamentalism is the natural consequence, especially in less wealthy societies." They go on further to state that as economies decline, less religious tolerance takes over as religion passion rises in meeting common concerns. This is most troubling. It certainly calls for a dispassionate soul search about democracy and its legitimacy in Tanzanian-type societies.

After all, democracy is fundamentally about the livelihood of the people. Where the people are poor and lack hope, they inevitably lose the sense and meaning of politics. Somebody once said that hunger was rage in the belly. This is probably correct. Tanzanians could easily resort to uncivil behaviour where they felt that democracy did not satisfy their fundamental human needs for an improved quality of life. Therefore, democracy should not only infer freedom in all its dimensions but should also and, importantly so, create and sustain equitable development and deliver the quality livelihood the people expect.

Mwalimu Nyerere had opted for the one party state because he genuinely and passionately believed that political pluralism in a poor country would militate against the very policies whose direction was to spearhead fast and improved development. Evidently, Tanzania could not return to the one party state system. However, the challenge is to conceive the wherewithal whereby a plural poor society can make a system of multiparty democracy take bold steps and measures to bolster the living standards of the people. Democracy as development should be the mantra of the day, the national slogan to galvanise Tanzanians to work harder and more intelligently to usher in a nation of opportunity, of hope, peace and prosperity.

Conclusion

I believe that the Tanzanian leadership does not suffer from any form of mental orthodoxy as to fail to respond firmly and positively to the realities that confront Tanzanians. We live after all in a complex and dynamic world. Therefore, the leadership has to be open to new ideas and to new thinking. Nothing is sacrosanct anymore. It is important to note, though, that democracy thrives where there is good governance. Without good governance, from its broad perspective, democracy, in the sense of political, social and economic pluralism, gets undermined. Moreover, whilst institutions of governance occupy a central position in ensuring good governance, history has shown that without good leadership, institutions become surrogate and even relegated to play second fiddle. It is thus imperative, especially during the period of political and economic transition, that good leadership, along with good governance, is ensured and sustained. I examine the leadership and governance challenge in the next section.

Chapter

16 THE LEADERSHIP AND GOVERNANCE CHALLENGE

—the decline in the quality of leadership is, in some respects, illusory—because the world fifty years ago was profoundly different from the world today. Then the great challenges could be clearly defined, and our best responses could be clearly articulated, within ideologies that were rooted in our cultures. Now, the challenges before us seem fuzzy and impossibly entangled with long-term, deep, and barely understood social, economic, and ecological processes. Effective responses cannot be simple and ideologically satisfying; they must instead be as complex as the problems they address, malleable in the face of rapid change, and ambiguous enough to permit multiple interpretations by the constituencies they are supposed to satisfy. No wonder our leaders seem inadequate.

-Thomas Homer-Dixon: *The Ingenuity Gap: How Can We Solve the Problems of the Future?*

Introduction

Professor Homer-Dixon (2001) raises a fundamental point about the state of leadership in a world that has become more complex since the emergence of the cold war at the end of the Second World War. In the last two decades, in particular, new global challenges, political, social, economic and environmental, have emerged and intensified. These challenges are largely driven by new democratic values based on neo-liberalism, by market fundamentalism, globalisation of finance and trade and the threat of terrorism. Under these new conditions and circumstances, the leadership question is once again in the ascendancy. In this chapter, I examines how leadership has become a major and critical factor in Tanzania's political and economic management and development. At the outset, I interrogate who should lead Tanzania. This question is deliberately posed as there are key lessons to be drawn from an examination of why the management of economic reforms that started in earnest in July 1986 faltered between 1990 and 1995, on the one hand, and why, on the other hand, the reforms have taken a more robust and bullish trend since 1997. These lessons point to what constitutes good leadership, especially in the context of the Presidency and what constitutes good governance.

I agree with Homer-Dixon that the paucity of leadership perpetuating the problems we face may seldom be the basis for the problems. The causes could often be located in the "scale, interdependence and perceived uncontrollability of modern economic and political life." Yet I still hold the view, based on the broader African experience, that leadership shares a large blame. The late Mwalimu Julius Nyerere's leadership legacy provides an interesting case for close examination as we debate the challenges of leadership in countries such as Tanzania. In this context, I begin by examining what I view as the characteristics that crucially underpin who should lead Tanzania. A brief but important historical context focussing on these characteristics would set the stage for discussing more extensively what constitutes the key attributes of a Tanzanian leader at the top.

The Context

Tanzania has achieved dramatic achievements in the management of the economy since 1997. As outlined in the overview at the beginning of this book, macro-economic performance has been admirable. Yet, it is important to observe that economic analyses of Tanzania's state of health before the change in the top leadership in late 1995 took place had shown that the country's economic performance had reversed dramatically. The notable gains initially achieved as a result of the economic reforms implemented between 1986 and then, as part of the structural adjustment and stabilisation programmes, supported by the IMF, the World Bank and donor countries, had virtually been lost. It was also evident that some of the notable gains that had been achieved under Mwalimu Nyerere's leadership, particularly in human development. social, equity, human justice and equitable distribution of wealth and welfare), had equally been sacrificed.

Interestingly, by 1995, the donor countries that had been in the forefront in assisting Tanzania and funding its economic reform programmes had equally expressed fears that Tanzania's economic management had become overly dominated by private interests at the expense of a national concern for the welfare of ordinary citizens. Those fears were made known to the Tanzania delegation that appeared before the Creditors Consultative Group Meeting. Paris Club) in Paris early in 1995. The degeneration in economic management raised serious questions about the role of top leadership in managing the process of economic transition and reform.

It is important to review at some length the national state of health, as it existed in 1995, in order to discern why leadership matters. It is noteworthy that several debilitating societal characteristics had emerged or intensified in the period between 1990 and 1995. Whether those characteristics arose from the inherent nature of the reform measures themselves or from implementation inadequacies or both is probably insignificant in the context of an evaluation of the performance of the national leadership. Adopting potentially problem-creating policies can be as bad, in leadership terms, as poor implementation of good policies. So which are the destabilising characteristics or, in Nyerere's parlance, the cracks in the Tanzanian national building that manifested themselves in 1995, some of which are yet to be adequately addressed?

The Erosion in Quality of Life

The quality of life and sustainable livelihood of the majority of Tanzanians, particularly the rural and urban poor, has deteriorated. Gauged against the dimensions of access to primary education, health care, sanitation, potable water supply and adult education, amongst other human development indices, quality of life, pushed up only recently, reflected a serious reversal from the 1983 achievements. Literacy was down from 90% in the early 1980s to 60%. Primary education enrolment had declined from 3,553,144 in 1983 to 3,373,362 in 1990. Though enrolment increased to 3,872,473 in 1995, the increase was marginal considering that average population growth was 2.8% per annum. What is notable is that in 2003, enrolment jumped to 6,531,769. On the health front, most rural health facilities were without basic medicines. The condition of rural women had also degenerated though they still continue to bear the brunt of poverty.

Secondly, rural urban migration had intensified particularly among the able-bodied youth to an extent that agricultural production suffered in many areas of the country, notably in the poorer Lindi and Mtwara regions. Besides, the migration imposed a serious employment crisis in key metropolitan centres especially Dar es Salaam where the size of population has more than doubled in ten years without an equivalent growth in salaried employment, physical infrastructure, housing, sanitation and sewerage, education and health facilities. This is one problem that, to-date, has not found a solution. According to the ADB/OECD *African Economic Outlook, 2004,* unemployment in Tanzania in 2001 was 2.1% or 13% of the total labour force. In Dar es Salaam alone, unemployment in that year was 46.5%. Massive urban unemployment has also precipitated a haphazard and environmentally unfriendly growth of informal business activities, growing criminality and armed robberies, drug trafficking, drug abuse and prostitution, with its concomitant fast spread of HIV/AIDS. It has also engendered an unfortunate racial intolerance. With the majority of organised and well-established trading businesses in major towns owned by a minority citizenry of Asian descent, some of the actions taken by the government against informal trading activities in the central parts of major towns have been viewed to reflect undue favouring of the minority citizen traders. Such perception has triggered racial intolerance and a lopsided clamour for economic empowerment of indigenous Tanzanians.

The Threat of Demagoguery

The intensification of urbanisation and the negative consequences resulting there from, ordinarily expected under society conditions now enveloping Tanzania, in mid 1990s, gave rise to the emergence of populist policies and political demagoguery in certain quarters of the political spectrum. This was a perturbing and dangerous development. The resignation of a leading political figure, Mr Augustine Mrema, from the ruling political party, CCM, early in 1995 was interpreted to represent the rise in such populist politics. Mr Mrema, a former Member of Parliament, Minister for Home Affairs, Deputy Prime Minister and, until his resignation, Minister for Labour and Youth, resigned from the CCM after being fired as Cabinet Minister at the end of February 1995 following an alleged infringement of the ethical code of ministerial responsibility. Mr Mrema had apparently used the floor of Parliament to castigate the government for failing to take drastic "political" action against an Indian national with investments in Tanzania for allegedly misusing debt conversion funds at a time when the issue had already been discussed at cabinet level, in his presence.

At the time of his resignation, Mr Mrema had already turned into a hero of the underclass, particularly of the poor urban unemployed and self-employed, because of his populist stances over several sensitive social issues. These cut across tax evasion, corruption, women maltreatment at the hands of husbands, informal kiosk business, street business hawkers and protecting residential communities through vigilante or militia groups. called "*sungusungu*"). His unconventional style and approach in addressing and tackling such societal problems often made some people's flesh creep. Generally, the opinion of many informed Tanzanians was that Mr Mrema's approach had probably trampled on people's rights of natural justice and abused administrative ethics. Nevertheless, Mr Mrema, who had then joined one of the opposition parties, called NCCR Mageuzi, stood as a Presidential candidate and was defeated. However, he was able to garner some 27.77% of the total votes cast. In other words, he proved to be a formidable candidate. That electoral achievement alone raised the fundamental question: what should the attributes of a Tanzanian President be?

Moral Decay and Social Fragmentation

Yet another characteristic of the state of Tanzania in 1995 was corruption. Corruption had taken root and, even today, Tanzania is still regarded by international observers like Transparency International as moderately corrupt. Corruption manifests itself across the entire fabric of society. This weakening of the social fabric and the emergence of moral decay within the leadership and among the people of all occupations, is a reflection of nascent social disintegration. There is a genuine concern that the unity of Tanzanians could be dampened precisely because the equality of its citizens would be shaken. Such disunity is reflected over colour, religion and wealth. In fact, the national thrust and commitment to eradicate poverty, disease and ignorance had particularly waned by 1995, replaced by a divisive thrust of everybody to oneself and God for us all. Even over religious faith, mudslinging each other's faith had become commonplace. Tanzanians used to pride themselves of their national identity devoid of tribal, racial, and religious differences. This was the pivot of their unity. The common national language of Kiswahili reinforced that unity. However, once again, as at the dawn of independence, Tanzanians have started to identify each other on racial and religious lines. Nyerere rightly warned, early in 1995, that Tanzanians would shortly begin to tribalise each other. Indeed, tribalisation is on the rise.

On the wealth divide front, rather than searching for effective state-driven policies and strategies to bridge the gap and to distribute opportunities for wealth sharing more equitably, racial sentiments have instead been allowed to swell and to threaten unity. The respected Indian social scientist Rajni Kothari aptly noted in this context: "failure to perform on the distributive dimension will produce a State that has ceased to be a nation." It is a presage to be taken seriously. A class of *nouveau riches*. the new rich class), emerged following the on-set of economic liberalisation, catapulted by a trade liberalisation policy that failed to ensure strict tax compliance. The opening up of consumer and capital goods imports was, in itself, a positive measure considering the poor state of domestic productive capacity and the low quality of locally produced goods. However, the policy was not matched by strict enforcement of effective tax collection systems on imports thereby undermining the resurgence of domestic industries and enabling accumulation of starkly disproportionate wealth by a few, fuelling ethnic envy and resentment among the poor majority. In this light, with large sums of black money at their disposal, a small class of people succeeded to ingrain a culture of corruption into the Tanzanian society. The preponderant perception amongst both the ordinary and the informed Tanzanian population was that this rich class was able to have its way, to evade taxes, to traffic narcotics and undertake shoddy deals, including short-circuiting the national legal system and due process.

The Demise of Spirit Of Self Reliance

The thrust of self-reliance probably treated more rhetorically during the reign of Nyerere much as the spirit of nation building was evidently deeply ingrained during the late 1960s and throughout the 1970s, has weakened in the two decades of economic reform. Part of the reason is that the past decade in particular has witnessed a major injection of aid and grants from abroad to support economic reforms. This is not a criticism because increased ODA has been driven by improved good governance and prudent economic management. Yet, a key component of any economic reform programme should be sustainability. In effect, this means building greater self-reliance. Unfortunately, the country has been implementing economic reforms as if aid and grants would continue to fall like manna from heaven. As a result, Tanzania today is placed in a quandary where, if suddenly aid and grants were to stop to flow in, for whatever reason, the country would find itself in a serious social and economic condition. This would be a dangerous outcome as it may lead the country to sacrifice some of its core principles.

As it is, some of the policies that the government has pursued in order to fulfil IMF/World Bank conditionalities for financial support and debt relief are viewed, in some Tanzanian quarters, as not being altogether in the national interest. It is argued, for instance, that the protection of domestic industries in the wake of trade liberalisation was for a long time not given due attention by the government until only lately, namely, between 2001 and 2003. For a considerable period of time, especially during President Mwinyi's second term, the presumed stand seemed to be that if domestic industries failed to stand up to competition from imports, then they should be allowed to die naturally or be privatised. That philosophy, centred on the "Washington Consensus," has been heavily criticised by leading economists such as Joseph Stiglitz and Jeffrey Sachs.

Leadership Frailty

The respect and defence of the Constitution and adherence to the rule of law and due process by top leaders of the country came to be viewed in bad light during the second term of President Mwinyi's administration. Mwalimu Nyerere, in particular, was in the forefront in orchestrating what he saw as a fundamental frailty in Mwinyi's leadership especially in upholding the sanctity of the constitution. Often in 1995, he pointed out that a President who swore at the time of inauguration to uphold and defend the Constitution and prayed to God for assistance should fulfil such sacred and noble duty at all cost. Three cases often cited as having brought about this criticism are: first, the failure on the part of the Union President to censure the unilateral decision of the Zanzibar government to join the *Organisation of Islamic Conference*. OIC). Second, the inconsistent position taken by President Mwinyi's government on the Union Question, notably on the motion moved by the Union National Assembly to have a government of Tanganyika established. Third, the alleged leeway Mr Mrema, as Home Affairs Minister, had been given to take the law into his own hands in dealing with law and order issues at the expense of the rule of law and the due process. All these shortcomings and reversals pointed to serious weaknesses in top leadership before Mkapa took over as President. Before I discuss what should be the desirable leadership qualities of a President, it is befitting to critically review Nyerere's vision for Tanzania after independence and contextualise the achievements and shortcomings of the strategies adopted to realise his vision. The aim of this exercise is to determine Tanzania's direction and how and what kind of leadership can move the country more effectively towards the new direction.

Nyerere's Vision at the Dawn of Independence

At the dawn of political independence in December 1961 and, subsequently through the medium of the Arusha Declaration, the founder President, Mwalimu Julius K. Nyerere, articulated a vision for his post-colonial nation. Prior to articulating his vision, Nyerere developed a deep insight of the reality as it obtained at the time of independence. Leading authorities on the subject of vision have pointed out that an insightful view of current reality is as important as a clear vision itself. In this light, it is important to examine what insights Nyerere had of the reality that obtained in Tanzania at the dawn of independence. Fundamentally, the reality was informed by the legacy of British colonialism.

The Colonial Legacy

The colonial legacy reflected the following conditions and characteristics:

i) the freehold land system that existed had the susceptibility to divide society into property owners and tenants. |The Africans who were poor would have been tenants whilst the immigrants, citizens and non-citizens, would have been the property owners. Such division would have led to an explosive situation.

ii) the Chiefdom system frustrated efforts to unify the country and give it a national identity.

iii) the economic divisions between rich and poor that coincided almost exactly with divisions between the races were a time bomb.

iv) the "underdevelopment" of Moslems *vis a vis* Christians particularly in relation to inequitable access to education undermined the potential to build national unity.

v) a divide in educational advancement between a few tribes. *Wachagga, Wahaya* and *Wanyakyusa*) where Missionaries had concentrated their education programmes, and the rest of the country's tribes, was a situation that could be exploited to stir up tribal animosity.

vi) multi-party democracy was inimical to unifying a newly independent nation towards the pursuit of a common destiny.

vii) scattered rural homesteads frustrated efforts both of nation building and of cost- effective delivery of social and economic services for rural transformation.

viii) African states were intensively balkanised to the point where it would be difficult to overcome poverty and insecurity.

ix) corruption existed to the point of undermining the confidence of the people in their government.

x) the society was capitalist oriented and the majority Africans were mere labourers.

xi) poverty, ignorance and disease were a massive problem.

xii) racial harmony and tolerance were fragile.

In the light of such realities, Mwalimu Nyerere proceeded to construct a vision that the new independent nation would work for in pursuit of a desired future. The vision centred on a Tanzania that would be:

a) united with a sense of common and shared destiny.

b) moral and ethical, devoid of corruption and other social ills.

c) racially harmonious and tolerant, where race, tribe and religion differences and diversities were irrelevant in pursuing national goals.

d) socially and economically egalitarian, wherein there was fair and equitable distribution of wealth. Such a nation could not have identification of race with a wealth divide.

e) a nation with its rural population living, not in scattered homesteads, but in community villages that became the instruments for rural transformation.

f) a welfare state wherein social services like education, health and water were largely freely provided by the state for free.

g) socialist and self-reliant.

h) united with or aspires for unification with other African nations.

It is not essential to discuss in detail the strategies that Nyerere adopted to bridge the gap between the reality he discerned at the time of independence and the vision that he developed for a future Tanzania. The purpose of articulating Nyerere's reality and vision is merely to put Tanzania's present social and economic challenges into perspective and to underscore why any social and economic strategy, implemented without an accurate insight of such reality and without a vision of a desired future stands to falter and to generate cynicism.

Nyerere's Strategies for a New Tanzania

Nyerere's implementation strategies were several. Some proved more successful in moving the country towards the desired future. Others were less successful. Some were even disastrous. The successful strategies included the abolition of the freehold land system and the introduction of leaseholds; the abolition of Chiefdoms, the establishment of the One Party political system, the nationalisation of education, and health services, the promulgation of a Leadership Code under which all political functionaries and senior public officials, both in government and parastatals, were prohibited from owning private businesses and being directors of private companies, the promotion of human development through a broad social service delivery system and, finally, the Union of Tanganyika and Zanzibar. The less successful strategies included the nationalisation of commanding heights of the economy, the creation of a state anti corruption squad, and the acquisition of privately owned rented properties. Strategies that failed include the villagisation programme. moving rural people into planned villages) and the Operation Retail and Wholesale Business. *"Operation Maduka"*) that was directed at socialising retail and wholesale trade to de-monopolise the control of such business on racial as well as private sector lines, the abolition of local government in 1972 and the Cooperatives in 1976.

It is important to note, however, that everything considered, Nyerere's vision was so compelling that it became people's power. Nyerere was able to use his shared vision to create a sense of commonality permeating the whole fabric of society. Socialism and Self Reliance became a shared aspiration. Nyerere succeeded in inspiring the people to share his vision because it resonated with the values that people lived by all the time. His vision was also endorsed because he was viewed by the people to be a leader who put principles ahead of politics, and the people ahead of self-interest. Thus, in spite of some drawbacks, Nyerere's strategies generally succeeded in getting Tanzania close to the articulated desired future. This success manifested in the realisation of:

i) national peace and tranquillity.

ii) unity, brotherhood and solidarity without regard to colour, tribe or religion.

iii) major expansion in and improvement of social service delivery. health, primary education, literacy education and water supply) provided free by the state.

iv) the development of a large state-owned industrial sector. particularly textiles, cement, sugar and leather) and a nation-wide state trading system which provided the means for equitable distribution of wealth and minimisation of the wealth divide on racial lines.

v) job opportunities for many people in urban areas.

vi) improved quality of life in rural areas.

vii) a culture of human dignity and respect irrespective of wealth differences.

viii) a national moral ethic. Leaders were trustworthy. Corruption existed but was minimal. Thefts and armed robberies were rare. Open public prostitution and drug trafficking were non-existent.

ix) the emergence of a Tanzanian national identity based on unity, respect for diversity and tolerance.

Many of these achievements have come under enormous pressure since the on-set of economic reforms. Indeed as at 1995, these pressures had precipitated a real threat to Tanzania's unity and integrity.

The Challenge of Leadership Choice

The social, economic and identity problems examined above from a historical and dialectical perspective and considered in the context of Nyerere's legacy, could not be properly or adequately grasped, tackled and addressed through mere populism and demagoguery that featured in certain political quarters of aspiring leaders in the 1995 elections. Rather, they point to the critical need for Tanzanians to gear up and wisely elect leaders that protect the country from the forces of disorder. Tanzania is still in ardent need of leaders who know what it takes to turnaround an economy in distress and offering the people a renewed hope for a better tomorrow through concrete, realistic and pragmatic poverty reducing policies and programmes. Since 1995, Tanzania can boast to have had a leader in President Mkapa able to confront the challenges Tanzania faces. His bold and courageous leadership was behind the success he made in pursuing prudent economic management of the economy and making Tanzania attractive to investors. Tanzanians now face the onerous challenge of contriving to elect a President in 2005 and beyond able to sustain the laudable achievements realised under President Mkapa and move the country to higher levels of success. Above all, they have to elect a President able to understand the challenges and dynamics of the global economy and what it takes to deal with globalisation. Therefore, who should lead Tanzania takes a pre-eminent position. I discuss this onerous question below.

Who Should Lead Tanzania?

The ability to learn is a defining characteristic of being human; the ability to continue learning is an essential skill of leadership. When leaders lose that ability, they inevitably falter. When any of us lose that ability, we no longer grow.

-*Warren G. Bennis & Robert J. Thomas:* **Geeks & Geezers: How Era, Values, and Defining Moments Shape Leaders.**

The. second) fallacy in the cry for strong leadership is its unspoken assumption that a style of leadership that worked in the past will work in the present or future. We are continually dredging up images from the past when we think about leadership-Roosevelt, Churchill, de Gaulle. Yet different civilisations require vastly different leadership qualities. And what is strong may be inept and disastrously weak in another.

-*Alvin Toffler:* **The Third Wave: The Revolution that will change our lives.**

Brave New World

The world in which Tanzania finds itself part of at the dawn of the 21st century imposes different demands on it in contrast to what prevailed in the 1960s and 1970s. Like most other poor countries, Tanzania, may be underdeveloped yet exists in and interacts with a highly developed world, thanks to information and communications technology breakthroughs. With globalisation taking root, matters that hitherto have been within the exclusive domain of national sovereignty are now increasingly dealt with or required to be considered on the basis of global governance parameters. Issues such as poverty reduction that constituted the core theme of the 1995 United Nations Social Development Summit in Copenhagen; the role, status, rights and empowerment of women which underlined the thrust of the UN Conference on Women held in Beijing in September, 1995, the monitoring, regulation and limiting of trade in arms, control of trafficking in narcotics, dealing with the HIV/AIDS pandemic, the protection of the environment, which was the theme of the UN Earth Summit in Rio de Janeiro in 1992 and in Johannesburg in 2002, the UN Millennium Summit that came up with the *Millennium Development Goals in 2000*, the WTO Doha Round of trade negotiations, managing migrations, the refugee problem, containing national civil wars, dealing with the debt problem, reforming the international financial system, reform of the UN, making NEPAD succeed, all these constitute international common responsibilities and decisions on them are increasingly taking or being influenced by an international global governance framework. However, in reality they are yet to be driven by principles of sovereign equality and the quest to create a global order of equity. As Francis Fukuyama has correctly observed in his recent book, *State Building: Governance and World Order in the 21St Century,* there is a tendency to erode the legitimacy of nation states, particularly over matters of a political character "without putting effective international institutions in their place."

This is the brave new world that confronts Tanzania and insularity is not an option. The Tanzanian leadership should thus be better able to understand and muster the logic and intricacies of such new world and seek to play a more insightful role. Such world is not for nation-state leaders who cannot make meaning of what globalisation is all about; leaders who cannot address an international conference on global economic inequities or face an international press conference on global issues on an *ex tempore* basis. In other words, Tanzania should have a leader with the leadership qualities that correspond to the current global challenges. In this context, Tanzania has been lucky to have President Benjamin Mkapa, a leader who has risen to enjoy global respect on global issues. His appointment as Co-Chair of the International Labour Organisation's World Commission on Social Dimension of Globalisation and member of Tony Blair's Commission on Africa is clear testimony of such recognition. He has also earned equal respect on the African front. Who would comfortably step into his shoes and sustain the record realised?

At another level, the immediate and central global challenge for the poor world is the promotion of South-South cooperation, at global, regional and sub-regional levels; the quest to achieve a common political platform and voice on global issues that impact poor countries. The Cancun WTO meeting held in September 2003 proved how important trade union of the poor is. Tanzanian leadership has to be seized of the importance of developing countries playing an influential role in global issues and promoting engaged relationships, as reflected, for instance, in the WTO Doha Round trade negotiations and providing exemplary leadership. It is imperative to provide a lead that poor countries have no choice but to cooperate and integrate. The leadership should be able to influence co-leaders, economic actors and the people generally to support measures and institutional arrangements directed at strengthening and diversifying South-South cooperation. Such leadership attribute has evidently become more complex in the wake of the changing economic structures of the South in which some of the countries have become emerging economies and some newly industrialising ones. However, recent attempts at re-awakening the Bandung spirit are comforting. Fifty years after the first Asia-Africa Conference held in Bandung, Indonesia, African and Asian leaders met again at the same venue in April 2005 to deliberate on new forms of co-operation in the post-cold war era. A declaration on "New Asian-African Strategic Partnership" framework was adopted directed at establishing a bridge between the two continents with focus on poverty reduction and broad based development co-operation. The establishment of a Joint Economic Commission between Tanzania and Indonesia in May 2005 may be viewed as one of the positive outcomes of the new Bandung spirit. Clearly though, it is critical that countries of the South move beyond rhetoric and embrace pragmatism in developing concrete economic partnership arrangements.

Principles and Development

In the brave new world it is increasingly becoming difficult for poor countries to exercise economic sovereignty. In the late 1960s, Mwalimu Nyerere promoted the idea of principles and development, arguing that it was better to be poor than to be a rich slave. In 1966, he directed the Federal Republic of Germany. FRG) Embassy in Tanzania to pack up and leave upon FRG's threat to withdraw aid because Tanzania had decided to establish diplomatic relations with the then Democratic Republic of Germany. GDR). To Nyerere, that decision was driven by principle. His was not only an act of boldness but of competence as well for it did not make sense to Nyerere for the FRG to try and run Tanzania's foreign policy. In contrast, Tanzania has, in recent years, suffered from the syndrome of "beggars are never choosers." Indeed, most poor countries and even those that are more developed within the Group of 77 have generally become surrogates of rich countries. Often, they have sacrificed core principles that underlie the trade union of the poor as well as principles of political significance over matters such as the struggle of the Palestinian people and the growing unilateralism in international relations, in favour of their own immediate national economic interests. Yet, at the same time, there are realities that have to be faced head on, that raise the question whether it is viable, in the conditions that presently underpin the global economic environment, for a poor country to exhibit the type of arrogance Nyerere displayed in making principles override economic support from rich countries. This question raises fundamental issues about leadership integrity and legitimacy. Nyerere was able to be arrogant because he enjoyed total legitimacy of his people. The people trusted him unreservedly and were prepared to suffer the consequences of Tanzania standing firm against the inequitable interests of the economic powerful. Thus, as we search for the right attributes of a national leader in this brave new world it is important to examine how Nyerere came to enjoy such adoration and trust of his people and to learn from these attributes as we ponder on who should lead Tanzania.

In the first place, Nyerere was a leader who had an unwavering commitment to principle; he was passionate about what was right and just; he was a person who upon being entrapped in any crisis-political, social or economic- never sacrificed principle. Instead, he searched for opportunities. Such leadership is not necessarily charismatic. Rather, it is leadership that inspires enviable trust and loyalty from the people.

Secondly, traditional symbols and metaphors of identity and cohesion are what enabled Tanzanians to rally behind Mwalimu Nyerere's leadership. Nyerere had the ability and capacity to interpret traditional concepts of living, of sharing and of equality of rights and duties and giving them meaning that crystallised into a national consciousness and a national identity. Politics was the engine of mobilisation and identity formation that together inspired a galvanised commitment to a desired political and economic order. The Tanzanian leader, today and tomorrow, should equally be able to use politics as the purveyor of socio-economic transformation. In the case of Nyerere, even when out of political office, his presence was felt in Tanzanian national life as he continued to prod the nation to treasure unity and tranquillity. Tanzania could no longer continue to take the unity of its people and the state of peace and stability it currently enjoys for granted. Indeed, in recent years, signs of social strife have emerged and these have to be effectively addressed and resolved, not through acts of populism or demagoguery, but rather through politics of identity consolidation that inspire a galvanised commitment to a shared national consciousness founded on brotherhood and respect for cultural and religious diversity. Tanzania needs a leader who would steadfastly and in earnest work to forge and solidify the unity of Tanzania as a nation and of its people across the tribal, racial and religious divides.

Nyerere also created an environment that enabled the people to exploit and expand their capacity. He viewed a socio-political system that would work for assuring minimum conditions for all the people and the means for their realisation through self-reliance as necessary in this context; a system that would work towards bridging the rich and poor chasm that had developed within the country. More than ever before, Tanzania today needs a President who would quickly work towards correcting the vast disparities of income, creating employment, promoting the role, rights and status of women, arrest the sharp and entrenching disparity between urban and rural by adopting policies that promote the productive employment of the poor and advancing environmentally sustainable development policies. Much has been done under President Mkapa's administration to address these challenges. Yet these challenges are of a long-term character and would thus remain to be of serious concern beyond Mkapa's term.

Compelling Vision

Tanzania today needs a leadership that understands that resisting change is as futile as resisting the weather; a leadership that knows that current global challenges demand that the best, the brightest and the committed work with the national leadership to provide a new guiding purpose for Tanzania's prosperity. In this context, the Tanzanian leader should be able to clarify the vision for a desired Tanzania future the way Nyerere did; a vision able to uplift people's hopes and aspirations and inspire them to pursue a larger purpose and then be able to set the goals and priorities in moving the country towards the realisation of that vision. Tanzania already has in place the Development Vision, 2025. However, the vision is yet to be a compelling one. In other words, it is yet to be used, in a powerful sense, to rally and galvanise the people behind its goals in the manner in which the Arusha Declaration was made to become a household rallying battle for a new development paradigm. Evidently, under the leadership of President Mkapa the economy has been put back into shape and kick started into a growth trajectory. With such pressure of attention, there probably has been little time for the administration to focus on promoting Vision 2005 in the same manner that the Arusha Declaration was promoted, much as the core policy and strategic direction of President Mkapa's administration has been in line with the Vision's key goals. However, the new President from November 2005 would have to embrace Vision 2025 more concretely and vigorously champion it. Such leadership style would demand that Tanzanians elect a leader who is well-educated, intelligent, worldly, creative, perceptive, risk oriented, bold and decisive, a person who is consistent and persistent in upholding goals and in pursuing the realisation of such goals. Such leaders should connect with the people and be able to communicate better the Vision and its underlying lofty goals.

Development Vision 2025 is in place but so is Nyerere's Vision of an *Ujamaa* society. The sensitive challenge that has developed in the Tanzanian society in the last ten years is how to apply the market to create an *ujamaa* society. Tony Blair likes to invoke, in this context, the distinction between the pursuits of a market economy as opposed to the creation of a market society. There is a major distinction. Tanzania's vision of development should be to use the market as a vehicle, not for building a market society but rather an *ujamaa* society. Many Tanzanians are now caught up, rather confusedly, between the ideology of the past, of using a socialist command economy to build an *ujamaa* society and the new ideology of the market economy to build the same society. They need a leadership that is able to clarify the distinction, a leadership that is truly committed to Vision 2025, to the market economy, and one that is able to connect with people in an effective way thereby influencing them to change their perceptions, for instance, about the role of the state and the market. Such leader should personify the new vision, the way Nyerere so passionately did with the Arusha Declaration.

Ethic of Service

Tanzania needs a leader committed to and who sustains an ethic of service. Looking around the Tanzanian political landscape, one often wonders how many Tanzanians that aspire to one or another high political office actually do so to make a difference to the lives of the Tanzanian people as opposed to making a difference to their own personal lives. The founder of the Children's Defence Fund, Marian Wright Edelman once said, "Service is the rent we pay for living." More so for leaders. The Tanzanian leader should openly display to the people that leadership is a responsibility, not a status or privilege and that the ethic of service involves genuine respect of the intelligence and efforts of the broad masses. President Mkapa's June 2003 Radio Address to the people on democracy and leadership, in which he clarified the role of TASAF and its link to participatory democracy, resonated well with such type of leadership. It needs no underscoring that this particular attribute of leadership, with the benefit of lessons of history in mind, is probably the most difficult one for many African leaders to fulfil. Yet Tanzania can ill afford to squander such attribute of leadership that constituted Nyerere's core legacy to Tanzanians.

Leadership and Learning

At another level, leadership, as a responsibility, means a permanent pursuit of knowledge. Learning is a critical factor in leadership development. One wonders though whether Tanzanian leaders seriously learn. It is pointed out by analysts of leadership that leaders are perpetual learners; they are voracious readers. In their profoundly pathbreaking book on Leadership, *Geeks & Geezers: How Era, Values, and Defining Moments Shape Leaders,* Warren Bennis and Burt Nanus posit that "Learning is the essential fuel for the leader, the source of high-octane energy that keeps up the momentum by continually sparking new understanding, new ideas and new challenges. It is indispensable under today's conditions of rapid change and complexity. Very simply, those who do not learn do not long survive as leaders." Those who knew Nyerere well would recall that his leadership qualities were enhanced by his habitual, almost serial, learning habits. To him, reading was pleasure. In contrast, many of our leaders today take reading to be some form of torture. President Mkapa has been a notable exception.

Leadership Integrity

Personal example of credibility, commitment, integrity and moral fervour is central to leadership. Nyerere once said that Tanzanians did not have to elect a Pope or a puritanical person as their President. In his view, the State House was neither a Church nor a Mosque to require a holy person as President. Yet it is imperative that a national leader be steeped in moral rectitude, always leading the fight against sources of national decay, particularly corruption, promiscuity, prostitution, drug abuse and exploitation of children, especially girls, alcoholism, criminal behaviour and violence on women. More critically, as HIV/AIDS decimates the African people, the President should be the role model in fighting this pandemic. On the question of moral standards of leaders, however, a caveat could be apt. It is said that when Earl Stanley Baldwin formed his first Cabinet in May 1923 and decided to drop Sir F.E. Smith. Earl of Birkenhead) apparently because of his marital infidelities, he commented, "So, gentlemen, we will remain a Cabinet of faithful husbands." Probably such a standard is too high to sustain. However, leaders who have concubines as a matter of routine style of living could find it difficult to uphold other ethical standards required of leadership.

Democratic Leadership

The attribute of democratic leadership manifests itself in several dimensions. The first relates to the nature of democratisation itself. In Tanzania today, there is too much politics of organised political parties. It is as if democracy means multi-partyism. This is an area that needs to be quickly reformed. The challenge is for leadership to promote autonomous centres of civil society and using them to deepen the democratic ethos and practice. The NEDLAC form of smart partnership has been earlier proposed for adoption in Tanzania.

The second dimension relates to the character of the democratic system where respect and defence of the constitution stands out as primary. Tanzanian leaders should uphold the sanctity of the constitution and invoke it only to promote the interests of the people. Defence of the constitution should never invoke dictatorial behaviour whereby the perceptions and wishes of leaders and those of their own political parties are taken to be God's will. Tanzanians should be allowed to discuss all constitutional issues freely. It is the people, either through their elected representatives, legally constituted civil society bodies or through the medium of a referendum, who should determine whether a particular constitutional dispensation should prevail or not.

A leader that seeks to frustrate the full force of democratic principles from taking their natural course is not the right leader for a democratic nation. This dimension of democracy is also closely linked to the respect for and the upholding of the constitutional separation of powers as well as of the respect for the rule and the due process of law. A leader who short circuits the due process, who becomes the law unto himself, the investigator, the prosecutor and the judge, should have no place in Tanzania. The habit of the executive to use and even manipulate the legislature to change laws in order to upset court opinions and judgements that respond to broad national interest simply because it enjoys majority parliamentary representation, conflicts with the fundamental principle of constitutional democracy. Moreover, over issues like the nature of the Tanzania Union, the President should be a person who, whilst committed to the sustenance of unity, should be sufficiently flexible to accommodate different views and opinions over the Union and to preside over the determination of a Union dispensation that meets the wishes of the majority of Tanzanians from both sides of the Union. In other words, Tanzania needs a Presidential leadership that pulls rather than pushes, challenges rather than manipulates and enables rather than constrains. Unfortunately, this is one area that remains a dark one for Tanzania. Surely, it should not, for example, be sacrilegious to be open about the inadequacies of the Union and to propose changes. Indeed, during the last week of March 2004, on a visit to London, President Mkapa was bold, in suggesting that Zanzibaris should be brought together to a round table and allowed to debate openly and freely about their future. In my view, such a debate cannot exclude the character of the Union.

The third dimension manifests itself in ensuring that politics of patronage and factionalism do not feature in the political process. There is growing concern in Tanzania, especially as the country gears itself for the 2005 General Elections, that such politics of patronage and factionalism, two key sources of national disunity, are taking root. Within the ruling party, CCM, there are already different factions, driven by all types of factionalisms, from religion, places of origin, and even tribe. Such politics are harmful especially to the election of a desirable and effective President because Tanzania needs a President who has a high tolerance for dissent, and adept at providing consensual resolution of issues, problems and conflicts. A national leader, even at the level of a political party, should be a unity builder. Factionalism creates sources of enmity and breed revenge. In the case of CCM in Zanzibar, such factionalism, which apparently resulted from the manner in which the Presidential candidate for Zanzibar in 2000 was nominated, could harm the party. Such cleavages, if they exist, should be resolved. In fact, being able to achieve unity of the party members should constitute one of President Karume's central legacies during his first term of leadership.

Respectful Leadership

When Mwalimu Nyerere elected to retire from the Presidency in 1985, he left behind a strong legacy of a leader who is sober, kind, firm and likeable. He admonished witch hunting-the disgraceful habit of blaming past leaders for the ills afflicting the country instead of searching for solutions to problems. This is the fourth dimension of democratic leadership. Tanzania needs a national leader who would give due regard and respect to past leaders, a person who tackles past mistakes and weaknesses in a dignified rather than maligning manner. Such a leader would divest himself or herself of prejudices of all types and promote reconciliation rather than confrontation with political competitors, within his or her own party and without, and would use all past leaders as resource persons for advice and exchange of ideas. President Mkapa has been a good example in this area. He has used former President Mwinyi, as well as past leaders, Prime Ministers especially, extremely well in performing various national tasks. Little wonder that as part of his legacy, President Mkapa has sought to establish a Council of Presidential Advisors to comprise retired Presidents from both the Union and Zanzibar.

Whether this evidently credible decision necessitated its being institutionalised by force of law as had been proposed in the 14th

253

Constitutional Amendment Bill, 2005, is debatable in as much as countries like Nigeria do have such a Council within the constitutional framework. In my view, the functionality and ultimate success of such council would hinge on the mindset of the President in power. If he or she chooses to lead without *formal* advice from former Presidents, that would be it. I do not believe that the law would necessitate the President being censured where he fails to consult the Council. However, following indications that Parliament would have rejected the bill, the government decided to withdraw it. The apparent reason for frustrating the proposal is that the council would have dissipated the indivisible authority of the President and that it would have been in competition with the Cabinet. Neither of these two reasons stands the test of credibility apart from the fact that giving the Council constitutionality would indeed have made it appear as having legal force considering that the Cabinet is also constitutionally advisory to the President. However, the Cabinet has a different level of mandate and moral authority from that of retired Presidents.

Conclusion

Tanzania still stands at a crossroad: either it vigorously pursues a future of peace, stability and prosperity or it precipitates economic disorder and social conflict. The critical determining factor in choosing the correct path is leadership, a leadership that has a correct insight of the social and economic problems that afflict Tanzanians and which has a vision of a better tomorrow. It is a leadership steeped in moral and public service ethic; respectful of the people and of their intelligence; prepared to work closely with the people; respects and upholds the constitution and the laws of the country, including the due process of law; promotes the unity, love and solidarity of all people across the racial, tribal and religious divides. Finally, it is a leadership able to rekindle the hopes and aspirations of all Tanzanians especially those who are disadvantaged and marginalised.

In his recent book, *Changing Minds: The Art and Science of Changing Our Own and Other People's Minds,* Harvard Professor Howard Gardner points out that leaders stand out in terms of three intelligences: First, as story tellers. As such, they have to be gifted linguistically. Leaders must be able to create a story, communicate it effectively and alter it where changes intervene. Secondly, leaders must be masters of interpersonal intelligence. In other words, they must understand other people, listen to them, motivate them and respond to their needs and aspirations. Thirdly, leaders have to have existential intelligence. This means that they must be comfortable with posing fundamental questions, notably putting forward their visions. These are difficult intelligences to possess or achieve. Most Tanzanians would agree though that Mwalimu Nyerere possessed all the three. Fair is fair, Tanzanians should also accord President Mkapa his due.

He has undoubtedly been an effective President. He has been able to bolster Tanzania's image abroad and to begin a key process in boldly transforming the Tanzanian economy and the mindsets of the people. How to sustain and build on the quality and effectiveness of Mkapa's leadership stands out as the central challenge that confronts Tanzanians as they ponder who should next lead them after Mkapa and beyond. In the next section, I turn to examine the challenge of good governance from a much broader perspective.

Leadership and Good Governance

Current efforts to improve governance in the newly globalised economy are heavily biased towards the interests of the governments, firms and peoples of the wealthiest of the world and this bias will not easily be overcome. Whereas there are signs that larger and potentially more influential developing country players in the global economy may eventually be admitted to global governance and decision-making councils, in the interest of their very effectiveness and efficiency, the smaller and poorer risk continuing exclusion.

-Gerald Karl Helleiner: **Markets, Politics and Globalisation: Can the Global Economy be Civilised?**

In recent years, good governance has taken the centre stage of national public management as well as inter-state and international relations. Many a country, especially in the developing world and the former Soviet Union " bloc" of countries, have come under extreme influence, even pressure, to embrace and adopt a system of public order described as good governance. At heart, good governance symbolises a State system that is democratic, in the western liberal sense, respects basic human rights, pursues a prudent economic management system and respects fundamental principles of the rule of law.

The underlying logic of good governance is that government is responsible and accountable to the people, who elect it, for their welfare and prosperity. Governance ceases to be "good" when it fails to rise to this objective and expectation. However, the judgement, as to whether governance is good or bad, is necessarily a function of what constitutes the primary role of government. In a country like Tanzania, which is in a state of transition, as far as the basic role of government in society is concerned, judgement about governance often suffers from the lack of clarity about the shift in role. Thus, the question regarding the responsibility and accountability of the government for the prosperity of the people is often responded to differently depending on the perception one holds about the role of government in society. The difference in perception could have serious implications on society. This point needs amplification. Under the monolithic political party regime and state capitalism. some would prefer to describe it as the socialist economic system), Tanzania "enjoyed" what the majority thought and believed to be a vibrant welfare state. That welfarism was characterised by "free" education. universal at primary level and lesser and lesser universal at secondary and tertiary levels), health services, water supply etc. There was a sense and mood of "freeness" all around! Subsidies were abounding, from fertilizers to seeds. Even commercial credit took the form of "subsidy," to the point where a culture ingrained in the minds of borrowing Co-operatives and marketing boards. not to speak of individuals) that the term credit was a misnomer. To day, the banking system is risk averse to lending partly because this borrowing culture remains rife. To the Tanzanian people, that regime represented what good governance is all about.

At the root of that perception of good governance were factors born out of mal-governance. Tanzania was heavily reliant on external aid and borrowing. Debts mounted. State owned banks, including the Central Bank, became the "blood banks" for a vampire - like public administration. Fiscal prudence was weak. Monetary policy was not independent of the government, such that domestic bank borrowing, exchange rates and interest rates were not managed prudently. An overvalued shilling undermined the growth of exports and promoted the development of a lacklustre, largely technology obsolete state enterprise system. Low interest rates fuelled money supply and inflation. A patronised and surrogate parastatal enterprise system became the prime driver of economic mismanagement and corruption. In sum, the "happy days" of the 1970s and 1980's were not supported by a viable and sustainable economic system. The government was good; not governance. Put differently, the government wanted to do good to the people. It had a vision of hope and prosperity. However, governance undermined the realisation of the set out lofty goals.

As criticism mounted about the poor state of governance, it was critical that a "new form" of governance be instituted. It would be unfortunate were Tanzania to find itself at this stage retreating from the present system of governance out of sheer populism and fast reverse to a past social and economic system that was unviable and unsustainable. It is important to underscore, therefore, that the present system of governance that champions policies of liberalisation, deregulation, privatisation and prudent economic management in an environment where there is rule of law flows from a fundamental shift in the role of government. Yes, the government remains responsible and accountable to the people for their development. However, this role has taken a different dimension. As opposed to the past system where a dependency syndrome became the defining relationship between the people and their government, the new relationship is one of partnership.

At the core of such partnership is the key role of the government in creating a more conducive environment necessary for the people to work for their own their prosperity. This assertion always faces a barrage of criticism because poor people are viewed to need the state to intervene directly in their condition of poverty and, literally, as in feeding a baby, the government is duty bound to unshackle the chains that entrap the poor. Clearly, the key point is missed in this perception. And it is not as if the importance of the government directing resources towards de-bottlenecking those factors that militate against the poor becoming more productive and improving the results of their labour are disregarded. On the contrary, as President Mkapa has often observed, it is in line with the basic objective of poverty reduction that debt relief funds, for example, as they become available, are directed at improving education access, health facilities, agricultural productivity, animal husbandry and fishing.

The key point is that at the heart of the new role of government is the creation of conditions that make economic and business activity a worthwhile enterprise. Evidently, such an exercise, as a *sine qua non*, requires the establishment and sustenance of a sound, stable and predictable macro-economic environment. Yet it is often surprising to hear political leaders and some Tanzanians question the extent of the importance of focusing on these conditions simply because money supply has been tightened and that the poor are worst hit. It is not money supply that drives an economy. Indeed, experience has shown in Tanzania that too much money supply has destroyed the economy. Time has come for Tanzanians to accept, collectively, that as the nation faces new realities, national and global and that irrespective of which political party gets into power, good governance would demand macro economic policy prudence. This cannot be a subject of political differences. Mudslinging such measures merely smacks of cheap populism. In fact, it reflects poorly on the quality of leadership that contends for power.

The new challenge of good governance and this can certainly constitute an arena of political differences, is how to move beyond sound macro-economic fundamentals and address micro-economic issues. President Mkapa has strived to better understand, with the support of stakeholders in the economy, what the micro-economic bottlenecks are and how they could be addressed in order to stimulate the whole economy and put it on a growth trajectory. The idea of dialogue between the government and stakeholders, as alluded to earlier, in itself, reflects good governance. Above all, there is a new confidence emerging that a new level of seriousness, of commitment, of greater understanding is taking shape in the direction of translating macro-economic gains into key drivers of economic stimulation and improvement of people's quality of lives.

Of course, it cannot all be rosy, the spirit and commitment to good governance notwithstanding. The economic paradigm shift Tanzania is traversing is not an easy one. New demands, for example, on the judicial front, still require difficult responses in an environment confronted by serious scarcity of resources. The regulatory framework is only in the process of being put in place and fine-tuned to respond to the challenges of a market economy. Moreover, an ethical business culture is yet to ingrain in line with a new environment of competition and the demands for self-regulated tax compliance. Clearly, it is not only governments that are required to abide to good governance. The NEPAD Peer Review Mechanism has pointed to the necessity of corporate governance to fit the same standards required of governments with respect to fulfilling robust standards of good governance. Good corporate governance is thus an absolute necessity. The corporate scandals involving *Enron, WorldCom* and numerous American and European companies, like *Parmalat*, between 2001 and 2003 are a case in point. Tanzanian enterprises are not immune from similar corporate malfeasances.

Tanzania should now speed up micro-economic reform as it continues to improve the support systems for a viable and efficient market economy and respond to the challenges of promoting an equitable and people-centred development. In this context, it is noteworthy that the government is taking the question of good governance seriously. In the new five-year National Strategy for Growth and Reduction of Poverty due to commence in July 2005, governance and accountability have been given pre-eminence. There is focus on the following areas:

- ensuring good governance and the rule of law.
- making leaders and public servants accountable to the people.
- deepening democracy, political and social tolerance.
- Cultivating and sustaining peace, political stability, national unity and social cohesion.

Good Governance is a Continuum

It is important to note, though, that good governance is a continuum. Its quest is an on-going process. In fact, developing countries are not the only nations engrossed in its persistent pursuit. During the decade of the 1990s, industrialised nations-the United States, Britain and Germany- to mention a few specific cases, have equally found good governance elusive. For example, President Bill Clinton's first term focused on re-inventing government. Tony Blair's "Third Way" policy framework and the subsequent *"The Modernising Government White Paper"* clearly attest to the challenges that continues to confront most nations, rich and poor, to enforce good governance. Alexander Pope, the English Poet, once provided the touchstone of such challenge: "For forms of government, let fools contest; whate'er is best administered is best."

It is imperative to draw attention to the need to view good governance from its broad and dynamic character. There exists a danger, which presently looms large, of treating good governance as overly representing incorrupt governance. Such perception has the unfortunate potential to constrict the attention that ought to be given to addressing the core causes of corruption rooted in weak governance. Indeed, taking the more perceptive perspective of corruption, the Report of the South Commission, *The Challenge to the South,* observes that corruption is a product of several governance inadequacies. The Report lists the following as some of the weaknesses: over-regulation, the absence of effective systems of public accountability, over centralisation, limited administrative capabilities, laxity of tax administration, authoritarian tendencies, excessive concentration of economic power in the hands of the government and the corporate sector, poverty, human insecurity and low pay of public officials. The Report pointedly concludes in this context: "regardless of these factors. outlined above), governments must bear a large part of the responsibility for corruption in the South. By and large, they have not regarded its eradication as a priority, despite its acknowledged economic, social and political costs. Higher standards of integrity in public life could do much to strengthen the people's confidence in governments and the sense of community and civic responsibility."

Good Governance and Vision

Many factors underpin good governance. In my view, good governance is first and foremost influenced by the existence of a national vision, a sense of direction and shared values that animate, inspirit and galvanise a whole people beyond the parochial and, at times, conflicting interests. This view is well captured in the Report of the Commission on Global Governance, *Our Global Neighbourhood.* It is stated in that report that "people have to see with new eyes and understand with new minds before they can truly turn to new ways of living." For over two decades, Tanzania had been guided by a national vision of *"ujamaa"* whose instrument of implementation was dominantly state enterprise. In the last decade, policies of liberalisation, deregulation and privatisation have stepped in. A new national economic system is in place, creating new social values, often in contrast to and even in conflict with what *ujamaa* stands or stood for. It is not yet clear if Tanzanians do indeed still enjoy shared values based on the new social, political and economic dispensation. Indeed, a good number of Tanzanians hold the view that the economic policies presently pursued are largely an outcome of conditionalities imposed on Tanzania by the IMF and the World Bank.

Little wonder that the lack of shared and compelling values about the new forces that should shape and drive Tanzania's development were to trigger actions such as those taken by few workers of the National Bank of Commerce in 1998 directed at stopping the bank's privatisation through court action. In fact, it could be generalised that a mood of anti-privatisation still lingers in our polity. It is as if some Tanzanians felt or even still feel threatened by the operation of a new development paradigm taking root. Therefore, a huge challenge confronts the Tanzanian leadership, in all sectors of society, for what a distinguished Bangladesh social scientist, Anisur Rahman, describes as the "recovery and reassertion of the core values and cultural elements of the people" if the new development paradigm is to become a shared vision. Indeed, the challenge is to make Tanzanians see with new eyes and understand with new minds if Tanzania will effectively respond to new ways of living, and accept new social and economic realities encapsulated in the new world economic order of globalisation.

Closely connected to this challenge of shaping a new mindset focused on a new compelling and shared vision, is the existence of a courageous, bold, competent and risk taking national leadership, a leadership that is infused with a social and moral ethic. In the Introduction to *Freedom And Unity*, Mwalimu Julius Nyerere posited that "whatever the size of society and whatever its institutions, the freedom and well-being of its members depends upon there being a generally accepted social ethic - a sense of what things are right, and what things are wrong, both for the institutions in relation to the members, and for the members in relation to each other. This social ethic has to change over time as people's consciousness changes and as physical circumstances change."

It is not easy for a national leader to constantly face the people and assure them that the grave social and economic conditions that they face because of their government implementing bold and difficult but necessary reforms would, eventually, deliver a promised land. Nyerere was fortunate to find himself in a more advantageous position by having been the liberator of Tanzania from colonialism. Thus he could easily be listened to and trusted, even at the height of Tanzania's adverse social conditions which Kenyans, at the worst period of Kenya-Tanzania relations, mockingly described as "man eat nothing society." Nyerere also enjoyed an advantage of ideological philosophy. His vision of *ujamaa* captured the imagination of ordinary Tanzanians. It gave them meaning and a compelling hope of a better life to come. The post-Nyerere leaders, on the other hand, lack such advantage. Their leadership attributes must stand out and be assessed. More onerously, leadership attributes should stand out at a time of pursuit of a development agenda that is in huge contrast and parallel to that of Nyerere. The current challenge of leadership is thus more pronounced. It is a challenge that demands courageous patience. How often do our leaders face the Indeed, to the point where he is often confronted with the question: "what can you show for results from your leadership?" In itself, this question, often viewed as unfair by leaders, reflects how much more needs to be done to reach out to and connect with ordinary people to make them better understand that the pain of reform is the necessary sacrifice Tanzanians should endure if a new dawn of prosperity is to emerge.

Governance and Corruption

An African Union Report last year. 2002) estimated that corruption costs Africa US$ 148 billion a year. Research by the UN Economic Commission for Africa shows, that Africans have stashed 37% of the Continent's wealth outside its borders. The comparable figures are 17% in Latin America, 4% South Asia and 3% in East Asia.

-Ross Herbert and Richard Stovin-Bradford: Stopping the Corrupt=KYC, ***Electronic Journal of Governance and Innovation.***

One of the critical factors of leadership is integrity. Good governance is almost singularly driven by integrity. To cite the Report, *Our Global Neighbourhood*, "the quality of governance depends to a crucial degree on policy makers and those in position of authority adhering to the highest principles and ideals." Yet integrity is in decline in Tanzania. The *Warioba Commission Report* vividly underlined that corruption had become the worst form of social pollution in the country. It subverts democratic governance and ordinary people are its worst victims; victims because the effect of corruption is waste, distorted resource allocation, reduced revenues and poor investor response. Corruption, in other words, undermines social and economic development. When President Benjamin Mkapa rose to the Presidency in November 1995 he immediately coined the catch phrase *"Zama za Uwazi Na Ukweli"*. The era of transparency and truth) to underlie the philosophy of his style and substance of governance. Mkapa was obviously not trying to be original in this policy direction. Throughout his Presidential campaign in 1995, he made a commitment to the people that he would take Tanzania back to its past moral ethic that had underpinned the national sense of pride, purpose, unity, solidarity, peace and stability.

Mwalimu Nyerere had articulated this moral ethic in a famous intervention in the Tanganyika Parliament on 17th May 1960. Debating the Budget, and in reference to corruption as an enemy of the people, Nyerere said: "Let us face it, Sir, we can talk all this idealistic nonsense about the right of the people to govern themselves and all that. You establish a government of the people. They have hopes, and during the whole struggle of the nationalist movement, we have been raising the expectations of our people. They have been expecting a government that is going to lift their standard of living. How? By raising taxes and using them to wage this war. against poverty, disease and ignorance). Our people hope they are going to have a government that is going to spend their taxes properly in waging this war. They expect they are going to have a government that is going to be determined to see that justice is done in this country. What is the enemy of that? What is the enemy of the expectation? Not merely poverty. We can do something about poverty. Not disease, we can do something about disease as long as honest men are carrying out the job. Not ignorance, we know that enemy too, we know we don't want people who are ignorant. But, if our people cannot have absolute confidence in their-government, in the people to whom they have entrusted their welfare, how, Sir, are you going to wage this silly war against poverty, disease and ignorance? You have got to have people with confidence in their own government and when I say in their own government, I don't mean in a few Ministers, I mean every man and woman in the country who is in a position of responsibility."

Mwalimu Nyerere went on further to demand that corruption be treated with the same ruthlessness accorded to cases of treason. Nyerere was right in his definition of good governance. The critical underpinning of good governance is almost certainly the existence of confidence and trust by the people in their government. Evidently, such confidence and trust is driven by the ethical character and integrity of those who constitute the leaders of government. What Mwalimu did not discuss, however, is what constitutes the source of corruption. After all, corruption, in the broad sense, includes abuse of authority, even where it does not involve money-changing hands. Moreover, in law, there is even a concept of corruption of public morals whose inference is sexual misconduct.

President Mkapa has gone some distance, through the *Warioba Commission Report*, to address the sources of corruption. However, the effort underlined by the seminal *Warioba Commission Report* has unfortunately been undermined by orchestrated sentimentalism and media frenzy directed at apprehending corrupt elements, placing undue emphasis on ends, not on the means that drive corruption. Some Tanzanians have wanted to see blood as proof of commitment to implement the Warioba recommendations. President Mkapa has also been put under much pressure from donors who have tried to drive the anti-corruption agenda focused on the short-termist objective of catching the thief and not in helping enough to address the underlying causes of such criminal and deviant behaviour Such attitudes beg the very question about the fertility of corruption, namely that the rule of law has to become the very vehicle to combat corruption and not to be subverted, instead, because of it.

Apart from the stance that the donors took over the Zanzibar Question. the ostensible CCM- CUF political quagmire), viewing it as a manifestation of the subversion of good governance, there has been little attention on their part and on the part of the World Bank to address good governance from its broad dimensions. As a result, many Tanzanians have come to adopt a very narrow and potentially retrogressive perception of good governance, viewing it as almost exclusively or dominantly synonymous with the absence of corruption. This is a dangerous approach. As a country in transition, politically, in terms of constitutionality and democratisation, on the one hand, and economically, on the other hand, good governance has to be viewed from its broader perspective or else some of its key elements may not receive the attention they deserve. This is not to say that corruption is not a serious problem. It is; it undermines economic development and subverts democratic governance. To that extent, ordinary people are worst victims of corruption. In fact, the tragedy is that they often do not even recognise the relationship between corruption and the quality of their own livelihood. Tanzanians should thus come to terms with the fact that weak and suspect governance is what triggers, fertilises and nourishes corruption. Moreover, to tackle corruption head on, they should address what underlies good governance. This is an onerous challenge. Short cuts would only create false hopes. Tanzanians may end up addressing the manifestations, not the latent causes of corruption. In this instance, it is a welcome development that the NSGRP is seized of the importance to institute more effective regulations and mechanisms to combat petty and grand corruption.

Media and Governance

The media is presently confronted with an onerous yet important challenge of identifying the larger national interest and explaining it. Tinkering at the margins of central issues such as good governance obviously sells newspapers. It has the potential of confusing and misleading, unwittingly as it may be. The role of the media should be to lead and educate the public. Greater clarity of thinking and articulation of ideas and issues is called for in this regard. As an organ of civil society, the media has critical role to play in articulating freely, accurately and fairly, what Rajni Kothari describes as the "convulsion of human consciousness" and transforming it into political action. The signal recognition of the media in all democratic societies as the Fourth Estate gives the media a special place and role in national governance, along with the conventional instruments of the state, the executive, the legislature and the judiciary. The media, not being part of the state, has the advantage of being able to exercise a greater role of checks and balance. This role underlies a functioning democracy, particularly so in Tanzania type of polities that are still in transition to real democracies in the sense of realising a constitutional order that truly respects the doctrine of the separation of powers. This doctrine represents a well-balanced constitutional dispensation that respects the authority of the people beyond the electoral and legislative process. In it, lies the foundation for realising a national ethic that supports human dignity, equality, freedom, tolerance and stability. Thomas Jefferson said that he knew "no safe depository of the ultimate powers of the society but the people themselves, and if we think them not enlightened enough to exercise their control with a wholesome discretion, the remedy is not to take it from them but to inform their discretion." The media should play the role of informing the people. It is their watchdog, their medium and platform for holding the instruments of the state to account for their policies, decisions, actions and omissions.

In many respects, the role of the media in good governance is an extension of democratic values, of pluralism. For good governance to thrive, democracy must pervade all levels of society. Some people would argue that democracy has nothing to do with development. The often-quoted example is the People's Republic of China that has been able to achieve annual average economic growth over the past decade and half of about 10%. Yet China is not a democracy in the western liberal sense. The point is obviously missed. The point is not the *relationship* between democracy and development. Rather, it is the *goal* of development itself. In this context, I am in agreement with the view advanced in the *Challenge to the South* that "a democratic environment which governs fundamental human rights is an essential goal of development centred on the people as well as a crucial means of accelerating development". Therefore, good governance should entail maximum participation by the people in the governance structures that determine their welfare and development. In Tanzania's specific conditions, the role and concerns of women in development for instance, take pre-eminence.

Law and Governance

Good governance also crucially means the existence of the rule of law, of enforceable law. It is not simply adequate to have a rule of law. Many people would proclaim that Tanzania has a rule of law. They could be right in the sense that there exists a well established judicial system and the constitution provides for a solid legal framework. However, the enforceability of the laws is what accords the rule of law its respect. Evidently, in this area much remains to be achieved. For instance, the legal and regulatory framework that underpins a market economy is yet to be fully put in place. One shortcoming is the labour law regime, a relic of the socialist era. The new labour law enacted in 2004 goes some way in responding to the needs of a new market regime. However, Tanzania still suffers from labour market inflexibilities, especially relating to freedom to hire skilled people irrespective of nationality and the industrial dispute machinery that is still politically influenced. This area should be addressed quickly as it inhibits investor confidence and fertilises corruption. Moreover, in spite of the establishment of commercial courts, commercial cases still take long to conclude and court injunctions have sometimes become a vehicle for corruption.

Evidently, inadequate allocation of resources to the judicial system has impacted it negatively. One would have thought that since one of the key pillars of the re-defined role of the state is the promotion and maintenance of the rule of law, this responsibility would have been accorded a high regard in terms of resources. However, this is not to be though, since fiscal year 2001, there have been improvements in budgetary allocations. In such an environment, how could Tanzanians not be surprised by the level of corruption that engulfs the judicial system! Good governance demands that, as in the case of the Tanzania Revenue Authority, the judicial and legal service would equally be well compensated, in pay and benefits, so that it better upholds the rule of law.

One of the linkages to promoting the rule of law is the existence of an independent system for public evaluation of government conduct. In this area, urgent need had existed for the reform of the Permanent Commission of Enquiry. PCE) to make it a free and fair ombudsperson. The PCE, as it was constituted and in its authority, smacked of the excess baggage of a past era of political hegemony. The PCE law had to be reviewed and recasted to transform it into a truly independent instrument for checking and exposing abuse of power and authority by public officials. Therefore, the enactment of a law in 2001 establishing the Commission of Human Rights and Good Governance was a welcome development.

Governance and Economic Management

Not many Tanzanians would associate good governance with economic issues. Yet, as a developing country that should quickly respond to the growing expectations of its people and to the challenges of making itself an attractive investment destination, good governance, at the economic level, is paramount. In this era, good governance is characterised by the existence of stable and predicable economic policies - macro and micro. It is difficult to point an accusing finger at President Mkapa's administration in this area of good governance. Evidently, much remains to be done to improve the micro-economic conditions that largely hinge on reducing the presently high costs of doing business in Tanzania. Yet, there is a will and a commitment to address these issues.

The task of informing and stabilising the micro-economic fundamentals has been an arduous one and its effects on the poor have been debilitating. Indeed, on this score, criticism has been levelled against President Mkapa. For instance, on why he has had to honour external debts when poverty and disease have been entrenching. Yet it is important to restate that the realisation of economic goals in Tanzanian-type of economic conditions could not be simple and painless. Good governance demands a leadership focused on the end goal, on the destination and not simply on the state of conditions to be traversed. It is a challenge of leadership of doing the right thing as opposed to merely doing things right. Mkapa has had to choose between moving the economy forward, to a growth and sustainable path, or be a short-termist populist leader with little to deliver to his people in the medium and long term.

There is another factor of good governance in economics to consider. In my view, economic growth cannot be confined to national statistics without there being visible improved conditions of people's livelihoods. In this context, *The Challenge To The South* has aptly underscored that the "concern for social justice has to be an integral part of genuine development. A faster distribution of income and productive assets like land is essential as a means of speeding up development and making it sustainable." The same thrust features in the Report, *Our Global Neighbourhood* that there is need to take deliberate efforts to "reduce gross inequalities, to deal with factors that cause or perpetuate them and to promote a faster sharing of resources". These concerns are pivotal to good governance. It is these concerns that lead to the root causes of social conflict and crime. The erosion of security of property and life in South Africa in recent years, for example, is a direct outcome of lost hopes at a time when equity and social justice are yet to feature as fruits arising from the destruction of apartheid. Discussing the crisis of human security, the renowned Pakistani and the man behind the UN Human Development Reports, the late Mahbub UI Haq, had this to say in his Barbara Ward Lecture at the 21st World Conference of the Society for International Development in April 1994: "There must be a search for models of development which enhance human life, not marginalize it; which treat GNP growth as a means, not as a end; which replenish natural resources for future generations, not destroy them; which encourage grassroots participation of people in the events and process that shape their lives. The issue is not growth per se but its character and its distribution."

Good Governance Requires Good Government

The qualities to govern well -wisdom, intellect, competence, character-qualities that made Mwalimu Nyerere such an affable and adorable leader, are in short supply in Tanzania. Good government, after all, does not merely mean the President. The President alone could not become the pillar of good governance. Good government thus embraces all leaders-political and the bureaucracy. It is in this context that there are elements of expediency in place that sometimes override rational decisions in Tanzania. Tanzania is yet to attract a significant number of individuals of intellect, competence and character into its public life, both government and civil society. Tanzanians would be failing in their basic and fundamental nationalist duty if they do not play a part in enabling good governance to take root. The establishment of a Ministry of State in the President's Office responsible for Good Governance is a positive move but could be merely symbolic. For this ministry to be a pathbreaker and a pathfinder, the government would have to be able to rely on the support and solidarity of the civil society, the media being an important part. The legislature has an even more vital role to play. It should not allow itself to be reduced to playing second fiddle or surrogate to the executive simply because the majority of parliamentarians are from the party in power. In a poor country, the role of a party whip has to be overridden by a broader national interest that the legislature should ensure. The legislature should not trade off good governance with privilege, prerogative and perquisites. Good government must inherently entail making the legislature and, indeed, all the registered political parties, more effective vehicles for realising good governance. These parties have to be well funded with state support if political corruption is to be arrested. The Public Service also has to be well rewarded and meritocracy should once again be championed.

To sum up, good governance is not a buzzword. It refers to well-balanced and focused governance. The government, the private sector, non-governmental organisations and the civil society have to work in unison and harmoniously share the responsibility of governance. At the end of the day, good governance means nothing more, nothing less than the promotion and protection of interests and the meeting of the basic needs of the people. It is when this objective is realised that corruption would wither and be seen to be a scourge to be avoided and admonished.

A discussion of the challenges of leadership and governance in Tanzania cannot be complete without reviewing the place and role of the late Mwalimu Nyerere. At no time was the centrality of Nyerere's role and ideas as critical in determining Tanzania's direction, as it pursued far-reaching social and economic reforms, as at the time when it was gearing itself for the first multi-party general elections in October 1995. Though Nyerere is dead, his vision of *ujamaa* still looms large and in many respects haunts the national leadership since it still enjoys a wide and strong followership. In the following sections, I closely analyse Nyerere's influence, as it featured in 1995, and as it continues to constitute the bedrock of ideological debate in the country.

Leadership and the "Ghost" of Socialism

The future direction of Tanzania's economic policies became a central issue in the period just before the October 1995 Presidential elections. Indeed, that debate or concern about the direction has remained ever alive in the Tanzanian political scene from the time when the country adopted a market driven economic philosophy. It is noteworthy that during the period just before the 1995 general elections, close watchers of the national political scene-academics, professionals, bureaucrats, industrialists and, even the IFM and the World Bank, were apprehensive about whether President Ali Hassan Mwinyi's market-based economic reforms would be sustained or deepened by the incoming Executive Presidency. It was a worrying question. It remains a concern as Tanzania now moves towards the third multi-party general elections in 2005.

Paradoxically, in 1995, the apprehension was focused more on Benjamin Mkapa's likely Presidency rather than on any of the opposition party leaders. One would have thought that such anxiety would not have existed following President Mwinyi's address on dissolving the National Assembly at the end of July 1995 to usher in the commencement the general elections electoral process. In that address, which highlighted his legacy, after 10 years at the helm, Mr. Mwinyi confidently affirmed that the infrastructure for a market economy had been solidly laid and that the regime after him, which he forecasted would be a CCM one, his own party, would in fact consolidate and improve upon his achievements.

Additionally, the anxieties were incomprehensible, at least within the CCM. The party had already set out its core economic policies. At Chimwaga, Dodoma in December 1992, the CCM's 4th National Conference adopted a programme that set out a new policy and strategic direction for the Party in the 1990s. That programme, which revisited the core tenets of the 1967 Arusha Declaration and also recorded continued commitment to the Arusha Declaration's principles, but only in so far as building a self reliant nation is concerned and not a socialist command economy, marked a major ideological shift by the CCM from the socialist framework of the Arusha Declaration, to wit that it shall:

> i) cease to be the principal entrepreneur and would instead become a facilitator, promoter and regulator of the economy.

ii) continue to intervene in the economy only where ownership of strategic economic activities. for instance, railways, harbours, posts and telecommunications, energy and water supply) is concerned.

iii) construct a "socialist" society based, predominantly, on private ownership.

It is interesting to note though, that the CCM government took bold steps after the 1995 and 2000 elections to privatise or prepare to privatise even the strategic economic activities such as the railways, telecom, ports and harbours, energy and water and sewerage. On the face of it, these actions would appear to contradict the CCM policy for the 1990s adopted at Chimwaga in 1992. The political changes, in themselves, have raised serious debate, rancour and semblance of political turbulence especially in the period between 2002 and 2003. Several CCM parliamentarians, during this period, questioned: the manner in which the telecommunications company, TTCL, was privatised, the award of the management contract of the power utility company, TANESCO, and the concessioning of the Dar es Salaam water and sewerage company, DAWASA, to a British company. Put differently, there is a disconcerting environment emerging that vindicates the concern whether Tanzania could not revert to socialism. This is the context behind the anxieties felt in 1995. The anxieties have resumed particularly as to whether the depth of economic reforms realised so far would be sustained and deepened after the 2005 Elections.

Relevance of the Anxiety

Clearly, pursuant to the new party policies the CCM adopted in late 1992, the state of disquiet about what economic policies a new CCM government would have pursued after the 1995 elections appeared frivolous and a deliberate creation of the opposition parties directed at discrediting CCM as a party lacking a clear a sense of direction. However, such a stance on the part of the CCM would have been overly simplistic and unscientific and could have damaged its electoral chances. There were two important reasons why those anxieties needed to be taken seriously. The first reason had a direct connection to campaign politics leading to the general elections and thus could have informed electorate behaviour. It is particularly important to take note of the scientific campaign approach that was adopted by the Civic United Front's Presidential candidate, Professor Ibrahim Lipumba. He slowly but consistently focused on economic issues and, to that extent, ideological economic issues remained central. The second reason had a direct bearing on the future of external support to Tanzania. In other words, it impacted the flow of foreign aid and investments and the confidence of domestic producers, whether peasants or manufactures, with respect to the sustainability of market-led reforms. Stability of good policies, after all, is the fuel that drives economic actors. Any form of apprehension about the continuity and stability of good policies creates instability in the economy; it drives business to mark-time, if not to halt; and above all, it promotes speculative business, including hoarding of consumer goods, and capital flight. The manifestations of such state of economic instability loomed large in 1995. They should not be dismissed even at this stage as Tanzania moves towards the 2005 elections. In fact, whether Tanzania likes it or not, there is an uncertainty within the donor community as whether Tanzania would sustain and deepen the reforms it has boldly and prudently pursued, particularly in the last ten years.

Why the Anxieties?

The fundamental question remains: why did the apprehensive mood in Tanzanian society and in the donor community arise in 1995? Was it reasonably believed that President Mkapa would have reinstated the Arusha Declaration, lock, stock and barrel? Nevertheless, that was precisely the question that loomed large in 1995. Personally, I did not think so, for three reasons. First, because Mr. Mkapa had the fortunate advantage of having being a cabinet minister in both the Nyerere government that pursued a socialist path of development as well as in Mwinyi's government that ushered in a market economy. Secondly, Mkapa is an intellectual of high order, with the capacity and capability to make objective assessments based on the costs and benefits of an economic system- socialist and market- and determine the most viable one to pursue. If anything, Tanzania has been lucky to have a person who, by virtue of his incisive insight and experience, has been able to determine the appropriate path of development for Tanzania to take. Thirdly, those who had worked closely with Mkapa knew him as a person who respected intellect and empowered colleagues and subordinates by involving them in decision-making processes whilst retaining ultimate effective decision. Rationality and pragmatism were seen to be his forte and the basis of his decisions.

However, my views about Mr. Mkapa may not have reflected the general mood as it obtained at the material time. In fact, the mood, in the view of some seasoned Tanzanian watchers, appeared to be conditioned by the central role the late Mwalimu Julius Nyerere, a person known and respected or revered for his abiding faith to socialism, played in the nomination process for the CCM Presidential candidate and in his unequivocal commitment to campaign for the CCM Presidential candidate. I shall review and analyse below Nyerere's role in the nomination process in some detail to explain the ostensible grounds that made the state of apprehension appear plausible in certain quarters of

Tanzanian society and in the donor community. Suffice it to state at this stage that the apprehension appeared to be influenced more by what was seen to be a close personal relationship between Mwalimu Nyerere and Mkapa than the actual reality.

Because of that relationship, there existed a psychological perception that the potential for Mr. Mkapa being intimately influenced by Nyerere to detour from market economic policies and turn back to socialism was great. That perception was reinforced by views of some influential thinkers deemed, at the material time, to be close to Mkapa. People like Jenerali Ulimwengu. In an article in the respected Kiswahili language weekly tabloid, *Rai*. August 31st to September 6th, 1995), Jenerali Ulimwengu, then Editor in Chief of the paper, and an outgoing Member of Parliament and a Member of the CCM National Executive Committee, observed that in spite of the fact that, for some time, right wing thinking within the CCM appeared to be in command the situation had not dovetailed a sustained and passionate debate on the CCM's political philosophies, both within the CCM and in the National Assembly. He further observed, "The nomination of Benjamin Mkapa as CCM's Presidential candidate, in one respect, is a reflection, that within the CCM, there is brainpower and energy which had not been given recognition because of the right wing dominance". In speculating the existence of stratification within the CCM top leadership based on ideological differences, Mr. Ulimwengu was proposing that Mr. Mkapa, as President, would move the CCM, once again, close to the fundamentals of the Arusha Declaration.

Nyerere's Legacy in the Anxiety

However, why should Nyerere have featured so prominently in the state of apprehension about the future of market economy policies? Political pundits postulate that since the onset of economic reforms, Nyerere had taken a back seat in Tanzanian politics. In fact, there was a general belief that Nyerere had deliberately been politically marginalised, with President Mwinyi entrenching his authority. Thus, the sudden return of Nyerere onto the political centre stage, towards the end of 1994, and the active role he played in the CCM Presidential candidate selection process, as well as in the 1995 Presidential campaign, raised the question: Why the renewed interest on Nyerere's part about politics? The logic behind the question was, whilst Nyerere had indeed committed himself to remaining an active CCM member after his retirement from the CCM Chairmanship in late 1990, he had apparently become anguished and disenchanted about CCM's policies and leadership particularly so from 1990. It was that state of disillusionment that made observers suspect that Nyerere could try to ensure that under President Mkapa there would be renewal of socialist philosophies to guide new social and economic policies. However, what could have been the cause of Nyerere's anguish? Four reasons stand out.

First, was the chipping away of the Arusha Declaration by the Mwinyi Administration through the market-led economic policies. Nyerere did not seem to accept the view that socialism was the cause for Tanzania's economic mess under his rule. Neither was he sold to the idea that a market economy was the best prescription for Tanzania's economic woes. Nyerere was particularly disturbed by the adoption of the Zanzibar resolution by the CCM national Executive in January 1991 that scrapped off the Leadership Code, a pillar of the Arusha Declaration that required national leaders not to be involved in capitalist activities. The Leadership Code was Nyerere's principal instrument for curbing the emergence of capitalist tendencies and practices within the Tanzanian leadership. broadly defined to embrace all CCM functionaries, and later every CCM member, senior government bureaucrats and senior officials of state-owned enterprises).

The thrust of the Zanzibar Resolution was that the Leadership Code was "out of tune" with new economic realities. The subsequent adoption, in December 1992, of the programme that set out a new policy and strategic direction for the CCM for the 1990s, reflecting a major shift from the fundamentals of the Arusha Declaration apparently constituted the last nail on the coffin bearing Nyerere's socialist economic legacy. Some observers would wish to believe that following Nyerere's stint with the South Commission, his passion for socialism had taken a more realistic posture. meaning that he had transformed into a social democrat than a socialist), particularly in the light of global political and economic changes. I believe, on the contrary, that Nyerere remained a committed socialist largely because he did not believe that poor economies could effectively be transformed through market or liberal economic policies without unity and peace being sacrificed.

Indeed, it is precisely because of such conviction that when Nyerere tossed the idea in a key address to the CCM National Conference in August 1990, that Tanzania should seriously consider reverting to a multiparty political system, he was unequivocal about his preference for a two party system modelled on the American one. However, he championed the case of both parties being socialist. He said, at the time, "I will be extremely happy if Tanzania will only have two socialist political parties". In that same speech, at which Conference he decided to retire from the CCM Chairmanship, Nyerere was emphatic in stating, "If our party. i.e. CCM) will disregard the principles of socialism, then it will be disregarding one of the key foundations of our national peace and tranquillity. We will undermine peace; precisely because we will have frustrated the aspirations of forging the type of development which upholds human dignity and equality"

At the time when Nyerere was delivering that speech, President Mwinyi's economic reforms were exactly four years old and had begun to show positive results. Probably in reference to Mwinyi's market-friendly economic reforms, Nyerere played the liberal by stating that it would be necessary, from time to time, to adapt policies, tactics and strategies in order to move forward. Yet his apparent liberal stance had an in-built caveat. later he on went to assert that where such adaptations were made, human dignity and equality would be ensured because peace and tranquillity in a poor country could never be sustained in the absence of social justice and equality. In Nyerere's view, barbarism. a loose translation of the Kiswahili word "unyang'au" which he used in his speech, but several other meanings could be ascribed to it, like "capitalism"), by definition, was inconsistent with respect for social justice and equality. Nyerere ended his speech with, "Long live socialism and self reliance".

Secondly, Nyerere was saddened by the way in which the Mwinyi government had failed to uphold the Tanzania Union constitution, ostensibly by "allowing" Zanzibar to join the Organisation of Islamic Conference. OIC). Under the Union Constitution, Zanzibar cannot, without the consent of the Union Government, become a member of an international organisation of whatever kind. President Mwinyi was seen to have failed to uphold the oath he had taken as President to safeguard and defend the Constitution.

The third issue that disturbed Nyerere to the extent of his demanding the resignation of the former Prime Minister, John S. Malecela and the former CCM Secretary General, the late Horace Kolimba, involved the sanctity of the Tanzania Union. In Nyerere's view, President Mwinyi's CCM and government leadership failed to effectively handle the Union Parliament's quest and resolutions for the establishment of a three Union government structure, away from the present two-government structure. Parliament had demanded that a government of Tanganyika be established because the Union structure, which comprises a Union government and a Zanzibar government, was inequitable in that in favoured Zanzibar, status-wise. Early in 1995, Nyerere came down harshly on Mwinyi and his senior colleagues accusing them of failure to uphold the CCM's policy of sustaining the two Union government structure. He described President Mwinyi as a "weak leader". However, he argued that his removal from power at that time would have unnecessarily disturbed the machinery of government and thus Mwinyi should be allowed to complete his term of office.

Finally, what appears to have particularly offended Nyerere was the erosion of the socialist ethic manifested by entrenching corruption and the disintegration of the social fabric. In two angry speeches, one made before a press conference at Kilimanjaro Hotel in Dar es Salaam early in 1995 and another in Mbeya during the 1995 May Day celebrations, Nyerere objurgated the Mwinyi administration for allowing the Tanzania nation to degenerate into a despicable political condition resembling a country struck by an earthquake. Nyerere castigated deep-seated corruption at high leadership levels, deteriorated social service delivery, particularly in the health and education sectors, the collapse of public ownership through unwarranted privatisation of profitable and strategic productive industries like textile mills, and the growing disunity depicted by emerging tribal, religious and racial sentiments. To Nyerere, those cracks in the national fabric appeared to be the consequences of market-driven policies pursued by President Mwinyi, on the one hand, and the absence of leadership ethics, on the other hand.

Nyerere: "God" Father Figure in CCM Politics

Tanzania close watchers point out that Nyerere's aggressive involvement in the CCM politics in 1995 was fuelled by the opportunity that he believed was in his grasp to address and redress all the policies and leadership weaknesses that had precipitated his anguish and tribulations since his departure from political office. Such mindset made Nyerere publicly pronounce, declare and threaten that if the CCM failed to nominate a Presidential candidate with the attributes acceptable to him, he would quit the CCM and even support a Presidential candidate from the opposition. In other words, from the beginning, Nyerere's position had been to play a frontal role in ensuring that a CCM Presidential candidate who fitted his expectations became President. Nyerere wanted change; change from an economic system, which, in his view, was breeding disunity and disorder, to a system that would re-build unity and foster peace and tranquillity in the country.

That message came out clearly from his short statement to the CCM Special National Conference in Dodoma on 24th July 1995. A sombre and visibly emotional Nyerere told the CCM Delegates that "only the CCM can produce the President of Tanzania" and that the Conference had an onerous task of literally choosing a person who would be the President. He went on to add that the CCM was a party of the poor, not of the rich. as if, amongst the three Presidential candidates awaiting electoral judgement, some were rich or pro the rich!) and that delegates should carefully select a person who would maintain that particular party core value. Then he condemned the entrenched state of corruption, tribalism and religious bigotry pervading the country. clearly referring to the candidates) and asked the delegates to vote for a candidate who would fight those scourges. What is interesting to note, in retrospect, is that Nyerere did not call upon the delegates to choose a socialist. In the past, he used to demand the election of leaders who were devout socialists. That was quite a departure. Was it because he knew that the attributes he underlined would lead to the election of a person he believed was a "socialist" in his view at the time?

At the same time, underscoring that he was for a good and clean leader, Nyerere appeared to have been more concerned about the re-focusing of development strategies so that they targeted the poor and created the necessary conditions for fostering unity, peace and tranquillity in a country that prided itself, for years, as being devoid of tribal, racial and religious differences than necessarily on the construction of a socialist society based on the wholesale principles enshrined in the Arusha Declaration.

The "Market" or "Governance"?

In the Tanzanian case, the reason why market reforms of President Mwinyi were viewed by people like Nyerere to have not been people- centred with the result that they adversely affected the poor was, in my view, primarily because the reforms themselves performed below expectations, a result largely attributed to ineffective governance. A few examples would confirm such conclusion. Take trade liberalisation to start with. The opening up of the Tanzanian economy to imports, per se, was a positive policy. However, Tanzanians know that imports trade liberalisation had been poorly managed specifically at the level of ensuring tax compliance. The result was unequal competition between imported goods and domestic manufactures. This led to the virtual collapse of key national industries and to de-industrialisation.

At the same time, because government revenues had fallen dramatically due to massive tax evasion at the level of imports, the social sector and, specifically, education and health, became hard hit. The government response to such evident tax collection deficit had been to borrow from the Central Bank with adverse consequences: high inflation, large government debt that was consuming a huge chunk of recurrent budget and further depriving the already bad social service delivery system with much needed finance and credit squeeze, which starved the very domestic industry that the government depended upon more than from imports for its revenue.

Secondly, poor government expenditure control. In spite of excellent recommendations put before the government by two separate Presidential Commissions, the Mtei and Mramba Commissions. of 1991 and 1994 respectively) embracing the introduction of better fiscal and tax policies, including the introduction of VAT, improved tax collection measures, controlling government expenditure, downsizing the government, improving financial accountability, compensating civil servants better, thus reducing rent seeking in government contracts and tax collection and generally promote higher productivity, government was ineffective at the level of implementation. Even in the case of privatisation, the government failed to distinguish between privatisation of assets that were inherently unable to regenerate and those that had fallen into trouble simply because the government had failed, in the first place, to manage well the imports trade liberalisation. As I have argued earlier, privatisation is a good policy but it is not a panacea.

A good example in this case, and this comment is made not in any way to disparage the subsequent privatisation measure that I fully endorse and whose success is to be proud of, is Tanzania Breweries. TBL). In 1993, TBL was loudly appealing to the government to reduce consumption taxes imposed on beer to enable it compete with beer smuggled in from Kenya. The subsequent lowering of taxes did not help TBL because the smuggled beer was being bought in Kenya at competitive export prices. In other words, the beer was being purchased duty and tax-free. So how could TBL's beer have competed unless the government chose to zero-rate the consumption taxes applicable on TBL's beer? So imagine a scenario where TBL had collapsed, and the writings were on the wall in 1993. The blame would surely have fallen heavily on the government. Of course, there were other more fundamental reasons why TBL could not compete with Kenyan beer, grounds, which justified TBL's privatisation. However, it is important to underscore the fact that poor management of trade liberalisation had its negative and often devastating impact on some domestic industries.

The interesting question is whether privatisation would have helped at that stage. My response is no. The problem that faced TBL as at 1993 had nothing to do with its inability to compete. Rather, it is the non- payment of *any* tax at all on imported beer that was the prime cause of TBL's financial blues. The solution centred on curbing smuggled beer. If TBL had been privatised without the smuggling problem being resolved, having, whatever the new firm taking over TBL would have faced similar travails, at least in the short term.

Nyerere and Mkapa: What Underpinned their Relationship?

What I have attempted to highlight is that the apprehensions about what would have constituted CCM's economic policies after the 1995 elections were genuine and important. Intelligent observers of the Tanzania political scene knew Nyerere well and what he stood for. They also knew that he favoured Mkapa to be CCM's Presidential candidate. The missing link was whether Nyerere, the committed socialist, expected Mkapa to "pay back" for his support by dovetailing the market reforms and taking Tanzania back on the socialist path. I have contended that in as much as Nyerere remained an abiding socialist, his concerns and tribulations about the then fragile political and economic conditions that obtained in the country were addressed somewhat through the promotion of a clean and effective leadership and governance. He was thus not encumbered by ideological-based economic policies of his choice. In my view, Nyerere saw in Benjamin Mkapa the kind of leadership attributes that could make market friendly policies work in the interest of the people much in the same way as they have done in the Scandinavian countries, in UK, Australia and partly in Germany. Moreover, Tanzania needed a strong government led by a person who knew the world, who was intelligent enough to know that static and dogmatic policies could not work in a world that was increasingly globalising in economic terms. Nyerere, the socialist, knew this and it would have been unrealistic for him to undermine that reality. Curiously, President Mkapa applied an almost similar strategy at the CCM Congress in Dodoma early May 2005 in literally leading the delegates to choose a candidate whom he believed in and had confidence in his ability not only to win the Presidential election in November 2005 but also to consolidate and deepen the economic reforms he has so admirably presided on and led.

Conclusion

The market reforms that President Mwinyi had effected were generally in the right direction. The distortions that emanated from them precipitating the sentiments in 1995 that a return to socialism could have been better, were not inherent in the reforms themselves as in the *consequences* of their poor management. We learn from the East Asian experience that a market economy works well under a strong state apparatus, sometimes even authoritarian. In the Tanzanian case, it is not a secret that elements of laxity and lack of strong accountability in President Mwinyi's government frustrated the performance of some of the market reforms. Governance failure also created an environment supportive of corruption and all types of bigotry. Professor Gerald Helleiner in his paper: *The Legacies of Julius Nyerere: An Economist's Reflections*, makes reference to this scourge of corruption during this period, describing it as having "reached the highest levels of the Government and party," and that the "central economic policymaking machinery was demoralised and in disarray". This comment is not intended to be a trial of Mwinyi's government. On the contrary, President Mwinyi should be hailed for his courage and determination to change Tanzania's path of development. The CCM supported his policies and adopted them as its own. It was a major achievement and it constituted his core legacy for Tanzania. The implementation problems that resulted from lack of effective governance are a useful lesson for future governments. Indeed, the challenge of the government in Tanzania since 1995 has been markets and good governance. In other words, sustain and consolidate market policies but ensure that those policies redistribute wealth and support programmes targeting poverty reduction and which uplift the living standards of the whole people through more effective and good governance. This is also the challenge facing the government taking over in November 2005.

Of course, there exists a great deal of controversy whether there is a direct correlation between good governance and good government. In the preceding sections, I have outlined the close connection between good leadership and good governance. I have also briefly touched on good governance connected to good government. In the following chapter, an attempt is made to show that good government is a central determinant in ensuring that effective leadership and good governance realise their set objectives. Indeed, I call for the re-inventing of government and a total overhaul of the public service system as necessary processes in enabling the achievement of radical economic reforms and improving the management government.

Chapter

17 RE- INVENTING GOVERNMENT

The performance of government depends on the role assigned to the state, the competence of public agencies, and the extent to which there is an enabling environment that facilitates and encourages growth-promoting activities by private citizens and honest behaviour by public officials.

-Pierre Landell-Mills: ***Governance and the External Factor***

Governance is the process by which we collectively solve our problems and meet our society's needs. Government is the instrument we use.

-David Osborne and Ted Gaebler: ***Reinventing Government***

Introduction

In the first serious interview that President Benjamin Mkapa gave immediately before being formally sworn in as the President of the United Republic of Tanzania in 1995, the President had the opportunity to address many policy issues falling within the broad framework of what he saw as his Vision for his first term of office. In response to a question raised by David Martin about the challenge of recreating the *esprit de corps* of the civil service that obtained during the British colonial administration, President Mkapa was unequivocal. He observed, "You do want to renew the values that characterised the proper civil service as we were told by the British". However, he was also quick to ramify that the achievement of those desired values crucially depended on the existence of factors such as a good remuneration system, a meaningful pension, good public service training and meritocratic recruitment, appointments and promotions. The President was right in his perception. It would be interesting to learn how he feels about the Tanzanian public service at the end of his ten-year administration.

Evidently, the challenge of re-inventing government, of giving government a more clarified and greater strategic focus and capacity, is not only a matter of urgent concern to developing countries such as Tanzania. On the contrary, leading industrial states of the world, such as the United States and Britain, are also engaged in searching for ways of getting their governments to respond more effectively to new challenges. This is as it should be. The contemporary world, as a whole, is in the throes of a massive social, political, technological and economic transformation.

The emergence of this new environment has given rise to major changes in global economic structures and relations. These, in turn, have had deep and far-reaching impact on how governments work and on the overall mindset of the people. Financial crises and economic meltdowns in Japan, Russia, East Asia, South East Asia and Brazil in the late 1990's and, more recently in Argentina and Chile, have raised questions, for example, about the efficacy of how governments to deal and regulate capital markets. Suddenly, the world is realising that globalisation has unleashed a Frankenstein in the arena of capital markets at a time when effective global controls are still not in place. Thus, whilst it is incumbent upon nation-state governments to respond to the myriad and catastrophic changes that necessitate the restructuring of the social order and better management of a constantly changing environment, the establishment of a new system of global governance is urgently necessary. The late British philosopher Isaiah Berlin was correct, in this context, when he perceptively posited, "any study of society shows that every solution creates a new situation which breeds its own needs and problems, new demands".

What is important to distinguish here is that the challenges confronting the performance of the Tanzania government system are too insignificant to be compared to those facing the British government apparatus. Yet what Tony Blair postulates about the British government and how his government should be re-invented, is equally applicable to Tanzania, the intricacies and magnitude of reform notwithstanding. In his policy pamphlet, The Third Way, Mr. Blair asserts, "What government does, and how well, not how much, is the key to its role in modern society". Clearly, in whichever context one considers, what government <u>does</u> should be informed by a vision of its role and purposes. Such vision is inherently derived from a national vision. In this context, I draw attention to some of the core values of Tanzanian society. It is these core values, I believe, that should underpin the process of re-inventing government. A public service reform that fails to anchor itself on such values could miss the ideal which Blair encapsulated in the phrase "what government does and how well".

Public Administration and Effective Governance

In a democratic polity, public administration lies at the heart of effective governance. Without it, a country faces an uncertain political future. Indeed, it could even constitute the root cause for social and political instability. It is imperative then that government becomes an instrument for the realisation and sustenance of society's core values. Tanzania is a country of great diversities: it is a union, and one that is faced by the trials and tribulations emanating from a nascent democratic system, and has heterogeneity of religions and race. These diversities are vulnerable to exploitation by different forces in society. In this context, the stability and prosperity of Tanzania lies in a strong government that enjoys integrity and which above all provides democratic guarantees against forces of division and destabilisation. It should also be added that the very democratic ethos that informs the form and style of public administration should ensure that the power of governance is well devolved to bring it closer to the people.

At another level, as the Tanzanian economy intensifies its accord of a greater role to and influence of the operations of the market, which is a fact of life to be embraced since Tanzania is not going to be an island cut off from the rest of the world, the role of the public servant is going to become more rather than less important. There is a debate about this view and it has engrossed many social scientists. The preponderant view is that, with the intensification of the market economy, governments would have less and less to do. This is probably correct. However, this is not the central question. As Tony Blair has noted, it is not how much the government does that is central any more; it is what it does and how well. The "how well" is more pertinent. Indeed, in the Tanzanian situation, this has become the major challenge.

The entry of the market now means that Tanzania requires a more resourceful bureaucracy, better able to offer policy direction and advice, in keeping with the national economic interest. At the same time, there is need for a bureaucracy that can administer legislation more efficiently and perceptively whilst ensuring the maintenance of high standards of public accountability. These new requirements demand that central roles directly played by public officials in the market arena be re-examined. An example would validate this point. Presently, the government has in place a Competition Law administered by the Ministry of Industry and Trade. Clearly, in a competitive environment where the government is required to fix and regulate the rules of the game, a senior public official could not exercise impartiality and fairness were he or she to sit on a Board of Directors of a Company whose products compete with similar products produced by competing firms. Ethical governance would not allow such situation to take place. The Commissioner for Competition is under the Ministry of Industry and Trade who's Permanent Secretary has been sitting on Boards of sensitive companies. This is prejudicial and should be corrected.

In my book, *Management of Public Enterprises in Developing Countries: The Tanzania Experience*, I argued that it was wrong to appoint Members of

Parliament, Ministers and Permanent Secretaries in Boards of Directors of state institutions. The reasons were varied. There was conflict of interest, diffusion of separation of powers and putting political leaders in invidious positions where they had to defend in the legislature the actions of the very state institutions they were part of. Mwalimu Nyerere was quick to see sense in these views and in 1983 decided to remove all these parties from state Boards much to the anguish and anger of the affected parties. The point is this: we must return to that system if we are serious about promoting good governance.

Yet another example of an antiquated decision making authority in a typical market environment was the overriding power exercised by the Minister for Labour and Youth over labour disputes. Tanzania has had an elaborate judicial system for settling labour disputes and the decisions of the Labour Tribunal should clearly be final and conclusive. They should not be overridden by a political functionary in the name of a Minister. Such overriding power is a travesty of legal process and merely undermines and subverts the lofty principle of separation of powers. Markets operate well in an environment where the sanctity of the law is recognised and respected. The new Employment and Labour Relations Act No 7 of 2004 marks a huge departure from the revoked Security of Employment Act, 1964. The legislation, which is supported by the Labour Institutions Act, 2004 under which a Commission for Mediation and Arbitration, a Labour, Economic and Social Council and a Labour Court. a labour division of the High Court) are established, revokes the powers of the Minister for Labour and where any Ministerial powers are exercised under the Act, they are subjected to exclusive jurisdiction for review by the Labour Court. All industrial disputes are now referred to the Commission for mediation and arbitration. Upon failure of mediation, disputes are referred to the Labour Court. Overall, these new labour legislations establish a new regime of freedom of association, employment standards and entitlements, systems for termination of employment, role of trade unions and employers associations, collective bargaining, strikes and lockouts, dispute resolution and adjudication. They have gone a long way in creating more conducive management-labour relations in line with international labour standards.

Entrepreneurship in Government

I perceive a major challenge in re-inventing government when consideration is made on the challenge to balance the spirit of entrepreneurship in government with the imperativeness of strategic management of risk embodied within the framework of public accountability. I do not believe that there is a contradiction in these important two roles. However, there is a major task in the selection of public officials best able to balance the need for a facilitatory system whilst ensuring a well functioning regulatory system. Training public officials and attaching them in best managed private sector business organisations for brief periods, every now and then, would go a long way in inculcating a balanced spirit of entrepreneurship that respects the boundaries of government role in assuring equity and social justice. In this context, it would be expected, for example, that the leadership of the Tanzania Revenue Authority would approach its onerous tasks in a spirit of business mindedness and not simply in the spirit of mechanical revenue collection. Nobody doubts the centrality of TRA core responsibility. Yet, it is conceivable that it could succeed in performing its responsibilities with greater excellence were its approach and management style driven by greater entrepreneurial culture.

Knowledge-based Clusters

The clear move of the government towards creating value through knowledge- based services and through people that are well motivated and compensated is a commendable one. We have already witnessed how the Tanzania Revenue Authority has been able to transform itself into an intelligent enterprise and to deliver excellent results. The creation of similar service clusters in the government, particularly in those areas where there is presently significant loss of public funds and weak performance is necessary. I have a case in point. Annually, the government loses billions of shillings of public funds through poor procurement, and even outright misappropriation from procurement of goods and services for the government. Evidently, there is urgent need for the government to create another TRA or TANROADS-type of organisation to take responsibility for procurement. It should be noted that the central government procurement in Tanzania, pursuant to a study: *Public Procurement: Lessons from Kenya, Tanzania and Uganda* by Walter Odhiambo and Paul Kamau, was in 2000/2001 estimated to be about 8.5% of GDP. This makes public procurement critical in promoting transparency in government. The adoption of the Public Procurement Act in 2001 was a step in the right direction in making government procurement transparent. However, the agency charged with the responsibility for managing public procurement should ideally not be the Central Tender Board under the Ministry of Finance. An independent executive agency to perform such an onerous and specialised task is called for. In Uganda, the government privatised its procurement responsibility by appointing a private firm to take total responsibility for such role. *The Presidential Commission of Enquiry on Corruption in Tanzania.* the Warioba Commission) came close to making a similar proposal as a measure towards curbing deep-seated corruption in government procurement. There may be other services within the government system which could be brought under a similar approach. These should also be put under an independent government agency or services outsourced from private agencies.

In conclusion, it is evident that the government, as the executive arm of the state, has been at the centre of trenchant criticism for failing to adjust quickly and effectively to the demands of changed and changing social, political and economic circumstances. It is important that the ongoing reform of government and of the public service in particular responds to such concerns and demands. In the next section, I examine the challenges that exist in modernising the state, its institutions, structures and, more critically, the public servant.

Modernising the Tanzanian State

An Australian joke about public servants serves a useful opener to a serious discussion about the effectiveness of the Tanzanian State. Two Australian friends go hot air ballooning. Suddenly, a very thick fog engulfs them and they are left drifting helplessly in a haze. After a while, almost unexpectedly, there is a break in the clouds and they could then see a man walking a dog in the field below.

"Where are we?" yelled one of the Balloonists.
"About 200 metres in the air", came the reply. With that, the fog closed in once again.
"Bloody Public Servants" said the exasperated Balloonist.
"But how do you know he was a Public Servant?" his colleague quizzed.
"It is obvious. What he said was completely correct and of absolutely no help".

Public servants occupy a central position in the levers of the state. Indeed, it is in this context that, as early as 1964, in a speech when opening the Dar es Salaam University College campus, Mwalimu Nyerere was unequivocal in stating that the United Republic could not afford to carry "passengers" in its government services; that it could not afford to be "sentimental". He added, "Our public service must be efficient and imbued with a sense of the urgency of our national need for revolutionary change." This was not mere rhetoric. The Nyerere Administration, for all the failings attributed to it in the area of economic policy, succeeded to build a strong public service driven by a social and political ethic.

Nyerere succeeded to "socialise" public servants and to use them as an effective tool for promoting and safeguarding socialism and self-reliance as lofty principles and for implementing socialist programmes. So successful was the process of initiation and imbuing the public servant that it was never difficult for Nyerere to shift public servants into political assignments with positive results. In fact, with the benefit of hindsight, it is generally upheld today, in a negative sense, that the public service mindset and orientation is still so deeply anchored in an era long overtaken by global changes. For this reason, Development Vision 2025 affirms the necessity of re-orienting the role of government and the enhancement of its core competencies in providing effective leadership. Evidently, some Tanzanians would claim that something is happening within the state in improving the quality of public services. For example, it is observed that the Public Service Reform Commission, for years, has been undertaking a review of the public service system in order to transform it to fit the needs and challenges of a new era and generally to improve government accountability. In this context, effort has centred on retrenching excess personnel, streamlining government ministries and departments, and creating executive agencies.

Mindset of Public Servants

Yet, effective reform cannot simply be structural. The mindset of public servant has also got to be addressed. In this light, a state of frustration was perceived in a statement of lament from the Head of the Public Service himself about the dysfunctional mindset of public servants. *The Sunday News. Tanzania)* of March 28, 1999 reported the Chief Secretary as saying, "it is unacceptable that with all efforts by the government nothing visible comes out of our ministries, departments and institutions by way of improved performance." The Chief Secretary castigated the "business as usual" attitude entrenched in the management of government and warned that such attitude would not be tolerated since the government could not invest in reform efforts that were a wasteful exercise. Evidently, since 1998, the government has been implementing a robust public service as outlined in the following chapter. However, this programme has not specifically targeted the transformation of the mindset of the public servant. Little wonder that even President Mkapa has, in recent years, continuously underscored the importance to change the mindset of the bureaucracy if economic reforms are going to bear ultimate benefits to the people.

Key Institutional Reforms

At the same time, the effectiveness of the state cannot emerge from mere improvement of public service. The challenge is much broader. *The Challenge to the South* addressed this issue in a more holistic manner when it called for the modernisation of the state as a prior condition for its being able to fulfil its varied development responsibilities. The Report outlined five institutional reforms that constituted key factors in the modernisation of the state. These are:

First, the need for a national vision arrived at through a process of democratic consensus, which sets out the goals and purposes of development. Second, the imperativeness to establish institutions that would promote people-centred development. Third, evolvement of a political participation system that is underpinned by "an ethic that allows all ideas to contend" and views participation in the political process to embody "much more than the opportunity to exercise the vote." Fourth, the realisation of a system that promotes accountability to the public, through the rule of law and judicial review of administrative action, transparency of government activities, including freedom of and access to information, and an independent and fair judiciary. Fifth, the need to clarify the roles and responsibilities of government bodies, especially central and local government.

Like most developing countries, Tanzania, is at the threshold of change and transformation, not necessarily by choice but, more significantly, through force of circumstance and new reality. As the World Bank's *World Development Report of 1997* noted, the new millennium portends great promise of change and reason for hope. However, such promise of change and reason for hope crucially hinged on what the World Bank describes as "a fundamental rethinking of the roles of institutions and the interactions between citizens and government." The large question then is how the Tanzanian state has positioned itself in the context of the institutional reforms put forward by the South Commission Report and the World Bank. Three measures need to be effected: First and foremost, it would be necessary that the reforms and the new policies and directions pursued be encapsulated into a national vision which the people, as a whole, can make reference to and rally behind. Such vision is an important tool for cultivating a new public service ethic. In fact, civics or social studies school curriculum which is a vehicle of national conscientisation for young men and women would need to focus on such vision. Although Development Vision 2025 is in place since the end of 1999, it is yet to be effectively disseminated and introduced in the national school and college curriculum.

Secondly, the legislature and the judiciary should approach their tasks from a clarified position of what constitutes the principal pillars of the state. Presently, legislature and judicial oversight of the executive is still weak, mainly because the concept of separation of powers and how it should be concretised remains hazy. For example, judicial independence in managing the dynamics of the rule of law is still compromised in the sense that, where the judiciary has interpreted the law from the vantage point of the law as it is, the executive, in turn, at least on few occasions, has driven the legislature to change the affronted laws. It is also important for a rounded modernisation of the state to take place, allocation of resources to the legal and judicial system and the legislative branch be enhanced. Much has been done since 2000 in allocating more resources to these branches of the state. However, the allocations are far from being adequate given the relative importance of the legal and legislative systems. I have in mind, for instance, the shortage and poor state of court buildings around the country. A modern state needs to have more courts to ensure speedy enforcement of the law and adjudication of disputes. On the legislative front, MPs lack basic services like offices where they could work from supported by well-equipped library facilities.

Thirdly, local government has to be empowered much more to enable it to play the role it used to prior to the introduction of the Decentralisation Programme in 1972. It is regrettable that local government is still perceived in the context of ward electoral politics rather than in the roles and responsibilities that local authorities have and should exercise in order to promote development at local levels and people's participation in national affairs. The inadequacies of tax revenue sources and central government subventions, though notably on the rise since 2002 but still grossly low, have contributed to this deficit of effectiveness. The idea of constituting a Finance Commission similar to what India has, as suggested earlier, would go along way in enabling a more equitable allocation of resources from the centre to local government.

Conclusion

Modernisation of the Tanzanian state should therefore be given greater priority. Tanzania should move beyond viewing the process of state modernisation as an exercise in mere civil or public service reform. Yes, public service reform is important because the day-to-day functioning of the state takes place at the level of the public service. However, even such focus of reform is yet to realise the envisioned benefits precisely because the reform of the public service has centred more on institutional arrangements and power structures than on addressing the challenges of transforming the mindset of public servants and government political functionaries.

How such mindset transformation should be undertaken is the greater challenge facing public service reform. In my view, a process of de-briefing the key cadres and to establish specialised training institutions able to produce public servants who fit the new environment have to be given more serious and urgent attention. It is noteworthy that the government has being sending its regional commissioners and senior public servants to the Irish Management Institute in Dublin for specialised capsule courses targeting mindset change. However, not only is the programme costly, it also cannot replace the need for specialised institutions being established in Tanzania to provide similar training and probably more relevant to Tanzanian circumstances. Institutions like our Universities, unfortunately, are not catered for providing such specialised training for the public service.

Chapter

18 PUBLIC SERVICE REFORM AND THE PRIVATE SECTOR

Innovation and quality are concepts not frequently associated in people's minds with government. Too often, government is seen by citizens, the media, and sometimes by public servants and political leaders themselves, as plodding, inefficient, bureaucratic, change-resistant, incompetent, unresponsive, or corrupt. Citizens often complain that governments provide services that are inadequate, inappropriate, inferior, or too costly of their hard-earned tax payments. Frequently, people see government officials to be acting in their own interests rather than responding to the needs of citizens. In many countries, the claim that "we are from the Government and are here to help you" is met with popular derision.

-Dennis A Rondinelli: *Reinventing Government: The Imperatives of Innovation and Quality.*

The contemporary world is in the throes of a massive transformation. Science, technology, and the emergence of globalisation have catapulted major changes in the global economic structure and relations. These changes have had a deep and far-reaching impact on how governments work and on the psychological mindset of the people. Responses to these changes in terms of restructuring the social order and in managing the constantly changing environment vary from country to country. However, what is not in dispute is that management of rapid change has taken the centre stage of human concern in all countries. Public service reform, anywhere, makes meaning only where it is anchored within such a broad framework of management of change. For reform is not a static activity. It is dynamic. Thus, public service reform has to take a dynamic mode, constantly responding to the changing demands of the social, economic and political environment. Importantly, it should not be viewed simply as a mechanistic restructuring of the roles and functions of government, invariably involving the reduction of personnel, bolstering compensation and creating greater efficiencies and effectiveness through new fad strategies such as re-engineering. Public service reform has to embody a deeper context and purpose. At root, it should shape a new vision of government. At his *Inaugural Address in 1991*, California Governor, Pete Wilson, had this to say in this specific context: "We will not suffer the future. We will shape it. We will not simply grow. We will manage our growth. We will not passively experience change. We will manage change. But to shape our future, we will need a new vision of".

Ideological Shift and New Role of the State

Evidently, since the on-set of economic reforms in the early 1980s and especially after 1984, Tanzania has witnessed a development paradigm shift of fundamental ideological implications. The social and economic policies pursued in the last decade and a half are market-oriented. Tanzania has seen a gradual but consistent dismantling of the state-owned sector of the economy. Numerous policy statements have been made about the new role of the state and several measures have been taken in the direction of re-defining and re-constituting the role of the state. For example, the *CCM Programme on Policy and Direction for the 1990s,* adopted in December 1992, clearly articulated the new role of the state, declaring that the role had shifted from that of dominant state entrepreneurship and intervention to that of a guide, facilitator and enabler.

At the level of concrete measures taken to reflect the new role of the state, several examples can be given. They include the privatisation of state-owned enterprises, the promotion of private enterprise as the new dynamo of development and the injection of cost recovery and cost sharing mechanisms in some areas of social service delivery. It has also been clarified that the state will now be responsible for ensuring:

i) national defence and security;

ii) law and order;

iii) revenue collection,

iv) social and economic infrastructure; and

v) a conducive and enabling environment for economic activities, including quality regulation, and

vi) protection of the disadvantaged groups in society.

A New Vision of Government

There is little doubt, that congruence between the development ideological shift and the re-defined role of the state is being struck. What remains uncertain is the new role of the state underpinned by a new vision of government, a vision that shifts government's role from *"rowing"* to *"steering"*, to borrow bullet terms from David Osborne and Ted Gaebler. In their pioneering book, *Reinventing Government - How The Entrepreneurial Spirit is Transforming the Public Sector*, Osborne and Gaebler postulate a new vision of government that is characterised by "less government but more governance," meaning that there is less money allocated for government for "doing" things and more money for governance and for "leading" society and galvanising. It is such new vision of a catalytic role of government along with the new responsibilities of the state outlined above, that should inform public service reform. In other words, as the government increasingly adopts a *catalytic* role and embraces a re-defined role of the state, new organisations and systems within the government should be developed, including placing right kind of people in key positions that are better disposed to leading rather than doing. However, for any such vision to be effective, the vision should be a shared one. In other words, those impacted by policies and strategies adopted in the name of the vision should have an effective say in the formulation of the vision itself. In this specific case, the vision of a catalytic role of government and of the new role of the state should also benefit from the ideas of the private sector.

The central question in crafting a government vision is why the private sector should at all be concerned about public service reform? Several reasons can be adduced. But the key reason is that the performance of government crucially depends on the extent to which an enabling environment that encourages and facilitates growth-promoting activities by private actors in the economy exists. Public service reform should address itself to how best to transform the government to become business oriented. There are several other reasons that have a bearing on private sector development and these should be considered in reforming the public Service. These reasons are examined below.

Private Sector and Public Service Reform: The Context

The New Political-Economic Environment

It is important to recognise that Tanzania is undergoing a major political and economic transition. A new thrust of political and economic pluralism is driving social and economic development. New challenges, of globalisation and regionalism, are fast emerging and are affecting the Tanzanian polity. These new realities are putting to question the capacity and competency of institutions of state, particularly the public services, to support the economy and to enable economic agents to exploit available opportunities. The public service, as the executing arm of government, has been at the centre of trenchant criticism for failing to adjust quickly and effectively to the demands of changed and changing economic circumstances.

The question that looms large is whether the public Service, as it presently constituted, can be equal to the challenges of high growth, low inflation, higher investment and intensified competition. There is fear, not wholly misplaced, that the public service is fashioned on the premises of a previous era characterised by a political oligarchic system and state capitalism. At that time, the public service was the archenemy of the corporate private sector. The critical question is whether the public service has shed off the ideological baggage of that previous political era and embraced a managerial and technocratic ethos that is more private sector-oriented. Les Metcalfe and Sue Richards have put the public service reform in proper perspective as follows: "The anxieties of the 1970s about governmental overload and economic failure have crystallised into reform efforts directed towards reducing governmental demands on scarce resources and increasing the value for money obtained from resources actually deployed".

Government Structure Out of Tune

Admittedly, the structure of the Tanzanian government is still overreached: its present burden of responsibilities far exceeds its capacity to perform cost-effectively. Even though there has been a development paradigm shift necessitating an overhaul of the structure and system of government and several recommendations were made in this regard by the Presidential Commission chaired by Basil Mramba back in 1994, the structure of government has not changed much since the socialist era. Yes, in recent years there has been a positive move towards the establishment of Executive Agencies. The aim of these agencies is to shift management of key agencies of the state from the typical bureaucratic structures of the past and promote value for money from resources deployed. The government has also established regulatory authorities in keeping with the thrust of getting the government out of direct control. These changes are in the right direction. What is yet to be tested is performance and cost effectiveness. One could comment, however, as a brief example of the deficit in reform of government, by citing the case of the Ministry of Labour. This Ministry to-date is modelled on the socialist era with focus on labour relations and issuing of work permits to expatriates. Yet the challenge of the day is the creation of jobs and assuring full employment with abundant social security. Tanzania needs a Ministry of Employment, not of labour! I am not also sure that that the Ministry of Planning should have a privatisation portfolio in those terms. Privatisation is a mere action. What underlies it is the policy promotion of the spirit of enterprise, both public and private. The Ministry should thus be named as Ministry of Planning and Business Development. The term "economic development" is inappropriate because it is too omnibus, cutting across several Ministries.

A New Regulatory System

The government continues to have excessive controls within its system with some regulatory agencies still enjoying wide discretionary powers susceptible to caprice, arbitrariness, rent seeking and corruption. The *Warioba Commission Report* identified these agencies and recommended measures to reform the regulatory system within the government in order to generate transparency in decision making processes and thereby build confidence of investors, business, and the people as a whole. Public service reform cannot end at merely changing structures and personalities. Institutions are important in promoting greater government effectiveness. On this front, there has been significant progress in the past decade, especially with the establishment of several regulatory agencies. These include the Chief Government Chemist, Tanzania Communications Regulatory Authority,. TCRA), the Business Registration and Licensing Agency,. BRELA), Tanzania Food and Drug Agency. TFDA), the Surface and Marine Transport Regulatory Authority. SUMATRA), the Tanzania Government Aviation Regulatory Authority. TGARA), the Energy and Water Regulatory Authority. EWURA), and the Fair Competition Law Commission.

However, there is need to ensure that the systems and procedures of decision-making of these authorities and other executive agencies are modern and depart from the bureaucratic systems that ruled in government in the past. Experience with systems and procedures of decision-making in some government organs, such as the National Food Control Commission, the Chief Government Chemist, the Labour Department, the Tanzania Bureau of Standards and the Municipal Health Offices under Local Authorities, shows that having regulatory agencies in themselves may not result in improvements in regulating the performance of market institutions. This is because some of the decision-making procedures in these institutions have remained nebulous and, in some cases, are in conflict with constitutional rights of natural justice that economic and business actors expect and are entitled to. It is also not clear to whom the regulatory agencies are responsible to for their acts of commission and omission. They seem to enjoy wide authority. Clearly, it is essential to build in checks and balances on their work, a role that should be vested in the judiciary and the legislature. The Indian jurist H.R.Khanna once observed, "the liberties of the citizens face real danger in insidious encroachments by men of zeal, well-meaning but lacking in due deference for the rule of law."

Public service reform should thus ensure that the vast powers of public servants are cushioned with adequate safeguards for the rights of individuals and that any infringement by those in charge of administration is rectified by an agency independent of the administration. To what extent the Commission on Human Rights and Good Governance would exercise authority over such abuses of administrative discretion and authority would also be a test for the institution's legitimacy and credibility. At the same time, however, the establishment of Consumer Consultative Councils under each regulatory authority is a welcome development. However, these councils require adequate support of the government if the spirit behind their establishment is to be realised. It is essential that consumer interests that directly come under the oversight of the regulatory authorities have the right of presenting their cases and resorting to judicial review.

A central area of concern within the government is adequacy and competence of people to deal with regional and international trade and investment issues. Presently, the capacity is low. Yet the competitiveness of the private sector in terms of exploiting market access and trade preferences crucially hinges on such capacity being developed in the government. For example, the negotiations of the EAC Customs Union Protocol between 2002 and 2004 had to depend more on capacity that existed in the private sector, and especially in CTI, than in the government. Public service reform should thus urgently address such shortcomings and also rationalise decision-making structures that currently cut across the economic ministries, especially those responsible for planning and privatisation, finance, agriculture, co-operatives and marketing, trade and industry and foreign affairs and international co-operation.

Poor Ethics in Governance

There is still massive waste in government as evidenced by the Annual Reports of the Controller and Auditor General. The central weakness contributing to such waste is the failure of government to escape from old ideas and embrace new ones, alluded to earlier, like outsourcing services and privatising the procurement function. The government is the single largest consumer in society. Yet the systems and procedures that govern procurement are such that annually the government loses billions of shillings from all kinds of leakages. Another area infected by a deadly virus of corruption is the award of contracts. Obscure and illegal transactions badly affect private sector development because the private sector gets pushed to partake in corruption whose root cause is weak public accountability systems. The 1994 Mramba Commission Report had addressed this problem but it fell short of boldly recommending privatisation of the procurement function within the government by contracting out.

Improvement of Social and Economic Infrastructure

If the private sector is to succeed in today's intensely competitive environment, it needs the highest quality inputs and raw materials it can get. These include the most knowledgeable workers, cheapest capital, top rate infrastructure and breakthrough research. Unless our schools and colleges are improved and training systems upgraded; unless we improve health services, agricultural and industrial research, energy, water, telecommunications and transport infrastructure and make available equity capital financing, private sector development would be stunted. In all these areas, there is need to have greater government role of rowing rather than steering. Public service reform should ensure that these roles of government are given greater attention in terms of effective organisation as well as resources- human, physical and financial.

With the level of fiscal contraction Tanzania has witnessed in the 1997 due to excellent expenditure control, it is imperative that public service reform also embraces the search for market solutions to the government's role in the social sector. The conventional notion that health and education are public goods that require a leading and strong role of the government at financing and delivery levels cannot be sustainable. Already, in 2003/04 government expenditure to priority sectors falling under poverty reduction strategy reached 46% of total expenditure. Much as this achievement is a welcome development, it is also evident that it is foreign aid and grants that enable such a level of expenditure to be made. Clearly, such overreaching on external support is worrisome. Therefore, Public/private sector partnership should be vigorously promoted in supporting the financing of poverty reduction programmes.

Policy Making In Government

The machinery of policy making in the government suffers from the following characteristics:

a) over dependency by government Ministers on the bureaucracy.

b) existence of stakes of the bureaucracy linked to non-transparent and non-institutionalised business lobbies sometimes override political demands.

c) intense manipulative capacity of the bureaucrats enables them to keep Ministers in check and enables them to enjoy a firm hold on the overall functioning of government.

d) bureaucracy is not adequately and directly answerable to Parliament on policy making and thus reducing Parliament to what Professor Rajni Kothari has described as "inept spectators of the processes of policy making and implementation".

It is in the context of this huge authority that the bureaucracy seems to enjoy in the executive arm of the government that the private sector, in recent years, has decided to work more closely with Parliamentarians in promoting its concerns and interests.

Rigidities in Government

Public service reform should remove organisational rigidities in the government. This is a real time world and the private sector expects responses and actions from the government that are consistent with real time demands. Greater accountability of bureaucrats is called for. The lack of effective inter-ministerial linkages outside the cabinet framework often contributes to policy conflicts and competing approaches to dealing with critical development and investment policy issues. Reference was made earlier to policy clashes between investment promotion and maximisation of tax revenue. Thus, more co-ordination is needed to ensure, for instance, that a decision to allow the exports of raw cashew nuts does not militate against the objective of promoting value-added exports through processing of such cashew nuts in the country, an objective that also bolsters manufacturing employment.

Government to Leave Business Decisions to Business

The government is still heavily involved in an intricate array of business decisions or decisions that impact business. For instance, the Minister for Labour retains wide powers over labour market issues, from employment of expatriates to industrial relations. It is unfortunate that the Minister should exercise more authority in determining the disciplinary conduct of workers in a given organisation than the Chief Executive Officer of that organisation. Private sector development thrives in an environment where powers over discipline and productivity are exercised at the work place. Where there are appeals relating to industrial disputes they should be resolved judicially and not politically. As observed earlier, public service reform should address such troubling hangover from a past labour market regime that has since lost relevance and legitimacy.

Deficit In Entrepreneurial Ethics

Experience in Tanzania shows that both the public system as well as many of the people who work in the government lack a clear understanding of private sector development. Three problems stand out. First, there is the problem of applying out-dated ideas in government. In other words, the use of yesterday's tools to apply to problems or situations of today. Second, is the inappropriateness of a problem-solving culture. Third, the cultural ethos in the government is predominantly negative in its orientation. The challenge is to realise a shift from an ethic of power to an ethic of service within the bureaucracy. Business-school-type of training is necessary for bureaucrats. The bureaucracy should also learn to work in partnership with those outside the government, particularly the private sector.

Improving Public Service Management

Is there a new vision of government in Tanzania? Moreover, is it possible to transfer the skills of the private sector to the public service? John Banham, in his book *The Anatomy of Change: Blueprint for a New Era* argues that the management style and traditions of public service are simply not compatible with the demands of a competitive marketplace. He posits, "The hallmarks of the public service include concerns for fairness rather than results, process rather than outcome, language rather than analysis, economy rather than value for money, avoidance of risk and mistakes gather than reward, appearance rather than reality, consensus rather than conflict". In his view, therefore, public service is allergic to management and that it is futile to try and reform such a system. Banham proposes the following solutions to improving the performance of the public service:

a) completing the privatisation programme.

b) contracting out as many services undertaken by the government as is possible.

c) decentralising operations with maximum authority delegated to local officers.

d) hiving off activities into independent organisations.

e) increasing the number of people recruited from outside the government and the interchange of staff between the government and the private sector.

Finally, it is critical that the compensation package of the civil service is increased. Otherwise, this could be a source for sustaining and reinforcing corruption in the public service. In this context, it should be acknowledged that the salaries of public servants, much as they are still lower than those in the neighbouring countries such as Kenya and Uganda, have improved a lot, especially in the period between 1997 and 2004. The improvement is seen in the gross salaries of all public servants shooting up by more than 200% from Shs. 154.1 billion to Shs. 464.06 billion between 1995/96 and 2003/04.

Part Five

RELIGION AND POLITICS

The great hope of the liberal imagination, that politics could be superseded by economics, replacing public good with private choice, was bound to fail because economics as such offers no answer to the big questions of `Who` and `Why`. Religion does, and that is its power in the contemporary world. The politics of ideology may have died, but it has been replaced not by `the end of history` but by politics of identity.

-Jonathan Sacks: ***The Dignity of Difference-How to Avoid a Clash of Civilisations.***

Chapter

19 RELIGION AND POLITICS: THE FEARS AND THE REALITY

By the side of every religion is to be found a political opinion, which is connected with it by affinity. If the human mind be left to follow its own bent, it will regulate the temporal and spiritual institutions of society in a uniform manner, and man will endeavour to harmonise earth and heaven.

-Alexis de Tocqueville: *Democracy in America.*

Introduction

The emergence of political pluralism in Tanzania has not only promoted free expression, particularly through the print media, but has also given birth to what is proving to be a new but potentially destabilising phenomenon, namely the rise of religious involvement in matters of a social, economic and political character. Much as religion is emerging throughout the world as the political language of our time, questions are being raised whether the active and high profile role religious groups are now playing in society is not a violation of secularism. In addition, questions are also asked whether secularism, in itself, infers that religious leaders should not express opinions of a political character or, whether, in fact, it merely means the non- involvement of religion in the formation and organisation of political parties. The central question that features in this debate is what constitutes politics for which religion should be restrained from involvement? Where does one draw the line, for example, between issues that concern a state of deepening poverty, that is entrenching, on the one hand, and politics properly so-called, on the other? And what is politics, "properly so-called"?

As political pluralism deepens in Tanzania and as questions of race, ethnicity, tribalism, poverty and wealth redistribution take the centre stage of political debate and election manifestos, the role of religion in society could not be simply brushed aside in the name of secularism. Both the state and religion would have to re-examine the fundamentals of secularism in the context of a new pluralistic environment- domestic and global- and also re-define the rules of the game.

The Emergence of State-Religion Differences

It is difficult to determine whether any fundamental differences or even conflict arose between state and religion under Julius Nyerere's one party political system. If it existed, then it was centrifugal. In a way, in spite of the socialist policies of Nyerere that embraced the nationalisation of schools and hospitals, owned and managed by religious groups in 1969 and 1972 respectively, little or nothing surfaced in terms of open criticism of those policies. Those were the days when there was no free press. It is therefore possible that if any criticisms existed, they were muzzled.

However, in recent years and especially since 1994, there has been increased interest in the role of religion in initiating and promoting far-reaching changes in society. Whilst Christian groups have taken the lead in this new role, Moslems have not been left far behind. Notable interventions in this context have been the Dodoma and Bagamoyo Declarations of Lutheran Bishops in the 1990s. However, it is the Bagamoyo Declaration released in March 1994 titled, *The Democracy of Politics and Economics. Demokrasia ya Kisiasa Na Kiuchumi*) that set the pace, in terms of timing and radicalism. In the main, that Declaration postulated, "We as Church leaders cannot avoid being involved in various issues embracing economic, political, social and spiritual issues since this constitutes the mission of the Church. Moreover, we agreed that, since in its very functioning, the Church recognises the freedom of expression of every human being so as to forge development, unity, love and solidarity across the religious, racial ethnic, gender or ideological divide, there was need to educate the public on problems which face them."

In detail, the Bagamoyo and Dodoma Declarations encapsulated the following:

- the Tanzania economy was promoting the interests of foreigners and foreign capitalists who, after benefiting, nothing behind and forced the government to accept stringent conditionalities as a basis for getting assistance thereby eroding national economic freedom.
- economic and political democracy was not adequately transparent as to enable all the people to enjoy the fruits of their labour, to be better protected by state organs in order to enjoy better social services delivered by the state without their resorting to offering bribes and to enjoy equal access to education, commerce, health services, energy etc.
- for political pluralism to benefit the people, there was need to have few and strong political parties. Such parties should seek to unite where possible to ensure that political opposition was strengthened.

- political parties should recognise that opposition was not confrontation. Therefore, they should build a culture of tolerance and mutual respect.
- a single government was the only structure that could represent the interests of both sides of the Union. Where such structure proved difficult to achieve, a three-government structure should be adopted.
- effective democracy could not be achieved where repressive laws remained in place. In that regard, the Nyalali Commission recommendations on repressive laws should be implemented.
- to preserve peace and tranquillity, the ruling party should stop the monopolisation of state organs such as the Radio Tanzania for its own benefit.
- the ruling party should not lead political change without taking into cognisance people's opinions and wishes especially in respect to the call for holding a national conference to draft a new Constitution.
- corruption was a cancer at all levels of national leadership.
- the national interest had not been safeguarded in the allocation of land citing the Monduli land Loliondo Scandals where the Maasai had complained about their pastoral lands being offered to foreign nationals to be turned into beef ranches and for game hunting.
- peddling narcotics constituted a serious threat to the nation. The greed for getting rich quickly had made some businesspersons turn Tanzania into a market for narcotics.
- trade liberalisation had reinforced economic and social stratification. Evasion of taxes and customs duties had become the order of the day; so was the importation of commodities unfit for human consumption.
- government leaders should uncouple themselves from being overly influenced and manipulated by the rich in society.

Many of the concerns raised above may have lost relevance today. However, in addressing the more fundamental question about the looming threat to secularism, they are outlined here to provide the framework for discussion. The key question is whether the "interventions" by religious groups are political in the secular sense and thus constitute a legal or constitutional trespass. At least in so far as the Dodoma and Bagamoyo Declarations are concerned, President Mwinyi found them, to an extent, to constitute a trespass. In a National Address on 4th August 1994, President Mwinyi observed as follows: "I recognise that religious leaders are nationals and, in that capacity, have as much right as any other nationals to air their views on political matters. I do not intend ever to refuse the

Bishops this fundamental right. However, they should refrain from using the media and instead either use face-to-face deliberations with the state or send their views by post to respective political leaders." This statement is troublesome in the sense it does not unequivocally pronounce a verdict on whether Clerics have a role in national politics or not. In contrast, however, during the CCM 28th Anniversary celebrations in Dar es Salaam, in February 2005, the Tanzania Vice President, Dr. Ali Mohamed Shein warned about the rising tide of religion in politics. He called upon religious leaders who wished to be in politics to quit their religious positions and form or join political parties. The Vice President's strong remarks were made in response to reports that about 20 odd Moslem clerics, or Imams, of Dar es Salaam mosques had joined hands to campaign for a specific Moslem Presidential candidate, ostensibly in order to promote Moslem interests.

Religion and Democracy

Between 1995 and presently, there have been several cases where religious leaders and especially those of the Christian faith, who, in their personal capacities or through conferences and religious occasions, have expressed views and concerns about the state of politics and development in Tanzania. For instance, the Episcopal Conference has, on several occasions, been vociferous in pointing out that the government was not effectively addressing poverty and corruption. It would also be recalled that in the immediate period prior to the holding of ward and village elections towards the end of 2004, both the Episcopal Conference and the Christian Council of Tanzania issued declarations calling for free, fair and peaceful elections. The declarations condemned continued prevalence of corruption and the culture of politicians not to readily accept electoral defeats.

In such an environment, what should be brought to the fore is the question: since religion is a faith and faith has the potential to ignite fanaticism, passions and even perverse perceptions amongst followers within religions, is it advisable that Bishops, Reverends, Rabbis, Sheikhs and other religious leaders should raise or discuss political issues at religious sittings and settings and make resolutions on them either against a legally constituted government or simply about the state of politics in the country? Believers know that religious faith knows no democracy. Those who have studied theology and have been ordained are supposed to help the believers to understand the Word of God through teachings in Churches, Mosques and other places of worship, not through political platforms or turning the "pulpits" into platforms for making political statements. Politics knows no Bible or Koran in a secular state; neither is it led by a Bishop or Sheikh. This is why politics is managed through democracy, requiring the will of the people through the ballot box. One wonders where Tanzaniawould be had opinions of religious leaders coincided, for example, with those of political parties. It is a situation that would spell instability.

Tanzania recognised the danger of mixing religion with politics quite early. That is the reason why, at the time of the promulgation of the multiparty system in 1992, the government prohibited the establishment of political parties based on religion. Concomitantly, it would be absurd to debar political parties founded on religion to be established and at the same time proceed to allow religious groups to intervene in politics as they pleased. Yes, the government needs religious leaders to identify and castigate evils and wrong doings in society. Thus, to condemn corruption is their right. So it is to raise concern about the erosion of the moral fabric in society. However, for religious leaders to criticise, for example, the structure of the Union of Tanzania and to denigrate the Union Constitution at religious sittings is to transgress the boundaries of their mission as spiritual leaders.

Is there a Boundary: Where is the Boundary?

This upsurge in religion involvement in politics poses the inevitable question whether a boundary indeed exists between religion and politics and where that boundary line runs. Is it possible, in modern society, to have a precise and clear-cut boundary between religion and politics? In fact, President Mwinyi admitted in his above-cited national address that what had dismayed him about the Dodoma Declaration was not so much what was contained in it or that the Bishops held such views as contained in the declaration, as the methodology that the Bishops had used to communicate their views, namely using the media. The President had wished that the views of the Bishop should have been submitted directly to the government. The President isolated two issues from the Bishops' Declaration, which, in his view, were clearly of a political character: the legitimacy of the Union Constitution and the structure of the Tanzania Union. The political views cited are contained in two paragraphs of the Bagamoyo Declaration. Paragraph 1.12 states: "With respect to the Union of Tanzania, we the Bishops assert that in order to have a Union structure which will be representative and which will equitably promote the interests of both sides it is necessary to have a one Union government structure. If the implementation of this proposal would be impossible, then it is imperative that there be a three Union government structure." Moreover, under paragraph 1.2.5, it is asserted as follows: "the ruling party should not take the reigns of spearheading democratic pluralism in defiance of the views and opinions of the people regarding the holding of a national conference to draft a constitution."

At the same time, it may be noted that sometime in 1994, the Chief Sheikh of Tanzania Mainland threatened "Jihad" had the government proceeded with the enactment of a new inheritance law that sought to introduce the right to matrimonial home by a wife, a concept not recognised under Islamic law. In late 2004, the Imams in Zanzibar also put up a proposal before the Minister for Constitutional affairs recommending the introduction of Islamic law or Sharia in Zanzibar, a country that is constitutionally secular.

Clearly, the contents of the Bishops' statements as well as the clamours of the Imams in Zanzibar are of a political character with serious political ramifications. Yet, did the Bishops and the Imams disregard the boundary between state and religion in putting forth their views? Do religious leaders, like elected politicians, represent, by definition, the views of the people in that sense of "representation" where they make declarations and proposals of the type cited above? In this context, there is a strong body of opinion, ostensibly centred on secular philosophies, that holds that religious groups should seek ways and means of defending and promoting democratic values *without becoming embroiled in political activity* and even partisan debate. President Mwinyi appeared to belong to the group that holds such philosophy. In espousing such philosophy, President Mwinyi has cited Jesus' call in *Mathew: 22.21* "to render therefore into Caesar the things which are Caesar's; and into God the things that are God's," as sufficient evidence of the divine separation of religion and politics.

The opposing body of opinion, on the other hand, points to the danger of a rigid separation between private conscience and public activity. It is contended that when religious groups abdicate taking positions on public issues, such a stance may reflect that religion only addresses the concerns of private life; that it is confined to issues of private morality. Under such circumstances, it is argued, society would inevitably run the risk of living with public policies that violate moral principles. In this light, religion has the right to impart the *sacred* character to democratic values. In other words, it should intervene between the individual and the state. Indeed, in response to *Mathew 22.21* and in this specific context, Professor Kenneth D. Wald, in his book *Religion and Politics in the United States* observes that the cited verse "does not define precisely what it is that humanity owes to the state and to church. Depending on how responsibility is allocated between God and Caesar, that biblical injunction may be interpreted as a call to revolution or, at the other extreme, as a plea for servility."

The Role of Religion in Society

Whenever caught up in a political or economic philosophical problem, Tanzanians have established for themselves a culture of resorting to the views of the Father of the Nation, the late Mwalimu Julius Nyerere, for clarification. What then does Nyerere offer on the subject of religion and society or politics? In my opinion, he offers a pathbreaking analysis and opinion. In a brilliant speech to the Mary Knoll Sisters in New York in October 1970, titled, *The Church and Society*, Mwalimu Nyerere cogently analysed the role of the Church. read religion) in the development of man. He observed that for a long time the Church had been guilty of preaching resignation; viewing social, economic and political conditions as immutable and thereby taking an innocent bystander stance when the victims of poverty and oppression rebelled. Nyerere further noted that unless the Church participated actively in the rebellion against social, economic and political structures that condemn people to poverty, humiliation and degradation, it would lose its credibility and thereby become identified with injustice and oppression.

Nyerere further argued that development of people involved economic development, social development and political development and that the Church had a crucial role to play in all these facets. To quote him: "For the purpose of the Church is man - his human dignity, and his right to develop himself in freedom. To the service of man's development, any or all of the institutions of any particular society must be sacrificed if this should be necessary. For all human institutions, including the Church, are established in order to serve man. And it is the institution of the Church, through its members, which should be leading the attack on any organisation, or any economic, social or political structure which oppresses men, and which denies to them the right and power to live as the sons of a loving God." In reference to secularism, Nyerere noted that his position was not that the Church should abdicate its spiritual functions by becoming associated with political parties or political doctrines. Rather, that it was important for the Church to refuse to be identified with unjust political and economic power groups. He ramified, "The Church must stand up for what it believes to be right; that is its justification and purpose." Indeed, Nyerere was of the view that the role of the Church could sometimes demand that Church leaders involved themselves in nationalist freedom struggles and be part of social movements that worked in opposition to established authorities and powers.

In addition, Nyerere postulated that the Church should participate actively in initiating, securing, and creating the changes that aim at promoting social justice. One may pose here and ask the question: Was Nyerere going too far in his interpretation of religion as a force for change? This question is pertinent because Nyerere was advocating these radical views at a time when he wielded massive, almost unchallenged political power in Tanzania under the one party political system. At that time, no political opposition was allowed to operate. In fact, Nyerere had even banned the powerful All Muslim National Union of Tanganyika immediately after independence apparently because of its political inclinations. In its place, he promoted the establishment of what a section of the Muslim community view as a surrogate national religious representative body, BAKWATA. *Baraza la Waislamu Tanzania*), ostensibly, as a calculated and strategic move to put Muslims under close oversight by the state. The reasons can be speculated. Islam has throughout history been a religion that has had difficulties with the concept of secularism. The difficulties involved in the attempt by western powers to "democratise". in the liberal sense) countries of the Middle and Near East are adequate evidence and may partly explain the fears Nyerere may have had.

Yet what Nyerere postulated about the role of religion in society makes sense. In this context, stark realities around the world show that religious groups are taking a frontal role in politics, even more pronouncedly than Nyerere could ever have perceived. For instance, *The Khaleej Times,* a leading United Arab Emirates Daily Newspaper, of Friday 11th November 1994 featured a news headline, cited from Reuters, titled "Evangelicals claim victory credit" in the US Congressional and State elections. It is of interest to quote the feature story fully: "The right-wing Christian Coalition, a growing force in the Republican Party, claimed much of the credit — for the Party's dramatic victory in US Congressional and state elections. The Christian Coalition, which says it has one million members organised a major get-out-to vote effort for the elections, distributing some 33 million pieces of campaign literature, much of them through churches. It said that an exit poll it commissioned showed that religious conservatives accounted for one- third of all votes cast in the elections, compared to only 18% in 1988, and 22% in 1992. Of these, 68% backed Republicans in Senate races and a slightly higher proportion in Governors' races." The same feature story went on to report that the Christian Coalition "pushes moral issues such as prayer in schools, family values and fervent opposition to abortion. But increasingly, it has also been campaigning on more mainstream themes, such as lower taxes and smaller government".

The United States of America is a secular state by its constitution. How then are religious bodies like the Christian Coalition allowed to take openly active political role in society? And thus when the United States preaches liberty and democracy, should nascent democracies like Tanzania not view the role of religion in politics as relevant? Of course, the United States could be a bad example to cite in examining the relationship between religion and politics. The US, after all, is dominantly a Christian nation, its diverse Christian denominations notwithstanding. In other words, the direct role that the Christian Coalition plays in politics may probably not cause the same level of rancour and concern as it would in a country such as Tanzania where there exist two dominant religious faiths, Islam and Christianity. The consequences of such religious faiths pursuing opposing electoral objectives as appears to happen in the United States, would be alarming. This could be the reason why President Mwinyi had responded harshly to the Bishops' Declarations. Naturally, he feared the threat of religion becoming a vehicle of electoral politics and choices. Be that as it may, it may not have been possible for him to debar religious groups from merely expressing opinions about political, social and economic issues. What should be disallowed is religious groups becoming directly involved in promoting the interests of political parties and contestants in elections.

Conclusion

Religion is emerging as an inevitable political factor in the Tanzanian political scene. The underestimation of this phenomenon for a long time had been due to two main reasons. First, the mistaken belief that secularisation of Tanzanian life was inevitable. Secondly, the "superficial" homogeneity of the Tanzanian society that has been ingrained in society since independence through a hegemonic political party system and by socialism. However, times have now changed with the on-set of political and economic pluralisms. In a liberal political and economic environment, the sacredness of the concept of a secular state has increasingly confronted the ideal, constitutional, secular state. In this context, I agree with Yale Professor, Lamin Sanneh, who, in an article titled, *Religion and Politics: Third World Perspectives*, posits "the proximity of religion and politics in practical situations modifies any rigid separation of the two, and, conversely, the instrumental nature of politics implies at least a national distinction between them. Ideally, there are as sound religious grounds as there are pragmatic ones for not confusing religion and politics, though, in practice, it is risky to attempt splitting the two."

Tanzanians should therefore openly discuss and debate the relationship between religion and politics if they are to deepen their understanding both of this emerging phenomenon in their society and its impact on national unity, peace and stability. More importantly, and especially in electoral politics, it is pertinent that government exercises greater restraint and tolerance over national issues raised by religious leaders. Government and political leaders should apply dialogue and guidance instead of a confrontational approach in the public domain that could be counter-productive, and unnecessarily fuel tension and inevitable instability. This is important as Tanzania, like the rest of the world, continues to come face to face with the fear factor about terrorism and its association with Islamic fundamentalism, a subject that I turn to next.

Chapter

20 ISLAMIC FUNDAMENTALISM AND TERRORISM

The underlying problem for the West is not Islamic fundamentalism. It is Islam, a different civilisation whose people is convinced of the superiority of their culture and are obsessed with the inferiority of their power. The problem is not the CIA or the U.S. Department of Defence. It is the West, a different civilisation whose people is convinced of the universality of their culture and believe that their superior, if declining, power imposes on them the obligation to extend that culture throughout the world. These are the basic ingredients that fuel conflict between Islam and the West.

-Samuel P. Huntington: ***The Clash of Civilisations and the Making of World Order.***

In the West, Islam remains more than something of an enigma, an alien cultural force to be treated with considerable suspicion. Increasingly, the popular tendency is to associate it with terrorism, no matter how much scholars may deny that this is sanctioned by Islamic doctrine or representative of the faith in general.

-Stuart Sim: ***Fundamentalist World: The New Dark Age Of Dogma.***

Colonialism tried to deform all the cultural traditions of Islam. I am not an Islamist. I don't think there is a conflict between religions. There is a conflict between civilisations.

-Mohamed Sid-Ahmed, ***Cybernetic Colonialism and the Moral Search.***

It is amazing how much solid scholarship has gone into Islam and the subject of Islamic fundamentalism, from the political perspective, in the past two decades. Numerous books, many written especially by western authors, in the USA and Western Europe, have featured this subject with varying concerns and conclusions. In August 1998, during a study visit to Germany, the late Tanzania Chief Justice Francis Nyalali, the Speaker of the National Assembly, Pius Msekwa and myself brainstormed with the "brainpower" of the German Institute of International Affairs-an NGO think tank based in Bonn on several issues concerning Africa.

Interestingly, one of the burning subjects raised concerned the state of growing Islamic fundamentalism around the world. Reference was specifically made to the bombings of the US Embassies in Nairobi and Dar es Salaam which had just occurred, as a manifestation of the "globalisation" of a new threat, namely that of Islamic fundamentalism, which, in post 9/11 period, has changed parlance into "Islamic extremism or fanaticism". In the media and academic articles, terrorists are now called "Islamic terrorists". There is also what is described as "Political Islam." Yet, are terrorists not simply terrorists? At the height of the Irish Republican Army. IRA) "terrorism," one never heard of "Christian terrorism"! So what could the difference be? Moreover, what *is* "Political Islam" in the wake of the type of terrorism associated with *Al Qaeda* or the terrorism that occurred in Madrid in 2004 and in London in July 2005? This topical subject forms part of a brilliant book review essay by Professor Mahmood Mamdani, *Whither Political Islam: Understanding the Modern Jihad,* published in the Journal *Foreign Affairs* of January/February 2005. Moreover, Professor Mahmood Mamdani has contributed an insightful treatment of this subject in his book: *Good Muslim, Bad Muslim: America, the Cold War, and the Roots of Terror.* In sum, Mamdani debunks the thinking in western societies that mere reading of religious texts translate into suicide bombers and other forms of terrorism. He caricatures the distinction between good Muslim and bad Muslim, positing that the presented fault line is ridiculous. A Muslim is simply a Muslim. In amplification, he notes that "Political Islam, especially radical political Islam, and even more so, the terrorist wing in radical political Islam, did not emerge from conservative, religious currents, but on the contrary, from a *secular* intelligentsia. In other words, its preoccupation is *this*-worldly, it is about power in this world. To take only the most obvious example: I am not aware of anyone who thinks of bin Laden as a theologian; he is a political strategist and is conceived of in precisely such terms".

Tanzanian Secularism

Tanzania is a secular state. Secularism has played an important part in ensuring and sustaining the unity and peace that is nationally enjoyed. Yet it is important to heed that the demographic religious divide between Christians and Moslems in Tanzania almost cuts at its centre. One could thus ask: is there a potential societal conflict based on a *"clash"* of core values of Islam and those of Judeo- Christianity in Tanzania? Could there be a threat to Tanzanian secularism? Why then should we be concerned about a threat arising if Tanzanian constitutional secularism embodies the gratification of the desire for both the spirit of freedom, liberty and pluralism as well as the spirit of religious faith and freedom. These questions should be carefully addressed in order to fertilise the unity of a people across various diversities, including religion. In addressing these questions, it is important to take into account the increasingly drummed up threat of Islamic fundamentalism or extremism and its association with global terror and test the existing predispositions and arguments against the objective realities as they obtain in the Tanzanian society. It would be recalled that when the Mwembechai "religious" clashes with the Police occurred on 13 February 1998 in the Mburahati area of central Dar es Salaam, a section of the media and public opinion was quick to point an accusing finger at Islamic fundamentalism as the precipitating cause. In other words, Islamic fundamentalism was viewed and is probably still viewed, in some quarters of Tanzanian society, to be a threat to peace and stability. Is this a correct perception?

It is important to address the so-called threat of Islamic fundamentalism or extremism in a dispassionate manner. The objective should be to determine its roots and interrogate its *prima facie* attribution to terrorism. In this context, it is important, at the outset, to ask what exactly is "fundamentalism". A Jesuit publication titled *America* defines fundamentalism as "a reactionary emotional movement that develops within cultures experiencing social crisis." Yet another definition of fundamentalism, in the eyes of the US magazine *Humanist,* embraces authoritarianism, intolerance and compulsiveness about imposing oneself upon the rest of society. In sum, fundamentalism is perceived as a mindset that sees everything in black and white and for which the virtue of compromise is alien.

Religious Fundamentalism Pervades Religions

Evidently, fundamentalism, by definition, cuts across the religious divide. It is not mono-religious. Writing on the rise of Christian fundamentalism in the US in an article titled, *The Spirit of Liberty and The Spirit of Religion,* Adam Wolfson posits that "religious conservatives' vision of the common good has sometimes seemed a thinly disguised and narrowly conceived sectarian grab for power, and their political agenda to involve little more than proclaiming the USA 'Christian Nation'". In his book *The Megatrends 2000,* John Naisbitt sheds more light on this aspect of religious fundamentalism. He observes that the world is experiencing "a multi-denominational revival" at the dawn of the third millennium. He refers to American baby boomers as "setting a fundamentalist or mystical trend" and cites figures, in millions, of "fundamentalist" Christian groups in the US.

The Waco tragedy, in 1993, and the Oklahoma Bombing in 1995 were circumstances that clearly manifested such religious revival of the fundamentalist variety, revival to the point of its taking violent and even "terrorist" dimensions. Naisbitt's conclusion is that, contrary to predictions of the mid-sixties that religion "would wither away with modernity" there is, on the contrary, a revival in all religions. In the US, the Christian Right, represented by the Christian Coalition, openly and vigorously rallies behind the Republican Party to the point of playing a significant role in federal policy formulation. The so-called "hawks" within President George W. Bush Jr's administration which include the Vice President and the Defence Secretary, are fundamentalist Christians. Paul Wolfwitz and Douglas Feith are Jewish neo-conservatives. The former Attorney General, John Ashcroft has been described as a "Bible-thumping evangelical". It is also widely recognised that the House of Representatives' Majority Whip, Tom DeLay, leads the Christian Right forces in the law making machinery of the Bush Administration. Little wonder that such religious extremism is even posing a threat on the sanctity of the law. The recent Terri Schiavo case involving a brain-damaged patient in the United States has been hijacked by religious groups supported by fundamentalist Christian politicians who attempt to violate the spirit of the law in the name of God. Writing in the International Herald Tribune of 30 March 2005, Professor Paul Krugman posits in an article titled *Extremism at the top* that "one thing that is going on. in the US) is a climate of fear for those who try to enforce laws that religious extremists oppose."

In the book, *Fundamentalist World,* Stuart Sim goes further in pointing out that the "Christian Right has come to have effective right of veto over Republican Party policy, and no aspiring politician in the party can run the risk of clashing with that constituency." In the view of the US Christian Coalition, the spirit of religion should override and, indeed, determine the spirit of liberty. Thus when the former US First Lady, Hilary Clinton entertained Muslim leaders at the White House in 1997 to mark *Eid Ul Fitr,* an Islamic festival marking the end of the holy month of Ramadhan, the Wall Street Journal saw in the invitation evidence to the effect that the friends of Hamas, the Palestinian "Islamic extremist" group, had penetrated the White House. That is how Islam had come to be viewed in some key sectors of the US society. In other words, to many fundamentalist American Christians, Islam was viewed as a terrorist religion. Such perception is yet to change in spite of the frequent populist statements by the American leadership to the contrary, notably that it is not Islam but Islamic fanatics that is the enemy.

Terrorism and Violence Distinguished

In the context of the rising tide in Islamic fundamentalism, it is imperative to distinguish violence and terror, on the one hand, and resurgent deep religious faith on the other. It is difficult to avoid this definitional question. Indeed, the recent UN Report of the High level Panel: *A more secure world: Our shared responsibility* takes an almost similar position when it observes that the search for an agreed definition of terrorism could not avoid the view that people under foreign occupation have a right to resistance and a that the definition of terrorism should not override such right. The caveat that the report makes, however, is that occupation should not justify the targeting and killing of innocent civilians. The evident reference here is to Palestinian Intifada's suicide bombers. However, such example could tantamount to begging the question about what resistance means in the context of a military occupation as had happened in most of the lands under the control of the Palestinian Authority especially between 2002 and 2005. Take also the case of Iran. The Shah was deposed through the leadership of Moslem clerics. The Shah had symbolised corruption, abuse of power and the kind of social liberalism which, to Islamic devotees, was contrary to and undermined the letter and spirit of the Holy Qur'an. Though Islamic Iran has repeatedly been accused of exporting terrorism, there has never been any clear and conclusive evidence to justify the accusation. The *"fatwa"* imposed on Salman Rushdie for his book *"The Satanic Verses"* could not, in itself, be viewed as an act of "terrorism" because it was publicly pronounced to all and sundry. To Iranians, the *fatwa* is judgement based on Islamic law. Nevertheless, the Iranians subsequently waived the decree against Rushdie. Many Muslim scholars may dispute the legal rationale of the *"fatwa"* from the legal positivist theory. But Iran practises Sharia law.

At the root of the suggested link between Islamic fundamentalism or extremism and terrorism is the perception in the Western world as suggested, for instance, in the book, *The Great Reckoning*, that Prophet Muhammad had replaced Karl Marx in the new world order. Until 1989, Marx, the architect of communism, was considered the common enemy of both the West and Islam because of the irreligious ideology of communism. With the disappearance of communism, the authors of this book argue, Islam has emerged as the new threat to western civilisation. This theme is further advanced by Harvard's Samuel Huntington. In his book: *The Clash of Civilisations And The Remaking of World Order,* he argues that the collapse of communism left the West and Islam with a "perceived major threat" to each other. The controversial feature in Huntington's analysis is located in his postulation that "the underlying problem for the West is not Islamic fundamentalism. It is Islam, a different civilisation whose people are convinced of the superiority of their culture and obsessed with the inferiority of their power". This view, which dismisses the validity of the claim that Islamic fundamentalism is a movement, finds support from a respected African scholar and a Muslim, Ali Mazrui. In an article titled *Islamic and Western Values*, the Kenyan intellectual observes that Islam is not simply a religion, "it is a civilisation and a way of life." In contrast, however, Professor Mazrui does not postulate that Islam is a problem to the West.

What explains the rivalry between the Christianity and Islam, in

Huntington's view, is "the nature of the two religions and the civilisations based on them. A central characteristic of the inherent conflict centres on the relationship between the State and Religion. The Muslim concept of Islam as a way of life transcends and unifies religion with politics. The Christian concept, on the other hand, sees a clear divide between "the realms of God and those of Caesar." However, this view is challenged in several quarters. For instance, in reference to a lecture at the University of Oxford on 24 May 2004 delivered by Chris Patten, published in an *Editorial of the Financial Times* of May 25, 2004 it is argued that "the idea that the world was hell-bent on a clash of civilisation, and in particular on an inevitable conflict between the Islamic and the so-called western world, is wrong, and dangerously so. Samuel Huntington's thesis may have had a certain academic attraction 10 years ago. Since then, however, it has been seized upon by Osama bin Laden and his supporters to justify their terrorist attacks." Surely, this position begs the question whether Bin Laden's "terrorist struggle" was inspired by Huntington in the first place as opposed to Huntington's reading of Bin Laden's fanaticism being inspired by a clash of civilisations. It seems to me that Huntington's thesis is attacked simply because the "clash" has come to manifest itself increasingly in acts of terrorism. The civilisation aspects of the clash are omitted, almost deliberately. Could the Egyptian Marxist columnist of Al-Ahram Newspaper, Mohamed Sid-Ahmed be far from the truth in postulating that "colonialism tried to deform all the cultural traditions of Islam. I am not an Islamist. I don't think there is a conflict between religions. There is a conflict between civilisations".

Islam and Liberal Democracy

Some Western scholars have argued that Islam is dominantly opposed to democracy and that the terrorism taking place around the world is dominantly driven by the desire and struggle to subvert Western liberal democracy and impose, in its place, a global Islamic State. Yes and No. Yes, because Islamic states that have had a non- monarchical system, notably Iran, overran the Shah's "democracy" and imposed their own "democratic system" much as many people would regard the distribution of power in Iran as manifestly unequal and probably unjust in the light of the monopoly of power that resides in a few Clerics. No, because in Algeria, the Islamic Salvation Front. FIS) which had been legally constituted as a political party in 1990, swept the country-wide local elections and appeared to be on the verge of winning the 1991 Parliamentary elections as well had those elections not been postponed. Expert opinion indicates that the FIS victory had been propelled more by a broad-based protest against alleged corruption on the part of the ruling party and not so much on a move to impose Islamic mores. In the case of the 1987 Egyptian parliamentary elections, a coalition dominated by the "fundamentalist"

Muslim Brethren emerged as the biggest opposition party. In Jordan, as well, in 1989, the so-called Islamic fundamentalist parties captured the lower House of Parliament in the general elections.

These democratic electoral results from Islamic countries do not render much credence to Huntington's theory that the underlying problem for the West is not Islamic fundamentalism but Islam itself. Islamic fundamentalism also features in Islamic societies themselves. As argued by Martin Kramer in his article *Islam Vs Democracy*, fundamentalism "is destined not to disappear but to triumph, because it is the yearning for democracy in Islamic camouflage". Professor Mamdani also sees this phenomenon more in the context of "the clash inside civilisations." Indeed, we may be witnessing a situation where the struggle to impose liberal democracy in the broader Arab world actually backfiring. For how then do you stop Islamicist political parties such as the FIS from taking part in the democratisation process and even taking over political power? Concomitantly, the political uncertainty in Iraq marked by religious groups taking the centre stage of the political and constitution making process, or even undermining such process, may not augur well for a stable and unified Iraq.

As to Islam as a way of life and thus anti-modernity and that thereby lies the ostensible "clash of civilisations" between Islam and Christianity, we perceptively learn from Ali Mazrui that "one can escape modernity by striving to transcend it as well as retracting from it into the past". Mazrui calls for the Muslim world to explore its suggested path, that of "searching for post-modern solutions to its political tensions and economic woes, and pursuing the positive aspects of globalisation without falling victim to the negative aspects of westernisation." Evidently, this is a difficult challenge to respond to and to pursue given the delicate balancing act required. Professor Benjamin Barber, in his book *Jihad Vs McWorld,* has put this delicate balancing act in clearer perspective. He postulates that "unlike democracy, which can be compatible with religion, modernity is tantamount to secularism and is almost by definition corrupting to all religion, above all to that religion that assures the *comprehensive* and *universal* nature of the message of God as presented in the Qur' an".

From the foregoing, I clearly discern the lack of a causal linkage between Islam and Islamic fundamentalism, on the one hand, and Islamic fundamentalism and terrorism, on the other hand. Osama bin Laden is accused of terrorism. It is debatable, however, that his terrorist activities are necessarily rooted in Islamic fundamentalism or the religious philosophy of Jihad pursuant to the Holy Qur'an. Thus, it could be asked whether there are other reasons behind his "fanatical struggle" probably in the same lines as those that had led him to support the US in arming and fighting on the side of the Afghan Mujaheedin to throw out the Soviets from Afghanistan. In fact, Mahmood Mamdani takes the view that "jihadist Islam, which embraces violence as central to political action, cannot be fully explained without reference to the Afghan jihad and the western influences that shaped it." Within such perspective and logic, it would appear illogical to argue that the tragic events of September 11, 2001 have a causal linkage or relationship with Islamic fundamentalism.

The Tanzanian Religion Challenge

So, where do Tanzanians place themselves in this whole question? Of particular importance is the fact that Zanzibar, a constituent part of Tanzania, is almost wholly Muslim, 99% of it. On the Mainland, and reliable statistics are unavailable, it is generally assumed that Muslims and Christians may be 50:50. So how does Tanzania respond to the emerging Western grave concern about an "Islamic" threat to global peace and security? Does it accept that such a threat is real? In turn, does it have a strong enough national creed of tolerance and respect for religious and cultural diversity to overcome a drummed up or real threat? Tanzanians have always prided themselves about the centrality of a unifying culture in their society that transcends their religious divide. However, how deeply is Tanzania committed at sustaining and reinforcing such a culture of unity and tolerance that has galvanised its national cohesion and stability since the dawn of independence in the light of globalisation of terror increasingly linked to Islamic fundamentalism?

Evidently, one could not stop the growth of fundamentalist beliefs in religions. What could be done is to arrest intolerant beliefs from emerging by unifying people and making the community more open and egalitarian in its relationships. Such a "democratic community", to borrow an expression from Professor Barber, is "defined by imaginative artifice, by achieved values, common work and chosen ends". Evidently, it is a formidable task and an onerous challenge to the Tanzanian political, civil society and religious leaderships to build such a community in a world that is increasingly more open and mobile. But it is a goal worth striving for.

Conclusion

Tanzania is not an island onto itself. Tanzanian leaders should therefore wrestle with the difficult challenge that lies before them, of being sensitively seized of the fact that future peace and stability of Tanzania crucially hinges on how the country holistically addresses what Huntington outlined as an emerging *"clash of civilisations"* in the new global society. It is foolhardy, in our view, to dismiss such a "clash" summarily, in the manner in which many leaders of the western and even Islamic world have done. At a special colloquium at UNESCO in Paris on 4 April 2005, on the theme, *Dialogue Among Civilisations,* both former President Khatami of Iran and Bouteflika of Algeria denounced Huntington's thesis of a "clash" in civilisations. However and paradoxically, they observed that the world was in urgent need of a dialogue between Islam and Western civilisation in order to promote greater understanding and tolerance. In a speech at the Nobel Institute in Oslo on 7 April 2005, His Highness The Aga Khan equally made reference to the "clash" idea, refuting its thesis and positing, instead, that the world was facing a "clash of ignorance," especially between the Judeo-Christian and Muslim worlds. The Aga Khan never came up with a suggestion on how to bridge such a clash of ignorance. One may also quiz: what "ignorance" was the Aga Khan referring to, if not on differing "civilisations"? In my opinion, it is unavoidable not to think in terms of a clash and thus the necessity to search for an appropriate dialogue. Such dialogue has to be situated within the framework of how to construct societies that are more democratic, egalitarian and prosperous In this light, the key challenge in promoting such a dialogue is to change the mindsets of the people the majority of whom are mired in the past and who are mentally driven by conventional thinking about many of the issues that are potentially exploitable by those that seek to destabilise societies for reasons of all forms of extremism, be they religious, political or economic. The new mindset has to engender a future of hope and prosperity to the majority of the people. It is in this light that the Report of the World Commission on Social Dimension of Globalisation, *A Fair Globalisation: Creating Opportunities For All,* has aptly observed, "A fair and more prosperous world is the key to a more secure world. Terror exploits poverty, injustice and desperation to gain public legitimacy. The existence of such conditions is an obstacle in the fight against terrorism." It is thus incumbent upon Tanzania to address the conditions that feed on all forms of fundamentalist ideas and behaviours. In the next chapter, I examine some of these conditions and the challenges they pose within the broad context of the theme of development vision and mindsets.

Part Six

DEVELOPMENT VISION AND MINDSETS

We do not live in a time of vision-no dream of a better world to come, and no image in my mind of a dynamic new world order or transcendent technologies. The future will not be filled with the fulfilment of promises and dreams, but with something better: surprises.

Peter Schwartz: **The Art of the Long View.**

Chapter

21 COMMITMENT AND CHALLENGE TO SUCCEED

We have learned—that good answers to the pressing questions of economic development are not sufficient to engender the change needed to reverse the tides of poorly performing economies. Individuals will often accept intellectual arguments, understand their need to change, and express commitment to changing, but then resort to what is familiar. This tendency to revert to the familiar is not a cultural trait per se, but it is indicative of some of the deeper challenges faced by those who wish to promote a different, more prosperous vision of the future.

-Stace Lindsay: ***Culture, Mental Models, and National Prosperity***
Commitment

Commitment, defined as the mindset of people to persist with their broad courses of action in order to realise their set goals is the driver of social, economic and political development. A nation lacking in commitment would inevitably lose direction and finally disintegrate. This question of commitment is addressed precisely because the majority of Tanzanians, 48% of whom survive below the poverty line, are today anguished by a deepening poverty. Whether it is in urban areas or in rural Tanzania, there is a state of hopelessness. Above all, there is a state of growing despair.

Yet the economic achievements realised so far are hugely commendable, marked as they are by rising economic growth. However, they have not yet translated into improved standards of living for the broad masses. Indeed, Tanzania is witnessing some backlash from this economic deficit in the form of erosion in commitment to development. The *'bongo'* culture, a behaviour or attitude for survival at any cost, is one such backlash. The large migrations of youth from the rural areas into townships could also be explained by this sense of despair and erosion in commitment on the part of the rural youth, on the one hand, and their refusal to continue to live in economic and social conditions that have deteriorated beyond tolerance, on the other hand. So what has gone wrong? What is the source of such poor state of commitment? Can it be salvaged and given a new life?

In searching for some answers to these pertinent questions we should, inevitably, take a historical perspective of this virtue-commitment. In the Introduction to his book, *Freedom and Unity*, Mwalimu Julius Nyerere posits, as a conclusion, that for those with the courage to aspire, to believe, and to work, Tanzania is a challenging and exciting land. Even prior to the final decolonisation of Tanganyika, in December 1961, Nyerere was very clear in his own mind that in the struggle to overcome poverty, ignorance and disease, the only weapon available in such struggle was the people's determination and their effort. Nyerere was cognisant of the fact and the reality that effort and determination was not like *manna* from heaven. It had to be worked for. Thus, from the outset of political independence, a massive mobilisation work was undertaken to promote, strengthen and channel social attitudes that were conducive to national progress. At the same time, there was a deliberate fight against the intensification of an attitude which militated against the national pursuit of human dignity and equality. Slogans such as *Uhuru na Kazi.* Freedom and Work) and *Uhuru ni Kazi.* Freedom is Work) were coined and used to serve as symbols and metaphors to galvanise the people and mobilise them to confront the poor state of their development. Those were the rallying calls for a commitment to nation building, self-help, self-reliance, selflessness and anti-imperialism Thus, the late 1960s and part of the 1970s witnessed the rise of a huge national ethos and drive towards national goals. The people were made to understand that failure to link commitment to hard and productive work entailed loss of freedom; in other words, re-colonisation.

The Arusha Declaration and Commitment

The birth of the Arusha Declaration ushered in a new spirit of commitment. People from all corners of Tanzania who walked hundreds of miles in support of the declaration helped to intensify the spirit of commitment of the people because it manifested a demonstrable pursuit of shared goals of realising unity, social justice, people's participation and the prudent utilisation of resources and management of institutions. This was the period when Tanzania saw the ascent of man. In other words, man became the centre of development. A new sense of national purpose and mission emerged. In this direction, Nyerere demonstrated powerful leadership at mobilising the people to embrace commitment and to view it in the context of a mindset of self belief and abiding faith in national goals. So deeply ingrained was this new sense of commitment that when it came to responding to the 1974 Nyerere's message of *Kilimo cha Kufa na Kupona.* Producing adequate agricultural commodities as a matter of life and death), the response was overwhelming and even overzealous such that even golf courses were invaded by government authorities and turned into agricultural farms. In sum, the Arusha Declaration set out a vision of national human development. It embodied deep-shared values that created a strong bond in society and underlined commitment as a powerful weapon in realising its core values. At a different level, the commitment to the goals of the Arusha Declaration became the essence of and the manifestation of national productivity. In fact, the power to ingrain and catalyse commitment underpinned the effectiveness of development programmes.

However, it is also noteworthy that even at the height of implementing the vision of the Arusha Declaration, a commitment gap began to emerge. The dissolution of local government in 1972 and the Cooperative Societies in 1976 left the broad masses in rural Tanzania with grass without roots, a phenomenon that ate into the vitals of their commitment. Local Government and the Cooperatives had constituted the pillars of popular participation at local levels from the time of the struggle for political independence. Their dissolution undermined a vital part of the people's commitment. Equally, the implementation of the *"Villagisation"* programme in rural areas between 1973 and 1976 destabilised the traditional habitat of the people and resulted in even deeper frustration and disillusionment. Unwittingly, the large role played by the state from mid 70s to early 80s in social and economic development also played a part in weakening the commitment of the people since the self-help spirit was undermined. It remains a paradox that rather than promoting a commitment to the collective pursuit of development, socialism and self-reliance should instead have undermined the very root of commitment itself. The welfare state system had evidently gone too far.

The Market Economy and Commitment

It is important to examine how the people have behaved in response to the changes ushered in by the economic reform and the entry of the market economy, away from the socialist system. Evidently, Tanzanians entered this period of economic liberalisation with a mindset still anchored on the aid syndrome that had entrenched during the 1970s. The syndrome sow seeds of mental destruction in so far as commitment to self help and self reliance are concerned. In other words, Tanzanians lost the sense of being masters of their own game. It is not clear as yet what vision of development informs the national political following the implementation of liberal market-led reforms. What is in place, and often confused as the vision itself, is a market-led economy. However, the market is a mere instrument. A vision, on the other hand, is the big live picture of a future and the direction that must be taken towards the new society to be built. What core values can the people relate to and identify themselves with under the new social, political and economic dispensation? The challenge is for the political leadership to mobilise the nation to determine the basic pillars of such new vision and mobilise the people's acceptance and support. We should heed the wisdom of Jacob Bronowski, who, in his book, *The Ascent of Man,* observed as follows: "We are all afraid - for our confidence; for the future, for the world. This is the nature of the human imagination. Yet every man, every civilisation, has gone forward because of its engagement with what it has set itself to do. The personal commitment of a man to his skill, the intellectual commitment and the emotional commitment working together as one, has made the Ascent of Man."

President Benjamin Mkapa and future leaders should galvanise the personal, the intellectual, and the emotional commitment of Tanzanians and set out what they wish to do and achieve. Election Manifestos are not a vision. They are a mere portfolio of policies and strategies. In other words, what I am proposing is that the task of getting the people to be committed, in whatever activities they are engaged in, is the responsibility of top leadership. The commitment gap presently characterised by a state of apathy and despair in society demands a focused and committed leadership. So much is depended on them. As Jesus preached, "For unto whomsoever much is given, of him shall be much required and to whom men have much committed, of him they shall ask the more."

In sum, commitment is underpinned by a social ethic - a sense of what things are right, and what things are wrong, to borrow Nyerere's words. The key challenge of national leadership today is to create the social ethic based on historical experience and on the new realities in the domestic and global environment. The first step in moulding this social ethic is to accept the wisdom that to build a nation is to build the character of the people and the attitude of mind that fosters hard work, creativity, unity, social justice and tolerance.

The Challenge to Own the Development Agenda

How often do Tanzanians sit back and seriously ponder what it takes for their nation and for every one of them to be challenged to pursue a better quality of life and prosperity? Are they at all insulted by their continuing condition of deprivation, squalor and poverty? Whatever happened to the rallying battle cry for political independence and for the fight to vanquish poverty, disease and ignorance? Who is responsible for this war of economic liberation: is it only the government or is there a way in which the burden of responsibility can effectively be shared in line with the ardent realisation that, at the end of the day, the individual has the ultimate responsibility for his and her own development and prosperity? There is much talk today about poor countries "owning" their development agenda, a wake up call from what has come to be seen as the "imposition" of a conventional wisdom charted out and prescribed by the Bretton Woods institutions. Yet, do Tanzanians translate such ostensible imposition to a personal and national challenge to "own" the development agenda and work to make it succeed? Put simply, are Tanzanians challenged at all by the urge to succeed in whatever that they do? Are they sufficiently cognisant of the determinants of success? How much attention have they placed on this question?

In a book by Anthony Robbins titled, *Unlimited Power*, one is animated by its power of ideas about the challenges involved in the quest to succeed in whatever one is involved in. I have been animated by the power of ideas encapsulated in the book. The ideas that Robbins churns out respond to many of the questions that surround the national and individual state of deprivation Tanzania is presently cocooned in. For instance, he poses a familiar question that keeps popping up in Tanzania, "What do we do when we try everything we can and things still turn out wrong?" Robbins' answer to this question underlies the thrust and logic of the rest of his book. He asserts, "People who succeed do not have fewer problems than people who fail. The only people without problems are those in cemeteries. It is not what happens to us that separates failure from success. It is how we perceive it and what we do about what 'happens' that makes the difference." Put in context, as far as Tanzania is concerned, it is how the people perceive and understand their current social and economic problems and going about doing something about them that underlies the capacity to reverse mal-development and bringing about change for the better. How do Tanzanians then go about ingraining such capacity to perceive, to understand and to act? This is not an obvious or simple question as many Tanzanians may think. It is a question that critically defines the underlying mindset problem largely responsible today for stifling and undermining the birth of a renaissance in society.

Mindsets, Beliefs and Change

I have often wondered, in this context, to what extent, for example, economic reforms, liberalisation, deregulation and privatisation, have contributed to changing the mindset in the country. Can Tanzanians confidently assert that they are consciously moving in the direction of a market orientation? Are the '*Machingas*'. street hawkers), for example, in a mere 'survival' economic activity or are they consciously creating a new base of market - driven entrepreneurship? I am not sure if the latter is the case. The question of perception is central to the challenge for national renewal. Robbins explains this phenomenon by quoting the English Poet, John Milton: "The mind is its own place, and in it self can make a Heaven of Hell, a Hell of Heaven." Paraphrased, this means that the world we live in is the world we choose to live in. If we choose bliss, that is what we get. If we choose misery, we get that too. Therefore, the challenge is to transform the perception of our condition. This we can if we ingrain what

Robbins describes as the belief of success. Robbins identifies seven beliefs. However, I have focused only on four core beliefs.

The first belief is that "everything happens for a reason and a purpose, and it serves us." Put differently, adversity, as in cases where El Nino rains wreaked havoc on crops and infrastructure, followed by spells of drought, should be viewed both as a challenge and as an opportunity. Evidently, not all adversity is God-driven. Indeed, most of it emanates from the frailties of humankind. For example, there are Tanzanians who would ascribe some of the current economic adversity to the consequences of the collapse of public ownership, the dissolution of the Cooperatives in 1976, and the villagisation programme. What is clear though is that it is foolhardy to lament about such adversity. Instead, the challenge is to ensure that the adversity "serves" the nation as a lesson of experience demanding fresh insight and new policy perspective. Robbins posits that Israel found itself with a desert that was a serious adversity to her. Yet she boldly moved to transform it and create a promised land. The belief in "possibility," in being able to achieve, is therefore a critical factor for success.

The second belief is that "there is no such thing as failure; there are only results". This philosophy is underlined by Warren Bennis and Burt Nanus in their book titled *Leaders: The Strategies for Taking Charge*. In that book, the authors present their discoveries from studies of leaders. One such discovery is that "leaders put all their energies into their task. They simply do not think about failure". Recalling some of the best leadership attributes of Mwalimu Nyerere, one sees that he was a leader who, in whatever he did whether in politics, economics or international relations, it was the task, the policy, the decision, the principle, the mission and the goal, based on a vision, that stood out as paramount. Thus, he never regarded the drawbacks experienced from public ownership and the villagisation programme as failures. Yes, he admitted of and accepted "mistakes" having been committed. But he never embraced failure. Throughout his leadership, Nyerere acted as he believed. He read all the works of William Shakespeare and was almost certainly in agreement with Shakespeare, from *Measure for Measure*, where he posited, "Our doubts are traitors, and make us lose the good we oft might win, by fearing to attempt." This philosophy has wider application beyond leaders. Everybody should imbibe the underpinnings of this philosophy. Our whole attitude: to work, to starting business, to borrowing capital for an economic venture, to deciding to retire to a village rather than remaining in misery in an urban township, has to imbibe risk in which success is the goal and not just the subject of fear or failure. There is something to learn from what Aristotle said, "We are what we repeatedly do. Excellence, then, is not an act, but a habit." And if we go by Stephen Covey's definition from his book, *The Habits of Highly Effective People*, "habit" is driven by the "intersection of knowledge, skill and desire."

The third belief is that "whatever happens, take responsibility". Taking responsibility is not exclusive to leaders. It applies to everybody who is tasked to doing something that makes a difference to his or her life. Humankind generates experience in real life situations and learns from it. The challenge of development hinges on a belief that one can create different and better set of circumstances. Yet, the common drawback that often presents itself in Tanzania is characterised by the attitude that we are at the mercy of circumstances. As Robbins contextualises it, it is as if "things just happen" to us, and we seem to accept becoming the "object" and not a "subject" of circumstances. Such mindset should be changed if Tanzania is going to succeed to take control of its people's lives and environment from which livelihood and prosperity depends upon. More importantly, Tanzanians should liberate themselves from the common lament that for what happens to them, it is the government that should take responsibility. Tanzanians appear overly disposed to finding fault and not to proposing solutions. However, the reality is that there are several things and circumstances that happen to them, which, they are capable of taking responsibility for and doing something that is right.

Finally, it is the belief that abiding success comes with commitment. North Americans have the common powerful expression about commitment: to *"walk the talk"*. It literally means acting resolutely on what one pronounces. At the heart of commitment lies effective communication. The people should be mobilised to support a vision and make a success of it. If *Ujamaa* succeeded in the 1970s, it was because Nyerere "walked the talk" and created a flood of lieutenants to spread the *ujamaa* gospel. Even before the Arusha Declaration was enunciated in February 1967, Nyerere had already prepared Tanzanians mentally on what *Ujamaa* was all about. In addition, after the promulgation of Arusha Declaration, Nyerere went to great length to build commitment to *Ujamaa*. Regrettably, there is no equal commitment in propagating the philosophy and benefits of the market economy. However, commitment alone could not result in the improvement of quality of life. You need, in addition, to have a challenge to succeed. As Stace Lindsay has observed in his article, *Culture, Mental Models, and National Prosperity*, "We have learned—that good answers to the pressing questions of economic development are not sufficient to engender the change needed to reverse the tides of poorly performing economies. Individuals will often accept intellectual arguments, understand their need to change, and express commitment to changing, but then resort to what is familiar. This tendency to revert to the familiar is not a cultural trait per se, but it is indicative of some of the deeper challenges faced by those who wish to promote a different, more prosperous vision of the future".

In the Tanzanian case, the question is what is its vision of the future? What should constitute the critical underpinnings of that future? In the next chapter, I examine at length the background to Tanzania Development Vision 2002, what it encapsulates and the challenges it faces in realising its goals.

Chapter

22 DEVELOPMENT VISION 2025: A RENAISSANCE?

A development strategy needs to set forth the vision of transformation, what the society will be like 10 to 20 years from now. This vision may embrace certain quantitative goals, such as a reduction in poverty by half, or universal primary education, but these are elements in our targets for the transformation process, not the vision of the transformation itself.

-Joseph E. Stiglitz: *Towards a New Paradigm for Development: Strategies, Policies and Processes,* 19 October, 1998.

Historical Overview

It is evident that few Tanzanians doubt the fact that for a considerable period since the on-set of economic reforms in 1986, the Tanzanian economy has drifted along, though, in recent years, especially since 1997, it has begun to move in the right direction. For sometime, Tanzania lacked a defined, compelling and coherent vision of the kind of society it sought to build. Many Tanzanians still hold the view that the Arusha Declaration spells out such a vision, which, to them, remains valid and appropriate. This is a highly debatable issue. In its basic intent, the Arusha Declaration sought to create a socialist and self-reliant society. This means the realisation of a society committed to human equality and dignity in which, to cite Nyerere from his publication *The Purpose is Man*, "it is wrong for one man to dominate or to exploit another" and where "material wealth for its own sake" is rejected.

The Arusha Declaration adopted state control of the economy as the vehicle to construct such a society. In the absence of that vehicle, exploitation of one another and the "rejection of material wealth". though we do not clearly understand what exactly Mwalimu Nyerere meant with the phrase "for its own sake", in the context of the modern world of the Bill Gates and people of his kind) seem implausible. Evidently, it is still possible to promote social justice in the absence of state control of the economy. Tony Blair, in his pamphlet *The Third Way: New Politics for the New Century*, views social justice as being "founded on the equal worth of each individual whatever their background, capability, creed or race." Blair posits that his "new politics" stands for a "modernised social democracy, passionate in its commitment to social justice and the goal of the centre-left, but flexible, innovative and forward - looking in the means to achieve them." In important ways, however, social justice should recognise that there is no progress where there is no shared and fair distribution of the fruits of prosperity. Without it, society risks the danger of social exclusion, apathy, social unrest and conflict.

Tanzania has shifted from state control of the economy to the market. It probably did so because it realised that the economy was in a crisis from the early 1980s. At the same time, it is also indisputable that Tanzania made the ideological shift primarily because it assumed that it was the only way in which it could have obtained external assistance necessary to re-stabilise its economy and put it on a recovery and growth path. Yes, there was also the so-called *"End of History"* intervention with the collapse of communism and the Soviet-type socialism as a lesson to be considered. Clearly though, Tanzania was confronted by the stark and harsh realities that Nyerere succinctly captured in his essay, *Principles and Development*: "We have to understand our own objectives, and then assess the best way of reaching them. This will sometimes mean running straight ahead and fighting those obstacles; at other times it will mean manoeuvring to find a better and easier way through." What emerges from this analogy is the pertinent question: was Tanzania clear about its objectives, 'a la Nyerere, when it decided to liberalise the economy, foster competition, and allow privatisation and deregulation to step into the economy? In other words, why did Tanzania precisely adopt the shift to the market? If I could borrow an interesting question posed, in this light, from Daniel Yergin's book *The Commanding Heights*, was the move to the market irreversible? Put another way, "What will be the consequences and prospects- political, social, and economic- of this fundamental alteration in the relationship between government and marketplace?"

The Market and Social Justice

It is broadly accepted that the market, in itself, is not an end state or condition. In other words, it does not describe a specific societal condition. Could Tanzania's end state from pursuing a market economy be the same as that envisioned by the Arusha Declaration? As alluded to earlier, the answer could be yes and no. The market does not understand the language of non-exploitation. However, given clear values, the market can promote social justice. Blair posits in his essay, *The Third Way*, "A critical dimension of the Third Way is that policies flow from values, not vice versa. With the right policies, market mechanisms are critical to meeting social objectives, entrepreneurial zeal can promote social justice, and new technology represents an opportunity, not a threat." The critical question to be asked in the Tanzanian case is what are the values that inform market-led policies?

Tanzania Development Vision 2025, which I examine at length in the next section, sets out how the market, amongst other driving forces-social, economic cultural, technological and ecological-can be harnessed to deliver a compelling and shared aspiration for Tanzanians. The vision recognises that if, as a country, Tanzania is not clear about its goals and values, then the market model of development would most likely widen inequalities as the economy grows and becomes more industrialised. As a consequence, the present widening gap in incomes, knowledge and, even power, could be accentuated. The market would then trigger social turmoil and instability. Today, many ordinary Tanzanians still cry out for the return of *"ruksa"*. "anything goes") policies of President Ali Hassan Mwinyi's administration. To them, the skewed and unregulated liberalisation of the late 1980s and the early 1990s somehow reflected a vision of better times. This response was to be expected. After the collapse of state capitalism, an economic philosophy that had offered ordinary people hope and had made them rally behind the idea as an economic liberating one, Tanzanians had been left wondering what social and economic values drove their economy. Vision 2025 is meant to help them rekindle their hopes. In promoting Vision 2025, it was as if the CCM government was taking a cue from Tony Blair's powerful message: "Politics is first and foremost about ideas. Without a powerful commitment to goals and values, governments are rudderless and ineffective, however large their majorities."

Democracy shares many attributes with social justice and its development and deepening rests significantly with a vision of society. Indeed, if we could revert to Mwalimu Nyerere's aversion of material wealth "for its own sake," it is possible that what Nyerere had in mind in using that phrase was self-indulgence and the disregard for altruism among the wealthy. Interestingly, this subject has recently attracted the attention of learned social democrats. In an excellent book, *The Hungry Spirit: Beyond Capitalism - A Quest For Purpose In the Modern World*, the British social critic Charles Handy contends that new democracy would not for long tolerate unbridled capitalism. He argues, "A society that does not recognise the morality of 'enough' will see excesses arise which merge on the obscene, as those who have first choice of society's riches appropriate them for themselves. Democracy will not long tolerate such an abuse of the market." Giving a concrete example, Handy warns, "A society in which the top 1% earn more, collectively, than the bottom 40%, will not long be tolerated in a democratic state."

Such radical views provoke a deductive question: What does it require democracy to work? In his brilliant book, *The Future of Capitalism*, MIT Professor Lester Thurow responds to this question by positing: "To work, democracy needs a vision of utopia - a route to a better society - a vision of what it is that transcends narrow sectarian self- interest." In the absence of a compelling vision of a better future, Professor Thurow adds, "everyone starts trying to impose their personal micro agendas for raising their own personal income or wealth. Without an agenda, political parties splinter and political power shifts from those who want to do new things to those who want to stop things from being done. Governments lose their ability to impose costs on particular citizens and to accomplish tasks that would make the average person better off." Thurow's conclusion is that the only way to bridge the split between "democracy's belief in equality of power" and the "market's growing generation of great inequalities of economic power" is to forge a vision that is exciting enough for the people. It is has to be a vision that "they will want to make sacrifices and forget their narrow self-interests in order to reconstruct the economy to produce different results."

There are other important challenges that confront the democratic impulse. All such challenges demand the deepening of democratisation. One of the critical tests was the manner in which the CCM government that enjoyed parliamentary majority dealt with Judge Kisanga Committee's Report following the debates of the Constitutional Reform *White Paper*. Of course, many Tanzanians would have wished that major constitutional changes of the nature put before the people through the Kisanga Committee would have been put directly to them through a referendum as a testimony of commitment by the government to the quest to deepen democratisation. After all, the decision to move the capital from Dar es Salaam to Dodoma, an issue of lesser importance to the interests and constitutional freedoms of the people, had enjoyed a quasi-referendum process!

The point I am making is this: a people's government should respect the control by citizens of its affairs. In this context, I totally agree with Charles Handy that electorate responsibility exercised once every five years in a polling booth "is so minimalist as to be meaningless." For governments, on the other hand, to say "elect us and leave it to us to act, always, in your best interests" is equally tantamount, in Handy's opinion, to "turning democracy into elected paternalism, or less generously, into an elected dictatorship."

Poverty and Rural Development

Finally, and only briefly, there is the question about addressing poverty and rural development. Based on the Vision of the Arusha Declaration, Tanzania had a defined policy framework for attacking rural poverty, namely *Socialism and Rural Development*. The underlying framework of that policy was the recognition that, as at 1967, "the growth of urban centres and of wage employment" was insignificant with only 4% of Tanzanians living in towns and less than 340,000 people working for wages, out of a total population of 5 million.

Over time, life in urban areas has come to represent opportunities for advancement, excitement and better social services. *Socialism and Rural Development* had sought to destroy the myth about town conditions and to promote a family production structure and social unity consistent with the growth of socialism. However, rural socialism is effectively dead! The market has now penetrated rural economic life. On the other hand, the erosion of the welfare state and the poor state of local government have meant that social service delivery in rural areas has suffered serious setbacks though admittedly, basic education has seen robust and phenomenal government support since 2001. Peasant agriculture has until lately been virtually neglected by the state in terms of being supported with the much-needed infrastructure and institutional support, such as research and extension. Since 2003, the government has instituted support measures in the form of subsidised fertilisers which is a positive development. Generally, however, the vision of rural socialism is yet to be replaced by an equally powerful and compelling vision underpinned by the market. It is a situation which the South Commission's Report, *The Challenge To The South* captures in the following words: "Such neglect almost always meant stagnant or worsening conditions for the rural poor, and generally resulted in food output and peasant incomes falling to keep pace with population growth. The outcome was often a drag on all development efforts, in particular on attempts to industrialise. Far industries need markets and people who can afford to buy their output, and can hardly flourish when the mass of the people remain poor."

Vision 2025: A Tanzanian Renaissance?

In September 1999, Tanzania adopted a new vision of development called *Development Vision 2025*. It was worked out over two and half years by a non-partisan group of Tanzanians, comprising men and women, from both the Mainland and Zanzibar, people who enjoyed the respect of Tanzanian society for their intellect, independence of mind and love for their country. The Vision team worked in earnest to craft a vision based on a social compact with the aim that it may energise Tanzanians to jump-start their future by marshalling their skills, talents, concord, peace and stability and resources to make it happen.

What is a vision? Put simply, it is one's articulation of a realistic, credible and attractive destination. There is no more powerful force for driving a country toward a shared prosperity and human happiness than an attractive, plausible and realisable vision of the future. Thus, Tanzania Development Vision 2025 articulates a future that is considered better, more prosperous and more desirable than the present. It provides that by 2025 Tanzania should have eradicated abject poverty, illiteracy and infectious diseases. It espouses that Tanzania should attain the moral and material standards that would enhance national pride. Specifically, the vision postulates that Tanzania should by 2025 aim at attaining the level of development equivalent to that of a middle-income country. The characteristics of such a level of development include, in the main, the following:-

- food self-sufficiency,
- a learning society,
- absence of illiteracy,
- a strong and diversified economy which is regionally and globally competitive and enjoys macro-economic stability and low inflation,
- universal primary education,
- good and adequate physical infrastructure,
- high level of tertiary education in tune with national needs and demands for high level human resources,
- ecological balance,
- access to quality primary health care and reproductive health services for all,
- a strong rule of law regime,
- reduction in infant and maternity mortality rates by three-quarters of the current levels,
- moral and cultural uprightness,
- mass availability of safe water,
- absence of corruption,
- life expectancy comparable to the level attained by typical middle income countries,
- gender justice and
- absence of abject poverty.

Post-independence Challenges

Tanzania gained political independence in December 1961, inheriting a legacy of poverty, disease, ignorance and a social and economic system that stratified the citizenry on the basis of wealth, largely along racial lines, educational opportunities and on gender. The post-independence government led by the beloved Founder President and Father of the Nation, the late Mwalimu Julius Kambarage Nyerere, was seized, from the start, of the acuteness of the challenges that confronted the new nation.

In the formative years, Nyerere used the private sector as the driving force in addressing the problems of development. At the same time, he was mindful of the fact that liberal policies, both political and economic, were critical to attracting foreign direct investment. Although in 1962, Nyerere had crafted his vision for Tanzania from both the political and economic angles, as encapsulated in his seminal papers: *Democracy And The One-Party State* and *Ujamaa-The Basis of African Socialism*, it was only in 1965 and 1967 that he translated his vision into concrete measures. Thus, the introduction of the One Party State in mid 1965 and the promulgation of the socialist blueprint, the *Arusha Declaration* in February 1967.

Nyerere's optimism about foreign direct investment had waned by 1966. The intense politics of the cold war at the time did not help. It was believed then that the financial support of the Western nations crucially hinged on new nations rallying behind them in the cold war. Those were the realities of global realpolitik. On the other hand, it did not take Nyerere long enough to recognise that the organised private sector in the newly independent Tanzania was not only nascent but was also extremely fragile. It lacked a strong base, size, scope of ownership and capital to promote growth, sustainability and legitimacy. Those shortcomings prompted Nyerere to jump-start his political and economic vision. Apparently, Nyerere was also concerned that delaying the introduction of the one party state and socialism would have undermined the prospect of their subsequent successful introduction as political polarisation could have entrenched and that the taste of private wealth could also have built strong political resistance against public ownership.

What then was Nyerere's vision as encapsulated in his philosophies of the One Party State and Socialism and Self-Reliance? The vision sought to create a new society wherein the following core values would exist: -

- people-centred development,
- social and economic justice,
- absence of poverty, ignorance and disease,
- social safety nets would provide care for the disadvantaged and the disabled,
- ethical leadership and absence of corruption,
- human dignity, respect and equality and
- democratic form of governance through a one party system.

In his wisdom, Nyerere believed that these core values, the pillars, as it were, of a peaceful, stable and happy society, could best be realised in the context of the political, social and economic conditions that prevailed at that material time, conditions whose driving forces were:

- public. or State) ownership of the major means of production, exchange and distribution;
- collective rural development. villagisation); absence of political opposition. enabling a more focused approach to tackling development problems confronting the country),
- support for the liberation of African countries still under the yoke of colonialism and minority rule, and
- The quest for realising African unity.

Nyerere's vision had a historic and significant impact on Tanzania. Importantly, his compelling vision has resulted in Tanzania's national unity, peace and stability. Thus, in the whole African region, Tanzania today stands at the pinnacle as a model of self-determination in a post cold war era and of peace and stability. It is a haven for political refugees and its role in African conflict management and resolution is exemplary. The Nyerere vision and the resultant legacy should inevitably act as the launching pad for the Tanzanian spacecraft as it takes off to the next stage of its journey envisioned in Vision 2025.

Natural Endowments of Tanzania

Tanzania is rich in human and natural resources. If effectively harnessed and utilised, these can ensure, for all the people, a reasonably high quality livelihood measured in terms of human happiness, material well being, ethical values, gender justice and environmental sustainability. All these life chances can also be realised within an environment of peace, harmony and broad-based pluralism. One clear example of the benefits of such environment is Tanzania's ability to transit from a monolithic political system to a multiparty system in a peaceful and orderly fashion, notwithstanding the political fracas that presently bedevils some of the opposition parties. However, in spite of this rich resource endowment, Tanzania has not succeeded to eradicate abject poverty, ignorance and disease. In fact, the challenge to address these scourges has become more arduous and urgent. Evidently, there is reason for deep introspection and critical appraisal of the factors that underlie incapacity to reduce the intensity of these scourges.

Since 1982, whilst Mwalimu Nyerere was still in power, but more especially since mid 1986, serious efforts have been embarked upon to identify the underlying causes of Tanzania's economic stagnation and to put in place appropriate measures to arrest the condition, whilst, at the same time, getting the economy onto a growth trajectory. In this context, several social and economic fundamentals have improved significantly. Paradoxically, these macro-economic improvements have not effectively translated into improved quality of livelihood of the people. Poverty shows signs of deepening and illiteracy is abating only slowly. Infectious diseases, on the other hand, have become more rampant and more devastating in human life. About half the Tanzanian population lives below the poverty line, with an income of less than one United States dollar per day. As if these problems were enough, new problems, of different form and seriousness, are emerging, making the national development challenge even more complex and demanding. Problems such as the fragmentation of the social fabric, characterised by concerning levels of corruption, violent crime, drug trafficking and prostitution. Growing urban unemployment and poor habitat and sanitation conditions manifest and reinforce declining quality livelihood in rural areas prompting more energetic youth to flock the urban centres in search of better conditions of life.

This social and economic environment is untenable. It is not in line with the dream of the independence movement and of Nyerere's vision for post independent Tanzania. Therefore, time had come for Tanzanians to soul-search and craft a new vision that more effectively responds to new challenges and which can unshackle them from underdevelopment and economic misery. This was a task of profound proportions. In constructing Development Vision 2025, the underlying factors that have been major impediments to the realisation of the goals of development in the past have been identified. These are the following: -

- a donor dependency syndrome and a dependent and defeatist development mindset,
- a weak and low capacity for economic management,
- failure in good governance and in the organisation and production and
- ineffective implementation syndrome.

Tanzanians, as a people and as leaders, have succumbed to welfare dependency from the state and from donors. They have lost their sense of pride, dignity and the spirit of self-reliance. should take. The discipline of hard work has largely been replaced by a culture of *"bongoism,"* making it in life whatever the means! Even the educational system, from primary to university level, has also unfortunately jumped onto the bandwagon of *bongoism*, undermining, on the way, the ethos of professionalism and the spirit of academic excellence.

Until sometime around 1996, at both the political and bureaucracy fronts, the national leadership had not quickly enough and adequately adapted to the changing social and economic conditions of a domestic and global character. What were viewed as good reforms, invariably suffered at the level of sustainability precisely because decision-makers were not sufficiently responsive to and bold enough at mastering changing conditions. At the same time, policy analysis and policy formulation capacity, for a considerable period of time, was weak such that key sectors like agriculture, had not, until lately, received the level of attention necessary to transform them. Equally, there could have been a more timely exploitation of growth-promoting economic sectors such as tourism and mining, which the *1998 African Competitiveness Report*, prepared by the World Economic Forum and the Harvard Institute for International Development, viewed to be Tanzania's key assets for extricating the country from underdevelopment and for making Tanzania a stronger and more sustainable economy. Evidently, serious efforts on the part of the national leadership have been made to improve the investment climate for mining and tourism since 1997 and for agriculture since 2004.

Conditions Propelling Vision 2025

The underlying impediments to Tanzania's development success were examined from the standpoint of the changing domestic and global conditions. From such a review that new driving forces for bringing about viable changes were identified. These conditions were the following:

- political and economic pluralism had set in.
- public ownership, villagisation and the application of administrative controls in the management of the economy had proven ineffective.
- individual initiative and the private sector are the central driving forces for building a strong, productive and renewing economy.
- state welfare responsibilities should focus on cost-effective ways of enhancing access and quality of social services.
- market and technological conditions were fast changing.
- post cold war geopolitical factors influence international economic relations.
- nation-state economic behaviour is being transformed by globalisation and regionalism trends thus undermining inward looking economic policies.

The impediments to change and the new domestic and global conditions that are permanently in a state of flux pose new challenges to Tanzania. These challenges demand that Tanzania identifies new driving forces for moving itself forward. Past driving forces had evidently failed to respond to new demands. In this context, therefore, Vision 2025 identified three key driving forces for the realisation of its goals:

- a developmental mindset.
- competence and competitiveness.
- good governance and the rule of law.

We learn from the distinguished Yale University Professor of History, Paul Kennedy's book, *Preparing for the Twenty First Century*, that "a society which desires to be better prepared for the 21st century will pay a price to achieve the transition; it will need to retool its national skills and infrastructure, challenge vested interests, alter many old habits and perhaps amend in its governmental structure." Tanzania's effective preparedness for the 21st century and realising the goals of Vision 2025 critically hinge on the three driving forces outlined above. These forces can be seized in three ways:

First, Tanzanians should liberate themselves from a dependent and defeatist developmental mindset. Poverty is an attitude of mind to most Tanzanians. It is not a condition imposed from external factors. Thus, abject poverty can be mainly eradicated by radically changing the culture of work and the technology of production. Equally, the majority of Tanzanians, unlike their brethren of Asian origin, lack entrepreneurship and a culture of saving and investment. They are dominantly consumptionist-oriented. They cherish materialism. This culture should change. Tanzanians should honour hard work, creativity and entrepreneurship. It is important that the education system is reformed to make it the vehicle for mindset transformation, to promote these new entrepreneurial virtues and inculcate a spirit of self-development through continuous learning. However, self-development, hard work and excellence should be rewarded if they are to act as role models in society and at the workplace.

Secondly, competitiveness is central to ensuring decent standards of living, good education, reasonable health and leisure. Such competitiveness can best be achieved where the nation does a number of key things:

- fosters sound economic management,
- develops adequate and reliable infrastructure,
- promotes science and technology education,
- masters new technologies,
- effectively manages demographic changes,
- ensures sustainable growth through environmental protection and management,
- utilises domestic resources fully,

- optimally transforms the economy towards greater productivity and competitiveness, especially in the fields of agriculture and agro-industry,
- develops the capacity to anticipate and respond to domestic and global changes.

Thirdly, the rule of law should be treated as the basic postulate of a democratic society. Democracy is inseparable from and cannot survive without the rule of law. Good governance and the rule of law should become the central instruments for the promotion and realisation of development, fair play, social virtues, equity and concord. In this light, it is imperative that the power of the market and of the private sector be unleashed. The balance of roles, between the state and the market, should be effectively delineated and their roles well defined and clarified, particularly the role of the state in investing in infrastructure and the social sector of the economy and in enabling an effective dialogue with the private sector and other stakeholders in society to be institutionalised and put to work. Democratic and popular participation should also be effectively promoted at all levels of the society. A Union constitution that enjoys popular support and acceptance of the majority of the people is an important vehicle in the realisation of the goals of Vision 2025.

The Role of Leadership

Experience drawn from other countries that have had a compelling lesson on visionary directions, countries like Singapore and Malaysia, clearly shows that leadership lies at the heart of success in implementing a vision. In support of this view, the British management guru Charles Handy pointed out in his book *Beyond Certainty* that sacrifices by the people are made voluntarily "for goals and ideals we believe in and when we have confidence in those who may lead us there." Thus, whilst Vision 2025 is a historic framework for realising sustainable and robust national development it requires a committed and insightful leadership to effect it. Mwalimu Nyerere was able to "move mountains," sometimes to the point of causing hardship on the people but without attracting any visible dissent or disturbance of peace and stability because he was a role model in whatever that he said and did. He was always able to convince the people that the one party state, socialism, and self-reliance were proper vehicles for the people's own social and economic emancipation and for realising their improved livelihoods. Tanzania needs a Nyerere-model of leadership to sell Vision 2025 to the people and to inspire them with a new hope. Vision 2025, a product of broad national consensus by any standards, within the limits of the possible in a participatory democracy, is Tanzania's new dream of a better and more prosperous future. It needs the acceptance and support of all Tanzanians across the political and other divides. Its success hinges on the commitment and zeal of the people to work for its goals. It can be done, if everybody plays a part. However, it evidently faces challenges driven by dogmatic thinking. Many Tanzanians still believe that we live in a world where what happened yesterday informs what we do today. They are not able or refuse to accept the fact that we live in an age of unreason. In the following section, I address this perception and its dysfunctions.

Vision 2025 and the Age of Unreason

Immediately following the adoption of Development Vision 2025 views were and comments on the vision were invited. Unfortunately, there was a disappointing response from the public. Tanzanians appeared to be more concerned about their social and economic predicaments than getting involved in lofty issues about their country's future. It was a disappointing situation for a country once proud of being highly socialised and participatory, that it should appear to be so apathetic a time when political pluralism had set in. Nevertheless, there was a notable exception. In three separate essays, published in *The African Newspaper*, Walter Bgoya, a leading Tanzanian social critic and a publisher made an incisive contribution on Vision 2025. His essays which were driven by an ideological thrust raised fundamental questions. A central theme underlying the thrust of Bgoya's essays was that Tanzania did not need another vision because it already had one, in Arusha Declaration's socialism and self-reliance. In his view, "the so-called" Development Vision 2025 was nothing less than an exercise in rhetoric and romanticism. In other words, it was a high-sounding nothing. Bgoya cited the French adage to underscore the irrelevance of Vision 2025, that "the more there is change, the more it is the same thing."

Let me address Bgoya's core theme first. In my view, Bgoya belongs, ideologically, to what may be described as the Tanzanian *ancien regime*, the class of people, to borrow a phrase from the French Revolution, who have learnt nothing and forgotten nothing about the imperativeness of change, in this case, about Tanzania's ideological shift from socialism. In other words, whatever change that has taken place and is taking place, at social and economic levels of society, is not *particularly* meaningful to people of such character. To Bgoya, there was only one road to prosperity for a poor country like Tanzania and it was through socialism or public ownership, not even a mixed economy. Nyerere's maxim on socialist *status quoism* that "if you turn your head to look back at where you are coming. meaning the capitalist past) from you would turn into stone" appeared to be still fresh and valid in Tanzanians with Bgoya's mindset. Bgoya was evidently overly *status quoist* as to where Tanzanians had come from considering the social and economic changes Tanzania was embracing, changes that informed the ethos of Vision 2025. Surely, the French expression about the nature of change that Bgoya referred to is dated. In his book, *The Age of Unreason*, Charles Handy, informs us that "thirty years ago most people thought that change would mean more of the same, only better". He adds, yet changes are now different; they are discontinuous. In other words, changes today no longer form part of a pattern as before. Charles Handy further ramifies: "today we know that in many areas of life we cannot guarantee more of the same, be it work or money, peace or freedom, health or happiness." How true.

Development Vision 2025 recognises these realities. We do live in an age of unreason and we cannot continue to assume that what worked well in the past would continue to work well in the future when most of our philosophies, past can legitimately be challenged. Vision 2025 challenges the logic of people "turning into stone" if they soul-searched their past and promote the need for a collective mental national adaptation to changing conditions. After all, it was Mwalimu Julius Nyerere, Bgoya's protégé and mentor, who, in his *Introduction* to the book, *Freedom and Unity*, cautioned that the choice for Africa was between changing under its own conditions and being changed by the impact of forces outside its control. Actually, the world is increasingly moving from mere adaptation to change to coping with "surprises," a more formidable challenge.

The second dimension that informed Bgoya's views concerns ownership of development goals. In Bgoya's view, public ownership was the key vehicle for the realisation of Tanzanian values and that, to him, these values were a product of socialism and self-reliance. I have a problem with such line of reasoning. How could socialism and self-reliance constitute "the codification of Tanzania values"? My understanding is that Nyerere had a vision of a new society that he wished tô create, a society of equals endowed with equity and respect that eschewed exploitation and thus enjoyed social and economic justice. Nyerere also believed that socialism and self-reliance was ideal for the realisation of such societal values. Put differently, it was the envisioned values that Nyerere strived to realise that brought about that necessitated the adoption of socialism and self reliance and not vice versa. It does not necessarily follow, therefore, that such values could only be realised through socialism. In this context, Ljubo Sirc, in his article *Socialism and Ownership*, which appears in the book *The Socialist Idea: A Reappraisal*, argues that the view that the private ownership of the means of production is the root cause of all evil. Bgoya castigated the market for discriminating against women and the uneducated; for erosion of jobs, and exploitation of peasants as unacceptable. He posits, "To my mind, the experience of the last fifty years has undeniably shown that evil does not stem only from greed but can also be the consequence of the lust for power, sexual drive, irrationality, sheer madness and possibly other human properties. Greed itself is not necessarily a result of private ownership of the means of production."

The traditional concepts and values that constitute the socialist idea, specifically public ownership, are going through a major transformation in the light of historical experience and emerging realities. It is only by realising such reality that we can rationally locate the ideological shifts that have taken place, for example, within the Labour Party in Britain and in the socialist and social democratic parties in Western Europe.

The third issue Bgoya has taken Vision 2025 to task on involves the role of the state. In Bgoya's view, the pre-eminence of the market in the economy and society subsumed a weak State. He thus questioned how a weak State could be able to create an enabling climate for the private sector to thrive whilst, at the same time, containing the struggle between the oppressed and the oppressors. This is a mistaken position. Vision 2025 is quite clear about the need for a strong state. The vision does not signify or postulate the entry of *laissez-faire*. On the contrary, under the section on institutional framework and organisation of development, the vision articulates three principles that underlie the role of the state in a market economy. One of these is the harnessing of power of the market in allocating resources and the dynamism of private sector development to achieve *shared* and sustainable growth. It is further provided that "to ensure that the resulting growth is shared it will be necessary to promote an efficient government which is consistently committed to development and a sufficiently strong government to facilitate and regulate the development process, influence and facilitate strategic investment and prudently provide selective industrial support".

Vision 2025 is equally emphatic about the role of the state over governance and the rule of law, clearly stipulating that governance should be made an instrument for promoting development, equity, unity and peace, buttressed on the rule of law and the mobilisation of public participation in the war against corruption and other vices in society. Above all, Vision 2025 recognises that markets do not work where human cost of failure is unacceptable. Thus, yes, Bgoya was right that the entry of the market did not support Fukuyama's thesis of the *"End of History."* It would be overly simplistic to think that the market could be an end all for humanity's social, political and economic problems. Neither could Fukuyama have envisioned such a conclusion!

Moreover, the weak and the vulnerable in society clearly need State protection. The market has its limits and unintended impacts. As Charles Handy has noted in his book, *The Hungry Spirit: Beyond Capitalism*, the market "is only a mechanism, not a philosophy. It should therefore be subjectable to flexible application. What is important to note is that the market itself has nothing to do with the protection or disprotection of the weak. The market is a means, not the end." In clarifying the point, Charles Handy posits, "capitalism, efficiency and markets have their flaws, but also their uses. They are neither the complete answer to our dilemmas nor the only cause of them. They provide some of the context of our lives but not the purpose".

Walter Bgoya made a useful and serious contribution in getting the debate on Vision 2025 onto the public domain. Yet, it should be pointed out that some of the major impediments to developing and pursuing a future direction for Tanzania revolve around issues, policies and past ideological positions that continue to dominate the mindset of many informed Tanzanians. Such positions confine and sometimes cloud the vision. They are based on the view that change is more of the same, a view that allowed many post-independence African leaders to embrace idealism; an idealism which, for sometime, made meaning but which, over time, did not work well, over time, in advancing the cause of development. The mindset of many African political leaders has now changed. It is no longer focused on disagreements over ends. Rather, the new realities, global and national, have helped transform the mindset. Peter Drucker in his book *The New Realities*, has argued that the task of political leadership is thus now directed at organising "around agreement over ends, indeed to mobilise the consensus on ends." In other words, the means, which constitute the instrumentality of the market, are given. As Mwalimu Nyerere indeed told the Vision 2025 Team of Experts that met him to dialogue on their work, capitalism was now inevitable. "It is futile to knock your head on the wall" against capitalism, Nyerere remarked. More important, Nyerere further ramified, was to ensure that capitalism worked for the broad interests of all the people. This, in my view, is the underlying philosophy of Development Vision 2025. However, the realisation of Vision 2025 also crucially hinges on the state of the mindset of the broad masses. What is the present state of this mindset?

The State of the Mindset in Tanzania

Change comes from small initiatives, which work, initiatives, which, imitated, become the fashion. We cannot wait for great visions from great people, for they are in short supply at the end of history. It is up to us to fight our own small fires in the darkness.

-Charles Handy: *The Empty Raincoat: Making Sense of the Future*

Time has come for Tanzanians to challenge their thinking and determine the critical driving forces that can enable Vision 2025 to succeed. In this context, I am reminded of a rare statement a deceased friend once made over a few drinks in Dar es Salaam in 1974. The late Leonard Kopa Tarimo had this to say, "This country that I have come to love and admire has now gone to the dogs; if I were to become the President, I would turn it into a company incorporated and run it on business lines".

The year 1974 marked the watershed in putting socialism at the centre of all economic activities. The Villagisation programme had then started. However, famine was also threatening people's lives. It was the year of "Kilimo cha kufa na kupona". Agricultural production as a matter of life and death), as Nyerere described it. Seven years after the promulgation of the socialist blueprint- the Arusha Declaration, Tarimo was already sensing the serious dangers of economic malaise that were begin to afflict the country and of the need to change course by promoting market capitalism. Since 1986, the government has attempted to practice what Tarimo had in mind. Two decades after the initiation of economic reforms and liberalisation, Tanzania is yet to get out of its miseries of poverty, ignorance and disease. Has the government, as the conceiver and implementer of the reforms clearly determined what should be done better to improve the state of the economy, not just in GDP growth terms but more importantly in improving the quality of life of the broad masses?

Admittedly, some of these questions are addressed in Vision 2025. Nevertheless, a key driving force that would crucially underpin the success of the vision is the state of the mindset of Tanzanians in government, in business, at household levels and as individuals. How then does one get into instilling into the minds of Tanzanians the challenge of change, the challenge of being one's own master and vehicle for personal and national economic advancement and the challenge to reject poverty, ignorance and communicable diseases?

It is indisputable that a deep-seated state of lethargy pervades the Tanzanians' ways of life in many ways:

- the culture of discipline has waned;
- the ethic and ethos supportive of hard work that manifested itself in the nation building and self-help spirit era of the 1960s and the early 70's has weakened;
- a detrimental syndrome of resignation and helplessness and the attitude that the government and "wafadhili". donors) would always step in to alleviate destitution has stepped in.

So pervasive is the mindset that it has deeply permeated the societal fabric. A poor example but which manifests such mindset is that top football clubs can no longer sustain themselves without aid and grants.

A mercenary culture has so deeply ingrained itself in this field of sports as to undermine the spirit of sports. Under socialist rule, Tanzania regrettably funded its welfare state largely through foreign aid. This made a mockery of its drummed up objective of self-reliance. It even made the people believe, falsely, in the capacity of their government to deliver free and quality social services. Today, ordinary people at village levels and even the better-exposed University students fail or refuse to understand the rationale of policies like cost recovery and cost sharing. The University students' strike in 2004 against the proposed funding of part of their education through a soft loan arrangement offered by the government was a clear manifestation of this skewed perception. These Tanzanians still live in the past; a past that was illusory because the Welfare State had never been sustained by domestic resources. It was a system that was incapable of self-sustenance.

Nothing is more dangerous to peace, stability and unity than holding on to illusory past successes. Yet such expectations have become a national psyche; they are taken for granted when, in fact, they have ceased to be relevant. Thus the task of designing a vision, a shared vision, is only one side of the coin. The other side is how to see the vision through the context of the present attitudes of the people. This is the more difficult challenge. In Malaysia, there has been a collective ethos about Vision 2020. Every Malaysian, from the taxi driver to the Kuala Lumpur prostitute sings Vision 2020. They know that the mission of the Vision is to create wealth and more wealth, which would be equitably distributed to build a more humane, united and peaceful Malaysia. However, Malaysia did not have as pervasive a socialist past as Tanzania did. Mindset transformation, in their case, has thus not been an impediment. In contrast, the majority of Tanzanians are still blinded by philosophies such as state ownership even when experience elsewhere has clearly shown that governments have no business being in business. If it is a question of promoting direct ownership by the people then this is possible through broad ownership of privatised assets or through greenfield investments. Indeed, the stock exchange has been constituted in Tanzania precisely to enable such broad ownership to be realised.

Another area of mindset transformation relates to the broad attitude about the place of business and about the role of the private sector in the Tanzanian economy. It is regrettable that business activity is still viewed in certain quarters of the society with a negative perception. A simple example is the paradoxical negative reaction of the media and some Members of Parliament to the smart partnership that has developed between the government and business. For example, the 1997/98 Budget which, to some extent, was influenced by the National Business Lobby, was described by the media and MPs as being pro-business and thus anti-people, as if business did not work for the interests of Tanzania and its people. Surely, if business is able to lobby the government successfully to have taxes reduced in order to boost demand and thus raise more revenue for the Exchequer, why should a positive response on the part of the government be viewed as anti- people? Such attitudes are only symptomatic of an anti-private sector mindset, a hangover from the discredited past economic policies. Such mindset should change or else it would undermine Tanzania's attractiveness to investments. In particular, the government should respond to the challenge of change. Central to such change is getting the government to play a catalytic role in igniting the forces of efficiency, creativity and competitiveness in the private sector. The process involves a major de-briefing on the part of the bureaucracy and re-inventing the government. Bureaucratic bottlenecks that still constrain and shackle investments and effective operations of business because of the attitude of mind of bureaucrats as opposed to entrenched bureaucratic rules and regulations should be transformed. The operating culture of the government is supposed to have changed dramatically upon the revision of the role of the state and upon the private sector becoming the new engine of development. This change is emerging only slowly emerging due to a robust public service reform programme under implementation.

At another level, the mindset of the private sector should equally change to reflect the growing confidence being placed on it in the development effort. In this direction, the private sector can partly help to transform the negative mindset that exists against it. One way is for the private sector to develop a socio-economic code of conduct that reflects socially responsible behaviour. This it can achieve if its main actors in the economy quickly realise the importance of their being part of business lobby associations where business ethical standards are promoted and enforced through censure. The attitude of everybody to himself and God for us all in business would only balkanise the private sector making it more difficult for the government to work with it. The correct path is for the private sector to operate ethically, to pay taxes and stamp out corruption. Tanzania has the potential to become an economic powerhouse in its own right. However, to be able to harness and exploit such potential, it should deconstruct its mindset-in politics, government, business and civil society. It must swiftly adjust to the challenges of development that confront it. Habits of the last three decades that have somewhat enabled Tanzania to subsist, may now be a recipe for deepening poverty and social instability. Tanzanians have to crystallise the new vision, mobilise nation-wide support for change and adapt to the challenges of globalisation. Commitment, discipline, self development, continuous learning and hard work are some of the critical tools for promoting such social and economic transformation. The mindset is thus a key ingredient for enabling the Vision to succeed. It has to be factored into the vision.

Factoring in the Mindset in Vision 2025

Professor Issa Shivji of the University of Dar es Salaam has a conceptual problem with the words "mindset" and "mindsets". Those who closely know Shivji's "mindset",. a devout Marxist, teaching law) his position is simply consistent. At a Symposium of the Society for International Development on Globalisation in 1998, he cynically attacked the use of the term "empowerment". Professor Shivji and the Indian Social Scientist, Rajni Kothari, share a common distrust of what Kothari describes as "fashionable conceptions like 'conscientisation', 'empowerment' and 'mobilisation' of the people". To Kothari, these terms merely tend to be populist or paternalistic; arguing that there could be no people's action except by the people themselves and that others can, at best, facilitate and catalyse that process. My view, to cite from the American Philosopher John Dewey's 1930 book, *Individualism Old and New* is that: "As long as we limit ourselves to generalities, the phrases that express ideals may be transferred from conservative to radical or vice versa, and nobody will be the wiser. For, without analysis, they do not descend into actual scene nor concern themselves with the generative conditions of realisation of ideals".

In this context, it is important to clarify the concept of the mindset and how it fits into the overall ethos and the challenge to realise to realise Development Vision 2025. In its Report, *The First Global Revolution,* The Club of Rome observed, "The pressure of the facts is that we must either change or disappear. To meet priorities that require immediate action and begin managing change without losing time, a true transformation of mindsets and behaviour is imperative". Reference may also be made to one of the leading architects of the concept of vision, Peter Schwartz. In his pioneering book, *The Art of the Long View,* he posits, "changing public beliefs can pivot the direction of history more swiftly and irrevocably than money or military power".

Much closer to the Tanzanian environment, we learn from Mwalimu Julius Nyerere who, in his earlier writings after independence, addressed issues anchored on "an attitude - a social ethic," which to him underlined the institutional framework of a vision and its purpose: namely equality, freedom and unity and mutual respect and obligation that bound society together. In the powerful introduction to his book, *Freedom and Unity*, Mwalimu Nyerere underscored the challenge to fight the intensification of the attitude where rights of the individual overrode the need for human dignity, an attitude that would eventually nullify the need for human dignity and equality. He called for the establishment of a social organisation that would reduce personal temptations to a minimum and averred that "the spreading of such attitudes and the introduction of such institutions" should constitute an important part of the policies of the government.

There is no misnomer in the word 'mindset' and its relevance in society and in the dynamics of societal transformation. The question of attitudes, public beliefs and behaviour, encapsulated in the word 'mindset', should thus occupy a central place in any discussion about change processes, whether human or institutional. It is in this specific framework that I discuss the concept of mindset, its place and its role in the realisation of Vision 2025.

Mindset: Seeing with New Eyes

The French novelist Marcel Proust once wrote, "The real voyage of discovery consists not in seeking new lands but in seeing with new eyes". These are powerful words. In a way, the realisation of the goals of Vision 2025 somewhat hinge on the philosophical wit of Proust. Put differently, it is not the form and substance of the new development paradigm reflected in Vision 2025 that may, in an overriding way, enable the realisation of the vision. Rather, as experience around the world has shown, the challenge of bringing about change and achieving transformation, whether social, political, economic or even technological, depends profoundly on the people's ability to *"see with new eyes"*. The state of the people's mindset their thinking, habits, beliefs, attitudes, values, behaviour and their approach towards matters that directly impact and bear on their survival, welfare and well being, have an important bearing on enabling them to rise to new challenges of change and development; change that is discontinuous and permanently in a state of flux.

In order for Tanzania to effectively address and cope with the challenges of the twenty first century and specifically with those posed in Vision 2025, it would need to possess or develop a state of mind that is in tune with current global realities and those that lie ahead. The success or failure in achieving the goals of Vision 2025 critically depends on such state of the mind. An objective analysis of whether Tanzania, as a people and as organisations or institutions, possesses the appropriate mindset or mindsets as vehicles for effecting and managing the needed perception change and transformation is required. So is the need to determine how the mindset could be shaped to conform and respond to the new demands and challenges deemed necessary and appropriate in mastering the challenges that Vision 2025. In this context, the following three questions are examined.

First, which mindset is necessary for realising the goals of Vision 2025? Second, what is the state of the current mindset and how does it constitute an obstacle to the realisation of the goals of Vision 2025?

Thirdly, what are the challenges and tasks of transforming the mindset so that it can act as a driving force for the realisation of the goals of Vision 2025?

At the outset, it is important to observe that Vision 2025 has been crafted within the context of the concrete realisation that the national, regional and global economic conditions have changed dramatically in recent years and continue to change. Some of these contextual realities are the following:

- political pluralism and democratisation is taking root in the society.
- state sector -led policies have not been sustainable; they are largely becoming reformed and in many ceases abandoned.
- the forces of the market and of individual initiative are driving most social and economic activities.
- the 'Welfare State' is being pruned and new approaches in social service provisioning and delivery, which are market driven, are taking shape and dominance.
- changed and changing market conditions and technological developments are taking place at a fast pace making economic competitiveness the only route to success.
- economic nationalism or isolationist nation-state economic behaviour is increasingly being undermined by regionalism and globalisation.
- a New World order centred on US military and economic power has replaced the geopolitics of the Cold War.

It would be foolhardy to behave, like an ostrich, and discount such realities. These realities have serious implications on state behaviour and on how a people can tackle their problems of development. In many respects, the ability of nation-states and people to master these challenges crucially depends on the state of their mindset. Given the goals of Vision 2025 and the challenges, which, of necessity, should be confronted, there is little doubt that a major mindset formation consistent with the challenges and tasks that lie ahead of Tanzania and its people. Unfortunately, these realities are not seen with the same eyes by all the people. To that extent they raise different, often opposing, responses about the challenges that inform Vision 2025. At the centre of such divergence of opinion is the understanding of the relevance of *"ujamaa"* in the current environment. There are those who link Mwalimu Nyerere's philosophy of socialism to some kind of *"papal infallibility"*. Nobody has said that socialism as an ideal end goal has failed. Nyerere did not say so; we have not. Yet one has to be clear about *Ujamaa*, as a way of life and as a social value, in contrast to *Ujamaa* as an economic vehicle, the latter having failed almost everywhere. In fact, Nyerere publicly admitted this latter failure. However, it is also failure that catalyses a bold response.

Often the failure of the Tanzanian socialist economic system is blamed on implementation. Such a stance would tantamount to saying that all countries that practiced socialism failed to make the system succeed simply because of failure of implementation. That would be absurd. Clearly, in terms of a vision, and I believe that Nyerere had a credible desired future of Tanzania, I do not discern any departure of what Vision 2025 envisions from what the Arusha Declaration envisioned as a future society for Tanzania. The point of departure is in the expression that the means do not justify the ends. We could, of course, debate whether capitalism can be "socialised". Even then, you still have credible "welfare states" in Scandinavia and the social market economies in Germany and Singapore that have achieved, with varying degrees, social justice through capitalism.

In this light, I view a mindset that regards perception as an opportunity for innovation as being extremely important. When a change in perception, what Proust described as the process of "seeing with new eyes" *takes* place, the facts, the physical state of things, do not change. Thus, the form and extent of poverty, the state of demographics and environmental degradation exist in their given form. What change in perception does is merely to give meaning to those facts. In other words, one is able to make sense, for instance, of what poverty is all about, its causes and its effects. Equally, it better informs issues such as impacts of over-population and environmental dislocation in development.

In the same vein, the value for work is a key ingredient of such perception. The realisation of the vision requires values that view hard and productive work as well as thriftiness, obedience, perseverance and social harmony as essential vehicles for social and economic transformation. The role of leadership, its competence and integrity also has an important role to play in generating and shaping a mind shift in society. Leaders should be able to develop the capabilities of the people by helping them to break out of conventional and out-mode patterns of thinking and unquestioning attitudes. Nyerere was a model in this instance. Though *Ujamaa* is viewed to be one of his key legacies, yet he is one who ventured to help Tanzanians break out of the *Ujamaa* "economic ideological" when he genuinely felt that new global realities had set in. Thus, the role of leadership is of great importance in helping the people ingrain in their minds a culture of accepting and embracing change and using such culture to their advantage. Charles Handy perceptively noted in his book, *The Age of Unreason*, "those who realise where changes are headed are better able to use those changes to their own advantage".

An important area that requires mind shift centres on the question of ownership. Today, Tanzania needs a mindset that celebrates investments rather than the mere form of ownership. Foreign investments, Greenfield, or through a process of privatisation, are not necessarily incompatible with the promotion of national ownership. On the contrary, they promote national development. Economic empowerment of nationals has to be viewed in a broader context particularly that of fast changing ownership structures, from predominantly private family ownership to broad ownership through publicly -held companies. At both the levels of leadership and society, the realisation of Vision 2025 significantly depends on a mindset ingrained by positive beliefs, morals, ethics, values and attitudes rooted in the country's history and culture. *Positive* is the key word because witchcraft is a belief, but is a negative one, much as it may be rooted in many tribal cultures. Confucianism in East Asia has had a positive role to play in economic change because of its emphasis on education, hard work and meritocracy. This is a positive cultural value. An important transformational attitude relates to the adoption of science and technology as the base for realising social and economic revolution, particularly in the field of agriculture, mining and broad-based industrialisation.

The realisation of science and technology revolution hinges not only on the economic sector but also on the government. It is imperative that the government becomes entrepreneurial at using and allocating resources in ways that heighten both efficiency and effectiveness. Incentives should be enabled to flow to the private sector to speed up the adoption of modern science and technology and training for technical skills. The role of an entrepreneurial government should extend to dynamising the private sector to become more attuned to investment, employment creation, entrepreneurship and skills development. On its part, the private sector would have to imbibe an ethical behaviour and a sense of corporate responsibility and citizenship if it is going to gain national legitimacy and thereby become a crucial force in the realisation of Vision 2025.

Finally, but not least, the realisation of Vision 2025 envisions a mindset that is gender and youth sensitive. The challenge is to mainstream the role of women and youth in all walks of social, cultural, political and economic life of the nation. A critical element is the promotion of equal opportunity for women and youth. In the next two sections, I focus on the mindsets that are critical in making the vision succeed as well as the mindsets that have to be arrested as they constitute enemies of the Vision.

Mindsets That Constitute Driving Forces

In the context of the changed and changing national and global economic realities Tanzania should identify mindsets that constitute key driving forces for the realisation of Vision 2025. Evidently, some mindsets are more important than others. The following are paramount mindsets in propelling Vision 2025:

First, a mindset that accepts and honours broad participation and injects confidence in the people's intelligence and their aspirations. In his book, *The Empty Raincoat: Making Sense of the Future,* Charles Handy has aptly written, "where no one knows the future with any certainty, we have the right to dream. But for anyone's wishes or dreams, to be accepted without enforcement, some form of Chinese contract. which he defines as compromise and trust as a prerequisite of progress) will be necessary, on which the interests of all parties, both now and in the future, are heard and heeded." It is this mindset that is hugely connected to the form of leadership Tanzania has in place at all levels- national, society, community and corporate levels- a leadership that promotes people's pride in themselves as worthy human beings, possessing self-esteem to give their best and most creative and humane response to the challenges of development that confronts them.

The second type of mindset embodies the morality of compromise in the national leadership. The new national and global challenges of the 21st century do not easily respond to a "one right answer". There are also numerous wrong answers. What is relevant to appreciate is that social, economic and political conditions, behaviour and problems are much too complex to admit a straightforward "right answer". Compromise cannot, therefore, be reduced to the choice between right and wrong, or, indeed, to the choice between right and right. Invariably, compromise involves sacrificing one principle for another viewed to be greater. In a new era of deepening political pluralism, compromise becomes an essential factor in making democracy work more effectively. Compromise is also a beneficial attribute for leaders who aspire have able followers and not sycophants.

The third mindset is one that constantly unlearns the past, not by necessarily abandoning all past lessons and experiences, but by applying those lessons considered relevant and useful. The aim is to abandon what represents excess baggage and allow only past strengths to bolster capacities that empower ability to confront the future. A critical element to take note is that Vision 2025 encapsulates a mindset driven by the challenge of forging a positive future outcome notwithstanding the state of limited opportunities and resources and other constraints, national or global.

The fourth mindset is focussed on knowledge rather than income and wealth as the key driving force of social and economic transformation. The protection of intellectual property rights under the framework of the World Trade Organisation. WTO) provides sufficient evidence about the centrality of knowledge in global economic competition. Evidently, poor economies are at a disadvantage in this light and need to negotiate with a greater collective voice and purpose if they are to strike more balanced and beneficial outcomes from new global arrangements. However, this situation does not nullify the centrality of knowledge and the importance poor countries should attach to promoting it. Alvin Toffler aptly captured the importance of knowledge in his book, *Powershift* in these words: "the control of knowledge is the crux of tomorrow's world-wide struggle for power in every human institution."

A mindset that recognises the limits of government constitutes the fifth important attribute. The question increasingly asked today is not what the government *should do* but what it *can do*. This is a question that concerns the role of the state in a new social and economic environment. During the socialist era, the Tanzania government was more focused on what it should do as opposed to what it could do. It discerned that it was its responsibility to be the ultimate doer in society. But times have changed. The state now has to balance its role with that of the market, thereby selecting what it can best do. This change is inevitable because the government is becoming less and less the monopoly centre of power. New social, political and economic pluralisms are emerging and have emerged in some cases that challenge the traditional monopoly of power by governments. These pluralisms feature at the level of the individual, the political parties, the private sector, Non-governmental organisations, community-based organisations and the civil society. At the same time, it is important to note that it is when the role of government becomes downsized or rightsized that good governance also stands a better chance to take root. Good governance infers the promotion of social justice, fairness, rule of law, unity and peace. It also means transparency of decisions and the absence of corruption. In the emerging global economic order, or disorder, whichever way one views the character of globalisation and unipolarism, critical economic decisions taken by nation-states significantly shift from national levels to the level of global capital market and *"transnational corporations"*. Decisions relating to interest rates, exchange rates and allocation of capital are increasingly determined not on the basis of nation-state objectives but on global objectives that are essentially market-driven.

These transformations drive fundamental changes in the way national economies behave and operate and in how economic power of nation-states is exercised. As Francis Fukuyama noted in his article published in the US magazine *Commentary* titled, *Asian Values and the Asian Crisis,* there was no reason why, in the long run, the nations of Asia could not resume the economic trajectory they were on before the 1997 financial crisis. However, Fukuyama cautioned, "it is much less certain, however, that their economic and political institutions will be able to withstand the powerful forces of globalisation". It is for this reason that the mindset that views globalisation and regionalism as a reality and as and opportunity rather than as a choice or threat has to be ingrained. This is a mindset anchored on the pursuit of policies that are in tune with global capitalism but which also ultimately promote the interests of national economies. Consider the upside of globalisation that has emerged since the turn of the third millennium where increasingly we are witnessing offshoring and outsourcing becoming key drivers of globalisation of business. Driven by the quest to lower costs and enhance competitiveness, global companies are now shifting their headquarters and key offices from their home territories to foreign lands like China, Brazil, India, South Africa, Malaysia, Mexico and the Philippines in search of cheaper yet highly skilled human capital. At the same time, they are shifting their manufacturing operations and their research and technology development undertakings to these same countries which, by definition, part of the developing world. In other words, globalisation does not in all cases infer gloom and doom for poor countries.

The last mindset envisions a high level of national savings as a critical pre-requisite for economic take- off and for building a self -reliant nation. Self reliance does not entail turning Tanzania into an autarchy. Rather, by promoting a national savings habit, Tanzania should be able to liberate itself from the vulnerabilities of exogenous factors that normally erode and undermine national sovereignty. The attraction of foreign savings in the form of direct foreign investments and portfolio investments to supplement domestic savings remains a great priority.

Impediments to Achieving Vision 2025

Tanzania Development Vision 2025 also recognises the prevailing presence of a dysfunctional state of mindsets in the Tanzanian society, mindsets that constitute impediments to the vision's effective realisation. The vision postulates that there presently exists in the Tanzanian society a lack of purpose, a weakened sense of national pride and wounded confidence. The prevailing environment is characterised by an air of indiscipline, apathy, despair, cynicism, low level of accountability and an element of mistrust among the population of the government and leaders. The core reason for such mistrust is what the people view as inadequate improvement in their quality of lives. There is an abiding perception that the leadership has not been adequately sensitive and responsive to changing conditions in the domestic, regional and global environment that has given rise to a declining quality of people's livelihoods. The selfless leadership committed to the development of the people that manifested itself so clearly during the Nyerere leadership era is discerned to be in short supply. Vision 2025 draws attention to these shortcomings centred on attitudes and values.

Some of the shortcomings are examined here in order to propose what should be done to correct as well as to propose the types of mindset that can effectively support and drive Vision 2025 to success.

Growth of Materialism

In the earlier examination of mindsets that constitute driving forces, I identified a high level of national savings and investment as being one of the pivotal factors for Tanzanian's economic take-off and the achievement of economic self-reliance. Yet evidence is abounding that vividly shows that the ratio of savings to gross domestic product is low, as low as 14%. This rate has to move up to around 25 per cent if Tanzania is to accumulate adequate investible domestic resources to spur meaningful social and economic growth. Unfortunately, however, an anti-development consumption culture that is both conspicuous and ostentatious presently pervades the well to do and militates against the evolution of a robust savings and investment culture. More worrisome is the fact that even those that are not so well to do have also taken to wasteful expenditure. However, it is at the other end of the wealth spectrum, that of the new rich, that large speculative investments in real estate and motor vehicles have emerged and have taken an unfortunate dimension of competition for size, beauty and cost.

Evidently, economic liberalism has played its part in unleashing this state of growing materialism. However, this culture is a culmination of what was long time coming when you consider the fact that the Tanzanian mindset has been generally imbibed and ingrained in state ownership. For almost two decades since 1967, the state was the main saver and investor. However, in recent years, government has fallen victim to a mindset that views foreign aid as more or else a constituent part of domestic savings, taken for granted and thus a necessity rather than a complementing resource. In the early 1990s, this mindset triggered the emergence of a consumptionist culture within the government, including, inevitably, a culture of callous wastage and theft of public resources, a fact consistently reflected in the Annual Reports of the Controller and Auditor General.

This state of growing state materialism and conspicuous consumption coincides with an unfortunate emergence of a culture that devalues the importance of hard and productive work. As materialism has taken root, especially in the main Tanzanian townships, so has rural life and agricultural work become despised. Many young people have hit the road from the ostensibly "dying" rural communities into the hustle and bustle of urban Tanzania with its discos, television and the *"mambo poa"*. "cool") culture. The youth would now rather be street hawkers than lead dull rural lives. Even the young people born and brought up in urban areas would also now skip primary school and become "bell boys" at fish markets. This is the *bongo* culture of live and make live; the end, not the means, justifies life. Many youth have stopped to aspire for wholesome life that is so much dependent on education. What is disturbing is that it is this generation that is key to the success of Vision 2025.

There is yet another negative linkage flowing from the materialism that pervades the Tanzanian nouveau riches. It relates to the pervasive private sector short-term profit inclinations. Undoubtedly, the private sector is still in a state of transition in terms of the quest to acquire adequate confidence about its being recognised as the true new engine of development. This lack of confidence partly stems from the existence of a negative mindset within society about the new role of the private sector following the government's decision to roll back its role and to privatise state-owned assets. A pro-state sector mindset still enjoys broad credence. In this context, footloose investments, import trade and investments of the type which do not involve huge capital outlays and which have short payback periods still underlie investment choice and decisions. On a different dimension, even the best of the private sector firms in the country, including those taken over by leading regional and global firms though privatisation, have an aversion of and feel threatened by growing regionalism and globalisation. This attitude is characterised by consistent calls and demands for zero-sum nationalism in negotiations of regional and sub-regional trade protocols and customs union arrangements. It is an attitude fuelled by a perception that government is not well versed with the intricacies and implications of global and regional economic arrangements.

Bureaucratic Mindset

Some of these concerns about the new role of the private sector also flow from the existing negative mindset of the bureaucracy. As things stand today, you still have in the government an amalgam of beliefs, attitudes, assumptions and values more relevant during the socialist era. Such bureaucratic values have denigrated public service ethics and professionalism. They have also downgraded and undermined meritocracy, discipline and the importance of continuous training. Today, bureaucratic culture is still informed by conformism, a "standardised mindset," ingrained during the socialist era. Some change is evidently taking place, encapsulated in the public service reform programme. However, a great deal of damage had been done and professional public service training is yet to be adequately installed. Thus, whilst the government has expressed the desire to shift its role from "rowing" to "steering" by becoming more catalytic and facilitatory, the bureaucratic mindset, expressed in the styles of work and management, are yet to adequately fit such avowed role of steering.

President Benjamin Mkapa has in fact recognised the dysfunctional character of the bureaucratic mindset and culture that shackles the administration of the government. Immediately upon his taking over as President, he called for a mind shift in the bureaucracy. The President's rallying call has only borne few improvements. It is a tough task just as it is tough to generate a nation-wide mind shift. One could sense the state of desperation that afflicted President Mkapa in this context. On a visit to Arusha Region in 1998, little was said to the President by the masses about development. Most of the burning issues that featured centred on the destructive and corrupt mindsets of those who administer justice. The people have little confidence in individuals entrusted with administering justice and the rule of law. Yet it is not the system or the structures that are to blame. It is the attitudes of the people in charge of these instruments who are not driven by an ethic of service. Greed and corruption drives the. Surely, a vision of development cannot succeed where the rule of law is subverted by corruption.

Shortage of Inspirational Leadership

A central challenge that confronts Tanzania is the absence of a critical mass of inspirational leadership. A national President alone could not successfully lead a national transformation. The process involved in getting Tanzanians to move towards the realisation of Vision 2025 entails every person becoming a leader. This often involves the destabilisation of the *status quo*. Issues relating to the constitution, the character of the Union, the market economic system, the quality of leadership, the state of the bureaucracy and issues relating to moral integrity, all have to be confronted by a leadership and people whose mindset is open and not clogged by populist passions and the excess baggage of the past.

One of the shortcomings in the present leadership is that they have yet to come out as clearly and forcefully as Nyerere did during the Arusha Declaration era in creating the state of mind that guides the society. Yet a new political and economic philosophy has been hatched. How to commit Tanzanians to rally behind such a new philosophy in a different domestic and global environment from that of the 1960s and 1970s constitutes the key mindset challenge of the present leadership. For instance, did it really require Nyerere himself to pronounce that economic socialism had lost its relevance in Tanzania before most Tanzanians could realise the same?

Overdependence on Outsiders

Another characteristic of the mindset that pervades the national psyche today is the loss of indigenous sovereignty in self-expression and authentic development. For several decades, Tanzania had committed itself to practising and realising self-reliance as a form of self-determination and as a means for economic emancipation. That spirit has waned. Tanzania is now overly nourished by financial and technical assistance from the North. Under this "offer of hope for prosperity", to borrow the phrase of the renowned Bangladesh social scientist, Anisur Rahman, most Tanzanians have come to be classified as poor and as objects of sympathy, paternalistic intervention and assistance. Professor Rahman (1993) describes the consequences of such state of dehumanisation as "internalisation of a negative self image," of feeling inferior and subject to being developed by others viewed to be more superior. It is economic impoverishment and the erosion of identity that have catapulted this state of helplessness and dependency in Tanzania. The work of PSRC, the Public Service Reform, TRA, LART and even the work of crafting Vision 2025 have all had to be financed by donors. Evidently, the support was needed at the stage when the country was implementing several structural adjustment programmes. These reforming institutions and activities would not have realised set objectives without external donor assistance.

However, what is more perturbing is the fact that dependency on external aid has now percolated all the way down to the village level where the spirit of self-help and nation building, which Tanzania was once proud of, has also given way to a *"wafadhili"* or *"wahisani".* donor) syndrome. Cabinet Ministers now routinely take advantage of their peer positions to solicit aid, outside the framework of the government, from Ambassadors accredited to Tanzania, from the rich North and the Far East, for building secondary schools, health centres and water supply systems in their constituencies to bolster their own political ends. Leadership at the level of grassroots which has a leading role in mobilising the people to imbibe the spirit of nation building and self-reliance is also now surrendering to this dependency mindset and reinforcing it. In fact, the effectiveness of leadership at parliamentary constituency levels is increasingly being determined by success in getting as many *wafadhili* projects into one's constituency rather than by one's own creative and inspirational abilities to mobilise and promote self-reliance. No doubt, the idea of sourcing aid for development in rural areas is a good one. However, the means used to obtain such aid are the subject of concern as far as political ethics are concerned.

It should also be acknowledged that the dependency syndrome is in the process of being addressed. In the Finance Minister's Budget Speech for 2004/05, the government is seized of the concern and has outlined measures to move Tanzania towards budgetary self-reliance. This is a welcome commitment and all efforts should be directed at realising the goal.

Intolerant Leadership

Another impediment to the realisation of Vision 2025 is the shortage of tolerant leadership. Earlier in an examination of what constituted the driving forces for the realisation of Vision 2025, I observed that Tanzania needed a leadership mindset that honoured the morality of compromise and tolerance. Yet experience has shown, particularly since the onset of multiparty democracy heralded by the General Elections of 1995 and 2000, that the virtues of compromise and tolerance remain fragile in the new political system. Some leaders tend to view compromise as defeatism or capitulation, both of which smack of leadership weakness. Such mindset deficiency reminds us of a powerful assertion made by Brandeis University Professor, Eugence Goodheart in his book, *The Reign of Ideology:* "The person who claims to know the truth and is certain that others with an opposing view are the captives of illusion is a potential despot."

Mwalimu Nyerere once warned that there was nothing more obvious in the modern world than the fact that it was easier, from a political point of view, to fight than to talk. In his Dag Hammerskjold Memorial Lecture titled, *The Courage of Reconciliation*, Nyerere argued that a leader who refuses to talk about a dispute that undermines mutual trust refuses to face up to the basic dilemma of man and, "for his own freedom he needs unity with his fellows, and this requires from him compromise, tolerance, and a concept of justice". Mwalimu Nyerere went on to ramify that "the real enemy in the modern world is, in fact, the man who refuses to talk about the disputes in which he is involved". There is urgent need to build in the Tanzanian society a culture that encourages and celebrates courage to talk and criticise plainly and freely. The media, religious leaders and other organs of civil society have an important role to play in promoting this positive mindset. Despots would not galvanise and rally Tanzanians behind the challenges of realising Vision 2025. Thus, the choice of leaders should constitute one of the key underpinnings in enabling Vision 2025 to be realised.

Gender Inequality and Inequity

Finally, the prevailing mindset that does not give needed recognition to equal status of women and which disregards the potential role and contribution of the youth in development is a major setback. Women and the youth constitute the bedrock of any progressive society. In the Tanzanian society, they can be a moving force for realising development objectives. However, women and the youth are yet to be given their due recognition and are yet to be empowered and enabled through policies and the law to enjoy equal status. Some positive development has been achieved in the case of women at the political level in terms of parliamentary representation. The same has not been done for the youth.

However, women still endure abject poverty. Little is done to forge gender balance in sharing the burden of poverty. Customs and customary laws in many tribes still relegate women to positions of chattel and beasts of burden. The state is yet to address such customs and laws with the seriousness the challenge deserves.

I have so far been able to delineate what the state of the mindset is like in Tanzania, what are its driving forces and what are their impediments. But a critical task is also how to go about transforming the mindset so that it becomes the catalyst for change and transformation and locate the challenges that need to be addressed in such task.

How to Transform the Mindset

The current mindset is incapable of appreciating the complex and dynamic character of the major transformations now taking place around the world. An attempt has been made to identify what underlies the current dysfunctional mindset and the concrete examples that constitute the mindset impediments.

My focus now shifts to examining how Tanzanians, at all levels of society, can transform their mindsets and turn them into key driving forces for changing the quality of their lives and unleashing a propensity for wealth creation and shared prosperity. Tanzanians should quickly get over their apathy and become more creative and innovative. Creating a new, more positive sense of awareness and insight is the central challenge. They need to inculcate and ingrain a new way of looking at things, at their problems and challenges, always imbibing the confidence to ride the wave and achieve their goals. The achievement of Vision 2025 crucially depends on such fresh insight and confidence. Numerous ways exist in which Tanzanians, in and by themselves, and through being enabled and empowered, can create new awareness and insight. What are the policies and strategies then that can effectively respond to the challenge of creating a new Tanzanian able to face the new world and the immediate environment with self-confidence, dynamism, aggressiveness and entrepreneurial spirit?

Giving Power to the People

At the outset, it is important to note that one of the central underlying strategies in mindset transformation is for the nation, and particularly the leadership and professionals in government and in non-governmental organisations, to discard the notion, invariably a myth, that they are the repository of knowledge and wisdom necessary for assuring people's development. The experience gained from the failed villagisation programme is one clear proof that mindset transformation cannot be imposed. What is important, as an external intervention, is invariably to enable the people, in all occupations, to own and construct their relevant reality through popular social enquiry, anchored in core values and culture. Lack of concern for cultural values is recipe for apathy and even hostility. The role of 'external' agencies should be limited to contributing to the construction of specific aspects of reality; for instance, the application of modem technology in bolstering agricultural productivity and providing domestic incentives in support of agriculture. In other words, the people should be mobilised and stimulated to self-search and discover. Therefore, mindset transforming mainly rests on restoring the sense of identity and the collective self-expression of the people. After the miserable failure of the villagisation programme, the regrettable dissolution of local government and the Cooperatives, Tanzania needed to get back to the basics of what drive progressive rural life, productivity and development and then re-ignite the old spirit of nation building that thrived in the 1960s and the early 1970s. The corollary of such restoration of societal self-expression and the re-emergence of indigenous alternatives to confronting development challenges is popular participation in all facets of social, economic and political life.

In this context, the *Challenge to the South*, has perceptively posited, "enthusiasm and creative potential of the people" can only be mobilised if development is consistent with their fundamental socio-cultural values. The report further asserted that in order to involve the people as active participants and, thereby, "draw on large reserves of creativity and traditional knowledge and skills," development should be culture sensitive. What these perspectives show is that, on the one hand, a paternalistic approach to planning and execution of development programmes at all levels and involving both the government and NGOs, inhibits participation at the grass-roots levels. On the other hand, the absence of popular participation militates against the absorption of new ideas regarding appropriate technologies, processes, management and facilities. Thus, popular participation should be promoted as a vehicle for mindset change and for spearheading social, economic and political transformation. In similar vein, the Prime Minister of Singapore, Goh Chok Tong, in his address to the Singapore Parliament, sometime in 1997, observed, "We must change the mindset that only a few leaders at the top of the system need to think and take responsibility for social and national issues, while the rest of society can simply mind their own business and go about their daily lives — The government itself must be prepared to take a step back and perhaps even a back seat, especially on local community issues, and allow some free play to develop". Effective popular participation, particularly at rural level, demands the existence of a significant measure of decentralised authority and not mere responsibility as seems the case at this stage, as well as empowerment of local government and community -based organisations. The state of local government in Tanzania to day, to say the least, is fragile. In most respects, the central government is still the principal driver of development. local government plays second fiddle.

Changing the Perceptions of People

The next critical strategy in mindset transformation is to get Tanzanians to see the challenges of development that confront them "with new eyes". This task involves changing the people's attitudes and perceptions about their ways of life and the conditions they live in, a process that requires reaching out to the people through a conscientisation rather than a manipulative process, to enable the people to distinguish between the realities they are in and what such reality entails. Charles Handy has written in *Beyond Certainty* that "the search for the meaning of things" is the driving force of economics. An interesting real life example is the way the late Indian Prime Minister, Mrs Indira Gandhi, sought to improve the shelter conditions of the very poor in Bombay who resided, all their lives, inside sewerage pipelines. She had constructed low cost houses for these poor people to live in and get away from squalor. The poor accepted the houses but immediately proceeded to rent them out. They returned to their traditional shelters of squalor and filth. The policy failed because it addressed the fact or conditions, but not their meaning to the targeted people. It is only through change of meaning, values and perceptions about one's condition that positive transformation could result.

Equally, the villagisation policy failed precisely because it sought to change the facts, the rural scattered homesteads, and not changing the perception of the people about the dysfunctions of living in scattered homesteads. The villagisation programme was conceived based on the objective of enabling delivery of welfare services to be deepened and delivered more cost effectively. However, the programme failed to address the underlying anthropological factors like witchcraft and cattle theft that underlined the scattered character of rural homesteads. Similar questions and issues could be raised in relation to several other policy interventions. For example, the introduction of cost sharing in social service provisioning and the methodology of privatisation of parastatals could have been approached differently.

The key challenge is in getting Tanzanians to see these challenges with new eyes. On this issue, there are lessons from history. Mwalimu Julius Nyerere succeeded in developing a nationalistic mindset in Tanzanians through the *Ujamaa* policy. *Ujamaa* became the national symbol, the metaphor, the song, the culture and the national identity. However, many

Tanzanians accepted what was prescribed as given and did not challenge or question or seek to understand the underlying assumptions of the ideological prescription. Be that as it may, however, Nyerere achieved his objective. Indeed, the unity, peace and stability which Tanzania has enjoyed until now is primarily an outcome of the acceptance of Nyerere's prescription. However, given the current changed conditions, characterised by political and economic pluralism, Nyerere's prescription of political and economic oligarchy would face problems. A new mindset that approaches issues from an objective angle of alternative scenarios is more likely to promote within the people, particularly the informed ones, who are the movers and shakers of the political scene, greater creativity and innovation. In this situation, the challenge is to have a new breed of leadership that is enlightened, better understands the trends and discontinuities of different forces- social, political, economic, environmental, technological, and demographic- and able to create new dynamic spaces for development. Today, you need a credible leadership with ethical and political force to promote the virtues of the market and of individual initiative. You need the late China's Deng Tsiao Ping's-type of leadership that was able, within a decade and a half, to transform China's economy with the slogan: *It does not matter whether the cat is black or white as long as it catches mice.*

It has been repeatedly proven that leaders like Nyerere, Deng, Mahathir and Lee Kuan Yew, have had major impact on the mindsets of their people because they were able to win their confidence and trust over their visions of development and on policies that build unity and solidarity, peace and tolerance, human dignity and social justice. In other words, building the confidence of the people around a vision is a key driving force for mindset transformation.

Promoting Education and Pedagogy

A related challenge in transforming the mindset of Tanzanians is education. In the preface to Paulo Freire's book *Cultural Action for Freedom*, Joao da Veiga Coutinco outlines the following framework of education: "Education can be deconditioning because man, essentially a conditioned being, is also essentially a being capable of knowing what conditions him, capable of reflecting on his behaviour, and of perceiving his perceptions. The key to "perception", and hence to the recuperation of hidden or mystified reality, is problematisation. Problematisation which means both asking questions and calling into question is therefore a challenging attitude, is, at one and the same time, the beginning of an act of subversion to 'overdetermination', is that, subversion of praxis inverted upon man." This process of problematisation as a system of education for mindset transformation requires a "revolutionary educator" whose key task is to challenge the reality to be studied. The objective is to enlighten the people as a whole about the obstacles, physical and mental, that constrain them from a clear perception of reality. The educator referred here is not limited to the conventional school or college teacher. The meaning of educator is broad and encompasses the traditional teacher, the political leader, the community opinion leader, the leader of civil society and business, the religious leader and the media.

In this context, value judgement can be drawn from the following Nyerere's pedagogy in conditioning the mind of Tanzanians:

his education for self-reliance;
the various political slogans. *"Afya ni Uhai", "Siasa ni Kilimo"*, meaning health is life and agriculture is politics, respectively) that he coined,
his introduction of a compulsory political education curriculum in primary and secondary schools and
the socialist education he influenced to be imparted to political leaders at the "old" Kivukoni College.

All these pedagogic processes were part of Nyerere's strategy to create a new Tanzanian. Largely, the conditioning of the mind was internalised by the majority of Tanzanians. Nyerere succeeded to define the reality that ingrained the confidence in Tanzanians as well as in the new socialist institutions established to "unlearn" the capitalist past. The new breed of educators and institutions should also extend the process of conscientisation to the objective reality that the state has now redefined its role. The era of free social services is gone precisely because the government has little choice but to focus more on creating the environment that would enable the private sector-individuals and institutions-to become more productive and efficient and thus increasingly deliver goods and services to the market at more competitive prices. This process of conscientisation should be broad-based to the extent of building a national consciousness and a social compact on national goals of development. In other words, political parties, civil society, the bureaucracy and the people as a whole should be reached by such pedagogy of mindset transformation. However, the objective should never be to re-do the past or to ingrain a conformist mindset. The process should involve real conscientisation, not manipulation.

Another important strategy in changing the mindset of the people relates to the imperativeness of placing greater importance on knowledge as a resource in wealth creation as opposed to the current practice of over-relying on traditional resources, namely, labour, capital and land. Value and wealth are now created mainly through productivity and innovation, both of which require the application of knowledge to work. Thus, one of the main challenges in the realisation of Vision 2025 is going to be the promotion of productivity of knowledge work and of the knowledge worker. The majority of Tanzanians- rural and urban, peasants and workers- are yet to appreciate, in serious ways, this particular form of transformation, driven by education and science and technology. To transcend the problem is the central philosophical and educational challenge for Tanzania.

Arguably, the starting point is national commitment to achieving education for all. This commitment demands the allocation of more resources to education-formal, vocational, literacy, skills development and competence building. It is important that education and training become the vehicles for ingraining a mind that reflects a broad view of the *very* factors that underpin the creation of national and individual wealth, of which knowledge now take pre-eminence. Though the role of the government is central to knowledge development, the private sector also has an important role to play, particularly in promoting intra-firm training and formal training provided by training institutions. The mindset of the trade unions also crucially needs to change in tune with the centrality of developing knowledge workers as a factor in the advancement of workers as opposed to the current mindset that is overly focused on negotiating better wages and benefits for workers. Both education and training have important implications in discarding the destructive habits and cultures of the people. These habits relate to work culture and discipline, gender equality, protection of the environment, demography, and the development of the girl child. Whilst laws can help to have to enforce a new social order changing customary and other laws that denigrate women, such as genital mutilation, dispossession of women of their rights over matrimonial home, inheritance and custody of children, it is education that ultimately can cause cultural change.

Promoting the Savings Habit

When one raises the question about the poor level of household savings in Tanzania the invariable response is a witch-hunt. The witch is invariably Julius Nyerere who is accused of undermining the culture of savings because of the massive state control of the economy that he had instituted from the late 1960s. The basis of the criticism is that the people had no reason to save in the face of guaranteed state-sponsored "promised land." This is an evidently simplistic criticism. The truth of the matter, as Professor Ali Mazrui wrote a few years ago, is that the African. not just Tanzanian) is dominantly consumptionist by nature. Consumption takes different forms. In rural areas, it manifests itself in heavy liquor drinking and marrying many wives. In urban areas, it manifests itself in conspicuous consumption, ostentatious mansions, expensive weddings and funerals, luxury motor vehicles and several concubines. This culture is in sharp contrast to the lifestyles of overseas Indians and Chinese who now constitute important investors in their countries of birth and origin. The lesson is that Tanzanians should radically change their mindset about savings if they are going to be able to build a strong base of domestic capital to drive investments and growth. Some years ago, Cleopa Msuya, then Minister for Finance, spoke plainly to the effect that "every Tanzanian should bear his own cross". What he meant was that every Tanzanian should reap what he has sowed. That message of economic liberation should be spread around like the Gospel and the Koran. It should be popularised and made to constitute one of the driving forces in transforming the mindset of Tanzanians, to awaken them from the slumber of state dependency, subsistence and economic despondency.

Making Government Entrepreneurial

The government and all the instruments of the state should also transform themselves by putting on a new pair of eyes. There is so much talk, today, around the world, about governments re-inventing themselves, about the transformation of inept bureaucracies and creating innovative and entrepreneurial centres of public decision-making and accountability. The challenge is to move from the rhetoric to the practical. In addition, it should be recognised that the task to forge a mindset break from the present requires that the top political leadership becomes committed to enforcing change. It is possible to achieve such change if some of the following measures are adopted:

- introduce into selected and critical senior positions of government, on contract basis, private sector executives who have distinguished themselves. If the government cannot foot the bill, the private sector should support. Key private sector organisations like those in tobacco, beer, beverages and mining could be willing to underwrite such costs if the potential benefits are seen on the wall.

- Introduce a competitive compensatory and meritocratic system for personnel selection, recruitment, training and career development in the public service. Today, it is a liability to work in the government. The working conditions induce people to be corrupt and to moonlight. For a long time, promotions have been routinely based on "being known" to those that make promotion decisions rather than one's competence. Transparency in promotion decision making remains elusive. Training, formal and on-the-job is intermittent and not well structured.

The Institute of Development Management at Mzumbe, Morogoro, originally conceived as a Henley-type Staff College,. the famous British Civil Service Staff College), was transformed into a full fledged University in 2002. No problem about that, but, as a consequence, the government now lacks a training institution of a higher calibre for developing its senior cadre.

Changing Business Culture

The idea about seeing with new eyes is extensive. A segment of the Tanzania private sector is still mired in the old ways of doing business, ways that are symptomatic of the command economy era when private business faced uncertainty and insecurity because of the threat of nationalisation and lack of government support hanging on their necks. Thus, there is still in place a business culture anchored on short-term profit making, reflected in both investments that are both footloose and corruption driven. Social responsibility of business is viewed to be double taxation thus avoided unless political patronage is gained. In turn, where genuine private sector social responsibility crops up, for example, in the form of alleviating the traumas of the disabled or in helping the organised unemployed youth to secure better lives in the wake of growing urban joblessness, this is viewed, in certain political circles, as an attempt to win political leverage or constituency. Yet why should a businessperson genuinely committed to helping those less endowed in their midst be necessarily viewed as a platform for getting into politics or obtaining political advantage? In any case, how many millionaires around the rich world have attempted to seek political office and yet have been rejected by the electorate?

Conclusion

Tanzanians are on a voyage whose final destination is shared prosperity and well-being. However, the voyage is not mechanical. It is not based on conventional wisdom, attitudes and beliefs. Rather, it is a voyage demanding a new way of looking at the environment that surrounds them; of being challenged by the state of destitution, squalor and poverty surrounding them and of working together to create the understanding and the synergy that generates unity and shared purpose. If Tanzanians do not respond to these challenges and instead stick their necks into the sand like ostriches, if they do not, in other words, attempt the unattemptable and try, in the words of Proust, to see with "new eyes," they are likely to fail in realising the goals of their dreams and expectations. Numerous instances are proof of the centrality and realism of Proust's thinking in daily lives of Tanzanians. We learn from the scriptures that, "God is not mocked: for whatsoever a man soweth, that shall he also reap".. *Galatians 6:7)*

In Kiswahili, there is an equivalent adage: *Utavuna ulichopanda*. It is a simple Biblical philosophy about life, which, unfortunately, many Tanzanians have failed to imbibe. It is an adage founded on basic logic whether we think about the state or the individual. Without promoting a savings habit there could be no accumulation and thus no investment. And without investment there could be no social and economic development. Tanzania's Development Vision 2005 is primarily an intangible asset. To make it realise tangible outcomes, its ideas have to be translated into action. Mwalimu Nyerere was able to formulate a vision in socialism and self reliance and was bold in formulating actions to realise the ideas behind that vision. His legacy is open to surgical review. In this chapter, I have attempted to examine and propose tentative issues that should be addressed if Vision 2025 is to have the chance of success.

The next chapter, examines more specifically the challenges posed by the state of the mindset in the context of the brave new world of the 21st century.

Chapter

23 DEVELOPMENT MINDSET AND THE NEW MILLENNIUM

If a change in mindset is at the centre of development, then it is clear that attention needs to be shifted to how to effect [sic] such changes in mindset. Such changes cannot be "ordered" or forced from the outside, however well-intentioned the outsiders may be. Change has to come from within.

Joseph Stiglitz: **Globalisation and Its Discontents.**

At the dawn of the third Christian millennium, the world is still not at peace with itself. The powerful images of W.B Yeats' poem, *The Second Coming*, remain as relevant to-day as they were around the end of the First World War: "Turning and turning in the widening gyre the falcon cannot hear the falconer; Things fall apart; the centre cannot hold; Mere anarchy is loosed upon the world, the blood-dimmed tide is loosed, and everywhere the ceremony of innocence is drowned; the best lack all conviction, whilst the worst are full of passionate intensity". The blood-dimmed tide remains loosed in conflict, war, killer diseases and deepening poverty. The constant images of famine in Ethiopia and South Sudan, the ethnic cleansing in Bosnia Herzegovina and Kosovo, the endless conflicts in Burundi, Liberia, Sierra Leone, the Democratic Republic of the Congo, Ethiopia-Eritrea, Chechnya, India-Pakistan, Afghanistan, the Iraq insurgency and the endless conflict of all conflicts, Israel-Palestine, all of them reflect a state of anarchy in the world. The rise in the cases of terrorism, whose pinnacle was the tragic 11th September, 2001 incident in the United States, the train bombings in Madrid in March 2004, the bombing of the transport system in London in July 2005, the devastation caused by HIV/AIDS, and the recent Tsunami tragedy have all drowned the celebration of life.

The world is still pitifully haunted by the question Yeats posed at the end of his poem: "And what rough beast, its hour come round at last, slouches towards Bethlehem to be born?" There are many Christians around the world who could be at such a state of despair and that only the second coming of Jesus would bring to them salvation. Above all, Christians and Moslems alike, in their billions, are full of passionate intensity. They would welcome another revelation to liberate them from the present state of anguish, lack of self-determination and deprivation. The fundamental question in everybody's mind is whether the world's poor can afford to wait for a new salvation. Could they realistically hope for a new earthly conviction to emerge that would stop the hopelessness that looms large? How could such outcome be possible when "the drama of a free-running economic system" is reordering the world and its faith and beliefs? In a radical, pro-poor book, *One World Ready or Not -The Manic Logic of Global Capitalism*, the respected American editor of the *Rolling Stone* magazine William Greider (1997) has pointed out, in the context of the future: "I would estimate that the global system will, indeed, probably experience a series of terrible events - wrenching calamities that are economic or social or environmental in nature - before common sense can prevail. It would be pleasing to believe otherwise, but the global system so dominates and intimidates present thinking that I expect societies will be taught still more painful lessons before they will find the will to act." It was as if Greider was foretelling the tsunami catastrophe.

In a critical discourse, on the so-called logic of the market, William Greider observes that many intelligent people worship market principles as if they were some form of a religious code; that they "will carry them forward to millennial outcomes." He warns, that when faith in the market leads to failure, "as I think it must" then people around the world "may at last be free to see things more clearly again, and to reclaim responsibility for their own lives and begin organising the future in its more promising terms." It is interesting to note the similarity of views between Greider and Eric Hobsbawn, the author of *Age of Extremes: A History of the World 1914 - 1991*. In his book, Hobsbawn posits, "If humanity is to have a recognisable future, it cannot be by prolonging the past or the present. If we try to build the third millennium on that basis, we shall fail. And the price of failure, that is to say, the alternative to a changed society, is darkness." Is the market then the prescription for the economic liberation of the world's poor? Moreover, with respect to Tanzanians, where are they at the dawn of the third millennium? Have they set out for themselves "a recognizable future" that is neither based on *prolonging* the past nor the present? What are the "painful lessons" shall they be further taught by the global system before they garner the will to act? Are they disposed to seeing things more clearly and, perhaps, importantly, see them differently, and thus reclaim responsibility to shape their own lives and organise them better in future?

It is customary for individuals to commit themselves to New Year Resolutions. Sometimes, such resolutions, like stopping to take alcohol or smoke, have permanently changed people's styles, ways of life and of doing things. More often, however, the resolutions have failed to last even a year. Whichever way, New Year Resolutions constitute an interesting mental framework for creating meaning and purpose in life and for promoting a resolve to work for one's aims and ambitions. This sense of looking at the New Year by committing oneself to certain goals and to addressing the problems and challenges that confront you as well as driving yourself to seize the opportunities that present themselves is a step forward in creating a recognisable future. Most people tend to think strategically in determining New Year Resolutions. What about governments? Yes, every new year, Tanzanians are addressed by their President in what is known as the *"Salaam za Kheri za Mwaka Mpya"*. New Year good wishes). However, time has now come to transform New Year messages into statements that create a recognisable future, even if it is for a year. After all, Tanzanians had never had a "State of the Union Address" of the US-type until when President Mkapa decided to deliver one in 2000. President Mkapa has retained this formality which now also involves a Monthly Radio Address to the nation. Nevertheless, the key point I am making here is that, in the same manner that individuals make New Year Resolutions, so should the government.

In a broader context, it is pertinent to ask how Tanzanians as individuals and as a government are preparing themselves for the new century and the new millennium. It is ludicrous of course to think about what Tanzania would do in the next 1000 years, or, for that matter, in the next 100 years. However, they could surely think through the new global realities in place and how they would respond to them in the next twenty years. They could also think about the anticipated changes that would take place in the global system in the next decade and determine their implications. More importantly, they could think about their own economic condition in terms of mindset and the resources that are at their disposal for creating a recognisable and plausible future of well-being and prosperity.

Impending Transformations

The starting point in preparing for the new millennium is to be clear about the impending transformations that would affect Tanzania in one form or another. This is important. For as Professor Paul Kennedy aptly posed in his book: *Preparing For the Twenty-First Century,* "If we are being challenged by major forces of change, how can a society best 'prepare' itself for the coming twenty-first century? What characteristics, what strengths, are desirable for a people to possess in such fast-changing and unpredictable times"? Charles Handy has, moreover, captured this point more pointedly. In his book, *The Age of Unreason*, he postulates that "those who know why changes come waste less effort in protecting themselves or in fighting the inevitable. Those who realize where changes are heading are better able to use those changes to their advantage."

The Big Picture, Stupid!

To realise where global changes are headed remains a serious shortcoming for many Tanzanians, to such a point that where policies in line with new realities are adopted, they are often confronted by dissent or disquiet. Tanzanians tend to miss the underlying thrust embodied in Kennedy's and Handy's views. Many remain encumbered in the small picture syndrome. Such stance features prominently in policymaking, be it fiscal or economic integration. Tanzanians are not seriously asking themselves what characteristics and strengths they need to acquire in order to equip themselves sufficiently to face the challenges of globalisation and proceed to creating those capacities. It is important to note, in this context, that the challenges of globalisation would affect some nations more than others, positively and negatively. This is due to "the uneven pattern of change and of the human race's differentiated responses", as Professor Kennedy has put it.

Evidently, the first challenge that confronts Tanzanians in better understanding the dynamics of the fast-changing global system is to fix their mindset. Their will to act is critically predicated on liberating themselves from the domination and intimidation of current global thinking. It is clear, as Daniel Yargin (1998) wrote in his book: *The Commanding Heights - The Battle Between Government and the Marketplace that is Remaking the Modern World*, that the world is fast shifting from "an era in which 'State' - national governments - sought to seize and exercise control over their economies to an era in which the ideas of competition, openness, privatisation and deregulation have captured world economic thinking." However, as Yergin himself correctly argued, it is important for any country to clarify the boundary between state and market. The reason being that "the realm and responsibility of the state in the economy, and what kind of protection is the state to afford its citizens" should be more clearly spelt out.

How have Tanzanians performed on this critical point in terms of their thinking and values? It would be noted that the debate about *"Uzawa"* has emerged precisely because there is some fuzziness over the boundary between the state and the market. Indeed, much as I disown the idea of indigenisation and find the concept baseless as far as the broad thrust of economic empowerment of Tanzanians is concerned, I would caution against a simplistic wishing away of the idea. There are genuine sentiments and concerns in the Tanzanian society that drive the indigenisation agenda. These centre on the question posed by Daniel Yergin, namely, "will the market economies deliver the goods in terms of economic growth, employment, and higher standards of living, and how will they redefine the welfare state: will the results be seen as fair, equitable and just?"

Tanzanians are clamouring for indigenisation precisely because they perceive, wrongly, in my view, that the new market economy is not positively and quickly enough bridging the wealth divide that coincides with the racial divide. It is also not improving the quality of life of the majority of the people. The problem with this perception is that it is centred on a skewed view of cause and effect. What is it that makes the wealth divide be what it is? Who is responsible? Is it the government? In my view, the perception and the problem centre on mindset. Unless Tanzanians deconstruct their beliefs, values and ideas away from the traditional faith in public ownership and massive state support in different social programmes, and toward giving greater credence and confidence in the market, very much within the framework of Germany's "Social Market" or Britain's "Third Way", questions like indigenisation would subsist and ultimately could divide the society. The wrath would not end with the African versus Asian. On the contrary, the struggle may extend to why the Chaggas, for example, enjoy dominance in commerce or why the *Wapemba* merchants who are performing extremely well on the Mainland should not be "shipped" back to Pemba. Finally, and this would be the last nail on the societal coffin, the struggle may extend and embrace differences in religion. This stage would almost certainly destroy the country.

Thus, the central question that confronts Tanzanians at the dawn of the 21st century is whether they are sufficiently clear about what they must prepare for? Like all nations, there are impending social, economic, political and environmental transformations that would affect Tanzania. The impact would inevitably be uneven depending on the country's pattern of change and the quality of response. However, the starting point for Tanzania is to understand better the dynamics of the fast changing global system.

A Galvanising Mass Movement

The state of the mindset is a key driving force in understanding and appreciating such global dynamics of change. Tanzania has gone through radical economic reforms since 1986. However, the country continues to face lack of a cogent and coherent political philosophy capable, in the words of Roger Burbach et al, "of galvanising a mass movement". After the collapse of public ownership and the ideology that underpinned it, Tanzania is in a state of an ideological void. This situation has nothing to do, as some people would wish to conjecture, with political pluralism in place. The United States has a galvanising mass movement in capitalism, its political pluralism notwithstanding. Germany's "social market" is also entrenched in its Constitution. Rather, since the adoption of market reforms, or capitalism, Tanzania has lacked a clear political philosophy that underpins its new direction. In other words, what kind of society is Tanzania seeking to build?

This ideology void poses problems in terms of policymaking. The market economy, often spoken of as the new driver of development is not, in itself, a political philosophy. It is a mere vehicle. Thus, whither does the vehicle take Tanzania and what are the imponderables? There is the inevitable suspicion, cynicism, and mistrust about this void. Tanzania Development Vision 2025 has evidently attempted to address some of the concerns. However, Vision 2025 should be given a political philosophical framework that creates the labels and symbols that the people can relate to, internalise and help them to galvanise their efforts and commitment. For example, the British Prime Minister, Tony Blair, charted out New Labour's political philosophy as "The Third Way". In the booklet that espouses that philosophy, Blair asserts, "ideas need labels if they are to become popular and widely understood." He postulates that "Third Way" is the label for his new politics for Britain. It would be recalled that Mwalimu Nyerere had used *"Ujamaa na Kujitegemea"* as the label for Tanzania's politics of development Therefore, yes, Tanzania now has Vision 2025. Nevertheless, what is the label for this new politics of Tanzania represented by this vision? Is it *"Ubepari".* capitalism), *"Ujamaa wa kisasa".* modern socialism) or what? In other words, what is the political philosophy capable of "galvanising a mass movement" in the country? For without such a mass movement in place, it would be difficult for Tanzanians to reclaim responsibility to shape and organise their own future in the context of global change.

Another challenging global transformation for countries like Tanzania is the emergence of what is described as *"Connexity,"* meaning a connected world. In his book: *Connexity: Responsibility, Freedom, Business and Power in a New Century,* Geoff Mulgan observes: "a connected world defies the rules of zero sum games, where an advantage for someone else means a disadvantage for me. This is most apparent in economics. In an economy based on material objects, everything means less of another. An economy based on information and knowledge behaves very differently." Unfortunately, Tanzania's economy is not yet based on information and knowledge. Indeed, precisely because of this, there is growing fear in many developing countries about connexity since it conjures loss of economic sovereignty and the subversion of economic growth. Yet the reality centres on how such economies, even at the stage they are in, being predominantly material object - based economies, can and should adjust to the global fundamentals of connexity. We learn from Lester Thurow's book, *The Future of Capitalism* that "in a world of regional trading blocs, selling one's products if a country is not part of one of the trading groups is going to become increasingly difficult for developing countries. Market access will be a privilege that has to be earned and not a right that is bestowed automatically."

Integrate or Falter

This is the context in which South Africa concluded a bilateral trade agreement with the EU. The lesson to appreciate and internalise from South Africa's trade deal with the EU is that one needs to be a sizeable market to earn the privilege to have market access in trading blocs such as the EU and NAFTA. Yet when it comes to creating the framework for releasing such sizeable markets, amongst ourselves, we invariably tend to be more concerned about the economic disparities that exist between co-operating countries and the vulnerabilities we would be subjected to rather than the objective of creating the market capacity from economic integration itself to access globally dynamic and attractive markets. This is not a chicken and egg question as many would argue. Rather it is a question out of tune with global realities. Economies that continue to suffer from such mind block would regrettably falter.

In this context, it was not surprising that at the 2000 Southern African Economic Summit of the World Economic Forum held in Durban, the then US Deputy Secretary of Commerce in the Clinton Administration, Robert Mallett, warned that the global economy was already upon Southern Africa. Therefore, the region had to figure out more urgently how it could integrate itself into the global economy and avert being written off. So why zero-sum nationalism? William Greider captures the problem strikingly in his book: *One World Ready or Not: The Manic of Logic of Global Capitalism*. He posits: "the political power arrayed against reform visions is overwhelming, while the people who support these new directions are everywhere quite weak. The inertial momentum of the *status quo*-the insecurity of political leaders, intimidated as they are by the overbearing influence of business and finance - makes it quite difficult, if not impossible, to imagine that the alternatives will receive rational consideration and timely response". Yet do countries like Tanzania have a choice but to be part of regional economic blocks? How can they have a choice when in the global neighbourhood of which the world has become, to cite the Report of the Commission on Global Governance, *Our Global Neighbourhood*, "a sense of otherness cannot be allowed to nourish instincts of insularity, intolerance, greed, bigotry, and, above all, a desire for dominance. But barricades in the mind can be even more negative than frontiers on the ground." In other words, unless Tanzanians are able to see things with new eyes, they cannot adequately respond to the challenges that confront them.

Turning to another dimension of global transformation, we come head to head with what a CNN advert used to say: *"You are what you know."* This advert has since changed to *"Be the first to know"*. This is the reality. Global information and communications technologies have advanced so much that breaking news around the world is a 24 hours event for those who have access to such technologies. As a result, the world is experiencing a widening gap between those who are better informed and thus more sensitive and responsive to what is happening around them and those lesser exposed to such technologies and information. In such type of situation, the key question that emerges is how the latter can participate in the process of influencing the creation and realisation of equitable global governance. The Report, *Our Global Neighbourhood,* finds such hope a mirage, because the hope "would be a pious one were there not signs that future generations come to the task better equipped than their parents were." The tragedy, to day, is that parents, in countries like Tanzania, still appear to be better mentally equipped to face the modern world than most of their children! Professor Armatya Sen in a *CNN's Q & A* Talk Show early in 2000 saw education as central in equipping children and young people to confront new global challenges. This raises the question how Tanzania would leapfrog and dramatically improve the educational system to respond to the challenges of the new millennium.

Development as Freedom

Finally, the question about the relationship between development and freedom would feature prominently in the new century, particularly so in poor societies. *The Economist* of September 11-17, 1997 featured an interesting discussion on the relationship between economic freedom and development. It defined economic freedom as "the ability to do what you want with whatever property you have legally acquired, as long as your actions do not violate other people's rights to do the same." The Nobel Laureate for Economics, Armatya Sen in his brilliant book: *Development As Freedom* promotes the new thinking that what drives development is, at root, freedom in its broadest sense. Mwalimu Nyerere, in contrast, believed that people had to be helped or forced to do what was deemed. or what he himself deemed) to be in their best interests. The Villagisation Programme of the 1970s, for example, was based on this "positive liberty" theory. However, the project failed. In a powerful conclusion, the above referred Economist magazine posits, "things can go wrong, not just because of the acts of chance or God that vex viticulturalist, but also because of the many acts of man that, deliberately or in error, threaten our liberties and our freedom of choice, that are liable through false claims of certainty to send us in new and dangerous directions, even in the most mature democracies."

Tanzania has gone through a bitter lesson and transition where democracy ha sometimes come at the expense of development. In other words, it is a situation where Tanzanians have been made to choose what was believed to be good for them. The distinguished Indian economist, Professor Jagdish Bhagwati, in his Rajiv Gandhi Golden Jubilee Memorial Lecture delivered in October, 1994 titled *Democracy and Development: New Thinking on an Old Question* asserted that "the new thinking is that this trade-off. between democracy and development), or the crucial dilemma as I called it nearly thirty years ago, is by no means a compelling necessity, one may be able to eat one's cake and have it too: either democracy does not handicap development or, in the best of circumstances, it even promotes it." At the dawn of the new millennium, Tanzanians have to come to terms with making their quest for development an inherent component of their struggle for freedom. Democracy should increasingly be viewed in the context of enabling such freedom to drive the agenda of development. In this arena, the role of the private sector, reflecting the exercise of economic freedom at its best, takes pre-eminence.

The next chapter, examines some of the challenges that confront Tanzania in building a robust private sector especially in the context of its having been marginalised during the state party system. A number of themes are tackled in this process. They include: the growth of private sector lobby associations, business ethics, the relationship between the environment and economic growth and private sector role in building a culture of peace.

Part Seven

CHALLENGES OF PRIVATE SECTOR DEVELOPMENT

Private sector development is about promoting growth, reducing poverty and helping people improve their quality of life. It is a way of doing things across sectors. Private initiative, unleashed in competitive markets, is key to promoting growth and poverty reduction, in parallel with public sector efforts. Tax revenues generated by private markets are critical to support public expenditure programmes. All this has been the experience in developed countries and is now increasingly evident in the developing world.

The World Bank: ***Private Sector Development-Directions for the World Bank Group, April 2002.***

Chapter

24 GROWTH OF PRIVATE SECTOR LOBBY POWER

In the real world, neither business nor government gets all it wants from the other: government officials are usually dissatisfied with the economy's rate of growth, while businesspersons invariably argue that their profits would be higher if the government were more responsive to their needs. It is obvious whose advantage is greater.

-David Vogel: *Do Corporations Have Political Power?*

For several years, particularly following the adoption of the Arusha Declaration in February 1967 and up until 1988, business organisations in Tanzania acted as if politics were an exercise in crisis management. In other words, politics received their attention only after trouble struck in the business domain. Even when trouble arose, the obtaining political environment was such that business firms, particularly the private-owned ones, did not dare stand up and be counted. No doubt, Chambers of Commerce had existed, even under the socialist years; in fact, they existed at the national level and in few of the major business centres across the country. such as Mwanza, Arusha, Morogoro, Moshi, Tanga and Dar es Salaam). However, these representative organs of business existed mostly in body, not in spirit. They lacked strong leadership, largely because prominent business executives were wary of finding themselves face to face, ostensibly in a confrontational manner, with the national political leadership.

It is also important to note, that until the emergence of the IPP Group of Companies in the mid 1980s, most of the leading business firms in Tanzania were Asian-owned and many Asians, even those who are nationals, have been and indeed remain largely low profile-oriented over matters of national character and concern. If there was anything that they deliberately avoided, it was to feature prominently in society confronting the government. Above all, the weaknesses of the Chambers of Commerce during the socialist era centred on the inherent fragile structure of the private sector itself. It suffered from the following three major weaknesses:

- it lacked a clear mission and identity largely because the sector during the socialist era was seen, in the eyes of the government and the common Tanzanian, as the enemy of the people, an institution of exploitation and social stratification.

- it kept its plans and operations largely secret except to those that it sought financial resources from. e.g. banks) and to tax authorities from whom they had to obtain tax clearance in order to renew annual business licences and pay taxes.

- it lacked and even avoided professional, as opposed to own-family management in running the affairs of companies.

Until very recently, private-owned firms have been predominantly egocentric and balkanised to the point that they were directly responsible for their own alienation from anything like an effective collective form of business lobby association. However, it is important to observe that this situation was in many ways created by the obtaining political- economic environment. Resources made available to the private sector, especially bank credit, were extremely scarce as state owned banks favoured the state-owned enterprises as a matter of state policy; industrial licenses were secured after a great deal of difficulty and often after giving kickbacks; import licenses, backed by allocation of foreign exchange from the Central Bank, were a privilege and discretionarily given. Under such a rigid and bureaucratic resource allocation system, the private sector was put at the mercy of the government. As a result, what emerged from the private sector was a surrogate mindset driven by a business culture of "everybody to himself and God for us all". Whether by act of commission or omission, the government was able, through the instrumentality of discretionary resource allocation, to divide the business sector and deal with it on a company-by -company basis. It is through such resource allocation system that some of the leading Asian -owned firms grew to large sizes in the late 1970s and the early 1980s, even as Tanzania continued to espouse and entrench a socialist ideology. Notable examples are the KJ Group, Rajani Group, Sumaria Group and the currently almost moribund JV Group.

Growth of New Business Representation

In the early mid 1980s, few industrial associations like MEIDA. Metal and Allied industries Association) and the Textile Manufacturers Association emerged. These associations had been pursuing parochial interests and thus lacked industry-wide focus and solidarity. Because of such parochialism, the government had resisted making any concessions to them. As Harvard Professor David Yoffie has correctly argued, "no politician wants to help one industry if it means antagonising three others." It was in this light, that the government itself promoted the idea of the establishment of the Tanzania Chamber of Commerce, Industry and Agriculture. TCCIA) in the latter part of 1988. The establishment coincided with Tanzania hosting the Summit of Heads of State under the umbrella of the precursor of the Preferential Trade Area for Eastern and Southern Africa. PTA) now COMESA, in November 1988.

The early history of TCCIA is a sad one for the business sector in Tanzania. In its early years of establishment, the TCCIA became corrupted by greed for power, power of self, not of the collective interest. The elected founding President of the Chamber chose to use the organisation for his own political self-aggrandisement, resulting in the absolute abuse of the Chamber's constitutional authority. Thus, at the dawn of Tanzania's economic pluralism, broad business community found itself lacking an effective *national* umbrella platform to enable its extensive and important presence properly and effectively felt in government and society over matters of national development. Most of the leaders who founded the TCCIA left the organisation by 1990.

The Birth of the CTI

In many ways, the birth of the Confederation of Tanzania Industries. CTI) resulted from the initial failures of the TCCIA. Lessons had been learnt the hard way. CTI's key belief was that the economy should be honeycombed by industrial associations of different sub-sectors, and that, through the co-ordination of views and positions of such associations, through CTI, industrial policies and actions of the government could be shaped. Established on 20th July 1991, the CTI has made much headway in its nascent years in promoting this ethos and thrust. The CTI has taken the view that the government should be on tap, not on top. In other words, business firms should enjoy a privileged position in society because the nation has placed in their hands the task for investing and mobilising national economic and human resources for national progress. For it is business that primarily determines the country's resource allocation, be it industrial technology, employment, market-structure or employee compensation.

Since its establishment, the CTI adopted a strategy of political activism to push the interests of its members. This activism has not been confrontational. On the contrary, it has taken the framework of consultation, interaction and dialogue. Two elements have reinforced this form of activism. First, CTI has been in the forefront in ensuring that there is a united front and voice in the industrial business sector. Secondly, it has embraced the government as an ally rather than, as TCCIA mistakenly did in its founding years, as a foe. It is also CTI's philosophy and strategy not to practice *"cry baby capitalism"* using the government as a crutch.

Dialogue has been informed by objective realities and not the quest for favours. Through these two core strategies, in a short spell of time, CTI has been able to access key public officials and legislators and thereby leveraging industry visibility within the government. It has also been able to construct an agenda for dialogue and reform that has been appealing to the government. In sum, CTI has been successful in showing the government that the Tanzanian industrial condition and the industry's collective market position would suffer were the government to fail to intervene to protect local industries. Its major challenge, to-date, has been to influence the government to translate the objective of creating a fair level playing field into government policy.

With a membership of more than 200 companies in the industrial and service sectors, CTI's belief is that a key step in the process of building coalitions is to expand membership. Strong membership means strong lobby. However, it means more; it means that by bringing together a wide range of diverse industrial members under the umbrella of a single organisation, a structure and capacity is created for a more informed understanding of sub-sectoral interests, challenges and priorities. Thus, CTI is first a forum for intra-industrial membership consultation and dialogue and, only second, though more importantly, a medium to voice issues and concerns having a bearing on the viability and vibrancy of the industrial sector.

During its early years of institutional development, between 1991 and 1997, the CTI relied primarily on members of its Executive Council for generation and crystallisation of ideas and policy papers. Such thinking process took place both at the Council level and at Standing Committee Levels. Several standing committees were constituted: A Fiscal Policy and Research Committee; A Planning Committee; a Membership and Funds Mobilisation Committee and a Small Industries Committee. More committees were later formed, for example, on legal matters and on utilities. Invariably, the CTI Council involved its key members from various sub-sectors in subscribing views on issues of collective interest. For instance, faced with a request in 1994 from the Patron of the CTI, who is also Tanzania's President, to submit concrete views on what needed to be done to help industries, to promote foreign exchange earnings through tourism and transit trade, the CTI constituted a Task Force comprising both Council members and general members to undertake the assignment. That Task Force completed its work and the Report, titled: *Manufacturing Industry in Crisis: Measures to avert de-industrialisation* was submitted to the President in 1994.

The CTI was also able to embark on an ambitious project whose aim was to propose an industrial policy for Tanzania. With financial support from the United States Aid for International Development. USAID), the CTI appointed a leading Tanzanian economist, the late Professor Mboya Bagachwa of the University of Dar es Salaam to lead a team of consultants to undertake a thorough study of the problems and challenges that confronted the Tanzanian industrial sector, in the wake of the implementation of structural adjustment and stabilisation programmes, and suggest policy measures to be taken. The study gave birth to a Report, which, since 1997, has become the government's official Industrial Policy. Notwithstanding these achievements, the reality is that the private sector, as an institution, is yet to gain legitimacy in Tanzania. What then is behind this identity crisis? This question is examired in the next section.

Private Sector Identity Crisis

Following the radical economic reforms that commenced in 1986, there has been a great deal of rhetoric, on the political front, about the private sector having being elevated to the position of being the new engine of national development. Undoubtedly, the government has shown a great deal of commitment in enabling the private sector to rise and take a frontal role in driving the economy. In recent years, such commitment has translated itself into the creation of an enabling environment for the private sector to gain the necessary confidence leading to growth in investments from both domestic and foreign sources. Several pro-private sector policies and laws have been put in place. These include: a broad investment promotion policy, a specific investment policy to cater for the mining sector, the re-constitution of the Investment Promotion Centre into the Tanzania Investment Centre-a "one stop" agency for providing services to new investors, a new land law, a new Income Tax Act, fiscal incentives to bolster investments in the agricultural, livestock and fisheries sectors and a new labour and employment law. The government also established a commercial court in 2000 to enable fast track adjudication of commercial disputes.

The re-organisation of the revenue collection system leading to the establishment of the Tanzania Revenue Authority. TRA) in 1997 was also testimony to the government's resolve and commitment to ensuring that the private sector was better served by a tax machinery that was both efficient and business-friendly. Of course, there still exists a concern about the manner in which the TRA operates. Such concern is justified. It should certainly be possible to address and rectify work styles without the TRA abdicating its core responsibility. Since mid 2003, the government has more recently, been giving this concern a great deal of attention. Other concerns, however, are the product of a past era when there was serious laxity in tax administration and wide room for tax-induced corruption. Legacies do indeed die-hard.

At the level of decision making within the government and the regulatory agencies, much remains to be done to ingrain a new culture that is more entrepreneurial and risk oriented. The on-going Public Service Reform is cognisant of some of these bottlenecks and would, in good time, re-invent the whole system of government and make it supportive and facilitatory to the business sector than presently. Evidently, the private sector is still confronted by serious challenges with respect to the economic environment. This environment is yet to be comprehensively private sector promoting because high costs of doing business remain in place. Tanzania is still a high cost country especially over energy and transportation costs. Inadequate and erratic water supply also hurts industries, especially in the beverage, beer and chemical sectors. At the same time, the government appears caught in a difficult situation when it comes to striking a balance between maximising revenue critically required for supporting the social and infrastructure sectors and lowering consumption taxes in a regime characterised by a narrow tax base. Thus, Tanzania has the highest VAT rate in the East African Community and the SADC. These issues constitute the burning agenda of the government and inform the smart partnership that has been structured through the creation, in 2001, of the Tanzania National Business Council as an organ for promoting structured dialogue between the government and the business sector.

Legitimacy of the Private Sector

However, the effectiveness of the National Business Council or any other avenue of dialogue between the private sector and the government crucially depends on the character of the private sector and its mindset. Back in early 1997, President Benjamin Mkapa confronted us with the question whether Tanzania indeed had a private sector. It was a tricky question and different people could probably have responded differently. There are those amongst us who, even today, would use a racial criteria about the ownership character of the Tanzanian private sector to respond to that question and their answer would be 'no' simply because they equate the present organised private sector with a dominant ownership by a national ethnic minority. In their view, the private sector can only be legitimate, as a national private sector, if there existed broad ownership of private assets or if the majority Tanzanians were brought into the mainstream of wealth creation and ownership through deliberate, positive discriminatory. or affirmative action) policies and schemes. Another group of Tanzanians would hold a different view. As a start, they would discount the view that the legitimacy of the private sector hinges on the majority Tanzanians being effective players in the organised private economy. Indeed, they would associate the existing dichotomy, non-indigenous versus indigenous with historical circumstances, including the role played by the Arusha Declaration and the Leadership Code, and the present constraints in obtaining equity financing and working capital from the banks.

My approach to this question is different. Tanzania does not as yet have in place a private sector in the same sense that it had a state-owned sector within the framework of the Arusha Declaration. State owned enterprises were born, bred and nourished by the policies of the Arusha Declaration. Their vision was also clear. Whichever way you want to look at it, state enterprises had a collective and coherent policy framework and strategy. The owner parent was one. Parastatals also enjoyed a common culture and they were viewed by people as their economic liberator from the scourges of poverty, ignorance and disease. They were the major source of employment. Given this background, it is no surprise that privatisation of parastatals should be viewed by some Tanzanians with a sense of negative emotion and indignation. It is simply because the private sector lacks a similar visionary underpinning.

What we have in Tanzania today is a nascent organised private sector. It suffers from the lack of homogeneity. This is not necessarily because there is no national collective body for all private sector players, the so-called apex body with powers of a collective voice, to rally under. Rather, it is because private companies are not adequately coming out to be part of business associations that can represent their collective interests. This failure in getting all business players to join sectoral associations like the CTI, TCCIA, Chamber of Mines, Confederation of Tourism Industries and the Chamber of Agriculture is a major cause for the lack of mission and influence by the private sector with which to drive economic opinion and secure a win-win partnership with the government. Many business actors are free riders. They still make believe that they can be served free by those already organised or, indeed, that they can independently use their financial muscle to secure whatever positive decisions they want from the government. It is an attitude that fertilises corruption and weakens the power of the private sector as a whole. In saying all this, I do not seek to demean the role of the TPSF. I will revert to a discussion of the role of the TPSF later in this chapter.

The private sector could become a legitimate and strong private sector if it were able to galvanise various national business associations and all businesspersons who presently have voluntarily excluded themselves. To try to enforce compulsory membership as a strategy to create stronger and powerful associations, a system which some of the continental European nations. e.g. Germany and France) apply, would be to flout the constitutional right of choice: to associate or not to associate. At the same time, forced membership invariably leads to apathy, disinterest and lack of commitment. The work of business associations is primarily voluntary. It relies on a high spirit of commitment. What should therefore ingrain the minds of businesspersons in Tanzania is that unity at business sectoral levels is the only way that can enable the private sector to galvanise its resources, information, experience and judgement. Such collective wisdom and authority is what would transform the private sector and turn it into a powerhouse in the economy earning it both legitimacy and credibility on the way.

A disparate private sector, on the other hand, cannot meet the standard of being a private sector. Its role and impact in the economy and the society would lack the force and power necessary to play the role expected of it. At the centre of transforming an inadequately organised private sector, lies the challenge: what is it that can or should be done to inspire the enthusiasm and promote the commitment of private actors in the economy to rally behind organs established to work on their behalf and thereby engender a collective purpose and mission? it is agonising that almost twenty years after the formulation of the Economic Recovery Programme, the private sector is yet to develop strong and financially self-reliant membership organisations. Indeed, in certain key sectors of the economy, there have been no business lobby bodies to represent economic players in those fields. A national organ to represent the interests of farmers and peasants was only established in 2001. Even then, its capacity as an effective voice suffers in the light of weak Cooperative Unions and Societies. The Cooperatives, which, from the late 1940s to early 1970s, were strong and effective representative bodies of peasants, were dissolved by the government in 1976 to make way for the introduction of socialist oriented cooperatives based on village governments. That change came in the wake of the massive movement of rural populations, between 1973 and 1976 into what were described as planned villages. Since their re-establishment in 1984, Cooperatives have remained largely lame. The Federation of Cooperative Unions, the equivalent of a national body, is also weak. Clearly, with about 80% of private sector actors operating at the agricultural front in the form of peasants, it is incorrect to speak of the existence a dynamic collective private sector mission and thrust in the aftermath of the near moribund state business sector.

As the same time, with over 30% of the Tanzania gross domestic product coming out of the informal sector that is marginalised from the private sector lobby, the identity of the private sector remains fuzzy. What should be asked is whether this informal character of what is presently a thriving business of a broad dimension, justifies its marginalisation? There are attempts, driven by President Mkapa, with the support of the Norwegian government and the technical and professional advice from Hernando de

Soto's organisation, to empower this sector. However, the success of this effort would significantly depend on how banks and micro-finance institutions respond to the challenge of accepting title of assets belonging to informal sector players as adequate security for credit. However, for these informal players to have a voice in influencing public policy they have to be mainstreamed in the private sector business lobby.

Disparate Private Sector Lobby Associations

If the private sector in Tanzania is to achieve the status of being a nationally organised institution that is broadly representative, then the challenge is to embark on a major task to get all private sector actors to rally behind business lobby associations. This can be achieved if bodies like the CTI and TCCIA deliberately help to organize the informal sector to establish its own "voice". There are no short cuts or alternatives in getting the whole private sector to have a collective mission and to play a more emphatic role at the national policy front. For this objective to be realised, the need of strength in numbers and strength in resources cannot be over-emphasised. This is the immediate challenge that faces private sector actors in trade and in industry in Tanzania.

There are other reasons why the private sector is still facing problems. We touched upon such issue earlier in reference to the private sector being owned and controlled by a national ethnic minority. With privatisation and the opening up of the economy to foreign investment, different sentiments also cropped up. Privatisation is viewed not only in the context of selling off the family silver but also in the entrenchment of the wealth divide on racial lines. Greenfield investments by foreigners, for example, are viewed as the antithesis of constructing a sustainable national economy. In other words, the private sector that is emerging in Tanzania is viewed not to be nationally representative; that it is like a deck of cards easily collapsible when one card is disturbed.

Clearly, these views are farfetched. They are oblivious of the changing nature of global economics. It is thus important to mobilise the people to appreciate that any form of productive investment, irrespective of ownership, benefits Tanzania. Jobs are created, taxes are paid, which contribute towards enabling the government to meet the social welfare needs of the people and for building infrastructure; technology is transferred and skills are developed. In this context, it is also important to inject quickly the concept of broad ownership of business through the stock market. This can be achieved at the individual level and through pension funds such as Parastatal Pensions Fund. PPF), the National Social Security Fund. NSSF) and the Local Government Pensions Fund. At the same time, the government and the better established private sector firms need to establish as many venture capital funds as possible to enable more national players to secure equity finance and thereby enter the wealth creation process.

Finally, there is a great deal of criticism levelled by the private sector against the bureaucracy for not being adequately business friendly. Yet, the private sector is equally to blame for the negative image it paints of itself in the eyes of the people. Therefore, the Tanzania private sector needs a fundamental shift in attitudes. It needs to be more sensitive at developing and embracing a sense of community, *vis a vis* what Charles Handy has described in his book *Beyond Uncertainty,* as "instinctive individuality that seems to have run amok." In this period of social and economic stress, there should be more to the well-being of all Tanzanians than mere money and riches. More agitating, especially to the urban poor, is to see the level of conspicuous and exhibitionist materialism the Tanzanian *nouveau* riches display. The private sector should transform this culture if it is to gain legitimacy and credibility. Above all, the private sector should rise above image destruction activities such as tax evasion, corruption and drug trafficking.

Tanzania is yet to have a cohesive private sector informed by a common purpose and mission. The government has a role to play in enabling the emergence of such a collective entity. The birth of the National Business Council would go a long way in kick starting this process. However, ultimately, the private sector players themselves hold the key in forging the type of private sector that can truly replace the state sector and prove to be the new dynamo of social and economic transformation. How to dynamise this private sector is the challenge I examine next.

Dynamising the Private Sector

Does dynamising the private sector hinge on the creation of an apex body for all business associations to rally under? My view is an affirmative "no." The reason for this stand is that such approach is tantamount to putting the cart before the horse. Surely, the more immediate challenge, as I see it, is to get all the key economic sectors better organised and allowed to mature. Such maturity of sector specific associations is imperative because it is associations that are the brainpower of the private sector. In this context, a focused priority in organising the private sector demands that sectoral associations be made strong as a necessary building block. There could be no simple short cut in which an apex business lobby organisation could garner the required strength. This is because, by definition, an apex body is largely a co-coordinating institution. Strength does not emanate from co-ordination of weak parts.

Role of Tanzania Private Sector Foundation

Evidently, collective actions of business associations, and I have witnessed quite a few over the past ten years, specifically on fiscal and budget issues and generally in the areas of policy advocacy and participation in investment policy making, ideally demand a structured pattern of interaction and synergy. This form of synergy validates the logic behind the establishment of an apex *co-ordinating* body, namely the Tanzania Private Sector Foundation. TPSF). However, synergy initiatives of this type could fail to meet stakeholders' expectations. Indeed, in the context of other experiences, such initiatives have never gone beyond perfunctory sessions.

I am an optimist. Yet it is often said that a healthy dose of scepticism helps to challenge conventional wisdom. In the case of the TPSF, it is paramount for this institution to distinguish in its work what constitutes *real* opportunities from mere mirage. Going by the unfortunate experience of the Ugandan Private Sector Foundation, we learn that the initial burst of enthusiasm about the Foundation petered out as soon as donor funds extended in support of the Foundation began to dry out and upon national business associations increasingly being required to cough up more funds than before to support the "apex" body. Here then lies the critical issue. Would the TPSF achieve sustainability in the medium term? Yes, donor assistance would be made available in the medium term, to support the Foundation in the belief that the government would also live up to its word to use the TPSF as the vehicle for promoting a structured dialogue through the National Business Council. But for how long would such aid continue? In the absence of donor support, it would be inconceivable that the presently fragile and financially weak business associations would support the TPSF. The TCCIA, for example, has for more than a decade survived on Swedish grants rather than on the subscriptions of its members and membership support activities of the association. The CTI is more or else self reliant, but at low levels of capacity. The capacity building drive engineered in 1997 through the support of DANIDA and managed by the Confederation of Danish Industries, CTI's cooperating partner, has a time limit. Whence would the TCCIA, CTI and other business associations achieve, for themselves, comfortable sustainability?

Notwithstanding the foregoing, the way the TPSF operates and functions would also determine its sustainability and legitimacy. The TPSF should approach its tasks and responsibilities from a balanced perspective. For instance, there is an orchestrated view that the TPSF should become the *apex* body of the business sector in Tanzania. The term "apex" is obviously misleading. It is simply impracticable and, in fact, outrightly outrageous and ludicrous, to expect the TPSF to become an apex body. Such a status merely subverts the very meaning and purpose of creating the TPSF, namely to act as a co-ordination point of reference for the whole business sector especially with respect to assuring smart partnership between the private sector and the government through the TNBC.

In this context, I would like to suggest that the major challenge, indeed the key factor of success of the TPSF, is to appreciate where the real synergy opportunities lie in the Tanzanian business sector while avoiding clashes with its shareholders on issues best and more cost-effectively dealt by them. The TPSF is not the equivalent of a monolithic, diversified organisation. Thus, the usual benefits of shared expertise, shared resources, pooled negotiating power, co-ordination, mergers, and acquisitions, which are commonplace in typically business conglomerates, are not part of the TPSF. In an article published in the *Harvard Business Review* titled: *Desperately Seeking Synergy*, it is posited that there are four biases which often distort the thinking of those who view synergy as the end game for achieving goals. These biases are as follows: the *synergy bias* underlined by an overestimation of the benefits and the underestimation of the costs of synergy. The second bias is *parenting bias* which is focused on the belief that synergy will only be captured by cajoling or compelling business units to co-operate. Then there is the *skills bias* driven by the assumption that whatever knowledge is required to achieve synergy would be available intra-organisationally. Lastly, is the *upside bias* which causes synergy bodies to concentrate too much on the potential benefits of synergy such that they overlook the downsides. The cumulative lesson from these biases is that synergy may appear to be more attractive and more easily achievable than it truly is. TPSF should learn from these biases about synergy and chart out a more realistic representational ethos.

Towards Focused Roles of Business Associations

The Tanzania Chamber of Commerce, Industry and Agriculture. TCCIA) may, by its constitution, claim to be a representative body for the industrial and the agricultural sector. Clearly, in so far as the industrial sector is concerned, this is a portfolio that falls squarely under the CTI. In the case of the agricultural sector, the TCCIA knows well that it has never *effectively* represented agriculture. Even if it intended to represent the agricultural sector, it would not have been able to fulfil such a role simply because the TCCIA, from inception, has not been a sector specific representative organisation. Indeed, one of the immediate challenges that face the process of organising the private sector is to get the TCCIA to restructure itself into a sector specific body, namely, to transform itself into a National Chamber of Commerce and Trade with the specific responsibility for promoting trade and commerce. The agricultural sector.

excluding agro-industry, which, as a process and as a manufacturing industry, would necessarily form part of CTI) has since 2001 constituted its own Chamber of Agriculture. At the same time, there is also the need for the CTI to review its Constitution to reflect its broad industry representative structure. The form and structure of the Confederation of British Industry or the Confederation of Indian Industry would be ideal for the CTI. The concept of CTI as dominantly a manufacturing lobby association is dated. The service industry is now taking leadership and there is a blurring line between manufacturing and service because of the importance of value chain in business. Another challenge is the need for the CTI to bring into its fold small industrial enterprises that presently lack effective representation. It would be necessary, in this context, for the CTI to assist small industrial enterprises to constitute their own national body that the CTI can work with closely.

The restructuring of existing associations and the establishment of new sector specific bodies would not necessarily lead to the emergence of an organised private sector. Such process would, as in all institutional representative organs, require resources- human and financial-if the institutions are to perform their tasks effectively and achieve envisioned objectives. There is little doubt that such resources are available. What are missing are private sector players ready and willing to associate themselves with the respective associations by becoming paying members. Strength in numbers of committed members ultimately would bring about financial viability and organisational capacity to the private sector in Tanzania.

Chapter

25 BUILDING SMART PARTNERSHIPS

I believe passionately that Africa will get far if it develops, nurtures, and exploits fully the immense potential of the partnership between government, workers, and employers in developing strategies that can contribute to the improvement of the quality of life that our people deserve.- the essence of "Smart Partnership" in today's world is not conformity or control. It is unity in diversity. Smart partnership is about the determination of the common interest in tripartite or multiple relationships. It is a shared commitment to adaptation, not to mutual resistance. It is the desire to work together for mutual benefit. We eschew the "us" versus "them" dichotomy, in favour of an acknowledgement of a shared destiny. We either swim together, or we drown together.

- Benjamin W. Mkapa: ***Opening Speech at the SADC Employment and Labour Sector Meeting of Ministers and Social Partners, March 2003.***

Introduction

From 26-29 July 1998, the Second Southern Africa International Dialogue was held in Swakopmund, Namibia. The theme of the dialogue was *"Smart Partnership for the Generation of Wealth in Southern Africa"*. Several Heads of State and Governments from Southern African,. SADC) countries and from East Africa attended the Dialogue. The Dialogue was focused on how to strengthen cooperation between governments, business and labour through smart partnership for realising long-term win-win gains for countries and businesses.

What is Smart Partnership?

The concept of smart partnership is new to many Tanzanians and people of other countries in the developing world. As such, an attempt is made, at the outset, to define and clarify it. The concept has its origin in the creative and innovative thinking of the former Malaysian Prime Minister, Dr. Mahathir Mohammed. In his wisdom, global prosperity is predicated on peace, stability and solidarity. With the intensification of globalisation under which the role and economic sovereignty of the nation-state is increasingly becoming undermined, Mahathir advocated a new dispensation that could assure a more equitable shared prosperity.

At first, smart partnership partners were limited government, business and the trade unions. However, at the 1997 Third Langkawi International Dialogue in Langkawi, Malaysia, Dr. Mahathir, in his opening keynote address, added political parties as new partners. In his view, which has now become part of the smart partnership framework, a national social compact or consensus could not be achieved where the traditional structure of political polarisation between ruling and opposition parties was extended to the level of determining issues such as national development vision and how countries respond to the global debt problem. Mahathir advocated the importance of treating all political parties as smart partners in the development challenge.

Participants at the Swakopmund Dialogue challenged the narrowness of the partnership framework in the light of the objective conditions and realities existing in poor countries especially those of Southern Africa. This challenge occurred during the interactive session moderated by the Tanzanian President, Benjamin Mkapa, under the theme: *Mobilising all Stakeholders: Smart Partnership in Action*. In his introductory remarks, President Mkapa challenged the participants with question whether the participating countries had ensured that all the national and regional stakeholders were on board the smart partnership boat. The response was a clear "no." It was noted, for instance, that the framework as it existed was somewhat elitist in the sense that the "poor and the landless" were excluded from the 'dialogue' process at all levels: global, regional, national and local. Thus whilst it was necessary for the poor to be mobilised and organised through their own grassroots movements, thereafter they needed to be "linked" to national organisational systems where they could also play a role in determining the future of their countries or participate in activities of national interest. A relevant example here relates to the traditional militia in Tanzania called *"sungusungu"*. This is a militia born out of a spontaneous grassroots movement. It featured in the public domain in the 1980s as a rural response to ineffective state law enforcement machinery especially in dealing with increasing cases of cattle theft. For a while, the movement worked well and even advanced into main urban areas in the form of neighbourhood night vigilante patrols against crime. However, because the movement was not well linked to the state law enforcement system, like the police, its effectiveness could not be sustained. Clearly, if a smart partnership had been developed between the movement and the state, positive results would have emerged on a sustainable basis.

Growing the Smart Partnership Ethos

Tanzania has few examples of state-induced destruction of grassroots-based smart partnerships, ranging from the abolition of local government in

1972 to the abolition of the co-operatives in 1976. Those measures seriously marginalised the rural poor. In spite of the reinstatement of local government and the co-operatives in 1982 and 1984 respectively, these organs are yet to recover the organisational strength and capacity that characterised their role in national affairs in the 1960s and the 1970s. It is noteworthy that only recently, in 2001, peasants and farmers have been able to organise around a national body that may constitute their collective voice and platform for forming partnerships with other stakeholders in society.

The Swakopmund Dialogue also called for the involvement of the public service in the smart partnership framework. The term government was found to be too restrictive as it had come to imply the political leadership. The public service, also described as the bureaucracy, was singled out as a key player in promoting shared prosperity. Yet, in many nations, the public service has proved to be a bottleneck in enabling economies to change and to respond rapidly to new imperatives driven by deepening globalisation, market-led policies, the roll back of the state and good governance. President Mkapa quizzed at Swakopmund: "Is the process of smart partnership owned only by us who participate in these dialogues, or is it increasingly being internalised and owned by the Ministers, Permanent Secretaries and the rest of the politicians and Civil Servants in our countries? Are we satisfied that they understand this concept and are ready to be facilitators rather than obstructionists? Do they feel and act as owners of the process who are keen to see it succeed"?

One of the directions towards transforming the mindset of the public service is located in getting it to be a 'smart partner'. This is in the belief that smart partnership creates the space for agility of mind and action. An ethos underlies it. In Tanzania, we have experienced from the Tax Review Task Force which the Government appointed in 1998 to assist in clarifying fiscal policies and tax measures that could be considered for underpinning the annual fiscal budgets, has been able to facilitate a meeting of minds between the bureaucracy and the private sector. Of course, to get the bureaucracy to think in a truly "win-win" way with the private sector remains a huge challenge.

Globalising Smart Partnership

One area that continues to elude smart partnership and which President Mkapa alluded to in his introductory remarks at Swakopmund, is the question of bringing global and regional stakeholders on board the smart partnership framework. There was genuine concern at Swakopmund that sub-regional economic cooperation arrangements such as SADC and COMESA were not informed by an ethos of smart partnership because political leaders behind their establishment were dogmatic about the uniqueness of distinct roles of such bodies. The on-going divide between COMESA and SADC is unhealthy and is not in line with the goals of smart partnership. These two organs should move towards integration in the interest of acting as a model for Africa-wide economic integration. There is also the question where the East African Community fits in this forest of integration arrangements? Tanzania is a member of SADC but not of COMESA. Yet Uganda and Kenya are members of COMESA not of SADC.

On the other hand, a SADC and SACU member, namely South Africa, has a bilateral trade and development agreement with the European Union. At a time when the whole ACP bloc concluded the Cotonou Agreement with the EU in 2000, an African powerhouse that vigorously promotes the smart idea of *"prosper thy-neighbour"* and the *"African renaissance"* has gone solo in negotiating an international protocol for its own prosperity. Is this smart partnership? How would NEPAD function as a vehicle of African smart partnership when some African countries negotiate their own bilateral agreements with the EU and even with the USA? President Mkapa was thus right to raise the issue of regional smart partnership and of the importance to get all the regional stakeholders involved in promoting such partnership. We should avoid idealistic rhetoric about the goal of integration and more seriously embrace more pragmatic and concrete ways of translating smart partnership into viable alliances that produce win-win environments and mutual gains.

There is also another dimension in getting all stakeholders involved. This concerns donors and international multilateral financial institutions. Are these agencies not stakeholders in our economies as well? Are they 'smart partners' or are they regulators and discipline enforcers? Yes, our economies could be in distress and need external support. However, does this condition demand a subordinate, master and servant relationship, or should it call for a more civilised form of relationship, that of "unequal equals?" *The Challenge To The South,* addressed these questions in a clear and cogent manner. The Report observes, for instance, that whilst the logic for a building new international development consensus, "a pact of global solidarity between South and North," exists it is imperative "to set up arenas and forums in which exchanges and negotiations can take place" if an environment favourable to development is to emerge. Thus, there is a challenge, at national and regional levels, to sit together with donors, the IMF and the World Bank, in particular, involving all national stakeholders and not just governments, to discuss the state of our economies and what could be done to improve them. It is the people, through their various stakeholder organs along with their governments that should own the development agenda. This form of participation should be promoted.

Fitting Trans-national Corporations into Smart Partnership

Getting trans-national companies involved in dialogue is also important. With globalisation, liberalisation and privatisation taking root, the role of transnational and multinational companies is increasingly becoming intense. Thus, as President Mkapa asked in Swakopumund, "how do we organise ourselves to ensure that foreign partners fall in line "within the framework of smart partnership?" He conjectured "foreign ownership, local control" as one approach to take in building such smart partnership. Interestingly, this idea has in fact taken root amongst the leading world management gurus. In a most invigorating article in the *Harvard Business Review* titled, *The End of Corporate Imperialism*, Professors C. K. Prahalad and Kenneth Lieberthal discuss this very issue. To cite them: "Leadership of a multinational's venture in an emerging market requires a complex blend of local sensitivity and global knowledge. Getting the balance right is critical but never easy. MNCS frequently lack the cultural understanding to get the mix of expatriate and local leaders right." The authors point out that in India, because of the availability of a good cadre of engineers and managers as well as a good command of English, many multinational companies have appointed Indian managers rather than expatriates to lead their organisations. This is smart partnership in action. Smart partnership should also extend to embracing a commitment on the part of investing multinationals to train local people to take up senior management positions in their firms.

Who Mobilises and for What?

On the face of it, it would appear that the task of mobilising all the stakeholders under the banner of smart partnership could be straightforward. In reality, it is not so. The process, invariably, is challenged by questions such as who mobilises and for what? Obviously, the whole society should be capable to mobilise. However, such capacity is crucially dependent on the state of democratisation in a country. Put differently, the people, as individuals and as collective members of society, should be free if they are to articulate their own interests and the interests of the nation. They have to be free to organise to further their common interests. Such freedom is a critical characteristic of smart partnership in the sense that those who govern and those that are governed should have a similar understanding of what freedom encompasses. Smart partnership cannot emerge in an environment where governments are not responsive to the people's freely expressed views. A quick example is the style the Tanzania government adopted in getting the constitution revisited in 1998. In putting forward a *White Paper* before the people highlighting the government's opinion on the form the constitutional reform should take was presumptuous. It was contrary to the spirit of smart partnership. The government sought to lead and control rather than to promote and enable an open-ended interaction. The subsequent appointment of the Special Constitution Review Committee to collect views of the people, based on the *White Paper*, was thus like putting a cart before the horse. The *White Paper* itself should have been informed by the Report of the Committee. The bedrock of smart partnership is real democratisation, in every sphere of life: social, economic, political and corporate. Without it, smart partnership becomes a facade, a gimmick to satisfy narrow, power-based interests.

Therefore, it is important that the question, who mobilises is taken seriously since the act of mobilisation should respond to the inevitable question "for what?" We learn from *The Challenge To The South* that, "the State is best able to perform its demanding functions where there is a national consensus on the goals and purposes of development, and on the apportionment of the costs as well as the benefits of development. Democratic institutions, which allow full participation and through which such a consensus can be reached, are therefore not only an objective of people-centred development, but its very means as well". In other words, smart partnership works well when a government or, for that matter, an NGO, a company or a political party, is able to unite around a powerful vision with a sustaining meaning. This is the message that Lester Thurow also propagates in his book, *The Future of Capitalism*. Professor Thurow postulates that "if there is no story to tell, leaders have no agenda and no self confidence in what they are doing. To hold together there has to be a utopian vision that underlies some common goals that members of society can work together to achieve". Smart Partnership needs a road map to a better society, a vision, and to cite Thurow, "that transcends narrow sectarian self interests".

The Leadership Challenge

In sum, who mobilises should be one with an agenda, a vision. It should be a person able to get a compelling and shared vision to be developed around which the people can galvanise and rally behind because it is credible, realisable and with worthwhile benefits. This is a serious challenge for leadership at all levels of society and institutions. John M. Richardson, Jr. once wrote that when it comes to the future there were three kinds of people: those who let it happen; those who make it happen and those who wonder what happened. Translating vision into reality requires leaders who can make the future happen; indeed, those who can even jump-start the future. The key attribute of such leaders is the ability to brew consensus among those they lead or would lead. Such ability, to cite from J.M.Kouzes and B.Z. Posner's book, *The Leadership Challenge: How to Get Extraordinary Things Done in Organisations*, emanates from a deep understanding of the collective yearnings, a sensitive ear to quiet whisperings, attendance to subtle cues, sniffing the air to get the scent, watching the people's faces and getting a sense of what they want and value, as well as what they dream about. Developing and achieving smart partnership critically depends upon the availability of this quality of leadership.

Vehicles for Mobilisation

Of course, the whole process of mobilisation of key stakeholders crucially requires vehicles, leadership being one of them. These days we hear of so many vehicles: the different sectoral associations of business, civil society organisations, NGO bodies, gender networking groups, youth organisations, trade unions, political parties and employers' organisations. Some of these vehicles exist at micro level, at meso. or middle) level and at macro. or national) level. The establishment of the Tanzania Private Sector Foundation as a focal point for the private sector to galvanise a collective position and resolve conflicts fits in well with this objective. The Foundation provides capacity for the private sector to engage and dialogue with the government at the level of the Tanzania National Business Council from a more informed and collective position.

The point to be underscored is that it is first class drivers who can drive vehicles to reach planned destinations. In other words, there is no short cut. Yes, democratic institutions are necessary. However, in themselves, they are not enough. Powerful and transforming visions are realisable only through equally powerful and visionary leadership. Here then lies the rub. To be able to meet the challenge of building a development consensus, whether at national or corporate level, through smart partnership, quality leadership is central.

Conclusion

The concept of smart partnership is in vogue and its benefits are real. Democratisation, regionalism and globalisation are the new realities. Smart partnership seeks to enable these realities to make meaning to nations and peoples. It seeks to ensure that relationships- social, political and economic- are based on a win-win formula. However, smart partnership is not an end in itself. It is an instrument; an approach derived from successful practice and intended to build trust and cooperation as well as to open up spaces that create and enable equitable sharing of wealth and prosperity.

Chapter

26 BUSINESS ETHICS - WHAT ETHICS?

An unattractive featur of private industrial development in many
underdeveloped countries is its tendency to shortsighted selfishness. Some
private industrialists have established a pattern of operating in antisocial and
sometimes dishonest way. They pride themselves upon devious methods of book
keeping so that they can evade axes. They fail to disclose facts of their business
to any unsuspecting investors who may have bought shares in their enterprises.
They assume no responsibility for community development. They adopt anti-
labour attitude. Such businesspersons are the foes of any legitimate and socially
acceptable private industrial development and much of the hostility to private
enterprise in many countries is due to their approach.

-Murray D. Bryce: *Industrial Development: A Guide for Accelerating*
Economic Growth.

Introduction

The philosophy underlining business ethics and corporate responsibility has been in vogue in the Tanzanian economic environment largely in the past decade. Near three decades of a socialist command economy created the notion and the perception that, given the dominance of the state-owned enterprises, viewed as *"Mali ya Umma"*. people's assets), the idea and the concern about business ethics and corporate responsibility appeared somewhat foreign and of passing significance. The logic was equally unquestionable. For what was considered owned by the whole people could not, surely, be stolen from the people. How could you steal what was considered yours? There was a characteristic moral ethic in the ownership system, that was somewhat taken for granted. Thus, even the question about corporate responsibility, in the sense of parastatals behaving as exemplary corporate citizens and all the time responsive to the needs of society beyond those ordinarily provided for by the state, also appeared frivolous. Parastatals served the people, period. It is significant to note, in the context of this assumed ethical and socially responsible value system that existed within the state-owned enterprise regime, that the emergence of vices likes corruption, waste and misuse of state assets and resources inevitably escaped serious attention. This was a regrettable situation. Indeed, with the benefit of hindsight, what undermines state enterprise was partly rooted in this wrongly assumed state of ethical and best practices systems.

Parastatals and Business Ethics

The government itself, as the organ directly accountable for the performance of state enterprises, fell victim to a weak and unethical management system that subverted the very health and viability of the parastatals. There is little doubt as to the generally accepted principle of business management in both public and private-owned enterprises that the realisation of reasonable surplus or profits is central. However, blatant derelictions on the part of the shareholder, the government in the case of parastatals, and corporate management in the case of private business in ensuring that the resources of the enterprise were directed towards the business of business as opposed to the business of political popularism and patronage, was not singled out as unethical or contrary to good business practice. The ruling environment that existed in the era of the socialist command economic system inhibited such derelictions. Indeed, the mindset of the society was heavily influenced by the dogma that state enterprises belonged to the people and thus worked purely for the interests of the people. It was a powerful belief that ingrained in the society's thinking. So powerful was the mindset about the inviolability of the state enterprise system that, even today, few Tanzanians are able to invoke a realistic context to what has befallen the parastatal system following the opening of the floodgates of liberalisation and deregulation.

Evidently, in the state and condition in which they were in, few parastatals could have valiantly confronted the competition that emerged. In a somewhat characteristic way, many Tanzanians, some very well informed, at least in terms of their levels of formal education, mentally refused to come to terms with the reality about the fragility of the parastatals that existed prior to the onset of liberalisation. They continue to carry the excess baggage of the primacy of public ownership. They suffer from a fixed mindset that sees only evil, inequity and social injustice in the system of private ownership. Not surprisingly, therefore, privatisation of state-owned enterprises constitutes, in their view, an unethical policy direction. Paradoxically, they are not able, at the same time, to advance forceful arguments against greenfield private investments which have a greater impact in the "privatisation" of the whole economy. However, in recent years, sensitivity has grown about the drummed up take over of the economy by South Africans. One is therefore left somewhat confused as to where the problem lies. Is the problem the *form* of privatisation or its *substance*? In other words, is the problem centred on whom parastatals are sold to or is it the *very* idea of privatising the so-called family silver? Evidently, there is nothing particularly ethical about either of these decision choices. Both centre on responding to varying economic realities.

New Expectations on Business Ethics

I raise these issues mainly to provide a useful context for an objective discussion of business ethics and corporate responsibility as perceived in the current, market-driven economic environment. At the centre of this contextual background, is the present inevitable public interest in ethics being at a historic high. In addition, there are obvious reasons for this interest. Particularly during the past decade, Tanzania has witnessed major transformations in its political and economic life. Both the political process and the economic system have been democratised and liberalised. Inevitably, ethical questions of a political, social and economic character have taken the centre stage of public affairs. Moreover, with the emergence of the private media, it has become easier to perceive the society as being ethically and morally deficient than it actually is. Of course, it would be unscientific to draw judgment about such perception.

It is clear, though, that the ethical standards applied to corporate and political behaviour and conduct have risen exponentially. Whether these standards have raised the average rectitude of business enterprise, of politicians and public officials remains a matter of conjecture. The conclusions of the *Warioba Commission Report* would appear to point out that the ethical problem has intensified and has probably become one of the critical problems confronting the nation.

At the level of corporate responsibility, on the other hand, the reform of the welfare state, characterised by the elevation of the private sector in welfare provisioning, has raised a different form of societal expectation from the private sector. A new development paradigm is emerging that requires the private sector to play a role beyond the traditional one of being a mere taxpayer. Economic liberalisation and privatisation have catapulted a difficult transition for the majority of Tanzanians. Purchasing power has fallen and jobs have been lost. Moreover, there are only a few new jobs being created as more and more young people come out of educational establishments. Self-employment is a mantra that is more passionate than realisable. It needs entrepreneurship, risk taking and working capital as well as availability of business premises, neither easily or readily obtainable. In this situation, the inevitable question is to what extent the corporate sector can step in and play the role of corporate citizen beyond the traditional role of contributing to the people's welfare through taxes. As Charles Handy has perceptively asked in his book: *The Empty Raincoat: Making Sense of The Future:* is business a purely wealth-creating instrument best left alone to do what it has to do, or does it mean that, "precisely because of its social compact, it has to recognize a wider accountability than making its owners seriously rich"?

The Mantra of Business Ethics

An attempt is made here to address some of the key issues on business ethics and corporate responsibility. At the outset, it is important to point out that business ethics and corporate responsibility are closely related. Sometimes, the terms are used interchangeably. However, for ease of addressing them, they are discussed here independently. The central question that surrounds the philosophy of business ethics is whether there is indeed such an animal as an ethical business enterprise. In other words, can business firms possess developmental ethical attitudes that are demonstrable at the levels of their relationships to employees, to the consumer and the society as a whole? In addressing these questions, I have been influenced by the approach taken by the distinguished Harvard Business School Professor Kenneth Andrews. In a trail-blazing article published in the *Harvard Business Review*, titled *Ethics In Practice*, Professor Andrews poses the following central question underlying business ethics: "Why is business ethics a problem that snares not just a few mature criminals or crooks in the making but a host of apparently good people who lead exemplary private lives while concealing information about dangerous products or systematically falsifying costs?"

In the view of Professor Andrews, there are three main characteristics to the problem of corporate ethics. These are: the development of the executive as a moral person; the influence of the business enterprise as a moral environment; and the actions needed to map a high road to economic and ethical performance. The development of the business executive as a moral person starts from the standpoint that unethical conduct or behaviour in business is often regarded as individual failure. As Professor Andrews puts it, "a person of the proper moral fibre, properly brought up, simply would not cheat". Yet, in real life situations, social or business, morality and ethical behaviour is influenced by factors not necessarily linked to one's upbringing. Increasingly, we see a kind of split personality in the way business executives and owners of business enterprises conduct themselves, almost in line with the Dr. Jekyll and Mr. Hyde personality syndrome. If the development of a person, not even necessarily a business executive, as a moral creature underpins one's ethical behaviour, then humans would be exemplary at the religious leadership level. However, this is not to be.

The world is witness to numerous cases of religious leaders going against God's Commandments. In business, equally, there are business people that live two contrasting and contradictory life styles. On the one hand, they are God fearing in their religious beliefs. Thus, some Moslem business people pray five times a day. They even leave their business premises to physically go to mosques to pray, rather than praying in properly set aside areas within their business precincts or offices. On the other hand, however, when it comes to business, they totally forget Almighty God. They cheat or under deal. This behaviour applies to business people in all other religious faiths. They cheat, they steal, they evade and avoid taxes, they corrupt and they even kill to make money and more money. Saint Augustine has taught us, "In ethics, to mistake the means for the ends is to be turned in on oneself, one of the worst of sins."

A distinguished lawyer and former Indian Minister for Law, Justice and Company Affairs, Mr. Ram Jethmalani, shared his insight on a visit to Tanzania in 1998 about the centrality of ethics in society. He posited that, as societies embrace, almost inevitably, the virtues of the free market, they tend to lose sight of the fact that the free market can only thrive where morality and social values predominate. If the free market were allowed to impose a free market society, as if it were an end, a goal, then society would almost certainly crumble in the face of temptation. Indeed, he argued, that a society of "free robbers" would ensue. Here then lies the central thrust of my argument. The socialist command economic system had fallen prey to an assumption that the means reflected the ends. It was obviously a wrong assumption, though the ends remain valid. Now that Tanzania has embraced the free market system, the critical issue is the one that Professor Kenneth Andrews posed, namely the influence of the business enterprise as a moral environment. In his view, the total loyalty of business, "to the maximization of profit is the principal obstacle to achieving higher standards of ethical practice." He further argued that the promulgation and institutionalisation of ethical policy in business is not as difficult as "escaping the compulsion of greed."

In my judgement, the on-set of the free market system in Tanzania has largely unleashed unethical business practices. It is almost as if liberalisation and deregulation have become symptomatic of and, indeed, embody unethical business behaviour. This is the challenge that confronts business as a moral environment. Tanzania has now come to the point where unethical corporate conduct undermines and subverts the well-being of the economy and of the people. The de-industrialisation that took place from the late 1980s to mid 1990s had been singularly propelled by unethical business conduct. Greed in the imports trading business community overrode the national economic interest. That community never cared, still largely does not care, about the collapse of domestic industries, about the loss of jobs and about the loss in tax revenue to the government. Enriching themselves is all that matters. In addition, as if tax evasion had not caused enough damage, dumping into the economy of sub-standard products, often at prices way below cost of production, added salt to injury. Yet the International Monetary Fund, conveniently ignorant of such unethical conduct of the trading business sector influenced the government to lower import tariffs ostensibly to stimulate the economy when in fact the level of the tariffs, to all intents and purposes, did not, at that time, have much impact on revenue growth because of massive tax evasion in place.

The logic of business competition is ethical business and this translates into fair trade practices. Where business subverts such logic, it gives business a bad name and image. At a different level, one notices that business ethics in Tanzania is eroded by the excess baggage of yesteryears when, to succeed in private business, one had to grease the machinery of government decision-making. In other words, a great number of business people continue to think and behave with this philosophy in mind, namely to succeed in business, you have to circumvent and cut corners around the decision-making system of the government. It is such unethical business culture that led to the *"mafuta na minofu"*. edible oil and fillet fish processing) scandal in 1996. The then Minister for Finance had to quit his post as a result. What is regrettable about such business culture is that it smacks of corruption, whether real or perceived. Whichever way, it definitely smacks of non-transparency and subverts good governance.
Two comments are called for. First, it is clear that the promotion and the realisation of business ethics crucially hinges on ethical governance. It takes two to tango. Ethics is about values. Without a clear preference for right over wrong, ethics cannot thrive. The government should lead the enforcement of ethics by practising good governance, ensuring transparency and promoting the rule of law. Corruption breeds unethical business conducts and vice versa. The government should come up with a forceful message to the business community that it would only listen to their problems and concerns when presented through relevant business support organisations, not individual companies, unless the problems are company specific.

The whole system governing the relationship between government and business should be transformed from a personalized one to a collective one. This point reminds us of what President Mkapa mentioned at the CTI Annual Dinner in January 1997, namely that the *Warioba Commission Report* observed that one of the sources of corruption in Tanzania was the intimate closeness that existed between political and government leaders with leading businesspeople. The President, jokingly, wondered if his presence at the dinner where there were over 200-business people would not have been misunderstood in the context of *Warioba Report's* perspective! Yet, the *Warioba Report*, on this stance, was not far from the truth. What it pointed out was that part of the decision-making system in the government fertilised the ground for corruption by making it necessary for the concerns of business to be addressed at personal levels.

Second, the business community is not able to achieve unity and strength and thus engage the government more effectively over policy issues precisely because many business people still believe that they can achieve what they want by dealing with the government on their own. Such situation explains the present organisational weaknesses of business associations like the CTI and the TCCIA. The new Private Sector Foundation would almost likely be an even weaker one under the prevailing circumstances. What is currently taking place is that only a handful of business firms keep business associations afloat and with great difficulty. Most businesses are free riders; they reap what they do not sow.

As the government increasingly works closely with these associations, the paradox is that the result is an even higher number of free riders. The win-win situation for members of business associations and non-members alike in the business-government dialogue is the height of unethical business behaviour in the Tanzanian business community. It is an insult to the image and credibility of business. There is simply no way that the Tanzania business community can successfully map a high road to economic and ethical performance if such a situation persists. The challenge to promulgate and institutionalise business ethical conduct also importantly rests with building strong business associations.

Conclusion

The imperativeness of making the market system acceptable as a means for building better quality of lives of Tanzanians is the ethical call to business. As Charles Handy has put it in his book, *Beyond Certainty*: "If free enterprise and the market is seen to be a license to corrupt and exploit, then the West will have betrayed its standards. Capitalism is, or should be, the means to a better life, not an end in itself." In the Tanzanian context, the market economy should mean humanisation of capitalism. If business fails to become ethical, the market would inevitably lose its legitimacy and credibility. And private enterprise would, in turn, be despised.

Chapter

27 ENVIRONMENTALISM: IS IT RUNNING RIOT?

Growth is not the enemy of environmentalism. It is in fact necessary if the environment is to be improved. It is only with growth and higher standards of living that people become interested in the environment. In the jargon of economics, environmental goods like clean air and pure water are luxuries.

-Lester Thurow: *Creating Wealth.*

The poor, the hungry and the diseased cannot be expected to put the preservation of their environment above the struggle to survive this very day. For them it is not the quality of life that is at stake, it is life itself.

-Benjamin William Mkapa: *Survival is the Poor's Priority*,
September 2002.

Overview

The importance of the physical environment and the threats posed to the environment are increasingly becoming evident to Tanzanians. The National Environment Management Council. NEMC) has enabled this sensitivity about environmental concerns to take the centre stage of politics and policymaking. Since 1997, Tanzania has witnessed a dramatic green zeal propelled by NEMC through the enforcement of cleaner and non-polluting manufacturing processes, around the country and especially in Dar es Salaam. In this context, a number of industries were closed down in the late 1990s, if only for sometime, as a clear move in enforcing environmental rules and regulations and thus putting the government at the heart of a new and serious effort to promote and protect the environment. Enforcement of environmental safeguards marked a wake up call to Tanzanians that promotion of environmental sustainability had become a key dimension of public policy.

The environmental movement is quickly gaining support largely within the context of a well drummed-up logic that the gains to human health from strict enforcement of environmental standards and clamping down on polluters, far outweighed the benefits of industrialisation. At the same time, however, for a developing economy that increasingly relies on industrialisation as the bedrock of economic growth, of tax revenues to support the social service delivery, infrastructure development and creation of jobs, the logic about the gains to human health requires a dispassionate and balanced examination. Otherwise, Tanzanians may pride themselves of being very green but at the same time very poor. In this context, *The Challenge to the South* has aptly cautioned, "the countries of the South will need to take specific steps to guard against environmental degradation while continuing to pursue rapid economic growth." In other words, the centrality of balance is imperative in pursuing and enforcing policies that promote and protect the environment whilst enabling industrialisation to deepen. In the late 1990s, there was serious concern whether the green movement could achieve such a balance given the fact that NEMC chose to unilaterally go on a rampage, closing down ostensibly polluting industries. At the same time and in fairness, however, NEMC had felt that the pollution situation had reached such grave proportions as to demand shock treatment.

Based on the lessons from the 1990s and as Tanzania's industrialisation picks up momentum, it is imperative to search for ways and means that would control environmentalism from running riot. In this regard, it is important to bring to the fore two complementing views about the delicateness of this balance and how public policy should handle it. The first view, well articulated in the *Economist Editorial* of August 8, 1992 posits, "Once governments have decided their environmental priorities, the best way to attain them is usually by looking for ways to harness the force of the market. The more companies can be given incentives to come up with technical answers to environmental problems, the more cost effective those answers are likely to be. Broadly speaking, any given level of environmental virtue can be delivered more cheaply by using green taxes or other measures that harness market endeavour than by using regulation." The second view holds that environmental sustainability needs a mindset rooted in and sensitive to environmental issues. A forceful approach to enforcing environmental safeguards is more likely not to succeed whilst greater use of education about the dangers of environmental degradation and its causes, at industry level, on the other hand, has better chance of success in promoting a new environmentally friendly production process.

Shared Vision of Environmentalism

The emerging thesis here is that the vision and mission of environmental sustainability in Tanzania has to be widely shared if it is to succeed. Up to a point, regulation through forced closures of polluting industries may work. In the long run, however, it is bound to fail. In his book, *Pedagogy of the Oppressed*, Paulo Freire cautions that a revolution or any other major social or economic transformation is achieved by unshakeable solidarity of leaders and the people. Invariably, this is the most effective route to take in realising a shared mission. In his magisterial new book, *Collapse: How Societies Choose To Fail Or Succeed,* Jared Diamond underscores the importance of a people's mindset in forging a changed view about issues such as environmental sustainability. He points out, for instance, that "businesses have changed when the public came to expect and require different behaviour, to reward businesses for behaviour that the public wanted, and to make things difficult for businesses practising behaviours that the public didn't want. I predict that in the future, just as in the past, changes in public attitudes will be essential for changes in businesses' environmental practices."

Unfortunately, not all leaders have sufficient courage to engage the people on needed bold and radical changes. As a result, they tend to become inflexible and, in the words of Freire, they "treat others as mere objects; instead of nurturing life they kill life." Freire's view is that there is a mechanistic view of reality in the world that if one fails to perceive the concrete situation that conditions the consciousness and the attitudes and the ways which people use to deal with reality, failure to change the false consciousness of reality would result. Thus, it is incumbent upon NEMC to transform the "false consciousness" of Tanzanians and especially industrialists about the reality of environmental fragilities. It is such an approach that is bound to promote positive change. This is also the view advanced in *The Challenge to the South.* It is postulated in that Report, that the realisation of environmental sustainability "requires the concerned involvement of all citizens" in order to create "a broad consensus of the actual or potential hazards threatening the country's environment and what the people themselves can do to reduce them."

In the specific context of the task involved in striking a delicate balance between environmental sustainability and industrialisation and economic growth, the challenge is for NEMC and business associations to constitute a consultative *Business Council For Environmental Sustainability* as an exclusive forum for constant and structured dialogue on policy and strategies related to environmental issues. Some voices of business present clear positions on the environmental question. For example, the CTI addressed the question of environmentally friendly industrialisation in its Industrial Policy Proposal submitted to the Government in May 1994. That Proposal, which later informed the drafting of the *National Sustainable Industrial Development Policy. 1997),* clearly outlined the need for industry to "be environmentally conscious in terms of disposal of wastes and other dangerous chemical substances in order to minimise environmental pollution." The proposal had also called for the adoption of "a positive environment management outlook that will allow for cleaner and safer operating of local industries while at the same time ensuring industrial reliability and maintaining a competitive edge in the internal and external markets." Finally, the CTI Proposal went further and addressed the legal regime required to respond to specific environmental issues at industry level. CTI was particularly concerned that legislations relating to industrial safety, health and the environment had been passive. The legislations included the *Factory Ordinance. Cap297)*, which is 1950 legislation; the *Public Health. Sewerage and Drainage)* law. Cap 336), also a 1950 legislation, and the *Water Utilisation Act 1971.* amended in 1981). These out-dated laws with an environmental link were dysfunctional in the context of modern realities and the physical conditions that existed, for example in relation to dilapidated sewerage and drainage in most urban areas.

- form of environmental regulatory standards needed to direct industrial performance.
- types of voluntary initiatives the business sector could adopt to protect the environment.
- how prices of goods and services could recognise and reflect the environmental cost of production.
- identification of factors that encourage or discourage industries from improving environmental performance.
- industrial processes that promote environmental sustainability.
- types of tax credits the government could offer for investments in energy saving and anti-polluting production processes.
- relevance and form of environment taxes. polluter pays- type of taxes) that could be imposed.
- role of the business sector in protecting and promoting the environment, for example over issues such as exploitation of tropical forests and fishing resources.

Conclusion

It would be foolhardy not to acknowledge that industry can be the predator and the environment the prey. At the same time, it is also clear that for industry to treat the environment as a strategic resource rather than as prey, a delicate balance should be struck between the lofty objectives of harnessing, nurturing and protecting the environment, on the one hand, and the equally important goal of promoting rapid economic growth, on the other hand. Such balance is achievable, not through environmentalism running riot, but rather through a clear headed, rational and objective environmental protection and promotion policy and legislation that produces both economic gains and helps Tanzania to become more competitive. A participatory approach with an in-built mindset transformation process and application of market incentives for arresting environmental pollution is what should characterise such objective and well- balanced framework. Such balance should not be limited to discussing legislation on the environment much as this process is important. Indeed, the business community and other stakeholders have been closely involved in discussing the new environment protection and management law adopted by Parliament early in 2005. My point is that dialogue between government and its organs, especially regulatory agencies, and stakeholders in the polity should be embraced beyond episodic exchanges. It has to be a cultural philosophy.

Chapter

28 THE PRIVATE SECTOR AND A CULTURE OF PEACE

Peace embodies a far more complex reality: it is, by principle, a dynamic process. What we are striving for is `positive peace` which, in the famous words of the philosopher Spinoza, `is born out of fortitude, concord and justice`. The culture of peace therefore presupposes a degree of sharing in order to attenuate imbalances in human development, eradicate poverty and bring to an end the exploitation of human beings, particularly of women and children. We are convinced that the greatest danger that threatens us today is the triple gap that is widening between the countries of the North and those of the South, between the countries of the South themselves and between the very rich and the very poor within a given society.

-Federico Mayor & Jerome Binde: ***The World Ahead: Our Future In The Making.***

Introduction

Tanzania has been hailed as a haven of peace. Indeed, one can venture to say that for several decades since Independence, peace has become a culture within the Tanzanian society. This culture has manifested itself in several forms: national unity, national language, racial and religious tolerance and harmony, de-tribalisation and a collective purpose and resolve to build a nation that respects human dignity, equality and the principles of social and economic justice. From the dawn of independence, the leader of the independence movement, Mwalimu Julius K. Nyerere, was seized of the reality that Tanganyika, and later Tanzania, could only prosper if it was at peace with itself and with its neighbours. At the home front, he knew that unless he worked to ensure national peace, sustainable development could not emerge. On the external front, on the other hand, he linked Tanzania's achievement and sustenance of peace with the existence of peace in other African states, especially those that were still colonised and under minority rule. It was clear to him that Tanzania's peace and stability would be vulnerable because of country's firm and bold stand against colonialism and minority rule. In promoting Pan Africanism, Nyerere was equally mindful of the fact that the inherited colonial borders were not only artificial but also constituted a danger to peace and stability.

As such, he viewed African unity as a bedrock strategy to promote peace, stability and development.

Nyerere's Culture of Peace

Nyerere was cognisant of the challenges Tanzania faced if real peace were to be achieved. His vision for a new nation and society which finds place in his *Presidential Inaugural Address of* December 1962, in his publications *Democracy And The One Party State, Ujamaa: The Basis of African Socialism* and in the *Arusha Declaration* characteristically underscored the importance of pursuing socialism and self reliance under a national governance system controlled by a monolithic political party. In this context, Nyerere effected several measures directed at curbing the emergence of a capitalist class and inequalities in the national social fabric. These measures included:

- nationalisation of the commanding heights of the economy in 1967,

- adoption of the Leadership Code of 1967,

- nationalisation of education in 1969,

- conception and implementation of ujamaa villages and villagisation policies in the late 1960s and early to mid 1970s,

- acquisition of rented properties 1971, the nationalisation of health services in 1972,

- abolition of local government in mid 1972, and

- abolition of Cooperatives in 1976.

It is also significant to note that even when Tanzania was under a dominant state enterprise system, Nyerere was still concerned that the state bourgeoisie could end up pursuing interests that were more personal than national. Thus, in 1970, he introduced a system of Workers' Participation in state-owned enterprises, followed by the adoption of *"Mwongozo wa TANU"*. TANU Ideology Directive) in 1971 which, *inter alia*, clarified managerial responsibility *vis a vis* the rights of workers and admonishing *"unyapala"* and *"ukaripiaji"*. bossy attitudes). Reinforced by the *Security of Employment Act*, 1964 the measures embodied in the system of workers' participation and *Mwongozo* heralded the victory of workers' rights over those of management at the work place. All these policies and measures constituted building blocks for promoting what Nyerere envisioned as the culture of peace for Tanzanians. In turn, presumably wittingly, the measures were building blocks for the virtual destruction of the spirit of private enterprise as well as confidence in the private sector in the national economy.

The culture of peace that Nyerere bequeathed to Tanzanians was a culture of peace based on a great hope, hope for better lives, human respect, human dignity, equality and social justice. It was a hope shared by all and sundry. Socialism and self-reliance sought to translate that hope into tangible outcomes. In many respects, socialism and self-reliance succeeded in promoting a culture of peace. The central question is whether the shift from state capitalism to market capitalism poses dangers to the sustenance of a culture of peace.

The Private Sector and the Legacy of Ujamaa

What challenge does the legacy of *Ujamaa* impose in the society in which the private sector has become the new engine of growth? The private sector under socialism was disparaged and maligned in Tanzanian society. Different types of slogans were used to demonise it. For example, "*Ubepari ni unyama*". capitalism is barbarism); the private sector is an instrument of exploitation. "*unyonyaji*"), and the private sector had very long "*mirija*". siphons) for sucking the blood, sweat and tears of the people. The private sector was not only destabilised following the adoption of the Arusha Declaration, it was reduced to insignificance in terms of its contribution to the national economy by mid 1980s.

The a well-orchestrated anti-private sector culture became ingrained in the minds of the people to such an extent that current economic policies, like privatisation, often face inevitably face feelings of indignation. There are still many Tanzanians who take privatisation to mean the selling off assets they consider their own and thus heralding a return to "*ubepari na unyonyaji*". capitalism and exploitation). Moreover, the private sector that has quickly emerged and grown since the adoption of economic liberalisation policies and measures, is often accused of or associated with massive tax evasion, profiteering motives, corruption of public officials and politicians, selfishness, indifference towards the poor, conspicuous consumption and vanity. In this light, the private sector faces a formidable challenge to win legitimacy, integrity and credibility. These challenges are reinforced by new economic realities that affect the Tanzanian economy and by the expectations in society from a private sector now expected to be the engine of economic growth. The new realities are both global, in the form of the influencing intense and fierce competition within a liberalised trade regime and domestic in the context of various policies and measures being implemented by the Government to restructure and stabilise the economy.

Especially between 1988 and 1995, the impact of these new realities and the measures the government took in reforming the economy, manifested themselves in de-industrialisation as more and more industrialists turned into trading to escape fierce competition that had emerged in the manufacturing sector as goods similar to those produced domestically became imported and at cheaper prices. They also precipitated closure of businesses, layoffs of workers, salary freezes, tax evasion, corruption, drug trafficking and speculative businesses. Less and less social responsibility on the part of the private sector became the norm. At another level, the erosion of the Welfare State in the form of declining state support to education and health services further aggravated the anti-private sector mindset.

All these circumstances undermined the capacity of the private sector's capacity to contribute towards legitimising a culture of peace. However, these new realities as well as the legacy of *ujamaa* itself are challenges of transition. Thus, destabilising as they are, the private sector should strive to address them quickly. How then does the private sector respond to these new challenges?

The Essence of Tanzanian Private Sector

The key challenge to be addressed centres on the legitimacy of the private sector itself. It could be quizzed at the outset whether a private sector exists in the first place. In fact, this discussion about the contribution of the private sector towards establishing a culture of peace could be premature in the sense that such contribution could only be logically nascent if a private sector is only beginning to emerge. This question needs further amplification. The years that saw the dominance of the state enterprise sector also saw the virtual demise of the small private sector that existed before 1967. What remained of the private sector after the adoption of the Arusha Declaration were few and small private trading businesses. It is also notable that the Chambers of Commerce that existed in few townships. they were no more than seven in the whole country) and which chose not to wind up, were very weak. They played no significant role in the economy. Moreover, the members of the chambers were almost wholly of a Tanzania-ethnic minority, in itself a phenomenon of colonial economic history. It is also significant to note that the period since the on set of economic liberalisation has witnessed the decline in the dominance of the state enterprise sector and the emergence of big private enterprises along with the formation TCCIA, CTI, the Chamber of Mines and other business lobby associations for agriculture and tourism.

It is important to distinguish the upsurge in private enterprise activity from the growth of a private sector. Unlike the state enterprise sector that comprised hundreds of parastatal organisations, possessing a collective purpose, mission and strategy in the context of the vision of the Arusha Declaration, the private enterprise sector, on the other hand, lacks an ideological underpinning. Above all, a large question keeps cropping up: who is the private sector in Tanzania? This question, predominantly influenced by racial overtones, has often precipitated the call for indigenisation of the private sector, a reflection of the negative perception that continues to exist that the private sector is dominantly controlled and influenced by an ethnic minority. Thus, the so-called private sector in Tanzania is not a unitary, homogeneous set of economic actors. It remains highly fragmented, lacking in common values and goals necessary to give it an identity and coherence. Parochial corporate interests underlie the behaviour of many enterprises. Membership in associations like the TCCIA and CTI is invariably driven and influenced by failure of individual enterprises to independently secure government support rather than by a broad aim of being part of a lobby association committed to working for and realising a common and shared purpose and mission. This is one of the factors that disempower the private sector from building a credible image of itself in the social milieu and thus militates against the private sector contributing to establishing a culture of peace in Tanzania.

The challenge is to get the fragmented private economic actors, big and small, in industry, services and in agriculture and across the racial and wealth divide, to constitute a coherent private sector in the same form and manner Tanzania had the state sector in its hey days. Enforcing membership in business associations by legislative means in respect of all business licence holders could be a quick solution to achieving such objective. Some continental European countries like Italy, Germany, France and Spain have such compulsory memberships. However, circumstances are clearly different in Tanzania. The European countries have had strong private sector economies for a century. In Italy, for example, the private sector has contributed to national economic growth even in times when no governments were in place. In these countries, companies feel obliged to be members of lobby associations and they honour their obligations. In the case of Tanzania, business associations would certainly benefit from higher financial contributions through a similar compulsory system. Yet, the central issue is not simply financial. It is the participation of the member companies in a business association that makes the difference. Thus if members still choose to be apathetic, as many of them are to day, Tanzania would still lack a coherent and effective private sector. It is for this reason that voluntary membership remains the rational choice. Private enterprise firms and individuals should, by their own volition, come to grips with the imperativeness to build private sector integrity and positive image. If they fail in not constituting a viable and purposeful private sector, they could ignite the sparks of social conflict and instability in the society. The culture of peace would be undermined.

Critical Underpinnings for Private Sector Role

Assuming that Tanzania, in the short term, builds a viable private sector, there is still the fundamental question about what constitutes the enabling environment those catalyses the private sector to contribute towards a culture of peace. Put differently, the private sector operates within a policy and regulatory framework set out by the government. Such framework should be conducive enough to spur the private sector to undertake activities that contribute towards the realisation of peace and stability. Several examples could be cited. Take, as a start, the question of savings and capital accumulation. High rates of savings and capital accumulation lend to high levels of social welfare and employment and thus to peace and stability. However, for high rates of savings and capital accumulation to be realised, fiscal and tax policies that promote a shift from conspicuous and ostentatious consumption as well as from rent seeking and speculative activities are needed. Tanzania's fiscal policies have not promoted a savings and accumulation culture outside the state itself. This environment is now changing. However, there is still need to create incentives in the form of tax breaks to induce people to save. Institutions like the Unit trust of Tanzania and NICO should be empowered by allowing individuals who invest in such institutions to enjoy tax breaks. India has offered such tax breaks with vibrant results.

Another example of a key element of a positive economic policy is a secure welfare system that sustains and develops the labour force. A secure welfare system promotes social peace in the sense that it blunts the gravity of distributive conflicts that are at the root of a private sector economic system. Such peace is characterised by low levels of industrial conflict and strikes. It is evident that strikes constitute a negative source of loss of economic welfare and efficiency in any enterprise. In addition, a secure welfare system promotes better education and health that are key factors for generating a more efficient workforce. Obviously, the government has the primary responsibility for providing such a welfare system. However, welfare policies should equally be at the heart of good corporate industrial relations. In this particular context, a key challenge for the private sector in promoting a culture of peace is to unleash a process that Alvin Toffler (1990) has described in his book, *Powershift: Knowledge, Wealth, and Violence at the Edge of the 21st Century* as the decolonisation of business through "corporate glasnost".

Towards A Culture of Industrial Peace

Toffler argues that industrial instability is often caused by the state of non-financial inequality; to use his words, the *"bwana"* and *"sahib"* mentality. It is important to clarify this process of decolonisation of business. Participation at workplace has hitherto been misconstrued and abused. In fact, in the past, it came to infer, what Rajni Kothari has described as the "process of involving everyone and reducing all to a common denominator." Clearly, instead of promoting industrial peace, this process undermines discipline, authority and productivity.

The form of participation that promotes industrial peace is one that creates institutional structures that allow diverse individuals to secure a sense of dignity and self-respect as human beings able to determine the destiny of the institutions in which they work. A stakeholder approach to the governance of business operations is one avenue towards establishing a culture of peace in work environments. In turn, it is important that the private sector forges a social compact with the trade unions. It can do this by developing a new system of industrial relations governed by a "business unionism." This is a partnership focused on promoting productivity and competitiveness of business rather than being dominantly focused on protecting jobs and higher salaries and benefits, totally unrelated to boosting productivity and overall business profitability.

Social Responsibilities of the Private Sector

Creation of jobs is central to the establishment of a culture of peace in Tanzania because it is a sure step towards realising greater equity. Rajni Kothari has correctly postulated in his article, *Redesigning the Development Strategy* that the "major source of injustice today is to be found not so much in a condition of general scarcity as in the fact of diminishing marginal utility of man as such, in the fact that millions of people find themselves idle and useless, often at their very prime of youth." Most of these millions are in rural areas and the only way that their lives could be transformed is by converting agriculture from an area of stagnation to a catalyst of growth. The private sector has a central role to play both at the level of injecting modern technology and in the provision of capital in the agricultural sector. Such role is not limited to banks and venture capital funds alone. For example, a Tanzanian firm that was owned by a Mr Balyagati successfully intervened in the cotton growing areas of Kilombero and Ifakara between the late 1990s and early 2000 by supplying peasants with fertiliser, herbicides, insecticides and good seeds and got paid in return through an agreed amount of seed cotton during the harvest period. This is evidently a risky business. Nevertheless, those that take calculated risks are the ones that make it in business.

What is important to underlie is the private sector's contribution to injecting a new identity of itself in the minds of the peasants. Legitimacy of the private sector would most likely emerge from such a new mindset. Secondly, by contributing towards an improved quality of life in rural Tanzania, the private sector would usher in a new urban social order that is not threatened by social strife and crime now emanating from an influx of young people flowing in from rural areas to urban areas to seek employment that is not readily available.

Another area that poses a major challenge to the private sector in promoting a culture of peace is education and training. Granted, the Government has the primary responsibility for promoting this sector. However, at the level of narrowing the gap in skills, which underlies the growing gap in income and, therefore, in equity, the private sector has an important role to play. It is disturbing to note that one major area of weakness in private corporate management in Tanzania, especially in regard to family-owned businesses, is inadequate funding for skills training and development. This deficit should be addressed. It undermines industrial performance and, in turn, evokes low morale and industrial conflict. More importantly, the private sector has to be more involved in supporting programmes that target entrepreneurship development.

Many young people qualify from vocational training centres but fail to start up their own businesses though the market exists for their services. This is simply because they lack venture capital. Banks are too risk averse to extend credit to budding entrepreneurs that lack collateral of any kind. Yet, the same young people, out of frustration, end up in organised crime, thereby destabilising the very culture of peace upon which the well established private sector crucially depends upon for profitable performance. The private sector should come up with supporting funds of venture capital-type that can easily be accessed on soft terms by young entrepreneurs. Extending financial support to TASAF could be one way to contribute to such effort.

The question regarding the relationship between business and the environment also has elements that relate to peace in society. The frequent conflicts that arise between pastoralists and peasants in different parts of Tanzania over ownership and use of land are proof about the close relationship between the environment and peace. In this context, in his address when inaugurating the First Sitting of the Third Phase Union Parliament in Dar es Salaam on 30th November 1995, President Mkapa said. my translation from the Kiswahili version): "Environmental issues are highly sensitive because the protection of natural resources and the curbing of misuse of chemicals and effluent discharges from industries are matters which, if not properly managed, can be a source of major conflicts within our society". Clearly, the protection of the environment is a major responsibility for each and everyone and the private sector should delicately balance the needs for economic development and job creation with those of promoting and sustaining a human supporting environment.

At another level, the relationship between the private sector and the scourge of corruption should also be addressed with commitment and vigour because it goes to the root of social stratification and social conflict. At the turn of independence, Mwalimu Nyerere had asserted that corruption and bribery constituted a great enemy to the welfare of people and could undermine the legitimacy of the government. The private sector is the major guilty party in parting with bribes and succumbing to corruption. The war against corruption would only be won if the private sector plays its part in refusing to be led into corrupt transactions. Of course, this is easier said than done. The legal and regulatory framework that governs the operations and decisions of many government agencies still leaves room for discretionary decisions. The *Warioba Commission Report* identified many of these weaknesses. Since 2000, the government has implemented many of the Warioba Commission recommendations. More effective regulatory agencies have been and are being established. The Public Procurement Act, which has been revised early in 2005 to make it more robust and supportive of local bidders for government contracts, has been in place since 2001 and is working, two commercial courts have been started and have already proven their integrity and capacity, and the Prevention of Corruption Bureau. PCB) has been revamped with more resources extended to it. Above all, a specialised ministry in the President's Office has been established to manage the whole process of good governance. With all these positive developments, the private sector should reciprocate by working closely with the government in improving their own and the national governance environments, especially in the direction of curbing corruption.

The Private Sector and Politics

The 1995 and 2000 multi-party general elections were a revelation as to the dangers of private capital influencing electoral choices by the electorate. In the absence of a clear regulatory framework governing private funding of political parties and of candidates, it would not be possible to put a check on what can be a serious subversion of electoral fairness and national governance. Such a situation should not be allowed to take root since it contains the seeds of national division and strife. The private sector, in particular, should take the lead in promoting a non-partisan stance in national and local government elections and must avoid funding any party or individual unless such support falls within the framework of the law. Equally, with the growth of privately owned media, the independence of the private sector in national politics takes an even sharper dimension. The media should strictly adhere to the code of ethics that governs its operations. As the fourth estate, it must act for and on behalf of the people and not be manipulated by political interests, or for that matter, the interests of private business.

Conclusion

A major challenge lies before the private sector, the government and the people of Tanzania in translating into reality the culture of peace based on hope for a better future of everyone. Hope is not timeless. If it is not sustained or crystallised, it wanes and is finally extinguished. The social and economic conditions as they are today pose danger to the sustenance of the culture of peace. Different people may offer different interpretations and reasons for this threat. However, Professor Ahmed Mohiddin probably offers a plausible conjecture in his article, *Tanzania In Transition: From Ujamaa to Ujangili?* He postulates: "The transition from a proven society of persistent poverty to a hopeful one of sustainable affluence may be riddled with serious difficulties. It could, rather, be one from *Ujamaa*, an admittedly poor but peaceful and united society, to *ujangili*, a society of the survival of the fittest, admittedly pregnant with potentials for economic growth but also fraught with insecurity and disharmony". It is in the context of the kind of apprehension Mohiddin presents that the question about economic empowerment has emerged. A culture of peace would be sustained in the Tanzanian society as the market economy entrenches if social and economic justice would also be promoted. In the following chapter, I discuss how Tanzania can effectively manage the transition from state capitalism to a market economy without provoking social tension. This can be realised if the project of economic empowerment of majority Tanzanians is handled pragmatically.

Part Eight

ECONOMIC EMPOWERMENT
OF MAJORITY OF TANZANIANS

In countries with widespread poverty and a market-dominant minority, the dream of upward mobility is largely a non-starter. It is extremely difficult to believe in the possibility of market generated upward mobility if you and everyone around you is mired in intractable poverty and the only wealthy people in the country appear to be members of a different ethnic group. The truth is that among the impoverished indigenous majorities of the developing world, exceedingly few believe that free markets will enable them to go "from rags to riches." For this reason, anti-market backlashes are much more common.

-Amy Chua: ***World On Fire: How Exporting Free Market Democracy Breeds Ethnic Hatred and Global Instability.***

The illusion of compensation for disadvantages too often ignores the reality that those individuals most likely to be compensated are often those with the least disadvantages, even when the groups they come from may suffer misfortunes.
Thomas Sowell: ***Affirmative Action Around the World: An Empirical Study.***

418

Chapter

29 ECONOMIC EMPOWERMENT: REALITIES AND CHALLENGES

When I wrote the Malay Dilemma in the late 60s, I had assumed that all Malays lacked the opportunities to develop and become successful. They lacked opportunities for educating themselves, opportunities to earn enough to go into business, opportunities to train in the required vocation, opportunities to obtain the necessary funding, licences and premises. If these opportunities could be made available to them then they would succeed. Admittedly, a few of them were serious and some succeed. But the majority contributed nothing to the National Economic Programme target ... Why has this happened? The answer lies in the culture of the Malays. They are laid back and prone to take the easy way out. And the easy way out is to sell off whatever they get and ask for more. This is their culture. Working hard, taking risk and being patient is not part of their culture. To succeed the Malays must change their culture ... changing culture is far more difficult than changing the policies of Government. It is easy enough to propose affirmative action but it is not easy to implement it. The recipients must have the right attitude if the results are going to be obtained.

-Dato Seri Dr. Mahathir Mohamad: *The New Malay Dilemma, July 2002.*

The context

During the past decade, a politically driven economic empowerment philosophy has been taking root in Tanzania. Its underlying thrust is the objective to create a structure of wealth creation and wealth ownership that transcends the social, economic and racial divides that had been inherited from the colonial system of governance. In Tanzania and countries such as Malaysia and the ex-apartheid regime such as South Africa, social cohesion, peace and stability and the quest for victory over social prejudices and bigotry of all types, has been crucially predicated on the pursuit of a national development paradigm that cherishes, promotes and sustains social economic empowerment. The philosophy is born out of the stark reality and the realisation that a viable attack on poverty and other social ills that afflict their societies significantly depends on economically empowering the majority of a people.

Different countries, inevitably, have approached the challenge of formulating economic empowerment philosophies and measures differently. Social, cultural, economic and political conditions of each nation have logically determined the distinct form and substance of such philosophies and measures. In Malaysia, for example, an economic empowerment philosophy that was adopted was termed *"positive discrimination"*. It was a policy that was adopted following violent racial riots that took place all over Malaysia, in 1968, organised and executed by the *"indigenous"* Malays. called the Bumiputra) targeting the more economically prosperous minority Malaysians of Chinese ancestry. The core thrust of the Malaysian policy, which was adopted in early 1971 and titled the New Economic Policy, was to create conditions and facilities that would "jump start" the indigenous Malays in the wealth creation and ownership structure of Malaysia. In effect, the policy was directed at transferring 30% of all corporate stock in Malaysia to the Malay population, either individually or to the government acting in the name of the Bumiputeras. As at 1969, Malays owned less than 2% of the country's corporate equity. Malaysian nationals of Chinese descent controlled most of the manufacturing, banking and distribution business outside the state sector.

Mahathir Mohammad was least bothered about few Malay elites becoming beneficiaries of the affirmative action. In his view, "with the existence of the few rich Malays at least the poor can say their fate is not entirely to serve rich non-Malays. From the point of view of racial ego and this ego is still strong, the unseemly existence of Malay tycoons is essential." Stanford Professor, Thomas Sowell, in an excellent book, *Affirmative Action Around the World: An Empirical Study,* has pointed out that it is indigenous Malay business people and virtually all of whom had Mahathir's political party connection who ended up being offered preferences in obtaining licences, credit and government contracts. Closer to Tanzania, in Uganda, the late dictator Idi Amin Dada took a fascist stance in promoting economic empowerment of majority Ugandans. In 1972, Idi Amin literally ethnically cleansed Uganda of the minority Asians almost in the same manner the scriptures write about how the Jews were kicked out of Egypt. However, since the rise to power of President Yoweri Museveni in the early 1980s, Ugandans of Asian origin, few as they are, have returned to Uganda and have been offered the assets they owned before their expulsion.

In post-apartheid South Africa, on the other hand, economic empowerment has taken the form of a constitutionally legislated affirmative action policy. Its rationale appears simple and logical. A minority white population had dominated South Africa, an African country, politically and economically, since the adoption of the 1913 Native Lands Act and the Group Areas Act. Such economic domination was not achieved out of special or distinctive economic might and greater economic insight and entrepreneurship on the part of the whites. On the contrary, it was fostered by a most repressive system of racial discrimination. In a new constitutional regime of equal rights and opportunities to all, such economic domination by a minority white population could not be allowed to continue. Neither could it remain viable and sustainable. Therefore, black economic empowerment as a deliberate policy to mainstream the majority *African* South Africans in wealth creation and ownership constitutes a logical prerequisite for fostering national reconciliation, balanced development, social justice and stability. The challenge confronting South Africa is how to ensure that companies controlled by whites are opened to broad ownership across the racial divide. The Black Economic Empowerment law establishes the means and the process for enabling the empowerment to be realised. It is also important to underscore that black economic empowerment in South Africa largely involves the creation of structures and conditions that would empower the blacks to enjoy equal opportunities over wider access to education and training, especially business entrepreneurship training, access to credit, better shelter conditions, health facilities, power and potable water supply.

A close examination of the Malaysian and South African experiences shows an important distinction between the Malaysian system of positive discrimination in favour of the indigenous Malays and the South African policy of affirmative action. The former system was not driven by the need to address an apartheid-type system of discrimination. The South African system, on the other hand, has been, through and through, driven by the policy imperativeness to reform an economic system that favoured one racial segment within the society against all others, not simply in business but in the broader socio-economic and political system. However, in recent times, black economic empowerment in South Africa has increasingly become unpopular amongst the poor blacks. The reason, as in Malaysia, is that the system has come to be viewed to favour a few elites who have had close connections with the ruling African National Congress Party. This development does not augur well for the policy. Structural changes should be introduced to ensure that the policy benefits the majority of the black people.

In the Malaysian context, Mahathir Mohammad also came to realise that that there existed other key social and economic attributes that had to be formed, created and inspired if the indigenous population were to be better able to seize and exploit economic opportunities. Mahathir was cognisant of the reality that exploitation of economic opportunities largely depended on the existence of an entrepreneurial mindset. A key focus of economic empowerment was thus the extension of accessibility to quality education for the indigenous Malays.

In Tanzania, to the common person, economic empowerment has come to portray *"Uzawa"* or indigenisation. What this concept means, what it entails and the parameters of its intentions, remains a matter of debate in Tanzania. However, when it first featured in the public domain, in 1992, the late Mwalimu Julius Nyerere, Tanzania's Founder President, quickly dismissed it as *"reverse apartheid."* At that time, Nyerere cautioned about the dangers of identifying social and economic problems and the wealth disparities confronting Tanzanians and how they could be redressed through racial distinction. His view was that such a race-driven distinction could ultimately extend to tribal and religious distinctions and that Tanzania's unity and peace could be undermined.

This chapter examines the concept of economic empowerment and some of the key stirrings surrounding the idea of indigenisation as a strategy of economic empowerment. Tentative ideas on the way forward are proposed on how Tanzania, as a government and as a civil society, may proceed in objectively addressing the challenges of economically empowering the majority of Tanzanians.

Sources of the Indigenisation Question

The question about economic empowerment of the general populace in order to achieve social and economic justice has once again been in play in Tanzania. The ruling party, the CCM, committed itself in its Party Document, *"The Orientation of CCM Policies in the Years 2000-2010"* to develop strategies for the economic empowerment of the people. In fact, the policy was encapsulated in the Party's Manifesto for the 2000 General Elections. Its revival came in the wake of the promotion of the black economic empowerment programme in South Africa that culminated in the introduction in the South African Constitution of *"Affirmative Action."* The revival could also be viewed against the backdrop of more recent ethnic tensions in some of the South East Asian polities, notably Indonesia, where political turmoil also resulted in ethnic turmoil.

I use the term *revival* deliberately. Back in 1994, Tanzania witnessed the initial stirrings of racial tension, interestingly sparked by an alleged death threat, apparently made by a Tanzanian of Asian decent, on a leading Tanzanian businessperson of African origin. Those were the early days when the *"TV Station Ownership Wars"* were entering the centre-stage of business competition as economic liberalisation took root. Like a spark in the dry bush, the fire of racial passion spread so fast that Mwalimu Julius Nyerere had to intervene with a remark that left many people wondering whether they were right or wrong in espousing economic empowerment of African Tanzanians.

Until Nyerere's emotional intervention, urban Tanzanians were generally caught in frenzy about the need for economic empowerment to redress what they saw as a racial imbalance that existed in the wealth creation process as well as in the wealth ownership structure. There was a vociferous call and demand that the Government enables and forges the indigenisation of the economy. *"Seek thee thy political kingdom first"* dictum of Kwame Nkrumah was, in the current environment, dismissed as a fallacy and a gross mistake that the African leadership had committed over the years. Mwalimu Nyerere, in particular, was blamed for having shut off the doors, especially for the educated African Tanzanians, from doing business.

Unfortunately, many Tanzanians critical of Nyerere's "cruel" intervention in 1994 against *"uzawa"* failed to realise that Nyerere was not, in principle, against economic empowerment of majority Tanzanians. What had actually made him intervene with such strong condemnatory words was his genuine fear that the goal of economic empowerment was taking a racial rather than an economic route. Moreover, it is not as if Nyerere did not appreciate the underlying nature of the problem or the quest. On the contrary, he did. In a December 1959 article to the *US Africa Special Report* titled, *The Race Problem Demands Economic Action*, he had observed: "in plural societies of Africa, the economic divisions between rich and poor coincide almost exactly with the divisions between the races. Wherever extreme poverty exists beside a visibly high standard of living, there is the risk of bitterness; when the problem is linked to racial differences, it is far more potentially dangerous than in mono-racial societies. At present, the African can see that his quarrel is not with the non-African in his midst, but with the colonial system itself ... But, when Independence comes, we must tackle this economic complication quickly. If we cannot close the gap rapidly enough, so that the differences in economic status become less glaring and, above all freed from their former link with the racial divisions, there is a possibility that the potential danger might become a reality and the economic problem brings us back to the very 'race' problem which we claim to have solved."

At that stage, pre-independence, Nyerere saw the problem of the wealth divide on racial lines not as critical. It was then driven by a colonial system. However, in his *reply* to the Proposals for Responsible Self-Government in the Legislative Council in the same year, namely 1959, he was also quick to point out that one of the difficulties facing the emerging independent nation was "the distribution of wealth". He went on to posit: "the division of any society into the "haves and have nots", is sir, dynamite. Here it is aggravated by its identification with the racial division also. The 'haves' here are generally the immigrant minorities; the "have-nots" are the indigenous majorities. This, sir, is dangerous. This puts a stumbling block in our way. We must remedy this one, and we must remedy this as quickly as is humanly possible".

It was much later in his Presidential Inaugural Address in December 1962 that Nyerere more perceptively cautioned that the wealth divide on racial lines had "no short-cut solution." At the back of his mind, Nyerere already knew that the Arusha Declaration was going to provide a broader political framework within the context of a functioning democracy to correct the wealth imbalances. Indeed, in the Introduction to his book *Freedom and Socialism*, he had argued: "a political democracy which exists in a society of gross inequalities, or of social inequality, is at best imperfect, and at worst a hollow sham." However, it is important to underscore the fact that whilst Nyerere was seized of the challenge of the wealth divide on racial lines, his concern was much broader or deeper. His concern was more fundamentally with private wealth, whether it was in the hands of "whites" or "blacks". In this context, in a speech to the Afro-Asian Solidarity Conference in Moshi early in 1963, he categorically stated: "the moment wealth is divorced from its purpose, which is the banishment of poverty, there develops a ruthless competition between individuals; each person tries to get more wealth simply so that he will have more power, and more prestige, than his fellows. Wealth becomes an instrument of domination, a means of humiliating other people. The very basis of socialism is the rejection of this use of wealth."

Nyerere's aspiration was primarily to achieve "economic empowerment" of the majority of Tanzanians by creating a society of egalitarianism; a society where wealth would not be under the control of a few, whether blacks or whites. This is the context of the Arusha Declaration. The aim of the declaration was precisely to create economic structures that would enable such objective to be realised. Nyerere was particularly concerned about the potential emergence of an African capitalist class. To him, therein lay the seed bed of political power that could undermine the very goal of the struggle for political liberation from colonialism and imperialism. A broad public ownership system was thus the appropriate economic policy response to both the problem of wealth divide based on racial lines and the wealth inequality generally. Nyerere knew that he would not be undermining a particular race as against another through the policy of public ownership. Rather, the policy of socialism would build a viable system of social and political justice devoid of gross inequalities and social inequities.

Of course, Nyerere may not have used his socialist policy to expropriate the small businesses that were largely owned by Tanzanians of Asian origin. Indeed, he is often accused of not have gone the whole hog way in removing all the bases of inequality by not having nationalised all private business assets. In fact, those who champion the cause of indigenisation largely locate their case on this apparent policy deficiency and deficit. They postulate that whilst through the Arusha Declaration's Leadership Code, many educated, and thus, ostensibly, entrepreneurial, Tanzanians holding political and government positions were barred from ownership of private economic or business activities, Tanzanians of Asian origin were, wittingly or otherwise, left alone to create the base for their present economic dominance and prosperity.

This criticism against Nyerere with respect to the skewed character of the leadership Code is misplaced. In fact, the criticism misses the fundamental point, namely, that Nyerere had wanted the Tanzanian majority to hold political power and translate it into economic power; power not of the few or of the individual, but of the many. It is also my view that Tanzanians too easily forget that when it came to the decision to nationalise rented properties in 1971, Nyerere's axe fell on all property owners irrespective of their race. Even the *"operation maduka"*. socialisation of ownership of retail businesses) programme that was effected in 1973 did not discriminate Tanzanians on the basis of race. Put in perspective, had the "Operation Maduka" succeeded, it probably would have extended public ownership to the non-commanding heights of the economy; not by way of state ownership, but by way of ownership through the people's consumer co-operatives.

In contrast, it was difficult for Nyerere to fathom how the wealth divide along racial lines could be bridged by a policy other than wholesale public ownership that would not, otherwise, have been viewed as racially discriminatory! This could be the key reason why Nyerere probably out rightly rejected the concept of indigenisation. Evidently, Nyerere was and any well reasoning Tanzanian would be well aware of such fact, that the wealth divide as it exists in Tanzania today no longer coincides exclusively with the division *between* the races. The present divide also coincides with the division *within* distinct races and tribes and even religions. For this reason, Nyerere correctly cautioned, in my view, that the clamour for indigenisation could very well extend to attacking the more entrepreneurial "indigenous" Tanzanians such as *"Wapemba"* and *"Wachagga"*. Wapemba are from Pemba Island in Zanzibar and Wachagga are a tribe from the Kilimanjaro region in Mainland Tanzania). Subsequently, Nyerere further feared that the attack could extend to targeting wealth ownership along religious lines which would be a dangerous development for peace and stability.

Tanzania needs to face new realities. Racially driven sentiments, subtle and subdued as they may presently appear, are unfortunately taking shape in the Tanzanian society. Yes, the wealth or economic problem now faced is no longer the same as the one that Mwalimu Nyerere perceived in 1959 or which those who espouse "*Uzawa*" now drum up. Indeed, the economic problem in place is dominantly centred on the conventional divide; namely that of the rich versus the poor. This, in our opinion, is the problem that Tanzanians should assiduously recognise and address in the best way they can. David Landes, in his powerful book, *The Wealth and Poverty of Nations* refers to this problem as the big challenge of the third millennium. He describes it as the threat of the gap "in wealth and health that separates the rich and poor." In the context of the rich North, Landes argues that the central task for them centres on helping the poor to become healthier and wealthier. In his view, if the North fails to respond, the poor "will seek to take what they cannot make; and if they cannot earn by exporting commodities, they will export people".

The central problem that poor countries like Tanzania face is simply the crisis of the wealth divide. As Landes puts it, "wealth is an irresistible magnet". It thus inevitably attracts the poor, with the result that the rich now barricade themselves, turning their homes into virtual prisons! Indigenisation is not and cannot surely be the panacea for bridging such a wealth divide. The divide is beyond the *racial* divide. At best, again to borrow a phrase from David Landes, indigenisation could be described as an "ideological fantasy." The indigenisation issue is overly affected by what is called the Pygmalion effect. In other words, the power of perception over reality. Tanzanians should seek effective prescriptions that address *the reality* of the poverty that afflicts the majority of Tanzanians instead of being simplistic by espousing "*uzawa*".

The key question that keeps on popping up is what can practically be done? How can the wealth divide be addressed? Is affirmative action possible and how? Importantly, is this question still a racial one or is the more important question now centred on how to get the majority of Tanzanians to be mainstreamed in the wealth-creation process? How can they be made to feel that they are deliberately assisted and empowered to create wealth for themselves? What form of policy environment, as opposed to being offered special favours, subsidies and preferences, would be considered conducive?

Putting Indigenisation into Objective Perspective

It is equally simplistic and probably insensitive to try to reduce the clamour for indigenisation to poverty of aspiration, a clogged imagination, and a millennium dream. Indeed, the Report of the Commission on Global Governance titled *Our Global Neighbourhood* posits, "Empowerment depends on people's ability to provide for themselves, for poverty translates into a lack of options for the individual." This conclusion may not altogether be realistic, particularly in the context of poor countries such as Tanzania. Thus, I would go along with the view advanced by the respected British management guru, Charles Handy. In his book, *The Hungry Spirit: Beyond Capitalism - A Quest for Purpose In the Modern World*, Professor Handy tosses the view that "markets give wings to ideas" and proceeds to take a pragmatic stance that "there are huge structural impediments to individual wealth creation. Many don't have the know-how, or the initiative or the will. Somehow they must be helped to acquire these things, if the idea of personal sovereignty is not going to seem like some sort of obscene joke perpetrated on a permanent underclass".

Here lies the challenge, how to identify the impediments to individual wealth creation by individuals and removing them. The response process has to be inclusive. It could not segregate Tanzanians based on race. The next question is whose responsibility is it to dislodge the structural impediments? Is it the state, the individual or both? If both, what is the balance of responsibility? In addition, how would the task be undertaken? The starting point in searching for the correct path in empowering Tanzanians economically is to recognise, in the first place, that the idea of economic empowerment has emerged within the context of the ideological shift from socialism to capitalism. Hitherto, under socialism, economic empowerment, a concept largely capitalism-driven, had no room. The main reason is that the vehicle for realising a balanced, self-reliant development and social justice excluded capitalism. Economic empowerment was state-led; not individual-led. However, having embraced capitalism, howsoever it may be interpreted, Tanzanians may wish to define economic empowerment differently to suit their particular political platforms and constituencies.

It is clear why economic empowerment should come face to face with the objective realities and conditions of the market system. One such reality is that static economic policies have largely been dismantled. New market-driven economic policies that support economic empowerment of individual entrepreneurs have come on stream. However, as it has often been restated, it is never easy to emerge from the entrepreneurial breeding ground at the lower end of the economy. Indigenisation, in itself, could not be the effective driving force in such circumstances. Indeed, we learn from Paul Kennedy's outstanding book *African Capitalism: The Struggle For Ascendancy*, that "the one significant resource available to. African) entrepreneurs is their personal drive to succeed at all costs and the necessity to hang on to what they have already gained." This statement reminds us of and captures how Reginald Mengi of the IPP Group in Tanzania rose from a most basic start, making ballpoint pens in rudimentary fashion with his family in their home, to his present pre-eminent economic position of a media mogul.

There is another reality from the market. It is only by constantly directing new resources into production that investment can be empowered to grow. Yet, it is on record that many entrepreneurs of African origin are culturally predisposed to conspicuous consumption. In 1992, Professor Ali Mazrui presented a paper at a conference in Arusha, Tanzania titled, *The Liberal Revival, Privatisation and The Market in Africa's Cultural Contradictions*. In that paper, Mazrui argued that there existed in Africa's economic behaviour an all-pervasive constraint, that of the prestige motive. Whilst hailing the prestige motive behaviour for what he describes as "competitive philanthropy", citing examples of popular participation programmes such as Kenya's *"Harambee"*. meaning let us pull together) Mazrui castigated the ostentatious consumption and "self-indulgent exhibitionism" that characterise African capitalism. His conclusion would almost certainly provoke anger from the champions of *"Uzawa"*. He states: "When Westerners call upon African countries to privatise, they are expecting the profit motive to be given a free play. However, in fact, the problem in most Africa is not simply how to liberate and activate the profit motive, but also how to control and restrain the prestige motive. Arguably, the latter crusade is more urgent than the former in impoverished African countries."

Two important conclusions can be drawn from the postulations of Kennedy and Mazrui. The first one centres on the importance of entrepreneurship. Indigenisation or any programme of economic empowerment is empty without entrepreneurship. Indeed, where there is strong entrepreneurship, the clamour for indigenisation may be illogical. Indigenisation seeks a short cut to wealth creation. This could not work because entrepreneurship that creates value is non-existent. This entrepreneurship is defined as the pulling together of a unique package of resources that exploit available opportunities. Indigenisation, in itself, does not do that. Were resources extended to an indigenous person who is not entrepreneurial the result would invariably be failure. Mr. Mengi started with meagre resources on his own. He has succeeded largely because he has been entrepreneurial and not because he has been economically empowered by the state as an indigenous Tanzanian.

The challenge for economic empowerment then is not indigenisation. Rather, it is the building of entrepreneurship among the majority Tanzanians. The government should assist in this endeavour. Universities and Institutes of higher learning, including vocational education institutions should also play a role. Above all, wealthy Tanzanians of Asian and other racial origins and including foreign investors in Tanzania, should take this case as a worthy challenge and cause. They should fund entrepreneurship training. They should also deliberately involve Tanzanians of African origin in their businesses- at sensitive decision-making levels to enable them acquire entrepreneurship from experience.

The second lesson relates to Professor Mazrui's implicit apprehension about associating privatisation with indigenisation. His view is that people make it in business and economic life because they invest; they search for financial opportunities and they take risks. Privatisation that is driven mainly by an indigenisation policy can prove to be a recipe for economic disaster. For those who know what actually sparked indigenisation sentiments in the first place, they would recall that it was the government decision in the early 1990s to sell off state-owned enterprises to foreigners and Tanzanians with adequate resources. in other words, those who came to be mainly of Asian origin) that was the principal precipitating cause. Ali Mazrui has a valid caution against such sentiments. He is not the only critic in this sphere. His perception is shared by Paul Kennedy who ascribes the African conspicuous consumption to include house purchases, luxury imports "and building up a network of personal dependants including 'investment' in children through contracting several marriages". Africans generally may find these views wild and even insulting. But they are supported by research findings. The prestige motive is a prime enemy of successful business enterprise.

There is also another perspective to the privatisation question. What is deemed invariably as an inequitable system of privatisation is somehow never discussed in the context of the inequity that would also arise were the so-called "indigenous" Tanzanians to be offered preferential treatment in the privatisation process. Should the indigenisation policy be premised on economic empowerment of the many or should it be premised on the economic empowerment of the few? Is the wealth divide within the community of Tanzanian Africans more acceptable than that which exists between them with Tanzanians of Asian origin? From experience, those "indigenous" Tanzanians who have succeeded to buy privatised assets have done so as individuals and as close families. They are in no way different from foreigners and Tanzanians of Asian origin as far as the goal of bridging the wealth divide between the rich and the poor is concerned. Precisely for this reason, the philosophy of indigenisation misses the point. It is not *race* that is at issue; rather it is the wealth divide between rich and poor. Mwalimu Nyerere correctly argued in the Introduction to his book, *Freedom and Socialism,* that exploitation is not wrong only "when carried out upon the masses by people of a different race." Earlier, in his speech when inaugurating the University of East Africa in June 1963, Nyerere quizzed, relevantly in this specific context: "When does corrective action itself become discriminatory?"

Popular Capitalism and Empowerment

On this point about the irrelevance of *"uzawa,"* Mwalimu Nyerere had also challenged the doctrine of *"popular capitalism"* which Margaret Thatcher had championed to embody the ascendancy of a people's capitalism. What underlined popular capitalism was the sale of shares, in whole or in part, of state assets being privatised to individuals; ostensibly, *the whole people*. In Britain, the shares were bought either directly by individuals or by social security organisations. the likes of Tanzania's PPF and NSSF) and mutual funds, in trust for their members. However, Nyerere was not impressed by the logic of economic empowerment based on such forms of privatisation of assets, where a whole people are assumed to be owners. In his view, popular capitalism was and is for the few, those with the means. The majority of the people, on the other hand, remain economically marginalised. After all, less than 6% of the population constitute wage employees in Tanzania and total membership in the NSSF and PPF could even be lower than 5% of the national adult population.

In raising the relationship between privatisation and the ideology of popular capitalism, Nyerere sought to underline the point that the people should not be hoodwinked by modern economic slogans and measures that only seek to justify a new form of exploitation in the name of economic empowerment. For if economic empowerment or, even going by the concept that Nyerere admonished, namely "indigenisation," meant bridging the wealth divide in society, then popular capitalism could surely not be *"popular"* as it fails the basic test of being inclusive in its affordability and access. In fact, in Nyerere's view, which is convincing, popular capitalism tends to polarise society even deeper by widening the wealth divide within the *very* national majority ethnic entity that believes that the *"wrong"* wealth divide is that which is inter-racial and not intra-racial.

It is also important to raise the question about project finance. One of the central planks behind the clamour for indigenisation is the ostensible difficulty encountered by indigenous Tanzanians in not being able, in contrast to the national racial minority, to access risk and working capital. However, this problem is not a racial one. Indeed, during the whole period of public ownership, Tanzanians of Asian origin had been starved of credit by the state-owned banking system. On average, between 1968 and 1990, the period that saw a huge growth in business activities by Tanzanians of Asian origin, slightly over 90% of term lending and working capital went to public enterprises and the co-operatives. The wealth divide, along racial lines, would clearly have been wider had this not happened. This is piece of factual data that the arch promoters of the *"uzawa"* idea fail to point out. After all, access to capital today knows no colour. It only knows entrepreneurship, project viability and good management.

Evidently, Tanzanians of Asian origin are at an advantage because they have been in business for a much longer time than Tanzanians of African and other origins. They have also acquired adequate collateral. However, banks and financial institutions would not discriminate against Tanzanians of African origin simply because they were budding entrepreneurs. Moreover, to most good banks, collateral is traditionally secondary. Banks hate mortgage foreclosures because the legal process involved is long, costs money and, invariably, banks do not realise the full value of the money loaned. Thus, to most banks, a project has to be viable based on performance, not on collateral. One of the crucial underpinnings of economic empowerment is thus a clearer understanding about how banks and lending institutions operate. Business education for economic empowerment is of vital importance. It would be foolhardy to think that the on-going restructuring of the Tanzania Investment Bank into a proper development financial institution and the government move to establish an Agricultural Development Bank, as announced in the 2004/2005 Budget Speech, would, by themselves, create "softer" conditions for "indigenous" Tanzanians to access capital. Even the credit guarantee schemes that have been established by the government since 2002 and managed by the Central Bank to support small and medium enterprises, ostensibly owned largely by "indigenous" Tanzanians, have to be prudently supervised. Mwalimu Nyerere once said, in the early 1980s, "Even a socialist bank is a bank" and has to operate commercially!

Extension of Opportunities

The key thrust of the concept of economic empowerment is the extension of greater economic opportunities to all Tanzanians. In this context, it is correct to state, as the *British Commission for Social Justice* noted in its first Report in 1993, "we cannot help but regard a commitment to the extension of opportunities as a radical doctrine, and one that lies at the heart of social justice." At the same time, it is pertinent to determine, on the one hand, the form and nature of opportunities that are available and, on the other hand, how those opportunities can constitute a viable and effective means of economic empowerment. This is where the crux of the debate about economic empowerment should centre. Clearly, as I have alluded to earlier, in a market economy where the government is committed, and rightly so, to economic prudence, there could not be easy money available to the so-called indigenous people for investment and for doing business. The days of subsidies, of decisions based on administrative fiat and on what India used to call the *"licence raj"*, are gone. This is the reality. Tanzania is in a market economy environment. Self empowerment through institutions such as NICO is the right approach to take.

Structural Impediments to Empowerment

Reverting to the question raised earlier about the structural impediments to individual wealth creation, Tanzania should confidently start by establishing the key opportunities that have to be made available and exploited by majority Tanzanians. On this point, it is important to discard the conventional thinking that many Tanzanians still hold, namely that wealth is created primarily through what, in economics, is described as "factors of production"- land, labour and capital. Of course, the importance of such traditional factors or natural resource base of a developing country such as Tanzania cannot be discounted. What can be discounted, however, is the fact that Tanzania has had these factors, particularly land and labour, for over forty years since independence to little avail in terms of appreciable development. Indeed, part of the rationale for taking the public ownership route in 1967 was precisely because the private sector capital base was infant and inadequate and that, in order to mobilise resources more effectively, state entrepreneurship had to take command. Even then, the results, in so far as releasing a promising level of development, have not yet liberated Tanzania from the scourges of poverty, disease and illiteracy.

Recent experience of economic performance around the world shows, on the contrary, that land, labour and capital are not the key drivers of development. In the *World Development Report of the World Bank, 1999/2000* titled *Entering the 21st Century*, it is noted therein, "investment in human capital, including health and education, might become more urgent than investment in physical capital". In other words, knowledge is the more fundamental resource for development. Mwalimu Julius Nyerere was also aptly seized of this reality. In his brilliant Address on the 25th anniversary of the University of Dar es Salaam in July 1995, titled, *The Link Between The Economy, The Society And the University*, he observed as follows: "The most superficial study of comparative development over recent decades makes unavoidable the conclusion that, in the 21st century, knowledge will be of very much greater importance in determining the standard of living in a nation than will be its wealth in natural resources or its monetary capital".

Education and Health are Primary

This is not to say, however, that other resources are not as important as drivers in the specific economic environment of Tanzania. On the contrary, what is underscored is that focused intelligence which Charles Handy has defined in his book, *The Empty Raincoat: Making Sense of the Future,* as "the ability to acquire and apply knowledge and know how" constitutes the new and more vital source of wealth. Professor Handy further posits, "Where brains prevail, security lies not in the physical property but in the intelligence quotient." In his view, social justice and fairness in society is derived from everybody being offered the opportunity to acquire intelligence.

It thus follows that the realisation of social justice is principally predicated on investment in intelligence; in other words, the education of all people throughout their lives. In this context, Handy gives a telling example that characterises the problem that confronts those who preach the language of indigenisation. He postulates that many people in developing countries prefer to spend their money on buying or constructing houses rather than investing in intelligence creation. Citing an example, he points out that in poor Bangladesh 90% of houses are owner-occupied. In Switzerland, in contrast, only 33% are owner-occupied. Of course, this data may not be as convincing because of the massive differential in quality and cost of the houses. However, the message is clear. Poor countries tend to invest in assets that do not produce significant wealth. Tanzanians should clearly appreciate the relevance of this example. Some of the leaders of the indigenisation movement are indeed the very people who own expensive villas and flats in Dar es Salaam, Moshi, Arusha and Mwanza. They are the ones who drive expensive *"Shangingis"*. the 4 x 4 luxury vehicles). Some of them probably have huge foreign currency accounts stashed away abroad, probably lying virtually idle, apart from earning meagre interest.

Professor Handy is right. One of the big structural impediments to the economic empowerment of the majority Tanzanians is the state of the mindset; the mental bloc in appreciating what critically underpins wealth creation. What underpins it instead is education; and it is health as well. As Paul Streeten has asserted, "a healthy, alert, vigorous, well nourished, well educated population is a source of production and productivity." In an article, *Social Development in Africa: A Focus on People*, Professor Streeten points out that "Africa's largest under-utilised resources are its people. It is on them for them by them that a successful strategy for Africa's renewal has to be built". The government should play a bigger role than presently in promoting a better system of education and delivering better health services. So should all Tanzanians, especially those who mis-invest or under-invest their own personal wealth.

Economic empowerment should also focus on breaking the cycle of the culture of poverty whose roots are located in the cultural milieu, presently driven largely by ignorance and gender inequality. Literacy and universal minimum quality education are the preconditions for a cultural attack against this dysfunctional culture. More importantly, it is imperative to give special attention to the education of the girl child and women. *The*

Challenge To The South, correctly captured this goal when it observed, "a nation cannot genuinely develop so long as half of its population. notably women) is marginalized and suffers discrimination." In addressing the economic empowerment of women, it is also important to reform the laws that are vital in integrating women in the mainstream of the economy. Ensuring women rights to social justice and equity are central to such legal reform. As Nobel Laureate for Economics, Amartya Sen has written in his book *Development As Freedom,* "development consists of the removal of various types of unfreedoms that leave people with little choice and little opportunity of exercising their reasoned agency."

Youth and Agriculture

It is also important to recognise that young people make up the vast majority of the population. They constitute a major dynamic force that needs to be harnessed and empowered for development. The exodus of the youth from rural areas, witnessed in recent years, is not a simple whimsical rejection of rural life on their part. There are strong appeals of modernism that attract them to urban life. However, the problematique of rural-urban migration has to be objectively located on other more fundamental premises. One such premise is the reality that the economy is increasingly becoming more consumerist than production oriented. Economic reform policy and process have focused more at the macro level, with notable success. Unfortunately, they have not yet forged critical micro transformations in the structures of production, especially in the agricultural sector. The result is that the so-called *"machingas"* are not only unproductive, they are also alienated from the very social production structure that constitutes the pillar of economic empowerment and economic liberation, namely agriculture.

With 75% of the Tanzanian population employed in the rural sector of the economy, the focus of economic empowerment should seriously centre at the rural level. Such thrust of empowerment thrust should be driven by human capital formation especially that of the girl child and women, a social group that presently bears a disproportionate share of poverty. Empowerment focused on better education and health delivery is also central to transforming the agricultural sector from the present poor state to one of being a catalyst of higher national economic growth. Equally, an urgent change in attitudes should generally emerge, attitudes such as the role of women in society. The present technological, economic, social. particularly reproductive behaviour) and institutional constraints that impede increased food production and agricultural labour productivity are driven more by a state of poor education, nutrition and health, particularly of women, than by voluntary poverty that has socially been accepted as a living evil.

There is often a tendency to criticise government policies and programmes, particularly in the social sector. The challenge is to be fair and objective. In the context of revolutionising rural development, the villagisation programme that has been maligned, probably not too fairly, was actually intended to be an economic empowerment strategy for the rural sector of the economy. Its implementation was evidently disastrous. However, its policy thrust was correct and focused. It never was and it never will be viable to transform the lives of the rural population in a poor country without transforming the structure of rural settlement. I am therefore in total agreement with Mwalimu Nyerere that the critical underpinning of economic empowerment, namely the cost-effective delivery of quality education, health, water supply and other social services, agricultural extension and the introduction of agricultural seed and technology innovations, has been and continues to be undermined by the existing skewed structure of rural settlement. A radical strategy of economic empowerment necessitates the revival of a villagisation strategy, necessarily based on popular participation as opposed to the coercion and force used earlier, as well as on a massive mindset transformation of Tanzanians about entrepreneurship across the board.

Job Creation

Generating sustainable employment for the ever-increasing unemployed and under-employed labour force is a fundamental driver of economic empowerment. However, the creation of jobs comes out of good economic policies that stimulate investments and economic growth. The government has a key role to play in economic empowerment of majority Tanzanians by creating the enabling conditions that stimulate job-creating activities. It is for this reason that the government should now give greater attention to improving the micro-economic conditions of the economy; reducing the costs of doing business through lowering power tariffs and business transaction costs, like payroll taxes, and catalysing agricultural production through the extension of support in the areas of agricultural research, extension services and rural infrastructure.

State Intervention in Promoting Empowerment

Sometime in April 1999, the Ministry of Industries and Trade issued a statement, through the Information Services Directorate, setting out what appeared to be a new policy framework that would regulate business ownership in Tanzania. The statement listed twenty four types of businesses, dubbed category A, which would come under exclusive ownership of Tanzanian nationals and thirteen types of businesses, dubbed category B, which would require joint ownership between foreigners and Tanzanian nationals, provided that the nationals owned at least 50% of the equity stake. Those decisions were to take effect from 1st May 1999. It is important to note that the policy was subsequently not implemented, though the Shipping Agency Act of 2002 can be summed up as a manifestation of that particular policy.

Many Tanzanians, at that time, appeared to have welcomed the step taken by the government. To them, it ostensibly made both economic and political sense. It would be recalled, that early in 1990, when the Tanzania investment policy was initially being crafted, a policy that was to inform the framework of the legislation that later that year was enacted as the *National Investment. Promotion and Protection) Act,* Mwalimu Nyerere had intervened with a public statement to the effect that the policy was overly foreign-investment driven. Mwalimu Nyerere had asserted that no country could develop by predominantly relying on foreign investment. In his view, self-reliant development could only be realised and sustained if there was a deliberate and massive mobilisation of domestic savings and the building of human capacity. In theory, Mwalimu Nyerere was right. In its publication published in 2002 titled: *Foreign Direct Investment for Development: Maximising Benefits, Minimising Costs,* the OECD, on this point, notes, "FDI-like official development assistance-cannot be the main source for solving poor countries' development problems. With average inward FDI stocks representing around 15% of gross domestic capital formation in developing countries, foreign investment acts as a valuable supplement to domestically provided fixed capital rather than primary source of finance. Countries incapable of raising funds for investment locally are unlikely to be beneficiaries of FDI."

Nyerere's intervention led to the setting out of reserved areas of economic activity which only nationals could be allowed to invest in and areas that could jointly be owned by foreigners and nationals. It is significant to note, however, that neither the 1990 investment legislation nor the new one enacted in 1997 encapsulate legal provisions that translate the 1990 policy on reserved economic activities into law. Actually, some, if not many of the enterprises owned by foreigners that were ostensibly covered under Group A and B, in the policy framework, enjoy the status of "approved enterprises" under the 1990 and the 1997 investment promotion and protection laws. Thus, the decision taken in May 1999 to implement the 1990 investment policy, which had not been given the force of law, was clearly *ultra vires.* The government had attempted to enforce a measure through political fiat with serious consequences to the sanctity of the law and the confidence of investors in the stability of the country's legal regime. In retrospect, the subsequent reversal, in not effecting the decision, was rational. Nevertheless, that decision needs to be examined within the broad context of determining what form of economic empowerment policy framework is appropriate.

In my view, the measure that the government had sought to effect in May 1999 totally missed the point. Those few foreigners that were and are still involved in what are seemingly regarded as "pedestrian-type" of businesses are engaged in them simply because they have realised that Tanzanians themselves have failed to take them up, probably not for lack of wishing, but almost certainly for lack of inventiveness. *If wishes were horses beggars would ride* is the probably the relevant metaphor or analogy to cite for this specific situation. It would be ludicrous to try to argue that the reason why Tanzanians are not involved in owning ostensibly small business activities that were categorised for national ownership is because foreigners crowded or crowd them out or that they stand a small chance to compete. The issue here is not the nature or size of business activity. It is entrepreneurship.

Wishes and Horses

Tanzanians should not trivialise the importance of quality of products and services offered by foreign owned small enterprises be they Chinese restaurants or furniture industries. After all, what are the expectations of discerning Tanzanian consumers tourists, visitors and members of the foreign community working or investing in Tanzania from such products or services? There is a price that any country must pay in terms of the quality of its products and services including from specialised restaurants that cater for Chinese, Mughlai, Thai or Japanese cuisine or from fast food chains like South Africa's "Ocean Basket" or the US's Burger King. When you lock out such type of foreign investment in the name of allowing local ownership, you inevitably isolate yourself from more substantive investments as well as discerning consumers. It is a complex world we live in. It teaches us that public choice is not politically driven.

The rationale and manner of implementation of the government policy was also wrong. It is doubtful that the type of enterprises that had been reserved would, in any case, have increased the employment of Tanzanians simply through the indigenisation of the economy. I can understand the logic of creating jobs for nationals. However, the struggle for jobs should not be as cooks of Chinese food. Nevertheless, Tanzanian ownership, in itself, could not have changed the situation much in terms of improving employment levels. Equally, it is debatable if the attack on poverty had anything to do with such policy. On the contrary, Tanzania's present level of domestic savings, at 14% of GDP, is too low to support a massive programme of "indigenisation" of the economy. In addition, the capacity of the banking and financial institutions to offer risk capital is still low, not to speak of the banks' risk averseness to lend for different reasons later explored in this book. Thus, as a government and as a people, Tanzania should be cautious and realistic about how it approaches the economic empowerment question. It should strike a delicate balance between its objective to attract FDI and promoting policies that may cause potential backlashes thereby damaging the FDI objective. One appreciates that the government decision in 1999 may have represented some form of a political weapon to wage a war in promoting economic empowerment of majority of Tanzanians. However, the position taken reminds us of a story, probably concocted by an Englishman. The story goes that an Englishman and a Frenchman were travelling together. The Frenchman asked the Englishman why the English waged war. The reply was for gold, raw materials, markets and territory. Then the Englishman, in turn, asked the Frenchman what made the French go to war. The reply came: for liberty, equality, fraternity and honour. The Englishman was quiet for a while and then said, "Perhaps, each nation goes to war for what it does not have."

Tanzanians should thus be clear about what economic war they wage for, whatever the circumstances. If not, the country could end up valiantly fighting for equity as a lofty political objective without actually realising economic empowerment in the end or, worse, undermining investor confidence and thereby economic growth. Exposing freewheeling equity to the people may indeed evoke high expectations. However, in the absence of effective and realisable *real* economic empowerment, the rising tide of expectations may instead give rise to a tidal wave of disappointment, disillusionment and even anger. People who are miserable in an environment of stark wealth divide and one that coincides with racial lines can often direct their anger on those who look better off. In his address to *The Third, 2003 National Conference on Science, Policy and the Environment*, Jan Pronk aptly pointed out: "Poverty does not lead straight to violence. Poverty without any perspective whatsoever, plus the experience of exclusion and neglect, the perception to be seen as lesser people with inferior culture, to be treated as dispensable by those who have access to modernity, to the market, to wealth and power, all that together will lead to aversion, resistance, hate, violence and terrorism."

This is the possible danger that could emerge from adopting an ostensibly lofty economic decision that is implemented through a political rather than economic weapon. In sum, it would be a tragedy were the government's new economic empowerment programme to be driven by the politics of the wealth divide and the role of foreign investment rather than by the need to address the underlying causes of the entrepreneurial deficit afflicting many Tanzanians. Such an empowerment programme, catalysed by politics, would merely end up in reinforcing the adage: if wishes were horses, beggars might ride. Tanzanians may indeed end up continuing being beggars! This is the lesson Tanzanians should learn as they effect the new law on Economic Empowerment. It is also a useful lesson for institutions like NICO as they plan on how best to further mobilise people's savings and investing them in shares and new projects.

Conclusion

Tanzania is still a prisoner to survival. Food self-sufficiency and food security remain elusive. The scourges of poverty, ignorance and disease, which the father of our independence movement and Father of the Nation, Mwalimu Nyerere so eloquently challenged all of us to defeat with every bit of our energy and intelligence, are still in place and are proving to be ever more challenging. How a passionate clamour for an economic policy driven by indigenisation overtones in the form in which it presently features in the public domain can address and tackle these national ills baffles wisdom, intellect and reality. The call for the democratisation of the economy and the broadening of participation by Tanzanians of African origin in the wealth creation process is certainly animating. However, building a real stake in the economy amongst the indigenous Tanzanians could surely not be undertaken through political fiat. Moreover, the wealth divide no longer coincides *exclusively* with the racial divide, much as many Tanzanians perceive it differently. David Landes reminds us in his magisterial work, *The Wealth and Poverty of Nations:* "History tells us that the most successful cures for poverty come from within ... what counts is work, thrift, honesty, patience and tenacity. To people haunted by misery and hunger, that may add up to selfish indifference. But at bottom, no empowerment is as effective as self empowerment."

If *"Uzawa"* or indigenisation is a form of economic empowerment, then let it be a strategy of self-empowerment. Tanzanians of African origin should begin by putting their money where their mouths are. This means embracing entrepreneurship and investing in productive, not consumption assets. It means reinforcing government efforts in educating children, especially girls, and improving health services, both through protection and curative measures. Economic empowerment of the majority Tanzanians is possible, not through indigenisation, but rather through a new mindset driven largely by a challenge of self-development.

Chapter

30 FINANCE FOR ECONOMIC EMPOWERMENT

A focal point is needed to engage commercial banks and private investors. Historically, commercial banks have avoided targeting poor people and the vast informal economies they support. The microfinance industry has now achieved sufficient momentum to establish viable partnerships with the banking sector, but it is a direction that remains, for the most part, uncharted.

Centre for Global Studies, Victoria, British Columbia, Canada: *The Need for a Global Microfinance Facility.*

Role of Private Banks

It is evident that considerable progress has been made over the past few years in restructuring and liberalising the domestic banking system. The lofty objective has clearly been to unshackle a hitherto severely repressed financial system. However, much remains to be done in the area of reducing interest rate distortions *vis a vis* the declining rate of inflation and in promoting the growth of the capital market, particularly the broader opening up of the equity capital market. The more notable worrying trend is that the liberalisation of the banking and financial sector is not adequately providing the envisioned sound foundation for the stimulation and growth of the national economy.

This chapter addresses some of the elements embodied in these shortcomings, which have to do, partly, with a conventional monetary policy stance the Bank of Tanzania has pursued in recent years. Suffice it to state that conventional monetary policy that guides the direction of the economies of industrialised nations invariably distances itself from issues such as job creation and consumption stimulation. However, it is noteworthy that faced with shrinking corporate lending and faltering consumption, the Bank of Japan has in recent years shifted from such a conventional monetary policy stance by directly injecting more money into the private sector and funnelling its own loans to companies through commercial banks. According to an article, *Japan's leaky pump*, published in *The Economist* of November 21, 1998, criticism was levelled against the Japanese Central Bank for taking such steps rather than for the *form* of the steps taken in the sense that non-credit worthy companies could equally benefit and thereby undermining corporate adjustment and recovery of banks. In Tanzania, the recent introduction of the export credit guarantee facility by the Bank of Tanzania marks the only occasion when an interventionist stance has been witnessed on the part of the Central bank, in this case to stimulate the economy and bolster exports growth. However, for a considerable period, Bank of Tanzania monetary policy has overly focused on promoting price stability, often to the detriment of having more commercial credit being directed to the productive sector of the economy.

Addressing the financial sector specifically, it is notable that a central characteristic of the investment portfolio of banks and financial institutions in Tanzania has been their focus on liquid assets. The relationship of these assets to total assets is such that the economy is rid of much-needed working and productive investment capital. A July 1998 survey of the leading commercial banks reflected the following picture: Citibank had 81% of its total assets in liquid and risk weighted assets, namely, treasury bills and fixed deposits. The weighted risk of these assets is zero. Standard Chartered and Stanbic banks, on the other hand, had 73% and 65% of their total assets, respectively, in risk-weighted assets. Of the foreign banks then, only the defunct Trust Bank had 55% of its total assets invested in liquid assets and apparently the bank was performing well in spite of its high level lending exposure. The closure and subsequent bankruptcy of that bank appears to have had little to do with its gearing. However, times have changed since 1998 and this is well captured in the following table involving the status of the six largest commercial banks as at end of March 2003:

(In Shs. billion)

Bank-	Customers' Deposits	Loans, advances & Overdrafts	Investment in Bonds
NBC	310	100	130
CRDB	270	39	150
Stanchart	230	110	20
Stanbic	135	74	3
Citibank	160	74	18
Barclays	70	78	12

From this table, it would appear that Standard Chartered Bank was more risk oriented in that a significant part of its deposits base was applied towards lending rather than in investments in more secure treasury bills. 47.8% of total deposits went to lending. However, with a lower deposits base, Stanbic has a ratio of 54.8% of lending to deposits and is thus the high flyer in this overall banking scenario. As a much newer bank, on the other hand, Barclays has performed well on the lending front, evidently using some external resources to boost its operations. In the case of NBC and CRDB, they still have significant part of their assets in a more secure portfolio, namely treasury bills and bonds. Given the overall picture, however, more needs to be done by the banks in order for the economy to be bolstered through allocation of higher volumes of credit.

Role for the Central Bank

In the context of the foregoing scenario, has the monetary policy stance of the Bank of Tanzania not reached the critical mass of having exhausted the mopping up of excess liquidity in the economy necessary for promoting price stability and reducing inflation to a desirable level? In my view, it is because the Bank of Tanzania continues to flog the secondary securities market with rosy returns on treasury bills to finance government expenditure that the credit market is crowded out. How else it could be when the Bank of Tanzania, paradoxically, pursues what is a perplexing policy stance on treasury bills and bonds. The average weighted return on these securities in April 2003 was 5.9%. Though lower than in the past, banks and social security funds have still had dominant recourse to them as safe havens. But why should this be the case when the economy is growing? It could mean that banks are constrained from lending because of structural problems. Thus, it is the responsibility of the Central Bank to advise the government to remove such structural bottlenecks that largely lie in the land law regime and court process in contracts enforcement.

Challenging Banks and Financial Institutions

The structure and size of the financial sector plays a critical role in promoting sustained economic growth in any economic system. I attempt here to review the status of the Tanzanian financial system that underpins economic growth and analyse, at some length, some of the impediments that affect the realisation of a wider and deeper financial system and what can be done to redress or change and improve the situation.

The Current Status

Financial depth or development arising from financial and banking sector liberalisation enhances the allocation efficiency of capital. productivity of capital) by diverting credit to the sectors where returns are highest, or shifting risk to those that are more willing to bear it. This shift increases the savings rate and promotes higher investment rates. Financial sector development is an essential prerequisite for economic growth and its widening and deepening must thus precede mobilisation of resources for realising faster growth. As part of financial reform and unleashing of competition for loanable savings, development financial institutions. Dfis) have shown a preference to operate as universal banks. As a result, the role of these institutions is diminishing and so is lending to the productive sector of the economy. Currently, there is inadequate access by the poor to financial institutions and banks to save and invest. New private, foreign-owned and Tanzanian-owned banks, whilst dominating the domestic market, are overly involved in retail banking and concentrating service provision to the large corporates. Though they have opened up flows of international capital from parent banks, their lending is limited because their marketable assets are largely derived from short-term. 1-2 years duration) deposits. An extract from the *Financial Sector Reform Study, 2001*, shows that almost 85% of total lending of these banks was in short-term instruments. Only 15% of the lending is directed to medium and long-term finance. There is thus what is called "funds mismatch". Small and Medium enterprises. SMEs) are largely outside the "credit market" of these banks because of what they describe as the relatively high fixed transaction costs of lending to small and numerous borrowers.

Microfinance institutions. MFIs) are on the increase in Tanzania. With the establishment of a regulatory and supervisory framework in 2004 following the enactment of the Financial Laws. Miscellaneous Amendments) Act, 2003, and the institution of operational guidelines and standards for Savings and Credit Cooperative Societies. SACCOS) in place in June, 2004, Mfis are bound to increase even more. However, many Mfis suffer from liquidity problems despite the very high loan repayment compliance, on average, in excess of 98%. Mfis need more funds and from a wider pool of providers. Social security and pension funds are loaded with funds, even after huge outlays in real estate development. According to the *Annual Reports of 2002* of two of the four leading pension funds, namely, the National Social Security Fund. NSSF) and the Parastatal Pension Fund. PPF), their 2001 aggregate portfolio size was as follows: total assets: Tanzania Shillings 234 billion of which current assets. i.e. short term investments) amounted to Tanzania Shillings 68.6 billion. This picture has changed dramatically since then. According to the PPF Annual Report for 2004, its accumulated fund was Shs.198 billion as at December, 2004. The accumulated fund of NSSF, on the other hand, was Shs.350.8 billion as at June 2004

However, the portfolio investment management of these Funds is focused on risk free assets such as bonds and securities and short-term buoyant shares in the stock market. Thus, for the fiscal year 2002, the NSSF investment portfolio mix was 30.6% for real estate; 32.4% for government securities, 11.5% for fixed deposits, 4.1% for corporate bonds. exclusively of East African Development Bank), 0.3% for loans. in relation to long term investments) and only 7.5 % for equities. The portfolio picture is quite revealing in terms of non-participation of the NSSF in promoting viable productive economic activities in Tanzania. Recently, there has been some change, a welcome one that should be deepened. In mid 2004, the NSSF allocated Shs 5.0 billion to finance EPZ textile-based projects. Nevertheless, it is my considered view that NSSF is not in the business of lending. This is a professional banking task and is best left to banking professionals. I have argued below that funds of this kind should be lent to development banking institutions like the Tanzania Investment Bank for on-lending purposes. Such strategic alliance in better and more effective utilisation of portfolio funds is the ideal avenue to take.

In the case of the PPF, the picture is equally negative in terms of the Fund's role in promoting economic development via the productive sectors of the economy. Its portfolio mix is as follows: 8% for long term government securities, 52% real estate. which can be quite risky), 3% loans, 4% on equities. Most of the short-term assets are in bank fixed deposits, to the tune of 32%. Based on this mix, one could sum up that the PPF is too risk averse. By having 32% of its total assets invested in fixed deposits whose returns are ever dwindling, and which presently do not exceed 3% per annum, compared to lending rates averaging 14%, appears to be poor investment judgement. Analysing the PPF figures from its 2003 Annual Report, one finds that short-term investments, at Shs 55.16 billion, still constitute 37.3% of the accumulated fund of the institution. In other words, the risk averseness is unabated. A much newer player, the Local Government Pensions Fund established in 2000, had investments, in 2002, in different portfolios totalling Shs. 52.6 billion. How these funds are being invested remains unclear. Of course, one may appreciate the risk involved by these Funds in extending loans to banks and financial institutions such as the Tanzania Investment Bank and TDFL for onward lending to the productive sectors of the economy including export finance. Yet the troubling question is whether attempts have been made to determine the nature of such risks and what could be done to reduce or hedge against them.

The depth and liquidity of the capital market, on the other hand, remains low because Tanzania has yet to mature into a full-fledged capital market. It is still at secondary market level. Tanzania is yet to have a capital market vehicle for raising non-debt equity finance. by floating new issues of shares) for greenfield projects and business expansions. Part of the problem is that even the more successful family owned private enterprises still shun becoming publicly held companies because of fears stringent disclosure stock exchange requirements for listing. Not many Tanzanian private firms comply either with corporate governance standards which, in many countries, like South Africa, are now standard for all registered companies.

Financial Deepening: Impediments and Solutions

In the context of the obtaining financial sector environment in Tanzania, the present "backseat" role of the government in the financial sector raises the fundamental question whether the government should or should not intervene in the financial sector to leverage its more efficient functioning and deepening. This is a fundamental policy question but also a highly sensitive one. In Tanzania, its experience vindicates Professor Joseph Stiglitz's view that, in financial markets, the failure of the market mechanism to allocate resources effectively is highly prevalent, especially in transitional economies, largely due to imperfections in the market structure. due to monopoly activities) and incomplete or missing markets for many financial services. The *need* for intervention is not as debated around the world as in the *form* of intervention. Stiglitz, of course, argues a case for even directed credit and maintenance of low interest rates through a system of financial repression. For policy makers, the challenge here is to design acceptable forms of policy interventions. For example, nowhere in the world do purely market forces determine the interest rate. Since interest rate is a strategic variable, the Bank of Tanzania could influence its level through monetary instruments at its disposal.

Secondly, in India, the government has intervened at the level of directed credit. On the face of it, this goes counter to the liberalisation process based on market principles. Tanzanian monetary policy since the mid 1990s has been not to influence the direction of credit in the economy. Such policy has had its dysfunctions, particularly in so far as credit allocation to priority sectors like agriculture, SMEs and to economic projects that target poverty reduction. Some form of monetary policy that forges a balanced credit management in the economy could have helped to get the unorganised sectors of the economy on their feet. What is fundamental in such a policy alignment is the determination whether directed credit encourages *efficiency* and *productivity* in the economy contrasted to the situation that existed in the 1970s and 1980s when directed credit was, *prima facie*, intended to promote socialist construction irrespective of the results emanating from the beneficiaries of credit. This is one of the reasons why the NBC performed poorly leading to its inevitable privatisation.

There are only two development financial institutions *proper* in Tanzania today: TDFL and Tanzania Investment Bank. TIB). TDFL is private, well capitalised and is able to access loanable funds from its foreign shareholders. However, TDFL is not able and cannot meet the capital needs of an economy whose growth crucially depends on long-term finance. 5-10 years). The gap filled by the few Venture Capital Funds that have emerged in the past decade is extremely small. Moreover, the direction of their loans may not coincide with what the government views as priority sectors. It is in this context, that the role of the TIB takes pre-eminence.

Two policy questions are pertinent to examine. First should or should not the TIB be privatised? There is a body of opinion within the Treasury and the Bank of Tanzania that TIB should be privatised. It is argued, that the government should seek out a "strategic investor" to take up majority shares in TIB and manage the Bank. The national political leadership should tread carefully on such a proposal. It should first ask itself: where would long-term finance come from? How would the priority sectors of the economy, like agriculture, be developed? What would TIB's privatisation promote? These questions also emerged during 2003 with respect to the privatisation of NMB.

However, TIB is a different kind of banking institution from NMB. It has the know how and the experience to deal with medium and long term lending which is what is needed , for example, to transform agriculture. Small, short-term loans for peasants can always be made available where a broad-based, national system of credit and savings societies is established, which then benefits from group loan allocations from mainstream banks such as CRDB, Akiba, EXIM, NBC and even NMB, whichever form of ownership NMB finally takes. To expect these types of banks to offer micro-credit directly to small borrowers is to dream. It could never work.

Second, and this would follow a policy decision that TIB is indeed a necessary state-owned vehicle for promoting the development of the priority sectors of the economy and thus should not be privatised, the government should ask: how do you then "empower" TIB to fulfil its role as a development bank? In this context, TIB put up proposals to the Treasury in 2001 and 2004. Central to the proposals is the imperativeness to re-capitalise the TIB. This could be done, for instance, by way of government raising capital through bonds, the way the East African Development Bank was able to do in 2000 and 2001 through the DSE. Through such a process, the government can raise immediate and adequate cash flow. The outflow, overtime, will be in the form of interest payments and phased amortisation of the bonds. Such re-capitalisation of TIB would provide the bank with the much-needed long-term funds as well assist the bank to clean up its few contingent liabilities in contrast to government taking over huge non-performing assets of TIB as it had done in the case of the NBC and the NMB.

It needs no amplification that a TIB with a strong capital structure would be able to raise its own additional finance for lending to the productive sectors of the economy through the issue of bonds in the secondary market. However, in its present financial position, TIB would probably not attract buyers of its bond due to the inevitable doubts about its balance sheet ability to redeem the liabilities on maturity dates as well as doubts about its future as a state-owned bank.

Why Low Credit Off-take?

Another dimension is the reality that Tanzania has a serious problem of low credit off-take. In 2004 the rate of credit to the private sector declined to 30% from 43.2% in 2003. This problem is explained by several factors: a low entrepreneurial bias; a history of high non-performing assets; lack of clear property rights and weak legal contract enforcement machinery especially in enforcing mortgages and debentures. The present judicial process is still viewed to favour borrowers and there have been cases that have reflected judicial abuse over the sanctioning of ex *parte* injunctions. The judicial process is also still lengthy and costly. Clearly, there are numerous areas, both legal and bureaucratic, that require immediate governmental intervention if the financial sector is to improve and contribute more effectively to economic growth. Credit off-take, in particular, stands to benefit from the following measures and decisions:

i) subjecting ex *parte* injunctions to rigorous criteria. Applications for injunctions should be heard and determined in the presence of all parties concerned. Right of appeal should automatically be availed where an *ex parte injunction* is issued and enforcement measures should be stayed.

ii) transfer cases of a commercial character from present courts of jurisdiction to commercial courts to speed up adjudication.

iii) vest enforceable rights to land in use by deeming it a productive asset.

iv) implement a fast and large-scale titling programme so that people have title to the assets they own. Contract out to private sector the role of surveying, mapping and registration of titles. The routine roles of the Registrar of Titles should be decentralised to lower levels of the central government, leaving the Registrar with the responsibility of signing title deeds. Presently, the government has a low capacity to undertake this function efficiently. The existing system is lengthy, cumbersome, riddled with the corruption-driven *"njoo kesho".* come tomorrow) syndrome.

v) allow transfer of rights over titled land through an *"automatic"* arrangement in order to boost productive investment in agriculture. China has made a success of this arrangement. It should be noted that title ownership in and of itself is not adequate for accessing credit. Only those who can use property titles for productive investment access credit. This is why easy transferability of titles is paramount.

vi) Tanzanian banks should become more entrepreneurial by marketing for credit. For example, why cannot our banks borrow a leaf from a Kansas USA experience? Their cattle are preferred collateral for bank credit as long as ownership is verified. e.g. through special tattoo on the cattle). Indeed, one of the strategic avenues to be applied in mobilisation of savings is to allow the "capitalisation" of assets such as cattle.

vii) improve the liquidity of Micro-financing institutions. Micro-finance is a new enterprise in Tanzania and whilst Mfis are growing in number, they are still nascent. Their major problem is liquidity and not a failure rate in loan repayments. In fact, as noted earlier, the record of loan repayments is as high as 98% and above. This record is partly explained by women being the major borrowers. Women have proven to be more reliable and operate based on trust. Equally important, is the fact that Mfis generally lend to groups and not to individuals. This system, in itself, inculcates a self-regulating or policing culture, in assuring loan repayments.

For policy makers, the key question is how to enhance the liquidity of Mfis? If one considers Mfis' excellent record of loan recovery and at premium interest rates which are presently higher than those charged by mainstream banks, one could ask why institutions such as social security and pension funds are not channelling some of their resources to them in the form of credit lines? Another question is how to institutionalise credit registers that can provide a collective platform for Mfis to share information about small borrowers and small enterprises. Mfis themselves should consider the establishment of such vehicles. However, this requires capacity-building support.

Addressing poverty effectively crucially means deepening access to finance to majority Tanzanians. To realise such deepening, Mfis have to shift from group lending to individual-based lending. To achieve such shift, the need for collateral emerges. In this regard, the role of government is central in enabling the people to acquire legal titles to their physical assets, including squatters. The uncoupling of extralegal assets into fungible assets would unlock the potential for many Tanzanians in accessing credit where they come up with bankable projects. As Hernando de Soto has posited in his book, *The Mystery of Capital*, "the crucial stage. has) to do with adapting the law to the social and economic needs of the majority of the population." It is "squatters", which de Soto describes as "extralegal settlements" that constitute, in most urban Tanzania, the principal source of investment capital. Such physical assets represent an important component of national savings and capital formation structure. Participation in wealth creation has been constricted by the failure of public policy to reform the real property legal regime. This area is now receiving serious government attention under a project managed by the de Soto Foundation. I examine below the context and the nature of work Hernando de Soto's Foundation is undertaking in Tanzania.

Mystery of Capital

The existence of prosperous enclaves in a sea of poverty conceals an abysmal retardation in a nation's capacity to create, respect and make available formal property rights to the majority of its citizens.

-Hernando de Soto: **The Mystery of Capital: Why Capitalism Triumphs In the West and Fails Everywhere else.**

In October 2003, a close friend, a Tanzanian Cabinet Minister, was on an official visit to France. At a dinner in my house, he confronted me and my wife with the question whether we owned any shares in companies listed on the Dar es Salaam Stock Exchange. The question was like a bolt from the blue! He went on to amplify that he had personally mortgaged his immovable assets with a bank, raising capital that he subsequently invested in stocks. The result was that he not only comfortably serviced his bank loan from dividends earned, but was also left with more than a comfortable monthly income that may not even necessitate him to continue working full time. The conversation did not end there. He went on to say that he knew of the two properties we owned and wondered whether we had title deeds on them and whether we had valued the properties. We responded by saying that we had title deeds but had not valued the assets. His concluding remark was that *"tunakalia uchumi"*. meaning that we were unproductively sitting on wealth). Paraphrased, he told us that we were economically stupid. The moral of this story is that many Tanzanians have assets that could be translated into capital and wealth. Yet their assets are not put to economic purpose. Two scenarios emerge from this situation. First, the basic lack of assets that have legal force in the form of title deeds or incorporation in the case of a business. The second is the state of the entrepreneurial mindset of appreciating the translation of a property right into capital. Both scenarios fit into what

Hernando de Soto calls, "the mystery of capital." So how can a country like Tanzania empower its citizens economically in a situation where the scenarios mentioned above constitute the cultural environment?

Promoting Economic Empowerment

In its policy and strategy programme for 2000–2010, the ruling political party, CCM, defined as one of its core mission the promotion of economic empowerment of the majority of Tanzanians. CCM was seized of the reality, captured by Hernando de Soto in these words: "no nation can overcome the legal apartheid between those who can create capital and those who cannot." For a long time, and especially in the period when economic reforms became deepened, manifested by privatisation of state-owned enterprises, the Tanzanian economic environment has become pregnant with the notion that the majority of Tanzanians are "disenfranchised" from wealth creation and ownership. There is a strong perception that only a few Tanzanians, of a racial minority, are enabled, allowed and promoted, even if unwittingly, as principal creators of wealth. This mindset has given birth to the clamour of *"uzawa"*, meaning the need for the government to apply economic affirmative action or positive discrimination policy in favour of "indigenous" Tanzanians. CCM saw this development, and particularly its "racial overtones", as retrogressive. In fact, before his death, Mwalimu Julius Nyerere had described *"uzawa"* as "reverse apartheid". It is in response to the emergence of this potentially social destabilising phenomenon, that CCM developed a well-defined policy and strategy on economic empowerment of the majority of Tanzanians. The aim of the policy is to open up opportunity horizons and spaces that Tanzanians, across the racial divide, can seize to create wealth and improve their livelihoods.

The foregoing provides the backdrop to the decision taken by the Tanzanian government to sign, on 10 October 2004, an agreement with the Norwegian government whereby the Norwegian Government is extending to Tanzania a grant of Shs. 7.0 billion to finance a project titled, *Property and Business Formalisation Programme*. PBFP). The management of this programme has been assigned to the *Institute for Liberty and Democracy*. ILD) based in Lima, Peru. ILD is under the leadership of Professor Hernando de Soto, the world famous Peruvian author of the book, The Mystery of Capital. ILD, described by UK's leading magazine, *The Economist*, as one of the two most important think tanks in the world, was responsible, through World Bank financial support, for managing several initiatives, laws and regulations that modernised Peru's economic system between 1992 and 1993. In Peru, ILD's role was management of the property rights system. Its work led to the issuance of registered title deeds to immovable assets involving more that 1.3 million properties. It also enabled the movement of about 380,000 businesses from the informal sector into legally incorporated businesses. Overall, the project resulted in increased tax revenues of US$ 400 million a year between 1993 and 1995 and creation of half a million new jobs. During this same period, Peru's net wealth increased by US$ 9.4 billion, about equal to the present GDP of Tanzania.

ILD's Economic Philosophy

The work of the ILD has been inspired by de Soto's novel thinking about the wealth and poverty of nations; in other words, why it is that some countries become rich and others remain poor. Hernando de Soto's core thesis is that the underlying cause for such a contrasting condition centres on insight about what drives the capitalist system and what constitutes the basic foundation of human progress. In his view, the driving force of capitalism is the ability to produce capital and capital is largely a product of an integrated formal property system. This is reason why real estate accounts for 50% of the national wealth of rich countries. In poor countries, on the other hand, it accounts for almost 75% of national wealth. The distinguishing characteristic, however, is that, in poor countries, this "national wealth" has not been translated or converted into capital and making it available to promote development. In other words, the wealth exists in the form of what de Soto describes as "dead capital." As a result, economies of poor countries are grossly undercapitalised. Think of a business that is undercapitalised. It is a recipe for bankruptcy. It is this poor understanding of the key dynamic of the capitalist system that explains why the market economy in poor countries is not a success in spite of implementing broad economic reforms.

Poverty of Entrepreneurship

What in fact is happening in most poor countries like Tanzania is that citizens actually own assets that could be used to make capital and, in turn, create wealth. Yet, they predominantly hoard or sit on such assets, appreciating them for their aesthetic rather than economic value. Houses are something of social value, a status symbol. Ownership of property, in other words, is driven largely by what Ali Mazrui has described as the "prestige motive" and "self-indulgent exhibitionism". The same can be said of ownership of land and farms. In these circumstances, capital exists yet is not realised or appreciated to exist. It is a clear picture of entrepreneurial poverty. In contrast, in rich countries, every piece of land, every building, equipment and movable assets such as motor vehicles and inventories in houses and shops constitute assets deployable to create capital and wealth.

In the context of what constitutes entrepreneurial poverty on a national scale, I examine ILD's work in Mexico and Egypt. When ILD was invited, in 2002, to work for the Mexican Government with the support of the World Bank, they found a despicable picture of what could only be described as poverty of ideas. 80% of the Mexican population was in the extralegal. or informal) economy. In other words, they did not pay taxes. They owned 11 million buildings, 6 million businesses, and 134 million hectors of land. The total value of all those assets was US$ 315 billion, equivalent to 7 times the value of all Mexico's oil reserves and 29 times the value of foreign direct investment. FDI) inflows since Spain left Mexico as a colonial power. Closer to the African context, what the poor owned outside the law in Egypt in 2002 was 92% of all buildings, 88% of all enterprises with a total net worth of US$ 248 billion. This translates into 55 times the value of all FDI Egypt has received since Napoleon Bonaparte left Egypt, 35 times the size of total market capitalisation of the Cairo Stock Exchange and 70 times the bilateral aid. ODA) Egypt has received for all time.

Unveiling the Mystery of Capital

The Peru, Mexico and Egypt examples clearly exemplify that unveiling the mystery of capital constitutes one of the profound prescriptions to attacking poverty. Important as economic reforms pursued by poor countries are, because it is essential that any economy should have its macro-economic fundamentals right, good infrastructure, well functioning regulatory and judicial institutions and enabling conditions that attract investments and bolster business to prosper, ultimately what unlocks the national economic potential is the ability to "globalise" capital to benefit all citizens. How to capitalise the citizens of a country then is what crucially makes a market economy viable, sustainable and successful. Indeed, the state of deepening informality witnessed in poor countries to the extent of its constituting up to 50% of GDP in some countries. in Tanzania it is estimated to constitute 30%), is primarily a result of a system that militates against such broad process of "capitalising" citizens to take place. Admittedly, other negative contributory factors play a part in promoting informality. For example, the cost of legal compliance often outweighs the benefits of formality. At the same time, business start-ups face serious hurdles in registering businesses due to up-front payment of tax requirements, strict urban health safety regulations and the requirement of registered address of business premises. These difficulties are accentuated by corruption-driven conditions attached to securing land allocation for constructing a residential or business building. Inevitably, the nightmarish requirements to obtain land allocation officially have resulted in the squatters that envelope most cities of poor countries. Clearly, it is viable to address these encumbrances where a well-established system of property rights is in place.

The Role of ILD in Tanzania

The role of ILD in Tanzania is to enable the country to move beyond macro-economic reforms and realise a broad based social and economic transformation. Such role proceeds from appreciating the reality, that economic reforms on their own, are not enough to cause deep economic transformation with social justice where they do not integrate the majority of the citizens into the national legal system which enables them to use their resources in the competitive market. Thus, ILD's work is directed at showing poor countries that it is the poor who constitute the dominant constituency for national transformation to a market economy. The work involves putting in place a system of property rights so that the assets of citizens are "uncoupled" from their present "rigid and physical state" and turned fungible, that is, usable in securing loans and credits and thereby creating capital that can be invested in business, stocks and secondary securities. Over time, such system creates a domestic capital base that is robust enough to underwrite a major part of national development. It also crucially scales-up poverty reduction by giving the poor better access to financial tools of wealth creation and ultimately enabling citizens to take effective charge of their nation's destiny.

It is important to underscore that what ILD is undertaking in Tanzania also importantly involves ingraining the culture of investment. It is noteworthy, that a widespread perception exists in many poor countries that, in the absence of a culture of capital formation and investment, formalisation of property rights, of itself, could be of little significance. Arguably, this perception could have constituted the context that informed the view, advanced in *The Challenge to the South,* the report of the South Commission that "the broad environment for the effectiveness of capital formation is a society's culture". In fact, it is often posited that many Tanzanians bred under the ethos of the Arusha Declaration still carry the excess baggage that views capital as not being the foundation of development. "fedha si msingi wa maendeleo"). As a corollary, such mindset is perceived to inhibit the process of capitalising the citizenry. On this point, Hernando de Soto's view is succinct. He notes, "formal property is more than a system of titling, recording and mapping assets – it is an instrument of thought, representing assets in such a way that people's minds can work on them to generate surplus value". In other words, a property rights system contains a cultural dimension. It could thus be concluded, as Newsweek's Fareed Zakaria has put it, that a property rights system shaped by new "political and economic forces" also shapes new "cultural attitudes." Put differently, it logically follows that the birth of a culture of entrepreneurship would be catalysed by having a system of property rights in place.

The year 2005 has been declared the UN International year of micro-credit. The declaration is in recognition of the fact that rapid growth of strong micro-credit and microfinance would serve the needs of poor people and bolster the realisation of the Millennium Development Goals that primarily target the eradication of poverty. In the last few years, Tanzania has witnessed the growth in micro-credit institutions, mainly in the form of savings and credit cooperative societies or SACCOS. Some of the mainstream commercial banks like CRDB, EXIM and AKIBA have taken a lead in providing microfinance facilities to these SACCOS. However, the realisation of a robust access to micro-credit, beyond the present weak system based on group lending, trust-based relationships and other informal means, greatly depends on establishing an effective and broad-based system of property rights. In this light, the promotion of the Property and Business Formalisation Programme in Tanzania could not be timelier. This programme would almost certainly catalyse Tanzania's economic growth and offer the opportunity to all Tanzanians to exploit their entrepreneurial creativities to be wealth creators and thereby promoting higher living standards.

Deepening the Capital Market

There is urgent need to deepen the capital market from its present secondary market character to a primary market if Tanzania is serious about widening and deepening the structure and size. liquidity) of the financial sector in Tanzania. The primary capital market, beyond the present securities market and buying and selling of shares in companies listed on the DSE, would enable more effective mobilisation of savings and channelling them into investments. Such a market would enable entrepreneurs to raise non-debt equity financing. Admittedly, Tanzania may presently lack the requisite equity culture to make a primary capital market have a quick impact. However, such a culture would come from confidence generated by the participation of renowned local and foreign firms in the capital market. A key challenge may be to what extent the Capital Markets and Securities Authority is well positioned, in terms of capacity, to appraise projects and prospectuses of firms before they are allowed to float public issues on the stock market?

Part of the reason why the financial system is also deprived of long-term finance is the manner in which the fund management of social security and pension funds is undertaken. Commercial portfolio fund management is new to our part of the world. This is because the market economy is still infant. For as long as social security and pension funds continue to operate as if they were under a socialist environment, portfolio management will be retained as part of management of the Funds. The present commercial environment demands that portfolio management be undertaken by fund professionals.

The growth of IPOs on the DSE in recent years has bolstered the shares market. But to what extent investments of pension funds in Tanzania Breweries and Tanzania Cigarette Company, for instance, actually contribute to higher national economic growth is debatable. Yes, the funds constitute savings of individual workers and their interests in terms of secured returns on such savings should thus be protected. However, public interest and the interests of the owners of those savings would demand that the savings be more professionally managed and invested. Such a direction would demand that PPF and NSSF hire investment professional firms to assist them. I know that in South Africa and Namibia, private-sector professional investment management firms manage pension funds, including public service pension funds. Evidently, the state of the economy would determine sources for investments. This is a point to consider in determining the cost effectiveness of hiring independent investment advisory firms to manage pension funds.

It should also be observed that with the planned privatisation of the National Insurance Corporation and the deepening of the insurance business following the deregulation of the industry in 1998, insurance premiums will be an additional buoyant reserve fund for supporting economic growth. An area where these insurance funds could be channelised is mortgage finance, currently virtually a non-existent in Tanzania following the demise of what was largely a perfunctory Housing Bank, the state-owned Tanzania Housing Bank. When supported by a modern system of legal property and mortgage contract enforcement, mortgage finance would create the vital wherewithal for converting property assets into capital and thereby empowering more and more Tanzanians to invest in projects that positively affect economic growth. The Land. Amendment) Act, 2004 enables such finance to take a bullish role.

Social Security Funds for Economic Growth

One other key issue to consider in the overall question about how to deepen the structure and size of the financial system is the way social security and pension funds invest what is deferred compensation of workers invested for their retirement or death. Must an institutional investor undertake the investment of such funds cumulatively? Can it not be possible for a contributor to the fund to borrow, using his or her own contribution to the Fund as collateral? The loan could then be used to construct a house. in itself a *"fungible"* asset that could be applied towards raising additional capital for investment) or could be used to buy TBL or TCC shares. which become their own and not those of PPF or NSSF, who, at this stage, pass over to their contributors only something like 4% return overall vis-a-vis much higher dividend returns they earn for themselves)?

There are, of course, bottlenecks involved in the process where an individual contributor is required to go through a broker. at a cost) and buying a minimum set of shares. which could be higher than affordability of the shares). However, such bottlenecks should not be exaggerated in terms of cost and thus constitute ground for exclusion for people with small savings. It simply needs to be accepted that a contributor could borrow from the Fund itself or from a bank in order to buy shares or invest in other assets.

Such flexibility in the management and investment of funds of institutions such as PPF, NSSF and even insurance companies requires a deeper commercial and risk management mindset. It could, however, have a major impact within the broad objective of mainstreaming many Tanzanians in the wealth creation process and wealth ownership. I believe, in this light, that the move to establish a Unit Trust of Tanzania. UTT), a government sponsored investment scheme modelled on the Indian one, is most welcome. UTT was formally enacted into law in mid 2003. Through such a Trust, if well managed, Tanzania should be able to increase the propensity of the middle and lower income groups to save and invest. Between 16 May and 29 July 2005, the Fund would sell shares to the people. The Trust would then be able to use such savings along with what the government has reserved for the Fund from government shares in Tanzania Breweries Limited. 2%), and Tanzania Cigarettes Company. 1%) to the tune of Shillings 11.57 billion. which includes earned dividends of Shillings 634.33 million) for acquiring, holding, management and disposal of different types of securities as well as tradable shares. The Fund can invest in shares only to the extent of 30% of its total fund portfolio with the balance investible in government securities, corporate bonds such as those of EADB and in bank fixed deposits. UTT has launched the Umoja Fund as an investment vehicle for raising savings of Tanzanians. Its contribution in channelling savings of the small investor into industrial and agricultural development is thus immense. It is noteworthy, in contrast, that the Unit Trust of India, set up in 1964 by Act of Parliament, today occupies a central position in the Indian capital market. This Trust does not have any share capital and operates on the principle of "no profit, no loss" since all income and gains, net of all costs and development charges, ultimately accrues to savers and investors in various schemes established by the Trust. It is such type of Trust that can become the key driver of economic empowerment of majority Tanzanians. UTT has a huge challenge, in this context, to rise to the expectations of ordinary Tanzanians.

Promoting Equity Capital Financing

Competitive and export-promoting industrialisation occupies a strategic position in accelerating Tanzania's pace of social and economic development. Yes, agriculture continues to be a strategic sector of the Tanzania economy. However, experience shows that in many poor countries, jump-starting change in the agricultural sector is not easy. Decisions involving technological change are not easily implementable in the rural sector. On the other hand, export-driven industrialisation increases market size thereby inducing a faster process of technological change in agriculture by withdrawing labour from that sector for industrial employment and by promoting innovations in agricultural processes and production methods. It is difficult to promote and sustain export-driven industrialisation in a poor country without an active role of the state especially in developing an institutional and policy framework suited to the stage of development in place. TIB was originally established in 1970 as a strategic vehicle of the government for financing socialist industrialisation. TIB can and should now be supported by the government to spearhead private sector industrialisation. This has to happen for several reasons:

First, at the present stage of Tanzania's development, there are economic activities that the government may consider to fall within the overriding objectives of the state to develop and which may not meet conventional or strict commercial criteria for lending.

Second, the commercial banking and financial sector in Tanzania is still nascent. In addition, the financing made available from most banks is largely short-term. Term finance is still scarce. Under ideal circumstances, development banks like the TIB should be able to capitalize themselves for robust lending by borrowing and issuing bonds and debentures from the capital market. However, the capital market itself is still infant. Moreover, the level of savings is low. This is evidenced by the low contributions made to the NICO financing programme. In spite of months of mobilisation to get Tanzanians to buy shares, the response was not as robust as expected. Of course, there is the mindset problem involved, for it is not as if people simply lack money to invest. They have the money. But the culture to buy shares and entrust somebody else with your money is yet to be adequately imbibed. In countries like Japan, Korea and India, for several decades since the 1960s, borrowing by development banks was facilitated either by the government or by the central bank through issue of bonds and other securities. Such facility induced commercial banks to subscribe to the bonds of development banks. A similar facility has now been put into place through the DSE since 2000. But it is yet to be deepened.

Third, the government is committed to a policy of economic empowerment of the majority of citizens of the country. There are sensitivities about this programme especially among those that feel that

African Tanzanians should, *in particular*, enjoy affirmative action. Polemics aside, economic empowerment demands the availability of a sizeable pool of resources for financing business-oriented projects. Therefore, adequate term finance is essential. Tanganyika Development Finance Company Limited. TDFL) and the Venture Capital Funds in place cannot presently cope with the magnitude of financial requirements expected for meaningful economic empowerment. What is suggested is that development financial institutions such as the TIB require direct financial support from the government in enabling them to build adequate liquidities that can be utilised for equity finance. This support should not be in the form of subsidies. Rather, it should be in the form of additional equity injection and offering guarantees for lines of credits securable from outside Tanzania.

It is noted that under the *Second Financial Institutions Development Project.* FIDP II) funded by the World Bank, TIB is listed for privatisation. On the face of it, privatisation of TIB could lead to the deepening of its liquidity and enhancing its capacity to lend more. At the same time, however, it is feared that if the privatisation of TIB is not well structured, whereby the government fails to maintain a reasonable, and not necessarily a controlling shareholding, TIB could find itself unable to play the pivotal role it should in addressing some of the development challenges embodied in Tanzania Development Vision 2025. These challenges include that of economic empowerment of the economically disadvantaged Tanzanians.

Chapter

31 WELFARE AND SOCIAL SECURITY

The welfare state of the future is based on a social contract between citizens. The relationship cannot simply be one of give by the state and take by the recipient. It must encompass rights and duties.

-Tony Blair: **Speech to the Confederation of Indian Industry, Bangalore, 5 January 2002.**

Overview

The welfare state, whose central policy framework is social security, which John Naisbitt in *Megatrends 2000* defines "as a government that spends funds to help protect citizens and promote their social well being" is now in a state of uncertainty. Around the world, in the industrialised capitalist economies and in poor countries as well, the fundamental philosophy that underlies the welfare state is going through a serious debate as welfare increasingly becomes viewed as a right rather than as a privilege. Welfare of the people has become so critical as to constitute one of the central factors responsible for increasing unemployment and the erosion of economic competitiveness. Welfare and social security reforms are now buzzwords in the US, Britain, France, Germany and even the Scandinavian countries where the welfare state, as an ideological paradigm, has been a dominant system of social justice since the end of the Second World War. The mantra now appears to be "the end of pension's pretensions" in what is increasingly becoming a developed world of the aged. There is the worrying expectation that individuals, especially the young workers, rather than the state, would have to shoulder more for their own pension and health burden as well as that of the aged.

The 1998 German elections witnessed social security constituting an important electoral plank for the successful Social Democratic Party. Tony Blair has also focused his social policy around the process of reforming the *very* concept of welfare. In his words, as enunciated in his pamphlet, "The Third Way", "the welfare state is one of the great creations of this century. It lifted many people out of poverty, and offered new opportunities to millions. To provide for those at the bottom is in some ways the essence of the good society. However, the ways in which we help people need to change. It is essential that we offer adequate services, not just cash benefits; we give greater emphasis to partnership between Public and private provision, that we recognise the need to relate subsidies to need, particularly where -as with university fees - a failure to do so would result in fewer opportunities and lower quality provision all round. We must also recognise the implications for the welfare state of change in labour market and family patterns - for example, the strain on contributory benefits that arises from regular and/or prolonged spells of unemployment. In addition, there are new needs to be met, such as long-term care for the elderly." In sum, what Blair contends is that "the provision of equal opportunities does not imply dull uniformity in welfare provision and public services". Recent proposals in Britain on the promotion of "Foundation Hospitals" and introduction of "Top up Fees" for University education indicate that the process towards the reform of the welfare state has picked up momentum. At the same time, on July 1st 1997, the US also witnessed what was described as the "end of welfare" as the Americans have known it. On that day, President Clinton assented to a federal legislation terminating a 62-year-old federal entitlement and creating, for the first time, a limit on how long a person could receive federal welfare assistance. In an article, titled *Why Welfare Reform is Working* published in the influential American magazine, *Commentary,* Daniel Case argues, "by eliminating the certainty that one will be paid whether or not one works or seeks to work, we have already taken the most important step on the road toward the end of welfare and of liberalism as we have know them."

The most important element of welfare, namely, social security is thus undergoing a barrage of criticism. Its focus is the apparent failure of the huge and rapidly growing programme to provide an adequate level of economic security for the beneficiaries. In the Scandinavian countries, especially Sweden as well as in Germany, personal tax rates, income taxes and private citizens' contributions to social security are viewed as highly excessive and a de-motivating factor for employment and productivity. In the US context, on the other hand, Thomas Duesterberg has pointed out in his publication *Reforming the Welfare State,* that social security benefits expanded 23 times between 1935, when the Social Security Act was enacted, and 1997. In 1999, social security benefits totalled US$ 375 billion, paid to 44.6 million people. However, payroll taxes required to fund such benefits have only grown from 2% to 12.4% of the first US$ 65,000 earnings between 1935 and 1997. His conclusion is that it is doubtful that "Social Security would provide an acceptable level of retirement security." A major debate has inevitably emerged in the US whether social security is indeed a good retirement investment. Based on a Presidential Commission Report in 2002, it is estimated that by 2018, the social security trust fund would be in severe financial crisis. It will experience an annual cash deficit as the annual benefit payments would exceed the amount collected in payroll revenues.

With respect to Tanzania, it is notable that the country has been undergoing a major social and economic transformation. The welfare state as we have known of it under the heydays of socialism has somewhat been chipped away as the market has taken over as the driving force of social and economic development. Evidently, a return to some form of a welfare state has been seen in recent years, particularly since 2001, as a positive aftermath of Tanzania's qualification into HIPC. Thus, primary and secondary education as well as health service have benefited significantly with lesser cost sharing burden falling on the people. Cancellation of primary school fees in 2003 is notable proof.

It is important to observe though, from the perspective of history, that the US adopted the welfare state system in the mid 1930s in response to disillusionment with the functioning of the market economy. Yet, today, there is growing disenchantment in the US and throughout the industrialised economies with the welfare system and, particularly, with the way the social security system is structured, funded and managed. It may be pertinent to ask whether there are any lessons Tanzania could learn from the global. This is the context in which Tanzania should address the role of social security and economic development and come up with a policy that is coherent and purposeful.

Background to Social Security in Tanzania

An objective treatment of the role of a welfare state and of social security in social and economic development in the Tanzanian context, necessarily embraces historical underpinnings. The philosophy behind such underpinnings vitally informs the debate about the relevance and direction of welfare policies in their broad sense. Mwalimu Julius Nyerere believed that there could be no human dignity in extreme poverty, disease, and ignorance. This was his core philosophy of social justice. Thus, from the outset of the attainment of political independence, Nyerere was seized of the challenge to create a new society founded on the lofty principles and social conditions of human dignity and equality, and the absence of deprivation, illiteracy and disease. In his book, *Freedom and Unity*, he aptly postulates, "the very purpose of society, its reason for existence, is and must be the individual man, his growth, his health, his security, his happiness." This philosophy of promoting the welfare of all Tanzanians, men and women, children and the old, able and disabled, living in unity and peace characterised Nyerere's dominant vision.

Throughout the period of his leadership, Nyerere vigorously and steadfastly pursued a social and economic policy whose underlying philosophy was the people's welfare. Indeed, even prior to the promulgation of the Arusha Declaration in February 1967, Nyerere had already created the foundations of a welfare state. Education and health services were already free to all citizens even prior to their acquisition in 1969 and 1972 respectively. In October 1964, the Nyerere government enacted a law to establish the National Provident Fund. NPF) to provide for contributions to and payment of benefits in respect of retirement, death, invalidity, sickness, withdrawal for statutorily provided reasons and for unemployment. The adoption of the NPF statute marked the entry of a limited form of statutory social security into Tanzania even though, at that time, there already existed a Government Pensions Ordinance that provided for a non-contributory retirement benefit scheme for government permanent and pensionable civil service employees.

The central organisation of welfare provisioning in Tanzania has been the delivery of free social services, covering health and education, delivered by the state. Evidently, tax revenues have underpinned such service delivery. It is thus incorrect to regard the service as having been fully free. Nevertheless, it is important to underscore that in it its broad sense, welfare was provided free to all Tanzanians. Job creation was also, in a way, viewed to be a state responsibility. Interestingly, though the NPF legislation covered unemployment, the phenomenon of unemployment in the sense of absence of jobs or of one not being able to secure a job after having lost one, was quite rare in the 1960s and 1970s. Indeed, even the whole idea of old age pension did not feature in its current meaning precisely because the welfare state had assured every citizen - in villages and in towns - of free education for all school going children, from primary to university level and of free medical and health services for all. This situation had changed dramatically. Since the on-set of economic liberalisation in mid 1986 and until fiscal year 2000 as earlier alluded to, Tanzanians witnessed the gradual but consistent reduction in budgetary allocations for social service delivery. The market increasingly drove government social service delivery policies and the citizenry was slowly but consistently called upon to share the burden of the cost. Cost sharing and cost recovery schemes were put in place then in the social economy. It was a policy shift, from welfare statism that characterised the Nyerere era.

For Tanzania, the quasi-rolling back of the state from social service delivery posed serious threats to human security. Mahbub Ul Haq in his 1994 Barbara Ward Lecture at the 21st World Conference of the Society for International Development titled, *New Imperatives of Human Security* painted a grim picture of the kind of human insecurity developing nations face from such a policy framework: "It is reflected in shrivelled faces of innocent children, in the anguished existence of the homeless, in the constant fear of the jobless in the silent despair of those without a hope." The threat to human security in the face of an eroding welfare state should seriously be addressed. It could not be addressed by mere condemnation of the policy shift. That would be ineffective since stark economic realities stare the country in the face. Tanzania cannot fail to be mindful of the fact that social service delivery costs have risen steadily, in real terms. Equally, budgetary resources available for health and education services are limited. As a principle, however, it would be foolhardy not to come to terms with the need to move towards making all those who can afford to contribute towards promoting and maintaining their own health, to be responsible for the cost of their medical treatment as well as the cost of the education needs of their children.

Social Security in the Global Context:

What is social security? Briefly, it is a protective mantle. It provides protection for loss of income when people work, lose jobs and when they have to depend upon the work of others. A leading US authority on social security, Merton Bernstein, in a book titled *Social Security: The System That Works* has described social security as a system that "protects us against the economic calamity that accompanies the personal tragedy of a parent's death, or severe disablement. Social Security benefits replace a portion of former earnings to sustain our family and us. When age compels our parents to cease working, social security provides them with income and Medicare provides a major portion of medical care. When one older parent dies, the survivor continues to draw social security benefits and obtain medical care under Medicare. And when we ourselves reach retirement age, Social Security provides at least a basic income to sustain us and Medicare assures that medical care, hospitalisation, surgery or convalescent care will be forthcoming".

In all countries where it is practised, the philosophical logic of social security is located in the pervasive problem that every member of the society irrespective of occupation depends upon current earnings. Such earnings are derived either from current jobs, business or other forms of economic activity, or from the support of a family member such as a parent. However, humanity is susceptible to the vagaries and calamities of life that include unemployment, ill health, injury, death and retirement. Such risks threaten and undermine income stream. Social security, as an insurance scheme, provides a partial contingency for lost income when such hazards of life strike.

As an insurance scheme, those who participate in social security be they employees or self-employed individuals, in all occupations, pay contributions. Some employers pay all the required contributions. In other schemes contributions are shared between employers and employees, at equal amounts, or at such variable amounts as are set out in the applicable or approved social security schemes or laws. One of the key assets of a social security system is that it frees workers to change jobs as opportunities present themselves. In this context, the general perception is that an economy functions well where working people can be re-deployed in line with their skills and professional inclinations. Such adaptability is a great strength in a dynamic economy. For this reason, many industrialised countries now undertake welfare reform to make job avoidance a far less attractive option for people. For example, in the UK, the over extension of welfare is viewed by the Labour government in the context of growing skills obsolescence in the wake of globalisation, technology breakthroughs and intense competition. Thus, the vast majority of the unemployed who are welfare recipients lack the repository of skills to enter the job market on their own. In other words, there is lack of a critical mass of skills that can provide the basis for worker adaptability. In this context, the Blair government has been directing sizeable funds towards job training and re-equipping the unemployed to be able to work. In the US, on the other hand, the Clinton Administration had also come up with a US$ 3 billion *Welfare- to- Work-Programme* with similar objectives to those of Britain's Labour government. In sum, the conventional welfare system is slowly but surely being dismantled in the rich world.

Welfare and Social Security in Tanzania

This section examines the welfare policy framework in Tanzania and the role social security funds play in supporting it. While it is correct that the job market in Tanzania has contracted in the wake of the restructuring of the economy, it is equally true that the skills demands of a new market-driven economy are in short-supply. Private Banks and some of the large economic players like the breweries, cement, cigarettes, insurance, hotel and beverages companies, find it difficult to recruit skilled personnel. In this context, there is urgent need to review and adapt education and training programmes to fit them to current challenges and needs. Measures being taken to reform the secondary education curriculum announced early in 2005 indicate that the government is now seized of the weaknesses that exist in the educational system. Though there is controversy about these measures, what is important is to come to terms with are the demands of the marketplace and the need to create the capacity for individuals to be self employed. This is a welcome development and it should be extended to include a major overhaul of college and university curriculum as well.

Tanzania may inevitably face a problem of unemployment, by default, more because of lack of shortage of appropriate skills than the non-availability of jobs as such. This may sound an exaggeration, viewed in the context of current job realities. However, few years down the line, as the economy gets a boost from new private investments, it may not be so. The important question will then be whether social security would develop sufficiently to fund those that lose jobs. At this stage, the Parastatal Pensions Fund. PPF) is not involved in providing unemployment benefits. Thus, this question is more relevant to the National Social Security Fund. NSSF) which is empowered by law to become a broad based social security fund. Regrettably, NSSF appears to have withdrawn from providing unemployment insurance. For whilst the NPF Act Section 29. 2) catered for a temporary and permanent withdrawal benefit to those who find themselves unemployed for at least six months, the new NSSF Act omits such benefit from the list of benefits it covers. Difficult as it is to manage, Tanzania needs to move in the direction of extending unemployment insurance to those who can insure for it.

At another level, whilst social security in the industrialised and some of the newly industrialising nations of East Asia and Latin America caters for a universal health insurance and pensions system for all. The PPF does not cater for such universal system. However, the National Social Security Fund Act has introduced the benefit of a *universal* health Insurance and pensions system for all. except for parastatal and government employees). It also covers both an employee and the self-employed. The NSSF Act provides: "Every person who is self employed or who is employed in the private sector, other than in a body which is a parastatal organisation under the Parastatal Pensions Fund Act, 1978 shall be registered as an insured person". It is also noteworthy that the Parastatal Pensions Act is not a comprehensive social security scheme since its benefits extend only to pensions benefits on retirement and upon death as a death gratuity, payable to dependants. The PPF scheme does not provide the broad spectrum of benefits that the NSSF does namely, retirement pension, invalidity pension, survivors' pension, funeral grants, maternity benefit, employment injury benefit and health insurance benefit.

It is interesting to note that in 1998 the Tanzania government tabled in Parliament a Bill titled, *The Government Pensions Act, 1998.* That Bill became law in 1999. The legislation repealed the colonial Pensions Ordinance and introduced a social security scheme for government employees under pensionable service within the public service of the United Republic. The scheme, a contributory one, in the sense that both the employer and employee contribute, respectively, at the rate of 15% and 5% of the employee's salary, provides broader benefits than those presently provided by the PPF and they are closer to those provided by the NSSF. A *Local Government Service Pension Scheme or Fund* was also established in 2000 in the same form as that for the public service. The benefits under this scheme include retirement pension, death gratuity, sickness benefit, invalidity benefit and a withdrawal benefit.

The age of retirement is also an important question to address. In 2000, Parliament endorsed the retirement age of 60. Under a new law, passed in Parliament early in 2005, this age limit has now been extended to 65 in respect of High Court Judges. However, the extension to 65 years is yet to be applied more broadly and especially to University teachers. It is critical, in my view that the age limit be extended because 60 is too young an age for a University Professor to retire. In my view, for Judges and University Professors, the age for retirement should be 70. In the rich world, some of the reputable academic dons invariably retire only when they die. The logic of extension of retirement age should not be linked to questions of equity. It is not as if young people are deliberately delayed from taking over the highest positions in the land. On the contrary, this is a question about how best to use scarce expertise and experience to the optimum level in the interest of the nation. Obviously, the merit of the individual should determine whether a public servant should or should not continue to work for the people irrespective of age. At the age of 77, Mwalimu Nyerere was intellectually vibrant and still worked for the people with energy and excellence.

Conclusion

Time has come for the government to develop a clear policy on how Tanzania is going to build a society in which social justice prevails. As the country increasingly entrenches market-led policies to govern the management of social and economic development, the majority of the people would find their well-being in jeopardy and not cared for. That would be tragic and would inevitably undermine social cohesion, peace and stability. A modern welfare state rests on the efficiency and effectiveness of social security. It is social security rather than direct government budgetary allocations to the social sector that assures the well-being of the citizens of the industrialised nations.

Evidently, for poor countries like Tanzania, the government should have its priorities right. Investments and recurrent budget allocations in education and health must be given greater priority. Due to HIPC dividends and the loans and grants secured from donors and the World Bank, efforts have been directed at addressing social policy deficits. As a matter of deliberate welfare policy the government has to put its money where its mouth is. A well-planned and broad-based social security system that covers the whole population should be considered if the well-being of Tanzanians, in sickness, in unemployment, in retirement and on death, can be assured and sustained. The NSSF legislation provides the base for moving in this direction. However, Tanzania needs an umbrella legal regime that creates the framework and the enabling conditions to support such a broad social security system.

Part Nine

EDUCATION, KNOWLEDGE AND YOUTH

It is certainly self-evident that prosperous nations are also highly educated ones: any compendium of statistics shows that to be the case. But can we conclude that the education caused the prosperity, and that spending on schools and universities spills over into general well being? The short answer is "No". The experience of the developing world actually makes it all too clear that education cannot guarantee growth. It is certainly not enough on its own. The more interesting question is whether it is even very relevant.

-Alison Wolf: ***Does Education Matter? Myths about education and economic growth.***

Chapter

32 EDUCATION FOR CITIZENSHIP

To free ourselves from habit, to resolve the paradoxes, to transcend conflicts, to become the masters rather than the slaves of our own lives, we must first see and remember, and then forget. That is why true learning begins with unlearning.

-Warren Bennis: *On Becoming a Leader.*

The Context

Questions about the state of national values, social distinctiveness and citizenship are in vogue around the world. President Bill Clinton's political plank during the campaign for his second term was the regeneration of family values in an American society afflicted by social disruption. The "Asian Crisis" in 1997, on the other hand, raised questions regarding the overextension or abuse of social capital based on Confucian values. It was argued, that the very values that had been considered the driving force for the economic success of East Asian economies, namely work ethic, respect for authority, paternalistic government and communitarianism, had become the cause of financial crisis and economic meltdown. There was a preponderant view that those values had led to a financial system that had become overly influenced by nepotism and non-transparency. Put differently, crony capitalism had become institutionalised.

However, it is debatable whether the Asian crisis was indeed caused by the so-called "Asian values". In fact, Francis Fukuyama, in an interesting article in the magazine *Commentary* titled *Asian Values and the Asian Crisis* fails to see any direct link between the so-called Asian Values. which in his view, are, at any rate, not homogeneous even within a given nation-state like Singapore or Malaysia) and the financial and economic crisis of 1997. Fukuyama locates the crisis in other factors like excessive state intervention and "crony capitalism" a reference to the making of business decisions outside the realm of market criteria.

Tanzania is increasingly becoming sensitive and concerned about certain trends in its society that point towards some form of a crisis in its social, cultural and political distinctiveness and identity. Whichever interpretation one gives to the *Mwembechai Disorder* that took place in Dar es Salaam in February 1998, a fracas that manifested itself in civil clashes with the riot police following Friday prayers, leading to injury and loss of lives, the incident, in my view, was precipitated by several factors beyond religious fanaticism. Of course, there those who point a finger at law enforcement organs as having deliberately targeted Muslims, ostensibly a calculated attack on growing Islamic fundamentalism. They are entitled to their opinion. However, deepening poverty in Tanzania's inner cities, disconcerting "voices" of intolerance from all corners of the religious divide, acute shortage of jobs for the youth and poor education in urban centres stand out as the principal causes of religious passion wherever it occurs in urban Tanzania. The unavoidable question is whether Tanzania is witnessing the beginnings of social and cultural fragmentation.

Colonialism and Colonial Values

It is important and timely to commence a serious conversation within the Tanzanian civil society about the emerging sources of intolerance and social fractures. A national debate about the state of national values and the role of citizenship in re-building a united, peaceful and resourceful Tanzania in a new era in which capitalism and political pluralism may be the very sources of social instability should be brought onto the public domain. The spirit of citizenship is one of the key driving forces of a stable social and economic order. The British government strategically promoted such spirit of citizenship under its colonial administration in the then Tanganyika precisely to promote its colonial interests and authority. The distinctive division of the people on tribal lines, with the role of tribal chiefs celebrated and the chiefs offered all kinds of privileges, enabled the colonial administration to effectively divide and rule the country. At the same time, by promoting more and better education opportunities in predominantly Christian parts of the country, the colonial administration assured itself that the lesser educated Muslims would not undermine the Christianity crusade which British colonialism was partly founded on.

To entrench its national culture and attitudes, British colonialism used education as the primary instrument. In lower classes of education, in primary and middle schools, the critical stage for the formation of attitudes, civics was introduced as a political education subject to glorify the British Empire, the King or Queen and its systems of governance. The impact on people's attitudes was generally awesome and overwhelming. National identity became "colonised". Therefore, education is a critical vehicle in forming the mindset. Almost everything in society- stability and change- are influenced by education. This is the reason why Tanzania's Founding President, Mwalimu Julius Nyerere recognised very early on in the immediate aftermath of independence that without addressing the philosophy and purpose of education it would be difficult to build a new citizen whose mindset was decolonised and whose values were consistent with the challenges of constructing an independent, peaceful, unified and developed nation. In this regard, Nyerere wrote a booklet titled *Education for Self Reliance* in 1967. In that publication, he cogently argued, that in the pursuit of education, before and post independence, Tanzania had never "stopped to consider why we want education, what its purpose is".

Education for Self Reliance

In justifying the adoption of a new philosophy of education, Nyerere posited that the purpose of education was to transmit from one generation to the next the accumulated vision and knowledge of the society and to prepare young people for their future membership of the society and their active participation in its maintenance and development. His view was that colonial education had inculcated the values of the colonising state as well as its interests. Those values had to be overturned. The underlying philosophy of Education for Self Reliance was: the transformation of Tanzanian education to promote co-operative endeavour, equality and responsibility to give service, counteract intellectual arrogance, prepare young people to work anywhere in the service of the nation, promote the ability to think independently, interpret issues "through the democratic institution of our society" and encourage the growth of socialist values.

This is not the place to critique Nyerere's philosophy of education, much as there is a body of opinion that holds that Education for Self -Reliance has failed and that it has contributed to what is now perceived to be poor education standards. My quick response to this view is that in matters of philosophy we should always distinguish between what Karl Popper described in his work, *Conjectures and refutations* as "methods or techniques" and the "sensitivity to problems and a consuming passion" for those problems. Put differently, Nyerere did not prescribe the curriculum for education for self-reliance. He merely gave the curriculum a philosophical underpinning based on a consuming passion and sensitivity to a new societal environment. I have referred to Nyerere's Education for Self-Reliance because its philosophy has relevance in moulding a new Tanzanian.

Inevitably, Nyerere's philosophy of education was informed by the kind of future society he envisioned for Tanzania. The new society embraced the following attributes: social and economic justice, absence of abject poverty, human dignity, equality, self-reliance, ethical behaviour and caring for the disadvantaged and the disabled. It was to be built primarily through non-pluralistic political and economic systems, namely a one party state and public ownership of the major means of production, exchange and distribution. Thus political education, which replaced the colonial "Civics," introduced as part of education for self reliance and taught in primary and secondary schools and even as a cross-cutting subject in all faculties and institutes in the university and institutions of higher learning, was singularly informed by Nyerere's Vision of the new Tanzania.

Education for a New Era

Since 1986, however, Tanzania has been going through major changes of a political and economic character. The multiparty political system has stepped in and so has a market economic system. In such circumstances, it is inevitable to ask whether Nyerere's philosophy of education is still relevant and appropriate and whether a new philosophy of education for ingraining a new mindset that is in tune with such environment and the new global political and economic realities is needed. In addressing such question, about the challenges of a new era, I should concede being inspired by recent debates in Britain, under Tony Blair's leadership, on the role of education and its specific relationship with the development of a new breed of citizenry. In a Report on *Democracy and Citizenship in Schools in Britain* by the Advisory Group on Education for Citizenship and Teaching of Democracy in schools, chaired by University of London Professor Bernard Crick and released in September 1998, it was pointed out that lessons on how to be a good citizen should form part of the national curriculum in order to combat "apathy, ignorance and cynicism" about public life. Whilst underscoring the need for safeguards to prevent indoctrination, the report recommended that schoolchildren should:

- be taught about socially and morally responsible behaviour;

- learn about becoming helpfully involved in the life of the community and encouraged to do voluntary work;

- be given more instructions political literacy and on how to make oneself effective in public life, including knowledge about conflict resolution.

Reviews of the Report point to the fact that no part of British education had been as dangerously neglected as "citizenship", about what it meant to be citizens in a modern state. Interestingly, there is a great deal of meeting of minds between the philosophy behind the British Report and Nyerere's philosophy of education. The only point of departure is probably what has taken place in Tanzania between Nyerere's retirement from the highest office of State in 1985 and presently. Two major transformations have taken place in Tanzania that makes the ethos of the British Report inspiring for the country. These are the emergence of political and economic pluralism. For whatever Tanzanians may say in hailing these inevitable transformations, they should take cognisance, at the same time, of the underlying social fragility that engulfs the Tanzanian society. In other words, the Tanzanian society may not have been well prepared to embrace such changes.

The manifestations of such fragility are thus vivid. At the level of multiparty politics, the people agonise at and are concerned about the extent of political immaturity that pervades political tasks. Indeed, it is even debatable whether effective political opposition exists in Tanzania today. At another level, secularism, which, for many years contributed to national unity, peace and stability, has increasingly become undermined by bigotry. Could its source be attributed to the growing state of despair and poverty in the inner cities of urban Tanzania? In my view, anti-secularism is much deeper and has a colonial background as outlined earlier.

At the same time, there is general apathy in the people towards playing a greater role in the democratic process beyond participation in elections. The spirit of participation, of nation building, so fired up in the 1970s, has significantly waned. The youth, who also once constituted a revolutionary cadre with a vanguard mindset, have now reverted to money seeking activities, or *"bongoism"*, with minimal interest in voluntary work and nation building activities. Tanzania faces its worst disenchantment with politics of development in decades. It is a tragedy for political pluralism and for the positive economic reforms under implementation. On the other hand, economic pluralism has catapulted the characteristic tensions of a transition from a socialist or welfare state system that assured people of jobs and welfare to a market system largely lacking in the kind of social safety nets that could render legitimacy and credibility to the new economic system. Thus, there is a perception, often misleading, that economic liberalisation and privatisation would worsen the economic condition of the broad masses. These new transformations constitute a radical shift from some of the core philosophies that informed Nyerere's education for self-reliance. Even then, many of the societal attributes that Nyerere sought to realise remain relevant. It is the human and institutional means for their realisation that are changing. These vehicles are bound to dramatically change in the future. Thus, Tanzanians should be clearer in their minds of the social revolution that engulfs them. It is a revolution that Charles Handy described in his book, *The Hungry Spirit,* as "the switch from a life that is largely organised for us— to a world in which we are all forced to be in charge of our own destiny". Yet, it is these new institutional means that conspire to sow the seeds of social and cultural fragmentation as well as instability.

Tanzanian school curriculum has now dropped political education and a new curriculum called "social studies" has replaced it. It would be dangerous were this change to be treated simply as a mechanistic response by educators to the new realities in Tanzania. Tanzania should re-visit the philosophical underpinnings of Education for Self-Reliance and, in the context of a new vision that responds to the national and global challenges of a new millennium, develop a new philosophy of education. Fostering a new generation of responsible citizens enriched by the core values that have enabled Tanzania to be peaceful, stable and united, is a lofty goal to pursue and sustain. Without such a new breed of citizenry, the new vehicles of social and economic transformation, namely political pluralism and the market, may fail to build the envisioned new social and economic order. Here then lies an urgent and critical challenge for the political leadership and philosophers of education. Equipping men, women and children with a new citizenship mindset through education, as opposed to indoctrination, should constitute the central and urgent task of the education system. As Federico Mayor *et al* writes in the book, *The World Ahead: Our Future In The Making,* "It is first and foremost, through education that the values of non-violence, tolerance, democracy, solidarity and justice, which are the very lifeblood of peace, can be passed on to individuals at the very early age. Education should promote open-mindedness, which is vital in a world where the interdependence of nations and peoples and their interactions are becoming increasingly important day by day. The task is not to combat what is different but to explain and understand it."

Chapter

33 PROMOTING A KNOWLEDGE SOCIETY

Poor countries-and poor people differ from rich ones not because they have less capital but because they have less knowledge. Knowledge is often costly to create, and that is why much of it is created in industrial countries. But developing countries can acquire knowledge overseas as well as create their own at home.

-World Development Report 1998/1999: *Knowledge for Development.*

Since 1984, when Tanzania began to rethink its development philosophy and strategy, a new intellectual ferment driven by a progressive and nationalistic rethinking has been taking root in the Tanzanian body politic. Current social, economic and political ideologies and directions drive this ferment. It has also featured in the context of the constitutional and democratic system and in the social service delivery system. There is growing concern in the Tanzanian society about the state of the education system. It is a growing concern because, around the world- developed and developing- educational systems, public and private, are now generally considered to be lagging behind the transformation in learning that is evolving outside the school system. Increasingly, knowledge work now underpins the competitiveness of national economies and economic growth. The conventional factors for promoting economic development, namely labour, land and capital, whilst still important, are considered not as critical. It is knowledge and information that now stand out as the prime drivers of development.

The leading American management guru, Peter Drucker, aptly captured this new dimension of development by asserting that the challenge of development now centres on moving from producing an "educated person" to creating a "knowledge person". Put differently, the central challenge that confronts educational systems if they are to become pivotal in transforming quality of lives is to create knowledge in societies.

New Challenges for Education

Here then lies the central area of concern for Tanzania. The education system in place is primarily geared at creating an educated person, not a knowledge person. Creating knowledge remains secondary. Because of such skewed focus in the educational system, the product, namely the educated person is not well equipped to absorb and apply new technology and new management best practices. Many Tanzanians, including those considered the best and the brightest are largely deficient in imagining the future. In other words, they are not able to build the strategic architecture so critical for the country to develop based on its own resources.

Mwalimu Julius Nyerere had considered good leadership a central factor of development. Many Tanzanians read such "leadership" in its common parlance. Yet, Nyerere saw leadership primarily as knowledge. To him, leadership was people-wide. This is the reason why he focused so much on literacy development; not to create an educated person, but, rather to use it as a vehicle for imparting knowledge. And knowledge that would create broad-based good leadership in the social, economic and political life of a person and the nation as a whole. As Tanzania considers the state of its education system, greater focus should be placed on what should be changed and achieved. The world has already entered the era of knowledge. The new mantra is the creation of knowledge societies and of promoting knowledge-based industries. Indeed, a new meaning of education and learning is in vogue. The inevitable challenge is to explore such knowledge and how it can be created quickly, and transferred and applied more effectively and productively. However, knowledge does not come cheap. Many developed countries spend about one fifth of their GDP on the production and dissemination of knowledge. In fact, knowledge formation constitutes the largest single investment in most developed countries. Moreover, about one-tenth of GDP in rich countries is spent on funding schooling of young people even before they enter the workforce.

In exploring what knowledge is and how to use the education system to create it, it is imperative that the educational bureaucracy in Tanzania adapts and quickly responds to new needs of training, especially in fields such as information and communications technology. More importantly, both the government and industry should view education and training as the most important competitive factor in national development. They should move from regarding education and training as a mere issue of social policy and treat it instead as a prime economic policy question.

Key Features of a New Education System

Some of the key features of such an economic policy-driven education and training system are the following:

First, there is need to set high standards of educational achievement at all levels of education and training. Wide access to education being implemented under the Primary Education development Programme should not lead to lowering of standards. The government should ensure that educational and training institutions, particularly those in the private sector, promote high standards of educational and training excellence. It is regrettable, for example, that the growing number of modern hotels and lodges in Tanzania are disappointed by the quality of people produced by most Tanzanian Hotel Management Schools. The same goes for many institutions offering computer training. The system used to approve accreditation of institutions of higher learning should be extended to all registered institutions that provide education and training at different levels.

Second, it is imperative that teaching be once again elevated, as it used to be in the 1970s, as a *valued* and *prestigious* profession. The quality of teacher training should be improved. This, of necessity, requires improvement of pay and benefits offered to teachers.

Third, student education should involve more and more practical orientation. It is a setback, in this context, that Mwalimu Nyerere's sound philosophy of education for self-reliance that incorporated a curriculum involving practical orientation should have been so poorly interpreted and implemented. In the context of the current economic environment, practical orientation should embrace basic education foundations such as computing, business writing and foreign languages.

Fourth, more technical and professional colleges with high standards should be promoted by the government and the private sector. It is unfortunate that professional institutions of higher learning such as the Institute of Development Management. IDM) and the Institute of Finance Management. IFM) should transform themselves into Universities. In Germany, many technical and professional institutes are as prestigious as Universities.

Fifth, it is important that the government creates the enabling conditions for the private sector to invest in education and training of the workforce. A radical review of current high payroll taxes is necessary if employers are to be motivated to create more jobs and invest more in training for productivity growth.

Tanzania Development Vision 2025 incorporates, as one of its central goals, the creation of a well-educated and learning society. By year 2025, it is envisioned that Tanzania would be a nation with a high level of education at all levels; a nation with people well equipped with appropriate knowledge to confront national development challenges. The central challenge is how to chart out concrete strategies that would enable this goal of to be realised.

Chapter

34 CHALLENGES FACING THE AFRICAN UNIVERSITY

The African university ... must move away from the traditions of Western Universities and evolve a different approach to its task. The truly African University must be one that draws its inspiration from its environment; not a transplanted tree, but one growing from a seed that is planted and nurtured in the African soil.

Ajayi, Ade et al: ***The African Experience with Higher Education.***

During the past two decades, numerous countries, especially those confronted by serious challenges of underdevelopment, have attempted to redefine and even re-configure their social, economic and political policies to fit the new realities that the 21st century is expected to unleash. The common cliché has been how to get poor nations to move beyond managing change to leading change; in other words, how to stay ahead of change.

The late Mwalimu Julius K. Nyerere wrote in the Introduction to his book, *Freedom And Unity* that for Africa the choice was not between change and no change; rather it is between changing and being changed; changing its lives under its own direction or being changed by the impact of forces outside its control. At the dawn of the new century and millennium, it is important to reflect seriously whether Africa is truly leading change or is, instead, being changed by forces external to it. Otherwise, why should Africa now be engrossed in the seemingly valiant quest for a renaissance that Thabo Mbeki has paraphrased as the "new birth of Africa"? Is Africa dead, philosophically? Moreover, whatever has happened to the role and contribution of African intellectuals and intelligentsia? Has the purpose and mission of the African University lost its mantle or has it become skewed, not properly focused? Is the African University lacking an in-built dynamic suited to the form and pace of global change and to its own African challenge of development? Why is Africa, more than 40 years after independence, still mired in extreme poverty, ignorance, disease, civil strife and conflict? Indeed, is it not true that Africa is poorer today than it was in 1957 when Ghana became independent? These are pertinent questions to consider in examining the mission and vision of the African University.

Let me put these questions into relevant context. At the formal ceremony marking the commencement of the Faculty of Law of the then University College of Dar es Salaam in October 1961, Mwalimu Julius K. Nyerere, then Prime Minister, had this to say, "We are in the process of building up a Tanganyika nation. Valuable as is the contribution which overseas education can give us, in the long run, if we are to build up a sturdy sense of nationhood, we must nurture our own educated citizens. Our young men and women must have an African-oriented education. That is, an education which is not only given in Africa but is also directed at meeting the present needs of Africa. For while other people can aim at reaching the moon, and while in future we might aim at reaching the moon, our present plans must be directed at reaching the villages."

Later, when inaugurating the University of East Africa in June 1963, Nyerere was more specific on the mission of the African University. Acknowledging the importance of the University being more concerned with the year 2000 and beyond, which would have constituted a University vision, he went on to underscore the importance of the present at that material time. To quote him: "It is *now*. emphasis his) that we have to engage the three enemies. that is poverty, ignorance and disease) whose names have become a cliché, but who oppress us more than ever— Our problems will not wait. We must, and do demand that this University takes an active part in the social revolution we are engineering." Those that seriously study Mwalimu would know that Nyerere's philosophical consistency of vision and mission was his greatest forte. In June 1966, when opening the *General Assembly of the World University Service*, Mwalimu restated the mission of the university. He said, "there are priorities, and we have to look at the immediate future, and the immediate present, and decide what it is that the University in our kind of society can at present most usefully give to the world of which we are a part - I do not believe that they can at this stage pursue 'pure research' and 'knowledge for its own sake' without neglecting other functions which are for the time being more important".

Many of the new African universities came into being at the same time as the birth of the independent African state. Therefore, it is inevitable to ask why the promise of modernisation has eluded Africa. Why has the purpose and mission of the African University, so well articulated by the founding fathers of Africa's independence, failed to rise to the challenges of poverty, ignorance and disease? *The Challenge to the South* postulated interesting observations in this context. Arguing from the standpoint that countries of the South have generally failed to adequately adapt higher education to development needs, especially in the context of a failure to foster a science and technology culture, the *South Commission Report* concluded that "education has too often continued on the lines set in the past, and has been too academic and unsuited to the scientific, vocational and other needs of societies in the process of modernization." Specifically in the context of University education, the Report further observed, "Under pressure to accommodate more students, universities have tended to neglect quality". The Report called for a university expansion programme that is carefully planned and linked to development needs and priorities. It would be interesting to find out how the African University has responded to the South Commission's view and advice, a decade and a half after the release of its Report.

At the level of the University of Dar es Salaam, we may wish to be self critical about the objective rationale of the strategic transformation programme 2000 and determine to what extent the programme addresses the question of quality of the university product. For those in industry, manufacturing and service sectors, they would agree that there is a widespread view that the quality of Tanzanian graduates today is lower than that of Kenya and Uganda. This shortcoming should be addressed. At a conference on Academic Freedom at the University of Dar es Salaam in mid February 2005, the question regarding "marketisation" of the university arose. A predominant view prevailed that knowledge and standards had become devalued in the interest of producing more graduates. Academic research has suffered due to shortage of state funding and the quality of teaching has inevitably diminished.

Whilst acknowledging the broad shortcomings of the mission of the African university to-date, it is also important to recognise that, like the rest of the world, Africa is in a state of social and political flux. As Professor Furedi has aptly observed, the world has gone through a major transformation from competing political philosophies that offered contrasting visions of society during the 19th century to a political landscape at the end of the 20th century that is marked by an impotent politics that is neither ardently committed to the free-market philosophy or to a robust "revolutionary" transformation. This environment imposes a new set of challenges on the African university. Until about a decade ago, most of Africa was shackled by political and economic philosophies anchored in the one party state, military dictatorship, state capitalism, and a fear of the market. Indeed, ethnic conflict and other forms of civil strife continue to bedevil nationhood, peace, and stability in several African states. Evidently, a new era is now emerging. A political and economic paradigm of a new African society is taking shape. It is ostensibly a paradigm of shared destiny encapsulated in what is called the African renaissance, well captured in the birth of the African Union and NEPAD. The attributes of the vision are a deep sense of African confidence and pride, a sense of competence to make Africa prosper and take care of its own problems, democracy, good governance, social inclusion, moral virtues, including an ardent attack on corruption, peace and stability, tolerance, gender equality and social and economic justice. How the African university would help to nurture and instil the ethics that engender and ingrain all these values and capacities clearly demands a new bold vision and mission for the African university. But can the African university rise to the challenge when one perceives a bewildering sense of powerlessness on the part of academics so well exhibited by Professor Shivji's lament about university mandarins having hijacked the core mission of the university and ostensibly undermining the university's radical political discourse?

Herbert Vilekazi, a Professor of Sociology at the University of Zululand, in an article titled, *The Problem of African Universities*, aptly asserted that, "like African civilisation itself, African Universities are in deep crisis. Indeed, the crisis of African civilisation, and of contemporary African societies, cannot but influence, in a larger sense, the shape, direction, and mental and spiritual life of African Universities." The question is who will liberate the other? In the view of Professor Vilekazi, the African university must become more and more "the dominant source of the guiding light of society". In other words, the new vision, that of the African renaissance, should be driven by what Mahmood Mamdani has described as "a re-awakening of creative thought" in the arts, culture, philosophy and social sciences. Thabo Mbeki equally sees Africa's rediscovery of its own soul as the critical underpinning for the realisation of African renaissance. The vision of the African university should thus be to enable Africa rediscover this soul. The key question is how it should go about enabling such process of rediscovery to unfold?

As a start, the mission of the African University could focus on creating what Paul Baran described as the "intellect worker" - a person who lives by his wits and works with his mind. More importantly, however, it should seek to create an African intellectual, a person who is restless in the quest to influence the nature and context of social and political change. Such person is a fearless social critic; one who moulds public opinion. He is also a person able to be creative and innovative in transforming his or her own quality of life and that of the nation.

It clearly follows that how the African university positions itself to meet the vision of the African renaissance demands visionary leadership, not simply at its helm, but also across all the focal points of the African university-wide leadership. The university needs a leadership that provides a commonsense of direction and taps the genius of knowledge. Such leadership is imperative if the African university is going to spearhead what Nyerere described as the social revolution that Africa is engineering.

Chapter

35 TOWARDS AN ENTREPRENEURIAL UNIVERSITY

At a time when cynicism is so prevalent and the need for reliable information is so important, any damage to the reputation of universities, and to the integrity and objectivity of their scholars, weakens not only the academy but the functioning of our democratic, self-governing society. That is quite a price to pay for the limited, often exaggerated gains that commercialization brings to even the best-known institutions.

Derek Bok: *Universities In The Marketplace: The Commercialization of Higher Education.*

T he lofty and pragmatic moves of attempting to transform the funding culture of the University of Dar es Salaam and to give the University a business orientation in recent years are of great interest and even concern. Time has come for all public institutions of higher learning to become entrepreneurial organisations if they are to cope with declining state subventions to fund their operations. However, there are, at the same time, several *ifs* and *buts*. At a time when heightened international competition demands higher educational standards and skills, it is important for countries like Tanzania to upgrade their systems of education and training. In the industrialised world, and indeed, in the newly industrialised countries, the general thinking in this area is that education and training, to cite Michael Porter from his book, *The Competitive Advantage of Nations*, "constitute perhaps the single greatest long-term leverage point available to all levels of government in upgrading industry".

The Challenges for Change

At the outset, I wish to address some of the common pessimisms advanced when an idea to inject a business orientation into a University is promoted. Professor Charles Bernstein of the University of New York at Buffalo in his article published in *Deadalus* titled, *A Blow is like an Instrument* takes a very cautious, almost negative stance, about the entry of the market into the United States University arena. His view is that, "the most salient values of the University are reflected by the fact that it is the largest and most vibrant non-commercial quasi-public space in the United States. The bright idea of managers and politicians to adopt commercial decision making on campus is almost always an erosion of the immutable value of the institution, destructive beyond measure." Professor Bernstein's major concern is that, in trying to make education more efficient, in market terms, it instead turns more deficient in terms of the quality of the core mission. This view is interesting and has some contextual relevance to what the University of Dar es Salaam is embarking on. At the same time, however, one has to be mindful of other ideas that have been generated in a similar context. Nobody in the academic world has probably written as much on the role and challenges that confront non-profit institutions, such as Universities, as the global management guru, Professor Peter Drucker. Reading his books, *Innovation and Entrepreneurship* and *Managing for the Future*, amongst several others, the common underlying message is that non-profit institutions are dominantly bogged down by outdated philosophies, such as "good intentions and a noble cause are all that is needed to produce results," or that having a good mission, in itself, is adequate when in fact "it spawns bureaucracy".

Drucker points out that management, in its business sense, invariably eludes non-profit institutions precisely because they lack a bottom line. In turn, the absence of a bottom line hampers the emergence or the existence of the discipline common to business or profit-oriented organisations. Put differently, Universities would find it tough to raise resources to meet growing costs if they do not adopt principles of management applied in business firms. Evidently, the reason behind the University of Dar es Salaam thinking about creating income generating activities is precisely because public funding of the university by the government has not only been fluctuating, consistently since the early 1990s, but has also been unpredictable in terms of amounts. Appropriations have fallen substantially below budget projections while unpredictability of adequate funding has also had serious implications on the efficient running of the University. In this context, academic semesters have sometimes been dislocated. Student research-based course work has also often suffered thereby adversely affecting normal systems of academic assessment.

In sum, the gap between budget projections and cost realities has heightened the economic pressure on the University. It is evident, at the same time, that public universities and state subvented institutions of higher learning are now generally under pressure to reduce costs. However, in the absence of a profit test, to borrow from Peter Drucker's words, "size is the one criterion of success for a service institution, and growth a goal in itself," the university is not adequately kept on its toes to perform and be accountable. With this new perception, the university is now expected to function more like a business and survive in a competitive context.

Are Income-Generating Activities Meaningful?

Given the present Tanzanian economic conditions, the critical challenge faced by public universities- of Dar es Salaam, Sokoine, Open University and Mzumbe- is how to realistically develop viable plurality of self-generated funding sources. The pertinent question is, can a public Tanzanian university pursue economic generating activities of any serious magnitude to enable it to bridge its budget shortfalls without sacrificing and undermining its basic mission? Equally, it could further be asked: how realistic would the objective of limiting the income generating activities to only those that are consistent with the basic mission, functions and aspirations of a university be? For example, should the University of Dar es Salaam not ask itself if, in fact, it is not being forced by the state into activities that would be inconsistent with its basic mission by failing to fulfil its most basic responsibility of providing adequate funding?

It would be recalled that one University-wide income generating activity initiated in the academic year 1997/1998 related to the decision to allow the admission of students who could privately fund their own tuition fees. In that year, 149 privately sponsored students were enrolled. That decision has not bore the expected results viewed in the context of the total number of students that qualify to be enrolled and yet not able to receive bursaries from the state to enable them pursue university education. In academic year 2002/2003, the University of Dar es Salaam received a total of 6403 applications for admission by qualifying students. However, only 3579 or 56% were admitted. Part of the problem for such low admissions is the acute lack of space for both lecture rooms and accommodation. However, this is clearly a chicken and egg paradox. The government should expand University facilities. Such task is way beyond the university's income generating capacity. Commencing the 1998/99 academic year, the University was forced to reduce tuition fees for privately sponsored students in an effort to bolster the number of such candidates. In 1999/2000, the number of these students rose to 384 and has been on the increase yearly.

Lessons of Poor Experience

The recent history of income generating activities at the University of Dar es Salaam has not been a rosy one. The University has presumably learnt the lesson from its past negative experiences. The story of the University Consultancy Bureau, for example, much as it's more recent performance results have been somewhat encouraging, is still not something to be proud of. Evidently, the Consultancy Bureau could be one of the university's key starting points in injecting a more focused business orientation. Presently, the Bureau is run largely on good intentions and a noble cause. It is more or else a one-person leadership organisation lacking in the most basic management and organisational requirements. Clearly, this is not the best way to run a business as a business. It is advisable that the Bureau learns from similar organisations elsewhere, such as the US Boston Consulting Group. There should also be several numerous examples to learn from in the developing world.

The Institute of Production Innovation. IPI) is yet another sad story. Though originally not created as an income generating unit, the IPI had the necessary seeds that could have effectively been fertilised to transform itself into a successful knowledge-based income-generating project. However, the success of the IPI was allowed to hinge more on external funding support, later to constitute the root cause of its demise, as aid vanished, than on the economic viability of its activities. In other words, the IPI should have clearly delineated its Research and Development. R&D) mission, an academic-focused mission, from its commercial objectives. The mixture of the two objectives, much as they were strategically complementary in terms of prototype technology development, over time they precipitated, over time, a non-commercial approach to resource allocation, technology commercialisation and market development. The idea of creating a University-wide Income Generating Unit. IGU), which the University adopted in 1999, was informed by lessons drawn from this past poor performance.

Towards a New Perspective

Certainly, one of the clear and immediate benefits of the IGU emanates from the need for the university to develop an investment stimulus programme that can make the university more attractive to investors. In the past, the university lacked a well-organised capacity to determine it's economic and investment interests and negotiate for "yes" with potential investors. As the University of Dar es Salaam continues to search more widely into how best its rich land endowment could be put to greater productive and economic beneficial use, the role of the IGU becomes more critical, more so since the university has been granted title to all its lands, a historic development since the university's inception in 1970. In the light of this development, negotiations of future investments involving, for example, the university owned Silversands Hotel and other land-use investments should be more beneficial to the University. Presumably, there are other income-generating activities that the IGU could develop. In this case, the role of University Faculties, Institutes and Departments would be important and essential in determining what economic ventures, from the vantage point of their own decentralised situations, would make economic sense. However, for the University to be able to effectively and efficiently handle and manage these new responsibilities that are outside its mainstream activities, it is important that it addresses what structure and system of management is best suited for the IGU. As a start, the IGU should be incorporated into a limited liability company and allowed to operate on commercial lines.

Promoting Entrepreneurial Ideas

I wish to underscore the imperativeness of decentralised centres of ideas formation and decision-making being given as much space as possible to propose what income generating activities should be adopted and the strategies that should be applied to make them achievable and profitable. What should be heeded in driving such objective and exercise is the recognition that income generation is a double-edged phenomenon. In a typical business, income can either be increased through growth or by cutting costs and raising productivity or both. Indeed, in periods of punctualised equilibrium, in other words, periods of economic uncertainties, as those that presently characterise the Tanzanian and global situation, income generation is often achieved by increasing productivity, downsizing activities, freezing salaries, selling off non-core assets, staff retrenchment and cutting back on operational costs such as energy and telecommunications. However, in my view, the University stands a better chance to succeed in its income generation task if it pursues the path of raising productivity and cost cutting. I say so from the vantage position of knowing intimately the serious constraints the University would face in creating meaningful returns from the obtaining highly competitive Tanzanian environment much as the IGU, with the close support of the knowledge-based organs of the University, could develop significant economically meaningful projects.

As alluded to earlier, there are opportunities to be seized in the consultancy area, from instituting programmes that optimise strong relationships with industry at the level of R&D, particularly involving the Centre for Continuing Education. CCE), the Centre for Entrepreneurship Development, the Computing Centre Limited and some of the science-based units as well as in jointly undertaken research projects. One concrete business development opportunity available to the university to exploit and which falls within its core competence and mission lies within the scope of the CCE. The university, as a business, focused on its core mission, means providing lifelong learning opportunities for Tanzanians. Presently, the university is not adequately tapping the available market niche. It should be possible for the university, like many universities in the United States and in the UK, to provide short-term, continuing education courses for business executives, professional and technical people. The university should also encourage employers and professional associations to access tailor-made executive graduate business programmes, whose admission standards would not necessarily require possession of an undergraduate or honours degree. Some of these graduate programmes could be made flexible in such a way that there is a compulsory class attendance of so many weeks of the course's duration and the balance undertaken through distance education. The University of Dar es Salaam through its Faculty of Commerce and management has started such Executive MBA degree programme, but it lacks in-built flexibility to enable a busy business executive to pursue it comfortably.

What is of particular importance is that the curriculum of these programmes, whether of short duration or of a graduate character, should be structured in such a manner as to meet the criterion of their being close to the market; in other words, they should be demand driven. Unfortunately, the University of Dar es Salaam is still mired in traditional business academic programmes. Greater innovation is required. The university is falling behind in terms of flexibility and versatility of academic education, attributes that are today of strategic importance in boosting university revenues and meeting customer demands. It should be noted, for instance, that Professor Issa Shivji, in February, 2005 raised criticism against the semester system which the university introduced in academic year 2002, describing it as "cutting up courses into bits and pieces, regardless of whether it makes pedagogical sense, to enable fee-paying students to collect necessary units to pass". This broadside was strange because the semester system has been in place in many universities around the world for almost a century. Even the more conservative British universities have introduced it. Little wonder, in this context, that when the ILO Representative in Tanzania in mid 2004 raised the question about the relevance of some of the courses offered at the university he was fiercely attacked for seeking to water down the quality of courses offered and for attempting the make the university surrogate to market demands. Yet he was right to observe that many of the course subjects and content offered, especially in economics and business fields, had seen their day.

Referring to a similar environment, Harvard Professor and former Harvard President and Dean of Harvard Law School, Derek Bok has aptly noted in his book, *Universities In The Marketplace: The Commercialization of Higher Education,* that, "Some faculty members will cry foul, claiming that teaching is simply not comparable to a piece of merchandise. But protestations of this kind cannot hide the fact that very few universities make a serious, systematic effort to study their own teaching, let alone try to assess how much their students learn or to experiment with new methods of instruction. Instead, faculty members invoke all manner of rationalisations-academic freedom, professional autonomy, privacy- to resist efforts to subject their teaching to outside scrutiny."

Productivity Improvement

So how could the University stimulate higher productivity and cut costs? I would like to suggest a number of ways in which the University could possibly pursue this objective. These include, first, the University being clear about the forces that are affecting its ability to fulfil its mission at the optimal level. The question to be asked is: are the forces internal or are they external? For example: to what extent has the University considered all possible avenues in improving its student-faculty ratio by going for larger classes held in the centre of the City of Dar es Salaam, at the Institute of Finance Management. IFM), where there is unutilised space? I do not perceive any justifiable reason why the teaching of many commerce and management courses could not be undertaken at available teaching classrooms at the IFM. Moreover, the Executive MBA degree programme could be offered outside the university precincts, since the university is located far from where the large pools of students come from. The university could also consider reducing its costs by retaining part-time lecturers who are outside the university but without necessarily sacrificing standards? What could the university learn in this context from the costs of teaching delivery of the Open University of Tanzania?

Secondly, the University could stimulate higher productivity by challenging itself to adopt entrepreneurial management and policies. Entrepreneurial management demands that the University undertakes the following: First, it systematically reviews and abandons whatever activity-academic, administrative or physical-that is irrelevant, unproductive, obsolete or outworn. The University needs to embrace what Peter Drucker describes as a "culture of greed for new things" which is achieved by treating existing services, processes and activities as short-lived. The central question that the university should consistently ask itself is what does it have to do to stop wasting resources in given undertakings or activities? For instance, is the degree programme in physical education and sports cost-effective? What is the tutor-student ratio? Is the university reaping the benefits of size? Would it not make greater economic sense for students wishing to pursue degree courses in physical education and sports to go to South African universities?

Conclusion

Evidently, it is not easy to translate a typical business enterprise experience onto a non-profit institution like the university. However, and as a conclusion, I should underscore the fact that businesses, profit and non-profit alike, do not reform simply because of some promising new ideas. They are compelled to do so because they have to survive. However, I am not optimistic that business enterprise development in the form of income generating activities could save a public university from serious vulnerability. Ultimately, the government should come to terms with the need and challenge to fulfil its core responsibility in supporting universities as Centres of Excellence. University's own income generating activities can only be a complementary effort, one that is focussed on linking theory and practice, even as it makes money, rather than being a typical business activity. Where business investments that do not over-extend the University's resources, academic and non-academic, present themselves or can be promoted, then they should be welcome and exploited. I do not believe that this is as simple an issue as to justify a sweeping view posited by Shivji that "universities are being transformed from sites of knowledge production to sites of hotel construction; from building lecture halls to pre-fabricating shopping malls." Surely, the University of Dar es Salaam Mlimani Investment Project need not necessarily dilute the University's academic excellence! If it were to be so, then many Universities in the US and UK would have lost their academic standing. Yet the challenge remains, namely how best to balance available resources from the state with funding sourced from University's own entrepreneurial opportunities and avenues.

Chapter

36 YOUTH: A TIME OF HOPE?

The idea that young people will one day `inherit` the earth should be dispelled;
their involvement today is necessary for achieving sustainable development.
Although their `expertise` in "youth issues" is evident, their input should not be
limited to this arena. Youth are both willing and capable of formulating
pointed criticism and action strategies; and therefore, should be involved in all
of the pressing sustainable development struggles facing the global community.

-Youth: Building Knowledge Societies, Final Report and
Recommendations to the Global Knowledge Partnership Online
Conference of Young People, January and February 2000,. www.iisd.org.)

Introduction

B
ack in 1990, Dr. Nafis Sadiq, in outlining the importance of looking
at young women's life choices in the context of the future of the
world's population, made an apt observation about youth. She
postulated, "Youth is a time of hope, expectation and excitement about
the future. This is also a period of constant change in one's life-physically,
emotionally and intellectually - a crucial period that can determine the
future". It is difficult to disagree with a characterisation that is, by
definition, valid and full of meaning. Indeed, around the world to day, we
witness, in many arenas, this hope, expectation and excitement emerging
and taking root. In all these arenas, where more and more younger people
are taking charge in politics and in business, a time of hope is nigh for the
youth. To be young is now to have huge opportunities open before you.
The challenge becomes how the youth are able to exploit available
opportunities to their advantage. In addition, it is not as if such "time of
hope" is only a monopoly of the industrialised rich countries. The newly
industrialised countries of China, South East Asia and the Far East have
witnessed many young people taking the lead in business innovations and
entrepreneurship. In India, the computer software revolution is indeed a
brainchild of young engineers. For these countries, youth does present a
period of expectation and excitement.

Building an Environment supportive of Youth Development

It is significant to note though that as an embodiment of the future, the
youth have to be able to translate hope into reality. This necessitates the

existence of an enabling environment, one that is enriched by culture, education, religion and parental and community values. It is not therefore coincidental to see fast economic growth trends in countries where culture, religion and social values are deep rooted. The highest levels of education, especially in mathematics and physical sciences are a typical phenomenon of the Far East and East Asian Countries. They far exceed those of the USA and Western Europe. These countries design and implement policies designed to improve the status of young people. They pay close attention to their needs and allow them opportunities to be innovative and creative. They provide them with new knowledge and the appropriate tools that help them to challenge the conditions they are in and to foster change.

If nations are going to sustain the achievements and gains of political independence, namely freedom, equality, development, unity and peace, they have to address the challenge of how to secure life choices for young men and women. It is the youth who shape the future. They can promote sustainable growth and national cohesion. Thus, in the case of Tanzania, can we confidently assert that we live in times that foster hope for the youth? Evidently, Tanzania has a youth policy developed by the government a few years ago. One wonders, though, whether the policy was conceived in a broad participatory manner or whether, indeed, it adequately responds to the challenges that currently confront Tanzania youth.

In my view, the youth in Tanzania face serious challenges. These include:

- poor quality of basic education,
- declining quality of livelihood in rural areas,
- acute shortage of formal employment opportunities,
- low wages which do not correspond to cost of living,
- inadequate and affordable housing,
- strict conditions attached to access to equity finance,
- HIV/AIDS pandemic,
- teenage pregnancies largely driven by urban poverty,
- low-status employment for young women, and
- poor reproductive health services.

All these conditions point to a tough time for the youth. Thus, is it really time for hope for them?

Who Should Drive Hope of Youth?

Should the youth sit back and hope, like manna from heaven, that their situation would change? Such attitude would be disastrous. Hope would only come through self-management and development much as the government has a role to create the enabling conditions for self management and empowerment to take place. Tanzanian youth would have to learn to manage themselves, whether in terms of engaging the government on how to create the conditions that foster hope or in indulging in creative and innovative pursuits that create wealth. In pursuing either or both these ends, it is critical that the Tanzanian youth embrace Mwalimu Nyerere's famous statement: "the basis of human progress throughout history has been the existence of people who, regardless of the consequences to themselves, stood up when they believed it necessary and said, 'that is wrong; this is what we should do."

For those who were part of the higher education system in the 1960s and the early 1970s, they would not find these remarks unreasonably critical when I posit that the above-cited Mwalimu Nyerere's statement no longer finds place in the minds and actions of many Tanzanian youth today in the same manner they did earlier. The youth of the 1960s and early 1970s were more revolutionary, much as there are those who would still describe the 1966 University students' demonstration against the National Service, a hugely distorted phenomenon, as reactionary! In spite of the ostensibly intimidating structure of politics in the form of the one party system at the time, the youth were still courageous enough to be engaged in and to challenge the politics of the day. Theirs was the spirit of boldness and daringness. After all, on the question of high salaries paid to public officials, the students' protest was positively received by Mwalimu Nyerere and led to slashing of salaries. In his recent article, *From Neo-liberalism to Pan-Africanism: Reconstructing an East African Discourse.* www.nu.ac.za), Professor Issa Shivji has described the slashing of salaries as "a precursor to the leadership code of the Arusha declaration."

Today, however, the political structure is different. Political pluralism has stepped in and civil society is wide open to provide a platform for different views to contend. There is also the choice either to be politically aligned or to stay out of politics. Such a choice did not exist prior to 1992. Thus, here lies an opportunity for the youth to identify and project themselves and their travails, in a bipartisan and collective manner, across the political divides. Tanzanian youth is today better placed to articulate its vision, address its plight and construct its common goals without reference to a political and economic agenda established or promoted by a government in power or by any of the political parties in the opposition. Yet this opportunity is not effectively exploited. The excess baggage of yesteryears, of the youth feeling privileged to be part of a youth organisation linked to a political party is still dominantly in place. No wonder there is always such fierce struggle to take up leadership positions in the CCM Youth Organisation, as opposed to the more important need for the youth to establish strong organisations within the civil society. The youth are essentially an important component of civil society and it is at that level of society's organisation that they can more effectively promote and realise their collective interests.

Not that there is anything wrong about the youth being aligned to political parties. On the contrary, the youth should create the future of the nation and political parties constitute an important avenue to realise such a goal. The thrust of my argument is that the state of the youth in Tanzania today is such that they require unity across its divides - political, cultural, ethnic and religious- if they are to make the difference. There is too much at stake for youth development for the youth to be disunited in any form. In this context, reported attempts on the part of the government to enact a provision within the new umbrella law on higher education institutions in Tanzania that prohibits university students from partaking in political issues within the precincts of their institutions are clearly out of line and are contrary to fundamental rights of people as enshrined in the Tanzania Constitution.

A Crisis of Collective Youth Identity and Resolve

The Tanzania youth today is not valiantly questioning what the government is doing to promote its interests and interrogating whether the Ministry responsible for youth is indeed effective. It would seem that Tanzanian youth have lost hope. Indeed, the life style of many urban youth appears to be driven mainly by the quest for bread and butter. Self-indulgence and economic self-interest override their collective interests. It is now almost impossible to identify the common threads that are supposed to unite the youth. Youth stratification has become deep seated. It is embracing education, ethnic, tribal, wealth, political and religious differences. Such stratification did not exist in the 1960s and 1970s. Tragically, the youth today seem to have lost their moorings and collective sense of mission and direction, except in political pursuits and this is mainly limited in CCM. The youth are now at the centre of being used to promote the social vices of society especially drug trafficking and organised prostitution. In many respects, Tanzanian youth has been turned into *"messengers of death."* At the economic front, it is the youth that principally migrate from rural to urban areas in search of greener pastures that do not exist. These circumstances lead me to ask: are the Tanzanian youth able to participate, *collectively*, in critical issues that affect them? What are the underlying missions of youth organisations and youth ideas-formation that help to empower them? Are the youth clear about their common national concerns that should unite them on a collective basis? Are we not actually witnessing the emergence of a dangerous state of youth polarisation that does not augur well for a future strong and united nation?

Such disturbing scenario takes place at a time when the social, political and economic challenges that face the nation, be they political apathy, joblessness or HIV/AIDS, largely gravitate around the youth. At the political level, the youth are yet to take leading leadership roles. Presently, they do so but in a dissipated form rather than collectively. In contrast, the Tanzania Media Women Association. TAMWA) has been able to mobilise young women and girls to stand up for their rights at the political front and their demands for fundamental human rights have achieved notable results. However, the base of their struggle has to be broadened across gender and be more focused on youth. Growing criminality and social instability are the consequences of growing urbanisation where unemployment thrives. Education, poor as it has become in quality, has lost its mantle. It is no longer as prized as it used to be and for good reasons. Education among the youth is now perceived to no longer open doors of opportunities. The *"Bongo"* culture has stepped in instead. It is a culture of making a quick buck.

Conclusion

So, is it time for hope for Tanzanian youth? Clearly, as the situation stands to day, the answer is uncertain. The youth themselves should be organised and search for plausible and viable ways to give themselves hope. The government, on the other hand, has to work towards securing better life choices for the youth and thereby safeguard the future generation from the ills that now devastate the lives of many young men and women. Much needs to be done in areas such as improved quality of education, a return to family and community values, the stimulation of the industrial economy so that it creates more jobs and, finally, the improvement of the agricultural sector. These are onerous challenges. The national psyche and culture are at stake demanding that the whole nation rises to these challenges in all ways and means.

Chapter

37 CHALLENGES FOR YOUNG PROFESSIONALS

We cannot always build the future for our youth, but we can build the youth for our future.

- Franklin D. Roosevelt.

In his book, *The Invisible Continent*, the Japanese management guru, Kenichi Ohmae asserts the following: "In this world, children may often lead, because their parents will be busy unlearning the heritage of the last century." This is a powerful statement. However, does it apply to children of the poor world, of Tanzania, for example? This chapter examines whether indeed Tanzanian youth "may often lead" as their elders muddle to understand what is going on around them in a world driven by cutting edge technologies happening at the speed of light. In his address to the University of Liberia in February 1968, the late Mwalimu Julius Nyerere cited Jesus Christ's famous sermon: "For unto whomsoever much is given, of him shall be much required; and unto whom men have committed much, of him they shall seek the more." Where do young professionals unto whom Tanzania has committed much in their education and training, fit in the context of this message?

Young Tanzanians: Back Seat Attitude

In Mwalimu Nyerere's view, Africa is an exciting place to live in because Africa's development offers an exciting challenge and for those that are the educated, they have the unique and enviable opportunity to shape and lead the response to such challenge. Many Tanzanian young professionals, regrettably, seem to be sitting back waiting for the future to happen. They are not leading the process to shape Tanzania's future. Yet the country is pregnant with challenges that await the youth to step in and lead. One does not have to occupy a political office to perform such a task. The youth should have the courage and the sense of mission to bring ideas onto the public domain and thereby build a critical mass of understanding and support. It is possible to achieve this goal as long as the youth take up greater responsibility in shaping the direction Tanzania should take.

494

One of the frustrations commonly faced is precisely to be in the position where you witness a laid back stance that pervades the character of young intellectuals and professionals in Tanzania. We keep on asking: where are the whistle blowers, the movers and shakers, the people prepared to "rock the boat" and stand up to be counted in Tanzanian society? What is it that young professionals and the youth generally seem to "fear," if fear is what they fear in interrogating what is not right in the social milieu and the polity as a whole?

The youth seem overly occupied with shaping their own personal futures. This is a serious drawback. It is a mindset problem. The youth appear to view the Tanzanian situation- social, economic, political, technological and environmental -as an unsolved puzzle that awaits an occasional genius, like what the late Mwalimu Nyerere used to do, to unlock its secrets. Yet what lies before them is an empty space waiting to be filled. In this light, an immediate challenge they face is how they transform their mindset and respond to seize the opportunities that present themselves, opportunities that could surely change the lives of the majority of Tanzanians. What is disturbing about this mindset is that it thrives in an environment where many of those in leadership positions- in government, business and in civil society- the old folks if you will, still monopolise the process and management of change. The youth lack a critical mass of leadership to lead and to be ahead of change. Part of the reason for this deficit is that many of the older people holding positions of authority are still hesitant to abandon yesterday. The focus of their leadership remains heavily centred on realising some economic change when, in fact, there are also other profound challenges that engulf the country, such as changes in demographics, pandemics like HIV / AIDS, in ideological philosophy and generally in world-view.

Youth: Challenge of Pathfinding

Who then would lead such change if it were not the young professionals? Yet to be able to lead change, young professionals have to imbibe an inquisitive mind and acquire the courage of a pathfinder. They should propel themselves to a level, in society, where they would influence the emergence of new policies, new values and new behaviour. They have to appreciate, as the Economics Nobel Laureate Amartya Sen (1999) surmised in his book *Development as Freedom* that "in a democracy, people tend to get what they demand, and more crucially, do not typically get what they do not demand." The emergence of such new policies and new values is a process that crucially hinges on the level and intensity of political and social dialogue. Public debates and discussions leverage the conceptualisation of economic and other needs. Above all, they constitute the correlates of democracy. Given extensive reach, to cite Amartya Sen again, "these dialogues and debates can also make democracy itself function better" However, the record of participation of Tanzanian youth and young professionals in society within special interest groups has until, lately, been glaringly poor. How then could young professionals "democratise democracy," to borrow Anthony Giddens phrase, and thereby help to shape a Tanzanian future, if they take a back seat in national affairs? Could it be that we are witnessing a laid back stance driven by a happy and, probably, satisfied type who, in the words of the most celebrated modern English philosopher Isaiah Berlin, "live under a discipline which they accept without question, who freely obey the orders of leaders, spiritual or temporal, whose word is fully accepted as unbreakable law?"

Professionals worthy their salt, young and old, have a major responsibility to consolidate and strengthen a new wave and breed of politics. Tanzania needs a political renewal and renaissance and the youth have the onerous task to create new political thresholds and new spaces of political and economic engagement. Young professionals, in particular, should rise above the political space currently rooted in electoral and legislative politics. They should escape from their secluded specialist preserves and incipient parochialisms and forge coalitions based on a clear perspective fitting Tanzanian conditions and realities. After all, Young professionals are largely the intellectuals of our country. Therefore, they have a strategic role and task of giving voice to the conscience of the nation. They have to stop, to use the words of Rajni Kothari, "treating knowledge as a process of accumulation unrelated to political tasks." Their challenge is to sacrifice their immediate professional benefits and advantages, and earn greater respect, based, not on status, but on intellect and its application to national tasks. I know that many young professionals would retort that they are at the beginning of their careers and even of family lives. As such, they would not, ostensibly, risk their economic stability for some hazy lofty ideal.

Such attitude is short-termist and self-interest centred. It is an attitude founded on a philosophy that the Tanzanian environment is not adequately supportive of the growth of alchemists, defined here as people who create wealth out of their own innovation, creativity and entrepreneurship, as opposed to people who pursue traditional careers. This attitude holds that the *status quo* should be allowed to rule as long as it enables a decent living to be earned. Tanzania cannot transform and develop to a level envisioned by the people if young professionals choose such a path of self-centeredness. They are the ones best placed to spur the emergence of a new political and economic environment. As Lester Thurow has cautioned in his book, *Creating Wealth,* "when societies aren't organised so that old vested interests can be brushed aside, entrepreneurs cannot emerge."

The choice before the young professionals and the youth generally is thus clear. It is a choice to lead new social groups in society, groups of peasants, workers, business, consumers, civil and human rights, youth, and women and opening up new spaces for them. They have a responsibility to imbibe constructive dissatisfaction not only to spot problems early but also to act as active whistle blowers. I am not oblivious of the poor conditions and the economic plight that affects most young Tanzanians, young professionals included. The conditions are evidently harsh. More money, in this case, is undoubtedly the means to a better life. However, money could not surely be the point of it. How could the quest for money be bolstered in an environment that is not conducive to wealth creation in the first place? It could not be. Therefore, we should not beg the question. For young professionals to have significant impact in the social, political and economic life of Tanzania, they should develop a critical mass of power and influence amongst themselves even before they proceed to constitute strategic alliances and partnerships with other national social movements or groups.

Youth Polarisation

There is today a serious polarisation between foreign-educated and Tanzanian-educated young professionals. The depth of the polarisation is such that the mindset and confidence-divide between the two groups poses a serious threat to the cohesiveness and stability of the future leadership of the country. Here then lies another important challenge to young professionals, a challenge to close ranks and promote a collective sense of purpose, of shared values and commitment among all young professionals, Tanzanian and foreign educated alike. There is urgent need to be organised and to forge such solidarity through constant interactive meetings and dialogue focused on topical issues of common concern. The poor English language command of many Tanzanian educated young professionals is partly at the heart of their low level of confidence. This problem should be addressed. It can successfully be addressed through greater intellectual socialisation of the two groups. However, this prescription should not be interpreted to mean that Kiswahili should not be used as a means of the interactions. On the contrary, Kiswahili can and should be used. However, the point I am making is that many of the issues of concern, from the national and global perspectives, are best expressed in English since the source of information is largely English.

In addition to this problem of polarisation, the young professionals, like their older folks, appear to suffer from a down-skilling syndrome. Whilst it is clearer today, than ever before, that knowledge is the new basis for wealth and power, we are witness to growing "illiteracy" among the educated class of our country. The common problem appears to be that young professionals and the educated class as a whole have become too absorbed in trying to get rich quickly to the point where there is a dominant illusion that there is a short cut to getting rich now, through self-owned business, as opposed to pursuing a conventional employment career and pursuing self- development. No doubt, it is possible for alchemists to emerge in Tanzania. The opportunities exist. However, whether Tanzania presently has the requisite wealth-enhancing knowledge environment is debatable.

Nevertheless, whose responsibility is it to create such an environment? Do young professionals have a role? At any rate, professionals would be making a mistake to think that becoming an alchemist is simple even where the environment is conducive. Tanzanians and Africans generally are accused of not valuing the culture of savings and investment. Professor Ali Mazrui has described such culture as "self-indulgent exhibitionism" centred on "ostentatious consumption". Therefore, how can we successfully promote the growth of capitalism with such a culture in place? Young Tanzanian professionals should liberate their mindset from this retrogressive consumption culture. Tanzanians can only develop their economy sustainably if they save and invest. Foreign direct investment could only be supplemental; it cannot be the reliable driver of national development.

Creating Alchemists in Tanzania

In his book, *The New Alchemists,* Charles Handy identifies three common characteristics of alchemists that our young professionals would need to ingrain: First, dedication, commitment, drive and passion. even obsession) in a business that one seeks to pursue. Second is doggedness that embraces hard work, determination and tenacity. Third is difference, a mixture of unique personality and talent for doing things differently and doing things that are different. This embodies a character that is intolerant to conformity and to assumed authority. The challenge before young professionals is to rise to these challenging attributes and create the conditions that propel them. However, the mindset of our young professionals is largely concentrated on trying to get rich quickly. As Africans, we are often accused of creating the environment that supports "brain drain". Yet, the greater problem that afflicts Tanzania and Africa is what someone has described as allowing "brains to go down the drain". The burning question then is how could knowledge form the basis of wealth creation if young professionals and the educated class in general fail to use their time to enhance their knowledge and skills and enlarge the scope of their talents? How many have the habit to read and read enlightening books? After all, self-learning is the main driving force of education. Employers could never satisfy the full demands of education and training necessary for employees to respond to new set of global challenges like cyber connections and challenges of "borderless" cross-national business. Globalisation is already in Tanzania and the competition for securing professional jobs in the new private economy is stiff.

In his book *Powershift*, the American social critic, Alvin Toffler, postulates that knowledge is the most democratic source of power. If this is so, then Tanzanian young professionals have the basic tools for society to "seek the more" from them. They would be well positioned to inspire and lead change in Tanzania. They would be the new source of power.

Part Ten

REGIONALISM AND GLOBALISATION

Companies that do not adapt to the new global realities will become victims of those that do.

-Theodore Levitt: *Globalisation of Markets*, Harvard Business Review, May -June 1983.

The tensions and inequalities thrown up by globalisation and innovation require a political response. If we cannot innovate new institutions to govern the global economy cooperatively, to promote greater stability, more equitable development and much wider access to trade and education, then the disputes bred by globalisation will inevitably feed competitive political solutions.

-Charles Leadbeater: *Up the Down Escalator: Why the Global Pessimists are Wrong.*

Globalisation is seen through the eyes of women and men in terms of the opportunity it provides for decent work; for meeting their essential needs for food, water, health, education and shelter and for a liveable environment. Without such a social dimension, many will continue to view globalisation as a new version of earlier forms of domination and exploitation.

-ILO World Commission on Social Dimension of Globalisation: *-A Fair Globalisation: Creating Opportunities For All*, 2004.

Chapter

38 AFRICAN ECONOMIC INTEGRATION: A DREAM?

We are convinced that an historic opportunity presents itself to end the scourge of underdevelopment that afflicts Africa. The resources, including capital, technology and human skills, that are required to launch a global war on poverty and underdevelopment exist in abundance and within our reach. What is required to mobilise these resources and to use them properly, is bold and imaginative leadership that is committed to a sustained human development effort and the eradication of poverty, as well as a new global partnership based on shared responsibility and mutual interest.

- New Partnership For Africa's Development, October 2001.

In October 1995, the South Centre, based in Geneva, released a paper titled: *Enhancing South- South Trade: Contribution to an Economic Agenda for the Non-Aligned Movement.* The report underscored the imperativeness of South- South cooperation particularly in the wake of changing North-South economic relations-largely because of globalisation. It is noted in the Report that global economic relations spurred by globalisation's rapid technological breakthroughs, globalisation of world trade and intensive capital flows between regions have affected the role of the South in the global economy. The Report further observed that what appears to be growing global interdependence of national economies is in fact growing regionalism "associated with attempts to build large and powerful trading blocs". The Report cautions, that as these regional blocs strengthen, their impact on the functioning of the global economy and on the development prospects of the South countries would be staggering. In recent years, the trend towards the balkanisation of the South through the lure of joining North- driven economic and trade pacts has intensified. Post the immediate aftermath of the collapse of the Cancun trade talks in September 2003, to keep the Doha Development Round on track, the United States has been in the forefront to get some of the countries that led the Cancun debacle to negotiate bilateral trade pacts with it. It seems that the die has been cast.

Vision of Cooperation

It is in the context of the realities which the South Centre document above referred captured, that the Commission on Global Governance, in its Report, *Our Global Neighbourhood*, observed: that the "collective power of people to shape the future is greater now than ever before and the need to exercise it is more compelling." Referring to the challenges to make life in the twenty first century more democratic, more secure and more sustainable, the Report postulated, "The world needs a new vision that can galvanise people everywhere to achieve higher levels of cooperation in areas of common concern and shared destiny". In the industrialised world, this new vision is implemented through institutions such as the *European Union*. EU) and the *North American Free Trade Agreement*. NAFTA). In East Asia, on the other hand, a new regional dynamic is emerging and the idea of a Free Trade Area being promoted.

In fact, the world economy is witnessing an economic tripolar character with three centres of economic power: the EU countries, North America. which includes Mexico) and East Asia. China, India and Vietnam are also quickly entering the world economy arena with 2.5 billion people involved. Whilst India may form part of the proposed South Asian Preferential Trade Area, China and Vietnam along with the USA, Japan, Australia, Taiwan, Malaysia and other Pacific Rim countries may translate the *Asia-Pacific Economic Cooperation*. APEC) into a free trade area among the emerging economy members by 2020 and among the developed economies by 2010. Today, APEC covers 2.5 billion people and it accounts for half of world trade with a combined economic output of more than US$ 18 trillion a year.

Regionalism: Its Content

What does this growing process of regionalism mean in economic terms? Some of the important things to look at are the character of intra-regional trade. In the EU, for example, intra-regional trade in 2002 accounted for 62% of total trade. An *Economic Commission for Africa Report to a Committee of Experts on Economic and Social Conditions in Africa* dated May 2003 shows, on the other hand, that Africa's intra-regional trade, as a share of its total exports, was only 12% in 2002. In fact, according to a 2004 working paper of the Commission for Africa this share has declined to 8% in 2003. In contrast, according to an article by Martin Wolf, published in *Financial Times* of May 19, 2004 titled, *Asia needs the freedom of its own monetary fund,* intra-Asian trade in 2003 was 40% of that region's total exports. China exported 31% of its total exports to Asia. Clearly, Africa has to develop a bigger intra-African market for itself as a matter of deliberate policy if it is to bolster economic growth. What is encouraging is that intra-SADC trade is on the rise. According to the 2004 SADC Trade, Industry and Investment Review, such trade reached 24% of total SADC trade in 2003.

Another notable feature of regionalism is the growing intra-regional investment and financial flows. For Sub-Saharan Africa, there are positive indications on intra-regional investment flows *vis a vis* FDI from outside the region. According to the UNCTAD *World Investment Report, 2002*, more than 69% of total investment inflows into Sub-Saharan Africa in 2001, of about US$ 11.8 billion, originated from the region itself. Moreover, according to *Business Day Newspaper*. Johannesburg) of February 14, 2003, between 2000 and 2002, South Africa invested in the SADC sub region alone some US$ 3 billion out of the total investment inflows into the sub-region of US$ 7.72 billion over the period. In contrast, total FDI inflows to Africa in 2002 totalled a mere US$ 11 billion, constituting only 1.7% of global FDI flows in 2002 of US$ 651 billion.

In the view of the Report of the South Centre cited above, the growth in intra-South trade and investment, particularly in East Asia, "has tended to reduce economic dependence on the North, allowing for a more autonomous and regionally-centred growth process to emerge in some of these regions". As for Sub- Saharan Africa, the experience reinforces the reality which Thomas Callaghy has termed "post neo-colonialism". In fact, Callaghy, in his article: *Africa and the World Politics: Post Cold War Challenges* paints a bleak picture for Africa by positing a truism that foreign capital is highly sensitive to where it can be directed and invested. He concludes that it is "doubtful that Africa will play any significant role in current shifts in the pattern of production within the international division of labour." It is for this reason that Africa should deepen intra-African trade and investment flows.

Whither Africa?

So what direction is in store for the SSA? Can these countries afford to continue to sit back and lament? It would be recalled that following the adoption in June 1991 of the Abuja Treaty establishing the African Economic Community. AEC), a treaty described at its signing as a major milestone in the continent's quest for regional economic integration, the SSA have largely given lip service to regional integration. Frustrated African opinion is bewildered as to where the African dynamism so well manifested in the collective commitment to decolonisation and liberation has fizzled? Has SSA cooperation and integration been undermined by personal rule, military regimes, corrupt leaderships, civil wars and inconsistencies in macro-economic policies? Yes, since 2001 Africa has established the African Union. AU) and has adopted the New Economic Partnership for Africa's Development or NEPAD as the AU's development programme. Moreover, whilst the SSA countries have the Economic Commission for West Africa. ECOWAS), CEMAC, COMESA, SADC, and the East African Community. EAC), amongst other economic integration arrangements, it could not be adequate, surely, to have such institutions. Are they moving cooperation and integration forward? The record up to now is unsatisfactory. Intra-SSA trade in 2003 stood at only 8% of the region's total trade. As Arvind Subramanian and Natalia Tamirisa have pointed out in their IMF Working Paper *Africa's Trade Revisited*, some of these institutions, notably COMESA, do not even exhibit positive bloc effects in the sense that "countries within COMESA trade significantly less with each other than the average pair of countries." The authors attribute the shortcoming to the disparate character of COMESA membership. They conclude, "Preferential integration in the context of COMESA, may, therefore, be seriously re-evaluated."

The change in name from OAU to AU and the adoption of NEPAD would mean little without political will to integrate African economies. Such political will should be bold and galvanised from the standpoint that globalisation, as presently governed, does not offer a genuine and fair framework of partnership for Africa. If anything, globalisation has now fired the expectations of poor people in the third world for better lives and human rights through internet and the media. As such, globalisation has become, in itself, a catalyst for the destabilisation of poor countries, especially where leadership has failed to improve the living conditions of the people. Yet, by disturbing the old international consensus that led to the establishment of the United Nations, the Bretton Woods institutions. the IMF and the World Bank) and, more recently, the WTO, globalisation in its present form is undermining the capacity of poor countries to enjoy an equitable status in the global marketplace.

Globalisation: Need for A New International Consensus

The framework that underpins globalisation to day gives the industrialised nations, with their new regional set-ups, a position of authority. Since 1945, the world economy has been governed primarily by the instruments of the Bretton Woods institutions and by GATT, now WTO. However, these institutions were established to respond, not to globalisation, but to inter-state economic and trade relationships. The United Nations, on the other hand, has not had a clear mandate on regulating international economic issues. The UN Economic and Social Council. ECOSOC) has not been able to provide a global architecture for equitable governance of globalisation. It has been reduced into playing a mere co-ordinating role in global economic issues. In fact, it is the view of the UN High Level Panel based on their report, *A more secure world: Our shared responsibility that* it would be unrealistic to aim at making ECOSOC the centre of the world's decision-making on matters of trade and finance. On the other hand, the WTO, a product of free trade or globalisation, is already facing serious challenges. Its role is being tested and often undermined by its principal architect, the United States. Examples may be given of the 1995 US-Japan dispute over auto spares and, in 2002, the imposition by President Bush of steel tariffs that increased the cost of imported steel in the US by as much as 30%. Indeed, on 10th November 2003, the WTO ruled that that the steel tariffs were illegal, thereby opening the way for the EU to impose more than US$ 2 billion of sanctions on the US unless the tariffs were rescinded by December 2003. The tariffs were subsequently rescinded. It is in this context that Michael Hirsh, in an article in the *Newsweek* under the cover page title: *Does Government Matter? The State is Withering and Global Business is Taking Charge*, pertinently observed, "a brash new world economy is shoving the old statist structures aside; it is private, it is fast-paced and it is, by and large, averse to government meddling".

In that article, it was observed that during the 1980s the world's 37,000 transnational and multinational companies had been responsible for more in sales, US$ 5.8 trillion. 1992 figures) than all the world's trade exports put together. This point underscores the reality that the traditional rules of macro-economic policy that are nation-state based have been put to test. It is such impacts of globalisation that moved the South Commission to recommend in its Report, *The Challenge To The South*, the establishment of a new international system that would: -

- provide the framework for a rational, coherent and democratic management of international economic and political relations that ensure peace, stability, prosperity and human dignity within the global community as a whole,
- embody, as a central objective, support of the countries of the South to resume growth and to undertake a process of sustainable and self-reliant development.

The realisation of such a new international system lies in the fundamental reform of the Bretton Woods institutions and the United Nations. It also lies in clarifying the scope and operations of the WTO, particularly in the context of the attempts by the industrialised countries to continue to hold on to mercantilist philosophies, introduce labour standards, trade related environmental conditions and a competition policy, all of them prejudicial to the South's development prospects. The reform of these systems would provide an important window of opportunity for real cooperation, particularly for the SSA countries. In this context, as reported by the *Financial Times of July 6, 2004*, the British Government has released a trade and industry policy paper calling for the adoption of a new international trade policy. What underlines the policy is the proposal to move trade negotiations from the present mercantilist economic framework that drives the positions of most rich countries, to one that is more aligned to development policy with aid from the rich countries providing the catalyst for poor countries to make the much-needed adjustments in the face of liberalisation. This policy marks a major departure from the approach that has undermined the Doha trade round of negotiations. However, the success of these new initiatives crucially hinge on the unity and collective purpose of the developing countries themselves. These countries are increasingly becoming balkanised notwithstanding the stance reflected by the G20 of the South, specifically with respect to global trade negotiations.

It is also pertinent to mention Tony Blair's role in putting Africa's case at the heart of a new international initiative. In February 2004, he established the Commission for Africa with the following key objectives:

- to generate new ideas and action for a strong and prosperous Africa, using the 2005 British Presidencies of the G8 and the EU as a platform;
- to support the NEPAD and the AU to realise their goals;
- drive implementation of existing international commitments towards Africa.

The Commission had seventeen commissioners, nine of whom were from Africa. In its work, whose report was launched in March 2005, the Commission addressed problems of Africa's underdevelopment and recommend robust solutions. Some of the key issues addressed are: the state of the African economy, promotion of economic growth especially through investment in infrastructure) and poverty reduction, improving capacity for trade, total debt cancellation, governance and capacity building, investing in people or human development. from education, health and water and sanitation perspectives), HIV and AIDS, peace and security, challenges facing the youth, especially growing unemployment, and culture and participation. In sum, the salient recommendations of the Commission, framed within the MDG 2015 target date, are as follows:

- pump into Africa additional US$ 7-8 billion per annum to deliver education for all.
- improve and strengthen Africa's health systems through additional US$ 20 billion assistance annually.
- deliver annually additional US$ 10 billion for HIV and AIDS prevention, treatment and care.
- provide annually until 2010, US$ 10 billion and thereafter to 2015 US$ 20 billion to finance infrastructure development with specific attention to promotion of agriculture.

- developed countries to reduce progressively its tariffs to 0 by 2015 and removing non-tariff barriers. All trade-distorting subsidies to agriculture to be removed by 2010 and those on sugar and cotton to be eliminated immediately.
- Aid to be doubled in the next 3-5 years.
- Immediate 100% debt cancellation including debt stock and debt service in respect of multilateral debt.

Whilst Tony Blair's initiative should be hailed and supported, we cannot escape from the rude reality that over the years, there have been a number of commissions that have looked into the development predicament of poor countries ranging from Pearson, Brandt to the South Commission. The 2000 UN Millennium Summit which gave birth to the Millennium Development Goals was the pinnacle in this attempt to galvanise international consensus on how best to address the stark poverty that afflicts the developing world, and notably Africa. Regrettably, the rich world so far has not shown bold political will to extend meaningful assistance to Africa and the rest of the poor world. For instance, the Monterrey Consensus has not borne the results that had been envisioned. The British Government itself that is supporting Tony Blair's initiative is yet to exceed 0.3% of its GNI for development assistance to poor countries, way below the UN target of 0.7%. In the next chapter, I will examine recent developments in the rich world, notably the UK, in reversing this poor picture.

The Challenges for Africa

Overall, it is in the context of such lack of serious commitment on the part of the rich world to deliver on their numerous promises to get Africa out of poverty that Africa needs to soul search. SSA countries can only wait for each one of them to put its house in order before embarking seriously on cooperation and integration at their own peril. As Julius Ihonvbere lamented in his article, *The African Crisis, Regionalism and Prospects for Recovery in the Emerging Global Order*: "Africa cannot afford to be complacent or lackadaisical in responding to its marginalisation and relegation to the backwaters of global political and economic relations." Solid and sustainable cooperative and integration arrangements within groupings, at variable speeds and with a variety of focuses, informed by an overarching Africa-wide development framework, NEPAD, is the key foundation for creating a New Africa. This would be an Africa able to be heard and respected in the community of nations and to be a competitive player in the global marketplace. Having the AU as a political organisation even where supported by a development programme, NEPAD can only be rosy if empowered greater regional cooperation and integration.

In the case of SADC, one sees a certain level of seriousness in building a collective mission for shared development. The adoption in March 2004 of the *SADC Regional Indicative Strategic Development Plan* is a clear manifestation of the seriousness SADC attaches to building the social and economic infrastructure for making the SADC sub region the engine of growth in Sub-Saharan Africa. For the rest of Africa, however, time would tell whether political balkanisation and the intermittent instabilities that loom large would elicit from the new breed of African leadership the kind of impulse that is necessary to forge a more coherent and solid economic and political union.

East African Cooperation

Closer to the hearts of East Africans, is the deepening of East African cooperation and integration. It has been ludicrous to see Kenya and Tanzania undercutting each other to capture Ugandan business at the level of providing cheaper railway transportation and port services. Equally, it is sheer short-sightedness not to accept the logic of economies of scale, particularly involving the development of higher education, research and development and the acquisition of technology infrastructure and equipment. such as telecommunications, satellite television, energy, railway rolling stock, passenger aircraft, workshop facilities etc) in determining the direction of economic integration in East Africa. Above all, it is tragic, to say the least, that the East African countries have privatised and are privatising their state owned infrastructure enterprises such as airlines, telecommunications, including the licensing of cellular phone businesses, railways, ports and harbours and energy independently of each other. A more co-ordinated effort would not only have brought about greater benefits to East Africans but would also have ensured that these strategic industries are developed and managed on an East African basis, more in line with the situation that prevailed prior to the collapse of the East African Community in 1977. Until when it collapsed, the EAC was a model of economic integration to the whole world. Its revival in 1999, in the manner befitting present realities, would most probably make the EAC the leading catalyst for a more serious and committed pursuit to the realisation of the AU objectives and NEPAD spirit. Early in March, 2004, the East African Heads of State finally signed the East African Customs Union Protocol. The Customs Union was formally operationalised on 1st January, 2005.

So far so good. The overarching question for East Africans is what is the vision of the East African Community? It is simplistic, in my view, to talk about a political federation at this stage much as I believe that the move to constitute the Committee to fast track the EAC's process towards a political federation is important. At their current level of poverty, which, in itself, is a ground for the quest to promote stronger unity, it is inconceivable that such a vision could be pragmatic. Take the case of the EU as an example. Its attempt at formulating a Constitution which, at best, could provide pointers towards a political federation, has failed miserably to the utter frustration of pro-federation like the French Gaullists, notably Jacques Chirac. Thus, what the EAC should focus and strive on is first to make the East African Community a competitive sub-region with benefits being seen by ordinary people. It could, in this case, borrow a leaf from the EU Lisbon Process, started in 2000, and formulate a grand and ambitious strategy to make itself the most competitive economic region in Sub-Saharan Africa. The EAC has more advantages than any other sub-regional arrangement to realise such a goal. It has an advantage of history; of lessons of success and failure. The Southern African Customs Union. SACU), equally has a long history, but for a long time was apartheid driven. Since 1999, the EAC has embarked upon formulating strategies for developing the East African private sector, promoting industrialisation and putting in place an East African competition policy. These strategic policy initiatives are essential ingredients for enabling East African countries achieve robust economic growth. It is imperative, however, that the EAC establishes institutions that can enable the realisation of its vision. The East African Parliament and the Constitutional Court of Justice are important institutions in this case. However, it is at the economic front that the challenge is greatest. For example, regulatory convergence is essential if competition is going to be fair.

In this context, the creation of an East African Competition Authority, an institution for promoting flexible labour markets and another institution for undertaking joint promotion of FDI, especially for the infrastructure sectors. Equally imperative is the need for the EAC to promote democratic values and good governance in which the Peer Review Mechanism framework, as conceived under NEPAD and the AU, is a useful guide. Key areas to be given priority are building social cohesion, reinforcing and sustaining macro-economic stability and ensuring environmental sustainability.

Regionalism and Zero Sum Game

One of the important questions that keep on confronting the competitiveness of Tanzania, and one that often creates a sense of insecurity in the Tanzanian industrial business sector relates to Tanzania's place and role in regional economic co-operation arrangements. There is concern that Tanzania's involvement and accession to trade and economic protocols is prompted more by Pan-Africanist sentiments than economic interests. It is argued, for example, that Tanzanian stakeholders had not been involved in giving views about the SADC trade protocol. In the case of the EAC, the three East African governments were literally pressurised by the civil society and especially the business lobbies to postpone not only the signing of the Treaty establishing the EAC but also the fast tracking of the adoption of the Customs Union Protocol until East African stakeholders had had adequate time to air their views.

With specific respect to what initially dampened Tanzania's commitment to the conclusion of the East African Customs Union, several factors can be cited. First, the Tanzanian economy is dogged by deep-seated weaknesses: high taxes, especially VAT, high costs of doing business. e.g. energy) high transaction costs, tax evasion, poor infrastructure. roads, railways), high interest rates, and dumping. Secondly, given its low industrial production base, Tanzania was concerned about ending up being a mere market of Kenyan goods. Unfortunately, these factors hinge on the short and medium term. They overlooked, in my view, the fact that countries like Belgium and the Netherlands, predominantly agricultural, initially became members of the European Economic Community without a competitive industrial base. As members of the European Union, subsequently, they have been able to boost trade and investments by exploiting competitive advantages based on agriculture, agro-processing and good infrastructure, such as excellent ports and harbours, roads and railways.

Tanzania, in contrast, with a much lower industrial base than Kenya, is yet to define clearly what its comparative and competitive advantages are as an economy. It needs to be clearer about what it can promote in order to achieve the strategic benefits that would arise from being part of an economic block. Where comparative and competitive advantages are fallow or are undeveloped, the goal should be to enter an economic block with a clear goal that a fixed percentage of economic community resources and aid and investments, raised collectively or through aid and grants, would be directed towards developing those areas or centres of potential comparative and competitive advantage. This is what the EU has under what it calls regional development policy. Tanzania should appreciate that it might not be able, on its own, to raise the level of resources required to:

- improve its physical infrastructure,
- develop its agriculture through modern technology and skills,
- off load its excess energy capacity, once fully developed,
- promote competitive package tours for tourists who wish to visit and see its wildlife and other ecological wonders,
- expand educational facilities, especially at tertiary level.

After all, Tanzania enjoys a unique and strategic geographical location. This, in itself, is a competitive advantage for making Tanzania a logistics and transport hub of East Africa. Tanzanians who dismiss brusquely the opportunities that the East African Economic Community Customs Union unleashes and the additional opportunities that would arise from a common market and growl that Tanzania would be relinquishing its control over matters of vital and strategic concern to the Tanzanian people should remember that Tanzania is already a signatory to the World Trade Organisation. Thus, as far as international trade matters are concerned it has virtually relinquished national control. As an economic block, East Africa would be better able to face the WTO rules and regulations more formidably than as separate national entities. A major threat to a non-economic block member is its ostracisation from global markets. We learn from Lester Thurow who, in his book, *The Future of Capitalism* paints a black picture as follows: "In a world of regional trading blocs, selling one's products if a country is not part of one of the trading groups is going to become increasingly difficult for developing countries. Market access will be a privilege that has to be earned and not a right that is bestowed automatically."

In such an environment, developing countries would have to negotiate access to the world's wealthy markets. What happens then to countries unwanted in any trading group and are yet important enough to demand market access? Tanzania may have to face objective realities always mindful that whatever the pain its citizens undergo in the short term, in the longer term, it would be able to create more robust micro-economic conditions and thereby transforming itself into a more effective player in the EAC customs union and later the common market.

At this point, the question about the proliferation of Tanzania's memberships in regional economic co-operation arrangements requires examination. The World Bank's *Global Economic Prospects Report 2005* castigates the proliferation of regional trade agreements, which Jagdish Bhagwati has described as the *"spaghetti bowl"* effect, positing that their value for developing countries with small markets is questionable. The Report cautions that poor nations would suffer diminishing returns or even economic losses by rushing into deals, not only amongst themselves, but even with leading industrialised countries. In an editorial titled *Zero-sum Game: Bilateral trade deals risk doing more harm than good*, the Economist of November 17 2004 postulates that "deals between rich and poor countries are an unequal bargain, allowing the former to push their producers' narrow commercial interests. like investment protection agreements, strict intellectual property rules and abolition of capital controls) at the expense of weaker partners' welfare. Unfettered pursuit of Regional Trade Agreements also risks diverting political energy from the WTO, weakening its authority. Finally, preferential trade deals increase resistance to global liberalisation". Evidently, one could pick holes in this line of argument, especially with respect to the functioning of the WTO in the context of a globalisation that lacks clear and equitable governance systems that are fair and transparent. At the same time, however, it is evident that with SSA inter-regional trade at a low 5% in 2004, pursuant to the World Bank Report referred above, it is probable that regional trade arrangements have become more political than economic at this stage. Some order is thus called for. And here lies the critical challenge about how to improve the situation, even in the context of deals between the rich nations and the poor nations. I examine this question later in the context of the on-going negotiations between the EU and sub-regional groupings in SSA, like SADC.

In the specific context of East Africa, this sub-region constitutes a natural economic cluster for Tanzania. It has a long history of a strong economic community and it has useful lessons of experience about the strengths and weaknesses of an economic block. Moreover, East Africans are natural allies in language and ethnicity. There is personal rapport at various levels of political, government and civil society leaderships, with many of the leaders in these structures studied together. There are several opportunities to be taken advantage of under an EAC framework. These include:

- the exploitation and management of shared natural resources. e.g. Lake Victoria),
- dealing with common environmental problems,
- harnessing science and technology. e.g. telecommunications and civil aviation),
- promoting research and development in areas such as medicine, high yielding seed varieties suited to the East African climate and agro-diseases.
- exploiting economies of scale, in cost and effectiveness, at the level of tertiary education and vocational training.

I strongly believe that an EAC offers a strong economic unit to deal more effectively and profitably with the outside world as well as with the other parts of the African region, including Southern Africa, under the SADC framework, than any other African sub-regional block. Therefore, Tanzania should seriously consider where its immediate interests lie, and the same applies to Kenya and Uganda, considering that by 2008, the EAC members would be required, under WTO rules, to belong to only one customs union.

Africa's Economic Empowerment

In an article in the magazine, *African Forum* of March, 1965, the late Mwalimu Julius Nyerere wrote the following: "The man whose contribution merits a footnote in the history of United Africa will deserve more of the fortune than he whose obstinacy, fear or pride, prevents or delays the day when that history can be written. I believe that the people of Africa will be worthy of their great opportunity". The founding fathers of African unity, dead and alive, would have stood proud to witness how the spirit of Algiers, the *OAU Summit in 2000*, awakened to the beating drums that challenged Africa afresh to re-assert itself and to confront squarely the new global economic order that threatens to reinforce its marginalisation. Since its birth in 1963, the OAU has been an effective vehicle, the political and military force, for the political liberation of Africa. Such achievement could not be minimised by the new challenges of religion, ethnicity and tribal conflict that continue to afflict some African nation-states. Indeed, history has now shown that such strife is not exclusively rooted in the African continent. It also affects the European Continent, so badly manifested by the Basque insurgency. And we need not make reference to the Bosnia and Kosovo conflicts. Clearly though, civil and ethnic strife as well as civil wars pose a much greater challenge to Africa.

The Algiers Summit proved that these scourges, which include the instabilities caused by the subversion of constitutionalism and democratisation, should henceforth constitute the critical agenda for forging an African renewal and renaissance. This spirit was re-born in Durban in 2001 when Africa witnessed the transformation of the OAU to *African Union. AU)* and the adoption of *The New Partnership for Africa's Development. NEPAD)*. The UN Summit on the Great Lakes Region that Tanzania hosted in Dar es Salaam in November 2004 was equally a milestone endeavour in making Africa take responsibility, with the support of the UN and international community, for addressing its instabilities and searching for permanent solutions to promote lasting peace, stability and sustainable development.

Evidently, Africa's political turmoil and its political fragility remain largely rooted in its own state of deepening poverty and the erosion of hope, within the communities of the majority of African peoples, for a better quality of life. Thus, African renewal and African renaissance, of necessity, should give greater attention to how Africa can effectively liberate itself economically. Here lies the challenge of economic empowerment. This is not a new challenge. Economic empowerment has preoccupied African nation-states since the on-set of political independence. African leaders, like Nyerere, made commitments at the dawn of independence that their countries would achieve higher levels of economic development in ten years than what the colonial powers had realised for four decades. The thrust of political independence crucially hinged on the realisation of economic empowerment of the people, within national borders and across the borders of African nation-state. The logic behind some countries calling for delay to be granted independence was to enable a wider and collective realisation of independence. That move was driven by a vision of stronger African economic units. In other words, political federation was considered a driving force of economic empowerment. That spirit translated itself into the movement towards the realisation of an African Economic Community. The Abuja Treaty heralded Africa's commitment to creating such an African-wide economic powerhouse that transcended the levels of development disparities of nation-states.

Over time, that spirit of economic integration has waned. The earlier inspiration driven by the fathers of Africa's political independence, gave way to a parochial vision of seeking thee thy nation-state economic empowerment first and the rest shall follow. That goal, of economic nationalism, was not necessarily less important for the African nation state to empower itself economically. On the contrary, at the 1999 *Southern Africa Economic Summit* organised by the World Economic Forum whose crosscutting theme was *Responsible Leadership for Stability, Action and Growth*, it was made abundantly clear that nation-states had the primary responsibility to create strong economies focused on cost competitiveness.

The challenges in realising such competitiveness were set out to be lowering the costs of doing business, addressing high overhead costs, rewarding high productivity, deregulation and privatisation of utilities, lowering high transport costs and developing human skills, especially in technological fields. In this context, responsible leadership was interpreted to mean leadership that acted boldly and speedily in addressing these national challenges.

That said, the moving theme of that World Economic Forum centred on the pace of change needed in getting Africa to take the bull by its horns and speed up economic integration. The President of the World Economic Forum, Professor Klaus Schwab, admonished Africa and the African leadership for the absence of a luculent view of globalisation, considered a fact of life, and the commitment to economic integration as a strategic response to the challenges of globalisation. In his view, Africa behaved as if the rest of the world would stop or mark time to give Africa the chance to play catch up. He underscored that Africa did not enjoy the luxury of telling the world, in the words of a once popular tune, *'Stop the world, I wanna get off'*. Such option could not be an option for Africa. It would merely herald a lost cause. In this light, Professor Schwab cited how the South American Common Market, the Mercosur, which ties Argentina, Brazil, Paraguay and Uruguay. with Bolivia and Chile as associate members) had made commendable strides towards economic integration in a matter of few years. Intra-Mercosur trade in 1998 had increased by

157% over seven years, topping US$ 20 billion in 1997. At that time, this achievement reflected 20% of intra-Merscosur trade. Though the figure, according to the Centre for International Economy in Mercosur, declined to 16% in 2003, it is still reflects a better performance than most of the regional groupings in Sub-Saharan Africa.

SADC is the exception, having achieved about 24% intra- trade in 2004. However, this is the context that made Professor Schwab to lament about Africa's failure to rise above what Robert Reich has termed "zero-sum nationalism", a mindset that stifles and undermines an economic great leap forward. In his view, *patience* was the pandemic disease that devoured Africa's body economic. In his words, "patience is no longer a virtue." Rather, "impatience is the new virtue". The lesson here is that Africa should henceforth be driven by a sense of serious urgency, in its thinking and in its actions. African renaissance, the pinnacle of Africa's economic empowerment, would be but a dream or a mirage, were Africa to remain gripped in a psychological fear of globalisation and regional integration.

In a speech at Harvard University on September 17, 1998, the UN Secretary General, Kofi Annan, discussed the backlash against globalism and made reference to three dangerous reactions: Only the third one is cited here. He said, "The third reaction against the forces of globalisation has been the politics of populism. Embattled leaders may begin to propose forms of protectionism as a way to offset losses *supposedly* incurred by too open an embrace of competition and too free a system of competition and too free a system of political change. In this reaction, globalisation is made the scapegoat of the ills which more often have domestic roots of a political nature." As noted above, Tanzania often finds itself uncomfortable when issues about economic integration arise. I believe, however, in the same way that Mwalimu Nyerere did, that in the context of the new global economic realities, a speedier movement by Africa towards economic integration constitutes the key driver of their economic empowerment of the African peoples irrespective of the varying stages of economic development. In this context, *The Challenge to the South* observes, "If the world's people are to secure their future, they have now to move towards global unity through widening co-operation on an equitable basis".

If Africa's people are to secure their future, they should unite by widening economic integration. *The South Commission Report* underscored the aspect of equity because of the wide disparity in development between the North and the South. The same has no equal force within Africa. Yet Africa is a continent in poverty. The so-called disparity in development that now undermines a faster process of integration is often a disparity in levels of poverty. If equity is an issue, then it should underpin economic integration rather than being allowed to undermine integration as a principle.

Therefore, Africans should be clearer about what they are trying to do and achieve.

Africa is at crossroads. The choice for it is between, on the one hand, economic nationalism and resultant deeper marginalisation, and, on the other hand, broader economic integration, that respects variable geometry, and with resultant economic empowerment. This is what a viable African renaissance is all about. And if this were reckless politics rather than economic reality, as some people may hold, then history should be the judge.

Chapter

39 GLOBALISATION: SOLIDARITY OR MARGINALISATION?

—the goal of making further dramatic reductions in absolute poverty in developing countries is achievable with more successful integration of those economies into international trade and the global economy. With the right policies and approaches in these populous developing countries hundreds of millions of people could be lifted out of abject poverty in the next two decades, through globalisation not despite it. It may also be possible to limit the growth of inequality in the quality of life and longevity, in education and health, if not in income. Globalisation is an essential component of a poverty reduction strategy in the developing world.

-Charles Leadbeater: **Up the Down Escalator.**

External liberalisation policy in its various dimensions involves political, economic and social choices. The effects of such liberalisations and opening-up are not agreed and certainly are not uniform for all places and times. The challenge-both at the national and global levels- is, through conscious policy choices, to make the new globalised system work for maximum human welfare. The task before us all is make globalisation functional, to "civilise" it.

-Gerald Karl Helleiner: **Markets, Politics and Globalisation: Can the Global Economy be Civilised?**

Introduction

At root, globalisation is about revolutionary change, change that is both discontinuous and dynamic. Charles Handy has written that we live in an age of unreason and that nothing can any longer be taken for granted. Indeed, in a brilliant book by Will Hutton and Anthony Giddens, titled *On The Edge: Living With Global Capitalism*, we are told that what gives contemporary change its power and momentum is the technological, economic, political and cultural transformation summed up by the term globalisation. So how can we avoid talking and debating about a system that engulfs us, and which, if we cannot adequately respond to, could undermine our development? We are reminded, in this particular context, of the late Mwalimu Julius Nyerere's premonition which he articulated back in 1966. He wrote, in the introduction to the book,

Freedom And Unity, that for Africa to seize the opportunities that lay before it, it had to embrace change. In his view, the choice for Africa was not between change and no change. Rather, the choice was between changing and being changed; changing its lives under its own direction or being changed by the impact of forces outside its control. Today, globalisation constitutes the fundamental contemporary change. The choice for Africa is not between accepting and not accepting globalisation. There can be no trying to make believe that such change is non-existent or irrelevant. However, in determining the choice between being changed by globalisation or taking charge and mastering it, it is imperative to examine the attitude to adopt. For example, Professor Brian Van Arkadie, who has taught economics in Africa since the early 1960s, in an article titled *Globalisation and the East African Economies,* points out that "there is little **point** raising alarm about the dangers of globalisation when it is not even **clear** that African economies are participants in the globalisation process." Put differently, the question to be posed is why Africa should at all be bothered about the impact of globalisation when it is yet to enter the arena of global economics.

However, could Van Arkadie's view be inconsistent with reality? Is the central issue really centred on Africa being a participant, or is it, as Professor Paul Kennedy has more aptly described in his book, *Preparing For The Twenty First Century,* that globalisation is devoting "less attention to the prospect of a further marginalisation of four-fifth of the earth's population not well prepared for new commercial and financial trends?" In contrast, a powerful view has been advanced by two journalists of the Economist, John Micklethwait and Adrian Wooldridge in their book titled *A Future Perfect: The Challenges and Hidden Promise of Globalisation.* In that book, they argue that globalisation has a human face; that whilst it has few downsides, it generally works wonders. Clearly, this would not be the first time we come across the phrase, "with a human face." The Report of the ILO World Commission on Social Dimension of Globalisation also uses the phrase. It would be recalled that the IMF structural adjustment programmes came under severe attack in the 1980s for being anti-poor. Then somebody cleverly suggested that the adjustment programmes could have a human face. But how could globalisation have a human face when it is largely driven by faceless, profit-driven actors and not by governments? In this context, Nyerere was right. Africa and the poor world should get their act right.

Africa should itself appreciate and master contemporary change if it is going to control its future and its destiny. It should come to terms with what globalisation is all about and the impact it unleashes. What it unleashes has been well captured by William Greider in his book: *One World Ready or Not: The Manic Logic of Global Capitalism.* Greider views *globalisation* "as a free-running economic system and likens it to a wondrous machine strong and supple, a machine that reaps as it destroys. It is huge and mobile, something like the machines of modern agriculture but vastly more complicated and powerful. Think of this awesome machine running over open terrains and ignoring familiar boundaries. It plows across fields and fence crows with a fierce momentum that is exhilarating to behold and also frightening. As it goes, the machine throws off enormous mows of wealth and bounty while it leaves behind great furrows of wreckage. More frightening, there is not one at the wheel of this machine and neither does the machine have wheels nor internal governor to control its speed and direction."

Is Globalisation the Enemy?

There are six main drivers of this seemingly driverless machine called globalisation. The first one is the increased mobility in the location of industrial production resulting in a shift of significant industrial operations from traditional centres in the industrialised world. In recent years, this shift or offshoring has become intensified as transnational and large companies in rich countries seek to bolster their competitiveness and their bottom lines. The second relates to international financial markets increasingly eroding the capacity of national governments to pursue independent fiscal, monetary and foreign exchange policies. Third, is the intensification of transnational and multinational character of large business entities in the global marketplace. Fourth, is the growing hegemony of free market economics in the aftermath of the collapse of communism. Fifth, is the trend towards regionalism and all types of economic integration systems. Lastly, is the innovative technological entry of the "new economy" characterised by e-commerce powered by the internet.

In the context of this new global economic environment, it is pertinent to ask whether what Greider describes as the free-running economic machine and what drives it, has relevance to poor economies like those of Africa. Is the machine *truly* throwing off huge mows of wealth to rich nations and leaving the poor countries with only great furrows of wreckage? It may be politically passionate to be polemical about such evils of globalisation and thereby to have a sense of *deja vu*. Yet, paradoxically, the demonstrations against globalisation witnessed at Seattle and Davos, amongst other places, *in fact* have had more to do with globalisation's perceived ugly face in the industrialised economies than in poor economies. In addition, why should globalisation, in itself, be an enemy of the poor? Are the poor, *poor* because of globalisation and shall they necessarily become *poorer* because of it? Put differently, does Africa really matter *to* or *in* the global economy? The distinguished American economist Lester Thurow wrote in his book titled

Head to Head: The Coming Economic Battle among Japan, Europe and America that Africa South of the Sahara. excluding South Africa) is the world's economic basket case. Probably insultingly to many, he asserted, "If God gave it to you and made you its economic dictator, the only smart move would be to give it back to Him". This has been the dominant view held in rich countries. It is a view reflected in the policies of these countries towards addressing the plight of Africans and the poor around the world.

Africa's Marginalisation

Recent selected data shows deepening marginalisation of Sub Saharan Africa from the global economy. *UNCTAD World Investment Report. 2003)* shows, for example, that the African region's share in global FDI inflows declined from 2.3% in 2001 to 1.7% in 2002. In physical terms, the decline was from US$ 19 billion to US$ 11 billion. Over half of the 2002 inflows went to the oil industry. On the aid front, according to the OECD-Africa Development Bank Report, *Africa Economic Outlook, 2002/2003,* ODA to Africa declined from US$ 20 billion in 1996 to US$ 16.2 billion in 2001. In fact, Gordon Brown, the UK Chancellor of the Exchequer, has pointed out that aid to Africa has declined from $33 per person in 1993 to $ 20 per person in 2003. The United States government in 2002 spent only 13 cents a day per American in budget assistance for the poorest countries. EU annual aid to Sub-Saharan Africa, on the other hand, is equivalent to US$ 8 per person. Yet, according to the UN Human Development Report 2003, the EU annual diary subsidy in 2002 was US$ 913 per cow. This translates to US$ 2.50 per cow per day. The figure for 2003 is estimated to be around $3 per cow. Viewed from another perspective, whilst the total GDP of Sub-Saharan Africa was US$ 306 billion in 2001, total agricultural subsidies by all the OECD countries in the same period amounted to US$ 360 billion. Little wonder that average life expectancy in SSA has declined from 50 to 46 years between 1990 and 2003.

Evidently, following the adoption of the United Nations *Millennium Development Goals* in 2000, several efforts have been made to promote the idea of giving more ODA to poor countries. The UN International Conference on Financing for Development held in Monterrey in March 2002 and the consensus that came out of it was probably the high watermark in terms of commitments to address global poverty. The rich countries committed to make available an additional US$ 16 billion a year by 2006 to support poor countries. But this aid translates into only 0.26% of OECD countries' GNP, a far cry from the target set by the UN over three decades ago of 0.7%. Clearly, at this level of ODA, the realisation of the UN Millennium Development Goals, which seek to halve abject poverty in the world by the year 2015, appears to be a dream. This grim picture is captured by the World Bank Report, *Global Economic Prospects and the*

Developing Countries: Investing to Unlock Global Opportunities, 2003. The Report asserts, "Sub-Saharan Africa will continue to lag behind other development regions, and by 2015 the number of persons living on less than $1 per day is forecasted to rise by nearly 30%, from 315 million to 404 million." The Monterrey consensus has not borne the envisioned results. At the extraordinary AU Summit held in Abuja at the end of January 2005, the UN Secretary General, Kofi Annan, was unequivocal in pointing out his fears that African countries were way off in the quest to realise the MDGs by 2015.

It is to be seen, over time, whether Gordon Brown's International Finance facility. IFF) initiative would receive more concrete action than traditional passion. Chancellor Brown originally presented his views about the facility in the *Independent.* UK) on 21 September 2003. He officially launched it early in 2004. The initiative received significant support at a special conference held in Paris in April, 2004. 60 countries along with the World Bank and the IMF attended the meeting. The ambitious initiative seeks to raise US$ 100 billion a year between 2005 and 2015 in support of poor countries in their quest to achieve the MDGs by 2015. The facility targets education for all, HIV/AIDS, TB and malaria, debt relief, bolstering capacity for trade, increased ODA to reach the UN target of 0.7% of GDP. The UK government has already shown its commitment to making this initiative a reality by meeting the cost of the debt of poor countries, especially African, owed to the World Bank. It would be noted that it is the multilateral debt that has been the problem for poor countries because it does not fall under HIPC. So far indications are not promising. At the G7 meeting of Finance Ministers in London in February 2005, Chancellor Brown's IFF and modern Marshall Plan proposals were shot down by most of his colleagues for three main reasons. First, there is a view that the elimination of debt would not necessarily trigger a renaissance in poor countries. Second, it was contended that aid should be built up steadily, not suddenly, taking into consideration the absorptive capacities of recipient nations. Thirdly, it was underscored that aid to poor countries could not be treated on an omnibus basis; it should be directed to countries that have tolerant regimes and which have prudent economic policies.

At a different level, there is also the proposal put forward by the Presidents of Brazil and France early in 2004 to introduce a global tax on foreign exchange transactions. incorporating ideas around the Tobin tax), on multinational operations, arms sales, greenhouse gas emissions and aviation fuel. The proposal includes a global lottery. The proposal seeks to build a US$ 50 billion war chest to fight poverty. The US does not support this proposal arguing that global taxes are inherently undemocratic and uncollectible and that the real solution to fighting poverty lies in less government intervention, not more. At the World Economic Reform

Summit in Davos in January 2005, this proposal came under discussion and it would appear that it enjoys little support. Former President Clinton in commenting about the proposal noted that whilst it was sensible, it failed the crucial test of time effectiveness. He was pessimistic that governments would be able to reach a consensus on the proposal early enough and that in the meantime millions of people are dying from disease and malnutrition. It would be interesting to discover what would be reported at the Special UN Summit in September 2005 convened to assess how the MDGs have so far performed. Going by the current record, the world is in for a rude awakening. The situation cannot be otherwise. The Advisory Team of 265 experts, appointed by Kofi Annan in 2002, under the leadership of Jeffrey Sachs, to propose the means for making the MDGs realisable for 2005, presented its report in mid January 2005. In their report titled, *Investing in Development: A Practical Plan To Achieve The Millennium Development Goals,* they observe that for poor countries to achieve the MDGs by 2015, rich countries should dedicate about 0.5% of their combined GDP to ODA between 2006 and 2015. Such contribution would be about double what is presently offered. The pledge made by the EU Ministers of Finance and of International Development in Brussels on 24 May 2005 to double the EU combined aid to poor countries, especially Africa, from US$ 40 billion in 2005 to US$ 80 billion by 2010, reaching a 0.51% mark of Gross National Income is a welcome development and falls within the thrust of Jeffrey Sachs proposal. The EU countries have also committed themselves to bolstering aid to reach the UN target of 0.7% of GNI in aid by 2015. Of course, Denmark, Sweden, Luxembourg and the Netherlands have already achieved the UN target.

From Aid to Trade

In recent years, there has been a generation of much heat about trade taking an overriding position *vis a vis* aid. Rich countries have been preaching the idea that aid principally suffocates the will of the poor to develop. In their view, the economic future of poor countries lies in their being able to build capacity to produce goods and services that are exportable. This may be the right place to raise the implications of the total debt cancellation move of the G8. A view is emerging, notably from the United States, that such cancellation of the multilateral debt should be offset by a decline in ODA. In other words, the mantra may change from "aid to trade" to "debt cancellation less ODA". What is troubling is a view recently advanced by the IMF Chief Economist, Raghuran Rajan in an article, *Debt Relief and Growth* that debt cancellation, on the face of it, bolsters the confidence of investors because governments are not, thereby, placed in a position to overtax business profits to raise revenue for debt service. Rajan views the increased investments as a key justification for declining ODA. He could be right over the long run. However, in the medium term, such line of thinking is tantamount to putting the cart before the horse. It is informed by ideal conditions supporting attraction of investments which most poor countries are yet to attain and for which more ODA is required.

Based on the mantra, aid to trade, the way forward for poor countries is to become part of trade pacts. In fact, when President George W. Bush visited Africa in July 2003, he promoted the idea of concluding a free trade area pact with the Southern Africa Customs Union, SACU. And following the Cancun debacle, there have been further upsurge of interest within the Bush Administration to promote the Free Trade Area of the Americas, the apparent circumspection and hostility emanating from Brazil, Argentina and Venezuela, as manifested at the US-Latin America Summit in Monterrey, Mexico in January 2004, notwithstanding. It is in this context that Professor Jagdish Bhagwati in his think piece in the *Financial Times* of 15 July 2003, titled, *Bilateral trade treaties are a sham*, observed succinctly as follows, "America's tactic is weakening the power of poor countries in multilateral trade negotiations. Bilateral deals fragment the coalitions of developing countries as each abandons its legitimate objections to the inclusion of extraneous issues in trade treaties. Having abandoned these objections in a bilateral deal with the US, how can those countries pursue them in WTO negotiations"?

How these moves towards the promotion of what the WTO Director General, Supachai Panitchpakdi described, as *"a la carte regionalism"* plays out in the context of the AU objectives is a matter for conjecture at this stage. However, the EU is in the process of negotiating and concluding second generation bilateral Free Trade Areas based on reciprocal exchange of preferences with the Mediterranean and North African countries and also with the Mercosur with greater success with the former than with the latter, so far. In SSA, the EU already has a bilateral trade and development agreement with South Africa.

If more trade marks economic salvation for Africa, then available data is not comforting. According to the World Bank, Africa's share of world exports has dropped by nearly 60%, from 3.5% in 1970 to 1.5% at the end of the 1990s. This decline represents a loss of around 21% of Africa's total economic output and about four times the ODA at the end of the period. It is significant to note that Jeffrey Sachs in his recent book, *The End of Poverty*, has surmised that the mantra about trade not aid is flawed. In his view, poor countries need both aid and trade because trade alone would not suffice to move them out of the abject poverty they are in. His argument centres of the fact that "even if reforms would raise the incomes of the poorest countries by billions of dollars per year, only a small fraction of that would be available for funding the vitally important public investments needed to escape from the poverty trap."

Reform and Globalisation Effect

The tragic irony of all these statistics is that Sub Saharan Africa all along has been made to believe, by the so-called "Washington Consensus," that by pursuing fiscal discipline, financial liberalisation and deepening, privatisation, deregulation, democratisation, good governance and generally adopting market-driven policies, capital flows and trade would significantly increase. The record, unfortunately, does not match the economic logic. Indeed, in a recent book, *The Power of Productivity: Wealth, Poverty, And The Threat To Global Stability,* William W. Lewis clearly points out that under the Washington Consensus "one factor that was profoundly underestimated was the importance of a level playing field for competition in a country."

The acceleration in the annual average growth rates in Sub-Saharan Africa, which are attributed to positive outcomes of structural adjustment programmes, from 1.7% between 1980 and 1990 to 2 % between 1990 and 1996, with the average rate for 2003 being 2.8%, has not been accompanied by levels of investment necessary to sustain accelerated growth and reduce poverty. In accordance with the *OECD/ADB African Economic Outlook Report for 2002/2003,* on average, investment ratios of African countries in 2001 were between 16-22% of GDP. These are still below the UN Economic Commission for Africa's benchmark of 25% regarded as necessary for Africa to be able to achieve annual growth ratios of around 8% and to be able to achieve the goal of halving poverty by 2015. In its *Human Development Report for 2003,* the United Nations Development Programme estimates that Sub-Saharan Africa needs investment levels of around 38% if it is to reduce poverty by 50% by the turn of the century. In contrast, In East Asia, the average investment rate in 2001 was 31%. At the same time, in accordance with the *World Bank African Development Indicators, 2002,* Africa's average gross domestic savings in 2001 were around 16.1 % compared to East Asia's 33.5%. This means that Africa's capacity to save and thus to invest remains very low.

The Debt Quagmire

In addition, what adds to Africa's economic woes and deeper marginalisation is the debilitating debt quagmire. Total external debt stock of 40 Highly Indebted Poor Countries. HIPCs) with a total population of 600.8 million, was US$ 216 billion in 1996. Between 1990 and 2001, the external debt of Sub-Saharan African countries as a percentage of gross national income rose from 88.1% to 100.3%. Though the debt slightly declined to US$ 212.5 billion in 1998, debt service by the HIPC countries rose to US$28 billion per annum in 1998. In 2003, Africa's total external debt stood at US$ 217 billion, almost the same level as in 1996. Based on statistics released by UNCTAD in 2004, the 34 poorest African countries alone had a combined foreign debt of US$ 106 billion in 2002.

The impact of debt service payments on the economies of poor countries is devastating. The realisation of the Millennium Development Goals would be a mirage without the debt trap being resolved. The debt relief initiative launched in 1996, known as the Highly Indebted Poor Country Initiative. HIPC), has undoubtedly had some palliative impact on those countries that have succeeded to attain the qualifying standards for debt relief, about 22 of them in Sub-Saharan Africa, as at 2001. The debt relief dividend has freed some resources from debt payments. These have been directed at poverty reducing programmes within the framework of *Poverty Reduction Strategy Papers* prepared by the highly indebted poor countries themselves. However, the debt overhang continues to shackle the economies of poor countries in spite of creditor governments cancelling between 90 and 100% of the bilateral debt. The reason is that 80% of the total external debt of poor countries is owed to multilateral financial institutions, especially the World Bank, the IMF and the ADB, in the case of Africa. It is noteworthy that within the context of its proposal to the G8 Summit in February 2005 to launch a modern type Marshal Plan for Africa that encompasses Gordon Brown's International finance Facility proposal, the UK government decided to begin a process to meet part of the cost of the debt of poor countries to the multilateral financial institutions. Tanzania became the first country to benefit from that decision. 100% of the cost of its debt repayments to the World Bank, working out to about US$ 750 million of repayments due between 2005 and 2015 has been taken over. In his address to African leaders in Addis Ababa on 5 July, 2004, Professor Jeffrey Sachs noted that from the analysis undertaken by his Advisory Group to the UN Secretary General on poverty issues, "there is absolutely no way you. Africans) can make debt payments on debt and achieve the Millennium Development Goals." He went on further to make a most provocative suggestion that if the rich countries did not cancel the debts totally, that is 100%, "I would suggest obstruction-you do it yourselves." In other words, Sachs proposed that poor countries do exactly what Mwalimu Nyerere had suggested in the early 1990s, that poor countries refuse to pay debts owed to rich countries and to multilateral financial institutions

What continues to be worrisome is that the HIPC initiative thrives on the response of donors contributing to its Trust Fund. By 2003, the EU was the largest contributor. It had contributed 26% of pledged amounts and 30% of paid up contributions. The deficit remains wide. It is such deficit that contributes to the incapacity of the initiative to be deepened. However, as earlier noted in the overview, the G8 Summit in Gleneagles has made this problem irrelevant for the 18 countries from the poor world that would benefit from the debt cancellation decision. But the problem continues to afflict the majority of poor nations that have been excluded from debt cancellation. It is important to note that the reasons given for the G8 deciding not to approve wholesale debt cancellation do not make sense. Attaching conditionalities to a decision based on criteria that falls outside the powers of the suffering poor in affected countries flies in the face of the dominant human security considerations that should underpin such decision in the first place.

Bridging the Digital Divide

In considering further whether Africa really matters to the global economy, a few more facts need to be examined. Presently, there is much passion about the role of information and communications technology. There is a view being propelled, that like East Asia and now India, Africa could probably leapfrog economically by embracing IT. In a June 2000 article in *The Economist*, Jeffrey Sachs advanced the view that the poor of the world could be made to share the benefits of global growth by being connected to the world economy via information technology and that income inequality would be reduced. He noted, "A landlocked region, say Mongolia, surely would have a comparative advantage in IT-based service exports. software, data transcription, telemarketing) as against export-oriented manufactures." He further stated that the US had sophisticated industrial policy for the uptake of IT and that developing countries should exploit the available opportunity.

All this is easier said than done. Which developing countries is Mr. Sachs referring? Surely, they could not be Sub-Saharan Africa with its high levels of illiteracy, its low technology skills base, run of the mill basic education systems, especially in applied sciences, poor basic education infrastructure, and very low telephone line density. In 2001, there were only 23 million fixed lines for 800 million Africans. 90% of the lines were in the capital cities and main towns. Yet, on average, 70% to 80% of the population in SSA is found in rural areas. According to *Polymer Optical Fibre 2003 Conference Report*, mobile phone penetration across the African continent in 2002 was around 4%. This represented 65% of the total number of telephone lines in Africa. The Report further states that for Africa to reach a teledensity of 10% by year 2010, it would need an investment of US$ 11 billion per annum for the next seven years. In Tanzania, with a population of 34.5 million, there were only 300,000 fixed lines in 2004 with 148,360 subscribers. At the same time, there are four mobile operators with a total of around 2 million subscribers in 2004. Its teledensity. namely one telephone line per 1000 subscribers) in 2003 was 1.23. On the other hand, in 2003, there were only twenty three internet service providers with national coverage with 16,000 subscribers. In this context, the digital divide between the rich countries and poor nations is beyond definition.

At the World Economic Forum Summit in Davos in January 2004, the UNDP Administrator and Bill Gates jointly announced a partnership project to build IT and computer technology capacity and training in Africa as a way to bridge the digital divide. This is a positive response to the challenge posed by Professor Sachs because the capacity of poor countries to exploit the opportunity to uptake IT is hugely constrained by financial resources. Moreover, the challenge to bridge the digital divide is more onerous than perceived by UNDP and Microsoft. Except in few African countries, there is a serious drought of digital information champions, like Ghana's Nii Quaynor. "Digital leadership" is largely lacking in African countries. How many computers and internet hosts per 1,000 people does Africa have vis-à-vis East Asia or India. the huge Indian population differential notwithstanding)? *Data from Global Information, Inc 2002 Report on Africa* shows that in mid 2001, Internet uptake in Africa was a mere 5 million. It is a horrendous scenario! This is a manifestation of the deep social, economic and political North-South divide. Paradoxically, two economists of the World Bank, Carstein Fink and Charles J. Kenny, have questioned the logic behind the digital divide argument. In an article published in the *Journal of Policy and Strategy for Telecommunications,* titled *Whither the Digital Divide* they postulate that the size and importance of the divide are overstated. In their view, the divide is in fact shrinking. They postulate that the debate about the divide "is not how large it is, but how rapidly it is closing." They point out, first, that developing countries show faster rates of growth in network development than developed countries, and second, on income measure of access, developing countries already 'digitally leapfrog' the developed. They go on to dispute the prediction that disparities in absolute access to ICTs between countries would lead to reduced development prospects in poor countries. It is curious how World Bank bureaucrats should manipulate data about the ostensible high growth of telephone density and internet use in poor countries to paint such a distorted picture so distortedly. The fact that there is inequality of access in poor countries to IT facilities could not be the ground to advance the view that the digital divide is more of a symptom rather than the cause of inequality that exists between the urban and majority rural populations who lack the most basic infrastructure to accommodate IT.

The digital divide remains a huge challenge for Africa. It should be redressed if the continent is to be part of the movement towards the creation of knowledge, not simply information, societies. It is in such knowledge society that social inclusion, capacity building, empowerment and the sharing of equitable access to education and cultural diversity reside. In December 2003, the United Nations held a *World Summit on Information Society.* WSIS). The main objective of the Summit was "to assist governments, institutions and all actors of civil society deal with the new

527

challenges of the ever-evolving information society, specifically identifying ways to help close the gap between the "haves" and "have nots" of access to the global information and communication network." Africa can only hope, as with numerous previous UN Summits, that words and pledges would be translated into action.

The e-economy, on the other hand, would remain hype for Sub Saharan Africa for sometime to come. Africa is led to believe that any firm that fails to grapple with e-commerce is putting its future at risk. Yet, the key question is which African firm is referred to? One can appreciate the growth in the use of the internet as a source of broad-based information dissemination, especially in the arena of promoting distance and virtual education, democracy, business opportunities and multiculturalism. The same is not as evident in so far as the impact of the internet on direct African business transactions is concerned. I agree with the Editorial of *The Economist* of August 19th, 2000 that it is not as if the poor are shunning the internet for lack of financial capacity: "The problem is that they lack the skills to exploit it effectively. So it is difficult to see how connecting the poor to the Internet will improve their finances. It would make more sense to aim for universal literacy than universal Internet access." Even in the United States, according to *The Economist* of May 15th 2004, total e-commerce sales in the US for 2003 were estimated at US$ 54.9 billion, accounting for only 1.6% of total US retail sales, as much as these sales exclude items such as on-line travel and financial services, pornography, gambling and auction business.

There is another dimension to Africa's economic predicament and that is the state of the mobility of global capital. Africa is yet to feature prominently in the internationalisation of equity markets. Part of the blame lies on Africa itself. Countries like Tanzania, for example, until only in May 2003, were yet to come to grips with the need and importance of allowing capital account convertibility. Yet free flow of currency is a strong driver of globalisation, the setbacks arising from the East Asian financial crisis of 1997/1998 notwithstanding. This is why the IPOs on the DSE in Tanzania have not bee realising the best market prices. Indeed, it is for such reason blue chip African firms like South African Breweries decided to cross trade their stocks on the London Stock Exchange as well as in Johannesburg to take advantage of larger and more competitive pools of resources that leverage them to become truly competitive global players. Evidently, capital account convertibility has to be well managed. However, there should be no fear to unleash it. In his recent book, *In Praise of Empires: Globalization and Order*, Deepak Lal argues that "maintaining permanent controls, besides being an important denial of the economic freedom central to the efficient working of a market economy, it is also a denial of the associated efficiency gains." In allowing partial capital account convertibility in mid 2003, Tanzania took a bold stand in attracting foreign savings into its capital market.

Whilst the Malaysian experience following the 1997 financial crisis, is a good lesson in careful management of capital account liberalisation, we should at the same time appreciate that restricting taking money out of a country may not be as easy to manage. In his book, *Creating Wealth*, Professor Lester Thurow reports that in 1998, in spite of prohibiting free currency movement, Mainland China still lost over US$ 60 billion in currency reserves. As he puts it, "exporters just didn't bring their earnings back to China."

The African Mindset Dilemma

The foregoing analysis about Africa's marginalisation notwithstanding, it is also evident that Africa's economic malaise flows from its own mindset. Africa largely views its underdevelopment in the context of its economic relationship with the industrialised world. The emergence of terms such as marginalisation and the dominant perception that low levels of foreign direct investment and ODA are directly responsible for undermining Africa's capacity to accelerate structural change much needed to enable Africa's integration in the global economy seem to be at the heart of such mindset. Africa has somewhat failed to exploit the wisdom of people like Nyerere who have held that Africa must change by itself, under its own direction. NEPAD's ethos of making Africa work collectively in search of a lasting solution to the development challenges that confront it is in line with Nyerere's vision. The challenge is to get results from NEPAD's focus on infrastructure development, ICTs, energy, health, agriculture, environment and tourism, education, water and sanitation, science and technology, industrialisation, gender equality and governance through the Peer Review Mechanism.

In an article published in the *Journal of Economic Perspectives* by Paul Collier and Jan William Gunning titled: *Why has Africa Grown Slowly* the authors boldly tackle the African economic problematique. They admit that the deterioration in the terms of global trade for primary commodities has indeed adversely affected Sub Saharan Africa. However, they point out that the net aid inflows into Sub Saharan Africa since 1970, low as they have been, have been about 50% more than the income losses resulting from adverse terms of trade. More fundamentally, the authors locate Africa's underdevelopment on Africa's domestic policies that are largely unrelated to trade. They note for example, that African manufacturing, which can have significant value added export impact, suffers from a policy-driven, low-productivity trap. Such policy failure features in areas such as poor infrastructure, poor contract law enforcement, disenabling of firms to exploit economies of scale, low stock of skilled human capital, overprotection of industries from productive competition and the imposition of high costs of doing business. At the same time, the huge technology gap that contributes to the high level of industrial un-competitiveness is attributed to high cost of capital goods arising from a skewed taxation policy. As a result, Africa generally suffers from a low absorption of technological know how. This is a major setback. For as Thomas Friedman has correctly asserted in his book, *The Lexus and The Olive Tree,* one key reason in the distortion of globalisation is that "people don't understand that it is largely a technology-driven phenomenon, not a trade-driven one." Because of its technological backwardness, Africa is unable to integrate itself into the global economy.

Africa Cannot Feed Itself

Much can also be said about the poor state of African agriculture. A country that is not able to feed itself cannot even begin to think about how it can master globalisation and its impact. *The UNDP Human Development Report, 2003* asserts that between 1980 and 1995 per capita food production in Sub-Saharan Africa fell by 8% and that one in three Africans presently goes hungry. Of course, Nobel Laureate Amartya Sen is right in cautioning that the growth of food output should be viewed in the context of overall economic growth. Thus, yes, Singapore produces little food, if any, but its people are well fed. This is because its overall economy is strong. As Professor Sen correctly argues in his book, *Development As Freedom,* "the major feature of Sub-Saharan Africa's problems is not the particular lack of growth in food output as such, but the general lack of economic growth altogether. of which the problem of food output is only one *part)."* What is important to note is that Africa cannot wait for the rich countries to support it in feeding itself. The record of such external support is dismal. In his paper delivered at the Conference on Sustainable Food Security for all by 2000, titled, *What productive resources do the poor really require to escape poverty?* Professor Michael Lipton points out that aid to agriculture and rural development in the 1970s accounted for more than one third of total aid to the least developed countries. In the late 1980s, this figure had dropped to 24%. The figure in 2000 stood at 10%.

The food question has another curious dimension. Sub Saharan Africa's expenditure on imports of maize, rice and wheat has risen from US$ 514.3 million in 1973 to US$1.9 billion in 1985 and to US$2.5 billion in 1995. These figures exclude South Africa. According to the FAO, the value of food imports in Sub-Saharan Africa in 1999 was over US$ 8 billion. Moreover, food aid constitutes a major proportion of net food trade in Africa. In many of these countries, it constitutes more than half of net food imports. In Kenya and Tanzania, for example, food aid constituted two thirds of food imports in the 1990s. Sub Saharan Africa can ill afford huge expenditures equal almost to two thirds of its total annual FDI inflows. Africa should rise to the challenge of upgrading its economic productive capacities quickly enough; feed itself and then compete in global markets. This is why it is noteworthy that the *NEPAD Comprehensive Africa Agriculture Development Programme.* CAADP) plans an investment of US$ 240 billion by 2015 focussing on investments to improve agriculture, food security and trade balance. CAADP has a goal that African countries must, by 2008, allocate at least 10% of their budgetary resources to agriculture. Agriculture constitutes an important area that must receive more support from external sources.

Regional Integration is Fundamental

Poor countries themselves must seriously take charge of their economies through well-planned self-reliant actions. The peoples of the South must, by their own exertions, free themselves from poverty, underdevelopment and dependency and gain control of their economies and polities. In such struggle, their solidarity is of urgent and critical importance. The spirit of collective self-reliance should be fired up. Economics of aggregation must underpin Africa's renaissance. Africa should quickly overcome the fears of integration. Zero sum nationalism should give way to a lofty project of prosperity through integration. There is nothing to lose from integration but one's own chains of dependence and marginalisation. It is a often paradox that Africa should be less concerned about its being exploited by the industrialised world in trade matters, but feel exposed and undermined by cross-border trade! Africa should understand that its market of first resort is its own market. It is clear that North-South trade will not, in the near future, constitute the crucial engine or even provide the degree of stimulus for growth of poor economies. In this context, South-South cooperation has to be seriously addressed. China's bilateral agreements with 40 African countries concluded in 2004 which provide reciprocal most-favoured nation status and duty-free status to some goods exported by the least developed African countries is a positive pointer in this direction.

Solidarity of the poor or what the late Mwalimu Nyerere once described as the "trade union of the poor" is the inevitable choice for Africa's economic liberation. Such integration and solidarity is also imperative in ensuring that global institutions such as the IMF, the World Bank, the WTO and the United Nations are transformed to become more authentically democratic. Poor countries should help to reshape global economic relations in order to diminish the inequality that presently exists in North-South economic negotiations. This is a subject examined in the next chapter.

By taking charge of its own economies, Africa should realise that liberalising controls to market entry is not a panacea to attracting investments. Africa continues to be devilled by crime and political instability. A quick solution to such problems is paramount and demands robust improvement in national economic conditions. More seriously, however, especially to peaceful and stable polities like Tanzania, Africa faces the challenge of market risk. Market risk in the sense that basic marketing infrastructure is largely weak. Investors always seek a secure environment that allows profitable market penetration. Take the case of the insurance industry as an example. Overall, the emerging markets, of which only South Africa in the whole Sub Saharan Africa fits into the category, account for a mere 9% of global total insurance premium volume. According to the Speech of the Minister for Finance, Basil Mramba, to the Commonwealth-Tanzania Investment Conference in Dar es Salaam in May 2003, the contribution of the Tanzania insurance industry to GDP was 2.9% in 2002, up from 2.59% in 1998. Its gross premium income is expected to reach 3.42% of GDP by 2007. This is a low volume. Yet efficient insurance markets that have adequate depth in the economy to protect market risk and thus leverage profits, constitute important drivers for attracting foreign direct investment. They, in turn, leverage the integration of poor economies into the global economy. This means that unless African economies improve their marketing infrastructure, where it becomes easier to obtain reliable information about market potentials, many investors could be discouraged to plunge in.

Towards A New International Strategy

What is needed today is nothing less than a new consensus between alliances that are frayed, between wealthy nations and poor, and among peoples mired in mistrust across an apparently widening cultural abyss. The essence of that consensus is simple: we all share responsibility for each other's security. And the rest of that consensus will be action.

-United Nations High Level Panel Report: *A more secure world: Our shared responsibility, 2004.*

The *South Commission Report* had perceptively observed that "there cannot be either genuine peace at the global level or stable and secure prosperity in the North unless the South can accelerate its growth, overcome under-development and build a better life for its people." President John F. Kennedy had asserted, almost four decades earlier: "if a free society cannot help the many who are poor, it cannot save the few who are rich". I do not claim any originality in the many proposals that have been submitted in recent years in moving global relations from domination to building a strong partnership between the rich and poor countries. What clearly underlies most of the proposals made is the abiding concern about the marginalisation of countries like Sub-Saharan Africa and the dominant urge to integrate poor economies in the global economy. Only a brief summary of some of the most important proposals are made here.

First, there is little doubt that the progressive integration of the African economies into the global economy would demand for Africa longer waiver and transition period under *The Cotonou Agreement* and the World Trade Organisation in the specific context of the following:

- Protection against dumping and unregulated access of subsidised products into African markets;
- Agreement on a more careful and gradual relaxation of trade barriers erected by African countries on goods from industrialised countries;
- Preferential access to global markets for at least 20 years from year 2000;
- Cancellation of its total external debt.

The Burden of HIV/AIDS

According to the UN High Level Panel Report above referred to, about 30 million Africans have HIV/AIDS. This is a catastrophe beyond human imagination. *The 2003 Human Development Report* also shows that, in 2002, HIV/AIDS claimed an estimated 3.1 million deaths whilst 42 million people were infected with the HIV/AIDS, most of these in Sub-Saharan Africa. Health expenditure, as a percentage of GDP, averaged 2.1% per annum or US$ 38. in purchasing power parity terms) per person for selected HIPC countries in 2000. Tanzania spent US$ 27. PPP terms) per capita for health provisioning. In contrast, developed nations in 2000 spent, on average 5% of GDP on public health care. The figure for G 7 is as high as 6% of GDP and more than US$ 2,300 per capita. To address this major disease burden requires a complete change in international development and humanitarian strategy. Whilst global spending to combat HIV/AIDS has risen nine fold since 1996, at US$ 4.7 billion in 2003, it is still only half the annual amount needed to effectively tackle the pandemic.

According to Jeffrey Sachs, rich countries need to raise a minimum of US $ 10 billion a year in aid to poor countries for combating HIV/AIDS. This proposal has been endorsed by the UN High Level Panel Report, 2004. Yet, this amount translates into only $ 10 per person per year for the vulnerable 1 billion citizens in poor countries, the bare minimum to begin to make a difference in turning around the health and economic productivity potential in poor economies. President George W. Bush's May, 2003 HIV/AIDS law that put at the disposal of Africa and the Caribbean a US$15 billion Fund for five years was, on the face of it, a positive measure. However, political and bureaucratic procedures bedevil the realisation of the commitment. Whilst for the year 2003 President Bush requested allocation of US$ 3 billion, the House of Representatives, on 24 July 2003, approved only $ 2.0 billion. Of the approved amount, US$ 1.43 was directed to the global AIDS programme and the balance to general health spending in poor countries.

What is distressing about these grants is the complex conditionalities attached to their allocation, including conditions such as sexual abstinence. It is also not clear how much would feed into the *UN Global Fund* started by Kofi Annan. At any rate, the amount made available is still well short of Sachs' budget estimate. However, were such funding supported by much lower prices of antiretroviral drugs and the broader liberalisation of patent rules for the manufacture of generic drugs, Africa would probably confront the deadly pandemic much more successfully. The outlook appears negative given the strong lobby of US pharmaceutical companies on President Bush's administration especially in allowing the new generic combination drugs, containing all three drugs that AIDS patients in rich countries take separately, to be manufactured in poor countries. The WHO has argued a case for copyright protection over the three separate drugs to be waived to enable the manufacture of the combined drug which would lower costs and ease administration of treatment. Greater flexibility over the production of such a drug would make President Bush's $15 billion five-year commitment to fight AIDS in poor countries more effective. Some changes took place in mid 2004 enabling the manufacture of such three in one generic drug.

Moreover, conditionalities attached to the grant utilisation have been relaxed with respect to President George W. Bush's Emergency Plan for AIDS Relief. PEPFAR) set aside for selected 15 countries in 2004. For example, Tanzania, which has been offered US$ 65 million to address the AIDS pandemic, has had no conditionality imposed on the use of the funds for buying antiretroviral drugs. Coincidentally, the lack of such conditionality has come in the wake of the scientific finding, contained in the leading UK medical journal *Lancet* in June 2004 that the fixed dose of a combined three anti-retroviral generic drugs produced by an Indian pharmaceutical company, Cipla, called *Triomune* and costing US$ 20 for a month's prescription, was efficacious and effective. However, a different kind of problem, an ironic one, arose in Tanzania undermining early importation of the ARVs intended for a specified 44, 000 infected people. In an article in the *International Herald Tribune* of July 10-11, 2004, titled *Needless battle of brands vs. generics,* two health workers in Tanzania, Anne

Reeler and Joseph Sabe, reported that the delay in importation had arisen because Tanzanian health authorities held a dogmatic view that generic ARV drugs were cheaper which was not the case. Because of the help of some philanthropic institutions, some brand-name drugs were in fact cheaper than the generic ones. The "ideological" battle resulted in drugs not reaching Tanzania at the earliest stage.

Promoting Technology Collaboration

The third proposal relates to what Professor Sachs has described as the promotion of technology in poor countries bringing into collaboration the academia, government and industry of the industrialised world. The aim is both to promote technology cooperation between rich and poor countries and to assist education and research and development institutions in poor countries to develop technological capacity. Such cooperation necessarily embodies restraint on the part of the industrialised countries in exercising intellectual property rights. For as Lester Thurow has suggested in his book *Creating Wealth*, "increasingly the acquisition of knowledge is central for both catch-up states and keep-ahead states." Poor countries cannot afford to buy the knowledge they need to make it into the first world. They must inevitably copy knowing that such free riding would not destroy global R&D innovations. Globalisation, in other words, should embrace such flexibility over intellectual property rights.

Sleepless in Seattle, Davos and Cancun

A reviewer of a book titled *Globalisation and History: The Evolution of A Ninetieth-Century Atlantic Economy* in *The Economist* of January 8th, 2000 concluded, "Globalisation can sow the seeds of its own destruction." It would indeed be so if it failed to be an engine for progress of humanity. The UN Secretary General Kofi Annan, contributing in the *Special Edition of Newsweek*, December 1999 - February 2000, reflected similar concern when he wrote, that as much as globalisation brought forth new choices and opportunities, at the same time, to millions of people, it was viewed as an enemy of progress. In his words, globalisation is a "disruptive force that can destroy lives, jobs and traditions". Undoubtedly, globalisation is undergoing a crisis. The disruption of the World Trade Organisation meeting in Seattle, and in Prague, the fracas that featured during the meeting of the World Economic Forum in Davos, and the debacle of the WTO Doha Round of trade talks in Cancun in September 2003, all manifest a new challenge, and a growing one, to economic internationalism or globalism. As far back as 1990, *The Challenge To The South* had pointedly stated that "there cannot be either genuine peace at the global level or stable and secure prosperity in the North unless the South can accelerate its growth, overcome under-development, and build a better life for its people". Little did the South leaders who constituted the South Commission contemplate that their quest for a new global economic dispensation built around an equitable partnership and not an exploitative one would also constitute an agenda for social movements in the industrialised world. What featured in Seattle, Davos and Cancun was a paradoxical solidarity of all those who view globalisation as a trap rather than as a driver of prosperity. A Danish Diplomat, J. Orstrom Moller, wrote in the magazine *The Futurist* in March 1999 that tensions are growing around the world over the march toward the internationalisation of the global economy. He predicted a "clash" between the elite-the globaphiles-and the "growing feeling of ordinary people that internationalism lets them down and fails to provide an answer to the problems they face".

Yet globalisation is a reality. It is a reality in the sense of breakthroughs in information and communications technologies; 24 hour capital flows and depth of trade through transnational and multinational enterprises. Thus, globalisation could not be simply wished away or halted. At the same time, an economic reality need not subvert global peace and stability. Yet what globalisation portends is the expansion of prosperity in the North and the expansion of poverty in the South. Put differently, globalisation manifests an unacceptable contradiction. In his brilliant book, *Preparing For the Twenty First Century*, Professor Paul Kennedy argued that globalisation devoted "less attention to the prospect of a further marginalisation of four-fifths of the earth's population not well prepared for these new commercial and financial trends." Amplifying, he pointed out that it was difficult for developing nations to accept the logic of the global marketplace precisely because of "the structural obstacles that cramp" those nations.

Here then lies the central policy question: how could and should such structural obstacles be removed? One evident obstacle that stands out has to do with making the World Trade Organisation a more effective and truly global rule-based organisation driven by principles of transparency, multilateralism and non-discrimination. Yet, even *The Economist* of December 4th 1999 questioned whether rich-country governments, and especially the United States of America, were not to blame in propelling "legitimate fears that the WTO will take on a role beyond its proper competence." In clarifying this position, the respected British magazine observed, "Calls for the body. WTO) to develop a new agenda on the environment. trade-related) and on labour standards - demands that will push it into matters that, at best, belong in other forums, and which could easily end up hurting the poorest countries - have come from the United States". From the perspective of the South, the challenge is to transform, in a radical way, the international economic and political system that emerged in the post World War II era. Gamani Corea, the Sri Lankan former head of UNCTAD, wrote in *Global Stakes Require a New Consensus*, that the old consensus that gave birth to the Bretton Woods institutions and to GATT centred on assuring full employment; not on addressing the centrality of economic growth and development dynamism.

In spite of all the fanfare, the birth of the WTO has not propelled the merits of international regulation to stabilise commodity prices. It has failed to open up the economies of the developed world by removing market distorting subsidies, especially in agriculture, and to extend tariff preferences to exports of third world countries. Indeed, the Cotonou Agreement, the EU Everything But Arms. EBA) and AGOA that provide tariff preferences, are viewed, in a strict sense, to be a violation of WTO's free market rules. Of course, the WTO had sanctioned these trade tariff preferences on a temporary basis. The ultimate goal of the WTO is to engineer a global competition and investment policy regime that is driven by the market and applied equally, even among unequal partners! Poor countries expect a more equitable treatment from rich countries and the success of the WTO Doha round of trade talks when they resume in Hong Kong in December 2005 crucially hinges on such treatment.

At the same time, these realities constitute a wake up call for poor countries. Time has come for them to seriously close their ranks and galvanise their thinking and efforts behind the recommendations which the *South Commission Report* has made. Specifically, they should focus their attention on three areas. First, the need to transform the IMF into a World Central Bank with a limited but important role of establishing and managing the international reserve assets; ensuring stability of exchange rates and international interest rates and providing adequate international liquidity, especially to meet special needs of developing countries. Secondly, fine-tuning the WTO by making it more transparent, multilateral and non-discriminatory. Third, demanding the strengthening of the role of the United Nations in the management of the international system and in decision making on world economic and social issues. In this context, Samir Amin, in his book *Capitalism In the Age of Globalisation*, perceptively sees the development of "world organizational forms which are more authentically democratic" as being critical in "reshaping economic relations on the basis of diminishing equality". At Davos, in January 2000, President Clinton had also called for a more participatory approach to dialogue on global economic issues and even acceding to the involvement of NGOs and other social movements in deliberating global policy issues. This was a dramatic response to the growing challenge to internationalism! The Report of the UN High Level Panel on *Threats, Challenges and Change,* has gone to some length in making radical proposals to transform the UN system. It remains to be seen whether the major powers would be prepared to share responsibility in a world that is increasingly crying out loud for solidarity and equity.

As poor nations become more sensitive to the challenges and realities of globalisation so must they also re-kindle their spirit of collective self-reliance. There are three fundamental reasons to support this stance. First, the growing unparalleled power wielded by the North in economic affairs amply show that North-South trade would take a long time to constitute the key engine or even provide the degree of stimulus for growth of the economies of the poor South. Second, given the degree of industrialisation and the degree of complementarities of the economies in the newly industrialising countries of the South, the scope for South-South trade, based on fairer rules, is enormous. Earlier cited was the lead China has taken in promoting bilateral trade agreements with several African countries, offering a reciprocal most-favoured nation status. China has also concluded bilateral agreements with some African countries to encourage and guarantee investments and on double taxation avoidance. Third, South solidarity is critical in ensuring that global trade negotiations within the WTO framework protect and promote the interests of the South. Such solidarity was clearly reflected at the Cancun trade talks, even though signs of balkanisation driven by interests of the rich countries are fast emerging. World Bank President James Wolfensohn, speaking at the Annual Joint IMF/World Bank meeting in Dubai immediately following the collapse of the WTO Cancun meeting, saw the unity of the South at Cancun as something that signalled "determination to push for a new equilibrium" in a world which was "out of balance". In contrast, the then US Trade Representative, Robert Zoellick, wrote an article in the *Financial Times* of September 22, 2003 titled *America will not wait for the won't-do countries,* that "as WTO members ponder the future, the US will not wait: we will move towards free trade with can-do countries. In fact, liberal minded people like the" As threats of balkanisation loom large, what position do countries of the South do? Though I am not a pessimistic person, I fear that the acute disparities in stages of development of the countries of the South and the competing interests between the poorest and the emerging economies of the South in a globalised world, may undermine both the ethos of "trade union of the poor" as well as the drive for economic integration across the two groups.

In this light, it is critical and urgent that countries of the South, and especially poor Sub-Saharan African countries, take regional and sub-regional economic integration as a strategy of economic salvation, away from the apprehension driven by zero sum nationalism that national economies would falter from it. *Sleepless in Seattle, Davos and Cancun* is a wakeup call to poor countries to return to the basics of the quest for a new international economic order that is fair, equitable and democratic. This is the conclusion reached by the ILO World Commission on *The Social Dimension of Globalisation* in its report launched at the end of February

2004. The Report should be used by both rich and poor countries to move forward the agenda for greater equity in global economic and trade relations.

Chapter

40 GLOBAL TRADE AGENDA: CHALLENGES FOR AFRICA

All the developing countries I know are exasperated by the hypocrisy and double standards practised by industrialised countries in trade policy. This has reached a point that there are grave risks of a serious backlash. Not for decades has there been a greater possibility of a systemic breakdown. At a time when the world is facing great uncertainty on the geopolitical front, it is nothing short of a tragedy that the global economic system is being held hostage by the narrow and selfish vested interests of the rich countries.

-Professor Jean-Pierre Lehman: ***Protestations that Reek of Hypocrisy.***

Introduction

At the 2001 World Economic Forum Summit for Southern Africa that met in Durban, South Africa in the first week of June 2001, the crosscutting theme of the Summit was *"acting on realities, confronting perceptions"*. Put into context, the underlying message of the Conference was that Africa generally and the SADC sub-region in particular was confronted by two major challenges, at times complementary and, at times, opposing.

One of the challenges pertains to the fundamental question about appreciating realities- social, economic, political, technological, environmental- and seizing the opportunities which such realities present. There is concern, within and without Africa, that Africa may not consistently and affirmatively be acting on the stark realities that stare it in the face. For example, there is the dimension that Africa could only reasonably take a quantum leap in development if it vigorously integrated its own markets and economies. Yet deep zero sum nationalism presently militates against such objective. The second challenge relates to Africa's lack of or inadequate attention on confronting and addressing a myriad of perceptions about itself, from outside Africa and those located within Africa, including perceptions about each other as African nation states. Some of the perceptions are positive and are thus deployable as strengths. Others are negative, constituting weaknesses to be minimised or overcome.

With such a perception enigma looming large, the central challenge that Africa faces is one of leadership; a leadership prepared to be bold and frank, as well as capable of accepting that the negative perceptions confronting Africa are within Africa's capacity to transform.

An area that reflects Africa's dominant weakness in acting on realities and in confronting perceptions about itself, concerns how Africa, along with the rest of the poor world, gears itself and responds to global trade issues. Trade lies at the heart of any country's economic growth and Africa cannot therefore afford not to be mindful of it. In this chapter, I examine how Africa, and specifically Sub-Saharan Africa, acts on its realities and confronts perceptions about it within the context of the present global economic environment and the on-going WTO Doha round of trade negotiations.

The WTO Doha Development Round

It is wrong to characterise the Doha agenda, especially as it has evolved over the past two years, as a development round. Recent negotiations have not only failed to push an agenda that would promote development; they have included a host of issues that are of tangential interest, or even detrimental, to developing countries.
-Joseph E. Stiglitz: **It is time for a true development trade round.**

After the Seattle debacle, the WTO has held two trade rounds, in Doha, Qatar in November 2001 and in Cancun, Mexico, in September 2003. A key area for Africa's collective agreement, at both meetings, centred on the need for a new, full trade round of negotiations as opposed to limited negotiations on the WTO's "new issues", also known as the "Singapore Issues." These new issues relate to environmental and labour standards, competition policy, the multilateral investment agreement. MIA) and public procurement. Do Africa and the LDCs have a common position on all broad-based policies that surround the trade negotiations? The preparatory meeting of the LDCs that took place in Zanzibar in July 2001 reflected an attempt at forging unity of direction. At Cancun, such unity was more vivid, especially in outrightly rejecting the ostensible quid pro quo that the rich countries sought to strike as a trade off for acceptance of the "Singapore issues" in return for a more favourable position on agricultural subsidies.

However, it would seem that as far as Africa is concerned, several imponderables to address remain if unity of action is to emerge consistently and sustainably. Simba Makoni, Zimbabwe's former Finance Minister had cautioned, during the Durban meeting of the 2001 World Economic Forum that it was unrealistic to expect an African-wide capacity for collective action to emerge when there existed several constraints impeding national capacity in the first place. What are such constraints? A few of them are consider below.

Perceptions and Realities

Africa's capacity in advancing its position at Doha Round of trade negotiations crucially hinges on how it addresses its realities and at the same time confronts the perceptions over them. In this context, I should begin by painting the bleak yet plausible perception that prevails within Africa and especially within Sub-Saharan Africa. First is the preponderant perception about globalisation; that rather than spreading the fruits of economic growth and bolstering living standards of the poor, globalisation is in fact contributing to deepening poverty. Thus, the whole idea that Africa could be integrated into the world economy within the existing framework of global economic relationships is viewed to be illogical at best and illusionary at worst.

This dismal picture of Africa is orchestrated in the rich countries. The American economist Lester Thurow has described Sub-Saharan Africa. with the exception of South Africa) as "the world's basket case", as earlier alluded to. In such light, is it plausible that the present WTO trade regime and the framework of negotiations in place could effectively ameliorate Africa's grave economic condition? Does the WTO trade regime and negotiations recognise the real African realities? In addition, does it seriously address Africa's needs for broad-based development and economic transformation as a basis for realising a more equitable global trade regime? These are some of the pertinent questions that should underpin Africa's negotiating position at the WTO Doha Round of trade negotiations. The key question is whether such a collective African resolve can emerge? At Doha, in September 2001, it appeared that Africa largely spoke with one voice. The same happened in Cancun in September 2003. Following the Cancun debacle, the question is what happens next in the light of what appears to be a growing fracture in the trade union of the poor South? I amplify this point below.

Africa's Marginalisation

"Men are some time masters of their fate: The fault, dear Brutus, is not in our stars, But in our selves ..."

Cassius, in Shakespeare's Julius Caesar, may have exaggerated, in the context of Africa, about the cause of Africa's marginalisation. The fault with Africa's economic malaise does not simply lie with Africa itself. It significantly lies on the unequal state of the global economic system. In order to grasp the predicament confronting Africa within the context of the relevance of global trade negotiations, a deeper examination of Africa's economic fragility and how this weakness is not given the expected serious attention by the rich countries is called for. There is little doubt that market access, the buzzword of the rich to the poor, is definitely a strategic factor in trade issues. However, market access by itself begs the fundamental question about Africa's capacity, in the first place, to benefit from the so-called quota and duty free access preferences to the markets of the industrialised economies. OECD). According to the IMF, a repeal of all OECD countries' trade barriers and agricultural subsidies would improve global welfare by about $ 120 billion per annum. At the same time, an uplift of only 1% in Africa's share of world exports would amount to $ 70 billion a year, more than five times ODA and debt relief in 2003.

The Centre for Global Development and Foreign Policy Joint Report supports this view. Ranking the commitment to development goals, published in the journal, *Foreign Policy, May/June, 2000,* the report shows, that based on World Bank estimates, trade barriers in developed economies cost poor nations more than US$ 100 billion per year, roughly twice what rich countries give in aid. Worse, the industries protected include agriculture, textiles and apparel, the main sectors in which poor nations have competitive advantage. Farm subsidies alone in rich countries cost poor nations some US$ 50 billion in lost exports per annum. According to the US Department of Agriculture, in 2002, the US spent US$ 3.6 billion supporting 2,500 US farmers, less than 10% of total US cotton farmers. The US exported more than one-third its cotton production giving it about 40% of the world share of cotton market.

In an article in *The National Interest* of Summer 2003, titled, *Agrivation: The Farm Bill from Hell,* Professor C. Ford Runge points out that under the 2002 Farm Bill Programme, "cotton farmers. in the US) will receive direct payments of 66 cents a pound, a loan rate of 52 cents and a target price of 72 cents-all above global prices.. Across the ocean in Africa, cotton farmers in Mali will receive about 11 cents a pound this year)". Worse still, under the Federal Farm Subsidy Programme, the US extended some US$ 1.7 billion in 2003 to American agribusiness and manufacturers for buying already subsidised cotton. A report of the International Cotton Advisory Committee points out that during the cotton production year 2001/2002, subsidies to cotton growers in the industrialised countries, including the US, totalled US$ 5.8 billion. It is these subsidies that the Presidents of Mali and Burkina Faso cite in an article in the *New York Times* of 11 July 2003 titled *Your Farm Subsidies Are Strangling Us.* The total global subsidy equalled the size of cotton traded worldwide during that year. Such price distortions have grave impact on poor countries even considering that cotton production costs in the main African cotton growing areas such as

Mali, Burkina Faso, Benin and Chad are about 50% lower than those in the developed countries. Specifically, 10 million people in these poor West African nations are impoverished.

The EU appears to have some interest in reviewing this situation. It organised a special EU-Africa Cotton Forum in Paris from 5-6 July 2004 to promote a constructive dialogue on partnership over the cotton issue. What was the missing link was the non-involvement of the major cotton player in the global cotton market, the United States. Yes, a closer understanding of the respective cotton trade positions has probably been realised between the EU and Africa, at least in polemical terms. What is debatable is the effectiveness of such understanding in the broader context of the Doha Round of Trade Talks in which the question of subsidies to agriculture by the OECD countries lies at the heart and constitutes the central impediment to fruitful conclusions of trade negotiations. In sum, according to UNCTAD, between 1997 and 2001, Africa's primary commodities lost more than 50% of their purchasing power *vis a vis* manufactured goods.

However, at the same time, it is pertinent to interrogate whether improved market access is still Africa's panacea for higher export performance. Conversely, could it be concluded, unequivocally, that restricted market access and tariff barriers constitute the central factors undermining Africa's exports? How then could Africa defend itself, for instance, for being a net importer of food? Overall, Africa's trade performance has been poor. According to UNCTAD's October, 2003 Report: *Economic Development in Africa: Issues in Africa's Trade Performance,* Africa's share in global merchandise exports declined from 6.3% in 1980 to 2.5% in 2000. On the other hand, its share in world manufactured exports in 2000 was a little below 1%. Contrast this picture with that of Asia. Asia's share in global merchandise exports rose from 18% in 1980 to 22% in 2000. Its share in global manufactured exports between 1980 and 2000 increased three fold to 21%. What is more disturbing in Africa's case is the significant decline in its global share of trade in commodities. In their paper, *Is Africa Integrated in the Global Economy?* Arvind Subramanian and Natalia Tamirisa point out that this share has plummeted from about 8% in 1980 to 4.4% in 2000. It is not clear whether Africa's problems in exporting relate more to closed markets or to the lack of capacity for market penetration.

Thus, the jury is still out whether market advantage can be achieved when greater market access is extended to Africa. This is a fundamental point because it could be that rather than the OECD countries reinforcing the need for a new trade round of negotiations aimed at deepening global trade liberalisation, a strategy that now clearly favours the rich economies, they could, instead, shift attention and focus more on how to improve

Africa's capacity for integration in the global economy. In other words, meaningful global trade negotiations may have to flow from an economically stronger Africa. Peter Harrold's study titled *The Impact of the Uruguay Round on Africa* postulates that Africa's poor advantage on exports of industrial goods, for example, "has everything to do with domestic policies and little to do with multilateral trading arrangements". However, what Harrold's study fails to point out is that many Sub-Saharan African countries have prudently pursued domestic policies in line with the IMF/World Bank's conventional wisdom. Yet the levels of micro-economic results necessary for bolstering higher economic growth have not been realised. At the root of low growth is the fact that rich countries have largely been passive in extending adequate and the right kind of support for de-bottlenecking Africa's systemic economic problems. The result is that Africa has failed to stimulate sustainable economic growth able to exploit global trade opportunities offered by the industrialised countries. In effect, this means that if there is a global economic agenda demanding immediate attention it is how to transform the mindset and political will of rich countries. These countries have to become more responsive to Africa's economic fragility by extending more meaningful aid and investment targeted at elevating the economic potentials of Africa and enabling them to become global economic players. Moreover, UNCTAD's view, anyway, is that market access remains the central problem since most of the peak tariffs imposed by rich countries affect agricultural and agro-processed products. Average tariffs on agriculture are much higher than those imposed on manufactures.

No doubt, it is always tempting to fall prey to the mantra, "trade not aid". Indeed, an economic model developed by Christopher Adam and Stephen A. O'Connell in their work *Aid Versus Trade Revisited* shows that opening export markets through offering preferences to LDCs would bolster exports by around 6% over a five-year period and as much as 16% in a new steady global economic environment. In reality, however, such mantra about trade not aid is not an "either or" one. Yes, aid is critical in jump-starting economies of Africa and the LDCs by offering them the blood and sinews for effectively seizing the so-called trade opportunities made available through special trade preferences. On the other hand, what ought to be appreciated is that preferential market opportunities do not cover a wide range of products, especially in agricultural commodities. Moreover, there is stringent conditions- health and environmental- increasingly attached to many of the market access preferences thus militating against their optimal utilisation.

Agriculture: Africa's Mainstay

Africa's economic transformation and sustainable growth largely hinges on

545

enabling a massive transformation of agriculture. Earnings from primary commodities represent a mere 4% of Africa's GDP. Africa needs its own green revolution strategically linked to industrialisation. Yet, as a share of total lending of multilateral institutions, assistance to Africa's agriculture and rural development has fallen from 15% of total lending in 1997 to 10% in 1999. There has been little improvement since then because World Bank's support has concentrated on economic stabilisation rather than on directly inducing economic productivity at strategic sectoral levels, especially agriculture. Bilateral official development assistance for this sector also fell from US\$ 3.6 billion in 1981-83 to US\$ 1.4 billion in 1999-2000. Based on the *United Nations Economic Report for 2003,* the *US Farm Bill 2002* will extend US\$ 52 billion to US farmers in the next six years as additional subsidies to crops and dairies, this being 67% more than the subsidy given in 2002. The US based International Food Policy Research Institute released a report in August 2003 that revealed that rich country agricultural policies as a whole cost farmers in developing countries some US\$ 24 billion a year in lost incomes. The report further stated that elimination of trade-distorting subsidies and tariffs could result in tripling exports of developing countries to US\$ 60 billion.

To add salt to injury, whilst the prices of merchandise exports of rich countries have been on the rise those of Africa's primary commodities have been declining. Between 1980 and 2000 world prices for 18 major export commodities of poor countries have fallen by 25%. Some commodities have experienced worse price declines, for example: sugar. 76.6%), cocoa. 71.1), coffee. 64%), rice. 60.8%) and cotton. 47%). It would appear that world trade has shifted from traditional commodity exports to non-traditional products such as fruits, vegetables, fish and sea food, products that encounter high income elasticity and lower rates of protection because of strict environmental and health standards. But above all, data shows that in 1999 the European Union countries spent about 7% of their total GDP. almost US\$ 600 billion) simply to keep away cheaper products from entering its markets by imposing tariff escalations. In addition, the EU is procrastinating over the reform of its *Common Agricultural Policy.* CAP) that entrenches the notorious subsidies to European farmers. Could such situation change? Indications on the ground point to a lack of political will, especially on the part of France, to have the CAP reformed substantially. As it is said in France, *"nostalagie de la boue,"* meaning that farming is in the heart of France. Four fifths of France is rural. France is the European Union's biggest producer of cereals, sugar beet and poultry. Its farmland was 22% of EU's agricultural land, prior to enlargement.

The poor results in the regional and European Parliament elections attained by President Jacques Chirac's centre right political party, in March and June 2004 respectively, would intimate that the government in France may not easily be responsive to policy changes on agricultural issues. Nevertheless, the budget proposals put forward by the previous Romano Prodi's administration in Brussels for the period 2007-2013 do not either offer much hope of a radical reform of the CAP. Though the proposed budget proposes a "freeze" on spending for farm subsidies, the proposed budget for CAP itself is still at a high level of 36% of the total *enhanced* EU budget. Be that as it may, the collapse of the WTO Doha Round trade talks in Cancun have clearly underlined that neither the EU nor the US appear prepared to substantially reduce or totally remove the trade distorting farm subsidies extended to their farmers. How could Africa then win in such circumstances? Has free trade lost its logical underpinning, namely that competitiveness should be driven by rules and a level playing field? It is important, in this context, that the WTO Doha Round of trade negotiations move beyond negotiations that seek to impose the so-called Singapore "new issues". The negotiations should embrace the whole gamut of development issues essential in leapfrogging the performance of economies of poor countries.

On the other hand, and this is the larger question, would the reforms sought by Africa, in themselves, leverage Africa's export performance? Africa shuns this question in the name of pursuing a fair globalisation. Yet it is a fundamental question and an imperative one in informing Africa's priorities in the medium term over global negotiations to improve Africa's conditions for promoting speedier and more robust development. For Africa continues to face daunting supply side constraints for bolstering its agriculture as well as its manufactures. For this reason, support for Africa has to be a well-balanced mixture of both market access, unhindered by subsidies offered to rich farmers involving commodities upon which Africa has comparative advantage, and higher ODA for improving supply side factors, especially production-inducing infrastructure. In the next section, I examine more closely what Africa stands to gain from preferential market access and whether such preferences constitute a panacea to Africa's economic transformation.

Is Preferential Market Access Boon or Illusion?

The proposals encapsulated in UNCTAD's Bangkok Declaration and Plan of Action 2000, which centred on non-reciprocal quota-free and duty free treatment of primary commodities and industrial goods from LDCs in the OECD markets, on the face of it, have received a shot in the arm. Underline the words: "on the face of it". The new EU- ACP Partnership Agreement. Cotonou Agreement), 2000 and the US Africa Growth and Opportunity Act. AGOA), 2000, both point towards the underlying objective of the Bangkok Plan. However, both preferential concession programmes should fit into the WTO legal framework. The Cotonou

Agreement enjoys from the WTO a breathing space that would expire in 2007. After that, *Economic Partnership Agreements. EPAs*) concluded between the EU and the ACP countries, bilaterally and within the framework of sub-regional arrangements, would come into force. As for AGOA, it is also a time bound arrangement and ends in 2008 unless renewed. These concessions have to be examined in the context of the agenda before the Doha Round of trade negotiations that includes negotiations for multilateral tariffs on industrial goods, a cut down on such tariffs, the elimination of tariff peaks and tariff escalation and the expansion of tariff binding. There is also a proposal to eliminate tariffs on all industrial products altogether. After such measures are enforced, could Africa remain competitive in a global trade environment that already favours the rich countries? How can Africa withstand inequitable agreements, such as those on trade in services, intellectual property rights and a host of other issues subjected to multilateral discipline, like the multilateral investment agreement that would undermine Africa's comparative advantage in the production of manufactures?

The EU - ACP Agreement

This agreement, especially when coupled with the "everything but arms"(EBA) initiative that offers quota and duty free market access to commodities from the ACP countries into the EU, with the exception of sugar, bananas and rice, marks a positive direction. However, many beneficiaries have continued to utilise the Lome protocols that embodied less restrictive rules of origin than under EBA. Moreover, as Steven Radelet has aptly cautioned in his article, *Bush and Foreign Aid,* with respect to AGOA, namely that AGOA should hardly be trumpeted as the US "giving" something to the poor countries when in reality US legislation only slightly reduces barriers and leaves significant obstacles untouched, so should the ACP countries take EBA with some circumspection. The pernicious farm subsidies extended to farmers on both sides of the Atlantic remain in place and makes ACP agricultural exports less competitive even with the preferences.

Another important point to recognise is that the EU-ACP Agreement has an in-built condition for the conclusion of EPAs. These agreements will come into force in 2008 and last until 2020. Negotiations for their establishment are in full swing. However, the net effect of EPAs, probably not wittingly, is to "balkanise" Africa in its trade relations with the EU. EU's plan is to enable itself to deal with Africa, the Caribbean and the Pacific countries, individually and in groups, based on selected criteria. However, at the heart of the EPAs is the progressive removal of tariffs and non- tariff barriers to imports from the EU and enhance cooperation. A report by a Brussels based NGO called the European Solidarity Towards

Equal Participation of People. Eurostep) in cooperation with five partner organisations from ACP countries, released on March 31st 2004, points out that EPAs primarily focus on removal of tariff barriers. EPAs also seek to promote trade and investment reciprocity between the EU and the ACP, a move, according to Eurostep, that would "result in increased access for EU exports to the 77 ACP countries" and "pay little attention to non-tariff barriers that are the principal obstacle for ACP imports into the EU". EPAs do not extend assistance in addressing supply side constraints of the ACP countries. Moreover, ACP countries would continue to face rigorous and restrictive standards and regulations that hinder ACP exports to the EU in the first place.

A 2004 UNCTAD Report: *Trade Preferences for LDCs: An early Assessment of benefits and possible improvements* asserts that the Group of leading traders, namely the US, EU, Japan and Canada, provide preferential trade or duty free schemes to 49 LDCs. However, the preferences cover only two thirds of imports from LDCs. Moreover, two thirds of such imports actually receive relative preferential treatment given the difficulties in satisfying rules of origin conditions. Therefore, according to the UNCTAD report only US$ 4.9 billion or 43% of otherwise dutiable LDC exports to these leading trading nations worth US$11.5 billion enter duty free. In fact, effective January 2005, the EU is effecting new food safety regulations that would make it mandatory for all fruit and vegetables arriving in the EU to be traceable at all stages of production, processing and distribution. Fulfilling such strict conditions would entail higher overheads for farmers in poor countries and thereby eroding the competitiveness of their commodities. In sum, EBA and other preferences encapsulated in the EPAs have little effect in opening markets to commodities and other products from poor countries. This begs their relevance.

EPAs: Balkanising Africa?

One of the troubling questions about EPAs is that to the extent that they are focused on a group of few countries and sub-regional groups, like SADC, ECOWAS, CEMAC, COMESA and CARICOM, they fundamentally beg the relevance of the ACP, even as of now, as an institutional framework that the EU deals and negotiates with. Thus, whilst the EPAs would only come into force in 2008, it is noteworthy that the EU is already concluding or has concluded bilateral, trade, development and cooperation agreements. TDCAs) with countries such as South Africa. whose agreement came into force in January 2000, with the Free Trade Area provision coming into force in 2012). It is curious that South Africa, whilst not a member of ACP, but which has strong trade and investment dealings with ACP countries, is a member at the same time of preferential trade promoting organisations such as SACU and SADC. Thus, imagine a scenario, recently mooted, where India joins SACU. Where would that place the EU-South Africa TDCA? From a another perspective, as the SADC Secretariat Trade Policy Adviser, Regine Qualmann posed in Dar es Salaam on 7 April 2004, how would Tanzania treat the tariff reduction under the EU-SADC EPA arrangement *vis a vis* its other two partners in the East African Customs Union? It would be ludicrous were Tanzania to apply different external custom tariffs and rules of origin to the EAC Customs Union members from those applied to the EU-SADC EPA members. It would not work. The EU Commissioner, Peter Mandelson, has raised a similar concern in early December 2004, when he met a group of SADC journalists in Brussels. In his view, Tanzania was walking a tight rope in the EPA negotiations by its decision to negotiate as part of the SADC group as opposed to the EAC one. He also cautioned about the difficulties the other two EAC members had in negotiating the EPA whilst still part of COMESA given that the EAC is already a Customs Union. At any rate, under the WTO framework, a country can only belong to one customs union in terms of not sharing the preferences with other countries outside the union. Tanzania, Kenya and Uganda should make up their minds whether they wish to maintain the EAC or walk their separate ways under the SADC and COMESA frameworks.

The EU's objective is to conclude more and more TDCAs, with developing countries, the driving criteria being to build reciprocal preferential trade relations through Free Trade Agreements in line with WTO rules. The US is also pursuing a similar approach with Central American states and most of the Caribbean countries. In fact, on 28 July, 2005 the US Congress passed the Central American Free Trade Agreement. Australia and New Zealand are similarly moving in the direction of constituting a Free Trade Area with countries of the Pacific Islands. All the South countries are part of the ACP. In effect, therefore, the ACP Group in Brussels no longer has any teeth because the EPA negotiations taking place pursuant to the Cotonou Agreement are now outside the *collective* ACP negotiating framework. As a result, The ACP collective voice has been undermined.

In the specific African context, EPAs would come on stream at the time when Africa is seriously pursuing the NEPAD initiative. As such, it would be a mockery were Africa to allow itself to be balkanised at a time when NEPAD demands a collective resolve to addressing common African economic challenges. In formulating NEPAD, Africa has committed itself to fulfilling the dream of catapulting a renaissance and collective self-reliance. Pursued in a committed fashion and supported by the African Economic Union,. rhetorical as it may be at this stage) constituted at the Durban OAU Summit in July 2002, the NEPAD initiative could not have been timelier and imperative. Its objectives should be relentlessly and seriously pursued. The results of the Maputo AU Summit in July 2003 also point to a strong commitment to the birth of a truly powerful collective African voice and Africa's economic integration. EPAs may thus not be congruent with such development. If, at all, in the name of responding to variable geometry, they may, in fact, undermine Africa's desire to promote wider economic integration from the broad perspective envisioned in the AU's Charter and its Constitutive Act.

Is AGOA Sustainable?

The main thrust of the *Africa Growth and Opportunity Act*. AGOA), is the extension of the general system of preferences. GSP) to selected qualifying African countries. In essence, its GSP gives African exporters a 5% preference margin over the average Most Favoured Nation Tariff. MFN). 38 countries were declared AGOA eligible by December 2002. On the face of it, AGOA appears attractive. However, it has some drawbacks in so far as eligibility is concerned. To qualify for AGOA, an applicant has to fulfil a number of stringent set of criteria, particularly those relating to rules of origin applicable to textiles and clothing. The only African countries exempted from those stringent rules of origin conditions are those whose annual per capita incomes, based on 1998 figures, are less than US$ 1,500. There may be many such countries. Moreover, AGOA excludes some key products in its realm. These include leather goods, footwear, handbags, watches, and flatware unless special approval or waiver from the US International Trade Commission is granted which is a long and difficult process. Additionally, AGOA requires non-trade related conditions to be fulfilled. Some of them are susceptible to highly subjective interpretation by the US authorities and are difficult to fulfil. They include:

- proof of progress in reducing tariff levels and binding tariffs with WTO.. This is one of the contentious issues at the Doha Round).
- having a system in place to combat corruption.
- non-engagement in violations of human rights.
- elimination of barriers to US trade and investment.. This is a difficult condition to fulfil).
- adherence to international standards on protection of workers' rights.

The more pertinent question, however, is the timeframe of AGOA. The Bush Administration views AGOA as "the centrepiece of US policy toward Africa". On 13 July 2004, President Bush signed the extension of AGOA III to 2015 even though by the law that establishes it, the extension is supposed to end in September 2008. Yet, two questions are relevant here. Is the extension in line with WTO rules considering that the quotas on textiles and garments that had been fixed under the Multifibre Agreement.

MFA) were eliminated at the end of December 2004? Second, will the EU recognise AGOA after the lapse of the Cotonou Agreement in 2007? The lapse of the 30 year Multifibre Agreement poses serious challenges to poor countries and relevance of AGOA. In an article in the *Economist* of November 11, 2004 titled, *The Looming Revolution*, it is noted that trade associations from more than 50 countries actually signed the *Istanbul Declaration* requesting the WTO to extend the quotas on textiles and garments for an additional three years to buy more breathing space. Even then, as a WTO study has shown, China's share of the US textiles' market is envisaged to rise from 16% in 2003 to 50% in 2010.

Indeed, based on EU data, imports of T-shirts from China into the EU increased by 187% whilst imports of flex yarn rose by 56% in the first three months of 2005. The United States also faced similar surges in Chinese textiles. Both the EU and the US immediately threatened to impose restrictions. In response, on 20 May, China announced imposition of up to 400% export tariffs on 75 textile products. Textiles and apparels account for about 15% or US$ 19.6 billion of China's annual total exports. India is also close behind. The losers, inevitably, will largely be African and Asian countries. Already, the end of the Multifibre Agreement has undermined the efficacy AGOA. The Asian companies, mainly Taiwanese, Chinese and Mauritian that established textile and garments factories in Africa to take advantage of AGOA have hurriedly re-located back to Asia. Lesotho, whose textiles exports under AGOA accounted for 31% of Africa's total in 2003 and creating 50,000 jobs, has had six factories close down in the first four months of 2005. Other countries worst affected are South Africa, Kenya, Malawi and Swaziland. Even in Asia, some countries like Bangladesh are also facing similar dire consequences. An IMF report published in June 2004, cited in the Economist edition referred above, also shows that the potential loss to Bangladesh's textile exports arising from the removal of the MFA quotas, would, at the minimum, be 25%. In this light, yes Tanzania has somewhat benefited from AGOA. Its textile and apparel exports amounted to US$ 3.37 million in 2004. In contrast, Kenya's and South Africa's exports in 2003 were US$ 184 million and US$ 1.7 billion respectively. All said, however, according to *Africa News Report* of March 29, 2004 issued by the American Embassy, Paris, Sub-Saharan Africa's share of the total US apparel market was only 2.1% in 2003. Probably opportunities to expand the base for higher exports exist. However, the challenges confronting Africa in the emerging highly competitive global textiles and garments market are extremely daunting. How and to what extent the restrictions imposed by the US and the EU on Chinese textiles and apparels along with China's own imposed export tariffs would bolster Africa's textile exports remains a matter of serious concern.

In a way, what has happened in the textiles market, poses a rude lesson for poor countries like Africa, namely that there is nothing like a truly free trade regime in the world or, for that matter, a "fair" globalisation. It is a brave new world out there and Africa has to find ways and means to reach out to itself first as a step towards building capacity. Unfortunately, Africa is yet to realise such goal. Mwalimu Nyerere often warned that Africa had no "uncles" to depend or rely upon for its well-being. It must dominantly promote self reliance. Incentives provided by schemes such as AGOA, regrettably, would always be driven by the conditions of internal politics and the economic interests of the rich countries. For example, the manner in which the Bush Administration administers its *Millennium Challenge Account.* MCA) which it promoted in March 2002 with a budget outlay of US$5 billion spread over three fiscal years is a case in point. Notwithstanding the Fund's lofty objectives, it is not the needy that necessarily benefit from it. Poor countries have to fulfil a number of conditions set down by the Bush Administration, such as they must rule justly, invest in people and encourage economic freedoms before qualifying to receive assistance under the Fund. It is as if the poor that need such support have the power to make their governments fulfil the set conditions. Indeed, Madagascar is the only country that has so far secured a grant, of US$ 110 million and in April 2005 from the Millennium Challenge Corporation. The subjectivity involved in administering the criteria is evidenced in Tanzania's failure to qualify for the MCA development assistance in the initial phase in 2004. It is in the light of being subjected to such sovereign humiliation that Africa can ill afford to be complacent in moving forward towards promoting serious collective self-reliance.

Africa's Economic Problematique

Africa thus faces a daunting challenge in advancing its trade agenda. Its economic fragility lies at the heart of such challenge. A close examination of the economic condition of Sub-Saharan Africa manifests this reality. SSA's average GDP. excluding South Africa and Nigeria) dropped from 3.9% in 1996 to 3.3% in 2003. 50% of its population. of over 300 million) lives on US 65 cents a day, down from about US$ 1 per day a few years ago. In other words, Sub-Saharan Africa is getting poorer. The contribution of manufacturing industry to GDP in 1999 averaged 9%, down from an average of 18.8% in 1990. Average gross domestic savings. excluding South Africa and Nigeria) in 2001 were 16.1%, down from 20.2% in 1984. In comparison, South East Asia's average figure was 33.5% in the same period. The ratio of total fixed investment to GDP has also declined, from about 20% between 1970 and 1974 to 17.6% in 2001. South East Asia's figure in 2001 was 33.5%. In addition, only 10% of Sub-Saharan Africa's exports comprise manufactured goods. In his 1998 World Bank Study, titled *Can*

Africa Export Manufactures, Ibrahim El Badawi, asserts that, in the 1990s, Sub-Saharan Africa's manufactured exports accounted for only 2.9% of GDP. In comparison, the South East Asian manufactured export/GDP share in the same period was more than 30%. Worse, one in three adults, on average, is illiterate in SSA. In sum, Africa is economically gravely ill. Add the devastation of millions of Africans because of the HIV/AIDS pandemic, Africa has to become more committed to addressing its own plight

Building Africa's Capacity

These economic factors and realities raise fundamental questions about Africa's capacity to advance its trade and development agenda within the present framework of WTO trade negotiations. It is clear that Africa itself must begin by transforming and building its own internal capacity for economic growth as a strategic prerequisite for integrating itself into the global economy. A myriad supply side support is needed, especially to improve the policy environment and the capacity of economic institutions. Improving education and health delivery, developing better physical infrastructure and imbibing state of the art production and information and communication technologies are some of the important decisions to be effected. Africa's competitiveness in the global economy depends on these transformations. However, for these transformations to take a quantum leap, much depends on the emergence of a new global mindset. Here lies the rallying call for a complete new round of WTO trade negotiations which re-visit the Uruguay Round conclusions. Africa needs to place its core development interests at the heart and centre stage of future trade negotiations.

The rich world has a responsibility to share its wealth and resources to develop Africa if trade negotiations are to make any meaning at all. The South Commission Report, *The Challenge to the South,* was explicit on this point. It states, "a world in which a large proportion of the people is without enough food while a small proportion indulges in superfluous consumption; in which massive waste coexists with pervasive deprivation, at which the majority of the people have little control over their fates and futures, but are essentially at the mercy of trends, processes, and decisions in the centres of power of the industrialised world, such a world cannot be morally acceptable"

Part of Africa's and especially Sub-Saharan Africa's tragedy is that there is too much zero-sum nationalism. Such mindset weakens economic integration. The philosophy of win-win partnership in integration arrangements has been overplayed, probably to Africa's own detriment. Sub-Saharan Africa should come to terms with the reality, which the European Union and NAFTA went through, that dramatising the dysfunctions of uneven levels of development in determining the speed of integration never helps integration. The benefits of integration, in the medium and long-term, should outweigh the costs of short-term losses that result from integration. Africa must seize the big picture. There are clear and objective reasons for moving away from zero-sum nationalism. East Africa Community's recent move and effort commenced in September 2004, to fast track, not only economic and monetary integration but also the loftier goal of a political federation is in line with this view of downplaying zero-sum nationalism. It is a historic move for East Africa which should be championed by all foresighted East Africans.

The reasons for a radical and urgent shift from zero sum nationalism are simple. As a start, Africa suffers from inadequate inter-sectoral factor integration, particularly in economic and trade-related infrastructure and services such as investment capital that is essential in fostering industrial growth and competitiveness. Costs of infrastructure such as power, telecom and transportation are presently too high for individual countries to bear. At the June 2001 Durban World Economic Summit Forum, I had ventured to conjecture that that a fast track economic integration hinged more on accepting a different integration philosophy, that of "partial win, partial lose". I argued that *the* win-win mantra, after all, is not a means; it is an end. It would take time to be realised. In the European Union, the partial win, partial lose philosophy did not discourage or put off poorer countries of Europe, the so-called "backwaters" of Europe, from becoming members of the European Economic Community and later the EU. There was no immediate win-win situation for them. However, those countries that dared knew that, over time, they stood to benefit and that the "Structural Funds" set aside by the EU, as special annual support for them, was part of a deliberate policy measure to assist them to "catch up". Countries such as the Republic of Ireland, meantime, have become success stories under this framework. The 10 Eastern European countries and Baltic States that joined the EU in May 2004 have equally taken calculated risks because they are aware of such reality. Africa has much to learn from this EU model and experience in promoting viable African regional economic communities, so well evidenced by SADC and the EAC.

What is paramount to recognise for such a bold experiment is that it is fast track integration, with NEPAD as the key guiding development programme that would ultimately build Africa's collective self-reliance and drive the much-needed African collective momentum and voice in global negotiations. What the late Mwalimu Julius Nyerere clamoured for, namely the "trade union of the poor," would finally be in Africa's grasp. Africa cannot afford to continue to negotiate, as Nyerere put it in his address titled, *Unity for a New Order* at the Group of 77 Ministerial Conference in Arusha in February 1979, "as noisy and importunate supplicants". Instead, Africa should negotiate from a position of "steadily increasing power". Such power comes from economic integration and, ultimately, from an economic union. The Constitutive Act of the African Union provides for the coordination and harmonisation of policies between existing and future economic integration units as building blocks towards the realisation of the core objective of the African Union, namely Africa-wide economic union. However, the Constitutive Act is premised on voluntary accession by member states to the various institutions envisaged in the Act: the African Monetary Fund, African Investment Bank, African Central Bank, and the African Court of Justice. These are more difficult to realise than the establishment of political institutions such as the African Peace and Security Council, already established, and the Pan-African Parliament, inaugurated at the end of March 2004 in Addis Ababa with a Tanzanian Parliamentarian woman, Getrude Mongella, elected the first Speaker.

With respect to economic institutions, however, Professor Benno Ndulu, in his paper *From Vision to Reality of African Economic Integration: Priority Actions and the Institutional Framework for the Way Forward*, notes that the idea, for example, of establishing an African International Monetary Fund is "an ambitious undertaking by all judgements". He proceeds to list drawbacks against it, including unnecessary duplicity with the IMF and the potential lack of adequate funding to such institution that is supposed to have the capacity of being lender of last resort. Overall, therefore, the success of the AU's programmes would crucially hinge on political will, an attribute that has so far been in serious short supply in Africa.

Conclusion:

Africa is still troubled by a provocative question that lingers on. Would Africa continue to be the least prepared and equipped continent in the world to respond to the challenges that confront it? History is testimony to the fact that Africa was able to liberate itself politically, including through the barrel of the gun. Why should it therefore fail to liberate itself economically particularly when it is able to effectively rally behind NEPAD as well as seriously and speedily move towards effective economic integration? As President Mbeki's former Economic Advisor and now Head of the NEPAD Secretariat, Professor Wiseman Nkuhlu surmised at the Durban 2001 World Economic Forum Summit, "one cannot excite the rest of the world if one cannot excite one's own people." The African people want economic liberation and they cannot get it when Africa is economically balkanised. African leaders owe it to the African people to be bold in acting on Africa's realities and confronting the negative perceptions about it. Boldness should feature collectively and intelligently at WTO Doha Round of trade talks and beyond. Above all, such boldness should act as the poison to destroy the present culture of African zero-sum nationalism, the main danger militating against faster economic integration. Africa should take heed of Winston Churchill's wisdom: "The optimist sees opportunity in every danger. The pessimist sees danger in every opportunity." It is a huge challenge that should be seriously embraced and concrete strategies formulated to make Africa an integrated economy.

Part Eleven

GENERAL CONCLUSION

In democratic governance, the prerogative to govern emanates from the will of the people. Once you secure the right to govern, you can simply govern or, as I prefer, you can lead. If you simply govern it is tantamount to compelling people. If you lead, on the other hand, you counsel. It is not necessary to be a democrat to govern. Even colonialists and dictators govern. To lead, however, is to show the path, to be a role model, to make people feel satisfied that you are in the frontline and that they are followers. They follow not because of fear but because they trust you. Viable peace cannot be achieved through words alone but through your deeds, sense of direction and respect of the people.

Benjamin W. Mkapa: *Address to Parliament on the Occasion to Bid Parliament Farewell*, Dodoma, 28 July 2005.

Chapter

41 THE WAY FORWARD

An abiding concern with social justice must go hand in hand with the pursuit of economic efficiency. It is only through a commitment to social justice that the call to dedicated collective effort for development can be sustained, its objectives given a high moral purpose, and the spirit of human solidarity kept alive. The massive social and economic reforms needed to remove the scourge of mass poverty can succeed only if backed by a spirit of high idealism, self-sacrifice, and dedication. A self-sustaining economy is inconceivable in the long run if the society is not imbued with the integrative and cohesive spirit of social justice.

The Report of the South Commission: *The Challenge to the South*

In the last two decades, the realities of and challenges posed by a new world economic environment driven by globalisation, on the one hand, and a political order underpinned by an ethos of liberal democracy, on the other hand, have had significant influence on the direction of Tanzanian public policy and political mindset. Throughout this book, I capture what I have learned from the ideological paradigm shifts that have taken place in Tanzania because of these global realities. At its heart, the book espouses the idea that failure by Tanzania to adjust to the realities of a brave new world constitutes sure recipe for deepening poverty and social instability. Inevitably, the book discusses the debate about what some view as the dysfunctions of the ideological shift from the public ownership thrust of the Arusha Declaration to a market economy. The debate revolves around the thesis that the adoption of market-driven policies marked by the massive privatisation of state-owned enterprises is diametrically opposed to people-centered development and invariably leads to a destabilising wealth divide in society.

In contrast, the book argues that radical economic reforms informed by what Tony Blair describes as the system that works best, namely the market, is a rational and prudent policy choice in promoting national prosperity. However, it is argued, at the same time, that a strong State is essential in poor country pursuing a system of market economy. This is because social justice cannot be realised where the state fails to intervene prudently to provide social safety nets and to correct market imperfections through effective and efficient regulation. The de-privatisation of DAWASA in mid 2005 is a good example of prudent state intervention. However, in this area of regulation, more has to be done to ensure that an effective legal and regulatory environment is promoted and reinforced. Creating institutional arrangements alone as has been done so far is inadequate. These institutions have to be made to work, ethically and in response to changing conditions in the environment. It is important in particular that a culture of law that supports the rule of law through a credible, fair and honest judiciary and public service be ingrained. Overall, it is important, as a matter of deliberate public policy, especially in a poor country like Tanzania, that the role of the state and the market be more clearly defined and balanced. It is my view that the national political leadership needs to reach out to the people more forcefully in explaining the ideological shift from the Arusha Declaration. For whilst the objectives of the Arusha Declaration in terms of building a society that enjoys human dignity, respect and social justice remain, the vehicle for realising such objectives have radically changed. In this context, Tanzania Vision 2025 should be disseminated to the citizens with the same vigour as the Arusha Declaration was.

The book links success in promoting and realising promising macro-economic stability and higher economic growth to an equally successful democratic and governance system. Changes in the system of economic direction clearly demand a broad-based participatory approach in realising a national consensus and social compact. The experience in crafting Vision 2025 and the new National Strategy for Growth and Reduction of Poverty are proof of how closely democracy has been connected to formulation of development vision and strategy. At the same time, the question of bold and able leadership is given pre-eminence in enabling a nation to transform its economy and its politics peacefully and sustainably. Thus, the book underscores the point that populism and demagoguery do not lead to sustainable social and economic development. Nevertheless, effective leadership is best able to achieve its goals and tasks where the government is well structured, equipped and managed by people that are not only highly trained but who are also versatile and responsive to the fast changing global dynamic.

The book highlights several challenges that continue to confront Tanzania. It is important these be boldly addressed to assure higher and sustainable economic growth, improved quality of life of citizens and peace and stability. In this context, it is imperative first, that the current wave of economic reforms be pursued more vigorously and deepened. This is in recognition of the reality that it is the quality of domestic policies that determine how Tanzania would be affected or impacted by changing external realities. An important area to be focused upon is the modernisation of the agriculture sector. My position is that corporatisation of agriculture that is well structured and which involves and improves peasant agriculture and evidenced in the sugarcane industry, has to be given serious priority. Second and relatedly, greater impetus should be placed on bolstering agriculture-based value-added exports. Stimulation of investments in agro-processing needs to be given particular attention.

In the broad area of exports, much remains to be done to promote the brand Tanzania as a tourism destination of uniqueness and maximum enjoyment. Without embracing mass tourism, which is detrimental to the ecosystem, it is possible for Tanzania to realise higher revenues from tourism than presently. For example, opening up the Selous and Saadani national parks to environmentally friendly investments through improvement of physical infrastructure like roads and airstrips would give tourism a much needed shot in the arm. Equally, the maximisation of benefits that can flow from the exploitation of Tanzania's geo-strategic location for sea and land transportation and logistics has to be harnessed by improving Tanzania's seaports in terms of infrastructure and management and relaxing laws and regulations that presently constrict the participation of global shipping lines from investing. The overhauling the central railway system and improving its management would particularly constitute a major coup in making Tanzania a natural transport hub for East Africa and the Great Lakes Region.

Third, the high costs of doing business in Tanzania have to be significantly lowered if Tanzania is to bolster investments especially in manufactures. In this context, it is paramount that the government quickly addresses the future of TANESCO as a power monopoly. Along with this move is the necessity in the short term to find ways and means to lower power tariffs to comparable levels ruling in neighbouring and competing countries, notably South Africa, Zambia, Mozambique and Kenya. The serious shortages and erratic supplies of water, on the other hand, are a serious disincentive to investment inflow and a significant driver of low productivity in selected industries such as textiles and beverages. Another high cost of doing business lies in the low availability of workforce talent in Tanzania. With the growth in investments over the last decade, especially in businesses such as mining, tourism, banking and insurance, this shortage in highly skilled personnel has been keenly felt. Evidently, utilisation of expatriates instead of Tanzanians in staffing key positions in businesses distorts costs overheads and lowers profitability levels. The solution lies in improving the standards of the education system. But whilst there has been notable improvement in the basic education sector in terms of enrolment, the quality of education in Tanzanian still lags behind most African countries. This area poses a huge challenge to the country. It demands closer public-private partnerships in addressing it. The government alone cannot rise to the challenge. Specifically, more effort has to be placed in expanding and improving teachers' training. There is also the obvious weakness in the standard of English language which makes many young Tanzanians lack confidence in pursuing careers in new growth businesses like banking and insurance that demand an excellent command of spoken English. The government may have to consider adopting, for instance, a 10-year programme of recruitment of teachers from New Zealand, Canada, Australia, the UK and United States to teach a pool of teachers who would teach English in Secondary Schools. It is also important to note that tertiary, and especially university education, has not received sufficient state funding to enable it play a vanguard role in national transformation. Public universities have largely been under-funded with serious negative consequences on quality of teaching and research.

The fourth challenge concerns how to deepen democratisation. Evidently, a multi-party system of democracy has settled in well marked by two largely successful general elections in 1995 and 2000. The third general election will take place in October 2005. However, it is questionable to what extent the present first past the post electoral system, borrowed from the British, enables Tanzania to achieve a pronounced democratic system of representativeness. In those countries where a proportional representation electoral system is applied, it appears that a better balance of representativeness in parliaments is achieved because the popular vote determines the number of seats to be taken. I believe that time has come for Tanzania to review its electoral system and move towards the adoption of a proportional representation system which has so far worked well in South Africa, Mozambique, Namibia, Lesotho and other countries. It is important to note though that democratisation is not limited to or even well represented by electoral representativeness. It is more importantly realised through giving effective voice to all citizens through the framework of civil society and a well functioning and free media. However, civil society in Tanzania today is nascent and balkanised along special interest groups. Its trend has thus been to lean more towards lobbying than generally contributing to promoting policy reform of national implications and proportion and holding the government to account for its acts of commission and omission.

An important element of deepening democratisation is the question involving the Tanzania union. This question unfortunately remains a sensitive one and even a taboo to be discussed openly and in a radical fashion. Yet, it is evident that all is not well in the Union. And whilst no political union can be perfect, it should not, however, be a source of tension and continuous controversy. Democracy demands that citizens of Tanzania openly debate the Union Question and a better dispensation achieved.

In recent years, religious fundamentalism has emerged as a force of evil rather than of good. Whilst it is debatable that the upsurge in acts of terrorism has more to do with nihilistic tendencies and perversions of religion, especially Islam, and little, if any, with politics. whether of Palestine, Iraq or Saudi Arabia), it remains important to note that there has been significant involvement of religion in politics in many countries, notably the United States. Tanzania has also had its share of such involvement. This is a worrying trend given the state of global instability attributed to religious fundamentalism or extremism. In a poor country where the destitute and the extreme poor, especially the growing number of urban unemployed youth, can easily fall prey to the objectives of fundamentalist extremism, it is critical that the roots of bigotry of all types be sourced and brought under check. Citizenship education that fosters respect for diversity, across the various fault lines-tribal, ethnic and religious- has an important part to play in promoting unity within diversity. This is the fifth challenge that has to be given serious attention.

The sixth challenge is how to make Tanzanians have the appetite to make and achieve economic transformation. Evidently, self-empowerment is what should underpin such drive. However, self-empowerment is predominantly driven by the state of the mindset of the individual. In this connection, though the politics of economic empowerment are well placed, they cannot find light of day if they are not motored by a radical change of attitudes about the necessity of hard work, ingenuity, savings habit, simple style of life and investment. Much is said and written about the formalisation of the informal sector as strategy of economic empowerment and job creation. In this context, the project being undertaken in Tanzania by Hernando de Soto to formalize property rights in order to unleash capital formation that can, in turn, spur wealth creation is timely. Nevertheless, whilst capital is important in creating wealth, it is necessary that for a programme such as de Soto's to succeed, it has to be supported by the existence of an entrepreneurial culture. In my view, the primacy of this culture is diligence to hard work and thriftiness. This culture is in short supply in Tanzania. However, it can be stimulated through a massive national pedagogical mobilisation drive and the promotion of smart partnerships between well-established and budding entrepreneurs.

A challenge with major debilitating consequences involves tackling the HIV/AIDS pandemic. This challenge has a direct bearing on the livelihoods of citizens and the national economic well-being. Between 2002 and presently, the government and NGOs have done much to address the pandemic. Thanks to the intervention of President Bush's Global Fund, the Bill and Melinda Gates Foundation and the Bill Clinton Foundation, ARVs are now increasingly available to HIV/AIDS sufferers. At the same time, much effort has gone into educating the public about using protection. However, this challenge remains a case of so much to do yet so little done.

Finally, the book cautions against zero-sum economic nationalism in dealing with new realities of regionalism and globalisation. It argues that protection of special interests is bound to promote inefficiency in the economy and distort markets. Tanzania has and needs to attract regional and global best practice companies. These companies create more jobs; deliver higher wages and lower prices of goods and services. Tanzania can thus ill afford to be fearful of opening up its economy to the outside world and being intimately part of regional economic integration institutions such as the SADC and the EAC. Nevertheless, the book highlights the dark side of globalisation, especially its insensitivity to the need for a more democratic system of global governance and equitable sharing of global public goods. Thus, the book clamours for a fair globalisation.

The book has traversed a wide terrain of key economic and political issues and some of the central challenges that face Tanzania as it strives to confront new global economic and political realities. It proposes, as a crosscutting theme, that the capacity to address the outlined challenges centres predominantly on Tanzania having bold, courageous and well-informed leaders. In this context and as a closing remark, a statement made by the Brazilian President Luiz Inacio "Lula" da Silva reported in New York Times of May 31, 2003 come to mind: "I am fed up with meeting Presidents of Latin American countries who blame imperialism for the misfortunes of the Third World. That's nonsense. We are victims only of our own incompetence." Tanzania's economic reform experience in the last two decades and more specifically in the past decade vindicates Lula's assertion. Through a competent and bold national leadership under Benjamin William Mkapa, Tanzania has succeeded to overcome the economic malaise that severely afflicted it in the 1980s and early 1990s and achieve, by any standard, robust economic growth. From the heart of despair, Tanzania is able today to proclaim the hope of prosperity. This hope has to be sustained and given greater stimulus.

REFERENCES & BIBLIOGRAPHY

Adam, Christopher and Stephen A. O'Connell. *Aid versus Trade Revisited*, Centre for the Study of African Economies, Working Series No.129, July 2000.

Adedeji, Adebayo. Review of Progress on Economic Recovery and Long-Term Development in Africa, *Development; Journal of the Society for International Development,* Vol. 2/3, 1987, p.57-60.

Adedeji, Adebayo. From the Lagos Plan of Action to the New Partnership for African Development and the Final Act of Lagos to the Constitutive Act: Whither Africa? *Keynote Address* at the *African Forum for Envisioning Africa,* Nairobi, Kenya, 26-29 April, 2002.

Advisory Group on Social Responsibility: *Working Report on Social Responsibility,* April 30, 2004. (www.iso.org/iso/en/info/conferences/SRconference/pot/Working%20Rep ort%20%20SR. Accessed on 30th April 2005).

Adesina, J. *NEPAD and WTO Agreements: Linkages and Contradictions;* Presentation at the Regional Workshop on the Interface between Trade and Regional Partnership Agreements, Harare, 29-30 October 2002.

Adesina, J.O et al. (eds) *Africa and Development Challenges in the New Millennium: The NEPAD Debate.* New York: Palgrave Macmillan, 2005.

Ajayi, J.F. Ade *et al, The African Experience with Higher Education,* Accra; London and Athens, Ohio: Association of African Universities. James Currey and Ohio University Press, 1996.

Ahluwalia, P & Abebe Zegeye. Multiparty Democracy in Tanzania: Crises in the Union, *African Security Review,* Vol 10. No 3, 2001.

Aikman, David. The Great Revival: Understanding Religious "Fundamentalism," *Foreign Affairs,* July/August, 2003.

Al Barwani, Ali Muhsin, *Conflicts and Harmony in Zanzibar,* Dubai, UAE, 1997.

Albritton R. et al. (eds) *Beyond Market and Plan: Toward New Socialisms* London: Palgrave, 2003.

Amoako, K.Y. *African Universities, the Private Sector and Civil Society: Forging Partnership for Development,* Keynote Address at the International Association of University Presidents, Africa Regional Council Conference, Accra, Ghana, June, 1999. www.uneca.org/eca_resources/speeches/amoako/99/0609es_speech_univer sity.htm)

Amin Samir. *Capitalism In the Age of Globalisation: The Management of Contemporary Society,*. Cape Town: Institute for Policy and Social Research, Zed Books, 1997.

Amin, Samir. In favour of a Polycentric World, *Development: Journal of the Society for International Development,* Vo.1, 1991.

Amin, Samir. *Spectres of Capitalism: A Critique of Current Intellectual Fashions,* New York: Monthly Review Press, 1998.

Amin, Samir. World Poverty, Pauperization & Capital Accumulation, *Monthly Review,* October 2003.

Amin, Samir & F.Houtart. (eds). *The Globalisation of Resistance: The State of the Struggles* London: Zed Press, 2003.

Amin, Samir. The Political Economy of Africa in the global system, *First Conference of Intellectuals from Africa and the Diaspora on Africa in the 21st Century: Integration and Renaissance,* Dakar, 6-9 October, 2004. (www.ciad.org).

Amin, Samir. *Obsolescent Capitalism: Contemporary Politics and Global Disorder* London: Zed Books, 2004.

Anderson, Robert. *Just Get Out of the Way: How Government Can Help Business in Poor Countries,* Cato Institute, 2004.

Andrews, Kenneth. Ethics in Practice, *Harvard Business Review,* September-October 1989.

Anglin, Douglas G. Zanzibar: Political Impasse and Commonwealth Mediation, *Journal of Contemporary African Studies,* Vol. 18 No 1, January 2000.

Annan, Kofi. *Africa's New Spirit of Democratic Empowerment: Continent's Sobering Challenges,* Keynote Address at Harvard Kennedy School of Government, 25 April 2002.

Anonymous Zanzibari. Zanzibar: What is the Future? *Change,* Vol. 4, Nos. 7, 8 & 9, 1996.

Anyang' Nyong'o, Peter. (ed.), *Regional Integration in Africa: Unfinished Agenda,* Nairobi: Academy Science Publishers, 1990.

Anyang' Nyong'o, Peter et al. *NEPAD: A New Path?* Nairobi: Heinrich Boll Foundation, 2002.

Asiedu, Elizabeth. Policy Reform and Foreign Direct Investment to Africa: Absolute Progress but Relative Decline, *Development Policy Review,* Vol. 22 No 1, January 2004.

Arrighi, Giovanni. The African Crisis: World Systematic and Regional Aspects, *New Left Review,* Vol.15, May-June, 2002.

Attali, Jacques. (ed.) *Millennium: Winners and Losers in the Coming World Order.* London: Times Books, 1991.

Austin, James E. *Managing in Developing Countries: Strategic Analysis and Operating Techniques*. New York: The Free Press, 1990.

Ayittey, George BN. Combating Corruption in Africa: Analysis and Context in Ronald K. Hope et al. (eds) *Corruption and Development in Africa: Lessons from Country Studies*, London: Mcmillan Press, 2000.

Ayogu, Malvin D. Corporate Governance in Africa: The Record and Policies for Good Corporate Governance, *African Development Review*, Vol.13 No.2, December 2001.

Babu, Abdulrahman M. Wanted: A Third Force in Zanzibar Politics, *Change*, Vol. 4 Nos. 7, 8 & 9 1996.

Babu, Salma and Amrit Wilson. eds.), *BABU - The Future that Works: Selected Writings of A.M. Babu*, Trenton, NJ and Asmara: Africa World Press, Inc., 2002.

Bailey, C & J. Tuner. Social Security in Africa: A brief Review, *Journal of Aging Social Policy*, Vol. 14 No 1, 2002.

Bailey, Clive. Extending Social Security Coverage in Africa, *Social Science Research Network Working Paper* No 20, 2004.

Banham, John. *Anatomy of Change: Blueprint for a New Era* London: Weidenfeld & Nicolson, 1994.

Barber, Benjamin. *Jihad Vs McWorld* New York: Times Books, 1995.

Barbone, Luca et al. *Pensions and Social Security in Sub-Saharan Africa: Issues and Options,* World Bank Africa Region Working Paper No 4, October, 1999.

Bardhan, P. Decentralisation of Governance and Development, *Journal of Economic Perspectives*, Vol. 16 No 4, 2002.

Bardhan, P. Corruption and Development: A Review of Issues, *Journal of Economic Literature,* Vol. 35, September, 1997.

Barkan, Joel D. (ed.), *Beyond Capitalism vs. Socialism in Kenya and Tanzania*. Nairobi: East African Educational Publishers, 1994.

Bayart, J. *The State of Africa: The Politics of the Belly*. London: Longman, 1993.

Becker, Kristina. *The Informal Economy,* SIDA, Stockholm, March 2004.

Bayliss, Kate. *The World Bank and Privatisation: a flawed development tool,* November, 2000.. www.psiru.org/reports/2000 ll u WB.doc)

Benneh, George et al. (eds.), *African Universities, the Private Sector and Civil Society: Forging Partnerships for Development*, Accra: Ghana Universities Press, 2004.

Bennis, Warren and Burt Nanus. *Leaders: The Strategies of Taking Charge* London: Hutchinson Business Books, 1990.

Bennis, Warren and Robert J. Thomas. *Geeks and Geezers: How Era, Values and Defining Moments Shape Leaders.* Boston: Harvard Business School Press, 2002

Bennis, Warren. *On Becoming A Leader.* London: Hutchinson Business Books, 1990.

Berman, Bruce J. (ed) *African Capitalists in African Development.* Boulder: Lynne Rienner Publishers, 1993.

Bernstein, Charles. A Blow is like an Instrument, *Deadalus,* Fall, 1997.

Bernstein, Merton. *Social Security: The System that Works,* New York: Basic Books, 1998.

Bhagwati, Jagdish. Poverty and Reforms: Friends or Foes, *Journal of International Affairs,* Fall 1998.

Bhagwati, Jagdish. *In Defence of Globalisation.* Oxford: Oxford University Press, 2004.

Bhagwati, Jagdish. Don't Cry for Cancun, *Foreign Affairs,* January/February, 2004

Bhalla Surjit. S. *Imagine There is NO Country: Poverty, Inequality, and Growth in the Era of Globalisation,* Institute for International Economics, Washington DC, 2002.

Bigstein, Arne & Anders Danielsson. *Is Tanzania an emerging economy?* A report for the OECD project "Emerging Africa", May, 1999. www.oecd.org/dataoecd/40/30/2674918.pot)

Birdsall, Nancy et al. How to Help Poor Countries, *Foreign Affairs,* July/August, 2005

Blair, Tony. *The Courage of Our Convictions: Why Reform of the Public Services is the Route to Social Justice,* London: Fabian Society, 2002.

Blair, Tony. *The Third Way: New Politics For The Century,* Fabian Society Pamphlet No. 588, September 1998

Blasi, Joseph and Douglas Kruse. *The New Owners: The Mass Emergence of Employee Ownership in Public Companies and What it Means to American Business* New York: Harper Collins, Reprint Edition, 1992.

Bloom, David E & Joel E. Cohen. Education for All: an unfinished revolution, *Daedalus,* Summer, 2002.

Bloom, Harold. *Shakespeare: The Invention of the Human.* London: Fourth Estate, 1999.

Blomoncert, Jan. Intellectuals and Ideological Leadership in Ujamaa Tanzania, *African Languages and Cultures,* Vol. 10, No. 2, 1997.

Blond, Philip & Adrian Pabst. Shared Values: Why the West gets religion wrong, *International Herald Tribune,* July 8, 2005

Bok, Derek. *Universities In The Marketplace: The Commercialization of Higher Education.* Princeton University Press, 2003.

Bomani, Mark. Tanzania: The Withering Away Of The Union? A Rejoinder, *Change Magazine,* July 1993. (For an elaborate historical perspective on the Union and its travails, see Othman, Haroub. Tanzania: The Withering Away Of The Union in the same issue of *Change Magazine.)*

Brautigam, D. State Capacity and Effective Governance in Ndulu, B. & N. Vande Walla. (eds) *Agenda for Africa's Economic Renewal.* Somerset, NJ: Transaction Publishers, 1996.

Bromwick, David. *Politics by Other Means: Higher Education and Group Thinking.* Yale University Press, 1992 .

Bond, Patrick. From Racial to Class Apartheid: South Africa's Frustrating Decade of Freedom, *Monthly Review,* March 2004

Bryan, Lowell and Diana Farrel. *Market Unbound: Unleashing Global Capitalism.* New York: John Wiley & Sons, 1996.

Bryce, Murray D. *Industrial Development: A Guide for Accelerating Economic Growth.* New York: McGraw –Hill Books Co. Inc; 1990.

Business Associations in Developing Countries, *IDS Policy Briefing Issue 6,* February, 1996. www.ids.ac.uk).

CAFRAD*: e-Africa 2002: Building e-Governance Capacity in African Countries Project Proposal,* May 2002.

Callaghy, Thomas. Africa and the World Political Economy: Still Caught between a rock and a Hard Place, in Herbenson, John and Donald Rothchild. (eds.): *Africa and the World Politics: Post Cold War Challenges* Westview Press, USA, 1995.

Campbell, H and H. Stein. eds. *Tanzania and the IMF: The Dynamics of Liberalisation* Boulder: Westview Press, 2002.

Campbell Meaghan et al. Using Networks for Capacity Enhancement from Anticorruption Parliamentary Networks, *World Bank Institute Capacity Enhancement. Briefs No 10,* January, 2005 . www.parlcent.ca)

Campbell, John. Nationalism, Ethnicity and Religion: Fundamental Conflicts and the Politics of Identity in Tanzania, *Nations and Nationalism,* Vol. 5 No 1, 1999.

Cannon, Tom. *Corporate Responsibility.* London: Pitman Publishing, 1992.

Carnegie Corporation of New York et al: Higher Education in Tanzania: A Case Study, 2005.

Carrol, Jones. The Post-Humanist University: Three Theses, *The Salisbury Review,* Vol. 7 No. 2, December, 1988.

Caroll, James. Why Religion Still Matters, *Daedalus,* Summer, 2003.

Case, Daniel. Why Welfare Reform is Working, *Commentary,* September 1997.

Castro, Lucio et al. Regional Integration in East Africa: Trade and Revenue Impacts of the Planned East African Community Customs Union, *The World Bank, Africa Region Working Paper Series No 72,* Washington DC, August, 2004.

Cervantes, M. & Dominique Guellec. The Brain Drain: Old Myths and New Realities, *OECD Observer,* May 7, 2002.

Chachage, C. *Mwalimu Julius Kambarage Nyerere: A Tribute,* Centre for African Studies, University of Cape Town, 1999.

Chachage, Seithy L. Leadership in Civil Society, *Development Policy Management. DPMG) Forum,* Addis Ababa, 2002.

Chachage, Seithy L. *Environment and Politics in Zanzibar.* Oxford: African Books Collective, 2000.

Chachage, Seithy L. Globalisation and Democratic Governance in Tanzania, *Development Policy Management Forum, DPMG Occasional Paper No 10,* Addis Ababa, 2003

Chachage, Seithy L. Leadership, Civil Society and Democratisation in Tanzania, *DPMG Policy Brief Series No. 3,* Addis Ababa, 2002.

Chachage, Chachage Seithy L and Marjorie Mbilinyi. (eds.), *Against Neoliberalism: Gender, Democracy and Development,* Dar es Salaam: E & D Limited and TGNP, 2003.

Chachage, Seithy. *Makuadi wa Soko Huria.* Dar- es-Salaam, E&D Limited, 2002.

Chachage, Seithy L. Convernor). *The Dar es Salaam Declaration on Academic Freedom and Social Responsibility of Academics, 1990.*

Chachage, Seithy L. Academic Freedom and Social Responsibility of Intellectuals: Some Thoughts, the *Dar Graduate,* Vol. 3 New Series, November 2002.

Chambua, Samuel E. *Democratic Participation in Tanzania: The Voices of Workers Representatives,* Dar es Salaam: Dar es Salaam University Press, 2002.

Chambua, Samuel E Vincent Kihiyo and Gaudens P. Mpangala. (eds.), *Multiparty Elections and Corruption in Tanzania: With Special Reference to the 2000 Elections,* Dar es Salaam: Dar es Salaam University Press, 2002.

Chande, Ravi. *A Review of Business Environment in Tanzania,* a Report for the Tanzania National Business Council, November 2003.

Chande, Ravi. *Comparative Analysis of Prevailing and Emerging Macroeconomic and Sectoral Policies and their Impact on the Industry and Trade Sector,* a Report prepared for the Ministry of Industries and Trade,

November 2001.

Change Magazine. (editors). The Nyalali Commission Majority Opinion on the Union Between Tanganyika and Zanzibar, *Change*, Vol.7, July 1993.

Charles, Kathleen. *National AGOA Strategy Report for Tanzania*, East & Central Africa Competitiveness Hub, March 2005.

Chua, Amy. Making the World Safe for Markets, *Harvard Business Review*, August 2003.

Chua, Amy. *World On Fire: How Exporting Free Market Democracy Breeds Ethnic Hatred and Global Instability*, New York: Doubleday, 2003.

Clark, John. *Democratizing Development: The Role of Voluntary Organizations*, London: Earthscan Publications Ltd., 1991.

Clarke, J and D. Wood. New Public Management and Development : The Case of Public Service Reform in Tanzania and Uganda, in W. McCourt and M. Minogue. (eds) *The Internationalization of Public Management: Reinventing the Third World State*, Cheltenham: Edward Elgar, 2001.

Club of Rome. *The First Global Revolution*, New York: Pantheon Books, 1991.

Cohen, Adam. The Crumbling Wall Between Church and States, *International Herald Tribune*, July 5, 2005.

Collier, Paul and Jan Gunning. Why has Africa Grown Slowly, *Journal of Economic Perspectives*, Vol.13 No. 3, Summer, 1999

Commission For Africa: *Our Common Interest*, Report of the Commission for Africa, 2005.

Corlett, Angela, J. A Marxist Approach to Business Ethics, *Journal of Business Ethics*, Vol. 17, 1998.

Commission on Global Governance; *Our Global Neighbourhood*. Oxford: Oxford University Press, 1995.

Corea, Gamani. The Importance of South-South Cooperation in the Contemporary World of Globalisation and Liberalisation, *Cooperation South Journal*, Winter, 1996.

Covey, Stephen. *The Seven Habits of Highly Effective People: Powerful Lessons in Personal Change*, New York: Simon & Schuster, 1990.

Craig, John. *Privatisation and Indigenous Ownership: Evidence from Africa*, Working Paper 13, Centre on Regulation and Competition, University of Manchester, January 2002

Culbert, Samuel A. *Mind-Set Management: The Heart of Leadership*, Oxford: Oxford University Press, 1996.

CUTS Centre for Competition, Investment and Economic Regulation in association with Economic and Social Research Foundation: *Investment*

Policy in Tanzania - Performance and Perceptions, 2003. www.cuts-international.org/CR tanAB.pdf)

Daniel, John et al. It's the South Africans: Post Apartheid Corporate Expansion into Africa, *HSRC Review*, Vol. 1 No 3, September 2003.

Daniel, John et al. Post-Apartheid South Africa's Corporate Expansion into Africa, *Traders: African Business Journal* No 15, August-September 2003

Dasgupta, Partha. Economic Growth Often Accompanies a Decline in a Poor Country's Wealth, *New Statesman*, London, November 3, 2003.

Dau, R.K. Trends in Social Security in East Africa: Tanzania, Kenya and Uganda, *International Social Security Review,* Vol.56 No 3-4, November 2003.

David, Paul A and Dominique Foray. Economic Fundamentals of the Knowledge Society, February 2002, published in *Policy Futures In Education-An e- Journal* Vol. No. 1, January 2003. www_econ_stanford.edu/faculty/workp/swp02003.pdf).

Davidson, Basil. *For a Politics of Restitution,* in Adebayo Adedeji. (ed.): *Africa within the World: Beyond Dispossession and Dependence.* London: Zed Books, 1993.

Davidson, James and Williams Rees-Mogg. *The Sovereign Individual.* London. Macmillan, 1997.

Davidson, James Dale and William Rees-Mogg. *The Great Reckoning: How The World Will Change Before the Year 2000.* London: Pan Books, 1992.

Davis, Ian. What is business of business? *The McKinsey Newsletter,* McKinsey on Strategy, Second Quarter, 2005.

De Anda, Gustavo G. The State and the market: the Missing Link, *SD Dimensions*, April, 1997. www.fao.org/sd/redirect)

De Jong, Albert. *Mission and Politics in Eastern Africa: Dutch Missionaries and African Nationalism in Kenya, Tanzania and Malawi 1945-1965,* Nairobi: Paulines Publications Africa, 2000.

De Sardan, Olivier. A Moral Economy of Corruption in Africa? *The Journal of Modern African Studies,* Vol 37 No 1, 1999.

De Soto, Hernando. *The Mystery of Capital: Why Capitalism Triumphs In The West And Fails Everywhere Else.* London: Bantam Press, 2000.

De Soto, Hernando. *The Other Path: The Invisible Revolution in the Third World.* New York: HarperCollins, 1989.

Dewey, John. *Individualism, Old and New.* New York: Prometheus Books, 1999.

Dia, M. *A governance Approach to Civil Service Reform in Sub-Saharan Africa,* The World Bank, 1993.

Diamond, Jared. *Collapse: How Societies Choose To Fail Or Succeed.* New York: Viking, 2005.

Dibben, Pauline et al. *Contesting Public Sector Reforms: Critical Perspectives, International Debates.* Hampstead: Palgrave, 2004.

Drucker, Peter F. *Innovation and Entrepreneurship.* : Heinemann, 1985.London

Drucker, Peter F. *Management Challenges for the 21st Century.* New York: Harper Business, 1999.

Drucker, Peter F. *Managing For the Future.* London, Butterworth – Heinemann, 1992.

Drucker, Peter F. *Managing in Turbulent Times,* London, Pan Books, 1989.

Drucker, Peter F. *Post-Capitalist Society.* New York: Harper Business, 1983.

Drucker, Peter F. *The New Realities.* London: Heinemann, 1989.

Duesterberg, Thomas. Reforming the Welfare State*, Society,* September-October, 1998.

Duggan, William D. *Tanzania and Nyerere: A Study of Ujamaa and Nationhood.* London: Orbis Books, 1976.

East African Community: *Private Sector Development Strategy for the East African Community,* Arusha, 2003.

Easterly, William. The Lost Decades: Developing Countries' Stagnation in Spite of Policy Reform 1980-1998, *Journal of Economic Growth,* , 2001. Vol-6

Enderle, Georges, "Facing Globalization and Marginalization: Can Business Ethics Make a Difference?" in Kanyandago, Peter. (ed.), *Marginalized Africa: An International Perspective.* Nairobi: Paulines Publication 2000.

Fafchamps, Marcel. *The Role of Business Networks in Market Development in Sub-Saharan Africa..* Nairobi: Paulines Publications Africa, 2002.

Ellerman D. *Helping People Help Themselves: From the World Bank to an Alternative Philosophy of Development.* Ann Arbor: University of Michigan Press, 2004.

Ellis, Stephen. Religion and Politics in Sub-Saharan Africa, **Journal of Modern African Studies,** Vol. 36 No 2, 1988.

Fafchamps, Marcel. **The Role of Business Networks in Market Development in Sub-Saharan Africa..** www.economics.ox.ac.uk/members/marcel.fafchamps/homepapge/edicon f.pdf).

Evans, Mary. *Killing Thinking: Death of Universities,.* London: Continuum International Publishing Group, 2004.

Fairbanks, M and State Lindsay. *Plowing the Sea: Nurturing the Hidden*

Sources of Growth in the Developing World, Harvard Business School, 1997.

Farrell, Diana. The Hidden Dangers of the Informal Economy, *The McKinsey Quarterly,* Vol. 3. 2004

Feiffer, Jules, cited in Sadiq Nafis. Rethinking Modernism: Towards Human – Centred Development, in *Development,* Journal *of the Society for International Development,* Vol.2, 1999.

Fengler, Wolfgang. *Tanzania at Crossroads: The Conflict of the Union, Its Reasons and Its Consequences,* Friedrich Ebert Foundation, Munich, August, 1995.

Ferguson, Niall. Is Globalisation Doomed? *Foreign Affairs,* March/April, 2005.

Fink, Carstein and Charles J. Kenny: Whither the Digital Divide, *Journal of Policy, Regulation and Strategy,* Vol. 5 No. 6, 2003

Fisher, Thomas et al. *Beyond Microcredit: Putting Development Back into Microfinance.* London: Oxfam Publishing, 2002.

Folson, Kweku. Africa: One-Party State and Socialism, *Venture.* Fabian International and Commonwealth Bureau, October, 1963 p. 5-6.

Foucault, Michel. The Concern for Truth, in Foucault: Politics ,Philosophy Culture In Reviews and Other Writings 1977-1984, cited in

Pozen, Richard: *Public Intellectuals: A Study in Decline.* Cambridge, Massachusetts, Harvard University Press, 2001.

Freire, Paulo. *Cultural Action for Freedom.* Harvard Education Publishing Group, 2000.

Friedmann, J. *Empowerment: The Politics of Alternative Development.* Cambridge Mass: Blackwell, 1992.

Friedman, Milton. *Capitalism and Freedom.* 2nd Edition ,University of Chicago Press, 1963.

Friedman, Milton. The Social Responsibility of Business is to Increase Its Profits, *New York Times Magazine,* September 13, 1970.

Friedman, Thomas. *The Lexus and the Olive Tree.* New York: Farrar, Straus and Giroux, 1999.

Friedman, Thomas L. *The World is Flat: A Brief History of the Twenty First Century.* New York: Farrar, Strauss and Giroux, 2005.

Fukuyama, Francis. Asian Values and the Asian Crisis, *Commentary,* February, 1998.

Fukuyama, Francis. *State-Building: Governance and World Order in the 21st Century.* Ithaca, New York: Cornell University Press, 2004.

Fukuyama, Francis. *Trust: The Social Virtues and the Creation of Prosperity.* London: Penguin Books, 1995.

Fuller, Lon. *The Morality of Law*. Revised Edition, Yale University Press, 1977.

Furedi, Frank. *Where Have All The Intellectuals Gone? Confronting 21st Century Philistinism*. London: Continuum, 2004.

Galbraith, John K. Ideology and Economic Reality, *Challenge,* The Magazine of Economic Affairs, November-December, 1989.

Gardiner, Howard. *Changing Minds: The Art and Science of Changing Our Own and Other People's Minds*. Boston. Harvard Business School Press, 2004.

Gardner, John W. *No Easy Victories*. New York: Harper & Row Publishers, 1968.

Geiger, Susan, *TANU Women: Gender and Culture in the Making of Tanganyikan Nationalism 1955-1965*5. Portsmouth, NH; Oxford, Nairobi, and Dar es Salaam: Heinemann, James Currey, E.A.E.P, and Mkuki na Nyota, 1998.

Gibbons, David S. et al. *Financing Microfinance for Poverty Reduction.*. www.microcreditsummit.org/papers/+5gibbons_meeham.pdf)

Giles, Foden. *Zanzibar*. London: Faber and Faber, 2002.

Ginsburg, Tom: Book Review: Democracy, Markets and Doomsaying: Is Ethnic Conflict Inevitable? *Law and Economic Working Paper Series W/P No. LE04-002*, University of Illinois College of Law, 2004.

Goodheart, Eugence. *The Reign of Ideology*. New York: Columbia University Press, 1996.

Goodman, John. and Gary Loveman. Does Privatisation Serve the Public Interest? *Harvard Business Review,* November-December ,1991.

Gorg Hulger and David Greenway. Much Ado about Nothing? Do Domestic Firms Really Benefit from Foreign Direct Investment? *World Bank Research Observer*, Vol. 19 No. 2, 2004.

Gorham, EB. *National Service, Citizenship and Political Education.*. New York: State University of New York Press, 1992.

Governing Globalisation -Globalising Governance: New Approaches to Global Problem Solving, *Report of the Helsinki Process on Globalisation and Democracy*, Finnish Ministry of Foreign Affairs, Helsinki, 2005.

Government of the United Republic of Tanzania. *Report of the Presidential Commission on Single Party or Multiparty System in Tanzania*. also known as Nyalali Commission Report, 1992.

Greider, William. *One World Ready or Not: The Manic Logic of Global Capitalism*. London: Penguin Press, 1997).

Grenier, Louise et al. Exporting, Ownership and Confidence in Tanzania Enterprises, *World Economy*, Vol. 22, September, 1999.

Hamel, Gary and C.K Prahalad. *Competing For The Future: Breakthrough Strategies for Seizing Control of Your Industry and Creating the Markets of Tomorrow.* Harvard Business School Press, 1994.

Hampton , Paul. Commission for Africa: More Neo-liberal Capitalism, *Workers' Liberty,* London, 2005.

Handy, Charles. *Beyond Certainty.* London, Random House, 1995).

Handy, Charles. *The Age of Unreason.* Boston: Harvard Business School Press, 1990.

Handy, Charles. *The Empty Raincoat: Making Sense of the Future.* London: Arrow Business Books, 1995.

Handy, Charles. *The Hungry Spirit: Beyond Capitalism – A Quest for Purpose in the Modern World..* New York: Broadway, 1997.

Handy, Charles. *The New Alchemists.* London: Hutchinson, 1999.

Hardy Henry, (ed.) *Isaiah Berlin: The Proper Study of Mankind: An Anthology of Essays..*London: Chato & Windus, 1997.

Harper, M. The Role of Enterprise in Poor Countries, *Entrepreneurship, Theory and Practice,* Vol. 15 No 4, 1991.

Harris Curt J and Kishore G. Kulkarni. The Role of International Trade Policy in Economic Growth: The Case of Tanzania, *Global Business Review,* Vol. 5 No.2, 2004.

Harrison, G. Administering Market Friendly Growth? Liberal Populism and the World Bank's Involvement in Administrative Reform in Sub-Saharan Africa, *Review of International Political Economy,* Vol. 8 No 3, September 2001.

Hartley, Aiden. *The Zanzibar Chest: A Story of Life, Love, and Death in Foreign Lands.* New York: Atlantic Monthly Press, 2003.

Heilman, B.E and Kaiser J.P. Religion, Identity and Politics in Tanzania, *Third World Quarterly,* Vol. 23 No.4, 2002.

Helleiner, Gerald Karl. *Markets, Politics and Globalisation: Can the Global Economy be Civilised?* 10th Raul Prebisch Lecture, UNCTAD, Geneva, 11 December 2000.

Helleiner, Gerald. *The Legacies of Julius Nyerere: An Economist's Reflections,* University of Toronto, CIS Working Paper 2000-3, January 2000.

Herman, Edward. *Corporate Control, Corporate Power: A Twentieth Century Fund Study.* Cambridge: Cambridge University Press, 1981.

Himbara, David. The Failed Africanisation of Commerce and Industry in Kenya, *World Development* Vo. 22 No 3, March 1994.

Hirsh, Michael. Does Government Matter? The State is Withering and Global Business is Taking Charge, *Newsweek,* June 6, 1995.

Hobsbawm, Eric J. *The Age of Extremes: A History of the* World, 1914-1991.

New York: Vintage, 1994.

Hodd, Michael, *Tanzania After Nyerere*. London: Pinter, 1998.

Hood, John. Do Companies Have Social Responsibilities? *The Freeman*, Vol. 48 No.11, November 1998.

Hoekman, Bernard and Will Martin. (eds.), *Developing Countries and the WTO: A Pro-active Agenda*,. Oxford: Blackwell Publishers Ltd, 2001.

Hofstede, Grand M. Board. The Confucius Connection. From Cultural Roots to Economic Growth, *Organisational Dynamics*, Vol. 16 no 4, 1998.

Holmquist, Frank. *Business and Politics in Kenya in the 1990s*, Centre of African Studies, Occasional Paper, University of Copenhagen, 2002.

Homer- Dixon, Thomas. *The Ingenuity Gap: How Can We Solve the Problems of the Future?*. London: Vintage, 2001.

Howkins, J andR Valantin. (eds) *Development and the Information Age: Four Global Scenarios for the Future of Information and Communication Technology*, IDRC, Canada, 1997.

House W. Nairobi's Informal Sector: Dynamic Entrepreneurs or Surplus Labour? *Economic Development and Cultural Change*, Vol. 32 No 2, 1984.

Hulger, Hansen B. & Maj-Britt Johanssen. Eds) *The Challenge of the New Partnership for Africa's Development, NEPAD*, University of Copenhagen, North-South Priority Research Area, 2003.

Huntington, Samuel P. *The Clash of Civilizations and the Remaking of World Order*. New York: Simon & Schuster, 1996.

Hutton, Will and Anthony Giddens. *On the Edge: Living with Global Capitalism*. London: Jonathan Cape, 2000.

Hyden, Goran. AIDS, policy and politics: East Africa in comparative Perspective, *Policy Studies Review*, Vol. 12, Spring-Summer, 1993.

IFAD: *Sustainable Poverty Reduction Duilds on Self-help*, Presentation at a regional microcredit summit, October 2000. www.ifad org/pulo/other/rural e.pdf)

Ihonvbere, Julius. The African Crisis, Regionalism and Prospects for Recovery in the Emerging Global Orders, *The African Journal of Political Economy*, December 1993.

IMF. Africa: Turning the Corner? In *IMF World Economic Outlook*, 2005.

International Labour Organisation. *A Fair Globalisation: Creating Opportunities For All*, Report of the World Commission on Social Dimension of Globalisation, Geneva, 2004.

Jaffe, Tougeno D et al. *National Image and Competitive Advantage*, Copenhagen Business School Press, 2001.

James, P. Post-dependency? The Third World in an Era of Globalisation and Late Capitalism, *Alternatives*, Vol.22 No 2, 1997

Jameson, Boex and Jorge Martinez-Vazquez. *Local Government Reform in Tanzania: Considerations for the Development of a System of Formula-Based Grants*, March 2003. www.ideas.repec.org/plays/ispwps/paper0305.html)

Jelev, Jeliou. Education and Citizenship in the Twenty First Century, in Jerome Binde. (ed), *The Future of Values: 21st Century Talks*,. Paris: UNESCO Publishing, 2004.

Joseph, Richard. *Smart Partnerships for African Development: A New Strategic Framework,* Special Report, US Institute of Peace, May 12, 2002.

Jumbe, Abood. *The Partnership: Tanganyika and Zanzibar Union-30 Turbulent Years*. Dar-es-Salaam: Amana Publisher, 1994.

Jumbe, Aboud, *Tuishi Bila Kubaguana Kidini* , Dar es Salaam: Dar es Salaam University Muslims Trusteeship. Dumt, 2003.

Kaaya, Janet. Implementing e-government Services in East Africa: Assessing Status Through Content Analysis of Government Websites, *Electronic Journal of E-Government* Vol. 2 No 1, 2004

Kaaya, Janet. *The emergence of E-Government Services in East Africa: Tracking Adoption Patterns and Associated Factors,*. New York: ACM Press, 2004.

Kaduma, Ibrahim Mohamed, *Maadili ya Taifa na Hatma ya Tanzania: Enzi kwa Mwalimu Julius K. Nyerere,*. Soni: Vuga Press, 2004.

Kaijage, Frederick and Anna Tibaijuka. *Poverty and Social Exclusion in Tanzania*. Geneva: International Institute for Labour Studies, Research Series No. 109, 1996.

Kaijage, F.(ed) *Reflections on the Transition to Democracy in Tanzania,* University of Dar-es-Salaam, 1995.

Kanbur, Ravi. *NEPAD Commentary: the First Wave,* August, 2003. www.arts.cornell.edu/poverty/kanbur/NEPREV.pdf)

Kanbur, Ravi. *The African Peer Review Mechanism. APRM: An Assessment of Concept and Design, December 2001.*www.arts.cornell.edu/poverty/kanbur/APRM.pdf)

Kaplan, Robert. *Warrior Politics: Why Leadership Demands a Pagan Ethos.*. www.carnegiecouncil.org/viewmedia/php/prmTemplateID/8/prmID/80|1)

Kaiser, Paul. Multi-Level Analysis of Conflict Prevention Strategies: The Case of Zanzibar, *International Peace Academy Policy Report,* 2002.

Kaiser, Paul. Power, Sovereignty and International Election Observers: The Case of Zanzibar, *Africa Today* Vol. 46 No 1, Winter 1999.

Kanaan, O. Tanzania's Experience with Trade Liberalisation, *Finance and Development*, Vol. 37 No. 2, 2000.

Kanter, Rosabeth Moss. Desperately in Search of Synergy, *Harvard Business Review,* September-October 1998.

Kahane, Adam. Changing the Winds: Scenarios for People Who Want to

Change the World, *Whole Earth Review,* Spring, 1999

Kahane, Adam. *Scenarios as a Tool for Effecting Societal Change.* Beverly: Generon Consulting, 1999.

Keane, John. Democracy and the Media, *International Social Science Journal,* Vol. 129, 1991.

Kennedy, Paul M. *African Capitalism: The Struggle for Ascendancy.* Cambridge: Cambridge University Press, 1988.

Kennedy, Paul. *Preparing for the Twenty First Century.* London: Fontana Press, 1993.

Kerr, Clark. *Higher Education Cannot Escape History: Issues for the Twenty First Century,* State University of New York Press, 1994.

Khan, Mohsin S with S. Sharma. Reconciling Conditionality and Country Ownership of Programmes, *Finance & Development,* June 2002.

Khan, Mohsin S and Sunil Sharma. IMF Conditionality and Country Ownership of Adjustment Programmes, *World Bank Observer,* Vol. 18 No. 2, 2003.

Khandkar, S.R. *Fighting Poverty with Microfinance.* Oxford: Oxford University Press, 1998.

Khandwalla, Pradip. *Innovative Corporate Turnarounds..* New Delhi: Sage, 1992.

Khoo, Su-ming. The Millennium Development Goals: a Critical Discussion, *Trocaire Development Review,* Dublin, 2005.

Kibwana, K, Chris Peter Maina et al. (eds) *In Search of Freedom and Prosperity: Constitutional Reform in East Africa.* Nairobi, Claripress, 1996.

Kifle, Henoch. *A New Partnership for African Development: Issues and Parameters.* Uppsala: Nordiska Africa institutet, 1997.

Kilimwiko, Lawrence and Joseph Mapunda. (eds.), *A Handbook on the State of Media in Tanzania,.* Nairobi and Dar es Salaam: Friedrich Ebert Stiftung; Association of Journalists and Media Workers. AJM) and Eastern Africa Media Institute, 1998.

Klein, Michael and Bita Hadjirmichael. *The Private Sector Development: Entrepreneurship, Regulation and Cooperative Disciplines,* World Bank, Washington, DC, 2003.

Kothari, Rajni. *Politics and the People: In Search of a Humane India.* Vol. II. New Delhi: Ajanta Publishers, 1990.

Kothari, Rajni. Redesigning The Development Strategy, in K. S. Krishnaswamy et al. (eds.): *Society and Change,* Essays in Honour of Sachin Chaudhuri. Bombay: Oxford University Press, 1977.

Kotler, Philip and David Gartner. Country as Brand, product , and Beyond: A place Marketing and Brand Management Perspective, *The*

Journal of Brand Management, Vol. 9 No. 4-5, April, 2002.

Kouzes, J.M. and B.Z. Posner. *The Leadership Challenge: How to Get Extraordinary Things Done in Organisations*. San Francisco: Jossey – Bass, 1987.

Kramer, Martin. Islam Vs Democracy, *Commentary,* January 1993.

Krueger, Anne O.*Economic Policy Reform in Developing Countries*. Oxford: Blackwell Publishers, 1992.

Kulindwa, Kassim *et al, Mining for Sustainable Development in Tanzania*, Dar es Salaam: Dar es Salaam University Press, 2003.

La Porte, T.M. et al. Democracy and Bureaucracy in the Age of the Web, *Administration and Society* Vol. 34 No 4, 2002.

Lal, Deepak. *In Praise of Empires: Globalization and Order*. Palgrave Macmillan, New York, 2004.

Lambsdorff, Otto Graf. Religion and Global Politics: Three Corners of the World Try to Find Their Bearing, *International Herald Tribune*, June 22, 2005.

Landes, David. *The Wealth and Poverty of Nations: Why Some are so Rich and Others are So Poor*. New York: W. W. Norton, 1998.

Lang, Tony. *Scholars Renew Attempts to Explain Islamic Fundamentalism*, Carnegie Council of Ethics and International Affairs, 2005.

Le Roux, Peter et al. The Mont Fleur Scenarios, *Deeper News*, Volume 7 No 1. Emeryville: Global Business Network, 1992.

Lea, Jonathan S. *From the Postcolonial to the Global: The Testament of Julius Nyerere.*. www.global-partners.org/africa/2000/papers/jlee/jlee.pdf) .

Leadbeater, Charles. *Up the Down Escalator: Why the Global Pessimists are Wrong*. London: Viking, 2002.

Legum,Colin and Mmari, G.R.V. *The Influence of Nyerere*. London: Africa World Press, 1995.

Lendell-Mills, Pierre. *Governance and the External Factor,* Proceedings of the World Bank Annual Conference on Development Economics, 1991.

Lewis, William W. *The Power of Productivity: Wealth, Poverty, and The Threat To Global Stability*. Chicago, Chicago University Press, 2004.

Lienert, Ian. Civil Service Reform in Africa: Mixed Results After 10 Years, *Finance and Development,* Vol.35 No.2, June 1998.

Lindsay Stace. *Culture, Mental Models, and National Prosperity* in Hanson, Lawrence E. and Samuel P. Huntington. (eds.): *Culture Matters, How Values Shape Human Progress*. New York: Basic Books, 2002.

Lodge, George C. The Corporate Key: Using Business to Fight Global Poverty, *Foreign Affairs,* July /August, 2002.

Looney, Robert. The Cancun Conundrum: What Future for the World

Trade Organisation? *Strategic Insights*, Vol. II Issue 10, October 2003.

Loxley, John and Seddon David. Stranglehold on Africa, *Review of African Political Economy*, No. 62, 1994.

Ludgwig, Frieder. *Church and State in Tanzania: Aspects of a Changing Relationship1961-1994.* Amsterdam: Academic Publishers, 1999.

Lunde, Leiv. *UN Millennium Development Goals and the Role of Business*, Speech to the Nordic Global Compact Network, Oslo, 6 June 2005.

McDonald, David A and Eunice Njeri S. (eds) *The Legacies of Julius Nyerere: Influences on Development Discourse and Practice on Africa. The Politics of Self Reliance.* London: Africa World Press, 2002.

MacQueen, K et al. *Poverty, HIV/AIDS and Social Security*, Economic Policy Research Institute, Research Paper No.30, 27 January, 2002.

Magdoff, Fred. A Precarious Existence: The Fate of Billions? *Monthly Review,* February 2004.

Mahathir, Mohamad. *Globalisation, Smart Partnership and Government*, Kuala Lumpur, 2003.

Maliyamkono, T.L. (ed.), *The Political Plight of Zanzibar*, Dar es Salaam: Tema Publishers Company Ltd., 2000.

Maliyamkono, T. L. and M.S.D Bagachwa. *The Second Economy in Tanzania.* London, James Curry, 1990.

Mamdani, Mahmood. *Good Muslim, Bad Muslim: America, the Cold War, and the Roots of Terror.* New York, Pantheon, 2004.

Mamdani, Mahmood. Q&A Interview with Mahmood Mamdani, May 5, 2004.. www.asiasource.org/news/special_reports/mamdani.cfm.

Mamdani, Mahmood. There Can be No African Renaissance without an African-focuses Intelligentsia, in Makgoba, Malegapuru W. (ed): *African Renaissance.* Cape Town: Mafube Publications, 1999.

Mamdani, Mahmood. *Citizen and Subject: Contemporary Africa and the Legacy of Late Colonialism.* Princeton University Press, 1996.

Mamdani, Mahmood. 'Their Terror' and 'Our Terror': A Third World View, *Einstein Forum Conference: Terror International Law, and the Bonds of Democracy,* Postdam, March 4-5, 2004.

Mamdani, Mahmood. Inventing Political Violence, *Global Agenda Magazine,* 2005. www.globalagendamagazine.com/2005/mahmoodmamdani.asp).

Marong, B.M. Alhaj. Toward a Normative Consensus Against Corruption: Legal Effects of the Principles to Combat Corruption in Africa, *Denver Journal of International law & Policy* Vol. 30 No 2, 2002.

Martin, Ian. Adult Education, Lifelong Learning and Citizenship: Some Ifs and Buts, *International Journal of Lifelong Education,* Vol. 22 No 6,

November –December 2003.

Matlusa, Khabale et al. *The Role of the State in Development in the SADC Region: Does NEPAD Provide a New Paradigm?* Southern African Political Economy Series. SAPES, Harare, April 2002.

Mayor Federico and Binde Jerome. *The World Ahead: Our Future In The Making.* London, Zed Books, 2001.

Mayoux, L. (ed) *Sustainable Learning for Women's Empowerment: Ways Forward in Microfinance.* ITDG Publishing, 2005.

Mazrui, Ali. *Islamic and Western Values,* Foreign Affairs, September-October 1997.

Mazrui, Ali. *The Liberal Revival, Privatisation and the Market: Africa's Cultural Contradictions,* Paper Presented at the African Regional Conference on Liberalisation of African Economies and African Integration, Arusha, Tanzania, June, 1992.

Mazrui, Ali. Who Killed Democracy in Africa? Clues of the Past, Concerns of the Future, Keynote Address to Pan-African Conference on Democracy, Sustainable Development and Poverty Reduction: Are They Compatible? *Development Policy Management Forum, 4-6 December 2001.*

Mazrui, Ali A. Islamic and Western Values. www.alhewar.com/AliMazrui.htm).

Mazrui, Ali A. *Political Voices and the Educated Class in Africa,.* Berkeley, California University Press, 1978.

Mazrui, Ali, A. Tanzaphilia, *Transition,* Vol. 6, 1976.

Mbaku, Mukum John. Bureaucratic Corruption in Africa: The Futility of Cleanups, *Cato Journal,* Vol. 16 No 1, Spring/Summer, 1996.

Mbeki, Moeletsi. *Underdevelopment in Sub-Saharan Africa: The Role of the Private Sector and Political Elites,* CATO Institute, Foreign Policy Briefing No.85, April, 2005.

Mbeki, Thabo: *Address at the Conference of the Association of African Universities,* Cape Town, 22 February 2005.

Mbeki, Thabo. *Africa's Season of Hope: The Dawn of a New Africa- Asia Solidarity,* Address on the occasion of the 26th Singapore Lecture, Singapore, 21 April, 2005 . www.infor.gov.za/speeches/2005/05042114151002.htm)

Mbeki, Thabo. *Statement at the Opening of the NEPAD Stakeholders Dialogue,* Sandton Convention Centre, Johannesburg, 22 October 2004.

Mbelle, Ammon; G.D. Mjema and A.A.L. Kilindo. (eds.), *The Nyerere Legacy and Economic Policy Making in Tanzania,.* Dar es Salaam: Dar es Salaam University Press, 2002.

Mbilinyi, Marjorie. *Equity, Justice and Transformation in Education: The Challenge of Mwalimu Julius Nyerere Today,* HakiElimu Working Paper Series No. 2003.5, April 2000. www.hakielimu.org/WP/WPSeries5.pdf)

Mbogoni, Lawrence. *The Cross Versus the Crescent: Religion and Politics in Tanzania From the 1880s to the 1990s.* Dar-es Salaam: Mkuki na Nyota Publishers, 2005.

Mbogoro, Damas K., *Global Trading Arrangements and their Relevance to Tanzania Economic Development: Challenges and Prospects,.* Dar es Salaam: Friedrich Ebert Stiftung, 1996.

McCusker, Alison. (ed.), *Chagula: Speeches on Development,* Dar es Salaam: Tanzania Commission for Science and Technology, 1999.

Mchomvu, A.S.T et al. Social Security Systems in Tanzania: Phase I to IV, *Journal of Social Development in Africa,* Vol. 17 no 2, 2002.

McIntosh, Malcolm et al. *Corporate Citizenship: Successful Strategies for Responsible Companies.* London: Financial Times Management, 1998.

Metcaife, Les and Sue Richards. *Improving Public Management..* London: Sage, 1990.

Mhando, Harold S.. ed.), *Corruption and Drug Trafficking in Tanzania: A Social-Economic Analysis,.* Dar es Salaam: Popular Publications Limited, 1995.

Micklethwait, John and Adrian Wooldridge. *A Future Perfect: The Challenge and Hidden Promise of Globalisation.* London: William Heinemann, 2000.

Migiro, R.M. The Constitutional and Political Reform Process in Tanzania: Experiences from the White Paper Committee in R. Southall et al. (eds) *Constitutional Reform Processes in Eastern Africa,* Kampala: Friedrich Ebert Stiftung, 1996.

Mihevc, John. *The Market Tells Them So: The World Bank and Economic Fundamentalism in Africa.* London: Zed Books, 1995.

Milanovic, Branko. The Two Faces of Globalisation: Against Globalisation as We Know it, *World Development,* Vol. 31 No 4, 2003.

Ministry of Industries and Trade. *National Trade Policy – Background Papers: Trade Policy for a Competitive Economy and Export-led Growth.* Dar es Salaam: Dar es Salaam University Press, 2003.

Miraftab, F. Public-Private Partnerships: The Trojan Horse of Neoliberal Development? *Journal of Planning, Education and Research,* Vol.24 No 1, 2004.

Mkapa, Benjamin W., *Uwazi na Ukweli: Rais wa Watu Azungumza na Wananchi.* Kitabu cha Kwanza. Dar es Salaam: Mkuki na Nyota Publishers, 2003.

Mkapa, Benjamin W. *Uwazi na Ukweli: Rais wa Watu Azungumza na*

Wananchi. Kitabu cha Pili. Dar es Salaam: Mkuki na Nyota Publishers, 2004.

Mkude, Daniel *et al, Higher Education in Tanzania: A Case Study,.* Oxford and Dar es Salaam: James Currey and Mkuki na Nyota, 2003.

Mohamed, Ali Bakari. *The Democratisation Process in Zanzibar: A Retarded Transition.* Hamburg: Institut Fur Afrika-Kunde, 2001.

Mohamad, Mahathir Dr. *The New Malay Dilemma,* Address to the Harvard Club of Malaysia, Kuala Lumpur, July 29, 2002.

Mohiddin, Ahmed. Tanzania in Transition: From Ujamaa to Ujangili.? *Change.* (Tanzania) November – December 1993.

Mohiddin, Ahmed. The Challenges Of E-Democracy: Opportunities and Risks, *African Administrative Studies,* No. 62, 2004.

Mohiddin, Ahmed. *African Leadership: The Succeeding Generations-Challenges and Opportunities,* The African Foundation, Mombasa. (mimeo), November 1998.

Mohiddin, Ahmed. Perspectives On Civil Society in Africa, *Change,* Vol. 7, 8 & 9, 1996.

Moore, M and L. Hamalai. Economic Liberalisation, Political Pluralism and Business Associations in Developing Countries, *World Development,* Vol. 21 no 2, 1993.

Monthly Review Special Issue. Socialism for the 21st Century, *Monthly Review,* July-August 2005.

Morduch, Jonathan. The Microfinance Promise, *Journal of Economic Literature,* Vol. 37 No 4, 1999.

Morrissey, Oliver et al. A Critical Assessment of Proposed EU-ACP Economic Partnership Agreements, in Andrew Arnold.

(ed) *Challenges for Development Cooperation in the 21st Century.* London: Frank Cass, 2004.

Moshi, H.P.B and Warner Biermann. (eds). *Contextualising Poverty in Tanzania: Historical origins, Policy Failures and Recent Trends,* New Jersey:. Transaction Publishers, 1996.

Moshi, Humphrey P.B. et al. *Zanzibar: The Challenges of Globalisation and Poverty Reduction,* Zanzibar: Ministry of Finance and Economic Affairs and President's Economic Policy Advisory Unit, 2004.

Mosley, Paul et al. Aid, Poverty Reduction and the New Conditionality, *The Economic Journal,* June, 2004.

Moss, Todd. *Adventure Capitalism: Globalisation and the Political Economy of Stock Markets in Africa.* London: Palgrave Macmillan, 2003.

.Msabaha, Ibrahim. The Union with Zanzibar in Colin Legum and G.R.V Mmari, *Mwalimu: The Influence of Nyerere.* London: Africa World Press,

1995.

Msekwa, P. *The Transition to Multiparty Democracy*. Dar-es-Salaam: Tanzania Publishing House, 1995.

Mtemvu, Abdul. Islamic "Fundamentalism" and the Muslim Factor in Tanzania Mainland Politics, *Change*, Vol. 7, July, 1993.

Mukandala, Rwekaza, S. *Trade Unionism in Tanzania: The Case of the Tanzania Federation of Trade Unions. TFTU and Government*, Institute of Development Studies, Sussex, November 1999.

Mukandala, R.S. To Be or Not to Be: The Paradoxes of African Bureaucracies in the 1990s, *International Review of Administrative Sciences*, Vol. 58, 1992.

Mukandala R. The State of African Democracy, Presidential Address to the 13th Biannual Congress of the African Political Science Association, *African Journal of Political Science*, Vol. 6, No. 2, 2001.

Mukandala, R.S. *The State of African Democracy: Status, Prospects, Challenges*. Occasional Paper, Centre of African Studies, University of Copenhagen, December 2002.

Mulgan Geoff. *Connexity: Responsibility, Freedom, Business and Power in the New Century*. London: Vintage, 1998.

Mukandala, R. Decentralisation and Democratisation in Tanzania, in J.D. Barkan, *Decentralisation and Democratisation in Sub-Saharan Africa*, University of Iowa, 1998.

Mushi, Richard. Fiscal Impact of the Parastatal Sector in Tanzania: 1984-1995, *The African Journal of Finance and Management*, Vol. 9 No 1, July 2000.

Mushi, S.S and Mukandala, R.S. *Multiparty Democracy in Transition: Tanzania's 1995 General Elections*. Oxford, African Books Collective, 1997)

Mussonda, F et al. Constraints to Capital Market Development and Growth in Sub-Saharan Africa: The Case of Tanzania, *EAGER Policy Brief No 56*, February 2001.

Mutunga, Willy, "Constitutions, Law and Civil Society: Discourses on the Legitimacy of People's Power," in OLOKA-ONYANGO, Joseph. (ed.), *Constitutionalism in Africa: Creating Opportunities, Facing Challenges*,. Kampala: Fountain Publishers, 2001.

Mutahaba, G and Kithinji Kiragu. Lessons of International and African Perspectives on Public Service Reform: Examples from Five African Countries, *African Development* Vol.XXVII, No. 3 & 4, 2002.

Mvungi, Sengondo E.A. (ed.), *The Draft Treaty for the Establishment of the East African Community: A Critical Review*,. Dar es Salaam: Dar es Salaam University Press, 2002.

Mwambola, Ali. *Is NASACO's Future Bright or Doomed?* Business Times, Tanzania, 1999.

Mwandosya, M. J et al. (eds) *Towards a New Millennium; Perspectives on Tanzania's Vision 2025.* Dar-Es-Salaam: CEEST, 1998.

Mwansasu, Bismarck U. The Transition to Competitive Politics in Tanzania: The Agony and Predicament of the Opposition Parties, *Change,* Vol. 7, 8 & 9, 1996.

Mwapachu, Juma V, "Historical Overview of the Major University of Dar es Salaam Crises During its 25 Years," in MBWETTE, T.S.A and.Ishumi AGM. (eds.), *Managing University Crises.* Dar es Salaam: Dar es Salaam University Press, 2000.

Mwapachu, Juma Volter. *Management of Public Enterprises in Developing Countries: The Tanzanian Experience,.* New Delhi: Oxford & IBH Publishers,1983.

Mwapachu, Juma Volter. Operation Planned Villages in Tanzania: A Revolutionary Strategy for Development in Coulson A.. (ed): *African Socialism in Practice: The Tanzanian Experience.* Spokesman, Nottingham, 1979.

Mwapachu, J.V. Whither the Union of United Republic of Tanzania? *Change,* Vol. 7, July 1993.

Mwase Nkunde and Benno Ndulu. *Tanzania: Explaining Four Decades of Episodic Growth.* www.wcfia.harvard.edu/conferences/batesafrica/PaperPDF/MwaseTanzani a.pdf).

Mwilapa, Thobias, *Politics and Christian Relations in Tanzania.* www.ucip.ch/nv/tz), December 2002.

Nabudere, Dani W. The African Renaissance in the Age of Globalisation, *African Journal of Political Science,* Vol. 6 No. 2, 2001.

Nabudere, Dani W. *NEPAD: Historical Background and Its Prospects,* Paper presented at the African Forum for Envisioning Africa, Nairobi, Kenya, 26-29 April, 2002.

Naim Moises. Misguided Ideas in a Dangerous World, *Financial Times,* November 25, 2002.

Naisbitt, John. *The Megatrends 2000.* New York: William Morrow, 1990)

Nathan Associates. *Public-Private Partnerships for Integrating Small, Poor Countries into the Global Trading System,* Research Report for USAID, May 2004.

Ndulu, Benno J. and Wangwe Samuel. *Managing Tanzania's Economy in Transition to Sustained Development,* Mimeo, Economic and Social Research Foundation, Dar-es-Salaam, May 1997.

Ndulu, Benno J. *From Vision to Reality of African Economic Integration: Priority actions and the institutional framework for the Way Forward*, Reserve Bank of South Africa, 2002. www.reservebank.co.za/internet/Publication).

Ndulu, Benno J. From Stabilisation to Sustained Growth in Africa, in *International Politics and Society* No 1, 1998.

NEPAD: The African Peer Review Mechanism.(APRM). www.dfa.gov.za/au.nepad/nepad49.pdf)

Ndulu, Benno. Human Capital Flight: Stratification, Globalisation and the Challenges of Tertiary Education in Africa, *Journal of Higher Education in Africa*, Vol. 2 No. 1 Fall, 2004.

Ngara, Emmanuel. The African University and Its Mission: Strategies for Improving Delivery of Higher Education Institution, in *African Book Publishing Record* XXIII No. 2, 1997.

Ngware, Suleiman and J.M. Lusugga Kironde. (eds.), *Urbanising Tanzania: Issues, Initiatives and Priorities*. Dar es Salaam: Dar es Salaam University Press, 2000.

Nixon, Richard. *Leaders.* New York: Touchstone Books, 1990.

Njozi, Hamza M. *Mwembechai Killings and The Political Future of Tanzania.* Ottawa: Global Link Communications, 2000.

Njozi, Hamza Mustafa, *Muslims and the State in Tanzania,*. Dar es Salaam: Dar es Salaam University Muslims Trusteeship. (Dumt), 2003.

Nove, Alec. *The Economics of Feasible Socialism.* London: George Allen & Unwin, 1983.

Nunus, Burt. *Visionary Leadership.* San Francisco: Jossey-Bass Publishers, 1992.

Nye, Joseph S. Jr. Globalisation's Democratic Deficit: How to Make International Institutions More Accountable, *Foreign Affairs,* July/August, 2001.

Nye, Joseph. S. and John D. Donahue. *Governance in a Globalising World.* Washington DC: Brookings Institution Press, 2000.

Nyerere, Julius K. Democracy and the One Party State, in Julius K.

Nyerere, Freedom and Unity. London: Oxford University Press, 1967.

Nyerere, Julius K. Good Governance of Africa, *Daily News.* (Tanzania), November 22, 1998.

Nyerere, Julius, *Freedom and Development,* Oxford: oxford University Press 1973.

Nyerere, Julius K. *Freedom Socialism.* Oxford: Oxford University Press, 1968.

Nyerere, Julius K. The Link between the Economy, the Society, and the University, *Change.* (Tanzania), Vol. 3, No. 5, 6 &7, 1995, p. 46-47.

Nyerere, Julius K. *Uongozi Wetu na Hatima ya Tanzania.*
Harare: Zimbabwe Publishing House, 1995.

Nyerere, Julius K. *Our Leadership and the Destiny of Tanzania,.* Harare:
African Publishing Group, 1995.

Nyerere, Julius K. Leadership and the Management of Change, *Keynote
Speech at the Commonwealth Universities General Conference, Ottawa,
Canada* August 16, 1998, in the Bulletin ACU, Bulletin of current
Documentation No. 135, 1998.

Nyerere, Julius K. Are Universal Social Standards Possible.? *SEATINI
Bulletin,* Vol. 2 No. 2, 31 January, 1999.

O'Brien, Conor Cruise. *On The Eve of The Millennium.* House of Anansi
Press, 1994.

O' Brein, Donald B. Cruise. Satan Steps Out from the Shadows: Religion
and Politics in Africa, *Africa* Vol.70 No.2, September, 2000.

O' Brien, Donald B. Cruise. *Symbolic Confrontations: Muslim Imagining the
State in Africa.* . London: Hurst & Co, 2003.

O'Rourke, Kevin. *Globalisation and History: The Evolution of a Nineteenth-
Century* Atlantic *Economy,* MIT Press, 1999.

Odhiambo, Walter and Kamau Paul. *Public Procurement: Lessons from
Kenya, Tanzania and Uganda,* OECD Development Centre Technical
Papers No 208, March 2003.

OECD: *Anti-Corruption Action Plan: Anti-Corruption Network in Transition
Economies,* Paris, 2003.

OECD: *Improving Service Delivery Through Public Service Reform: Lessons of
Experience from Select Sub-Saharan African Countries,* KK Consulting
Associates, Nairobi, Kenya.. www.oecd.org/dataoecd/1/41/20601625.pdf)

OECD: *Outsourcing,* OECD Employment Outlook, 2005.

Ohiorhenuan, John F.E. The South in an Era of Globalisation, *Cooperation
South Journal,* No 2, 1998.

Ohmae Kenichi. *The End of the Nation – State: The Rise of Regional
Economics.* New York: Free Press, 1995, see also, Vincent Cable, The
Diminished Nation – State: A Study in the Loss of Economic Power,
Deadalus Vol. 124 No 2, Spring 1995.

Ohmae, Kenichi. Putting Global Logic First, in Kenichi Ohmae. Ed): *The
Evolving Global Economy: Making Sense of the New World Order.* Harvard
Business Review Book, 1995.

Ohmae, Kenichi. *The Invisible Continent: Four Strategic Imperatives of the
New Economy.*London: Nicholas Brealey, 2000.

Oloka-Onyango, J, K. Kibwana and Chris M Peter. (eds) *The Law and the
Struggle for Democracy in East Africa.* Nairobi: Claripress, 1996.

Ohmae, Kenichi. *The Next Global Stage: Challenges and Opportunities in Our Borderless World,* Wharton School Publishing, 2005.

Oloka-Onyango, Joseph and Maria Nassali. (eds.), *Constitutionalism and Political Stability in Zanzibar: The Search for a New Vision,*. Kampala: Kituo Cha Katiba, October, 2003.

Omari, C.K.(ed.), *The Right to Choose a Leader: Reflections on the 1995 Tanzanian General Elections,*Dar es Salaam: Dar es Salaam University Press, 1997.

Omari, C.K. (ed.), *Youth and Development,* Dar es Salaam: National Council of Social Welfare Services, 1981.

O'Neill, Onora. *A Question of Trust,* BBC Reith Lectures, 2002.

Onimode, Bade, *Africa in the World of the 21st Century,*. Ibadan: Ibadan University Press, 2000.

Oppenheim, Jeremy M. Corporations as Global Citizens, *The McKinsey Quarterly* No. 1, 2004.

Organisation for Economic Cooperation and Development. (OECD): Foreign Direct Investment for Development: Maximising Benefits, Minimising Costs. Paris, OECD, 2002.

Osborne, David and Ted Gaebler. *Re-inventing Government: How the Entrepreneurial Spirit is transforming the Public Sector.* San Francisco: Addison – Wesley, 1992.

Othman, Haroub. (ed.), *Reflections on Leadership in Africa: Forty Years After Independence – Essays in Honour of Mwalimu Julius K. Nyerere on the Occasion of his 75th Birthday.* Brussels:VUB University Press, 2000.

Othman, Haroub. *Tanzania: The Withering Away of the Union? Change,* Vol. 7, July 1993.

Othman, Haroub and Athumani Liviga. *Local Governance and Poverty Reduction,* Tanzania Country Paper for AGFV, UNDP, Dar-es-Salaam, May, 2002.

Othman, Haroub. Tanzania: Towards a New Constitutional Order? *Change,* Vol. 7, 8 & 9, 1996.

Othman, Haroub. Zanzibar's Political History: The Past Haunts the Present, *Change,* Vol. 2 No. 4/5, April-May, 1994.

Othman, Haroub. The Intellectual and Transformation in Southern Africa, *Dar-es-Salaam Alumni Newsletter,* Vol. 1 No.1, 1994.

Oxfam. *Oxfam: From `Donorship` to Ownership? Moving Towards PRSP Round Two,* Oxfam Briefing Paper No. 51. January 2004.

Page, Sheila. *Special and Differential Treatment or Divide and Rule? European Union Trade Policy Towards Developing Countries,* Overseas Development Institute, Development Research Briefings, No 3, 2004.

Patel, I.G. Employment, Growth and Basic Needs in Society , in K. S. Krishnaswamy et al. (eds.): *Society and Change*, Essays in Honour of Sachin Chaudhuri. Bombay: Oxford University Press, 1977.

Peter, Chris Maina. *Constitutional Making Process in Tanzania: The Role of Civil Organisations,* Institute of Development Studies, Sussex, December 1999.

Peter, Chris Maina and Saudin Jacob Mwakaje, *Investments in Tanzania: Some Comments – Some Issues.* Dar es Salaam: Department of International Law, University of Dar es Salaam and Friedrich Ebert Stiftung, 2004.

Peter, Chris Maina, *Racism, Racial Discrimination, Xenophobia and Related Intolerances in Tanzania.* Pretoria, African Association of Political Science, Volume 6 No. 2 Occasional Paper Series, 2002.

Petterson, Donald & Don Petterson. *Revolution in Zanzibar: An American Cold War Tale.* Westview Press, 2002.

Petras, James. The Third Way: Myth and Reality, *Monthly Review,* Vol. 51, 51 no 10, March, 2000.

Pfeffermann, Guy. *The Role of Private Enterprise in Developing Countries,* IFC, Washington DC, 2000.

Pfeiffer, Jeffrey. *Managing Power: Politics and Influence in Organisations.* Boston: Harvard Business School Press,1992.

Ping, Charles J. *Educational Imperatives for a New Era*, in Anne Holden Ronning and Mary – Louise Kearney: *Graduate Prospects in a Changing Society,* UNESCO Publishing, 1996.

Planmo, Marcus. *From Patron-Client to Client-Server: E-Democracy in Tanzania*? MA Thesis in Political Science, Uppsala University, Sweden.. www.cdt.org/egov/handbook/tanzania.pdf).

Popper, Karl. *Conjectures and Refutations.* New York: Harper & Row, 1963.

Porter, Michael. *The Competitive Advantage of Nations.* London: Macmillan, 1990.

Prahalad, C.K. and Kenneth Lieberthal. *The End of Corporate Imperialism,* Harvard Business Review, July-August, 1995.

Pratt, Cranford. Julius Nyerere: The Ethical Foundation of His Legacy. www.queensu.ca/snid/pratt.htm).

Preston, Paschal. *Knowledge or 'Know-less' Societies?* www.lirne.net/resources/netknowledge/reston.pdf)

Prewitt, Kenneth. Higher Education, Society and Government : Changing Dynamics, *Journal of Higher Education in Africa*, Vol. 2 No. 1, February, 2004.

Radelet, Stephen. Bush and Foreign Aid, *Foreign Affairs,* September/October 2003.

Rahman, M.D. Anisur. *People's Self Development.* London: Zed Press, 1993.

Rahman, Atiqur. *Financing Microfinance for Poverty Reduction,* Asia-Pacific Region Microcredit Summit Meeting of Councils. (APRMs), Dhaka, Bangladesh, 16-19February 2004.

Rajan, Raghuran. Debt Relief and Growth, *Finance and Development,* June 2005.

Rajan, Raghuram & Arvind Subramanian. Aid and Growth: What Does the Cross Country Evidence Really Show? *IMF Working Paper WP/05/127,* June 2005

Ramphele, Mamphela. The Role of Higher Education in Reducing Poverty and Promoting Prosperity, Speech Delivered to the *Conference, "Policies and Models for International Cooperation in Higher Education",* Bergen, Norway, October 6, 2003.

The Work of Nations: Preparing Ourselves for the 21st Century Capitalism. New York: Knopf, 1991.

Rifkin, Jeremy. *The End of Work: The Decline of the Global Labour Force and the Dawn of the Post-Market Era,.* New York: G.P. Putnam's Sons, 1995.

Robbins, Anthony. *Unlimited Power.* New York: Fawcett Books, 1996.

Rodrik, Dani. What Have We Learned from Twenty Years of Economic Reform? FORUM, *Newsletter of the Economic Research for Arab Countries, Iran and Turkey,* Vol. 7 No. 1, Spring, 2004.

Rondinelli, Dennis. Reinventing Government: The Imperatives of Innovation and Quality, 5th *Global Forum on Reinventing Government: Innovation and Quality in the Government of the 21st Century,* Mexico City, 3-7 November 2003.

Rondinelli, Dennis A. and G. Shabbir Cheeema. *Reinventing Government for the Twenty First Century-State Capacity in a Globalising World.* Kumarian Press, 2003.

Rodrik, Dani and Romain Wacziarg. *Do Democratic Transitions Produce Bad Economic Outcomes?* Working Paper, Harvard University, December, 2004.

Rugumamu, Severine M. *Lethal Aid: The Illusion of Socialism and Self-Reliance in Tanzania,.* Trenton, NJ and Asmara: Africa World Press, Inc., 1997.

Rushdie, Salman. *The Satanic Verses.* London: Henry Holt Publishers, 1997.

Rweyemamu, S. and T. Msambure, *The Catholic Church in Tanzania,.* Ndanda and Peremiho: Benedictine Publications, 1989.

Sachs, Jeffrey D. *The End of Poverty: Economic Possibilities For Our Time.* New York: The Penguin Press, 2005.

Sachs, Jeffrey D. Four Ways to fix America's failure on Africa, *International*

Herald Tribune, June 27, 2005.

Sacks, Jonathan. *The Dignity of Difference: How To Avoid The Clash of Civilizations.* London: Continuum, 2002.

Said, Mohamed, *The Life and Times of Abdulwahid Sykes. 1924-1968: The Untold Story of the Muslim Struggle Against British Colonialism in Tanganyika.* London: Minerva Press, 1998.

Said, Mohamed, Tanzania- The 'Secular' Unsecular State, *Change,* Vol. 2, No. 12, December 1994.

Saint, William S. Universities in Africa: Strategies for Stabilisation and Revitalisation, *Technical Paper No.194,* Technical Department, Africa Region, World Bank, 1992. Association for the Development of Education in Africa. (ADEA): Higher Education in Africa: The Way Forward, December 28, 2000.

Salih, Mohamed M. A. *The Potential Role of Democratic Political Education in the African Context..* www.ossrea.net/easrr/jan97/salih.htm)

Salleh, Abdul Latif H. Globalisation, Regionalisation and Localisation: The Challenging Roles of Higher Education Institutions in Economic Development, *Paper presented at an International Conference on Globalisation and Higher Education: Views from the South,* Cape Town, South Africa, 27-29 March 2001.

Sampson, Gary P. (ed.), *The Role of the World Trade Organisation in Global Governance.* Tokyo, New York and Paris: United Nations University Press, 2001.

Sanneh, Lamin. Religion and Politics: Third World Perspectives on a Comparative Religious Theme, *Deadalus,* Summer 1991.

Sarin Arun. Mobile Penetration Will Boost African Business, *Financial Times. (UK),* June 30, 2005.

Saul, John S. Poverty Alleviation and the Revolutionary-Socialist Imperative:Learning from Nyerere's Tanzania, *International Journal,* June 2002.

Saul, John S. Julius Nyerere: The Theory and Practice of Un Democratic Socialism in Africa, in McDonald D. and E. Sahle. (eds) *The Legacies of Julius Nyerere: Influences on Development Discourse and Practice.* Trenton: Africa World Press, 2002.

Saul, John. Radicalisation at the Hill, *East African Journal,* Vol. 7, 1970.

Saul, John S. and Colin Leys. Sub-Saharan Africa in Global Capitalism, *Monthly Review,* Vol. 51 No 3, July-August, 1999.

Schlesinger Jr, Arthur M. *The Cycles of American History.* New York: Houghton Miffin Co; 1986.

Schon, Donald A. *Beyond the Stable State.* New York: WW Norton &

Company, 1973.

Schneider, Leander. *Considering Tanzanian-style Rural Socialism: One More Time?* . www.arts.yorku.ca/african_liberation/confrence_papers/schneider_print.html)

Schwab, Klaus and Claude Smadja. *Power and Policy: The New Economic World Order*, in Ohmae Kenichi. (ed): *The Evolving Global Economy*. Harvard Business Review Book, 1995.

Scott, Gerald. Who Has Failed Africa, IMF Measures or African Leadership? *Journal of African Administrative Studies*, Vol. 8 No 1, 1998.

Schwartz, Peter. *The Art of the Long View.* New York: Doubleday 1991.

Sen, Amartya. *Development as Freedom.* New York: Alfred A. Knopf, 1999.

Sen, Amartya. Democracy as a Universal Value, *Journal of Democracy,* Vol. 10 No 3, 1999.

Shahin .Jamal B. The Internet: A Case Study for Global Governance, *Swiss Political Science Review,* Vol.5 No 1, 1999.

Shaw, George Bernard. *Man and Superman: A Comedy and a Philosophy.* London: Amereon Ltd. 1950.

Shivji, Issa G. Not Yet D*emocracy: Reforming Land Tenure in Tanzania,*. London and Dar es Salaam: IIED; Hakiardhi and Faculty of Law, University of Dar es Salaam, 1998.

Shivji, Issa G. Issa G. Hamudi I Majamba; Robert V. Makaramba; and Chris Maina Peter, *Constitutional and Legal System of Tanzania: A Civics Sourcebook*. Dar es Salaam: Mkuki na Nyota Publishers, 2004.

Shivji, Issa. *From Neo-Liberalism to Pan Africanism: Towards Reconstructing an Eastern African Discourse* in *Pambazuka: Weekly Forum for Social Justice in Africa,* 31 March 2005, www.pambazuka.org.

Shivji, Issa. Tanzania: What Kind of a Country are We Building? *Pambazuka News* 196. www.pambazuka.org), March 3, 2005.

Shivji, Issa. *The Second Great Boer Trek*, www.pambazuka.org .

Shivji, Issa. *Whither University?* Centre for Civil Society, University of Natal, March 2005, www.ukzn.ac.za).

Shivji, Issa G. The Beastly Face of Capitalism, 2005. www.pambazuka.org).

Shivji, Issa G. Debunking Nationalism from Haki ya Mungu to Haki ya Mzungu, *South African Centre for Civil Society, 2005.* www.nu.ac.za)

Shivji, Issa G. The Speaker Speaks: Editorial Commentary on the National Assembly Speaker's Interpretation on the Motion of Tanganyika Government, *Change,* August 1993.

Shivji, Issa. Towards a New Constitutional Order: The State of the Debate,

Change, Vol. 4 No. 7, 8 & 9, 1996.

Shivji, Issa. *The Experience of Constitutionalism and the State in Africa,*
American Council of Learned Societies, Appendix C of the ACLS
Comparative Constitutionalism Project Final Report. www.acls.org).

Shivji, Issa G. Critical Elements of a New Democratic Consensus in Africa
in Haroub Othman & M. Khalfani. (eds) *Reflections on Leadership in Africa:
Forty Years after Independence.* Brussels: VYB University Press, 2000.

Shivji, Issa G. Problems of Constitution-Making as Consensus-Building:
The Tanzanian Experience, in O. Sichone. Ed) *The State and
Constitutionalism.* Harare: Sapes Books, 1998.

Shivji, Issa G. *Intellectuals at the Hill: Essays and Talks 1969-1993.* Dar-es-
Salaam: Dar-es-Salaam University Press, 1998.

Shivji, Issa G. *Aid with One Hand, Guns With the Other, Q&A with Issa
Shivji on the G8 Gleneagles Summit* . www.panbazuka.org)

Shivji, Issa G. Globalisation and Popular Resistance, in Juma Mwapachu
et al. (eds) *Local Perspectives on Globalisation.* Dar-es-Salaam: Mkuki na
Nyota, 2002.

Sid -Ahmed, Mohamed. *Cybernetic Colonialism and the Moral Search.
Resurrection of the Religious Imagination.* New Perspectives Quarterly,
Spring, 1994.

Silcok, R. What is E-Government? *Parliamentary Affairs*, Vol. 54, 2001

Sim, Stuart. *Fundamentalist World: The New Dark Age of Dogma.*
Cambridge. Icon Books Ltd, 2004.

Simba, Iddi, *A Concept of Indigenisation*, Dar es Salaam, May, 2003.

Singer, Daniel. *Whose Millennium? Theirs or Ours?* New York: Monthly
Review Press, 1999.

Singer, Peter. *One World: The Ethics of Globalisation.* London: Yale
University Press, 2005.

Sirc, Ljubo. *Socialism and Ownership,* in *The Socialist Idea: A Reappraisal* by
Kolakowski L.. Ed.). London: Weidenfeld and Nicolson, 1975.

John Sivalon. Models for Understanding the Relationship of Religion to
Politics, *Change,* Vol. 12, December 1 1994.

Smith, Craig N. Arguments For and Against Corporate Social
Responsibility, in Laura P. Hartman. (ed) *Perspectives in Business Ethics.*
2nd Edition.New York: McGraw-Hill, 2002.

Smyth, Anne. *Tanzania: The Story of Julius: Africa's Elder Statesman.*
London: Fountain, 1998.

Social Security in Africa, *International Social Security Review*, Vol. 36 No 3-
4, 2003.

South Commission. *The Challenge to the South.* Oxford: Oxford University

Press, 1990.

Sowell, Thomas. *Affirmative Action Around the World: An Empirical Study.* New Haven. Yale University Press, 2004.

Sperling, Gene and Tom Hart. A Better Way to Fight Global Poverty: Broadening the Millennium Challenge Account, *Foreign Affairs,* March/April, 2003.

SRI International, Public Policy Centre: *The Higher Education-Economic Connection: Emerging Rules for Public Colleges and Universities in a Changing Economy,* American Association of State Colleges and Univer sities, Washington, DC, 1986.

Stevens, M and Teggeman S. Comparative Experience with Public Service Reform in Ghana, Tanzania and Zambia, in Levy, B and S. Kipundeh. (eds) *Building State Capacity in Africa: New Approaches, Emerging Lessons,* 2004.

Stiglitz, Joseph E. It is Time for a True Development Round, *Financial Times,* June 21, 2004.

Stiglitz, Joseph E. *The Roaring Nineties: Seeds of Destruction.* London, Allen Lane, 2003.

Stiglitz, Joseph E. *Whither Socialism?* London: The MIT Press, 1997.

Stiglitz, J. *Have Recent Crises Affected the State-Market Debate?* Public Lecture at Bangladesh Economic Association, March 1999.

Stiglitz, J.E. *Globalisation and Its Discontents.* New York: WW Norton, 2002.

Streatfeild, Jeremy E.J. An Examination of Regional Trade Agreements: A Case Study of the EC and the East African Community, *Trade Law Centre for Southern Africa, Working Paper No 11/2003,* November, 2003.

Streeten, Paul. Social Development in Africa: A Focus on People, *Development,* Journal of the Society for International Development, Vol.2, 1991.

Strengthening Private Sector Representation in Africa-BIAC Contribution to the OECD-Africa Investment Roundtable, Johannesburg, 19 November 2003.. www.biac.org/statements/nme/Africa III Final.pdf.)

Sturmer, Martin, *The Media History of Tanzania.* Salzburg and Ndanda: Afro-Asiatisches Institut Salzburg and Ndanda Mission Press, 1998.

Subramanian, Arvind and Natalia Tamirisa. Africa's Trade Revisited, *IMF Working Paper,. WP/01/33 ,* March 2001.

Subramanian., Arvind and Natalia Tamirisa. Is Africa Integrated in the Global Economy? *IMF Staff Papers,* Vol. 50, No. 3, 2003.

Sunstein, Cass. *Free Markets and Social Justice.* New York: Oxford University Press, 1997.

Sweezy, Paul M. Capitalism and the Environment Reprint, *Monthly Review*, June 1989 & October 2004.

Tandon, Yash. *University of Dar-es-Salaam: Debate on Class, State, and Imperialism*. Dar-es-Salaam: Tanzania Publishing House, 1984.

Tandon, Yash. Arguments Within African Marxism: The Dar-es-Salaam debates, *Journal of African Marxists*, No. 5, 1984.

Tanzania Commission for HIV/AIDS. *National Multi-Sectoral Strategic Framework on HIV/AIDS 2003-2007*, Dar-es-Salaam, January 2003.

Taylor, A.J.P. *The Origins of the Second World War*. London: Touchstone Books, 1996.

Temu, Andrew E. & Jean M. Due. The Business Environment in Tanzania After Socialism: Challenges of Reforming Banks, Parastatals, Taxation and the Civil Service, *Journal of African Modern Studies*, Vol. 38, 2000.

Teskey G and Rottouper. *Tanzania Civil Service Reform Programme: Case Study*, DFID, Nairobi, 1999.

The Economist*: Poverty and the Ballot Box, The Economist*, May 12, 2005.

The Economist: Doing Business in Africa: Different Skills Required, *The Economist*, June 30th 2005.

The Economist: Free Degrees to Fly: Marketisation of Higher Education, *The Economist*, February 24th, 2005.

The Economist Global Agenda: The G8's African Challenge, *The Economist*, July 6th, 2005.

The Editors, Monthly Review: Jobs Crunch: The Stagnation of Employment, *Monthly Review*, April 2004.

The King Report on Corporate Governance for South Africa, 2002. King II.

The World Bank. World Development Report 2005: *A Better Investment Climate for Everyone*, World Bank, 2005.

The World Bank. *The Poverty Reduction Strategy Initiative: An Independent Evaluation of the World Bank's Support Through 2003*, The World Bank, Washington DC. 2004.

The World Bank. *The* State in a Changing World, in *World Development Report, 1997*. Oxford: Oxford University Press, 1997.

The World Bank: *Building Institutions for Markets,*World Development Report, 2002. Oxford: Oxford University Press, 2002.

The World Bank. *Governance and Development*. World Bank, 1992.

The World Bank. *Tanzania at the Turn of the Century: Background Papers*, Country Study, February 2002.

The World Bank Institute. *The Right to Tell: The Role of Mass Media in Economic Development*, WBI Development Studies, The World Bank, 2002.

The World Bank: *Doing Business, 2005*, Washington DC, 2005.

Thomas, A.S & SL Mueller. A Case for Comparative Entrepreneurship: Assessing the Relevance of Culture, *Journal of International Business Studies*, Vol.31No2, June, 2000.

Thomas, Anisya S. & Stephen Mueller L. *Are Entrepreneurs the Same Across Cultures?* 1998. www.usabe.org/knowledge/proceedings/1998/22-Thomas.PDF)

Thurow, Lester. *Creating Wealth: The New Rules for Individuals, Companies and Countries in a Knowledge – Based Economy.* London: Nicholas Brealey Publishing, 1999.

Thurow, Lester. *Head to Head: The Coming Battle Among Japan, Europe and America.* London: Nicholas Brealey, 1992.

Thurow, Lester: *The Future of Capitalism: How Today's Economic Forces Shape Tomorrow's World.* London: Nicholas Brealey, 1996.

Tibaijuka, Anna Kajumulo. (ed.), *The Social Services Crisis of the 1990's: Strategies for Sustainable Systems in Tanzania.* Aldershot: Ashgate, 1998.

Tobin, James. Thinking Straight About Fiscal Stimulus and Deficit Reduction, *Challenge,* March-April, 1993.

Toffler, Alvin. *Powershift: Knowledge, Wealth, and Violence at the Edge of the 21st Century.* New York: Bantam Books, 1990.

Toffler, Alvin. *The Third Wave: The Revolution that will Change our Lives.* London, Collins, 1980.

Tostensen, Arne. Towards feasible Social Security Systems in Sub-° Africa, *Chr. Michelsen Institute Working Paper No 5, 2004,* ᴾ˙   ₊way.

Toynbee, Arnold. *A Study of History.* Abridge Editi   .. Oxford University Press, 1957.

Treichel, Volker. Tanzania's Growt₎   ₎₎ and Success in Reducing Poverty, *IMF Working Paper WP/05/35,* January 2005.

Tripp, M.A. *Changing the Rules: The Politics of Liberalisation and the Urban Informal Economy in Tanzania.* California University Press, 1997.

Tripp, Mari A. *Political Reform in Tanzania: The Struggle for Associational Autonomy* (www.essex.ac.uk/ecpr/events/jointsessions/paperarchive/mannheim/w3/tripp.pdf)

Tubiana, Laurence. Post-Cancun WTO: Focus on Objectives, Not the Means, *Bridges,* September-October, 2003. www.ictsd.org)

Tyson, Laura D'Andrea. *Who's Bashing Whom: Trade Conflicts in High Technology Industries,* Institute of International Economic Affairs, Washington DC, 1993.

Ul Haq, Mahbub. *New Imperatives of Human Security,* Barbara Ward Lecture, 21st World Conference of the Society For International

Development, 1994.

UNDP Human Development Report: *Cultural Liberty in Today's Diverse World*. Oxford: University Press, 2004.

UNDP & UN: *Public Service Ethics in Africa, Volume 1,* United Nations, New York, 2001.

www.unpant_un.org/intradoc/groups/public/documents/un/unpan000160.pdf)

UNDP: *Human Development Report: Deepening Democracy in a Fragmented World*. Oxford: Oxford University Press, 2002.

UNDP & The Prince of Wales. *Business and the Millennium Development Goals: A Framework for Action,* International Business Leaders Forum, London 2003.

UNDP: *Constraints on the Private Sector in Developing Countries,* in The *World Bank, Unleashing Entrepreneurship: Making Business Work for the Poor,* Report of the UN Commission on the Private Sector & Development. Chapter 2&3), April 2004.

UNESCO-International Catholic Centre For Cooperation with UNESCO. *The Merchandisation of Education*. Paris: UNESCO, October 23, 2004.

UNIDO: Industrial Development Report 2004: *Industrialisation, Environment and the Millennium Development Goals in Sub-Saharan Africa-The New Frontier in the Fight against Poverty*.

UN Economic Commission for Africa: *Youth in Africa: A Major Resource for Change*. www.uneca.org/adf/pre-symposium/issue_paper.pdf)

United Nations Conference on Trade and Development. (UNCTAD). *Economic Development in Africa: Issues in Africa's Trade Performance,* October, 2003.

United Nations Economic Commission for Africa: *Public Sector Management Reforms in Africa: Lessons Learned,* Development Policy Management Division, Addis Ababa, December 2003.

United Nations. UN Human Development Report, 2002:

United Republic of Tanzania. *Poverty Reduction Strategy Paper*. Government Printer, 2000.

United Republic of Tanzania. *Report of the Presidential Commission on One Party or Multi-Party System for Tanzania*. Nyalali Commission Report, 1992.

United Republic of Tanzania: *Tanzania Development Vision 2025*. Government Printer, 1999.

University of Dar-es-Salaam Convocation. *Why is Tanzania Still Poor 40 Years After Independence?* Proceedings of the 6th UDSM Convocation Symposium, 2003.

Van Arkadie, Brian. Globalisation and the East African Economies, in Semboja J, Juma Mwapachu & Eduard Jansen. (eds): *Local Perspectives on Globalisation: The African Case.* Dar Es Salaam, Mkuki na Nyota Publishers, 2003.

Van Ham, Peter. The Rise of the Brand State, *Foreign Affairs*, September-October, 2001.

Varley, John. Barclays is investing in Africa for Profit not Charity, *Financial Times,* July 8, 2005.

Vilekazi, Herbert. The Problem of African Universities, in Malegapuru W. Makgoba. (ed.): *African Renaissance.* Cape Town: Maguba Publishing, 1999.

Vogel, David. Do Corporations Have Political Power? *Dialogue,* No. 2, 1998.

Voight-Graf, Carmen, *Asian Communities in Tanzania: A Journey Through Past and Present Times.* Hamburg: Institute of African Affairs, 1998.

Wald, Kenneth D. *Religion and Politics in the United States.* Bombay: Popular Prakashan Publishers, 1992.

Wangwe, Samuel M. and Brian Van Arkadie. *Overcoming Constraints-Tanzanian Growth: Policy Challenges Facing The Third Phase* Government. Oxford: African Books Collective, 2000.

Watermann Jr, Robert H. *The Renewal Factor: How the Best Get and Keep Competitive Edge.* New York: Bantam Doubleday Dell Publishers

Weinstein, Michael M. *Globalisation: What's New?.* New York: Columbia University Press, 2005.

Westcott, C. Civil Service Reform in Africa, *International Journal of Public Sector Management,* Vol. 12 No. 2, 1994.

Whitehead, Martin. *Fighting Corruption in Sub-Saharan Africa: Can We Win the War?* Price Waterhouse Coopers, DA & I Africa Central.www.pwcglobal.com/gx/eng/cfr/gecs/Pwc_sub-saharan%20corruption_report.pot)

Widner, Jennifer A. Building the Rule of Law: Francis Nyalali and the Road to Judicial Independence in Africa. New York and London: W.W. Norton & Company, 2001.

Williams, Raymond. *Towards 2000.* London, Penguin Books, 1983.

Williams, Rowan Archbishop. This Media Tribe Disfigures Public, Speech at LambethHouse on Role of the Media, *The Guardian International Edition,* June 16, 2005.

Williamson, John. *Democracy and the "Washington Consensus",* World Development, Vol. 21, No.8, 1993.

Williamson, John. What Washington Means by Policy Reform, in J. Williamson, ed. *Latin American Adjustment: How Much Has Happened?*. Washington: Institute for International Economics, 1990.

Wilson, Ernest J III. *Economic Governance in Africa: New Directions for the Organised Private Sector in Africa,* Ibadan Centre for Public-Private Cooperation, 1998.

Wilson, Ernest J. III. Can Business Associations Contribute to Development and Democracy, in Ann Bernstein and Peter L. Berger. (eds.) *Business and Democracy: Cohabitation or Contradiction.* London: Pinter, 1998.

Wilson, Ernest J. III & Francisco Rodriguez. *Are Poor Countries Losing the Information Revolution?* Centre for International Development & Conflict Management,University of Maryland, USA.(www.cidcm.umd.edu/ibrary/papers/ewilson/apxc.pdf)

Wilson, Ernest J III and Kelvin Wong. *Negotiating the Net: The Politics of Internet Diffusion in Africa.* Boulder: Lynne Rienner Publishers, 2005.

Wolf, Alison. *Does Education Matter? Myths About Education and Economic Growth.* London: Penguin Books, 2002.

Wolf, Martin. *Why Globalisation Works: The Case for the Global Market Economy.* New Haven, Yale University Press, 2004.

Wolf, Martin. Aid Will not Make Poverty History-but it is Worth Trying, *Financial Times,* July 6, 2005

Wolfenhson, James D. *Foreword – The Right To Tell: The Role of Mass Media in Economic Development.* World Bank, 2002.

Wolfson, Adam. The Spirit of Liberty and the Spirit of Religion, *Commentary,* July 1995.

Wright, Anthony. *Socialism: Theories and Practices.* Oxford: Oxford Press, 1989.

Yang, Yongzheng & Sanjeev Gupta. Regional Trade Arrangements in Africa: Past Performance and the Way Forward, *IMF Working Paper WP/05/36,* Washington DC, February, 2005.

Yayha-Othman, Saida. (ed.), *Politics, Governance and Co-operation in East Africa.* Dar es Salaam: Research and Education for Democracy in Tanzania and Mkuki na Nyota Publishers, 2002.

Yargin, Daniel. *The Commanding Heights: The Battle Between Government and the Marketplace That is Remaking the Modern World.* New York: Simon & Schuster, 1998.

Yeats, W. B. The Second Coming in Finneran, Richard J. (ed.) *The Collected Poems of W. B. Yeats.* 2nd Edition, New York: Simon and Schuster, 1996.

Yieke, F.A. (ed) *East Africa: In Search of National and Regional Renewal,* CODESRIA, 2005.

Zakaria, Fareed. Culture Is Destiny: A Conversation with Lee Kuan Yew, *Foreign Affairs,* March-April 1994.

Zakaria, Fareed. *The Future of Freedom: Illiberal Democracy at Home and Abroad.* New York: WW Norton and Co. 2003.

Zakaria, Fareed. Islam, Democracy, and Constitutional Liberalism, *Political Science Quarterly,* Spring 2004.

Zeleze, Tiyambe et al. African Universities in the 21st Century, *CODESRIA, January 2004.*

Zemsky, Robert and Mass William. Towards an Understanding of Our Current Predicament, *Change,* November-December, 1995.

Zoel, Jean-Louis. *Globalisation, Growth and Africa's Pervasive Development Disorder,* Harvard University, May 2003.
www.wcfia.harvard.edu/fellows/papers02-03/zoel.pdf)

INDEX